Communings
of the Spirit

Mordecai Kaplan at the Jersey shore, ca. 1931.
(Courtesy Hadassah K. Musher)

Communings
of the Spirit

The Journals of
Mordecai M. Kaplan
Volume 1 1913–1934

Edited by Mel Scult

Wayne State University Press   Detroit
and The Reconstructionist Press

AMERICAN JEWISH CIVILIZATION SERIES

Editors
Moses Rischin
San Francisco State University

Jonathan D. Sarna
Brandeis University

A complete listing of the books in this series can be found at the back of this volume.

Manufactured in the United States of America.
04 03 02 01 00   5 4 3 2 1

Library of Congress Cataloging-in-Publication Data

Kaplan, Mordecai Menahem, 1881–
    Cummunings of the spirit : the journals of Mordecai M. Kaplan / edited by Mel Scult.
        p.   cm.—(American Jewish civilization series)
    Includes index.
    ISBN 0-8143-2575-0 (cloth : alk. paper)
    1. Kaplan, Mordecai Menahem, 1888—Diaries. 2. Rabbis—United States—Diaries. 3. Judaism—United States. 4. Judaism—20th century. 5. Reconstructionist Judaism. I. Scult, Mel. II. Title. III. Series.
BM755.K289 A3 2001
286.8'344'092—dc21   00-011802

Permission to reprint material from Mordecai Kaplan's diary has been granted by the Jewish Theological Seminary of America, which owns volumes 1–25 of the diary. Volumes 26 and 27 are owned by Reconstructionist College. Permission has also been granted by the Kaplan family.

With much gratitude
to
the Kaplan family
and
In memory of
Judith Kaplan Eisenstein
Naomi Kaplan Wenner
Sidney Musher
Joseph Goldman
Seymour Wenner
Saul Jaffe

We are particularly grateful to the Littauer Foundation
for its early and continued support of this project.

The Memorial Foundation for Jewish Culture
has been strongly supportive of this project.

"Only what is private, & yours, & essential, should ever be printed or spoken. I will buy the suppressed part of the author's mind; you are welcome to all he published."

—Ralph Waldo Emerson, Diary, Spring, 1853

"Of all writings I love only that which is written with blood."

—F. Nietzsche, *Thus Spake Zarathustra*,
quoted by Kaplan on the flyleaf of an early diary

Contents

❦

Chapter 2. May 30, 1915–August 14, 1918 93

❦

�

Chapter 4. September 22, 1922–April 16, 1925 165

❦

❧

❦

Chapter 7. November 25, 1928–March 9, 1929 283

❦

Chapter 8. March 10, 1929–July 22, 1929 314

❧

❧

Chapter 10. November 28, 1929–July 30, 1930 382

Contents

Chapter 12. November 17, 1931–December 19, 1932...457

❦

Preface

The originals of the first twenty-five volumes of the Kaplan journal are at the Jewish Theological Seminary. The last two volumes are at the Reconstructionist College in Wyncote, Pennsylvania. I am grateful to Dr. Mayer Rabinowitz, Dr. Ismar Schorsch of the JTS, and Dr. David Teutsch, president of the RRC, for allowing me to reproduce material from the volumes in their possession. I am also grateful to Rabbi Mordecai Liebling, the former director of the Reconstructionist Federation, for his help in preparing this volume, and to Mark Seal, the present director of the Jewish Reconstructionist Federation, for his support.

This published work exists only due to the generosity of Rabbi Kaplan and his family. First of all I am indebted to Mordecai Kaplan himself, who allowed me a very long time ago to have my own copy of the journals. There are many who have given support to this project. The Lucius N. Littauer Foundation gave generously at the very beginning of the project. Hadassah Musher also supported the publication from the beginning in a very generous way. Naomi Kaplan Wenner, Selma Kaplan Goldman, and Daniel Musher also have given generously of their resources. In addition I would like to note the generosity of the following supporters: Sidney and Dorothy Becker, Emanuel S. Goldsmith and Reba Rottenberg, Jack and Kaye Wolofsky, Dan Cederbaum, Benjamin Wm. Mehlman, Bert Linder, and Bliss Siman.

My friends and colleagues have been extremely helpful, though they are not responsible for my errors. First and foremost I want to thank my brother, Professor Allen Scult, with whom I have discussed many of the central issues connected with the journal and its meaning. Our conversations are unfailingly valuable. Professor Moses Rischin and Professor Jonathan Sarna have reviewed the entire manuscript, as has Rabbi Ira Eisenstein. Rabbi Jack Cohen has been a faithful and supportive mentor in all my projects, and I am grateful to him. My colleagues Professor Robert Seltzer and Professor Emanuel Goldsmith continue to be supportive and helpful on many levels. I am grateful to my son Rabbi Yehoshua Scult, who helped me with many of the rabbinic references.

The following colleagues and friends were consulted on specific issues: Judith Eisenstein, Rabbi Ira Eisenstein, Ann Eisenstein, Jethro Eisenstein, Miriam Eisenstein, Yaffa Eliach, Ed Feld, Avraham Holtz, Jonathan

Helfand, Seth Jerchower, Sid Leiman, Harry Mendelsson, Sara Regeur, Jane Rosen, Israel Schepansky, Jerry Schwartzbard, Baila Shargel, and Susan Winokur. I am also grateful to Elie Wise, the director of the Reconstructionist Rabbinical College Library, and to Julie Miller, the archivist of the Ratner Center at the Jewish Theological Seminary. The reference librarians at JTS and the New York Public Library have always been helpful. Sam Klein has been helpful with Hebrew references and with transliteration. I am grateful to Victor Kovner for his legal advice. Margo Stein and Chris Bugbee of the Reconstructionist Press have been very helpful. Finally, Sharon Polsky has been enormously helpful in preparing the diary for publication.

The material in this volume consists of approximately 25 percent of the journal for the period covered. Our principles of selection mirror Kaplan's major interests and focus. He lived in many worlds but is primarily known as an ideologue; thus a significant amount of space here is given to his thought on religion in general and Judaism in particular. Some mistakenly believe that Kaplan gave up God rather early in his life. The truth is that he thought about God and the belief in God all the time; that thinking is reflected here. We have given particular attention to issues and concepts that are not found in his published works.

Kaplan's journalizing changed over time. In the beginning (1913) the journal consisted almost totally of philosophical material—actually notes for his lectures and sermons. Kaplan functioned as a rabbi throughout his life, sometimes with a congregation and sometimes without. We have included some sermon outlines that dealt with the portion of the week or with holy days during the year. Kaplan's ideas also appear in casual conversations he had with different individuals, sometimes colleagues and sometimes unknown people who came to him seeking advice or counsel. He did not enjoy the ministerial functions of the rabbinate, but from time to time he did perform at a wedding or a funeral; some selections are included which describe his experience of these occasions.

Kaplan lived within a number of institutions, the most important of which was the Jewish Theological Seminary (JTS), where he taught in the Rabbinical School and where he directed the Teachers' Institute. We see him at faculty meetings, at Rabbinical Assembly (RA) conventions, and talking casually to seminary colleagues as he goes about his daily business. He never felt completely accepted by the seminary family, and his journal entries frequently reflect his anxieties and discomfort. Well-known seminary figures (Solomon Schechter, Cyrus Adler, Louis Finkelstein, Alexander Marx, Louis Ginzberg, etc.) are present here, as are many obscure rabbinical students and little-known rabbis whom Kaplan met in passing. Rabbi Ira Eisenstein, his most important disciple and his son-in-law, appears at the end of this volume and becomes important only in the years following 1934.

Kaplan was also associated with a number of synagogues, particularly the Jewish Center and the Society for the Advancement of Judaism (SAJ), both of which he helped establish. Selections on these institutions reflect many of the conflicts he had, as well as the programs he attempted to establish, and elucidate his thoughts on the place of the synagogue in American life. Through his journal we experience his struggle with the liturgy and his attempt to make it relevant for congregants, who were frequently oblivious to the service and its meaning. Kaplan was a radical innovator, and some of his attempts to vitalize the service by including new prayers are quite instructive.

Above and beyond everything else, the diary is a record of Kaplan's thoughts about himself. As we shall discuss in the introduction, the diary was profoundly important to his sense of himself as a person. It is here we begin to understand the nature of his self-doubt and his bouts with discouragement and despair.

There are not many comments on Kaplan's family life included in the journal. He loved his wife and children deeply, but they are present here in a very minimal way. The journal seemed to be a forum for "business"; family was another realm, in his mind. At times, however, we do get a glimpse into Kaplan's family life, with its inevitable complexities and conflicts. The most famous event regarding Kaplan's daughters is, of course, Judith's Bas Mitzvah (1922), one of the first on record. Unfortunately, Kaplan notes it only briefly; he intended to come back to it, but never did.

On the whole we have followed the journal itself in terms of the way it allots space. Some matters, though only briefly mentioned in the journal, are yet significant. Kaplan was a lifelong Zionist, though he was on the periphery of organized Zionist life in America. He knew many Zionists well, nonetheless, and spent time with Weizmann every time the Zionist leader came to New York; most of the selections on Kaplan and Weizmann have been included. Erez Yisrael was important to him, but he never really thought of following the example of his friends Judah Magnes and Henrietta Szold, who settled in the Holy Land. Zionists respected him and chose him to represent them at the dedication ceremonies of the Hebrew University. He was deeply moved by these events, and we have included his reactions here.

Kaplan was a keen observer of the Jewish scene in America. We have included here a multitude of miscellaneous reactions to passing events— a dinner at Felix Warburg's house, a Sabbath at Rockaway Beach, a rather unsavory gentleman who wants to run carnival on the Sabbath, and a Hasidic rabbi named Schneerson who comes to the Kaplans' for a Sabbath dinner and teaches Kaplan a new hasidic melody. Kaplan inevitably tells us a story with every diary entry, and frequently there is a healthy moral point as well, as when he meets Dr. Faitlowitch, the man who "discovered" the black Jews of Africa. Kaplan was profoundly moved by this man who came over for dinner one night. The Kaplan daughters apparently reacted rather strongly to Faitlowitch's physical unattractiveness, but for Kaplan the man radiated a divine aura. His devotion to the Falashas (black Jews) symbolized to Kaplan the real meaning of belief in God.

Kaplan's powers of observation are also reflected in his analysis of communities he visited. Before the age of easy air access, Kaplan traveled continuously throughout the country, giving lectures and holding conferences. Often he would describe the people he met and the communities he visited. We have included a sampling of this local history.

Titles given to the journal entries in this volume are my own, though the title of the volume itself is Kaplan's.

A few matters of style: The diary is not a finished product and was not prepared for publication. Some sentences are awkward. In all cases the language of the original text has been retained, except where there was a small, obvious mistake in Kaplan's original ("of" for "at," etc.). Punctuation has been corrected but original spelling for the most part has been retained. Capitalization has been corrected, but Kaplan's hyphenation has been kept. No indication is given when a selection ends in the middle of a paragraph or at the end of a sentence. Three dots indicate a selection that ends in the middle of a sentence. A given selection under a certain date is not necessarily the first paragraph under that date. If a selection runs to more than one day, the new date is indicated. A new title is given if a completely new subject for the same date is discussed. Each date contains many subjects. A person is annotated the first time he or she is mentioned; aside from this annotation, details about each person can be found in the glossary. If no death date is given, the person is still alive. If the death date is unknown, a "?" is listed.

Within the journal entries, square brackets are used for the editor and round for Kaplan. When an obvious word is omitted in the manuscript, it is supplied in brackets, with no comments—for example, "organized [life]."

Kaplan usually, but not always, wrote Hebrew words in Hebrew characters. Where a word was written in Hebrew characters, the note "Heb." appears. All Hebrew words have been transliterated and translated. Though in the twenties I imagine Kaplan pronounced Hebrew in the Ashkenazic mode, I have transliterated for the most part in the current Sephardic mode. Words such as "Golus" (Diaspora) are an exception. Kaplan did not look up the references he cited, thus minor errors did creep in. These errors have been corrected. The transliteration is designed to be consistent and accurate. Transliteration is underlined—for example, *Te-ehoz ba-zeh ve-gam mi-zeh* [Heb. Ecclesiastes 7:18 "(It is best that you) grasp one without letting go of the other"]. The portion of the verse that did not appear in Kaplan's Hebrew citation is given in parentheses within the square brackets. Kaplan most frequently rendered the name of God YHVH (the Tetragrammaton) as 'd in Hebrew, which we have retained.

Where Kaplan's spelling of the name of a person differs from the standard, Kaplan's spelling is retained in the text, with the accepted spelling used in the note. Archaic spellings, when not the name of a place or a person, are simply left—for example, "Yeshiba" instead of "Yeshiva."

Where the spelling of the name of an East European town differs from the standard contemporary spelling, Kaplan's original spelling is retained, with the present spelling given in brackets afterward.

Kaplan frequently wrote over passages. Where this was done the text includes the write-over without noting this fact. If the write-over is a significant change, the addition is listed in square brackets after the original text.

Introduction

A Universe of Words—The Diary of Mordecai Kaplan

The journal that Mordecai Kaplan kept from 1913 until the late 1970s is a remarkable document. It is extraordinarily long— twenty-seven volumes, each with 350 to 400 handwritten pages. The present volume represents about 20 percent of the journal for the period from 1913 to 1934.

The journal is certainly the largest by a Jewish person, and may even be one of the most extensive on record. Samuel Pepys's diary contains eleven published volumes. There are longer diaries (fifty volumes for Bronson Alcott) but the individual volumes are smaller than Kaplan's ledger-type volumes. Although Kaplan published a great deal during his lifetime, in his own opinion—and mine—the journal is his most significant work. Ralph Waldo Emerson, a compulsive diarist himself, realized the value of the private diary: "Only what is private, & yours, & essential, should ever be printed or spoken. I will buy the suppressed part of the author's mind; you are welcome to all he published."[1]

For me personally, the Kaplan journals are comparable to the *Yam HaTalmud* (the sea of the Talmud), always threatening to engulf me, yet carrying me forward; in reading them I was never quite sure where I would land or whether I would ever be delivered. Soon after I met Kaplan (in 1972) he permitted me to make a copy for myself. The family and those close to Kaplan undoubtedly wondered: "Who is this young man with the *chutzpa* (nerve) to expect a personal copy of the journal?" Fortunately, in the course of time their opinion changed, and I am deeply grateful to Kaplan and his family for their generous and steadfast support. Without a personal copy of the journal, this publication project would never have come to fruition.

Journal writing was common in the past. Recording the events of the day was particularly popular among the Puritans, who wanted to

---

1. Ralph Waldo Emerson Diary, Spring, 1853. *Emerson in His Journals*, ed. Joel Porte (Cambridge: Harvard University Press, 1982), 446.

scrutinize the moral quality of their behavior. Their "day-books" were often little more than a listing of events. In Concord, Massachusetts, during the 1840s, everyone kept diaries, even the children.[2]

Many people keep journals at one time or another, for many different reasons.[3] While traveling we try to capture the unique textures of our experience that so often go unnoticed in our daily routine. In times of crisis we sometimes keep a diary or write a memoir to unburden ourselves and clarify our emotional conflicts. The best example within the Jewish field is the recently published memoir of Henrietta Szold,[4] written after her rejection by Louis Ginzberg. This very brilliant woman, the founder of Hadassah, has given us a profoundly moving document which chronicles the joy and pain of her relationship with the preeminent Talmudic scholar of her time. In our own time a whole diary literature has emerged from the tragedy of the Holocaust.[5]

Today, although some people keep diaries, journal writing is no longer the habit it used to be. Aside, then, from traumas and travel, how are we to explain the case of Mordecai Kaplan, who kept a journal continuously for almost seventy years?

The first question we need to answer is whether Kaplan intended the journal to be published. When I first examined the diary in the early seventies, Kaplan indicated that he had shown the early volumes to other scholars interested in his life and thought. His daughters have also reported that from time to time he read them passages. He noted in his will that the diary should not be published for five years after his death, thereby implying that after that period it was permissible to publish it. Furthermore, he constantly reviewed the text and corrected it. If the diary was intended strictly for his own use, why correct it as if for publication? The diary's great length indicates that Kaplan did not view it in purely private terms. Yet, in the actual writing process, he probably did not think of himself as creating a public work. The extreme regularity of the enterprise underscores the fact that he often forgot that someone might someday read his journal.

Despite his ultimate ambivalence about publishing the diary, in his younger years Kaplan defended diary writing as a claim to fame. In 1922 he came across a statement that denigrated people who thought they could

---

2. See Paul Brooks, *The People of Concord—One Year in the Flowering of New England* (Chester, Conn.: Globe Pequot Press, 1990), passim. The year is 1846.

3. See Laura Arksey, Nancy Pries, and Marcia Reed, eds., *American Diaries: An Annotated Bibliography of Published Diaries and Journals* (Detroit: Gale Research, 1983). See also Lillian Schlissel, *Women's Diaries of the Westward Journey* (New York: Schocken, 1982).

4. See the volume edited by Baila Shargel, *Lost Love—The Untold Story of Henrietta Szold—Unpublished Diary and Letters* (Philadelphia: Jewish Publication Society, 1997).

5. See *Encyclopedia of the Holocaust* (New York: Macmillan & Co., 1990), s.v. "Diaries."

become famous through their diary or their memoirs. Kaplan responded in a note, found on the flyleaf of the second volume of his diary, dated November 22, 1922:

> Formerly only the famous men wrote their reminiscences; Today everyone who intends to become famous writes his memoirs. I do not see that there is anything wrong in intending to become famous. It is better to try and fail than not to try at all. The world is all the richer for the many who intended to become famous and did not succeed, much richer, no doubt, than if they had not made the attempt. Only carping individuals like the author of the above statement begrudge even the joy of an illusory prospect of fame. Besides may there not be other reasons for keeping diaries in addition to striving for fame? Some people like to converse about their experiences, others like to write them out. And everyone likes to go back to his own past and recall the things he has lived through. Keeping a diary affords enjoyment in one's later years.

Throughout most of Kaplan's adult life, journal keeping was a deeply ingrained habit. Kaplan started his journal in earnest as a way of writing first drafts of speeches he was presenting at universities around the country. Gradually the journal began to reflect the concreteness of his life, while continuing to record his theoretical speculations.

Usually Kaplan's journal keeping was spontaneous and lacked self-consciousness. He never thought of his diary as a conscious literary work. For Emerson, preeminent among diarists, the journal was primarily a "savings bank," a source of material for a later essay. Kaplan also used the journal for this purpose, but not as systematically as Emerson had. In his diary Kaplan thought through many issues that would later appear in his books; indeed, the journal often avoids the ponderous quality of his published prose.

Kaplan enjoyed keeping the diary; a period in which he did not make an entry made him uneasy, because he was convinced that the immediacy of the journal record made the writing more compelling. If he waited even a few days, he feared, an event which had loomed as important might become trivial upon reflection. In addition, after a significant time period he often felt the necessity of restructuring events. Because so much of the diary was written in close proximity to the events as they happened, this work projects a raw feeling—immediate and undiminished. Here is how Kaplan addressed the issue:

> Not having recorded my experiences since June 9, [This entry was made on June 25, 1929], all that I lived through and participated

in seems like a confused mass of fading impressions. If I should want to revive them I would have to exert mental energy for the purpose of giving them some logical order and proper evaluation to say nothing of trying to recall incidents that have sunk below the threshold of consciousness. That is asking too much. This is not meant to be literature, and does not deserve that mental strain and concentration which I ought to reserve for more serious tasks.

In view of the diary's apparent spontaneity, we have to consider the issue of self-censorship. Do we have an edited record? The answer is both yes and no. The journal brims with candid reactions; indeed, one of the great attractions of the diary is the impression it conveys of immediate access to Kaplan's inner life. On the other hand, Kaplan reviewed the text and often "cleaned" it up. In my opinion, his purpose was neither to remove ambiguity nor to conceal his thoughts; he was simply searching for the right expression.

The famous and the powerful often attempt to manipulate their image when they write. Some even destroy "negative" evidence that might tarnish their image. Fortunately, Kaplan's letters, papers, and journals do not reflect such manipulation. Indeed, the journal overwhelms the reader with its candor; we have an embarrassment of riches from which to reconstruct Kaplan's life, both inner and outer.

The one aspect of Kaplan's inner life that appears to be obviously missing in his journal is his libido. A product of a strict *misnagdic* [anti-Hasidic] Lithuanian family, and the father of four, Kaplan records nothing overtly sexual. There were surely some thoughts he would neither record nor let himself think.

At times Kaplan was critical of his own ruminations. When feeling sorry for himself, he often recorded his dissatisfactions with his depression. After noting some problems at the SAJ he wrote: "I have never felt so alone in the world. But I must learn to take my punishment like a man, and I shall try to refrain from self-pity."[6]

The diary in its motivation primarily partakes of conversation. Other than Samson Benderly, who was a close lifelong friend, Kaplan did not have many associates in whom he could confide.[7] In his workplace, the Jewish Theological Seminary (JTS), Kaplan always felt profoundly alienated, never having been close to the core senior faculty (Louis Ginzberg, Alexander

---

6. Kaplan Journal, December 29, 1924.
7. Samson Benderly (1876–1944), U.S. educator who was born in Palestine and served as director of the Bureau of Jewish Education of the New York Kehillah. A major figure in American-Jewish education and a dedicated Zionist, he was a Hebraist and a follower of Ahad Ha-Am.

Marx, Israel Davidson, Moses Hyamson). The administrators later consisted mostly of his students (e.g., Louis Finkelstein, Simon Greenberg, Max Arzt, Moshe Davis, etc.).[8]

In a momentary mood of depression in 1928, Kaplan voiced his regret that he had no one with whom to share his thoughts:

> I have been very much in the dumps of late. The longer I live the more alone I feel. I have not a single friend or companion in the world with whom I can share my interests and problems. What can wife and children do for me? They have their own lives to live. Of course they love me and I love them. But all they can do is to sympathize with me. What good can sympathy do me? In all the years that I have worked in the field of Judaism I have not succeeded in finding anybody who would be willing to collaborate with me on any project for the advancement or reconstruction of Judaism.[9]

We should not forget that Kaplan had many admirers, disciples, and students, with whom he was constantly in contact, but sharing his inner life with them was difficult.

More than once he compared writing in the diary to conversing with a friend: "As on previous occasions I shall resort again to this diary as though it were an intelligent friend to whom I could communicate what I am struggling these days to formulate."[10]

Conversation has become increasingly significant as a philosophical concept, particularly as related to the self. The self may be viewed either as a set of qualities that exist through time or as a series of stories we tell about ourselves. Conversations are events that carry forward our self-understanding, the unfolding of our selves. The stories are constantly changing. Journals, like conversation, become an ongoing configuration of the story. In the words of one contemporary thinker, "[the self is an effort] to interpret one's life by a subject that is continually refiguring itself through stories it appropriates as its own."[11] Conversation is a major component in this process, and for Mordecai Kaplan the diary and conversation function

---

8. Kaplan appreciated Cyrus Adler, but did not like him. Finkelstein, who became president of JTS in 1940, was active in the seminary administration from the late 1920s.

9. Kaplan Journal, April 12, 1928.

10. Kaplan Journal, July 3, 1929.

11. The ideas for this paragraph are based on the work of Paul Ricoeur, but the quotation is actually from the introduction to an anthology of his work, and the words are the editor's. Mark I. Wallace, introduction to *Figuring the Sacred—Religion, Narrative and Imagination—Paul Ricoeur*, trans. David Pelauer (Minneapolis: Fortress Press, 1995), 13.

in the same way. The diary does not simply record the events of the day; considerable detail is included, and writing in the diary is comparable to sharing concerns with an intimate friend.

One of the primary motives of conversation is the opportunity to clarify our thoughts. This urge to clarify is sometimes conscious but more often it is experienced as an inner tension which we seek to resolve. We want to "talk it out," but rarely do we in fact welcome the reactions of the listener. A diary does not interrupt or talk back and so gives the ultimate conversational pleasure. As Thoreau put it: "Says I to myself should be the motto of my journal."[12]

The inner life is often a dialogue in which we step back and look at ourselves. In the Kaplan journal this tendency to observe the self takes a rather unusual form. At one point, Kaplan wrote in the third person, and the candor which we have come to expect of Kaplan became even more illuminating. He was on a train headed for Schenectady, where he was to deliver a series of lectures. Musing on the matter of the "active self" and the "onlooker self" [Kaplan's expression], the one involved in the myriad of quotidian details, the other much more introspective, he lamented that people had lost the connection between the two. The onlooker ego, or the observing self, as we would say, only becomes real with cultivation. His mind then moved to the relationship between these mental processes and the larger universe. In the midst of these musings he began to write in the third person:

> One thing is certain that the onlooker-ego is much more the product of deliberate cultivation than the active ego. The onlooker ego transcends the limits of the body to which alone of all bodies it has entree to the same extent that the life process does which makes the heart beat and awakens the physical hungers. The question then arises "what relations subsist between the life's process and the mind process?" He [Kaplan here began to write about himself] began to grow dizzy as he contemplated the cosmic implications of his own ego and his mind reverted to his latest fad, filling his diary, postponing for some more leisurely hour the attempt to arrive at some working formula which might solve the metaphysical problem which he set before himself. He had a weakness for formulas. Never having had the fortune of experiencing

---

12. John C. Broderick, Robert Sattelmeyer, et al., eds., *The Journal of Henry David Thoreau* (Princeton, N.J.: Princeton University Press, 1981–), 4:177, as quoted in Leonard N. Neufeldt, "Thoreau in his Journal," in *The Cambridge Companion to Henry David Thoreau*, ed. Joel Myerson (Cambridge: Cambridge University Press, 1995), 115

the thrill of firsthand contact with things he lived in a universe of words.[13]

Writing in the third person serves the purpose of objectification. Conversation always serves this purpose. We need to bring ourselves out into the public space through speaking, writing, or some kind of creative activity. Through the process of speaking we come to name, and through naming to call into existence. Conversation not only reveals; it creates. Does the message exist if no one hears it? The hearing obviously is part of the creation. Yet we must also be confirmed. Kaplan had no doubts about the value of his message, but he needed to be heard; the diary was part of the process of creation and confirmation.[14]

It may also be that we come to know ourselves through speaking. Do we really know what we think before we have formulated our ideas in speech or writing?

Recording one's thoughts gives them permanence and indeed rescues the self from oblivion. At one point after Kaplan had been working on a précis of the rabbinic midrash on the *Song of Songs,* he put it down and turned to the diary. "Which was more important," he asked himself, "this literary work or the diary?" There was no contest. The rabbinic work could be written by another; "On the other hand no one but myself could write my diary. Whether what I have to say is wise or foolish, interesting or boring it is the attempt of a personality to save itself from inarticulateness and oblivion by the mere skin of its teeth. Its struggles are entirely its own and no other person in the world could know them and record them."[15]

On another occasion he put the question slightly differently. Which should be of more value, he asked, the record of one's inner struggles or one's theory of God? We might say today that they are one and the same—a "form of God-wrestling," as Arthur Waskow would put it. In Kaplan's formulation, "A detailed description, for example, of all the mental tortures I went through before and after the talk I gave last night should, it seems to me, be more interesting than my theory about God."[16]

Transience is obviously an inescapable aspect of the human condition, and we make heroic attempts to overcome it. Thus the diary redeemed Kaplan from the short-lived and the temporary: "After every such writing

---

13. Kaplan Journal, December 18, 1928. See chapter 7 for the full text.
14. Kaplan Journal, April 12, 1928.
15. Kaplan Journal, May 10, 1929.
16. Kaplan Journal, November 21, 1928. The expression "God-wrestling" is of course very ancient. Arthur Waskow used it in the title of his book *Godwrestling* (New York: Schocken Publishing Co., 1978). In recent years it has become a common expression among liberal Jews.

[in the journal] . . . he would experience a sense of calm as though he had succeeded in accomplishing something that had permanence to it, something, therefore, that rescued his life from the vortex of time."[17]

The process of objectification is a means of making the self more real. In order to exist fully we must enter the public sphere. A private event which never is objectified in any way in some sense does not exist—the dream we never tell anyone, the creative project that remains completely undone. These are not real. As one writer put it, "The individual biographies of all bees, a thorough retelling of all the dreams men and women have ever dreamed—these many hundred possible volumes do not belong even in theory to 'world history.' We will see that the truly private is a black hole that miraculously opens out upon other worlds. . . ."[18] All of us struggle mightily not to be drawn into this black hole; Mordecai Kaplan above all.

Kaplan was a congregational rabbi as well as a professor. When he experienced an insight, he "thrill[ed] with joy," but then, he wondered, whom should he tell? The congregation? They were a group of "simple untutored men and women . . . dull and lethargic," who would certainly not appreciate his ideas. Teaching at the JTS, alas, was not a solution either. Nor did he communicate his ideas to his wife and family.

The diary, then, became his "significant other," the mirror assuring him of his very existence. After a long period away from it, he would return with a renewed realization of its importance. Yet, the effort of "relating" in this way often tired him greatly. Having a significant other does demand work:

> The longer the period during which I fail to record my experience the harder I find it to resume the practice. But I must keep up the diary. It is the only evidence I have that I have existed. I need it to counteract the feeling of blankness with which I am often seized. My past is as though it was not so that I feel forced to turn the pages of the diary to convince myself that I have lived. I sometimes feel that we don't have to die to know what death is—in fact, it is then that we don't know. The time that we know it is when we are alive and we try to keep our own past from dying; yet no matter what we do it dies on our hands.[19]

---

17. Kaplan Journal, December 18, 1928. Here Kaplan was writing about himself in the third person.

18. Luther Askeland, *Ways in Mystery—Explorations in Mystical Awareness and Life* (Ashland, Ore.: White Cloud Press, 1997), 109.

19. Kaplan Journal, April 12, 1928. See the same entry for the remark about "simple untutored men."

When we externalize the self by writing a journal we create a legacy for our children spelling out our ideals for them. It is what Otto Rank, the psychological theorist, calls "an immortality substitute."[20] Kaplan, alas, was fully aware that using one's children in this way was fraught with danger, unfair to them and perhaps even to society in general: "In assuming that the children are sufficiently docile to render the process successful," Kaplan reasoned, "we are bound to reduce human life to a limited number of patterns which would keep on repeating themselves." If he were creative as an artist, he thought, he would have an obvious way to pass on his "self-aspect," but for him the diary was the only answer: "In my frustration, I turn to writing in this journal as the only means left me to externalize and render transferable that aspect of my being I experience as my soul, self or reason."[21] The journal thus became the repository of his self, his very soul.

The diary is valuable for other reasons as well. When we write something for publication, it is "cleaned up." All of the ambivalence that we might feel is eliminated. In a journal the contradictions remain. For example, who would question Kaplan's commitment to Judaism or Zionism? More than anything else he was the man "of Jewish Peoplehood"; his journal consistently gives evidence of his lifelong devotion to his people. Yet, when it came to his children his feelings were complex and multilayered. The following passage, in which Kaplan was contemplating his eldest daughter's involvement in Jewish life in general and Zionism in particular, is a glaring example of his ambivalence: "The more Jewishness I inculcate in them [his daughters] the more I am drawing them too into this fatal vortex. Today I purposely put into Judith's hands the lengthy debate carried on in the English pages of the Yiddish *Forverts* [*Forward*] concerning the Jewish prospect in Palestine. I am afraid that she [Judith] too is mesmerized by the romance and tragedy of the Jewish struggle. I want her to think for herself." Thus, encouraging her to question Zionism, Kaplan gave her some anti-Zionist articles from the *Forverts*. Yet, alas, "she seemed as ardent in her faith as before." [22] His ambivalence was certainly related to his pessimism and despair. So little was being accomplished that at times his dedication to Judaism and to Zionism seemed like a futile effort.

We are all dominated by myths that organize our lives, but rarely are we conscious of their power. Kaplan was aware of his personal myths, and they caused him much pain. "It has become clearer to me than ever that I am a veritable Don Quixote," he wrote. "Beguiled by the delusion that I can help to render Judaism permanent, or even temporarily safe, I fight against

---

20. Ernest Becker, *The Denial of Death* (New York: Free Press, 1973), 152.
21. Kaplan Journal, May 14, 1931.
22. Kaplan Journal, March 22, 1926.

windmills which always worst me. That is why I am the Knight of the long face, always grumpy, always in bad humor."[23]

He struggled despite the pessimism; he was the heroic pessimist. Even in his pessimism he was the rabbi and teacher. The journal and his life became a text for the religious and moral education of his followers. The Hasidim taught that Torah lies not only in Biblical and Rabbinic texts but in the lives of great men and women. In the Hasidic world the day-to-day deeds of the rebbe become Torah. In order to know how to live, the saying goes, you must watch the rebbe tie his shoes.

Kaplan himself had a sense of the religious value of biography. In 1929 he read a Hebrew biography of Isaac Nissenbaum, a religious Zionist who preached Zionism to the ultra-Orthodox with missionary zeal. This biography inspired the following comments:

> No less important than literature for the renascence of our people is the emergence of articulate personalities. No matter how humble or undistinguished the person be so long as he succeeds in giving an integrated account of his life he transmits as permanent record a body of experiences that is just as unique, interesting and valuable as a new book or poem, insofar as that account of his life represents a combination of experiences that cannot be duplicated by the member of any other people. If Jews of the past had sense enough to write autobiographies like Nissenbaum's what a wealth of historical material we should have possessed.[24]

The relation between text and life is also illustrated by Kaplan's explication of the biblical text. Kaplan was, of course, a very learned man with easy access to the classical Jewish texts. The journal is filled with rabbinic and biblical references that reinforce the connection between life and text. On one occasion, for example, he had been talking to faculty members at the Teachers Institute about the use of Hebrew as the medium of instruction. They were dedicated Hebraists, as was Kaplan. Yet, he would not preclude the use of English to explain a point that the students did not understand. In the journal he then cited a biblical verse that emphasized the human tendency to hold on to two competing positions: "Being a compromiser and a syncretist by nature, I try to abide by the principle enunciated in Koheleth [Ecclesiastes] *Te-eḥoz ba-zeh ve-gam mi-zeh*" [Heb. Ecclesiastes 7:18 "(It is best that you) grasp the one without letting go of the other."][25] Thus does his life serve as a midrash to Scripture.

---

23. Ibid.
24. Kaplan Journal, June 17, 1929.
25. Kaplan Journal, September 11, 1925.

In the journal we find attitudes and concepts only hinted at in Kaplan's published writings. For example, in print he rarely tackled the problem of evil directly. In the wake of the Holocaust, Kaplan has been severely criticized for this omission. Modern Jews are painfully sensitive to the violence done to the Jewish people in the recent past and to present threats of destruction. Any ideologue who fails to deal with the suffering of the innocents is suspect. His thinking seems to reflect the optimism of another era. Yet there are glimpses in the journal of a concept of evil which can be traced back to medieval thinkers. Kaplan tackled both the subjective and objective aspects of the problem. Personal sinning, he felt, led to personal suffering. He quoted the rabbis who reiterated that the reward of the mitzvah [commandment] is another good deed, whereas the consequence of sinfulness is an unending downward, disastrous cycle. While we might consider this belief somewhat naive, still we must recognize the ways in which immoral behavior can be self-destructive. General suffering, for Kaplan, was not a punishment for misdeeds, but was attributed to chance and circumstances that are not in God's power. Living in the post-Enlightenment age, it is obvious to us and to Kaplan that suffering is a result of natural laws and random happenings that cannot be controlled. If a child is brain-damaged, this is not a punishment inflicted by God, but a result of the birthing process and the accidental "luck of the draw." In our own time this concept of evil has been powerfully expressed by a disciple of Kaplan's, Harold Kushner, in his popular work *When Bad Things Happen to Good People*. Kushner studied with Kaplan, and the essence of his concept of evil may have been influenced by Mordecai Kaplan. Indeed, the following passage from the Kaplan diary reads as if it could have come straight out of Kushner's book:

> To me the very idea of a punishing God is perfectly abhorrent. All punishment is nothing but revenge and therefore belongs to the same class of evils as sin, suffering, cruelty, disease and death. I might as well think of God as deliberately sinning or committing cruelty as to attribute to Him the will to punish. God is not concerned in seeing to it that the consequences of sin shall be suffering. The consequences of sin are part of the sin that caused them, and like the sin itself possible in the universe because the domain of chance and accident still occupies a tremendous part of that universe and has not yet come under the dominion of God who is synonymous with what ever there is of order, purpose, intelligence and love in the universe.[26]

26. The quotation here is from Kaplan Journal, July 11, 1929. For Kushner, *When Bad Things Happen to Good People* (New York: Avon Books, 1981), see especially chapter 3

Just as the journal presents concepts not developed elsewhere, so does it offer insights into sides of Kaplan that were hidden from his students and friends. Though he never doubted the content of his ideas, he did question his ability to express them. One example: "Civilization is a heroic attempt to fit the confusion of human existence into the framework of a drama with purpose. The unfortunate thing is that most people are cast for parts for which they are not adapted. I am one of those people whom it is undoubtedly most difficult to cast for the proper part, because I belong to those whose reach far exceeds their grasp."[27]

To know a person is to know his demons. Kaplan had many demons, but that which plagued him the most was his sense of insufficiency and the possibility that all of his labor was in vain. In later years he was continuously incredulous that Reconstructionism had become a denomination and that a college existed that would perpetuate his thought. He doubted his ability but never the content of his thought.

Kaplan's journal entries frequently express his deep and sincere piety, a piety surprisingly embedded within the naturalistic framework of his thought. In one selection, written as Kaplan returned by train from St. Louis, having just finished a long entry into the diary before going to bed, he notes, "It is now 11:20 P.M. I want to note that with the help of God, the Life, the Love and the Intelligence of the Universe, I have been able to turn to good account the hours I am spending on this train. I thank thee, O God for the blessings which I enjoy. Amen"[28]

A pious man's religion helps him cope with the demons that plague him. The vitality of a religion, indeed, may be measured by the degree to which it helps individuals cope with their fears. Rabbi Nahman of Bratzlav used to say that all the world is a narrow ridge and that the essential point is not to be afraid. When Kaplan writes about fear he seems to be commenting on Rabbi Nahman's statement:

> Life for me is not just a pedestrian affair as it is for most people;
> neither is it a matter of climbing mountains to some pinnacle of
> attainment as it is for the privileged few, but a continual learning
> to walk on a tightrope. My task consists in having to control my
> personality and my experiences so that I might retain my mental
> balance and sanity. I am pretty successful when I perform in public

---

(Sometimes There is No Reason) and chapter 4 (No Exceptions for Nice People). For parallel ideas in Maimonides see Oliver Leaman, *Evil and Suffering in Jewish Philosophy* (Cambridge: Cambridge University Press, 1995), chapter 4 (Maimonides).

27. Kaplan Journal, May 9, 1931.
28. Kaplan Journal, January 3, 1929.

but when I am by myself I always slip. Fortunately there is always the net of habit to save me.[29]

Where there is fear, there may also be hope. After writing a sermon that dealt with fear and religion, Kaplan sought redemption from the crippling effects of this emotion: "All in all I do not regret having had to organize the sermon on Fear. It has helped me clarify my own ideas on the subject. May the time come when I shall be able to add *Darashti et 'd ve'anani . . .* [Heb. Psalms 34:5 "I sought the Lord, and he answered me, and delivered me from all my fears."][30]

The journal reveals not only Kaplan the man, but also the many-sided thinker. For scholars, Kaplan is generally seen as the pragmatic and sociological ideologue. This description is accurate but insufficient. All modern Jews confront the natural and the supernatural. Arthur Cohen, who used this distinction to great effect, always classified Kaplan as the "natural Jew."[31] A careful reading of the Kaplan journal, however, demonstrates conclusively that Cohen and others did not appreciate the "supernatural" aspects of Kaplan's thinking.

Kaplan dismissed the supernatural rather early in his career insofar as it referred to the miraculous, the divine origin of the Torah, and the notion of divine intervention in the historical process. In his later life he coined the term "transnatural" to characterize his own beliefs. The term transnatural is cumbersome, but will be helpful in understanding Kaplan, and in appreciating the fact that he was far from a theological naturalist.

Kaplan's theology centered around the concept of energy. At the very beginning of the journal Kaplan employed the concept of energy to define religion in general and Judaism in particular. The essence of Judaism for him was not found in any particular set of doctrines, beliefs, or values, but in the psycho-social energy that produced those values. In Kaplan's words, "the permanence of Judaism does not necessarily involve the permanence of its moral and spiritual values, but the continued identity of the ethno or socio-psychical energy capable of producing such values."

Kaplan's concept of God as "the power that makes for salvation" is familiar.[32] If we simply substitute the term "energy" for "power," as Kaplan did in his early formulations, we eliminate the unnecessary reification

---

29. Kaplan Journal, May 5, 1931.

30. Kaplan Journal, November 29, 1929.

31. Arthur A. Cohen, *The Natural and Supernatural Jew* (New York: Pantheon Books, 1962), chapter 3, part 3 (Judaism and Survival—Mordecai M. Kaplan).

32. See Kaplan's *The Meaning of God in Modern Jewish Religion* (Detroit: Wayne State University Press, 1995), passim.

which has plagued his theology. The phrase "Power that . . ." conjures up a nonpersonal force which is not far removed from traditional doctrine. Changing the term "power" to "energy" eliminates the question of how one might pray to a power. Prayer, according to Kaplan, is not petition but the mobilization of our energy to transcend ourselves. Thus, religion is a form of social energy and the divine is a form of ultimate energy, and the one is created to mobilize the other in order to help us be more fully human.

In the journal Kaplan spelled out these religious beliefs. At one point he outlined a conversation he had had:[33]

> Implications of modern conception of God—analogy of lightning and electricity
> a. God manifest everywhere and at all times
> b. God manifest in different degrees in different objects, persons and collectivities
> c. Religion should concern itself primarily with such knowledge of the relation of mind to body as enables one to achieve the supremacy of the spirit.

Again, instead of "God as the Power that . . ." Kaplan considered God to be identified with life-giving energies of the universe, energy that can also be identified with the creative efforts of our mind and our efforts to live life abundantly. Creative energy cannot, of course, be a supreme being. Kaplan explicitly rejected the belief in a supreme being: "I explained . . . that to me, God was not a being, but Reality viewed as an ordered universe. I believe with Spinoza in a *Deus sive Natura*. God was as much more than an idea as the ego is more than an idea representing the sum of psychic forces in the individual. In fact, Deus and Ego are related to each other as the body and apex of a pyramid. In prayer the Ego becomes conscious of God. Through this awareness it sets into operation psychic forces that are otherwise dormant. Hence the value of prayer."[34]

Another journal entry related the concept of divine energy to the individual, but also expressed Kaplan's difficulties in finding the answers to his quest.

> After all the years of thinking on the problem of religion I am still at a loss how to connect the conclusions I hold with the actual situation in which we find ourselves. I know very well what I mean by God. God to me is the process that makes for creativity,

---

33. Kaplan Journal, August 31, 1917. For the full text of the conversation, see chapter two.
34. Kaplan Journal, October 13, 1922.

integration, love and justice. The function of prayer is to render us conscious of that process. I can react with a sense of holiness or momentousness to existence because it is continually being worked upon by this divine process. I am not troubled in the least by the fact that God is not an identifiable being; for that matter neither is my Ego an identifiable being. Nor am I troubled by the fact that God is not perfect. He would have to be static to be perfect. Nothing dynamic can be perfect since to be dynamic implies to be in the state of becoming.

But how shall I relate all these ideas to the problem of Jewish religion? [35]

The journal is a revelation of Kaplan's inner life and of the complexity of his thought and of his own sense of incompleteness. It is also a record of his persistence in bringing his message to the Jewish people. In talking to a reporter, Kaplan once stated that all religious innovation should be measured by the standard of "spiritualized intelligence."[36]

Indeed, "the quest for spiritualized intelligence" might be a fitting epitaph for the life and mind of Mordecai Kaplan.

Mordecai M. Kaplan: His Life

Mordecai M. Kaplan began his life's journey within the confines of a small Lithuanian town on the outskirts of Vilna. He was born on a Friday evening in June 1881. Kaplan's submergence in a total Jewish atmosphere is illustrated by the fact that he knew his day of birth only by the Jewish calendar until he went to the New York Public Library as a young man to look up the corresponding date. Kaplan's family was a traditional one in every respect, and his father, Israel Kaplan, was a learned man. When Kaplan was a young boy he did not see much of his father because Reb Israel was traveling from one yeshivah to another. Israel Kaplan eventually received rabbinical ordination from the greatest rabbis of the day. In 1908, when Mordecai Kaplan was on his honeymoon in Europe, he visited his teacher, Rabbi Reines, was examined by him, and himself received rabbinical ordination.

In 1888, Israel Kaplan came to New York to serve in the Rabbinical Court set up by Rabbi Jacob Joseph, who had been appointed chief rabbi of the city. During that year of the great New York storm, Anna Kaplan and her two children, Mottel (called Maurice, then Max, then Mark, then

35. Kaplan Journal, January 15, 1931.
36. *American Hebrew*, October 14, 1927, 809 (unsigned editorial).

Mordecai) and Sprinza (later called Sophie), stayed with relatives in Paris, where Kaplan remembered playing near the Eiffel Tower, which was in the process of being built for the Paris Exposition of 1889. In July, the family came to New York to join Israel and settled on the Lower East Side. Israel Kaplan soon left the services of the chief rabbi, who had become embroiled in controversy, and served as a rabbinical supervisor at a number of local slaughtering houses.

Kaplan's most important teacher, with respect to his fine grounding in traditional Jewish sources, was his father. After the family came to America, Israel Kaplan was at home and studied Talmud and other rabbinic texts with young Mordecai. This continued on and off for many years. Kaplan also attended a yeshivah (Etz Chayim) and eventually a public school. About half a year before his bar mitzvah, he was admitted to the Jewish Theological Seminary of New York, a school for training rabbis. The Seminary, which was founded by forerunners of the Conservative movement, had a curriculum quite different from that of a regular yeshivah. Students studied Jewish history, books of the Bible, Hebrew grammar, archeology, Talmud, and medieval Jewish philosophy. Kaplan's teachers, most of whom were local rabbis, were modern Orthodox. Although they were observant of the Commandments, all of them had good secular educations. Kaplan briefly lived at the Seminary, which was then located on Lexington Avenue opposite Bloomingdale's Department Store. When the family moved uptown to the East Fifties, Kaplan moved back home. Because the Kaplan household was close to the Seminary, the rabbinical students frequently came to visit on Friday evenings. Old Rabbi Kaplan was a tolerant man, and frequently the boys were entertained by the conversation of a rather heretical Bible scholar named Arnold Ehrlich. Ehrlich visited the Kaplans because he wanted to use Rabbi Israel as a source to find out how certain key biblical words were used in the Talmud. Ehrlich shared his ideas with the family, and thus, at an early age, young Mordecai was exposed to biblical criticism and to the problems raised by a scientific study of the Bible. As a consequence, Rabbi Israel became annoyed with Ehrlich and hired a local savant (a maskil-enlightened Jew) by the name of Joseph Sossnitz to study Maimonides' *Guide for the Perplexed* with Mordecai.

At the same time that Kaplan was attending the Seminary in the afternoon, he was attending the City College of New York in the morning. There he studied the classical curriculum rather than the scientific, and thus had a heavy dose of Greek and Latin. He received his B.A. from City College in 1900, whereupon he began to take courses toward his M.A. at Columbia University. Kaplan's courses were mainly in philosophy and sociology. He studied philosophy with Nicholas Murray Butler, who became the head of the institution; with Frederick Woodbridge, the famous teacher of philosophy;

and with Felix Adler, the founder of the Ethical Culture movement. He studied the classical philosophers, as well as Spinoza and Kant, and wrote his master's thesis on a nineteenth-century utilitarian philosopher named Henry Sidgwick.[37]

Kaplan's philosophy has a strong pragmatic bent, and his thinking tends to be heavily sociological. Later in his life he was always talking about the way religious beliefs functioned and about the primary value of group life insofar as religion was concerned. It seems clear that his sociological bent was heavily influenced by his teacher at Columbia, Professor Franklyn H. Giddings. Kaplan took almost half his courses with Giddings, who was the first appointee in sociology in the United States. Giddings's approach to sociology emphasized a concept that later became central to Kaplan—the idea of like-mindedness, or consciousness of kind, as Giddings called it. Kaplan later referred to this idea as that of the collective mind. He came to believe in group consciousness as a source of values in general and religious matters in particular long before this idea received its classical formulation in the works of Emile Durkheim.

Kaplan's pragmatic emphasis may have been influenced by William James and his essays on pragmatism, which were published in 1907. His pragmatic tendency may also be traced to his involvement with the utilitarian philosophy of the nineteenth century, which looks to the results of an action in order to judge its ethical quality, and to the philosophy of Felix Adler. Although Kaplan had contempt for Adler because he had left the Jewish fold when he established Ethical Culture, he was drawn to Adler's thought, both in the classroom and through his publications. Adler emphasized a religion of obligation that is realistically related to the experience of those professing it. More than anything else, he felt that religion had to be in tune with the truths about the world as established by science. Adler's ethics centered on the notion of obligation or duty, which he related to society as viewed organically. According to this view, if each person is a part of a "living organism," he or she must be viewed as indispensable and irreplaceable and ought to be treated as such. Society viewed organically came to play a central role in Kaplan's thinking.

At the same time that Kaplan was studying at Columbia, he was also serving in one of the better-known Orthodox congregations in the city. He

---

37. Kaplan's master's thesis may be found at Columbia University. It runs to some ninety pages and is written in Kaplan's hand. It is entitled "The Ethical System of Henry Sidgwick" and was submitted on February 28, 1902.

The course with Felix Adler was entitled "Political and Social Ethics." Adler's lecture notes for this course are to be found among the Adler papers at Columbia University, Box 100–1900 E–1904 B, "Lectures for a Course at Columbia." The lecture notes are typed and dated.

came to Kehilath Jeshurun in 1903 and was appointed "minister" because at this point he lacked traditional rabbinical ordination. He had been graduated from the Seminary in 1902, on the eve of its takeover by Solomon Schechter. Kaplan was the first Seminary graduate to take a large Orthodox pulpit in New York City, and some of the more extreme among the Orthodox protested strongly. A warning was issued by a group of rabbis against any congregation taking Seminary graduates. Thus Kaplan, through no fault of his own, became the center of controversy within a short time after he was ordained. He continued to be controversial throughout his life. Solomon Schechter, who liked Kaplan, is known to have said that Kaplan gained more from his own *apikorsut* (heresy) than anyone else.[38]

At this point in his life (in his early twenties), Kaplan's views were virtually unknown. His private diaries and papers reveal that he was tortured within because his beliefs about the nature of religion and of Judaism conflicted with his duties as the leader of an Orthodox congregation. The people he served, for their part, were very happy with him, and his salary increased significantly during his relatively short stay, from 1903 to 1909. He was, however, unhappy, and looked for a way out of the rabbinate. He considered, at one time or another, a career as a lawyer, going into business with his brothers-in-law, or going into insurance. Thus, in 1909, when he was invited by Solomon Schechter to become principal of the newly created Teachers Institute of the Jewish Theological Seminary, he jumped at the chance.

The Seminary had instituted courses for teachers soon after Schechter's arrival. The first courses failed, however, because they were offered at the Seminary building, which by then was located on 123rd Street, far from the centers of Jewish population. The Teachers Institute (TI), which began in 1909 with a grant from Jacob Schiff, was directed by Kaplan from its inception until his retirement as dean in the 1940s, and until 1929 was located downtown at the Hebrew Technical Institute, in what is now called the East Village. Although students were few and standards were low at the beginning, Kaplan quickly became more selective as elementary Hebrew education improved.

Kaplan's contribution to Jewish education in America is immense. He was responsible for bringing into the field many people who later became the central pillars of American Jewish education. Men such as Alexander Dushkin came to serve the Jewish community because of Kaplan, and all those who held significant positions in Jewish education during the first half of the twentieth century were students of Kaplan, including Leo Honor, Samuel Dinin, Isaac Berkson, and Israel Chipkin. All of these men are mentioned in the journal many times.

---

38. Kaplan Journal, December 13, 1928.

During the first decade of his tenure as principal of the TI, Kaplan created a curriculum which was taught largely in Hebrew by outstanding Hebraists (e.g., Zvi Scharfstein, Morris Levine, and Leo Honor, who all joined the TI in 1917; Hillel Bavli, who joined it in the early 1920s; and Abraham Halkin, who joined it in 1929). Throughout this period, Kaplan was very active in the community at large. He served the New York *kehillah* (organized Jewish community) as a trustee of the Bureau of Jewish Education and worked closely with Samson Benderly, who was the director of the Bureau. He was quite active at the Y.M.H.A. on 92nd Street, and for a number of years he spoke regularly at the Y on Friday evenings and organized the religious activities. He strongly supported new educational ventures, such as the School for Jewish Communal Work and the Central Jewish Institute, an innovative educational institution located on Manhattan's Upper East Side. He also spoke widely before synagogues and organizations in the city and traveled to lecture to the Menorah Societies at Harvard and Yale. The opening selections in this volume are actually notes that Kaplan made in preparing these speeches.

At the point that the journal begins, Kaplan, without a congregation, was occupied with his work at the Teachers Institute and the Rabbinical School. His philosophy was just in the process of formulation. The notes for the speeches are actually the earliest formulation of his religious thought.

In his lectures, and even more so in his published articles, Kaplan's growing radicalism was becoming apparent. At a rather early point (1914) he made it clear that he accepted the major assumptions of biblical criticism, although he believed strongly that the scientific study of the Torah need not undermine its place in Jewish life: "Traditional belief as to the origin of the Torah is not the sole support of its supremacy. If this is found to give way, the one derived from its having rendered Israel the instrument of divine revelation is no less effective in maintaining its pre-eminence."[39] In 1915 and 1916 he published a series of articles in *The Menorah Journal* that clearly articulated his belief that religion in general and Judaism in particular could be understood best by the use of the new social sciences, especially sociology. He emphasized that religion must be linked to experience; otherwise it would wither and die. In his words, "A condition indispensable to a religion being an active force in human life is that it speaks to men in terms of their own experience," or, "To those who want to find in Judaism a way of life and a higher ambition, it must address itself in the language of concrete and verifiable experience."[40] Because experience changed, religion changed, and it

---

39. Mordecai M. Kaplan, "The Supremacy of the Torah," in *Students' Annual of the Jewish Theological Seminary*, 1914, 186.

40. Mordecai M. Kaplan, "What Judaism Is Not," *Menorah Journal* 1, no. 4 (October 1915): 215.

was important, Kaplan believed, to find ways in which beliefs and rituals could function today as they did in the past. To do this might mean changing a ritual, dropping it completely, or substituting something new.

It is important to note that Kaplan rejected Reform Judaism with as much vehemence as he rejected Orthodox Judaism. More than anything else, he perceived Reform as a radical break with the Jewish past. He decried its lack of appreciation (during this period) for ritual of any kind and its militant stand against Jewish nationalism. From his earliest years, Kaplan believed strongly in the Zionist cause. His growing sociological sophistication led him to have a strong feeling for the importance of group life. Judaism could not survive, he believed, if it was perceived merely as a set of beliefs. Rather, Judaism must be understood as the life energy of the Jewish people. When he looked around him, he perceived that this group energy was at an all-time low. Something new had to be done to foster group life in a way that would make sense in twentieth-century America. Kaplan's work at the Y.M.H.A. gave him the beginning of an answer. He saw the interest of the young men in all manner of activities, including sports, dramatics, and the arts. If only a religious dimension could be added to all this activity, he felt, perhaps Jewish life could be renewed.

The opportunity came in 1915 when a group of men who wanted to organize a new synagogue on the Upper West Side approached Kaplan for help. He told them of his ideas for a synagogue that would be the center of life for the community that it served. The founders were supportive, and Kaplan joined their initiative. A fine building was constructed which had not only a synagogue but facilities for sports and all other kinds of social activities. The synagogue was to be known as the Jewish Center. The group wanted Kaplan as their rabbi, and he finally agreed, although he warned them that he was not Orthodox and did not follow strict Jewish law. He stipulated that his salary be given to the Teachers Institute so that he could be free to express his ideas. His service at the center lasted until 1921, but the concept of the Jewish Center inspired a great many followers from that time on. There is much material in the journal about his work with the center. This material is instructive regarding the tensions that inevitably exist between rabbis and their congregations.

While Kaplan was at the center, he continued his work at the Seminary. Not only was he principal of the TI (his title was later changed to dean), but he also taught in the Rabbinical School. He began teaching at the Rabbinical School in 1910 and continued there until his retirement in 1963. Although officially he was supposed to deal with homiletics, or the art of giving a sermon, it was apparent to him from the beginning that he must deal not only with the mechanics of the sermon but also with the content. All of Kaplan's courses at the Rabbinical School, whether they dealt with philosophy, midrash, or homiletics, attempted to focus on the fundamental religious questions that face the modern Jew. Not every student was willing to follow in his philosophy, but every rabbi who studied with him was grateful for having been exposed to Kaplan and for Kaplan's having asked the right questions. Among his students may be counted all of the leaders of twentieth-century Conservative Judaism, including Louis Finkelstein, Max Kadushin, Simon Greenberg, Max Arzt, Robert Gordis, and Solomon Grayzel. All of these men, and many others, were significantly influenced by Mordecai Kaplan, and all are discussed in the journal.

Kaplan's energy always overflowed the classroom. He was forever forming one group or another which would meet at his house and devote itself to the study of fundamental questions. In 1913 a group of rabbinical students met with Kaplan and studied the philosophies of William James and Josiah Royce; another such group was formed in 1915. A few years later (1919–20) Kaplan organized his rabbinical colleagues into the Society for Jewish Renascence. This group was to meet regularly, with the following aims: "To interpret, in terms of present-day thought, the concepts of Judaism and the content of the authoritative Jewish literature. To revitalize the traditional Jewish practices, both within and without the synagogue, so as to make them the expression of the living spiritual experience of our people at the present time. . . ."[41] Among the members of this organization were Louis Finkelstein, Herman Rubenovitz, Solomon Goldman, Joshua Bloch, Jacob Kohn, and Israel Unterberg. At the same time that Kaplan was organizing the Society for Jewish Renascence, he published an article in *The Menorah Journal* that was highly critical of the Orthodox. "Nothing can be more repugnant to the thinking man of today," he wrote, "than the fundamental doctrine of Orthodoxy, which is that tradition is infallible."[42] The article, entitled "A Program for the Reconstruction of Judaism," stated that the only way to revitalize Judaism was to dispense with mythological ideas about God, to create a dynamic code that would guide Jewish behavior, and to establish a center for Jewish culture in the Land of Israel. The key to the whole program was a new way of thinking that Kaplan characterized as realistic rather than ideological, pragmatic rather than tradition-oriented.

The article was widely discussed throughout the Jewish community. Some of the more traditional Jewish Center leaders began to feel that they could no longer support Kaplan as their rabbi. After many meetings and negotiations, Kaplan, along with a sizable group of congregants, decided to leave the center. They established a new organization which would be a more

---

41. *The Society for Jewish Renascence*, n.d., p. 4.
42. Mordecai M. Kaplan, "A Program for the Reconstruction of Judaism," *Menorah Journal* 6, no. 4 (August 1920).

direct reflection of Kaplan's beliefs and philosophy. The new group, called the Society for the Advancement of Judaism (SAJ), eventually occupied a converted brownstone on West 86th Street in New York City, a block from the Jewish Center.

The SAJ allowed Kaplan free rein to explore his ideas and to implement his philosophy. At times he was boldly innovative in terms of changing long-established rituals. In 1922, for example, soon after the SAJ was established, he held a bat mitzvah ceremony for his eldest daughter, Judith. Kaplan always said that he had four good reasons for initiating the bat mitzvah ritual in the United States—his four daughters. It took a long time for American Jews to catch up with him in terms of bringing women into full equality with respect to ritual. Had he lived and written later, he would probably have modified his style and theological terminology to reflect his commitment to the equality of women. We would certainly expect there would be much material in the journal about this momentous event. Kaplan, however, mentions it in only a few lines, intending to discuss it at greater length, but never does. My sense from his remarks and from the fact that Judith was told about it only a few weeks before is that Kaplan did not actually give the whole matter much thought, but acted on a whim of the moment.

The other important innovation from this early period occurred in 1925, when Kaplan substituted Psalm 130 for the words of the Kol Nidre prayer.[43] The tune was kept. Both of these innovations beautifully illustrate Kaplan's desire not just to drop outmoded forms but to change them so that they become meaningful and functional.

Kaplan's growing radicalism made some of his Seminary colleagues uncomfortable. There is evidence that some supporters of the Seminary threatened to withdraw their funds unless Kaplan was terminated as a professor in the Rabbinical School and as head of the Teachers Institute. For his part, Kaplan was increasingly unhappy with the lack of support for his ideas, from either colleagues or the administration. Thus, when Stephen Wise invited him to the newly organized Jewish Institute of Religion, he was very tempted to leave the Seminary. Wise extended that invitation a number of times. In 1927, Kaplan finally accepted and tendered his resignation. There was, however, such a great uproar from the rabbinical students and from the Seminary alumni that Kaplan decided to stay.

Throughout the 1920s, Kaplan continued his activities at a vigorous pace. His diaries and journals reflect the fact that he traveled widely to speak to Jewish groups, both within congregations and at colleges and universities. Before the age of easy air travel, Kaplan not only made frequent trips on the

---

43. The Kol Nidre was restored a number of years later.

East Coast but also traveled to the South and the Middle West. In addition to his congregation, his teaching, his family life, and his speaking, he began to devote himself seriously to his writing. In 1926, he recorded his despair that he had reached the age of forty-five and had not yet produced a major published work.

By 1933, however, he had written what was destined to become a classic in American Jewish thought. He won a prize from the Rosenwald Fund for his manuscript and used the money to help defray the cost of publishing *Judaism as a Civilization.* The book was published in May 1934, when Kaplan was fifty-three years old. Kaplan's views were well known before the publication of his book, but here was a forceful and complete statement of his ideas on a wide variety of subjects, and it raised him in the minds of many to the first rank among Jewish ideologues.

As a direct result of his book and the attention it received, Kaplan and his followers launched a biweekly publication on topics of current interest to the Jewish community to serve as a forum for Kaplan to disseminate his views. The first number of the *Reconstructionist* appeared in January 1935 under Kaplan's editorship, with the aid of Ira Eisenstein. Eisenstein had been a student of Kaplan at the Seminary, became his assistant at the SAJ, and married Kaplan's daughter Judith. He continued to be Kaplan's most loyal disciple and assumed a primary role in the Reconstructionist movement.

During most of his life, Kaplan resisted the temptation to establish Reconstructionism as a separate denomination. He believed strongly that as a school of thought the movement could have significant impact on all types of Jews. He did not want to leave the Seminary, nor did he want to contribute to divisiveness within the Jewish community. Kaplan's overriding concern was always the creation of greater unity among the Jewish people. His ideas, however, have consistently drawn significant criticism. Indeed, one might say that his most important contribution has been to force others into defining their positions more precisely because they could not ignore the issues he raised.

Throughout his years at the SAJ, Kaplan was impatient with traditional rituals and prayers. He felt that the prayers rarely reflected the deepest concerns of modern Jews, and he was constantly trying new approaches. One lasting manifestation of his willingness to experiment is the Passover Haggadah that he, Rabbi Ira Eisenstein, and Rabbi Eugene Kohn published in 1941. It is hard for us in this age of freedom seders and feminist Haggadahs to realize the impact of the Reconstructionist Haggadah. Many were shocked because of what was left out (the Ten Plagues), because of what was changed (the language of the kiddush, where references to chosenness were removed), and because of what was inserted (historical portions on Moses, which are not in the traditional Haggadah). Kaplan's colleagues at the Seminary were outraged and wrote him a ten-page letter detailing their opposition.

Kaplan was never deterred by opposition. The criticisms of the New Haggadah did not stop him from preparing the Reconstructionist Sabbath Prayer Book, which was published by the Reconstructionist Foundation in 1945. The introduction to the prayer book details the many beliefs of traditional Judaism that Kaplan felt were not accepted within the Jewish community. Again he and his disciples dropped, changed, and added material, so that a new prayer book was created which reflected what Jews actually believed. The opposition to the Sabbath Prayer Book was loud and clear from many quarters. The senior professors at the Seminary (Professors Ginzberg, Marx, and Lieberman) criticized him strongly and publicly. In June 1945, the Union of Orthodox Rabbis of the United States and Canada issued a ban (*herem*) against Kaplan because of the prayer book. The *New York Times* recorded that his prayer book was burned during the *herem* ceremony which was held at the Hotel McAlpin in New York City.

Although Kaplan retired as dean of the Teachers Institute in 1945, he continued to teach at the Rabbinical School until 1963. As the years passed, long past the point when most people begin to think about retirement, his energy seemed almost to increase. In the 1940s, he made a number of trips to the West Coast and was instrumental in both the ideological groundwork and the actual setting up of the University of Judaism in Los Angeles. He continued to be active within the Conservative movement, hoping that Reconstructionism would be officially declared as the left wing of Conservative Judaism.

In 1949, at the age of sixty-seven, Kaplan published *The Future of the American Jew*. This large work again stated his basic approach, but more importantly, it spelled out his mature thinking on the chosen-people idea, the nature of religion, Jewish law, the status of women in Jewish law, and the way in which a reconstructed Judaism understood the basic moral and spiritual values. The 1950s and 1960s were years of great creativity for Kaplan. He continued to publish frequently and produced important works on Zionism, Judaism in the modern age, and ethical nationhood. His last book, *If Not Now, When?*, which is actually a record of his conversations with the theologian and novelist Arthur A. Cohen, appeared in 1973, when Kaplan was ninety-two years old.

Kaplan's goal of renewal led directly to the founding of the Reconstructionist movement. In Kaplan's determination not to be divisive, the movement remained loosely organized. The Society for the Advancement of Judaism was not only a congregation but also the focus for groups or even congregations who wanted to affiliate with the Reconstructionist philosophy. In 1954, the Federation of Reconstructionist Congregations and Havurot was organized. As the years passed, the number of affiliates grew, but it was not until the late 1960s that the movement actually became a separate denomination.

There were always people within the movement, particularly Rabbi Eisenstein, who wanted a separate and distinct identity rather than a group united by an ideology. In 1968, the Reconstructionist Rabbinical College opened its doors, with Ira Eisenstein as its first president. The school was located in Philadelphia, and Kaplan, although in his late eighties, traveled regularly to lecture there. The structure of the curriculum reflected Kaplan's approach, with each successive year devoted to a different phase of Jewish civilization (biblical civilization, the first year; rabbinic, the second; and so on). The school also reflected Kaplan's commitment to the world of secular learning. Each graduate was required to have a graduate degree from a secular institution. Many of the students took degrees in religion, education, or social work, particularly at Temple University.

A rabbinical school meant a new denomination. The divisiveness associated with a new stream in Jewish life was a stumbling block to Kaplan, but the success of the venture was not. The school has flourished, and in 1982 moved to a beautiful campus on the outskirts of Philadelphia in Wyncote, Pennsylvania. The Jewish Reconstructionist Federation likewise grew apace and in 1998 there were some ninety groups (fifty thousand people) affiliated with the movement. One very striking feature of these institutions is that the leadership is young. It should not surprise us that innovative and experimental modes continue to be the hallmark of Reconstructionism. The ideology of Mordecai M. Kaplan has not yet become a tradition in need of reconstruction.

In a sense, Mordecai Kaplan's life embodies the American Jewish experience of the first half of the twentieth century. The fact that he died in 1983 at the age of 102 means that, in a literal sense, he lived through the whole saga of the American Jew in our times. Arriving here as a boy, growing up in New York City, becoming thoroughly Americanized, he struggled to find ways of making Judaism compatible with the American experience and the modern temper. As rabbi, teacher, writer, and lecturer, he spearheaded the founding of new institutions and stimulated the reconsideration of long held assumptions.

1

February 24, 1913–May 27, 1915

Outline of Lectures That Were Delivered before the Harvard Menorah Society[1]

The Essence of Religion—A Talk at Harvard

MONDAY, FEBRUARY 24, 1913

Religion is primarily a social phenomenon. To grasp its reality, to observe its workings and to further its growth we must study its functioning in some social group. The individual and his development or perfection may constitute the sole aim of religion, but the fact and substance of religion cannot exist completely and exhaustively in an individual. We may for purposes of discussion consider the religion of an individual human being; we may be interested in the logical and psychological elements implied in it, but when we do that, we are arbitrarily cutting a piece out of the reality, and not studying the reality as a whole. We are in the habit of associating concreteness with individual things rather than with groups. The particular fox-terrier that happens to be our house-pet appears more concrete than the special dog.

But while this is the case with things that are objects of the senses, the very opposite holds good of matters that are the objects of the mind. Whatever concreteness these latter may be said to possess, depends not upon how intensively they exist in this or that individual mind, but upon how extensively they are distributed. Universality is a guarantee of the concreteness of an object of the mind, or perhaps identical with it, as individuality is a mark of concreteness of an object of the senses. A mental

---

1. This title is Kaplan's and is in the journal itself. All other titles were inserted by the editor.

The first page of Kaplan's journal.

object begins to gather reality or concreteness the moment it establishes a relation between two minds. Religion, like government and language, cannot even begin to be real with less than two minds. The two minds must, of course, be coordinate, in the sense that whatever the relation established between them be, it could, logically speaking, be reversed. Religion does not begin when an individual human being enters into relationship with a god; there must first be at least two human beings.

Religion as a social phenomenon is a form of the living energy which exists in all social groups. Whether nominalists be in the right with their view of general names as merely collective nouns, representing no reality other than that of the individuals included within those names, or the realists be right with their notion whereby they affirm a reality behind each collective noun, is immaterial in a discussion of the life of society. When we speak of society we do not mean simply a number of individuals that have some attributes in common as we do when we make mention of a term that denotes a species, but we imply a certain real and definite energy which is generated by the action and reaction of various individuals upon one another. Social life is not merely a metaphorical expression. It denotes a form of life no less real than that of any individual organism. This living energy which we term social life, manifests itself in various institutions, social habits, customs, standards, beliefs, and values.

Religion and Social Life

THURSDAY, FEBRUARY 27, 1913

But the main idea in all this discussion is that behind all moral and spiritual values there is a definite phase of social life, which for want of a better term, we designate religion.

SUNDAY, MARCH 2, 1913

If we will learn to identify religion as that form of social energy which is responsible for moral and spiritual values, we will abandon all attempts to formulate a definition of religion. What we may do is to look for its expressions and manifestations both in the individual and in society, but as for the substance of religion itself, nothing less than the exercise of intuitive sympathy will enable us to recognize it. We must ourselves share in that social experience which leads to the articulation of values that claim to derive their sanction from a source outside of the social unit, if we wish to realize what religion really is. As a phase of social experience, religion is a living thing.

The Essence of Judaism

MONDAY, MARCH 3, 1913

In accordance with this view, the permanence of Judaism does not necessarily involve the permanence of its moral and spiritual values, but the continued identity of the ethno or socio-psychical energy capable of producing such values. This ethno or socio-psychical energy is an ultimate fact and need not furnish any justification for its existence. . . .

Judaism cannot exist without the Jewish people. This which we have shown to be the case from a logical point of view has been quite amply demonstrated by the failure of the Reform movement. Not even the best friends of the movement can gainsay the fact that there is a marked want of content, a painful vacuity to Reform Judaism. The occasional relapses into a longing for the traditional ceremonies are symptomatic of this same feeling of hollowness. But no haphazard experimenting will lead to any permanent adjustment of Judaism to the modern environment. The work of adjustment must be begun all over again, in accordance with a method growing out of a clear understanding of the nature and substance of Judaism.

God as the Power that Makes for Righteousness

WEDNESDAY, MARCH 5, 1913

What Arnold says of God's will, if changed around, [might] serve as a definition of Judaism. "God," he says, "is the Power that makes for righteousness—not ourselves." "Judaism," we may say, "is the power in ourselves that makes for righteousness."[2]

---

2. For the elaboration of this concept in Matthew Arnold see *Literature and Dogma: An Essay Toward a Better Understanding of the Bible* (New York: Macmillan, 1924). For an elaboration in Kaplan, see *The Meaning of God in Modern Jewish Religion*, introduction by Mel Scult (Detroit: Wayne State University Press, 1994).

THURSDAY, MARCH 6, 1913

By the phrase "makes for righteousness" we should understand that Judaism has the tendency to evolve those moral and spiritual values which have endowed it with remarkable power of resistance.

Israel—The Chosen People

MONDAY, MARCH 10, 1913

The one evaluation which satisfies all these conditions has been that Israel is God's chosen people. Historically, it was this conviction [i.e., that Israel is God's Chosen People] which exercised incalculable cohesive influence upon the Jewish people. It was solely by force of this belief which had been instilled and drilled into them by the prophets that they were able to meet the shock of exile and reorganize as a people. Of course, this belief was bound to become more deeply rooted the moment it exhibited its efficacy, and the age of the second commonwealth is marked by a more detailed and intensive application of this principle to the entire life of the people than there was a call for at any time during the period of the first commonwealth. Ever since then, throughout the centuries of the Diaspora, their conviction and its logical accompaniment that God would restore Israel to its own has been responsible for the spirit of martyrdom which the most humble was ready to display when called upon to abandon Judaism. . . .

The next step is to determine whether the Jewish people regarded itself as chosen in and for itself apart from any further consideration or because of its actual or possible conformity to a type which it considered worthy. In other words, did this belief amount to a sort of unreasoned national conceit, or did it imply the contemplation of a general type which it was approaching or at which it had arrived? Did the Jewish people rise to the contemplation of an abstract type apart from its actual and present self? If there can not be the slightest doubt that this was the case, since the very chequered nature of its career was bound to impress upon it the realization of departure from the type, all that we have to do in order to get at the general value from which all the moral and spiritual values were derived, is to define the type of society which the Jewish people believed itself destined to realize. What that type has been may be stated as follows: a society or social group with all the opportunities for social and economic interaction that exists in a geographic group, knowing itself as constituting a society not by reason of propinquity, but by reason of God's commanding or sanctioning those of its laws which make for its life and well-being. . . .

Judaism thus assigned to God an entirely different function from that which any other of the ancient peoples assigned to their deities. While the deities of the nations served to furnish the sanction to the moral and spiritual laws, they never were regarded as the sole organizing principles or factors of social groups. The social group was a given fact. There was no further analysis of the social organism. This was in line with such a conception as that each social group was autochthonous. This new function which was assigned to the God of Israel was at the root of the strongly felt yet vaguely grasped truth that the God of Israel was *unique*. It was not his oneness that our fathers were first impressed by, but his uniqueness. In fact that declaration of Judaism which we have taken to be the slogan of monotheism was originally the war cry of the uniqueness of God. *u-mi khe-amkha ke-Yisra'el goy ehad ba-arets* [Heb. 2 Samuel 7:23 "And who is like your people Israel, a unique nation on earth"].

God the Bond of Unity

SUNDAY, MARCH 16, 1913

The majesty of "thus saith the Lord" is never dimmed in the slightest by the shadow of a suspicion that we are dealing with a cant phrase. Since God was Himself the bond of unity and stability of His people, the laws that made for justice and order were the very expression of His nature, the very manifestation of His character, and the sole means by which He served as the uniting force. Every violation of those laws was, therefore, practically a denial of His power and a challenge of His very character. Hence oppression and injustice were for the first time in human history denounced in accents which bespoke a conception of God that was destined to become the basis of true religion for mankind.

Democracy Is a Threat

SUNDAY, MARCH 30, 1913

The problem of Judaism is inherently the problem of how it is to meet modern life. No solution of this problem can be considered complete which fails to take into account the two elements that contribute to modern life, and which are bound to be elements of danger to Judaism so long as they are ignored. These are democracy and science. Democracy threatens the integrity of the Jewish social group. It tends to disintegrate the very social organization which is the bearer of Judaism and without which Judaism is inconceivable. This effect democracy exercises not by means of its doctrine of liberty or equality but by means of its fundamental principle of government, that the unit of political life is the individual, and that a nation is solely a group of individuals and not a group of groups. . . . In the face of this tendency Judaism will only be able to hold its own by creating social institutions which, while not interfering with the working out of that principle of individualism in the domain of political and economic life, will prevent it from encroaching upon the domain of the religious life.

God's Transcendence

MARCH 30, 1913

In common with other religions, Judaism acknowledged the transcendent nature of its God. But in contra-distinction to other religions, it gave new direction and significance to the doctrine of God's immanence. This it did, as we have seen, by consciously accepting God as the organizing factor of the social life. But while Judaism's characteristic contribution to religion consisted in the doctrine of divine immanence, it did not abandon that which was fundamental to and in common with other religions—the transcendence of God. The God of Judaism is one who is above as well as in the world. But His being a God in the world was due to His being a God above the world. The moment God is merely identified with the world and conceived as being immanent but not transcendent, His divinity is denied and He is dissolved into the world. This is the atheism and pantheism which religion so vigorously contends against. It will only verify the analysis we have suggested of the true character of the moral values and of the "ought" as being derivative from a source of sanctions beyond the social group to which these values are applied, to learn that in a system of logical Pantheism such as Spinoza's there is no room for any "ought." That which is is what ought to be. Religion, while not always clearly recognizing this danger in Pantheism, instinctively felt it and has insisted upon the transcendent phase of God being brought into prominence.

Religion and the Pragmatic Method

JANUARY 13, 1914

Perhaps the term that will best describe the method of interpretation that I am attempting to work out is pragmatic in contrast with the allegorical method on the one hand and the historical on the other. The historical method of interpretation proposes to reconstruct the meaning which was consciously in the mind of the writer; the allegorical method ascribes to the writer meanings which the reader arbitrarily wishes to find in the words of the writer; the pragmatic method[3] is concerned with the effect

---

3. Kaplan liked to call himself a functionalist rather than a pragmatist. On the pragmatic and Kaplan see *Judaism Faces the Twentieth Century: A Biography of Mordecai Kaplan* (Detroit:

that the words of the writer had on the inner life of the people or the way what he said worked. . . . The pragmatic method however, seeks to identify the direction which the thought first formulated by the writer has taken. It tries to get not at static truth but dynamic truth. It is this method alone which is of actual aid in the religious life of a people or group.

Zionism and Religion

SUNDAY, JANUARY 25, 1914

Abstract of lecture delivered this morning before the Jewish Institute at Kessler's Theatre. Subject: What has Zionism done for Judaism?. . . .

. . . there is one indispensable condition which must be fulfilled for religion to be at all possible, and it is this: that religion can only exist in a social group the members of which possess something else in common besides religion. It may be race-consciousness, a common history, a common national life, economic interests in common, or a culture to which all are attached and from which they draw their spiritual nourishment. . . .

And insofar as Zionism has been seeking to create this something [in common] it has been preparing the ground for religion and thus assuring a future to Judaism. With the fostering of an element like common nationality in Palestine, or of a common culture on the basis of the Hebrew language, the very ground and cause for the question why remain a Jew will be removed.

A Definition of Judaism

JANUARY 26, 1914

[We must behold Judaism] . . . not in any one doctrine or sum of doctrines but in the innermost life force which has vitalized the Jewish people and has made it the most self-conscious group of any upon the face of the earth.

A Club at the Seminary Discusses Religion

JANUARY 27, 1914

A number of students of the Senior Class at the Seminary have, at my suggestion, constituted themselves into a Homiletic Club. The experiment of my meeting them at the Seminary on Sunday nights did not prove convenient to most of them. They met, therefore, at my house last night

---

Wayne State University Press, 1993), 145–46. I do think that James was more important than Dewey. In rabbinical student discussion groups in his home at this time Kaplan read James.

at 10:15 P.M.[4] Present were Burstein[5], Sachs,[6] Feinberg,[7] Bosniak,[8] Alstat,[9] Halpern,[10] Teller,[11] Lebendiger[12] and Kohn[13].

In the course of my remarks I had occasion to refer to the absence in most of us of inner experiences that we could identify as religious. It would certainly be worthwhile to account for this remarkable change in the psychology of the Jew who from being a fervent seeker after God has become blase with regard to matters spiritual. Bosniak suggested that it might be a reaction to the overtime religiosity of our parents. I thought that this phenomenon might be more correctly described as one of psychical exhaustion, analogous to what occurs in the case of a parent of great genius giving birth to a mental defective. But the main reason undoubtedly appears to be the growth in the scientific conception of existence which gradually displaces the anthropomorphic conception of the Deity. Much if not most of the vigor possessed by the religious thought of our ancestors was due to their imagining God in terms of human experience. . . . In writing this I am reminded of James' treatment of this subject in his book on Pluralism[14] which is the best kind of introduction to Bergsonism. If his contention is correct—and I am very much inclined to believe it is—we will fare far better as far as the cultivation of the

---

4. Kaplan organized such student groups throughout his career. He continuously invited students to his house for additional study.

5. Abraham Burstein (1893–1966), rabbi; ordained JTS; editor, *The Jewish Outlook*. Here and below, *The Concise Dictionary of American Jewish Biography*, edited by Jacob R. Marcus and Judith Daniels (Brooklyn: Carlson Publishing, 1994) has been enormously useful in annotating Kaplan's diary.

6. Samuel Sachs (1893–?), graduate of JTS and Columbia; rabbi, Brooklyn, Portland, Ore., and Toronto; editor, *The Scribe*.

7. Louis Feinberg (1887–1949), rabbi; Yiddish and English author; active in the Zionist Organization of America (ZOA).

8. Jacob Bosniak (1887–1963), rabbi, Brooklyn; graduated Columbia; author; U.S. Marine Hospital chaplain.

9. Philip Alstat (1894–1976), rabbi; born in Lithuania; came to the United States in 1898; attended City College of New York and JTS, and received an MA from Columbia. For many years Alstat lived at the seminary and counseled rabbinical students.

10. Abraham Halpern (1891–1938), rabbi, St. Louis, congregation B'nai Amoona; active in the Zionist Organization of America; president, Midwest Rabbinical Assembly.

11. Morris Teller (1890–1966), attended Dropsie College and University of Chicago; rabbi, Chicago; contributing editor, *Jewish Monitor*.

12. Israel Lebendiger (1886–?), ordained JTS; prison chaplain, Woodbourne Correctional Facility , New York; officer, United Synagogue of America.

13. Eugene Kohn (1887–1977), rabbi; Reconstructionist and close disciple of Mordecai Kaplan; edited Reconstructionist prayer books with Kaplan and Rabbi Ira Eisenstein; rabbi in Baltimore and brother of Jacob Kohn, also a seminary graduate.

14. See William James, *A Pluralistic Universe: Hibbert Lectures at Manchester College on the Present Situation in Philosophy* (London: Longmans, Green, 1909).

religious sense is concerned not by thinking with Plato ideaward but with Bergson lifeward.

Seeking God

Februrary 11, 1914

The fundamental principle of religion in the future will be that the highest aim of each human life is to seek God, that is, to search among the various psychical experiences lived through, [for] that one which gives us an immediate awareness of God. . . . if any experience in the intellectual, emotional, or will aspect of our inner life is thought by us as furnishing us with the awareness of the Divine Presence we are in search of, it must lead to right conduct, to the exercise of justice and love. If it fails to do that, we merely delude ourselves in believing that it is God we are aware of. All that we are then aware of is a purely individual mental state.

Talking about a Religion of Experience at Yale

Thursday, February 12, 1914

On Sunday I went to New Haven to speak before the Yale Menorah Society[15] in the evening. I took as my subject "The Nature of the Present Crisis in Judaism." I defined it as being due to social and intellectual causes, both of which correspond respectively to the questions "Why" and "How" to Be a Jew? I was more definite this time, however, in reference to the problem "How to be a Jew?" by pointing out that the main difficulty is due to the elimination of the concept of the miraculous from our thinking. As the social condition for the maintenance of religion is the existence of a group that possessed something in common besides religion, so the indispensable intellectual condition is that the religion address itself to the actual experiences of the individuals in that group using the term experience in the widest sense of mental content. Intellectually, therefore, much of the content of Judaism violates this condition as far as the present generation is concerned. The solution, therefore, is not in merely setting the hands of the clock to correspond with the time indicated by other clocks, nor in forcibly getting the pendulum in motion but in examining the inner workings of Israel's history and spirit. In revaluation and interpretation of the historic Jewish values we shall meet with the solution of the intellectual problem in Judaism.

---

15. American campus organization and periodical begun by Henry Hurwitz. The Menorah Society sought to develop a positive intellectual relationship to Jewish tradition and belief. For Jews at Yale, see Dan Oren, *Joining the Club: A History of the Jews and Yale* (New Haven, Conn.: Yale University Press, 1985).

Two of the fellows met me when I got off the train at 7 o'clock and took me to the Taft Hotel near the college, and kept me company till the time scheduled for me to speak. They told me of the various difficulties they encountered before organizing, this being the first year of their organization. The main obstacle in the way seemed to have been the feeling that the segregation of the Jewish fellows which the organization would lead to, was not in keeping with the democratic traditions of which the college boasted. This is certainly an interesting fact that throws light upon the effect of the democratic spirit upon the social life of the Jews. The truth seems to be that if the so called democratic spirit at Yale had been more than a hollow pretension, as I inferred from the incidental remarks of the men, there would not even now have been a Menorah Society there. An argument which for a long time carried weight with most of the men against organizing a Menorah Society was advanced by a Jewish young man who happened to be on the editorial board of the college paper. He told of a cartoon that was sent into the paper immediately after a number of the Jewish boys had met a year or two ago to consider the proposition of organizing a Menorah Society. He naturally opposed the insertion of that lampoon into the paper, but in doing so he had to encounter the ill will of all the rest on the board of editors. Another interesting fact with regard to these men is that in accordance with their own assertions, it was Zionism that has swung them over to taking an interest in Judaism, and the political aspect of it even more so than the cultural, because of its more tangible form. The indebtedness of the revival in things Jewish to Zionism was also brought home to me the day after when I met the Jewish Harvard students.

Talking to the Mothers about Jewish Mothers

SATURDAY, FEBRUARY 14, 1914

This evening I addressed a mothers' meeting at 40 West 115 St . . . the Branch of the Uptown Talmud Torah. I introduced my remarks by referring to a cuckoo song which the children sang at the opening of the exercises as symbolic of Jewish effort at revival at a time that is so cold and discouraging as ours is. It is like the song of a bird that lost its way into a land where winter was still in its full force. I then contrasted the spirit of the meeting with the one of the Council of Jewish Women of Philadelphia. In the latter, they had reports of the great work they were doing on behalf of the poor children in the crowded sections and on behalf of immigrant girls in the way of religious education. Still as far as they themselves were concerned they wanted me to prove the value of religious education for their own children. At this meeting, however, not one of those present doubted for a moment the importance of religious education for their own children.

I commended Dushkin[16] for calling upon the mothers to help him in his task, because he was in keeping with the various teachings of the rabbis which emphasize the importance of the part that the woman takes in the religious life of the people. This attitude towards woman is in recognition of the truth that what a mother wants her child to be determines the weal or woe of the nation. Gave instances of spartan mothers, of Hannah[17] who is the type of Jewish mother. The extent to which this idealistic ambition of the mother [sentence incomplete] I illustrated by a story of one of the collectors employed by the Bureau. As he came to one of the families to collect the monthly tuition fee of the one dollar, the mother of the boy put him off by promising to pay him the next month. Upon his insistence that she pay at once, she told him that her husband was out of work and the grocer's bills had not been paid and they had to go without breakfast that morning. This so moved the young man that he took a dollar and gave it to the woman, saying to her that she could pay it back to him next month. As he turned to go the woman followed him and insisted that he take the dollar as tuition fee for the child.

Speaking on Ceremony and Community

THURSDAY, FEBRUARY 26, 1914

Last night I spoke before the young people's organization of the 85th Street synagogue[18] on the subject of Ceremonies, their Nature and meaning in Judaism. The following is the substance of what I said: Ceremonies in religion are usually represented as being commanded by God. As an object of study, however, they must be examined as a natural product of the inner or mental life of man, having their definite laws of rise, growth, and decay. Such a study of them in no way eliminates the divine that is in them any more than the realization of the extent to which the soul or the universe as a whole is governed by eternal laws lessens in any degree their dependence upon divine causation. The first fact that strikes us about religious ceremonies is that they are not at all unique and without parallel in the other phases of life. It is a popular error that ceremonies are limited to religion. Yet what is a handshake, or the tipping of the hat, or a salute or the wearing of a uniform if not ceremony? It appears then that religious ceremonial is s species of ceremonial in general which we may define as the conventional

---

16. Alexander Dushkin (1890–1976), educator; Ph.D. Columbia; communal educator New York City and Jerusalem; became an important disciple of Kaplan; responsible for bringing Kaplan to Hebrew University to teach in 1937 and 1938.

17. For story of Hannah see 1 Samuel 1–3.

18. Kehilath Jeshurun on East 85th Street in New York City was Kaplan's first pulpit, from 1903–9, and was a well-known Orthodox synagogue.

sign language of social relations. The main purpose of ceremonial is to give effective, dramatic and abbreviated expression to the various emotions that center about social relations such as deference, regard, fellowship. Being a language it will oft be as arbitrary as the particular words are for the objects which they denote. Religious ceremonies constitute the conventional sign language of those social relations which are regarded as divinely ordained. The differentiating character of religious ceremonies is the particular kind of social relations to which they give expression. To carry the matter one step further, we may define Jewish religious ceremonies as the conventional sign language of those Jewish social relations which are regarded as divinely ordained. A marriage ceremony is religious in character, because the bond which unites them is not merely a social convention but a divinely ordained institution. . . .

Ceremonial, therefore, is essentially bound up with the living of a religious life. But it is not a means, as has, hitherto, been believed, of bringing the individual into direct and immediate communion with the divine, either making the divine presence an immediate object of experience, or in some magic way obtaining divine favor that would, perhaps, otherwise have been withheld. The efficiency and functioning of ceremonial begins only when the community to which the individual is socially related in some way is consciously regarded as the medium whereby God and individual are brought close to each other. . . . To the believing Jew the common life that has been handed down from generation to generation of Israel of the past is a divinely constituted life. Every time the Jew puts on his tephilin or consecrates the Sabbath by means of the cup of wine or observes a festival he uses the sign language of Jewish social relations which is considered as divinely ordained. Furthermore, the hallowing of the person represents the sacred union into which the Jew must enter with the rest of his people that are contemporary with him. It is in that way that ceremonies such as those that pertain to the care of food and person are calculated to give expression to the belief that the bond which holds together all Jews of the same generation is not merely a racial or national one, but a spiritual and sacred one, that the Jews are still a "kingdom of priests and a holy nation."

A Rabbinic Conclave on Authority at the Jersey Shore

SUNDAY, AUGUST 23, 1914

The students of the Seminary published this year their first annual. Reluctant as I was I had to contribute the article on the "Supremacy of the Torah." It seems to have created some discussion among the graduates and to have aroused a few of them from their apparent indifference to the

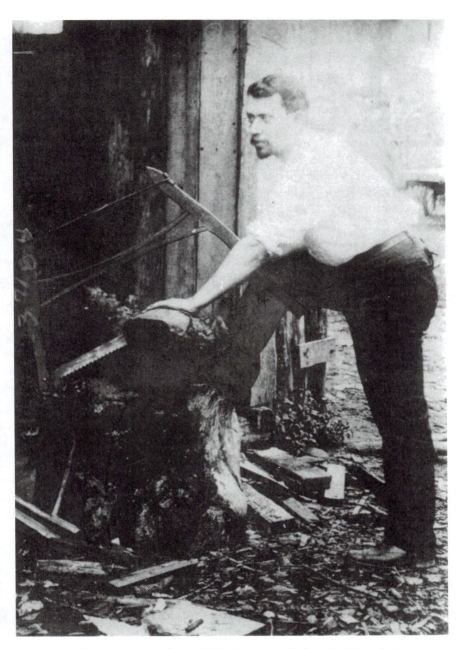

Kaplan cutting wood, ca. 1913. (Courtesy Hadassah K. Musher)

fundamental questions of Torah, revelation, etc. Rubenovitz,[19] with whom I had occasion about two years ago, while I was in Boston, to discuss the futility of most of our endeavors because they only touch the surface of our problems, came to Long Branch in the middle of July and asked me to invite a few of the leading graduates to an informal conference. We were going to confine the "conclave" primarily to those who approached the problem of Judaism with an open mind, but upon reflection such a procedure seemed likely to give offence to those who happened to be in and about New York [who] would not be invited. I sent out, accordingly, invitations to nearly all of the graduates that chanced to be in the East. The date was set for Wednesday, August 12, and was to last as long as the men would find it convenient to attend. . . . [At the meeting] Hoffman[20] read from a few notes that he had jotted down on traditional Judaism. He described tradition as a dynamic force which operated with the concepts and ideas of each age. Among the elements of the dynamic force he enumerated the cardinal principles of Judaism concerning God, the Torah, the selection of Israel Revelation, etc. . . .

Kohn[21] gave us his favorite principle of selection as to those laws which are binding and those the authority of which is no longer in force. . . . I presented my view of "authority." In the first place I took exception to Hoffman's identification of the cardinal principle as the dynamic force in Judaism. Only a living or moving thing can be termed dynamic. The dynamic force in Judaism is, therefore, none other than the socio-psychic vitality of the Jewish people. The problem therefore cannot be reduced to a question of preserving certain abstract concepts, whether they belong to the past or to the present. Our only concern is that the Jewish people be worthy of being Israel. This cannot be accomplished if we regard authority as something external. Authority may be based upon personal experience and conviction and yet not be subjective. It may possess the highest degree of objectivity, if the experiences and convictions are those which a normally constituted people share. There is an objective standard of beauty in spite of the fact that only that is beautiful which is immediately experienced to be so. The opinion of the critic is only authoritative in the sense of serving as a guide.

---

19. Herman H. Rubenovitz (1883–1966), rabbi and zionist; graduated JTS in 1908; a disciple of Kaplan and one of his strongest supporters; rabbi of Temple Mishkan Tefila, Boston, from 1910–46.

20. Charles I. Hoffman (1864–1945), Conservative rabbi and journalist; graduated JTS in 1904; a friend of Solomon Schechter and active in the Conservative movement; rabbi in Newark, New Jersey, for more than forty years.

21. Jacob Kohn (1881–1968), Conservative rabbi who served congregations in Syracuse, Manhattan, and Los Angeles. While in New York, Kohn served as rabbi of Ansche Hesed. He is the brother of Rabbi Eugene Kohn, a key disciple of Kaplan.

The reconstruction[22] of Judaism on the basis of natural human experience within reach of every one of us is not carried out to its legitimate length because we have little confidence in human reason and experience.

Abba Baum an Old Friend of the Kaplan Family

TUESDAY, AUGUST 25, 1914 [AT ARVERNE][23]

Mr E. is a slim, medium sized, sallow-complexioned man of about 45. He is not well-to-do and does not wield any influence because he lacks personality. He has at least some common sense and can be reasoned with. Outside of Joseph H. Cohen[24] he is the only member of my former congregation to whom I have ventured to speak openly on matters of belief. His wife is an American born woman, one of a large family headed by the late Abba Baum, now dead about twelve years, who was among the first Russian Jews to arrive in New York. When I was a little boy of about eight or nine Father took me over to his house which was at the time far out of the city; from this I conclude that he must have been an unusually kind man, as I do not remember anyone else to whom father ever took me in those years. Furthermore, from the description of him given by those who remember him as well as by his children, I gather that he was a saintly type of Jew, of the kind that one hears about as having been frequent in the old country, but that I have not had the good fortune of meeting in my own entourage. His children speak of the way he would bring two or three newly arrived immigrant Jews to the house from time to time, and ask his daughters to do everything to make them comfortable. These daughters he sent to Normal College—which was unusual among Russian immigrants at the time. This accounts for the generation of ignorant women that have grown up, who are even greater materialists than their husbands, and who are the cause of their husbands having but one ideal in life, to amass wealth. But Abba Baum was different. If his daughters were in any way inclined to smile at the crudities of the strangers he had brought to the house he would tell them that the strangers were learned men whom it was their duty to treat with the highest reverence. No wonder that he succeeded in bringing up a daughter like Esther Ruskay,[25] of blessed memory. (She died

---

22. Early use of this key term is significant.

23. Arverne: A resort community frequented by New York Jews near the Rockaways and Coney Island.

24. Joseph H. Cohen (1877–1961), businessman and philanthropist; manufactured men's clothing; the key figure in the founding of the Jewish Center.

25. Esther Ruskay (1857–1907), born in New York City; attended normal school and Columbia University; a writer, journalist, poet, and communal worker. Her home became a center for New York Jewish intellectuals. She was a member of Kehillath Jeshurun when Kaplan was rabbi, and supported him when others criticized.

about seven or eight years ago at the age of fifty.) To my sorrow, I must say that Judaism has not produced the like of her in this country, at least to my knowledge.

A Sabbath Afternoon on the Boardwalk at Rockaway

AUGUST 25, 1914

Mr. Unterberg,[26] who at first took part in the conversation, left us to go to Mincha service. When he returned the company broke up to take a stroll on the boardwalk. I accosted Mr. Unterberg. He told me that he had been over to see a certain (Mr.)Margolies, the man who was responsible for a carnival taking place on the Sabbath. Unterberg suggested that it might be advisable for me also to go over and talk to Margolies because the latter referred to me in rather deferential terms. I was glad to do what I could to prevent the public desecration of the Sabbath and I consented to meet the man. We walked on till we met him standing in front of his dance hall, and after being introduced to him I went over by myself with him to the porch of his house. The argument that he used was that, if the representatives of the (local) congregation had come to him when the announcement of the carnival was first made he would have been glad to change the date to please them. To do so now, less than a week before it was to take place, involved great financial loss. I could see that he was not altogether in the wrong. The observant Jews were certainly guilty of negligence. I, therefore, sought to persuade him to stand at least half the loss, while the other side should stand the other half.

Margolies and his confreres seemed to justify what H. said of them later in the evening when he came again to Mr. Unterberg's house, namely that they were not far removed from the "Lefty Louis" gang[27] and others of that type. [Margolies was] a big, heavily built man, short, thick neck, the big, fleshy face of a professional gambler. A cigar stuck out from his left side breast pocket, as a visible emblem of his being above the need of observing the Sabbath. Hyman who described him as a *"l'hachles ponim"* which shows what an *am-haarez* this Hyman is.[28] Hyman told us that Margolies makes it his business to

---

26. Israel Unterberg (1863–1934), wealthy clothing manufacturer and member of Kaplan's congregation at the SAJ; strong supporter of Kaplan; donated money for TI building at the JTS.

27. For more information on Jewish criminals of that time see Jenna Weissman Joselit, *Our Gang—Jewish Crime and the New York Jewish Community 1900–1940* (Bloomington: Indiana University Press, 1983).

28. Samuel Hyman (1870–1917), businessman, communal worker, New York City; one of the founders of the Jewish Center. The Yiddish word Hyman had in mind was *Lehakhes Ponim*, which would mean spiteful, but he mispronounced it, so Kaplan referred to him as a stupid, uneducated man (*Am-Ha-aretz*).

stand before his store on the boardwalk and to ask the Jews that come back from synagogue on Sabbath afternoon whether they "davened" a "minchele" for him too.[29] Though I had never met the man I remember his father who kept a wine store on Division Street. He was a rather clever *Baal Habayis* [Heb. head of the household or congregant] of the Lithuanian type, well learned, for a layman, in Talmudic lore. But as for bringing up children Jewishly he knew as much about [it] as a cow about Sunday. He changed for the worse as he grew older and died a poor asthmatic crank.

Harry Fischel[30]—The Russian Jacob Schiff[31]

WEDNESDAY, SEPTEMBER 16, 1914

A third regular attendant (at the congregation in Arverne) was Mr. Fischel my landlord in New York. Unlike the other two[32] who are representative of more or less extensive groups, this man resembles no one but himself. Yet the fact that he is a prominent figure in a section of New York Jewry seems to show that he has much in common with the people of that group. He came to this country about thirty years ago from a little town where he made his living as a carpenter. He must have been then about twenty. He married soon after his arrival, as I have heard it said, a girl who made her living by doing housework. Abstractly speaking there would be no reason why one who works as a servant girl should not be capable of a certain amount of refinement when the opportunity to cultivate it presents itself. But in practice, such is seldom if ever the case. There is a certain vulgarity which belongs to that class that is ineradicable, or to put it differently, among Jews, and probably among Gentiles as well, only those of a rather vulgar disposition are inclined to do housework. The Fischels worked hard and lived miserly until they saved up a small capital, which he by reason of his shrewdness knew how to invest and began to reap therefrom considerable profit. Rumor has it that he engaged in some shady deals whereby he had defrauded an employer of his who was a Gentile. He owes, however, his good fortune to the real estate boom that prevailed in this city before 1905 and he happened to stop speculating just before the reaction set in, and values went

---

29. The expression *Daven a minchele* means to pray the short afternoon service.

30. Harry Fischel (1865–1948), well-known philanthropist; member of the Jewish Center; supporter of Yeshiva University. One of the most important "givers" in the Jewish Community. Kaplan had contempt for him. For more information, see *Judaism Faces the Twentieth Century*, 65.

31. Jacob Schiff (1847–1920), financier and noted community leader; involved with virtually every major institution in the Jewish community.

32. The president and the vice president of the congregation in Arverne whom Kaplan had been describing.

down in a crash. He was estimated at that time as being worth $600,000.00, though conservative figures placed him at half that amount.

But all this pertains to the externals of the man. But what of the man himself? He is built rather short with ill-shaped usually closely cropped head and a red goatee beard, topped by a thin long moustache. His nose is straight and heavy, somewhat reddish and veiny at times. His eyes murky and bloodshot. Thus on the whole, he would be quite repellent were it not for the animation in his face which betrays a mixture of shrewdness and intelligence. These traits show themselves in his aggressive attitude towards whatever he is brought in contact with. In spite of these qualities, however, he cannot live down the inordinate vulgarity which urges him on to elbow his way to the front, regardless of the ridicule which he provokes. When years ago, for example, a number of representative Jewish citizens called on the Mayor Mr. Low, he made himself spokesman irrespective of his broad and foreign accent and uncouth form in which he expressed what he had to say. His love of display and self-advertisement knows no bounds. While he has been identified with an extraordinary number of philanthropic and educational societies, and gives quite freely to many a worthy cause, he makes sure that his generosity be cried from the house tops. It is characteristic of the man, that he explains his greed for publicity as a means of stimulating others to emulate his example. But all this would be forgiven him if he had been known to speak generally the truth. He is of the kind that find it easier to speak untruth than the truth. It is this in particular that makes him at times unbearable to the more sedate and earnest among us. Both his vulgarity and untruthfulness will take the form, for instance, of putting some cheap gilt brass bauble in his house to pass off as a valuable gold ornament. Or he would offer to make repairs for a charitable institution, and charge twice the usual price in order to have an opportunity to display his generosity by reducing the bill to 50%.

For these and similar exploits gossip has him well known. As he is quite well known downtown among the actor folk, by reason of his ownership of a building that was used as a Jewish theatre, a playwright took him a few years in a play on the Jewish stage known as "In the Mountains" in which he was spoken of as the "all-rightnik." The mountains referred to are the Catskills, to which many of our people resort during the summer. Fischel has a home in Hunter and there too he plays his part, whenever he stays there, in being forwardly and aggressively officious. He has contributed the synagogue building to the congregation that exists there, and, he therefore feels entitled to domineer over the local Jewish community. This naturally caused many an altercation with the result that last year they made it so unpleasant for him and his wife that this year he preferred to summer with his family in Long Branch. In their fracas, I am given to understand, his wife was more than an interested spectator.

Kaplan *"Discovers Dushkin and Berkson"*[33]

SATURDAY, OCTOBER 3, 1914

My interest in some of the city college men . . . brought me into touch with two young men to whom I was strongly drawn by reason of their alert mental powers as well as the elements of personality that seemed to be latent in them. These men were [Alexander] Dushkin and [Isaac] Berkson. The former happened to come to my house on a Friday evening to consult me about a program for the Menorah Society. I took that opportunity to sound him [out] as to what he expected to do after he graduated from college. He told me that he was himself uncertain but that in all likelihood he would follow up settlement work into which he had been drawn on account of his musical ability. His work, I believe, consisted of teaching music to some settlement group. At once I began to plead with him that a man like him who seemed to be interested in Jewish things ought not to waste his powers on so vague and un-Jewish an activity as settlement work. Forthwith I mentioned to him the new field that was being opened up with the establishment of the Bureau of Jewish Education; I argued that there was no reason why he could not make a career of Jewish work. I referred him to Dr. B. [Samson Benderly]—who then stayed, at that time in the hotel on 123rd Street between B'way and Amsterdam Ave; and it was not long before Dushkin was given charge of a class in the Preparatory School which met then in the rooms of the YMHA.

In the wake of Dushkin followed Berkson.

The Benderly Boys[34] — Future Leaders of Jewish Education

SUNDAY, OCTOBER 4, 1914

Both of these men took up the work with the bureau not merely to earn a livelihood but also to satisfy their more ideal ambition of being of service to the Jewish people. But upon their heels followed a number of young men of the same class at college who were attracted by the material opportunities which the new field of Jewish education seemed to offer. They were given a chance to earn a few hundred dollars a year and to pursue post-graduate courses at Columbia. This was certainly more than they could hope for from the Board of Education of the city which had reduced men's initial salaries to the pitiable sum of $720.

---

33. Isaac Berkson (1891–1975), U.S. educator and philosopher; director of the Central Jewish Institute in 1917; worked with the Bureau of Jewish Education in New York City and in Palestine from 1928–35, after which he received an appointment to the faculty at City College of New York; much influenced by Kaplan.

34. A group of young men who studied with Benderly and took special courses with Kaplan. The most important figures in Jewish education came from this group (the group included one woman). For more information, see my *Judaism Faces the Twentieth Century*.

All of these men were formed into a group. Dr. B. himself taught them Hebrew for two hours every morning during an entire summer. He had them read modern Hebrew literature and inculcated in them at the same time an enthusiasm for the general cause of Jewish education as he hoped to establish it. He also got a Dr. Shapiro to give them a more thorough grounding in grammar and composition. Later in the year about the middle of winter he asked me to give them some work and I took up with them the course in interpretation that I had been giving in the Institute to my regular classes. My work with that group did not constitute part of my duties at the Institute, but I carried it on for the Bureau. In June 1912 that group was turned over by the Bureau to the Teachers Institute. The work with them was then divided between Dr. Friedlaender[35] and myself. He was to give them instruction in Bible and history and I was to give them the principles of Jewish education. I gave them that course until February 1913 when I resumed once again the interpretation. Having concluded the book of Genesis with them last May (1914), I began with them the study of the Talmud.

In my heart of hearts I feel there is something wrong with the spirit that animates them in their work. I am not referring to their interest in it for what they can make out of it financially. Of that, I must say that there was till lately very little evidence. Even those who entered with a materialistic aim also acquired somewhat of a higher point of view. Whether it was sincere with them or not is of course hard to say. But the mere fact that a sense of "noblesse oblige" developed among them which shamed into silence any purely selfish pretensions is to me strong proof of the idealism animating Dr. B. himself.

All this afforded me keen satisfaction. But what I could never get myself accustomed to in those men has been their attitude towards Judaism. It was, of course, the reflection of Dr. B.'s attitude which in turn is that of Achad Haam.[36] I might, in fact, say that Dr. B. is perhaps the only man who is working out Achad Haamism in *Golus* [exile] in a systematic and organized way. I had always missed something in Achad Haam's conceptions of Judaism, but certainly its realization in practice I have always found jarring to me. It is wanting in appreciation of the indefinable religious longings and aspirations. It borders so closely on the clap trap soulless practical efficiency schemes that Carlyle so vehemently condemns in his "Signs of the Times." It is this spirit that has taken possession of the men

---

35. Israel Friedlaender (1876–1920), semitic scholar and community leader; born in Russia; in 1903 became professor of biblical literature at the JTS. He was killed in the Ukraine while on a relief mission. His philosophy has much in common with Kaplan's.

36. Ahad Ha-Am (Asher Zvi Ginsberg) (1856–1927), Hebrew writer and proponent of cultural Zionism. He edited the Hebrew monthly *Ha'Shiloah*, and was a prolific essayist. Kaplan was profoundly influenced by Ahad Ha-Am's thought, and was his most important disciple. SAJ paid for publication of *Ha'Shiloah* in the twenties. For more information, see *Judaism Faces the Twentieth Century*, 323.

and I have found them strange, unresponsive to the deeper appeals of Judaism, so that I have often wished that these men were drawn into the Seminary, where, while the religious spirit is lacking, it is at least not pooh-poohed, as is the case in nationalistic circles.

What a boon it would have been if the strongest men among them had seen that the only logical step for them to take was to combine the rabbinate with the function of the educator. The whole scheme of Dr. B. I believe is based upon a fallacy, viz., that it is feasible to maintain distinct Jewish groups in the Diaspora, that shall unite in themselves two coordinate cultures of a national character. In my opinion this can not possibly be realized. It can only have a short lived existence among the recently arrived immigrants and in their children, but not in the third generation. Only by giving Jewish culture a distinctively religious significance in the true modern sense of the term is there any hope of Jewish education being built up in this country. This means that only by maintaining the synagogue and vitalizing it by means of the Hebraic movement can the Jews hope to survive here as a distinct group. Only those, therefore, who will give a religious interpretation to Jewish culture will be entrusted with the care and supervision of Jewish education. The Talmud Torah system which is independent of the synagogue is only transitory and will in time disappear before the religious school system to be established by congregations. The abnormality which makes the T.T. system untenable is its eleemosynary character. It is maintained by the well-to-do for the children of the poor. There have so far been no schools of any account established by well-to-do parents for their own children. It is only when Conservative congregations are aroused to the need of establishing properly organized religious schools that the normal condition of self-support will be attained in Jewish education. This being the case it would have been wise for Dr. B. to induce his men to join the Seminary and become rabbis as well as educators. Instead of this he urges them to work for the Doctors' Degree in Columbia, expecting that when one of them will swoop down on an out of town Jewish community as Dr. So and So, the Jewish populace will be so overwhelmed that he will have no difficulty in carrying out his educational plans. This sounds well in theory but I do not think feasible in practice.

This tendency in the Bureau which I do not find to my liking is probably the main reason for the bitter antagonism which exists between Dr. Schechter[37] and Dr. Benderly. What to me is only jarring is to Dr. S. hateful and offensive.

---

37. Solomon Schechter (1847–1915), first president after 1902 of reorganized JTS; well-known rabbinics scholar who discovered the large cache of medieval Jewish documents in Cairo called the Geniza; primary force in creating Conservative Judaism in America; admired Kaplan but was critical of him. Kaplan saw Schechter as a father figure and thought Schechter had little confidence in him. See *Judaism Faces the Twentieth Century*, 107–8, for more information.

This accounts for their inability ever to get together. With a tendency such as this for an issue the difference is bound to be one that is rooted in temperament and therefore one which can hardly be overcome. The reason I can work with Dr. B. is probably because I am young and can adapt myself to what I see to be the need of the hour. For the time being he is to me the most positive force in Jewish life today. If I had any one else more like minded to turn to and cooperate with I would never have much to do with Dr. B. If for example I had found in Schechter a man who possessed a degree of efficiency that would assure general recognition for his point of view I would have surrendered myself heart and soul to him. But in my eagerness to live at least not as a parasite, and to do some constructive work in Jewish life, I have found Dr. B. the only man who could assist me.

But instead of the stronger men in that group turning to the ministry, the weaker men, weaker both in character and mentality, have grown displeased with their prospects in the Bureau, and have applied to me for advice with regard to entering the Seminary. This means that the rabbinate which is the only feasible form of effective Jewish spiritual leadership is to be in the hands of weaklings, while the better and stronger men who might have joined it, if not for the misguided fanatical tendency of Jewish nationalism, are doomed to become mere cogs in the philanthropic educational machinery.

Kaplan on His Own Religiosity

SUNDAY, OCTOBER 4, 1914

Two weeks ago to-day was the eve of Rosh Hashono. For the first time in eleven years I passed the high holidays without preaching anywhere. This had a very depressing effect upon me. It brought home to me that sense that there was no room for me in the only aspect of Jewish life that I look upon as having a future, namely the religious. I owe it probably to circumstances that I am an observant Jew, though in my beliefs I am a thoroughgoing radical. Otherwise I should have landed in the Reform movement. What is peculiar about my mode of life is that I do not hide my radical views from anyone; I state them freely to superiors, colleagues and students. My radicalism is, however, not of the usual kind, since it only relates to the outward forms of religion not to the fact of religion itself. I often feel particularly embittered because I am not able to give full vent to the enthusiasm for vital religion on account of the shackles which the outward forms and institutions impose upon me. This is the reason I refused the pulpit of the 85th Street Congregation [Kehilath Jeshurun] when it was offered to me last year by a committee of fifteen sent by the congregation to interview me. I have felt all along that Orthodoxy is the bane of Judaism. The only hope for Judaism is in the introduction of radical and sweeping changes to be made from the point of view of Catholic Israel. Still I had not the courage to tell them that I was not Orthodox[38] . . .

The Seminary and Jewish Scholarship

SATURDAY, OCTOBER 10, 1914

The Seminary had been scheduled to open on Thursday October 1. This does not mean that work was to commence and sessions to be resumed. The opening is a mere formality carried out in order that the Seminary not go on record as having commenced work considerably later in the season than the colleges and universities. Of course, the holidays interfere a great deal, and it would not be feasible to enforce attendance at this time but could not provision be made to reduce somewhat the term of inactivity at the Seminary which lasts from May 15th to October 15th? The trouble is that the leading men on the faculty regard their own scholarly work of more importance than giving instruction, which they look upon as a waste of time as far as they are concerned, and which they therefore restrict to as few hours as possible. The consequence is not only that the classes are undivided except into the two divisions — by far too few — in the case of Talmud instruction, and men of fourth year standing are made to do the same work as men who have recently entered, but the amount of instruction received is about half of what it should be. The men on the staff do not show the least desire to give themselves freely to the students if it is to be at the least sacrifice of time, and if it is liable to impair in the least the chance of writing some dry-as-dust article on some minute point in Jewish Science. I hold Jewish Science in proper respect, but I would not permit any but those who are crippled and maimed to pursue it, and I would compel men like Ginzberg, Davidson,[39] and Friedlaender who are men of brains to help build up a living Judaism with content to it.

Services at the 92nd Street Y—The Issue of an Organ

TUESDAY, OCTOBER 20, 1914

As for the services themselves,[40] they are so dull and monotonous that I can scarcely understand how they are tolerated by people who are constantly

---

38. Kaplan's practice changed as time passed, and he became less observant in the traditional mode. He prayed every morning until the late 1920s, and took box-fulls of sardines on a trip to Italy in 1922. For more information, see *Judaism Faces the Twentieth Century*, 29–30.

39. Israel Davidson (1870–1945), scholar of medieval Hebrew literature; born in Lithuania; taught at the JTS. His magnum opus is a four-volume thesaurus of medieval Hebrew poetry.

40. Kaplan directed religious activities at the 92nd Street Y for a number of years. He was at this point between congregations and succeeded Judah Magnes as the religious director at the Y. For more information, see *Judaism Faces the Twentieth Century*, 132.

clamoring for change. It [the service] is composed of a hodge podge of Hebrew and English congregational responses that make one think he is in a church and renderings in traditional music with all the fancy roulades of the *Elokeinu ve-elokei avoteinu* [Heb. God and the God of our Fathers].[41] They have no organ. Before I had anything to do with the Y.M.H.A. the services were entirely of the same kind as are held in the reformed synagogues, with organ. etc. When Mr. Felix M. Warburg[42] asked me to speak at the services on the high holidays four years ago I accepted only on condition that the organ be removed. At that time the Magnes[43] vogue ran high. Although I personally had no strong objections to an organ, I felt that I would shock my friends and folks if I would consent to officiate at the Y.M.H.A. so long as they retained the organ. Not long after Magnes became the chairman of the religious work in the Association, he raised the hopes of Warburg and one or two others that he would revolutionize conditions at the Y.M.H.A. and bring new life into its activities which had already then been lagging for some time. In consistency with his shutting down the organ at the Madison Avenue Congregation which he then held, Magnes insisted upon its exclusion from the services at the Association. He attempted to organize a congregation out of the young men but failed because he had neither the patience nor the tact to handle them properly. He handled them like children; this they resented. I was expected to help him conduct the services; and as the Association had no one to take charge of them I had to do most of the work. I tried various means to arouse interest, but it was of no avail. With the exclusion of the organ the services grew even more dull than before, and the young fellows were too glad to find an excuse for staying away from the services.

Older and Younger Members at Kehilath Jeshurun

SUNDAY, OCTOBER 25, 1914

This tendency to look upon the congregation[44] as consisting of two classes of members, those of the "old generation" and those of the "young generation" has been in vogue ever since they began to feel the need of taking

---

41. Kaplan was still traditional at this time and therefore wrote the name of God in the Hebrew with a "k" in order not to have the full name of God written out.

42. Felix M. Warburg (1871–1937), banker and philanthropist; born in Germany, emigrated to the United States, and became a partner in Kuhn Loeb and Company; especially interested in the Joint Distribution Committee and the Y.M.H.A. movement.

43. Judah L. Magnes (1877–1948), rabbi and president of the New York Kehillah; Zionist leader who later (1925) became the first president of the Hebrew University. Magnes and Kaplan were good friends but as time passed they became critical of each other. For more information, see *Judaism Faces the Twentieth Century*.

44. Congregation Kehilath Jeshurun, located on East 85th Street in Manhattan, where Kaplan served as rabbi from 1903 until 1909. He is the English-speaking rabbi that he mentions below. It was his first pulpit. See introduction for more details.

an English speaking rabbi. Such a rabbi was hardly thought of as being capable of being recognized [accepted] by the elder members since no one but a young man could fill that office and one who on account of his secular attainments was bound to be below the standards of knowledge of things Jewish—which standard included only familiarity with the codes particularly the parts bearing on ritual questions, and a pilpulistic [scholastic] knowledge of a few treatises. A rabbi of this kind was therefore to be gotten only to meet the clamorous demands of a few younger people who helped towards the putting up of a new structure—the one now on 85th St., the former one being a dingy little building on 82nd St.—and who having grown tired of the maggid [preacher] they had by the name of Peikes, wanted to complete the outfit by engaging a rabbi who would raise the congregation to the level of the fashionable ones which boast of English speaking modern rabbis. Of course, there was also something of the religious motive present in their eagerness to secure a man of that type but it was surely secondary to the social one just mentioned.

Kaplan on His Early Childhood

OCTOBER 28, 1914

I was a boy of eight when I came to this country and found father acting as Dayan [religious judge] in the office of the rabbi together with another man of small stature and still smaller mind, as I distinctly recall. Rabbi Jacob Joseph was brought over from Wilna, where he had been the chief preacher of the town, by an organization of congregations known [as] the *va'ad ha-kehillot* [Heb. Committee of Congregations] which undertook to pay his salary of about four thousand a year, an exorbitant sum for those people at that time. But those who brought him to this country had not the least intention of conferring upon him the office of Chief Rabbi for the purpose of establishing Judaism in this country. They had not the least conception that the life of this country would be the cause of problems and issues arising undreamed of before. They thought that the religious life in this city and country was to be merely a reproduction of what went on in the Russian towns they came from. It never occurred to them that the East Side ghetto was not a permanent one, that the life of the people round about would sooner or later penetrate their section of the city. Therefore, when they sent for Rabbi Joseph they only had in mind a man who would give rabbinical sanction for the various ritual regulations which the leading laymen would establish. It was not for the Rabbi to initiate anything. Some of the leading spirits seeing that the Rabbi was unacquainted with practical affairs took advantage of his ignorance to feather their own nests. A great part of the money contributed by the owners of slaughterhouses for the authorization to sell kosher meat was paid out in exorbitant salaries to these people. No accounts were kept. The Rabbi who was himself a good kind-hearted man and a great scholar unconsciously played into their hands. His own wife who like many of the wives of Rabbis of the old generation saw to it that the system of pious graft shall hold out as long an possible. All this irritated father a great deal and he revolted from the Rabbi and his clique. He suffered quite some persecution at their hands. . . .

Rabbi Moshe S. Margolies[45] *Speaks at Kehilath Jeshurun*

OCTOBER 29, 1914

Margolies rose to speak. I can surmise by this time what he has to say on occasions such as these. I have heard him repeat these speeches so often that I know them backwards. There is absolutely no connection in what be says, his language—i.e. his Yiddish is interspersed with English words, and he tries to make up for the lack of sense by being vociferous, getting red in the face and sometimes even stamping with his foot. These tricks ill accord with his general makeup and with his well combed white long beard. His followers listen to him with what might be called a sacramental attitude. They expect nothing new; what he says is a sort of liturgy with them and they are perfectly satisfied with whatever he says.

Students and Skeptics at the Teachers Institute

SATURDAY NIGHT, OCTOBER 31, 1914

Tomorrow will be two weeks since I gave the first lesson in the Course in Interpretation to the class of young men who belong to the graduating class of the Teachers Institute. I usually begin work of that kind by finding out the state of mind of the members of the class with regard to the fundamental questions of religion. These young fellows being between ages of 17 and 20 I naturally expected to find among them a great many whose minds were disturbed by questions that upset their implicit faith in Scripture. But before I asked many questions I found not only that every one without an exception was dissatisfied with the views that he had been taught to regard as infallible but that some went so far as to question the very existence of God. All these boys come from strictly observant homes, nevertheless they are in a fair way to develop into skeptics that want to have little to do with Judaism. This shows that the home training may do much for the inculcation of moral habits but by itself it cannot give to the child that which only a healthy and normal communal life is in a position to give. Hence the need of building up a communal life that shall meet the spiritual demands of the present generation.

---

45. Moses Sebulun Margolies (1851–1936), Orthodox rabbi and community leader; chief rabbi, Boston; rabbi Kehilath Jeshurun from 1906 until his death. Ramaz School in New York City is named after him.

From left: *Kaplan, his father, Judith, Lena (pregnant with Naomi), and Hadassah, August 1914. (Courtesy D. Naomi Kaplan Wenner)*

Daughter Naomi[46] *Is Born*

NOVEMBER 7, 1914
  Y.Ḥ. Marḥeshvan (Heb. 18th of Marḥshvan)[47] This morning at 12:46 Naomi was born.

Speaking at the 92nd Street Y.M.H.A. on Judaism and Community

TUESDAY, FEBRUARY 8, 1915
  Last Sabbath afternoon I spoke at the first Sabbath afternoon services organized at the Y.W.H.A. building. The services were scheduled to begin at four but very few people were present at that time, because the services had not

---

46. Naomi Kaplan Wenner (1914–97), third daughter of Mordecai Kaplan; psychiatrist, retired 1982, then full-time sculptor; married Seymour Wenner (1913–93), administrative law judge at several U.S. government agencies.
47. The Jewish month.

been sufficiently advertised. It took almost three quarters of an hour before a respectable crowd had gathered. In fact the trouble was that when the crowd did gather it consisted mostly of "respectable"; that is of people who came to see the services rather than to participate in them, of a couple of directresses and their husbands, and a few of my own family who came to hear me speak. Of the young folks there must have been about fifty or sixty. . . . Before coming to the main topic of my remarks I congratulated the workers on the installation of the Mincha services. I spoke of these services in connection with the forum as valuable in meeting the question "What shall the young person do on the Sabbath afternoon?" So far in most of the Jewish homes, even the most strictly observant the young people go to a matinee. They provide themselves with theatre tickets before hand and walk instead of riding so as to keep within the letter of the law. If some outlet for their social and intellectual desires were found that would be in keeping with the Jewish spirit, such violation of that spirit would not arise.

The topic I took for discussion was "What is Religion?" I defined it as being that phase of the life of a collective body or social group which makes for the subjection of the selfish to tho unselfish both in the individual and in the group. The two corollaries of the definition which I laid special emphasis upon were the following 1. We cannot think correctly about religion or arrive at any proper conclusions as to what our attitude towards it should be if we think of it in terms of individual life. 2. This definition rules out national patriotisms which are based upon the double standard viz. unselfishness as the duty of the individual and selfishness as that of the group.

Y.M.H.A. and Its Weaknesses

THURSDAY, MARCH 4, 1915

Another problem into which I have practically been led against my will is that of the Y.M.H.A. The position of that association is growing more anomalous every day. With the opening up of various recreation centers, many of the boys are beginning to desert the Y.M.H.A. I am taking advantage of every opportunity that presents itself at the biweekly meetings to impress upon the Board the futility of carrying on the work without a distinctively religious aim. I hold up to them the example of the Y.M.C.A. and am gradually bringing up before them concretely the issue whether its activities are to be carried on by men, who are scoffers at things religious or by Gentiles who are in no position to influence the boys even morally. They have e.g. a Gentile as their gymnasium teacher. In the Y.M.C.A they make it a point to have every gymnasium master familiar with the Bible so that whenever any occasion presents itself, they avail themselves of that knowledge. As an instance of how our boys who go to the gymnasium are without any kind of moral influence in the building I mentioned

Y.M.H.A. building, 92nd Street and Lexington Avenue, 1900–1920.
(Courtesy 92nd Street YM-YWHA Archives)

the case of the Purim festival at which a number of them were present. I learned that they indulged in the dirtiest jokes and stories conceivable right there in the building of the Y.M.H.A at the Purim dinner. These remarks I made the day before yesterday at the meeting down town.

Jewish Student Life at Harvard

MARCH 17, 1915

The group at Harvard Menorah to which I gave the talk consisted of about the same number of men as on the previous occasion. Before introducing me the chairman read some interchange of letters with Prof. Frankfurter[48] in reference to the Jewish students who have been stranded in Switzerland on account of the war. There are about 2,000 of them in Lausanne Basel, etc. Many of them particularly those who fled from Belgium are entirely homeless. Even the matriculated students are practically starving. In reference to this Frankfurter whom I have just named I have learned that he has achieved a phenomenal

---

48. Felix Frankfurter (1882–1965), American jurist and Zionist; Harvard Law School from 1914–39 and Supreme Court from 1939–62; good friend of his colleague Louis Brandeis.

career. He is only a man in the early thirties and a graduate of the N.Y. Law School in 1906. But so great is his reputation for having won various cases which he conducted for the U.S. Government that Harvard appointed him full professor of Law. . . .

But by far the most interesting part of the evening I spent in the discussion after the lecture. The usual practice is to go from the Phillips Brooks Hall where the lecture is delivered, to the dormitory room of one of the students and there a number of those who are interested put questions bearing upon the subject that had been dealt with in the lecture. The room is usually fitted up in the characteristic style of the college men with all sorts of pictures and college trophies and souvenirs, and the boys seat themselves in chairs and on tables and from out [of] the fumes of smoke which they puff out proceed sometimes clever, sometimes silly at times serious and at times frivolous queries on the matter in hand. One of the fellows I met there this year was present when I gave the series of talks before the society two years ago. His name is Brodsky and he is the son of a semi-modernized orthodox Rav in Newark. This student displayed quite some acumen both that time and this in the searching questions that he put to me, and judging from them one would conclude that he was an extreme radical. Yet the fact is that he was the first one to start last winter a daily minyan in the dormitory rooms of the college, which minyan kept up until the mid-year exams, and he intends to join the Seminary next year, as things look. The only, to me, discordant note was struck when I happened to make some slighting remarks about Sunday school teachers, and from the hearty laugh that it aroused I saw at once that quite a number of those who were gathered in the room were engaged in teaching in religious school. This I deplored in my own mind because it again showed me that only those who derive some sort of material benefit from Judaism can be gotten interested in it. I left for New York with the 12:00 midnight.

Trustees of the Bureau of Education Meet at Marshall's House

THURSDAY, MARCH 18, 1915

Last night I attended a meeting of the Trustees of the Bureau of Education of the Kehillah.[49] The meeting took place at Mr. Marshall's house. The only ones present were Mr. Marshall,[50] Dr. Magnes, Dr. Benderly and myself. The report which Dr. Benderly rendered pertained only to the moneys of the Bureau. The fact that stood out clearly was that Dr. Magnes was the mainstay

---

49. The Kehillah was the organized Jewish community of New York which Magnes helped found and which he headed.

50. Louis Marshall (1856–1929), lawyer and community leader; one of the founders of the American Jewish Committee; served for many years on the Board of the Jewish Theological Seminary; important spokesman for Jewish rights and a key figure of the German-Jewish elite.

of the Bureau. He has successfully solicited thousands of dollars from people who are completely estranged from Judaism.

After the discussion of the report Mr. Marshall touched upon the advisability of establishing an understanding with Dr. Schechter. He mentioned the fact that Schechter found fault with the Bureau on the ground that it leaned too much to the side of nationalism and paid little or no attention to religion. Dr. Schechter proposed that a man like Rabbi Jacob Kohn (his pet) ought to be on the Board or ought to have a hand at least in the work of the Bureau. Dr. Benderly replied that if Kohn would be admitted into the Bureau Orthodox and Reformed Judaism would also have a right to be represented. . . . What a confusion would then result. Dr. Benderly would have to spend ninety percent of his energy in politics and give only ten percent to the work. Both Benderly and myself than dwelt upon the unreasonableness of Schechter's attitude and the evil effect that it has upon all of us who naturally had a right to expect encouragement instead of opposition.

Dinner at the Unterbergs

Saturday night, April 3, 1915

On Thursday night, April 1 I attended the annual dinner given to Dr. Magnes by the Society for the Advancement of Judaism.[51] Like the two preceding dinners, it was given at the house of Mr. I. Unterberg who is the president of the Society. This Society consists of those who about four year ago organized themselves for the purpose of enabling Dr. Magnes to do communal work without being compelled at the same time to earn his livelihood by holding a pulpit. Those who belong to this Society contribute from $0 to $250 per year towards his support. The lion's share of that support however, comes from Mr. Felix M. Warburg. In all he receives about $7,500 per year.

Knowing beforehand the nature of the annual dinner, I was not at first in the mood to attend. But my better reason convinced me that no good can come from keeping aloof. When I arrived I found most of the guests assembled in the library room upstairs and after a little while spent in greeting and chatting we went down to the dining room where an elegantly set table running diagonally met our eyes. We were all duly "capped," we all washed our hands, and stood silently till the waiter came around with the "matzoth" in a silver tray, and all of us said the "Motzi"[52] in due form. We were as elegantly orthodox as we possibly

---

51. As the reader will see, the Society for the Advancement of Judaism which is mentioned here is not Kaplan's synagogue. The organization mentioned here was established for the express purpose of collecting money to support Magnes while he was head of New York Kehillah.

52. Matzoth are the unleavened bread of Passover. "Motzi" is the blessing over bread usually made before a meal.

could be so that I felt almost a heroic thrill when I dared to remove the cap after we got through with the meal—I certainly would not have thought of doing so while we ate—for no other reason than that it annoyed me.

I was seated next to Dr. Magnes. On the other side of me a place was reserved for Mr. Nathan Straus.[53] But he failed to appear and before we were far gone with the meal Mr. Felix M. Warburg came and took that seat. The first thing he did was to ask me to tell him who was at the table. I did so as well as I could. He proved a very interesting neighbor. He was brimful of jests and stories. There is no doubt that he is as democratic as it is possible for one in his circumstances to be. The only misfortune is that he does not seem to me to possess the depth of character that might have rendered him a power in Jewry. He is not interested in Judaism for what it means to him but for what it might mean to the masses whom it might keep out of mischief.

When the meal was over, Mr. Unterberg called upon Dr. Magnes to deliver his message. Personally I was very much disappointed. I heard practically the same thing numberless times before except that this year he said even less. He simply described the work of the various departments of the Kehillah far more prosaically with far less detail and less comprehensiveness than last year. As far as I can see he lacks executive ability and could not of his own accord carry out any piece of work great or small. I am sure that if not for the remarkable organizing talent of Dr. Benderly and the latter's insistence upon Magnes that he secure the money to run the bureau, things would have stood exactly where they stood five years ago. But little as I admire Magnes' ability—of which I am convinced he possesses very little, I do not believe that I am false to myself if I make it my business to sing his praises everywhere. In the first place, I do it because it is better that a man even of his mediocre ability should be given a chance to do whatever he can to build up the community than that no one should be entrusted with that task. In this vast Jewry there are no Jews who can be said to be popular. He is practically the only one who has achieved some degree of popularity. The consequence is that if his hands should not be upheld, there would be no one that would be entrusted with the leadership of the community and the chaos of communal life would become still more hopeless. Secondly, I apprehend that any disparagement of his work on my part might be due to a touch of envy rather than to a sincere desire to have the truth known. I therefore force myself both to see and show the side to his work which is beneficial.

After he got through Mr. Unterberg called on Warburg to say a few words. The latter spoke very smoothly and elegantly of what a privilege it was

---

53. Nathan Straus (1889–1961), department store executive (Macy's); public servant; legislator; officer, Jewish Institute of Religion.

to enable a man like Magnes to do this work for the community. I came in for a share of encomium together with Dr. Benderly which I must frankly admit I in no way deserve. He spoke for instance of what I did to improve tho moral tone of young men in YMHA while I know that it amounts practically to nil. This is an illustration of how people get credit for what they never do. But I am convinced that much more is gained by giving too much praise than by withholding where it is due.

I was called upon to speak next. I opened with a comment upon the distinction that M. drew between the content and organization of Judaism. He disclaimed all attempts to deal with the former. I pointed out that he was really teaching those present the content of Judaism by giving them a comprehensive view of the community. The sense of community is more than doctrine or practice the essential content of Judaism. I then spoke in praise of the patience and perseverance displayed by M. in building up that community. The story of the man who said that you can even carry water in a sieve, if you have the patience to wait till it freezes, was applied by me to the Jewish community. If we shall have patience enough till the forces that make for cohesion will set in, we shall have a Jewish community even under modern conditions. Friedlaender made the point that M. knew how to interest those "who do not know how to ask" and he compared him to Atlas. Benderly credited him with helping to create a cerebral Judaism, the present one being ganglionic.

God as the Power that Makes for Freedom — A Talk at the 92nd Street Y

SATURDAY NIGHT, APRIL 3, 1915

Last night I spoke at the YMHA services. The audience though far from filling the auditorium was fairly large so I was told, considering the lateness of the season. I noticed that very few if any of the old people that used to attend these services in former years were present. The audience consisted almost entirely of young men and women.

As introduction I took the passage from the Haggadah *Bekhol dor vedor* . . . [Heb. "In every generation (a person is obliged to see himself as if he went out of Egypt.)"] to point out the need of celebrating Passover not in the spirit of commemorating a past event but of noting an ever present truth. That truth is that Passover gives us the opportunity of learning what God is. It tells us that God is the power that makes for freedom. This is a more comprehensive conception than Arnold's because it includes a phase of human progress—conquest of inanimate nature which is not reckoned with in his definition of God as the power that makes for righteousness. Besides, God as the power that makes for freedom is less abstract and remote. It is a God each one can experience *ta'amu ure'u ki tov 'd* [Heb. Psalms 34:9 "Taste and see how good the Lord is"[54]] because each one has an immediate awareness of this inward striving to liberate himself from the besetting forces of earth and temptation. Men are not born free and equal, but are born to become free and equal. It is the goal of all social endeavor to bring about equality in the inequality into which men are born. It is the goal of spiritual endeavor to make man free. The tendency to retroject in[to] the past that which we hope to achieve in the remote future is a common one. The retrojection of the notion of the Garden of Eden into the beginnings of man's career upon earth instead of into the future of the race are cases in point. Freedom which is the reflection of God's nature is the freedom that is synonymous with personality, character and will.

The realization of such freedom is even more difficult in an aggregate of human beings than in the individual. The mob mind is even more of a slave to the hereditary and blind impulses of human nature and knows less of self-mastery than the individual. The Jews as a self-conscious group have proved to be the only exception, to the law of the crowd, because in them the God that makes for freedom made himself most felt. It was this self-mastery that gave the Jewish people exemption from mortality or the angel of death. Having that freedom which means national personality, the Jewish people was never totally bereft of that power of initiative and reflection which saved it from losing itself in its environment.

The Origin of the Jewish Center—A New Kind of Synagogue

SATURDAY NIGHT, APRIL 10, 1915

I find myself at the beginning of a new spiritual enterprise which holds out great promise. The very opening up of a new vista of possibilities is exhilarating. I refer to the new movement that has been started by some of my friends on the West Side to establish a Jewish communal centre. For the last three or four years I have been urging Joseph H. Cohen to induce his friends to establish an institution that would not only provide a place to worship for the elders and a school for the children but also an opportunity to all affiliated with it to develop their social life Jewishly. As a result of my general reading and thinking I have come to the conclusion that religion derives its vitality from the social activities with which it is bound up. Detached from social life it becomes an empty formalism and a corpse which no amount of tinsel can render attractive.

Cohen grasped my idea at once and took steps to have it realized. A little over two years ago he called together at his house a number of people and invited

---

54. Kaplan did not write in the name of God here but ended the sentence with ure'u. In general Kaplan did not write out the name of God, but rendered the Tetragrammaton as 'd, pronounced *adonai* when read aloud.

me to explain to them the kind of institution I wanted them to establish. In the meantime most of those who were present had became preoccupied with their own affairs, these years having been particularly strenuous, and the whole matter was left in abeyance. The various philanthropic and educational institutions in which Cohen and his friends are interested claimed all the attention that they could devote to things Jewish, and so nothing further was heard about my scheme.

Suddenly the undertaking was revived. Then I saw Cohen, Fischman[55] and Rothstein[56] at the Magnes gathering. I was told by Cohen that they had organized, and were determined to carry out the plan of having the kind of institution that I had been dreaming of. Since that day Cohen has been frequently in touch with me. I have had [the] most interesting discussions with him as to the attitude I ought to take if I am to identify myself with the movement. I told him that I had a definite conception of what Judaism ought to be. That conception was based upon the principle that one could only be a Jew by reckoning with the whole of Israel and not with any part of it merely. This principle supplies enough of the positive and constructive to permit considerable latitude in the form of worship without the possibility of injuring the essentials. For that reason I would leave the question of [the] form of [the] service to the members themselves. If they insist upon having the sexes seated separately, I shall certainly not object. And if they insist upon having them seated promiscuously I shall not oppose them either. If I am to have anything to do with that organization I should make it my business to prove that there are weightier problems that Judaism must deal with than those that have to do with the form of worship. . . .

Kaplan and Ginzberg[57] Clash as They Exit the Seminary Synagogue

SUNDAY, APRIL 25, 1915

Today I had a slight altercation with Prof. Ginzberg. Every time we go out from the Seminary synagogue on the Sabbath to the faculty room he makes it his business to make some cynical remark at the practice of having

---

55. William Fischman (1867–1959), cloak and suit manufacturer; an organizer of the Downtown Talmud Torah; active in the Union of Orthodox Jewish Congregations.

56. Abraham Rothstein (1857–1939), cotton merchant, labor arbitrator.

57. Louis Ginzberg (1873–1953), Talmud and Midrashic scholar; faculty, JTS; author; one of the founders of the Conservative movement. His relationship with Kaplan was complex, and they were critical of each other. Ginzberg was much more traditional than Kaplan. Their "jousts" at Rabbinical Assembly meetings in the 1920s were a source of major "entertainment" for Conservative rabbis. See entry below for June 1927. See also *Judaism Faces the Twentieth Century.*

each Sabbath a different student preaching before the congregation. Today he said in his nasty satirical squeak, "When will the students be done with their preaching?" My patience gave way and I said to him that I did not see why he favored having those sermons at all if they were such a nuisance. I then added that after all scholarship does little more than study sermons that have become 2,000 years old. His clever answer was a laundry bill of today you throw away, while one of Ashurbanifal's[58] time constitutes an important discovery. He was called away otherwise I would have answered him that his laundry bills are a greater care to him that Ashurbanifal's.

Schechter Lashes out at Seminary Faculty Meeting

MAY 27, 1915

[The scene is a Seminary faculty meeting.]

Then came the matter of scholarships for next year. There are at present seventeen scholarships for distribution. . . . One could see that a storm was brewing. One name was mentioned then another without aim or purpose. Schechter was at a loss what to do. He was reluctant to refuse scholarships to men who had received them before. When questions of that kind are discussed, Prof. Ginzberg usually leans back as far as he can in his chair in serene indifference to the situation, and puffs away at his cigar. This of course only adds fuel to the fire. Finally Schechter burst out. He fairly screamed at the top of his voice; he banged at the table; he jumped up and ran about the room hurling invectives. He aimed particularly at Friedlaender. "Do you think I am jealous of Magnes the *Manhig Ha-Dor* [Heb. Leader of our time] or of Benderly when I say that since they have come the Seminary has gone down? There used to be a group of about twenty people to whom I could come for money whenever I needed it. That has now become impossible because the 'Burau'[59] (so he pronounces it) has to have $300,000 a year. I need scholarships and there is no body to help me to get them. See what they are doing at Cincinnati. They give each man twice the amount we give. If we can't offer scholarships we can't have any students. There used to be times when I could approach a member of the board for money to buy some rare manuscript. That is gone now because the 'Burau' wants to swallow up everything. Unfortunately the last days of my life have become bound up with the Seminary and I hoped to see it before I die established on a firm footing. Instead of that it is going down and down. . . . I am really sorry that I have to speak out this way, but it hurts me and I can't help myself."

---

58. Usually written Assurbanipal (669 B.C.E.–627 B.C.E.); last powerful Assyrian ruler, and a patron of the arts.

59. Bureau of Jewish Education of the New York Kehillah (community).

2

May 30, 1915–August 14, 1918

Schiff Unhappy with the Bureau of Jewish Education

SUNDAY, MAY 30, 1915

I returned not long ago from a meeting of the Trustees of the Bureau of Education which took place at Mr. Marshall's house. The others present were Marshall, Benderly, Magnes, and Friedlaender. Benderly's report showed in what financial straits the Bureau found itself, and he made it clear that unless the Bureau were put upon a sound basis it is useless for him to go on. The discussion brought out the fact that Mr. Schiff was not as friendly (or well) disposed toward the Bureau as he used to be. In a lengthy conversation which he had with Benderly he wanted to make sure that the Bureau did not stand for Jewish Nationalism or Zionism. Benderly reported that he had said to Mr. Schiff that he was neither nationalist nor Zionist, but that he was mainly interested in the keeping of Israel alive in the diaspora. It is unfortunate and abnormal that so vital a work as that of education should depend upon the whim of a rich man whose ideas move in a narrow and limited groove. Today, (May 31) I learned from Friedlaender that Schiff had declared to Benderly that he would withdraw his support entirely both from the bureau and the Kehillah because he had been informed that the entire movement was planned with the end in view of organizing a kind of Jewish political party. Magnes also came in for a share of condemnation. Schiff disapproved of him as being a demagogue.

Kaplan at the Public Library—Becomes Depressed

TUESDAY, JUNE 1, 1915

Whenever I have to prepare an address I am in the habit of going to the Public Library to "brouse" among the books in the hope of coming across some striking phrases or ideas. It happens very often, however, that

I pick up some books that expose the untenability of professional religion. The effect which they have upon me is to awaken in me the suppressed and dormant rebelliousness at conventional religion. They make me realize the unnaturalness and abnormality of my own position in life. Every time I read such books I feel as though something true and good died within me. The humiliation which I experience is akin in painfulness to that felt when a bereavement occurs in the family. The depression lasts for a day or two then I go about my business, much as one does after a calamity which at the time seems overwhelming. The book which had that violent effect upon me yesterday when I went to the library to find some material for the address that I am to give next Sunday at the graduation exercises was Nordau, "Interpretation of History."[1]

Schechter Cautions Kaplan

JUNE 9, 1915

      Yesterday afternoon I spent more than two hours in the company of Dr. Schechter. He was quite genial and frank with me. For once he seemed to display some interest in me personally. He told me that I have a great future before me. I must not, however, commit myself to any views about the Bible, views which I might have to retract.[2] Instead of going on with the commentary, he said, I should finish the edition of Shir Hashirim Rabba upon which I have been at work on and off these last two years. As to the other that could wait till I am fifty.

TI Students Make Good-Natured Fun of Kaplan

WEDNESDAY, JUNE 30, 1915

      Last Saturday night the Graduating Class gave a class play at the auditorium of the Y.M.H.A. It was the first play given by the students of the Teachers Institute. The Graduating Class of 1914 had a play written but was not able to present it. It is remarkable that the students of the Institute should have been able to develop anything like an esprit de corps,

---

1. Max Nordau (1849–1923), philosopher and Zionist leader. The work in question is *The Interpretation of History* (New York: Willey Book Co., 1910), a philosophy of history which examines the advance from supernaturalism to community.

2. Kaplan had published an essay on the Bible in the *Students' Annual of the Jewish Theological Seminary* for 1914. It is entitled "The Supremacy of Torah." While Kaplan was in Europe on his honeymoon in 1908 he copied a manuscript of the Midrash on *Shir Ha-Shirim Rabba* (The Song of Songs), which he intended to use along with other manuscripts to publish a critical edition of this Midrash. He was also apparently working on a commentary to the Bible.

in spite of the fact that the Institute has as yet no home of its own. The play given last Saturday night was called "You'll Get There" based on Dr. Benderly's promise three years ago to the City College students whom he had invited, that if they would pursue the three years' course they would be provided with positions. Changes have taken place in the meantime, and the demand for man teachers is not very great. Consequently the men feel disappointed that Benderly failed to carry out his promise. I was very much amused by the play, particularly by the part where they caricatured my manner of teaching Bible Interpretation, which they designated "Biblical Interruption."

United Synagogue Convention—Ginzberg and Schechter Speak

FRIDAY, AUGUST 15, 1915

On Sunday, July 11, I went to Arverne to attend the meeting of the United Synagogue.[3] The gathering consisted of the Seminary Faculty, Dr. Adler,[4] about two dozen Seminary Graduates, a dozen delegates, and a few women. As a means of spending a vacation day, the convention was an excellent thing. In the afternoon nearly all the time was spent discussing the question whether or not to accept the invitation of the American Jewish Committee to send delegates to the Conference which is to take place about the beginning of November to consider what action to take with reference to the Jews in the belligerent countries. . . . In the evening a banquet was held. The usual string of talk about peace and harmony constituted the spiritual food.

Next day the business of the convention, or whatever there was of it, was concluded. In the afternoon and evening the alumni met. Ginzberg spoke on the Halacha as a source of history. It was a rather stimulating talk though in his usual style of administering a few sneering thrusts at speakers and at his colleagues on the faculty. His soul seems to be as small as his body and its music as squeaky as his voice. There is no room in it for spiritual resonance. I forgot to mention that Schechter preceded him with a talk on the function of the rabbi. He too managed to prove how small he could be by resorting to a veiled attack on Magnes as an illustration of what a rabbi should not be. He described him as a "rabbi at large," whose main business is collecting money to put down vice.

---

3. The United Synagogue, an organization of congregations loosely identified with the JTS, was founded by Solomon Schechter in 1913.

4. Cyrus Adler (1863–1940), major figure on the American Jewish scene; author; president of Dropsie College; president of JTS; founder of the Jewish Publication Society and the American Jewish Historical Society.

Kaplan Disgusted with the Y.M.H.A. Directors

SEPTEMBER 15, 1915

Yesterday I attended a meeting called by Herbert Straus[5] for the purpose of getting the directors and associate directors to engage in a house to house campaign for members. It was not so much the zeal for the institution that activated Straus as the desire to please F.M. Warburg who had expressed his displeasure at the failure of the directors to add to the membership list. The lunch that was served at the Manhattan Club, 26th St. & Madison Ave. consisted of oysters on shells and chicken. My stomach turned at the sight of some of our "Keiks," Shulman[6] among them enjoying their repast. There were not missing the two youngsters who are presented at every joint meeting of this kind as the product of the Y.M.H.A. and as samples of [what] the institution is turning out—like two well bred pups.

The Death of Solomon Schechter

SUNDAY, NOVEMBER 20, 1915

So Dr. Schechter is no more. On Friday, Nov. 19 at 3 P.M. he died from heart failure. It was a very stormy morning when he came to the Seminary to do his routine work. He felt bad and complained of neuralgic pains in the head and in his chest. He asked Prof. Ginzberg to take his hour with the students, while he himself remained in the office signing letters. Among the last letters he signed was one addressed to me. In reference to my taking part in the work for the classic series. When I saw him on Thursday he mentioned that I would be asked to translate the "Mesilath Yesharim."[7] I promised to undertake the work and asked him to give me in addition a somewhat more substantial task which he promised to do. The letter arrived seven o'clock in the evening, immediately after I had learned of his death. When I came to the house of the Schechters on Friday night I found but few people. Mrs. Schechter[8] was shut up in her room, and the children—Frank and Amie—were busy making arrangements with the help of Straus for the

---

5. Herbert Straus (1881–1933), merchant and business executive. The family owned Macy's department store.

6. Probably Rabbi Samuel Schulman (1864–1965), prominent reform rabbi, New York City; president, Association of Reform Rabbis; opposed Zionism but not Israel.

7. Mesillat Yesharim: *The Path of the Upright.* An eighteenth-century ethical treatise by Moses Hayyim Luzzato. Kaplan translated and annotated this work for the Schiff Classics series of the Jewish Publication Society. It appeared in 1936.

8. Mathilde Roth Schechter (1857–1924), born near Breslau, well educated, married Schechter 1887; Schechter home became a "salon" in London, Cambridge, and New York. Founded Woman's League for Conservative Judaism. See this author's "The Baale Boste Reconsidered: The Life of Mathilde Roth Schechter (M.R.S.)," *Modern Judaism* 7, no. 1 (February 1987).

Solomon Schechter, ca. 1902. (Courtesy Ratner Center, JTS)

funeral which was set for today at 10:30. The children intimated that their father as well as their mother had objected to the use of automobiles for funerals but their objections were overruled. This morning the funeral took place at 10:30. The body was brought to the Seminary building. Rabbi E. L. Solomon[9] delivered the eulogy. The crowd of people that had gathered though large (about 1,500–2,000) was by no means commensurate with the significance of Dr. Schechter to Judaism. We may now be prepared for changes of an eventful character.

Daughter Selma[10] Named after Solomon Schechter

DECEMBER 15, 1915

Selma *Shulamit* [Heb. Shulamit] whom we named after Solomon Schechter was born on Monday December 6, at 7:25 P.M. *L. Kislev* [Heb. 30th day of month of Kislev].

Setting Up the Jewish Center

SUNDAY, JUNE 18, 1916

The next matter I wish to record has to do with the Jewish Centre on the West Side. After the lapse of many months during which I had heard nothing about it the undertaking came to life again. The organization purchased ground on West 86 Street. J. H. Cohen put himself once again in touch with me with a view to having me take charge of the Institution when it was completed. As soon as I felt that I might actually be drawn into that position I regarded it as my duty to lay before Cohen my heterodoxical views. When, however, he asked me as to the practical form which these views would take on, if I were to assume charge of the position, (institution) I did not have the courage to go to the full length of what my attitude logically should have led me to state but I confined myself to the statement that I should be exempted from holding positive views about the seating of the sexes and about the organ. My contention was that there were more important issues than these in Judaism, and that if I were to insist upon these lesser issues, the more important ones would be obscured. Joseph H. Cohen, however, has been adamant to my suggestions. In spite of all my pleading he still insists that I ought to advocate the strict observance of the

---

9. Elias L. Solomon (1879–1956), rabbi and communal leader; born in Lithuania; graduated from the JTS in 1904; served the Conservative movement in a number of capacities, including president of the United Synagogue.

10. Selma Kaplan Jaffe-Goldman, fourth Daughter of M. Kaplan; worked in television production and syndication; married to Saul Jaffe (1913–77), attorney, radio and TV production; married to Joseph L. Goldman, M.D. (1904–91), chief, Department of Otolaryngology, Mt. Sinai Hospital.

traditional forms of worship. In the meantime, I have practically come to the conclusion that I could not give up either the [Teachers] Institute or the Seminary for the West Side Institution particularly for the reason that I can not have it conducted the way I should like to see it conducted. Cohen has been trying hard to sway me. He was to see me on the seventh day of Passover together with Fishman and Rothstein. But instead of flattering their orthodoxy I restated my attitude with considerable firmness. I learned from Cohen later on that they went away rather disappointed. On Saturday June 10 Cohen invited me to his house, and when after a long conversation in which we were later on joined by Rothstein, Cohen asked me whether he could propose me as a member preparatory to my becoming director, I refused to give him an affirmative answer. The suggestion to have me made a director had come from me when I had made up my mind that I would not become a salaried official of the institution. But now that I see that I may count upon a great deal of opposition to say nothing of the work that identifying myself with it would necessarily involve, I have grown cold to the idea of my having anything whatever to do with the institution. But as I have not taken any final step I may expect some interesting developments.

Kaplan Clashes with Jacob Schiff over Loyalty Issue

Friday, June 30, 1916

Practically the first time in my life that anything I had to say created something of a stir was when I delivered the address at the graduation exercises of the Seminary and Institute on Sunday, June 11. The "Times" of the Monday following gave the most prominent place to my address in the report it had of the graduation exercises. "Assails Doubters of Jew's Loyalty, Prof. Kaplan calls preaching patriotism to the Jews carrying coals to New Castle." The Jewish press both in Yiddish and English came out with the most laudatory editorials for the courage I displayed in taking issue with Schiff. The fact was that I did not have Schiff principally in mind. It was the general fashion that had become prevalent of late that I want to give a deathblow to, and I believe that I have been quite successful. I had been very much embittered by the boisterous patriotism of a man like Hyman, who had the impudence to tell his listeners at the dedication exercises of the Central Jewish Institute[11] that we should be Americans in public and Jews in private. Robison[12] of the Y.M.H.A. told me that whenever any of the

---

11. Central Jewish Institute, a uniquely American institution which combined a wide rage of social and recreational activities with a school at the hub. The institute "gave birth" to CeJwIn Camp.

12. Aaron G. Robison (1893–1936), rabbi, communal worker.

out-of-town Y.M.H.A. meetings takes place this is the everlasting theme. I was particularly indignant at the address made by Samuel Strauss[13] in the Educational Alliance[14] at the confirmation exercises which took place on the first day of Shabuoth, June 6, in the course of which he made the statement that it was more important to be a good American than to be a good Jew. The only thing I regretted was that some of the opponents of Schiff and the American Jewish Committee took occasion to make use of what I said to attack that crowd.

Bible Scholar Max Margolis[15] Complains to Kaplan about Adler and Schechter

JULY 18, 1916

At the memorial services in honor of Schechter, Adler gave an encyclopedic review of Schechter's life. I was glad when it was over and I made at once for home. I did not want to stay at the banquet which the congregation had arranged supposedly to celebrate the dedication of the synagogue[16] (it is almost a year since the synagogue has been in existence) but in reality to make some money to pay off debts. In the train I met Prof. Max Margolis of Dropsie College.[17] I had known him by sight for quite some time but I had never spoken with him for any length of time. I was quite pleasantly surprised to find him human and outspoken. Our conversation turned at once upon home politics. I alluded to Adler as the "Chief" and he spoke of the Seminary and Dropsie as the Dual Kingdom, by reason of Adler leading at present both of them and of his being likely to do so permanently. I could see that Margolis was one of those who after a series of futile struggles had settled down to a life of enforced assent to the inevitable. He had his little story to tell of silent persecutions at the hands of Schechter and Adler. The former bore against him an unaccountable grudge, as he did against any one of the dependent class of pedagogues who refused to flatter him.

---

13. Samuel Strauss (1870–1953), journalist, publisher, and author; worked with the *Des Moines Leader* before coming to New York City.

14. The Educational Alliance was established in the 1890s on the Lower East Side and became one of the major social and educational institutions aiding Eastern European Jews in their adjustment to America. Meetings, lectures, classes, a library, a gymnasium, and a roof garden afforded a wide range of activities.

15. Max Margolis (1886–1932), biblical and semitics scholar; held positions at Hebrew Union College and Dropsie College; author, with Alexander Marx, of *The History of the Jewish People*, which has become a classic.

16. The service took place at an Orthodox synagogue in Far Rockaway where the United Synagogue was holding its meeting.

17. Dropsie College was a postgraduate institution of Jewish and semitic studies located in Philadelphia. It was established in 1907 through the will of Moses Aaron Dropsie (1821–1905). Cyrus Adler was one of the founders and the first president.

Jewish Congress Debate at the Astor Hotel—Kaplan's Analysis

JULY 18, 1916

The day before yesterday (Sunday) I was present at the conference called by the American Jewish Committee to discuss ways and means of securing full civil religious and political rights for our brethren in all lands. The conference met at the Astor Hotel. I came as one of the three delegates of the United Synagogue. The most interesting part of the meeting was the colloquy between Magnes and Brandeis.[18] Brandeis had come with Judge Pam[19] and Ex-Judge Sanders[20] as a committee representing the Philadelphia conference that had convened in March and that had voted the calling into existence of a congress. Brandeis told the members of the conference that they were welcome to join the Congress movement and that there were purposely left vacancies in the Executive Committee for such representative Jews as had not yet joined the Congress movement.

Despite the fact that Brandeis is now one of the Supreme Judges of the U.S. he did not impress me as having made the appropriate kind of an appeal, particularly if his object was to bring about an understanding between the Congress people and the members of the Astor Conference. But I have my doubts whether that was really his purpose. I have the feeling that the issue between the two groups is one that has to do with the question as to what should be the course adopted by the Jews of this country. Those who favor the Congress are for the most part drawn from the Zionist ranks. What they want, therefore, is to establish here a semi-autonomous Jewish group life. They are using the Congress idea simply as a means of getting the Jews together for that purpose. They want to utilize the predicament of the Jews in Europe as a means of organizing the Jews of America. The conference people on the other hand who are of the better placed class dread nothing more than the furtherance of Jewish group life. Their interest in the Jews of Europe is based on philanthropic principles and they fight bitterly any attempt to convert philanthropic Judaism into national Judaism. This is why the debate during the greater part of the afternoon was waged about the question whether the Congress should be called for the sole purpose of obtaining rights for the Jews everywhere or whether the Congress should become a permanent organization.

Joined of course to the question of principle is the matter of personal

---

18. Louis D. Brandeis (1856–1941), U.S. Supreme Court justice, lawyer, and national Zionist leader.

19. Hugo Pam (1870–1930), lawyer, state supreme court judge, Zionist civic and communal worker.

20. Leon Sanders (1867–1937), lawyer, legislator, and municipal court justice; active in the American Jewish Congress.

ambition and love of power. Marshall, Adler and Magnes are jealous of the popularity of Brandeis and Stephen Wise.[21] The latter again wish to wrest the power from the moneyed interests. With all that the higher interests of the Jewish people would not be compromised by these squabbles—every people has similar ones—if we had some terra firma to stand on. The very need our Jews have of some outward calamity to bring them together and the total apathy toward any internal improvement is indication of the final dissolution. The very freedom which will be won for the Jews will help to put an end to Judaism. Symptomatic of the inner condition of Jewish life are the following remarks made by Philipson[22] of the Cincinnati College [HUC]. "For many years have I dreamt of Jewish unity. But it was only a dream. I find that I could not meet in convention with Zionists, or with Orthodox Jews or with socialists. But now thank God, I have found something that can unite us all, and that is the endeavor to secure equal rights for our brethren." Reduced to simple terms his statement amounts to the fact that he thanks God for seeing to it that the Jews be boycotted, discriminated against and hounded like wild beasts. Otherwise there would be nothing to keep the Jews together.

A Chance Meeting with Bernard Revel[23]—Head of Yeshiva

THURSDAY, AUGUST 24, 1916

On one of my return trips this week I fell in with Dr. Bernard Revel, the present head of the Yeshiba. Although he has been living in N.Y. in the same house with me we have never visited each other. I avoided him because I had been warned that he is not altogether trustworthy. Although I could have avoided him this time too, I did not do so. We had a very interesting conversation. He maintained that Judaism emphasized this worldliness as opposed to the other worldliness and soul saving tendency of Christianity. I took issue with him on that score because I believe that we cannot attribute to Judaism any particular philosophy of life. He spoke very intelligently and used a remarkably good English, although he stammered once in a while. This particularly surprised me in a man who on the one hand possesses a

---

21. Stephen Wise (1872–1949), outstanding liberal rabbi; Zionist; founder of the Free Synagogue and the Jewish Institute of Religion (JIR). Admired Kaplan and hoped he would be associated with the JIR, offering him a position there three times. In 1927, Kaplan resigned from the seminary to go to JIR but then changed his mind. For more information, see *Judaism Faces the Twentieth Century: A Biography of Mordecai M. Kaplan* (Detroit: Wayne State University Press, 1993).

22. David Philipson (1862–1949), rabbi, reform Jewish leader, author, and member of the faculty of Hebrew Union College.

23. Bernard Revel (1885–1940), educator, scholar, and author who reorganized Rabbi Isaac Elhanan Theological Seminary and founded Yeshiva College, later to become Yeshiva University.

reputation for Jewish learning of the kind one meets with only in Eastern Europe and on the other hand is quite familiar with the literature of Jewish Science. As we parted he said "This has been a revelation to me; I hope there will no more be any misunderstanding between us."

Kaplan Visits Mill in Paterson in Search of a New Career

TUESDAY, AUGUST 29, 1916

Today I went with my brother-in-law Edward Rubin to take a look at his silk mill in Paterson. The hyde[24] of materialistic ambition is not completely dormed [dormant?] in me. It asserted itself last Friday night when I had a talk with him. I dreamed once again of turning to the practical affairs of life, and when he suggested that I go to take a look at the mill, I gladly consented to do so. When I rode with him and his son Milton in the train this morning I had them both explain to me the business situation as it concerned him, and the details involved in the manufacture of silk. At one moment it appeared to me as an enchanting Romance at the other as a sordid aimless pursuit. This latter conviction gained on me when Milton took me to Paterson while his father remained in New York. From my conversation with him it was borne in upon me that Ed with all his wealth gets very little out of life that is worthwhile. He is not even laying the foundation of future happiness. He is squandering all his energies in money getting without the prospect of ever really enjoying what he will have amassed. When I came to the mill I was sorely disappointed. I had expected to see a sanitary well managed factory. What I saw impressed me as noisy, unsafe and unsanitary, with disorder and waste quite rampant. As I returned my heart was very much saddened at the hard pitiless grind of the average well-to-do Jewish business man, whose life is ill-organized empty and futile. In addition they have as wives women who have not the least conception of their husband's toil, whose greatest problem is that of getting upstairs girls and nurses, and who grow stout and neurasthenic for want of anything worthwhile to occupy their minds with.

Kaplan Hears Woodrow Wilson Speak

SUNDAY, SEPTEMBER 3, 1916

Yesterday I went[25] to hear President Wilson deliver his speech of acceptance of the nomination for re-election. I experienced some of that

---

24. *O.E.D.* indicates *hyde* as an archaic form and past of *hie*, meaning to strive, be intent or eager.

25. The word "went" is crossed out and the phrase "walked to xxxxx" is substituted, but Kaplan's destination here is illegible, so I have taken the liberty of keeping the original reading.

awe which was meant to be voiced in the blessing *asher ḥalak mi-kevodo* [Heb. "(Blessed art thou o Lord our God) who has given of His glory to mortal man"].[26] I could not help thinking of the contrast between the Jewish people, moribund and spiritless, and the American people in the prime vigor of youth. How happy the lot of those that lead the one; how wretched the lot of those doomed to stand by the deathbed of the other.

Kaplan at the Shore — Depressed

SATURDAY NIGHT, SEPTEMBER 23, 1916

I enjoy my stay in Long Branch whenever I recall how essential it is to the health and well being of my family to spend the summer out-of-town. Occasionally I also regale in the outdoor air and sunshine when I sit and work or read quietly on the porch. Most of the time, however, I experience here all the solitude and isolation of a prison. The days and the weeks are passing by without my achieving anything. When I am in New York I have at least occasion to interchange a word with somebody. Here I am all alone; not a human being who is interested in or troubled by problems similar to mine. But the less said the better.

The last few weeks I have had an interchange of letters with Adler and Marshall about the finances of the Institute. I have gotten to a point where I realize the futility of all my moanings about the hopelessness of the task in life to which I am tied down. I am simply resigned.

This morning I preached at the Long Branch Synagogue. There were but few people present but I was impelled to speak by a desire to redeem myself for a previous sermon that I had foisted on the same audience two weeks ago. I then forgot that I had before me a congregation that possessed but little intellectual background and I attempted to explain to them the significance of the personification of Israel. I could see that the thing fell flat.

Kaplan Reminisces when His Father Dies

TUESDAY, JANUARY 30, 1917

My beloved Father *HaRav Yisrael b'r' Noson* [Heb. Rabbi Israel the son of Nathan] died on Thursday night, the third of Shebat, 5677 (Jan. 25, 1917) at 10:15 P.M.

His biography is brief. He was born sixty-nine years ago [1848]—so at least I gathered from various remarks made by him now and then, for he

---

26. The blessing here is for seeing a ruler. The blessing is supposed to be "Blessed art thou . . . who has given (natan) of thy glory. . . ." The blessing on seeing a wise man is " . . . asher ḥalak miḥakhmato . . ." (" . . . who has imparted His wisdom . . ."). Kaplan apparently mixed up the language of the two blessings.

Kaplan's father, Rabbi Israel Kaplan. (Courtesy Judith K. Eisenstein)

never stated to me his age—in the little town of Silel Russia.[27] He was the second of five children, three brothers and two sisters. At the age of twelve he was sent to study in Wilna and there while quite young he received S'micha from R. Bzalel. He married my mother at Swenziane to which town R. Reines[28] was called not long after. He also received S'micha [ordination] from R. Reines. After having spent a year or so in Swenziane, father studied in Dunaberg [now Dwinsk], Volozhin and Kovno, Shavel [Shavli] and Ashshoc [Eishishok].

THURSDAY, FEBRUARY 1, 1917

At Kovno he received S'micha from R. Isaac Elchanan.[29] He was recognized as a Harif [sharp, brilliant] though he never resorted to pilpulistic[30] [scholastic] casuistry. He was noted for his sound reasoning. When he came back from Kovno he was urged to accept a rabbinate and R. Reines went with him to induct him into office in one of the towns near Vilna. When he got there he was displeased with the class of people that came to the synagogue and refused to be their rabbi. After that he went again to study, this time to Rishen, [Rasseyn] the Yeshiba of which was presided over by R. Sender Moshe of whom father spoke frequently as remarkable both for his learning and strength of character. In most of these Yeshibas father enjoyed privileges not accorded to other students. He was permitted to read something of Modern Hebrew literature and journalism, such was the faith reposed in his adherence to the traditional habits and beliefs.

In all these years of his study mother maintained herself by keeping a small grocery store that was patronized by Polish inhabitants of the town. The earnings were very small but even these were growing less as the Poles began to open up their own little stores. It seems that the boycott of which we hear so much nowadays began already at that time, that is during the eighties. It thus became more and more imperative for father to earn a livelihood. An opening presented itself when the position of Rosh Yeshiba in Taurigen [Tavrig] became vacant. He was recommended by R. Isaac Elchanan and others. When he came there and delivered his inaugural lecture he made a very excellent impression and the people escorted him back to his house

---

27. The town is most probably Silale in Yiddish Shilel, which is in Lithuania not far from Kovno.

28. Isaac Jacob Reines (1839–1915), rabbi; founder of Mizrachi; rabbi Swenziane from 1869; founded innovative Yeshiva in Lida; author.

29. Rabbi Isaac Elchanan Spector (1817–96), Lithuanian rabbi; founded noted yeshiva in Kovno. R. Isaac Elchanan Theological Seminary at Yeshiva University is named after him.

30. Forms of Talmudic reasoning which evolved to test the cleverness of students and scholars. They had been criticized as early as the fifteenth century, and came into disrepute in the early nineteenth century when new methods of Talmudic study evolved.

with music. But he took sick; he suffered, it seems, from some kind of lung trouble and after twelve weeks he had to give up the position and go to Konigsberg to be cured.

My recollection of father during those years is limited to that of the hustle and bustle in the house when he was expected to return from the different Yeshibahs wither he had gone to study. I remember his having brought me a whistle—that was when I was probably about four, and later on when I had begun to go to Heder he brought me a small set of Humesh[31] of which I was very proud; I begrudged any other boy looking into it together with me while we studied in Heder. I remember also father's taking me once to the synagogue on a holiday and the impression made on me by the Rabbi in his silk hat, which I then saw for the first time. Outside of these few incidents, I do not recall anything that a child might expect from his father under normal circumstances.

When father returned from Konigsberg affairs at home took a turn for the worse and poverty began to threaten. It was decided that father should go to America—(I recall having heard from mother that father had made an attempt to go to America one or two years before he actually left Russia, but got only as far as Hamburg. The accompanying letter of introduction from Samuel Joseph Fin to Alexander Kohut[32] belongs to that first attempt.) that is to New York—where one of my mother's brothers, Mendel Kruzansky, had lived for about three years, and to find there some source of a livelihood. In the meantime mother together with my sister and myself were to go to Paris when two of my mother's brothers, Joseph and Jonas Kruzansky had established themselves. This was in July 1888. I was then seven years old. As soon as father came here he was taken into the house of the Chief Rabbi Jacob Joseph.[33] He was given food and lodging and some pocket money for services he rendered in the way of deciding upon ritual questions and entertaining scholarly visitors with discussions on Talmudic lore. Mother, Sophie and myself came from Paris where we had been in sore straits on July 16, 1889.

It was not long before father broke with R. Joseph and his entourage on account of their unscrupulous methods in trying to get control of the kosher meat trade and of the resources which that trade might have yielded

---

31. Pentateuch, five books of Moses.

32. Alexander Kohut (1842–94), rabbi and Conservative theologian; Talmudic scholar on the faculty of JTS.

33. Rabbi Jacob Joseph (1840–1902), noted rabbi of Vilna; installed as chief rabbi in New York City in 1888 in order to bring some order into traditional community; died in poverty. Israel Kaplan came to America in his entourage. See *Judaism Faces the Twentieth Century*, 28, for more details.

for communal purposes. A number of butchers seceded from the organization and appointed father as supervisor of the kashruth in their shops. Each one of these butchers put out a sign in the window of his store which read *Be-hashgaḥat ha-rav Yisra'el Kaplan* [Heb. Under the supervision of Rabbi Israel Kaplan]. After a year or so the group that recognized him as supervisor became disorganized. After a great deal of struggling he obtained the post of supervisor in a slaughterhouse which yielded him ten dollars a week. Later he was given charge of the kashruth of an additional slaughterhouse. Altogether he earned fifteen dollars a week.

He spent his mornings during the last two decades of his life in attending to his supervision work. Afternoons he would usually take his nap. The rest of the time he would spend in studying Talmud and Poskim [Rabbinic codes]. He was weak and unfit for strenuous or persistent labor of any kind. In his luminous hours he was capable of deep insight into the various problems of human life. He had a poor ear for language and was never able to acquire the vernacular of this country. He read the Yiddish papers for general news. During the last nine years we conversed in Hebrew. In the beginning I gained considerable fluency in Hebrew in this way. I enjoyed particularly telling him the substance of some of my sermons or addresses. In former years—that is about eight to twelve years ago—his suggestions were very helpful to me at times. During the last few years, however, there existed very little of an intellectual character that was in common between us. As I would go up daily to see my parents I would find very little to talk about except the petty trifles that concerned my own person—matters that I detest to talk about except as they are drawn out of me. I viewed the widening gap between father and myself as a tragedy and I tried last year to close it up by studying Talmud with him. I have no intrinsic interest in the Talmud because its contents are for the most part of no relevance whatever to the problems and needs of Jewish life. But, unfortunately, it is expected of me and generally supposed that I have a good command of Talmud. It is in order to live up to this opinion that I take up the study of it time and again. As I knew that nothing could please parents more than if I would study with father, I used to come to their house in the evening quite regularly about 10:30 and study the treatise of Gittin [divorces] for about an hour and a half each time. We stopped when he took sick with broncho-pneumonia last April. Ever since then he has been very weak and was finally overtaken about two weeks ago by the illness that ended his life. On his death bed he would quote some passage from the Talmud for many of the incidents of the attendance upon him. In a spell of semi-delirium which he had two nights before he died reciting passages from the Talmud in his usual sing-song chant. Realizing that there was no hope of his recovery he said the Shma and

Vidui [deathbed confessional] the night before. He passed away Thursday night at 10:15.

Today I rose from "Shiba" [prescribed seven days of mourning]. I must say that my attitude toward its observance has changed. Whereas from the theoretical standpoint I had regarded the ceremonious visitations and the compulsory abstention from labor as a boring and burdensome experience now that I have had to go through it myself, I have come to look upon it as a useful and humanizing institution. The stream of people coming and going prevents futile brooding and the compulsory abstention from labor makes it impossible for the dead to pass out of mind with almost tragic swiftness. I felt as if the days of mourning with the visits of all kinds of people and the daily services had socialized me more Jewishly, had knit me closer to the body of Jewish life and traditions. It is such a feeling that I always identify as Jewishness or Judaism.

Rabbis and Preaching—A Class Discussion

FEBRUARY 4, 1917

The contrast between (Louis) Newman[34] and the students at the Seminary was brought out into strong relief through an incident that occurred in my classroom on Wednesday, January 3. A student by the name of Solomon Goldman,[35] who in knowledge of Talmud is among the best, and in other respects also quite superior to most of the class, was asked by me to read the sermon he had delivered from the Seminary pulpit but which the class had not had a chance to hear before. While he was reading I noticed that the students did not take what he said very seriously. When he was through I took advantage of their want of seriousness to point out the importance to a sermon of proper atmosphere. As that was lacking in the classroom I could account for their semi-frivolous attitude. As I was speaking I was interrupted by semi-jocular remarks of one or two students in disparagement of preaching in general. This aroused the indignation of Newman and rising from his seat his excoriated the students in relation to whom he described himself as an outsider for their cynicisms and cheap wit that they were in the habit of launching against the ministry. This tirade of his was applauded by a few but apparently resented by most of the men. The only answer that the students could give came from its punster and versifier,

---

34. Louis Newman (1893–1972), reform rabbi, Zionist, communal and civil leader; one of the co-founders, with Stephen Wise, of the Jewish Institute of Religion. At this particular time Newman was in New York and sitting in on Kaplan's lectures.

35. Solomon Goldman (1893–1953), Conservative rabbi, Zionist leader, and key disciple of Mordecai Kaplan; spent most of his professional life in the Midwest. See *Judaism Faces the Twentieth Century* for more information.

Abraham Burstein, who merely uttered a weak protest on the ground that
a stranger had no right to meddle in the affairs of the Seminary. I, for my
part, did not think it prudent to agree entirely with Newman, and I pointed
out that with the present conditions that made it necessary for the students
to work each by himself individually, and that prevented their developing
a spirit of cooperation and material helpfulness during their student years,
they could not but reflect the general opinion of ministers and ministry that
was prevalent everywhere, an opinion that was derogatory and discouraging.
Of course I could not tell the whole truth and that was that the one really
and truly responsible for the spiritual disorganization of the Seminary was
its former president, the late Dr. Schechter. Though himself an interesting
and even picturesque personality, he was too much interested in his own
reputation as a scholar and man of letters to throw himself heart and soul
into rendering the Seminary a spiritual lighthouse for American Jewry. It
was he that used to wither the souls of the students with his ill-timed jests
about rabbis and their calling and it was he that made it fashionable for all
scholars and near-scholars in and about the Seminary to turn up their noses
at the term "rabbi"!

What Is Judaism—A Talk in Minneapolis

FEBRUARY 4, 1917

On Tuesday, December 26, I left for the Menorah Convention which
was taking place at the Minnesota University, Minneapolis. I had been
invited to lead a forum on the question, "What is Judaism?" in view of
the interest aroused by the series of five articles I had contributed to the
Menorah Journal last year.

Never having traveled by myself before over so long a distance folks
saw to it that I should be made as comfortable as possible. As I stepped
off the train at Chicago I was met by a Mr. Black, a salesman for the firm
of Rubin Bros., my brother-in-law. He had been asked by Max to meet me.
He was together with a man by the name of Sachs from Philadelphia. They
both took me to a nearby hotel where I had sardines and coffee, my mainstay
in trefa-land. After the meal they saw me off to the train for Minneapolis.
When I arrived there at eight o'clock I telephoned to Rabbi Matt,[36] a former
pupil of mine at the Seminary to find out where the Menorah men were
stopping. His wife answered that he was still at the morning service in his
synagogue, a fact which surprised me very much, as I could hardly believe
that in the western cities enough people could be gotten together to form

---

36. C. David Matt (1887–1951), Conservative rabbi; officer, Rabbinical Assembly; Zionist;
editor of *American Jewish World* (Minneapolis).

a minyan on a week-day. I refer of course to communities presided over by the graduates of the Seminary. . . .

In the evening (Thursday, December 28, 1916) I delivered the address for which I had been scheduled. There were about 200 people in the audience, divided about equally between men and women. Among them were Rabbi Deinard[37] of Minn. and Rabbis Rypins[38] and Herman M. Cohen[39] of St. Paul. The last is a Seminary graduate and former pupil of mine. I spoke for nearly an hour and a half on "What is Judaism?" The following is an abstract: The question is implied in many statements to be found in our literature, which purport to be a sort of definition of Judaism. 1) *ma 'd sho'el me-imkha* [Heb. Deuteronomy 10:12–13 "What does the Lord your God demand of you? (Only this: to revere the Lord your God, to walk only in His paths, to love Him, and to serve the Lord your God with all your heart and soul, keeping the Lord's commandments and laws, which I enjoin upon you today, for your good)"]. 2) *u-ma 'd doresh mimkha* [Heb. Micah 6:8 "He has told you, O man, what is good, and what the Lord requires of you: Only to do justice and to love goodness, and to walk modestly with your God"]. 3) not clear[40] 4)*avodah zarah, gilui arayot,* . . . [Heb. idolatry, unchastity . . .][41] 5) Y"G *ikkarim* [Heb. Thirteen Principles].[42] Yet none of these definitions is adequate for our purpose, because we put the question in a way it has never been asked before. We do not ask Whose good is to be served by keeping the Torah and the Mizvoth ours or God's?; What in our religion is more important, ceremonies or ethics?; What is primary, our relation to God or to one another?; What is the minimum to which we must adhere even on pain of death?; What distinguishes our religion from Christianity or Mohammedanism? None of these questions has relevance to our problem today when Judaism is called upon to adjust itself not only to a new cultural environment but also to a new social environment that is radically different from any type of social environment with which Judaism has ever come in contact. The democracy of the environment which calls

---

37. Samuel Deinard,(1872–1921), educated in Jerusalem and Cologne, University of Pennsylvania and University of Chicago; rabbi in Minneapolis and faculty member at University of Minnesota.

38. Isaac Rypins (1862–1951), educated at University of Cincinnati; ordained Hebrew Union College; rabbi, St. Paul, San Francisco.

39. Herman M. Cohen (1888–?), rabbi, Des Moines, Kansas City, and Minneapolis; officer, Zionist Organization of America.

40. May refer to Sinai or to rabbinic statement "What is hateful to you do not do to your neighbor." Manuscript not clear.

41. Kaplan is referring here to the rabbinic dictum that a Jew is to martyr himself rather than violate the three commandments against idolatry, unchastity, and murder. See Sanhedrin 74a.

42. Kaplan is referring here to the Thirteen Beliefs formulated by Maimonides. These are found in the complete daily prayer book after the daily morning service.

for a redistribution of the very units of Jewish social life is the novum in the problem. With the solvent influence exercised by the social environment upon the beliefs and practices associated with the name Judaism we begin to suspect that Judaism can function only under certain social conditions. The question What is Judaism? therefore resolves itself into the question "How do these beliefs and practices function?" For the first time we try to get at the very essence of Judaism, for the function of a thing practically constitutes its essence.

The theory of both the Orthodox and the Reformed school is that the beliefs and practices of Judaism are intended to make each one of us a better man or woman. If that were the case Judaism ought to be able to function despite the social redistribution of Jewry which takes place in democratic countries. The study of religion, however, helps us to understand why Judaism becomes defunct wherever Jews are prevented from living in aggregates. It has made clear that a religion is primarily a group conscious- ness. Whenever through one cause or another the group consciousness is destroyed the religion which is its expression must also perish. The problem of preserving Judaism is therefore a problem of preserving the Jewish consciousness. The intrinsic value not of the beliefs and practices of Judaism is what we must recognize, but of the Jewish consciousness of which they are an expression. So viewed the following two inferences follow as to the relation of the Jewish consciousness to the beliefs and practices that go by the name of Judaism (1) The Jewish consciousness is the end whereas the beliefs and practices are only the means. The former is life and the latter are truth. (2) The influence upon character of the belief and practices of Judaism is not exerted directly but only through the medium of the Jewish consciousness which they set into operation. Their immediate function is to integrate the individual into the Jewish consciousness.

Kaplan on Ethical Culture

MONDAY, FEBRUARY 19, 1917

Last night I conducted, at Hunter College, a Forum under the auspices of the Inter-Varsity Menorah on the question Ethical Culture or Judaism—Which? There was quite a large attendance consisting for the most part of young men and women college students. To my surprise however all those who participated in the discussion displayed such limited understanding of the problem that I was not stimulated to fresh thought on the question. Most of those who favored Ethical Culture did so not because of the intrinsic merits of the movement but because of the dilapidated condition of Judaism particularly Orthodoxy. Orthodox Judaism was roundly denounced for its filth and its lack of consideration for the young, and for its ceremonies. Here and there some arose in its defense. Practically no one as much as mentioned Reform Judaism as an alternative instead of Ethical Culture. I, therefore, infer that only from young men and women that came from old fashioned Jewish homes are the Menorah ranks recruited, a fact that I had occasion to observe every time I came in contact with Menorah men and women. It seems that the time is now ripe for a religious campaign among the Jewish students of the various high schools and colleges. I suspect that the cultural interests which the Menorah societies are seeking to foster are too weak to make any definite or positive impression upon their lives.

I am not sorry, however, that I consented to spend the evening with the Menorahs. I got more out of the preparation I had given to the meeting, expecting that it would develop into a real intellectual tussle, than out of the meeting itself. It gave me an opportunity to discover the weaknesses of the Ethical Culture movement to such a degree that I shall no longer look back with regret to my not having taken advantage of an Adler[43] Scholarship that I could have gotten in 1903 upon the recommendation of Prof. Woodbridge.[44] I often thought that if I had been drawn into the movement I might have been more spiritually satisfied than in Jewish work. Of course, I always felt there was something organically wrong with its philosophy as well as with its potentialities, but I was never so convinced as when I made a study of it the other week. I discovered that its principal weakness is that it dare not commit itself to a definite program of social reform, for fear of alienating those of its members who are so situated that they are interested in having the status quo maintained. I realized that it lacks the main essentials of a true cause that can fire the imagination and thrill the heart. It cannot evoke loyalty which is only possible when the group is organized on the basis either of common interests and a common history or of a definite object, such as socialism, world peace or woman suffrage.

---

43. Felix Adler (1851–1933), founder of the Ethical Culture movement; taught at Columbia in the Philosophy Department; a major influence on Kaplan while he was working for his master's degree. Kaplan inherited his emphasis on ethics and his theological tolerance but had contempt for Adler because he left the Jewish fold. In many ways Kaplan came to imitate Ethical Culture. See *Judaism Faces the Twentieth Century* for a full treatment of this complex relationship.

44. Fredrick Woodbridge (1867–1940), American philosopher; taught at Columbia (1902–12) and was dean from 1912–29. Kaplan studied with him when he was working on his master's degree.

Students at the Seminary—Particularly Louis Finkelstein

MONDAY, MARCH 12, 1917

In the course of my conferences with Seminary students during the last two weeks I had occasion to learn of two men, Finkelstein[45] and Harry Cohen,[46] who are opposed to the attitude I take towards the Bible. Finkelstein is by far the more sensible of the two. I understand that he has wealthy relations and that he is therefore in a position to give all his time to study, instead of having to spend most of the time, as the other Seminary men do, giving lessons. His father is a rabbi, and, from what he told me, is a man who holds far more liberal views than his son. Finkelstein's contention throughout a lengthy discussion I had with him was that the existence of Judaism is endangered if the traditional conception of revelation and miracle be denied. Harry Cohen is a foolish fellow who has never had any real intellectual training and who is studying for the ministry, as he himself said, because he can do nothing else. Both of these men are taking courses in Semitics at Columbia, their main ambition being to get a degree; whereas, if the authorities of the Seminary were to be sincere about graduating the proper kind of students, they would see to it that men like these should have some kind of grounding in the general problems of philosophy and the social sciences.

Last night there was a house dinner (in connection with Purim which was last Thursday) given at the Seminary. F. M. Warburg was the host. It was the second that was given this year. Schiff was present this time. After dinner was over he was called upon to speak. The principal point he made was that the alumni should make the Orthodox Jews realize what good the Seminary is doing. The rest was palaver. Adler[47] was toastmaster and having very little to say, wanted to introduce the precedent he had established at Dropsie College dinners of having no speaking. But when he called for a vote quite a number of the students voted in favor of speakers. Warburg spoke next. He called the attention of the students to the need of doing something for their respective communities in the way of social and philanthropic work and advised them to familiarize themselves with the courses given at the Jewish Communal School. Goldman, the chairman of the students' welfare

---

45. Louis Finkelstein (1895–1991), Conservative rabbi; talmudist; author; president, JTS, 1940–72. Finkelstein respected Kaplan but they differed on a whole host of issues and had a difficult time with each other from the start. Finkelstein was Kaplan's student and became his nemesis in the 1930s and 1940s. They reconciled in the 1950s with the help of Moshe Davis. For more information on this very complex relationship see *Judaism Faces the Twentieth Century.*

46. Harry Cohen (1893–?), Conservative rabbi in Cleveland, Bethlehem, Pennsylvania, and Norwich, Connecticut; officer, Zionist Organization of America.

47. Cyrus Adler had become acting president of the JTS after Solomon Schechter died.

committee, was called upon to speak, but said practically nothing. What he did say was in bad taste and Adler sailed into him afterwards. Friedlaender spoke in his usually easy manner about his old theme of the need of an "atmosphere," and wound up by voicing the need of a dormitory[48] which sentiment the students heartily applauded.

A Victory for Jewish Education — The Talmud Torahs

TUESDAY, MARCH 13, 1917

Benderly called me up a few minutes ago to tell me that the Federation of Charities finally admitted the principal Talmud Torahs of this city on the same basis as its constituent organizations of a philanthropic character. This is, to my mind, an epoch-making event in American Jewry. It has broken the back of the assimilationist tendency. The precedent which has been established will be followed by the Federations which are about to be organized as well as by those which are already in existence. This means that collective Jewry will contribute toward Jewish education which will no longer have to depend entirely upon the handful of those who make the perpetuation of Judaism their one life's purpose. The one man without whom such a development would never have taken place is Dr. Benderly. All honor to this most constructive genius in Jewish social life of the present time! Had it not been for his ability to gather data and present concrete facts as to Jewish education, who would have given the least attention to Jewish educational needs?

A Talk at Columbia — Is Jewry a Sinking Ship?

FRIDAY, MARCH 23, 1917

I spoke last night before the Columbia Menorah Society. There were only about thirty people present. Almost half the number were Seminary men. I understand that the Columbia Society, unlike those at other colleges, leads a rather precarious existence. Although it is just where one would most expect a strong Menorah society Columbia has a large Jewish student body with sufficient leisure on their hands to devote to outside activities and with sufficient antisemitism to act as an incentive, this organization has fared very poorly. There is only one explanation. The Jewish spirit among the Jewish students there is at an ebb. I was convinced of this fact by the nature of the discussion that took place last night. The question was on The Conflict of Judaism with Modern Science. The discussion was led off by three Menorah

---

48. For more information on the matter of a dormitory and the establishment of a dining facility by Mathilde Schechter called "Students House," see this author's "Mathilde Roth Schechter: A Baale Boste Reconsidered," *Modern Judaism* 7, no. 1 (February 1987): 1–27.

members—Tannenbaum, Cohen and Gluck. The first of these has achieved notoriety as a I.W.W. [Industrial Workers of the World] leader. He led a rioting mob that broke into a church some time ago. Hearing him speak one would hardly believe him capable of violence. But there seemed to be something about him that betrayed a certain degree of personal power. He spoke a very fine English but with an accent that sounded very foreign at times. He told his religious biography, of his having learned Talmud with his grandfather before he was thirteen. When he arrived at that age or not much later, he said, he "parted company with God." This was about the only vile expression he used. The rest he spoke in a simple and unassertive manner. He analyzed religion into two elements, theological and ethical, and showed the inadequacy of both. He ended up by saying "I don't know and I don't care about religious truth. Why bother about conjectural worlds and beings when there is so much work to be done in a real world with all its joys and sufferings?" Gluck spoke in the same vein. In my summing up I stated that I accepted the "I don't know," but that I took exception to the attitude of "I don't care." I went so far as to deny that there was any such thing as religion or Judaism. There have been for a long time Jews with a particular mode of life without the term religion or Judaism. The mode of life has not been something fixed and unalterable. The real problem that should concern us is not what "religious" truth to uphold as what to do with and for the Jews whose moral wellbeing depends upon the maintenance of the collective entity of the Jewish people.

But of what significance are my words or my views in the face of the rapid dissolution of the Jewish cause that is taking place with ever hastening speed? How can one have the heart to prevent people from escaping a ship that is on fire?

Groundbreaking Ceremony at the Jewish Center

TUESDAY, MAY 22, 1917

This morning at 8:30 I participated in the ceremony of ground breaking of the Jewish Center on the West Side. It was to me a thrilling experience to watch the Italian laborers hauling the heavy derricks and getting the machinery ready to start building, while the passersby were hurrying to their shops and offices unmindful of the spiritual significance of what they were doing. It could never have occurred to them that the ancient spirit of Israel was once again seeking a foothold in the modern world despite the huge peace and war activities and interests that are threatening to crowd it out. The few men who have made the Jewish Center possible and who were on the grounds were at that moment simply obeying a mysterious impulse within them which has been driving them on to make every effort

The Jewish Center, ca. 1937. (Courtesy the Jewish Center)

to perpetuate the life of Israel. Do they themselves realize the nature and the direction of this impulse? Perhaps one or two among them. But it makes no difference. They are the tools of a will not their own and higher than their own.

I quoted in connection with the ceremony the following *az yashir yisra'el et ha-shirah ha-zot ali ve'er enu-lah* [Heb. Numbers 21:17 "Then Israel sang this song: Spring up o well . . .] and pointed out that it was not only a foundation that was being laid but a well that was being dug, a fountain of new and inexhaustible energy for living the Jewish life.

Jewish Boys Should Go Willingly into the Army

THURSDAY, JUNE 28, 1917

Last night I spoke at the Y.M.H.A. at a meeting which had been arranged by the director to urge the young men to go willingly when they will be drafted. Judge Lehman presided but did not say anything. Mayor Mitchel[49] was the principal speaker. I was surprised to see quite a poor attendance for a meeting of that character despite the fact that it had been heavily advertised and the Mayor himself was to speak. The audience was rather apathetic. The Mayor spoke the regular clap trap about the war being a contest between autocracy and democracy and wound up by a threat that if the men do not volunteer they will stand little chance of being exempted from the draft.

In my remarks I dwelt upon the idealism which is at the bottom of America's entry into the war, notwithstanding the selfish motives that may have actuated those who had invested a great deal of wealth in the Allies. This is a righteous war. Every war that our country fought had its detractors. The ideal for which we are fighting is to suppress the great bully and outlaw among the nations—the German government. Let us not delude ourselves by saying that it is no affair of ours. As long as wrong and injustice will obtain in the relations between nation and nation there is no likelihood of justice and law being established in the religions between one individual and another. The reason the fight against moral evil in human life has so far made but little headway is that moral evil has always been condoned in the higher circles or in the larger relations of mankind.

It is true that the Allies have been no less guilty of employing force to advance their purposes. But they have at least the saving grace of not raising to a principle the violence that they may have committed. Converting hate and lawlessness into a philosophy is Germany's distinctive trait. We Jews ought to know because we have been the victims of it. We had been hated

---

49. John P. Mitchel (1879–1918), mayor of New York City, 1913–17.

and persecuted for centuries but it was not before Germany came and called it antisemitism that Jew hatred became a philosophy.

As Jews, furthermore, we owe it to America to stand by her in her hour of trial.

Bernard Revel and the Forces of Reaction

MONDAY, JULY 16, 1917

My family left for Long Branch on Tuesday, June 26. I am trying the plan of staying in New York during the week and going out to Long Branch[50] only week-ends. Although I generally managed to do work when I stayed in Long Branch in past years, I always felt lost because I did not have the facilities to keep in touch with modern discussions of mooted problems in religion, nor would I have any one to converse with concerning these problems. Now that I have adopted a different plan of spending the summer I am no less restive than before. I feel mentally disorganized. Some of the things I have been at work on seem to have run to seed. And no matter how hard I am trying to pull myself together I do not succeed. I am very much disconcerted by the headway which reaction is making in Jewish life in this country. The advent of a young man by the name of Revel has given a new lease of life to the narrow minded bigotry that prevents Judaism from adjusting itself to modern thought and life. He is possessed of a good memory and had a good Talmudic training from his early youth. He married into a very rich and extremely Orthodox family—the Travises. He has an independent income and is extremely ambitious to assume leadership of Orthodoxy in this country. If I am to rely on rumor he is quite unscrupulous and no respecter of the truth. He has been able to gather around him not only the "old guard" but also some young men who either sincerely or insincerely play the part of protagonists of Orthodoxy. His official position is that of president of the faculty of the Yeshibath Elhanan. In that capacity he has been able to secure for it larger funds than it had ever commanded. He is very determined and aggressive in his purpose to outdo the Seminary by sending out graduates for whom the claim is made of being Talmudists. This entire movement resembles on a small scale that of the Jesuits who have saved Catholicism from imminent dissolution. The Seminary, on the other hand, instead of emphasizing the difference between the position taken by it and that of Orthodoxy truckles to that very element which is daily growing more pugnacious and self-confident in its opposition to the Seminary.

---

50. Long Branch is a shore resort in New Jersey where the Kaplans usually went during the summer.

The Meaning of Judaism—An Outline of a New Approach

FRIDAY, AUGUST 31, 1917

The following is the outline of the conversations I conducted with Cohen and Fischman on the meaning of religion in general and Judaism in particular:

Introd: Mind-picture of physical universe as contrasted with mind-picture entertained by the ancients

1. Altered conception of God
    a. Ancient conception—anthropomorphic
    b. Modern conception—psychic—mind force
    Suggested definition—God = that aspect of mind which gives one the courage to live.
2. Implications of modern conception of God—analogy of lightning and electricity
    a. God manifest everywhere and at all times
    b. God manifest in different degrees in different objects, persons and collectivities
    c. Religion should concern itself primarily with such knowledge of the relation of mind to body as enables one to achieve the supremacy of the spirit.
3. How the mind functions
    a. Association is the principle requisite to the development of the human mind.
    b. Universalism is the ideal condition necessary to make possible the complete development of the human mind.
    c. This ideal is to be attained through long process of evolution. Grouping along national lines the present stage in the process of evolution.
4. The extent to which collective mind has manifested itself in the Jewish people.
    a. This can be determined by adopting a criterion whereby we can tell the presence of mind and the difference between a less developed and a more developed mind.
    b. The criteria are
        1) Memory   }
        2) Imagination   } Self-consciousness
        3) Power of self-adjustment }
    c. The social mind of the Jewish people
        1) Memory—history and tradition
        2) Imagination—Messianic Ideal

      3) Power of self-adjustment as shown in life in different lands
         and eras
   d. The supremacy of the Jewish collective mind or Jewish soul proved
      by the fact that the greater part of humanity has had to resort
      to the Jewish people to acquire a soul. The Bible the basis of
      Christianity and Mohammedanism.
5. Manner in which the collective mind of the Jewish people must
   henceforth function.
   a. Mind whether individual or collective functions only through phys-
      ical organism. Hence the need of conserving the physical nation-
      ality. This can only be done in a Jewish land.
   b. Collective mind has to be made articulate through signs, symbols,
      language or ceremonies. Hence the need of conserving the tra-
      ditional customs until new life will give rise to new ceremonies.
   c. Until Jews will acquire center of national life it is necessary to
      1) Establish Jewish centers in the diaspora so as to conserve
         the Jewish organism
      2) Individualize the spiritual strivings of the Jewish people by
         bringing to bear upon each individual life the benefits
         of the mind's supremacy—social reform and mental
         healing.

The Meaning of Succoth—Return to the Simple

OCTOBER 9, 1917

     The following is the outline of the sermon I delivered on the First
day of Succoth.

     As soon as Yom Kippur is over the pious Jew is expected to build the
Sukkah. There is more than an accidental connection between the Succoth
festival and the season of Teshuvah which precedes it. Teshuvah has a
different connotation from that of repentance. "Repentance" implies some
kind of expiation as is shown by its etymology, whereas "Teshuvah" simply
means return. Return to what? The answer is given by the Sukkah, "Return
to the simple, the natural, the primitive and the primary sources of life."
le-ma'an yedi'u doroteykhem ki va-sukkot . . . [Heb. Leviticus 23:43 "In order
that future generations may know that I make the Israelite people dwell in
booths . . ."]. The principle of the Sukkah is an antidote and corrective to
the ever growing complexity of civilization. We have to go back in order to
go forward.

     Examine the whole of our early history and you will find that it is a
demonstration of the validity of the *Sukkos* [Heb. Festival of Tabernacles]
principle. On the one hand was the rich, bedigene [decked out, adorned] and

alluring civilization of Canaan. On the other the simple manners and faith brought from the wilderness. The only thing that prevented our ancestors from falling victim to the Canaanitish civilization was the recollection of its wilderness days which the prophets constantly strove to render vivid to them. (Cf. the Rehabites.)

The importance of resorting to the simplicity in which life had its beginnings is borne out in every phase of life. We seek to counteract the danger of the enormous growth of cities by urging people "Back to the Farms." In science—back to the physical realities instead of wandering among the mazes of futile pseudo concepts that had grown up in course of time. In philosophy—Descartes. In education—back to the child. In the life of the individual—back to the simplicity of the childhood years *mi yashkeni ma'yim me-bor bet lehem* [Heb. 2 Samuel 23:15 "(David felt a craving and said,) 'If only I could get a drink of water from the cistern which is by the gate of Bethlehem' "].[51]

Unless we retain the power of refreshing ourselves by contact with the original sources of life and reality civilization is bound to become a) fragmentary, b) artificial, c) sterile and d) parasitic. The fact that the apartment house has crowded out and rendered the Sukkah practically impossible is symbolic of the trend of modern civilization. Instead of plain living and high thinking which the Sukkah stands for, we have high living and plain, all too plain thinking.

The universal significance of the Sukkah is clearly recognized both in Scriptures and in rabbinic writings. It is the only Mitzvah that is assigned to the nations in the days to come *zot te-hiyeh hatat mitsra'im . . .* [Heb. Zechariah 14:19 "Such shall be the punishment of Egypt (and of all other nations that do not come up to observe the Feast of Booths)"]. There is a saying in Midrash (Yalkut in Ps. 29) that the Messiah will come mainly to give two mitzvot to the nations, *Sukkah ve-lulav* [Heb. Building the Sukkah and Lulav]. When the nations will in time to come present themselves before God to claim reward for what they have achieved, our sages say, God will say to them "Since you have done little for the spiritual life, what spiritual reward can you obtain? *mi she-tarah be-erev shabbat yokhal be-shabbat* [Heb. Avodah Zarah 3:a "He who toils before the sabbath will eat on the sabbath]. And to prove how incapable they are of spiritual achievement God will propose to them to make Succoth. (Cf. Avodah Zarah 3a.) It is a frame of mind which the nations are not qualified to maintain for long. Rome forgot her primitive simplicity when she conquered Greece and the Orient. America too is in danger of losing her puritan vigor, her insularity and her spirit of hospitality.

---

51. David was born in Bethlehem.

For us Jews today the *Sukkot* [Heb. booths] principle involves a return to the only source of our spiritual life that can prevent it from becoming artificial, sterile and parasitic, "Eretz Yisrael." To accept the dispersion as our normal condition is to forget the principle of Succoth. Let us not fail to be in contact once again with the life giving reality with a homeland of our own.

Yesterday I preached the following:

The holiday season is drawing to a close. Nearly everybody, men in business, housewives, school children, will be glad the holidays are over. This however is not the spirit in which we should conclude the holiday season. *Atseret* [Heb. Assembly][52] denotes reluctance at parting (cf. *na'atsrah na otakh . . .* [Heb. *Judges* 13:15 "(And Manoah said to the angel of the Lord, I pray thee,) let us detain thee . . ."]. God says *kash'e alai peridatkhem* [Heb. Rashi on Numbers 29:36 "Your parting is difficult for me . . ."]. *Atseret* is a term by which also the last day of Passover is designated. Why this reluctance? Because there is apt to set in a reaction. It is difficult to sustain the emotions in the valley of everyday existence that we experience on the spiritual heights to which we occasionally rise, especially at this time of the year. It is the reaction that Solomon had in mind when upon dismissing the people after the dedication of the temple he wished them *ve-hayah levavkhem shalem . . .* [Heb. 1 Kings 8:61 "And may you be wholehearted with the Lord our God (to walk in His ways and keep his commandments, even as now)"]. Even God himself said after the Israelites had been overcome by the glory of the revelation—Oh that they were of this heart always! The Talmud, it is true, finds fault with Israel for not asking God to grant them the heart that would sustain their loyalty and devotion to God, but the fact that this is a task which God has assigned to the human race—the task of inventing some means whereby we would be enabled to sustain the emotions and enthusiasms that we now experience only in rare moments.

The Jewish People: Stubborn or Strong?

OCTOBER 10, 1917

The fact that the Jewish will has become nerveless is due to the tendency to allow ourselves to be stirred to great enthusiasm without afterwards finding the means for carrying out the resolves conceived on those inspired occasions. Our enthusiasms are like strawfire. Hence the weakness of the Jewish will.

---

52. *Atseret* refers to the final day of Passover and to the eighth day of Sukkot. It is the concluding celebration of these holidays. For Kaplan's later interpretation see Mordecai M. Kaplan, *The Meaning of God in Modern Jewish Religion*, introduction by Mel Scult (Detroit: Wayne State University Press, 1994), chapter 8.

But are we not supposed to be a stiff-necked people? Is it not due to our stiff-neckedness that we have been able to hold out to the present day? We have a stubborn will but not a strong will. A stubborn will resists, a strong will persists; a stubborn will allies itself to tradition, a strong will to purpose; a stubborn will keeps to the past, a strong will builds for the future. We may have shown all the qualities of a stubborn will, but we do not know what it is to plan, to build, to reckon with the future. We grow enthusiastic about many undertakings that we never see through. The Agudath Yisrael, the Kehillah, the Congress movement. The Zionist Movement is the only one where there are some evidences of our ability to translate emotion into action. This is why it has a stronger hold on us than any other activity. Yet so many of those that I was addressing have little use for Zionism. So paralyzed has the Jewish will become that it can on the one hand be praying for *Geshem* [Heb. rain] in Palestine and on the other be entirely indifferent to the fact that the land to be rendered fruitful by the *Geshem* [Heb.] is in the hands of evil Arabs. Many a person that would give twenty-five dollars for the privilege of *Petiḥah* [Heb. honor of opening of the Ark] would not pay twenty-five cents toward the National Fund.

If the message of *Atseret* [Heb. last day of the holiday] meets with no response in us there is an appeal of the same kind from a source that we should scarcely disregard. It comes from those whom we have named in the *Yizkor* [Heb. memorial service for the dead]. The purpose of the memorial service as well as of the Kaddish[53] and A'M'R [Heb. Acronym for God Full of Compassion] is to redeem the dead. The notion that the dead are in need of redemption at the hands of the living is at the furthest remove from the worship of the dead. . . .

The popular imagination which has depicted the sufferings of the dead in terms of fire and brimstone gives but a faint notion of the genuine hell on the brink of which every soul of the departed trembles, the hell of futility, the hell so vividly portrayed by Koheleth in his *gam ahavatam gam sinatam* [Heb. Ecclesiastes 9:5–6 "(But the dead know nothing; they have no more hope, for even the memory of them has died.) Their loves, their hates, (their jealousies have long since perished . . .)"]. It is out of this hell that we are called upon to redeem them. By helping to perpetuate the community of Israel we are redeeming them from such a hell. The dead are not dead as long as the community that gave them spiritual life is still living. The purpose of the Kaddish is likewise to establish the fact that *yehei shmei raba mevarakh le-alam u-le-almei almaya* [Aramaic Kaddish "May God's name be blessed, forever and as long as worlds endure]. The future and not the past

---

53. Prayer for the dead.

is the keynote of all our prayers for the dead. Unless we shall give heed to this appeal of those whom we prayed for in the *Yizkor* the world will say *Yizkor* for the Jewish people and set up a statue for it as it has done for the vanished Indian. Only by being everyday Jews and not merely holiday Jews can such catastrophe be prevented.

The Seminary: New Developments and Old Problems

SUNDAY, NOVEMBER 11, 1917

On Sunday, October 14, the opening exercises of the Seminary took place. Instead of being held as they formerly were in the synagogue with only the student body and the faculty present, they were held this time in the lecture room where quite a large assembly was gotten together consisting in addition to the above of a number of alumni, a few visitors and two trustees. No doubt Adler is intent upon giving more éclat to the Seminary affairs than was hitherto his wont. From appearances he seems quite entrenched in his position as acting president. As for what was said by Adler, Marshall and Ginzberg I cannot but hold in slight esteem the sentiments they expressed. Adler's remarks were conventional and rambling. Marshall showed a want of ordinary common sense in finding fault with the Jews who claimed exemption from military service on the ground of being conscientious objectors. Every one of them, he thundered, gave some kind of ism as an excuse but not Judaism. And then he went on to denounce those who do not acquiesce wholeheartedly in the war policy of our government. This only shows how little imagination the man possesses. He can not realize that the Jewish young man, the more faithful he is to his people, would be the less likely to involve his religion in the blame that he is drawing upon himself by pleading exemption. Ginzberg too exasperated me with his arguments on behalf of the Talmud. The study of philology and of the different Aramaic jargons to be found in the Talmud figures most prominently among the reasons for knowing the Talmud. He had something to say about equivalents, as pointing to a method of utilizing its teachings, but the few living sparks of practical purpose were smothered by the ashes of his archaeological interests.

The courses at the Seminary this year are a vast improvement upon what they were in previous years. This is the result of the addition to the teaching staff of two instructors, Rabbi Morris Levine and Kotkov,[54] at a cost of about $2,200. The addition of these men has made it possible for the classes to be divided into smaller and more homogeneous groups. One can gain an idea of the inefficiency of the Seminary when one bears in mind that for fifteen years an annual expense of $50,000 was allowed to

---

54. Wilfred Kotkov (1885–1921), rabbi, instructor at JTS.

do one tenth of the service it could render, because of the reluctance to spend an additional $2,200 for tuition fee, instead of on all sorts of worm-eaten books and manuscripts. The library which has usurped the part of the building originally intended for classrooms and meeting rooms would itself be a great institution, if the students were taught how to utilize it, and if it were also to contain books of a general and human interest. But as it is conducted at present, it is like a sealed book to most of the men there. Only the few ambitious ones stumble upon the inexhaustible treasures that are hidden there.

At the beginning of the term the students sent in a petition to the faculty, asking them to call upon me to give a course which, for want of a better name, they designated practical theology. Two faculty meetings took place without the letter being read. When finally it was read it gave rise to the kind of discussion that one could expect from men who lack soul and vision. Marx[55] said not a word, Davidson pretended ignorance as to the kind of a course that was wanted, Hyamson[56] said "Alright we can trust Kaplan," Friedlaender played the double game of progressive and obstructionist, Ginzburg openly opposed my giving the course. Friedlaender, parliamentarian that he is, moved that the students be asked to explain more in detail what they wanted. Seeing that the faculty is opposed to my giving any courses, I have resolved that it were best for me to let the matter alone altogether and to proceed working out my ideas in book form so that these bats will have to come out of their holes.

The Jewish Center Opens for Services

SUNDAY, JANUARY 20, 1918

The Jewish Center of W. 86th Street was opened yesterday for services, despite the fact that the synagogue proper is still in the process of construction. The services were held in the auditorium which can admit about two hundred. The reason they inaugurated the services without waiting until the building was entirely completed was that Max Weinstein[57] one of the members celebrated the Bar Mitzvah of his son. Weinstein is not affiliated with any congregation and it occurred to some of the other members that if his son's Bar-mitzvah were made the occasion for inaugurating services at the Center, he would show his appreciation by

---

55. Alexander Marx (1878–1953), historian, librarian, and author; faculty member, JTS; largely responsible for making Seminary collection one of the largest in the world.

56. Moses Hyamson (1862–1949), rabbi and scholar; chairman Beth Din of British Empire; faculty member, JTS; taught Talmud and codes.

57. Max Weinstein (1878–1950), businessman, co-founder Daughters of Jacob Home and Hospital.

contributing liberally toward the building fund. As I understand it, he is one of the most successful cloak manufacturers in this city. As far as I can see his vulgarity measures up to his reputed wealth.

The spirit of the people who belong to the organization is clearly reflected in this action of theirs. Altogether I feel very much out of sorts about the whole business and I wonder what I can do to extricate myself from it. My distemper reflected itself in the lack of enthusiasm which marked the sermon that I delivered in the morning.

Kaplan Upset over the Center

SATURDAY NIGHT, MARCH 2, 1918

During the last three weeks I have been quite miserable. I am adrift again, tossed hither and thither by contrary gusts of passionate anger and disappointment. I have severed my relations with the West Side Center. The attitude of Cohen had been troubling me ever since I took an active interest in the undertaking. His dogged obstinacy in the policy of reaction became unbearable from the moment the activities at the Center began with the holding of Sabbath services. The things that annoyed me may seem exceedingly petty, but they were to me an indication of what I was to expect right along. He had his way in the construction of the synagogue with the women to be seated on the side in a kind of false gallery. He consulted Rabbi Hyamson and M. Z. Margolis[58] about the gallery not for the purpose of knowing the actual law, but how to be sufficiently within the letter of the law and yet please the members. In the auditorium the men sit on one side and the women on the other. Again in order to be within the law, or merely its letter, he has had a rope passed through the first line of chairs upon which the women are seated. The almemar[59] is on the platform in the front part of the synagogue. When the Torah is read he does not permit the reader to face the audience. All such trifles, in their cumulative effect, exhibit the man as a Pharisee in the worst sense of the word. I bore his fanaticism for a time, but my patience suddenly gave way and I cut loose from him. It all happened on account of something that apparently had nothing to do with questions of religious policy. It was understood that I was to engage an administrator to help me carry on the detail work.

---

58. Morris (Moses) Sebulon (Zebulon) Margolies (Ramaz) (1851–1936), rabbi and communal leader; Zionist; founder of Orthodox Rabbis of America; rabbi along with Kaplan at Kehillath Jeshurun. Margolis came in 1907 to the congregation, which put pressure on Kaplan to get the traditional rabbinical ordination. He did so in 1909. For more information, see *Judaism Faces the Twentieth Century*.

59. Pulpit where the Torah is read.

Kaplan and the Center: To Lead or Not to Lead

FRIDAY, APRIL 6, 1918

I am meandering once more. My relation to the community of the Jewish Center is again the same as what it was before I fell out with J. H. Cohen. Kauvar[60] came to the city on Thursday, March 7. He came to see me that same day and Cohen also came to meet him at my house. I cannot say that I was particularly happy over the fact that I felt myself being superseded in the leadership of the new institution, yet I had sense enough not to take myself too seriously by considering the unpleasantness I was experiencing as martyrdom. In fact I would like to forget the pettiness and the vacillation of which I feel I have been guilty these last weeks. My only object in recording the unmanly attitude which I have been taking is that I may have the more reason to rejoice later when I shall have at last found myself.

Kaplan Becomes Rabbi of the Center

SUNDAY, APRIL 21, 1918

Last night Judge Rosalsky[61] and Mr. Abraham Rothstein, who were appointed by the newly elected trustees of the Jewish Center as a committee to offer me the rabbinate, came to see me. While it had been generally assumed that I was to be the rabbi, this was the first time that a formal invitation was extended to me. It looks as though I have to make up my mind once and for all. I can by no means say that I am sorry that the state of uncertainty in which I have been living the last year or two will now finally and definitely come to an end.

The interview lasted between 9:30 and 12:30. No terms were mentioned. The length of the interview was due to Judge Rosalsky's long winded and circuitous method of speaking with now and then a tendency to give, as does Dr. Schulman,[62] resumes of speeches delivered on different occasions. I noted that he had quite a large vocabulary but that his grammar creaked. He is certainly a well meaning man. Despite his lack of general culture he is well versed in his own specialty as judge on the criminal bench. In the thirteen years that he has been sitting on the bench his decisions were appealed from 125 times and only in three cases were his decisions reversed, two of these reversals being on his own recommendation. He is a typical product of Jewish life on the East Side twenty and thirty years ago. His father was one of the foremost kosher butchers in Allen Street, of the kind

---

60. Charles E. H. Kauvar (1879–1971), ordained JTS; author; rabbi in Denver; president, United Synagogue of America; cousin of Kaplan.

61. Otto Rosalsky (1873–1936), lawyer, judge, philanthropist; fund-raiser, Yeshiva College.

62. Probably Samuel Schulman (1864–1955), rabbi and noted Reform leader; scholar; officer, Central Conference of American Rabbis; opposed Zionism but not Israel.

that took to that business because they possessed the asset of Jewish learning and respectability. The judge's parents were known as very hospitable and generous and these are the traits he seems to have inherited.

Rothstein, whom I have had occasion to describe before, chimed in with all that the judge said, and added with great emphasis that if they had not been sure I was going to accept the office of rabbi, they would not have gone on with the building; for they had been in a pinch more than once, and at one time had even contemplated selling the lots and it was only because they looked forward to my leadership that they persevered. Despite the fact that I cannot imagine a man like Rothstein speaking in hyperbole I cannot help discounting this statement of his.

With his quiet way of speaking and rather loud laughs he strikes off now and then some very clever remarks. "There are two kinds of Christians," he said, "bad and good. The bad Christians hate a Jew, the good ones don't like him." In speaking of the Center he said something that outclasses anything I have said about it. According to him the purpose of the Jewish Center is to render the environment safe for Judaism. Finding myself thus outdone by a layman I had to make my own contribution and amend his description by suggesting the word "democracy" in place of "the environment."

I was very much touched at one point in the conversation when he made the statement that the great regret of his life was that there was no such center fifteen years ago, because I knew that he referred to the unJewishness of his family.

SATURDAY NIGHT, APRIL 27, 1918
Last Monday night I was elected rabbi of the Jewish Center.

Will Center Members Return from the Shore for the Holidays

TUESDAY, AUGUST 14, 1918
Last Thursday night (Aug. 9) a number of members of the Center who live in and about Far Rockaway met on the porch of Schwartz's cottage. J. H. Cohen had told me beforehand that at a previous meeting he brought up the question of attendance on the High Holidays. This year the holidays come very early, at a time when nearly all of the members are still in their summer resorts. The possibility of having the synagogue more than half empty is by no means a remote one. Cohen in his tireless zeal for the Center could not contemplate such a possibility, so he had a meeting called for the purpose of urging the members to come into town for Rosh Hashana and Yom Kippur. He was not satisfied, however, with the spirit in which their consent was won. He wanted more. He wanted them actually to want to come. He therefore arranged for the meeting of Thursday night and summoned me to advance reasons for their coming into town.

By no means all who might have come showed up. The attitude of the greater part of the membership toward the Center is icy indifference. The men are busy making money and the women spending it, and they have no taste for the intangible realities which the Center is to further. I am sending Miss Aaronson[63] to make a canvass of the situation in order to have something to go by in organizing the work for the coming year and from her reports I gather that the Center holds little more than their marginal interest. Very rarely do the women reply to my request to make an appointment with Miss Aaronson and when she finally succeeds in being admitted to the presence of their highnesses, they make her feel as though she was intruding upon their important business of going to whist parties or automobiling.

Thank God, that I am now practically committed to the plan of having them contribute to the Teachers Institute $5,000 annually instead of paying me as they had intended $6,000 a year salary. I can afford now to be charitable with them. I feel that I am patient with their crass materialism not because I am being paid for it, but because I am serving the Jewish Cause. They can be the veriest roughnecks now, as far as I am concerned, the more reason for my loving the good that is dormant in them. But if I were to love them at so much per [text not clear] I would despise myself.

Kaplan Sings the Praises of Samson Benderly

TUESDAY, AUGUST 14, 1918

How marvelous the persistence and optimism of Benderly who is the prime mover in this attempt to build up a kehillah! How he keeps steadily at Magnes urging him on from task to task. Were it not for him Magnes would not only have resigned from the Kehillah but would have given up Jewish work entirely. Benderly is, I may say without an exaggeration, the sole constructive force in American Jewish life outside of Zionism. And the humility and self-effacement of the man! If we had five such men the Jewish future in the Diaspora would be assured. He has been and is to me the greatest inspiration in working for the Jewish cause. I do not know what I would have done without him. Rather I do know. I would have done anything in the world except work for the Jewish Cause which would then have appeared to me as hopelessly lost—so far as the Diaspora is concerned and what would Zionism have amounted to without provisional Jewish life for a generation or two in the Diaspora?

---

63. Probably Rebecca Aronson, one of the Benderly "Boys," who eventually married Barnett Brickner.

3

September 17, 1918–August 31, 1922

"I Only Come to High Holiday Services for an Hour or So"

TUESDAY, SEPTEMBER 17, 1918 (HEB. 11 TISHRI 5679)

The following are some of the types of Jewish life I have met or heard of recently: As J. H. Cohen was in the office of the Center poring over the chart of the synagogue there came in a man who asked him whether he was the sexton and explained that he was a manufacturer of synagogue and church fixtures. When Cohen told him he was not the sexton, the man noticing the chart asked whether the seats in the synagogue were being rented, and what was the price charged.

"We don't rent out any seats," said Cohen. "We give them to those who live in the neighborhood."

"If so let me have a few."

"Where do you live?" asked Cohen.

"On Central Park West corner of 84 St (no rents less than $2,500)

"We will let you have as many seats as you want but on one condition, that you attend the greater part of the services on the High Holidays," Cohen replied.

"Oh, I can't do that. I can come in only for an hour or so."

"I See by the Papers"—Kaplan Comments on the Jewish Press

FRIDAY, OCTOBER 4, 1918

I have had occasion to catch a glimpse of the disintegration of Jewish life from quite a different angle. The mere fact that in a Jewry of two million there should not be a single interesting and intelligent Jewish weekly is sufficient evidence of the ebb of Jewish consciousness in this country. A few weeklies of which the *Hebrew Standard* is typical are essentially advertising organs that have some inane stuff in the way of articles and editorials that might give the sheet the appearance of a journalistic endeavor. For a number of years there has appeared a colorless weekly under the name of *American Hebrew* which had the backing of the uptown German Jews. As soon as a downtowner moved uptown and became a trustee of an uptown congregation he became a subscriber to the *American Hebrew*. About a year or two ago it fell into the hands of a shrewd lawyer Edelhertz[1] who expected to make money out of it by engaging Herman Bernstein[2] as editor. Neither Edelhertz nor Bernstein is much interested in Jewish life or its problems. Bernstein has found a bigger field with the *N.Y. Herald* and his interest in the *American Hebrew* lapsed. The result is that the *American Hebrew* is fast approaching bankruptcy.

A similar fate is hanging over the *American Jewish Chronicle*—a paper of quite a different sort. It was established about two years ago by one of those rare idealists that now and then appear in Jewish life. Dr. Strauss[3] who was its original publisher is, from what I have heard about him, a highly intellectual man of the species "practical idealist." As a result of Prof. Gottheil's[4] machinations he was interned as an enemy alien. The *Jewish Chronicle* is without funds and without advertising and unless something be done immediately it will be discontinued. There is a possibility of Schiff saving it. But what will then become of its intensely Jewish and outspoken attitude? If it will continue to exist it will probably have to degenerate into a wishy washy sheet and be used for Americanization and the particular political purpose of its backers, something like the "Jewish World" of about a decade ago—a Yiddish daily fathered by the Uptown German Jews to make Republicans out of the benighted East Siders.

The Great War Is Over

MONDAY, NOVEMBER 11, 1918

This morning at 6 A.M. (New York Time) the Great World War came to an end.

As an insignificant sheltered spectator of this greatest of the world's tragedies, I have no right to say a word. Filled with bitterness and hate as my heart usually is against those who exploit their fellowmen, I did not know, when the war broke out, whom to hate and curse more, the Germans

---

1. Bernard Edelhertz (1880–1931), lawyer and assistant attorney general, New York City; director, American Hebrew Publishing Co.

2. Herman Bernstein (1876–1935), journalist, editor, and diplomat; founder of *Der Tog* and editor, *American Hebrew*; war correspondent.

3. Morris Strauss (1897–?), editor and freelance writer; officer, B'nai B'rith; Zionist.

4. Richard Gottheil (1862–1936), scholar and Zionist leader; faculty, Columbia University; one of the founders of the Jewish Institute of Religion.

with their arrogance and insolence or the Russians with their cruelty and superstition, or the capitalists of both the Allies and the Central Powers! The war made me a misanthrope. At the same time I am too much of a pragmatist to allow misanthropy to blind me to the spark of goodness and truth that with careful tending might in time become a flame consuming all evil and falsehood. It took me a long time honestly and sincerely to come to the conclusion that spark was with America and her allies. Harrison's Book on National and Social Problems and W. Trotter's *Instinct of Herd*[5] were eye openers to me and also Morgenthau's revelations[6] that now appear in book form.

But as I join in the general rejoicing I cannot help feeling that we are on the eve of a more terrible war than the one we have just lived through. I hear distinctly the rumblings of a new incoming storm. In place of wars of nations, we shall now have wars of classes. The human race, to carry out Trotter's analogy, is divided into wolf-packs and sheep folds. The war has sharpened the greed of the numerous profiteers and exploiters who have waxed fat on human sacrifices. The rich have grown richer and the poor poorer, and more helpless. But the poor have been taught to handle arms, which they will now turn against their oppressors. The exploiters can as little be reasoned with as the arrogant Prussians. The only argument that will prevail with them and against them is the argument of bullets and bayonets.

"Perhaps I Should Go and Live in Palestine"

DECEMBER 29, 1918

Ever since Palestine began to be spoken of seriously as a homeland for the Jews—which means, of course, since the British Declaration[7]—my longing for Palestine has been growing in intensity. I actually yearn to settle there with my family. This led me to inquire of the Zionist office in the city whether there could be found an opening for me whereby I could earn a livelihood for myself and family. DeHaas[8] who is the executive director of the Zionist Organization asked me to come to see him. I was to his house last Wednesday (Dec. 25) and he suggested the possibility of my going on a commission to report on the educational situation in Palestine for the

---

5. Wilfred Trotter, *Instinct of the Herd in Peace and War* (London: Ernest Benn, 1930).

6. Henry Morgenthau, *Ambassador Morgenthau's Story* (Garden City: Doubleday, Page & Co., 1918).

7. Kaplan is referring to the Balfour Declaration of November 2, 1917, in which the British Foreign Secretary Arthur J. Balfour declared that the British government favored "the establishment in Palestine of a national home for the Jewish people."

8. Jacob De Haas (1872–1937), Zionist leader; journalist; author; associate of Herzl; introduced Brandeis to Zionism; executive secretary, Federation of American Zionists.

purpose of advising the organization on the apportionment of its subvention of the educational work there. The mere hope of my beholding the land of my people has put new life into me. May God grant that my hope be realized, and that my lot ultimately be cast among those who will help rebuild the ruins of our land.

Does this mean ingratitude to America? To love America is simply to love myself, for it is only in this blessed country that I could have achieved that which I most value in myself, relentless honesty of mind. The Jewish people gave me the problem to work on, but America gave me the means, the leisure and the freedom to understand the problem. If I will go to Palestine, it will be for the purpose not only of helping to interpret my people to myself, but also of interpreting America to her own people. Very few of her own people understand her. The veil of Christianity is about them, obscuring their vision. It is only Judaism that will give purpose and direction to Americanism.

Kaplan the Social Revolutionary

TUESDAY, JANUARY 7, 1919

Like the "Sambation" of Jewish mythology, my soul is in a state of continual agitation. I am tortured by the restraints which prevent me from becoming an active participant in the Social Revolution which is in the air nowadays. As rabbi of the Jewish Center I am allied with the typical bourgeois Jews. I went into this alliance open eyed though with a great deal of reluctance and disgust. The only justification I could offer to myself for having affiliated myself with a class of people who for the most part belong to the class of exploiters is well expressed in the following which I came across the other day:

"Bernard Shaw once said that, under our present system, clergymen are nothing but chaplains of pirate ships. To which we may reply, 'Precisely so; and what ships have a greater need for chaplains?'" I thank God that I can conscientiously subscribe to this statement in view of the fact that I draw no salary from the Jewish Center.

Making the Jewish Center Democratic—The Forty-Hour Week

MONDAY, JULY 28, 1919

I am really surprised at myself that I have held on to the Center so long. I suppose it is due to the fact that I am beginning to age[9] and am commencing to realize that it is futile to measure one's strength against the world, especially when one's strength does not amount to much.

---

9. Kaplan was thirty-eight at this point.

The spiritual progress made by the families affiliated with the Center has been very slight. The few children—there are about thirty of them—that attend the religious school are probably the only ones that benefitted from the existence of the Center. Whether that is worth the forty thousand dollars that it cost to maintain the Center during the last year is another question. It all depends, of course, from whose standpoint we are to consider the money spent. From the standpoint of the members, the least wealthy of whom spends $10,000 a year on his living expenses, and the one of average wealth $20,000 to $30,000, the sum of forty thousand dollars is by no means large. But from the standpoint of the general community which is so poverty stricken, the good that could have been done with that amount is such that one is bound to consider the use to which it was put an economic and spiritual waste. The only part of the money that was well spent was the five thousand dollars which the Center contributed in my name to the Teachers Institute.

As a matter of fact not very much could be expected from the experience with the Center. The part of the building which was to constitute the new element in the reconstructed synagogue was not yet built up. So far there is really little more to the Center than the conventional auditorium for worship together with one for dances and entertainment. From the way matters stood at the beginning of the year I was very much afraid that they would not go on with the rest of the building. My fear was based on the apathetic attitude of the trustees. Outside of Joseph Cohen and Fischman not a single one of the trustees has the slightest comprehension of what the Center is really meant to accomplish. To be a trustee simply means to have the "privilege" of paying a thousand dollars annually as membership dues instead of the $200 to $250 that the other members pay. When it was found that the running expenses of the Center could not be met with only twelve trustees, they voted to add on six more.

On the other hand there are among the members a few, say four or five, who are genuinely interested in the Center. The question for me was how to maneuver so that these few members should be given an opportunity to become active in the furtherance of the general aims of the Center, especially in the completion of the building. I wrote up for the bulletin (Dec. 7, 1918) a statement in which I outlined a plan or organization whereby every member would be given a chance to take an interest in the work of the Center. I advised that the members who were not trustees should be organized into a House of Members, with a chairman of their own, and that the vice-chairman of each standing committee should be drawn from the general membership body, the chairman always being one of the Board of Trustees. Innocent as I was of any intention to wrest power from the trustees, J. H. Cohen strongly resented what he thought a move on my part and on the part of some of the members to make the trustees play second fiddle. This apprehension of his, I assume, was based on the fear that if the trustees be relegated to the background, the younger set would ultimately introduce reforms. Knowing as he does how anxious I am to introduce changes into the ritual, he suspects every move that I make.

The House of Members has by no means come up to my expectations. It has brought out two or three people who will contribute materially (I don't mean in a financial way) to the development of the Center. It is due to these few that the campaign for a loan for $150,000 from the members themselves was launched, and that it was finally decided to go on with the rest of the building. Contracts were placed some time ago and the other six stories are now in process of construction.

The following are the principal facts upon which I base my conclusion that the members of the Center are a very unpromising group spiritually:

1. At the beginning of this year some of the industries in which our people are interested were compelled as a result of strikes to shorten the number of laboring hours per week to forty-four. The time seemed ripe for a general movement to promote Sabbath observance by dividing the forty-four hours among five days instead of having the men work as hitherto, a half-day on Saturday. When the waist strike was on the point of being settled I made an attempt to introduce the five day week plan into the agreement that was about to be drawn up. I learned that a lawyer by the name Gordon represented the interests of the manufacturers. I went to see him, accompanied by J. H. Cohen. But no sooner did I see the man than I realized that my efforts with him would be in vain. He was far from reconciled to the idea of granting the workers the forty-four hour week, and was determined to fight them to the last ditch. With jaw firm and teeth set he hurled defiance at the workers with whom he said he was engaged in a bitter struggle. What cared he for Sabbath observance? He had no use for religion, anyhow. His father who was a religious man gave him an opportunity to see all that there was to religion, but failed to convince him that there was anything to it. I learned later that his father was the notorious firebug of the east side who was sentenced to seven years' prison in Sing Sing. I went away from the interview disheartened.

I then made arrangements for an open meeting to be held at the Center for the purpose of making propaganda for the five day a week idea. My purpose was to invite to the meeting as many of the leading manufacturers as possible, and to have Schiff, Magnes, Rosalsky and myself address them on the Sabbath question. The meeting was called for Tuesday, Feb. 4. In order that the outcome of the meeting be of a practical character I urged that a group of manufacturers who so far have kept their places open on the Sabbath come together preparatory to the meeting on Feb. 4 and work out some resolution to be presented at that meeting. The moving spirit of this conference was to be R. Sadowsky,[10] one of the wealthiest members of the Center. At the conference, from which I was advised to stay away, Jewish and spiritual claims had no weight whatever, and no attempt was made to press them by Judge Rosalsky who was the only man there that could have done so. The main obstacle to their favoring the adoption of a five day week schedule was the fear that if they would distribute the forty-four hours among five days the workers would soon come to ask for a reduction to forty hours. In the face of this difficulty there appeared no way for those men to favor the five day week scheme without prejudicing their material interests.

When the Tuesday night meeting took place, the members of the conference showed themselves benevolently neutral to the five day week plan that was warmly advocated by the speakers. A discordant note was strong by one "Col." Ginzberg who ranted some generalities about the efforts of what he called the "Jewish Church," to meddle in the labor problem. As far as I could see nothing of a positive character was accomplished. Schiff, who I hoped would take a leading part in the movement, refused to be troubled with it. Although the few who were anxious to see the cause of the Sabbath furthered congratulated themselves upon the successful meeting, we were no further than we were before.

Center Members Angry at Kaplan "The Bolshevik"

JULY 28, 1919

Finally, the reaction of the people to my preaching. Most of my intellectual activity last year was spent on the weekly sermons that I delivered at the Center. I succeeded practically each week in developing some striking idea and in making the idea popular. But from time to time I touched upon some of the vital political and economic questions and gave expression to views which I deemed both Jewish and just. Whenever I spoke in that vein I was accused of being a Bolshevik. Not that I am ashamed of being classed with the Bolsheviki. I would rather be classed with them than with the bourgeois profiteers. But what I object to in their charging me with Bolshevism is that such charge was to them sufficient reason for not taking my views seriously or analyzing them to see whether there was any truth to them. I had this experience with the series of sermons on Freedom that I delivered during the Passover season. A typical case was that of a wife of one of the members, a young woman in her thirties whose husband is just now growing rich on his investments in oil stock in Oklahoma. She complained

---

10. Reuben Sadowsky (1872–1944), manufacturer and banker; director of Beth Israel Hospital; active in the Federation of Jewish Philanthropies.

to Miss Langer[11] that she made up her mind to discontinue her attendance at the synagogue because of the type of sermon that I was delivering. The sermons so upset her nerves that she could not sleep nights on account of them. What truth there was in that statement I do not know but this report I got from Miss Langer who is the executive director of the Center.

With nothing left to preach or to teach and nothing that he can or dare change, what is there for the rabbi to do?

Magnes Not Strong Enough to Lead the Kehilla

JULY 28, 1919

The worst part of the situation is that I cannot for a moment lose sight of the fact that my troubles at the Center are due to the general state of demoralization in Jewish life which is growing worse every year. This was brought home to me about a month or two ago when at Benderly's insistence Friedlaender, Benderly and myself met with Magnes to consider the question of the Kehillah.[12] Benderly's heroic attempt to reorganize the Kehilla on the district plan turned out a failure, as I apprehended it would. Magnes' main interest is in the socialist movement. He is a radical and a sympathizer with the Bolsheviki. He advocates the cause of radicalism from the public rostrum. He has incapacitated himself entirely for Jewish work as a result of his new interests. But instead of cutting his connections with Jewish work he hangs on. He is after all a sentimentalist and he has not the heart to spurn an old love of his. We came together to talk Kehilla. Friedlaender did not mince matters and told Magnes that he ought to get out. I could not be quite as brutal. I advocated a completely new plan of organization. After a lengthy discussion we met again. I then saw that Benderly was steering the whole affair with the view of convincing Magnes to remain the head of the Kehilla. The discussion petered out. Again a meeting and another meeting but with no result. A few days ago I heard of an informal conference called together by Sadowsky and Rosalsky to ask Magnes as to his intentions with regard to the Kehilla. He told them plainly that he was not the man to organize N.Y. Jewry. He advised them to get some business man to head the Kehilla in the same way as Felix M. Warburg heads the Federation. In the meantime I heard that Benderly has gone into some kind of business. When I last saw him he told me that he intended doing something of that kind, though he would not discontinue to do Jewish work. He told me then that all he needed for business was five hours a day. The rest of the time he

11. Hajnalka Langer (Winer) (1890–1987), graduate of TI, who at this time was executive director at the Jewish Center. Later she was active in affairs at SAJ and TI Alumni.

12. Kehilla: organized Jewish community. The Jews of New York City engaged in an experiment to unite the community in one large organization. Judah Magnes was the head. It began in 1909 but had all but disappeared by 1918.

would spend in furthering the new scheme he has in mind of establishing a chain of institutions like the Central Jewish Institute throughout the city. He expects to interest Louis Marshall and get him to be the official head of the undertaking. I am afraid that he will be as little successful with the new scheme as with all of his schemes in the past. It occurs to me, that his mental make up as such disqualifies him for leadership in the Diaspora. He was born in Palestine, and it is only in modern Palestine that he might have succeeded. For the diaspora he lacks the religious note, which is only another name for that self-conscious Jewishness which a Jew in the Diaspora must possess if he wants to escape being absorbed by the environment. In the meantime the one man who I had hoped would hold out to the last has also surrendered. All this talk about his doing Jewish work in addition to his business duties is to me moonshine. If the Jewish community is in such a state that it has not enough work for a man like Benderly then it is in a mighty precarious condition from which a thousand tinkers [thinkers?] like myself are powerless to save it.

The Meaning of Golus [Exile]—We Have Not Yet Arrived

Tuesday, July 29, 1919

My topic was "The Meaning of the *Goluth*." I pointed out that by the side of the idea of the "Geulah" [redemption] Judaism lays great stress upon the idea of the *Goluth*. What *Goluth* means cannot be accurately defined because it is an emotional rather than an intellectual attitude, an attitude that is expressed by the minor key which is characteristic of Jewish music. Intellectually the *Golus* idea implies that one has not yet arrived. We note this idea running through the spiritual life of our people from the days of Abraham. In fact our people was in *Golus* even before it grew into a people. We were sojourners in another land before we had our own land. It was this *Golus* idea that differentiated our migrations from the migrations of the rest of mankind. All humanity is in a state of transit, but it is impelled by blind unconscious forces. Not so Israel. If it wanders it is because of or in the name of an idea.

This sense of "Golus" was kept alive until we were emancipated. The emancipation has broken us up into fragments, as a result of which we lost the sense of community. Losing that we lost the sense of *Golus*. We began to feel that at last we arrived. Not only the assimilationists among us, but the observant Jews who reduced Judaism to a formalism which is kept distinct and apart from life. To counteract such formalism we have to reconstruct the synagogue and make of it a center of Jewish social life. This is especially true of the synagogue in our summer resorts; if they had been made into centers of Jewish life it would not be necessary to send our children to camps where they not only have to violate the dietary laws, but where they are out of touch with Jewish life at the most important part of the year from the standpoint of their spiritual development. I pointed out that a center established at Long Branch could reach in its activities, which would by no means be confined to the Sabbath, the Jews of the various summer resorts all along the coast.

Kaplan Thinks about Going into the Silk Business

MONDAY, DECEMBER 8, 1919

As on a similar occasion previously I turned to my brothers-in-law for counsel and assistance to deliver me from my spiritual prison. After talking the matter over with them, Ed made the proposition that I should become interested in one of his mills which he was about to establish in Long Branch. After spending about a year in learning the manufacture of silk I might be able to take charge of a silk mill. Personally I would have been too glad to avail myself of the opportunity to learn a useful trade and make my way in the world as a worker instead of as a talker. But my folks cannot comprehend my struggle and my aims. All that they see in such a change on my part is an escape from the limelight into obscurity. They cannot bear the thought of my apparently throwing overboard all that I have acquired in the twenty-five years of my intellectual labors. I certainly cannot expect them to understand that if I were given the opportunity to live my own life I would be prepared to bring to the world the message of a religion less artificial and more normal than the one I am making a "forlorn hope" effort to maintain and develop in this country. With aims so vague and remote I cannot expect my own wife to sympathize, and certainly not my mother whose religiosity is of that unethical and hysterically fanatical type which can see nothing but sheer madness and folly in my struggle for the light and the truth. I am unfortunately too weak to fight single handed. As Heine said "I am not made of the stuff that martyrs are made of." I suppose I shall go on squirming and writing in spiritual agony for the rest of my days.

A Rabbi Should Have a Beard

(AUGUST 5, 1919) [TRANSCRIBED AT A LATER DATE]

Rabbi Solomon Goldman formerly of Brooklyn and now of Cleveland told me that he happened to come together one day in the same synagogue with a certain Rabbi Burak[13] who is a product of the Yeshiva. On leaving the synagogue Solomon Goldman got into a conversation with one of the older men of that congregation. When they got to talking about

---

13. Aaron Burack (1892–1960), rabbi, Brooklyn; faculty, Rabbi Isaac Elchanan Theological Seminary (RIETS); officer, Union of Orthodox Rabbis.

rabbis the old man said "To me neither you nor Burak is a rabbi. You have no beard. His is trimmed. One who is to be my rabbi must have a longer beard than mine."

A *Question [She'elah]* to Kaplan Concerning Cantor Rosenblatt

(AUGUST 20, 1919) [TRANSCRIBED MAY 12, 1920]

Isaac Cohen[14] came to me yesterday with a peculiar Sh'eloh [question on a matter of Jewish law]. Cantor Rosenblatt[15] sang at the Casino Deal Beach [in New Jersey] last Saturday night (Aug. 10) to a large audience. I understand that his singing was received with great applause. Toward the end of the concert the manager announced that as it is customary to have the artists who perform Saturday nights assist in the service Sunday morning, he had asked Rosenblatt to sing from the oratorio Elijah at the services the next day, and that Rosenblatt accepted the invitation. This announcement was applauded to the echo [text unclear] by the gathering two thirds of which were Christians. Deal Beach is known as a Methodist center, and the Casino is where the Methodists hold Sunday services.

When Garfunkel[16] heard about this incident he at once telephoned to Rosenblatt to back out from his promise. Rosenblatt gave indisposition as his excuse to the Casino manager. What Cohen wanted to know was whether Rosenblatt should sing on some subsequent Sunday in order not to give the goyim an impression that a Jewish cantor can not be taken at his word, or whether Rosenblatt should under no circumstances take part in a Christian service. My reply to Cohen was that Rosenblatt had no right to participate in a service the main purpose of which was the glorification of Jesus.

The Center Building Is Completed

JULY 27, 1920

I am still affiliated with the Center, that is, I am still their Rabbi. The preaching which I kept up regularly was good. Now and then I would touch upon the economic problem especially around Pesah time. Every time I did so I rubbed the fur the wrong way.

The building has been completed. The real test of the institution will be next year when the actual program of the Center idea will be put into

---

14. Layman from the center.

15. Joseph (Yossele) Rosenblatt (1882–1933), famous cantor, concert singer, and composer, New York City.

16. Morris Garfunkel (1875–1942), textile manufacturer, New York City.

Kaplan and family. From left: Kaplan, Naomi, Judith, Grandma Rubin, Hadassah, Lena, and Selma. (Courtesy Reconstructionist Rabbinical College)

effect. I am fortunate in having a good assistant in a man of about thirty-one, Emanuel Davis. I do not know what I would have done if Miss Langer hadn't gotten married. For all we know, Judaism may be saved because Miss Langer found a husband.

There is little to boast about the Center group. So far they have given little evidence of spiritual growth. They display no interest in the various pamphlets, questionnaires, books, etc., that are sent out from the office. Last January I saw to it that each one received a copy of Goodman's History of the Jews,[17] so that they might acquire some historical Jewish background. I can vouch that only J. H. Cohen and one other person looked into the book.

April 18 the Center held a dinner to celebrate the finishing of the building. The annual meeting was held at the same time. The dinner was noisy and drawn out. The dessert was hardly served when the young folks, they upon whom we stake all our hopes, rose as one man and walked down stairs to dance. This was too much for me. The lack of manners, the crassness that makes it possible for a banquet in the interests of a religious cause to be unattended by a word of prayer or blessing aroused my resentment to such a

---

17. Paul Goodman, A *History of the Jews* (London: J.M. Dent & Sons, 1921).

degree that I too walked out. No speeches were delivered that evening. Not that anyone took it to heart.

Kaplan Meditates on Friedlaender's Death and Benderly's Depression

JULY 27, 1920

Friedlaender's[18] death which the papers reported two weeks ago last Sunday (July 11) has a very depressing effect on me as I witness the evidences of futility of so talented a life and so noteworthy a character as his was. He went through so much, he was in contact with numerous cultures and absorbed the best that was in them, cosmopolitan in his sympathies yet intensely Jewish in his strivings, a man of facile pen and silver tongue, a master of wit and repartee, and yet a failure. That he should be cut off in the prime of his life by murderers' hands in a wild forest in distant Ukraine, that his body should wallow naked in the mud of a deserted road in Wild Russia, is something that my poor brain cannot grasp. I have long given up attempting to square life with the traditional conceptions of Providence, but such evidences of Unreason are to me staggering.

AUGUST 5, 1920

Dr. Benderly seems to have passed through a crisis both spiritual and physical during the last year. He is by nature very reserved and never speaks about his troubles though these may be weighing down ever so heavily upon him. But from a few remarks that his wife passed while I was speaking to her by 'phone in the course of my inquiring after his health—that was last March when he was sick with pneumonia—I gathered that matters had reached with him such a pass that he was ready to commit suicide. When he recovered from his illness he was a broken man, though he kept on repeating that he was himself again. Fortunately he succeeded in interesting a number of his friends in a Palestinian business scheme that necessitated his first going to Palestine and reporting on the prospects there. He left for Europe during the latter part of April.

Before his departure he was given a banquet by Unterberg to which a few of his friends were invited. A number of us delivered short addresses: Magnes, Marshall, Semel.[19] Magnes as usual was the master spokesman. But when Benderly replied he spoke in a manner that brought tears to my eyes. It was to me a most thrilling spiritual experience to hear him say that he was grateful for all that he had gotten out of life. He spoke like a saint. That he of

---

18. Israel Friedlaender was murdered by bandits in the Ukraine during a relief mission on behalf of the Joint Distribution Committee.

19. Bernard Semel (1878–1959), businessman, communal leader, Zionist, New York City.

all men should have been able to find some sweetness in the bitter cup of life
that he had been made to taste proved to me that the supremacy of spirit over
matter was not altogether a phantasy. I do not remember what any one of us
said. Even my own remarks I recollect but vaguely. I recall having stressed the
fact that Benderly taught the Jews of America to think of Jewish education
in communal instead of institutional terms. But what he said stands out
clearly in my mind. He began by saying that he disagreed with every one of the
speakers who pointed out in one form or another that the Jewish community
failed to appreciate what he did in the way of upbuilding Jewish education.
On the contrary, he added, he could not be grateful enough to God for all
the kindnesses he had been shown. He then went on to speak of the dreams
of his youth when from the Lebanon heights he mused of the land beyond
the Mediterranean, the land of golden opportunities for the Jewish people,
opportunities not of money making but of spiritual achievement—America.
What a difference in attitude toward this country between Friedlaender
and Benderly! The former always regarded this country as harboring a crude
uncouth civilization, inferior to the civilizations of Europe with their ancient
traditions, whereas Benderly loves his life here for the infinite opportunities
that it holds out to those who have spirit enough to turn those opportunities
to good advantage.

Finkelstein Gets "Infected" with the Scholarly Virus

THURSDAY, APRIL 21, 1921
Since January 1920 I have been in the habit of working out my
sermons together with Dr. L. Finkelstein of the Bronx Synagogue. He is
a scholarly young man, of fine character, but does not take his rabbinic
calling with sufficient earnestness. He has absorbed a good deal of the
scholarly virus of cynicism from the Seminary atmosphere. I have a hard
time getting him to realize that a preacher who fails to think out his ideas
clearly and genuinely comes under the category of " . . . *oseh melekhet 'd
remi'ah*" [Heb. Jeremiah 48:10 "(Cursed) is he who is slack in doing the
Lord's Work!"][20] and is to be condemned far more than a carpenter or
plumber who skimps his job. I can't get him to realize that without being
able to think in terms of present day psychology and philosophy one must
fall back upon the hackneyed unanalyzed abstract slogans of religion that
have brought religion into disrepute. Yet I hope that in time he will be won
for the cause of intellectual and spiritual honesty.

Is it not sad to find that our best men are devoid of the very sense
for intellectual honesty?

---

20. Kaplan omitted the word *cursed* from his Hebrew citation of the verse.

He is only a young man of twenty-five. Already his life is not his own. If he had his way, he told me the other day, he would have taken up law instead of the ministry. It was the pressure of home environment that forced him into the rabbinate. And with this state of mind a man is supposed to guide, advise and inspire Jewish life! His case is by no means exceptional. In fact, it is altogether typical of the effect of the abnormal existence that we Jews lead in Goluth where our spiritual interests have nothing to do with our practical affairs.

Finkelstein and Kaplan—A Problematic Relationship

WEDNESDAY, APRIL 27, 1921

Yesterday morning I received a letter from Finkelstein in which he stated that he did not care to continue working with me as he has been doing the last year and a half. He alleges in the letter that I had a tendency to make him "work in ways that are not natural to him." It appears that my expecting him to take up the work of the Renascence was the cause of his writing the letter. I replied that I wanted to discuss the letter with him. He came to see me today. I proved to him that he was entirely unjustified in assuming that I wanted to do his thinking for him, or that I expected him to undertake work uncongenial to him. We parted friends and decided to work jointly on the subject dealt with in the sermon "God the Liberator."[21]

The Brandeis-Weizmann[22] Controversy [23]

TUESDAY, MAY 3, 1921

Yesterday I learned from Magnes that he and Marshall had met Weizmann on Friday night and spoke to him of the advisability of having

---

21. Finkelstein and Kaplan met every week to discuss the weekly Torah portion while they walked around the reservoir in Central Park. The letter thanks Kaplan and requests they cease studying together. It is obvious from the letter that Finkelstein believes Kaplan is dominating him. When I interviewed Finkelstein I asked him about this incident and he denied feeling that Kaplan dominated him. After the interview I found the letter. For more facts, see *Judaism Faces the Twentieth Century: A Biography of Mordecai M. Kaplan* (Detroit: Wayne State University Press, 1993), 229–30.

22. Chaim Weizmann (1874–1952), Zionist leader; first president of the State of Israel; key figure in bringing about the Balfour Declaration; president in the 1920s of the Zionist Organization of America; knew Kaplan well and visited him every time he (Weizmann) came to New York.

23. This controversy refers to the conflict between Brandeis and Weizmann over the control of the Zionist Organization of America. It was "Pinsk vs. Washington" with a difference in policy as well as style being at the core. Weizmann believed a centralized Zionist organization was a necessity; Brandeis disagreed.

a number of Baale-batim [community leaders] who were anxious to do their duty toward the upbuilding of Palestine learn from him and Judge Julian Mack[24] the main issue of the present controversy in the ranks of the Zionists. They would not undertake to arbitrate. Their only purpose would be to obtain information. Weizmann promised to let Magnes know whether he would be willing to meet such a committee. Yesterday Magnes received a telegram from Weizmann who had left for Montreal the day before, saying that he would be ready to state his case before a group of Baale-batim on Thursday, May 19 or Friday, May 20.

I immediately got in touch with Judge Mack and obtained his consent to come before that group together with Weizmann.

Today Schmarya Levin[25] got in touch with me. I informed him of Mack's acceptance. Levin asked that Ussishkin[26] be also permitted to be present. I got Mack's consent to that as well. The understanding is that Mack would also bring someone with him who would be in a position to speak with authority on the Zionist work in Palestine. Mack stipulated with me that he be not forced as he had been once before to speak in German in order that Ussischkin might understand.

Drs. Weizmann and Mossinson[27] attended services at the Center last Friday.

Kaplan Alienated from His Congregation

THURSDAY, MAY 5, 1921

Last night the annual meeting of the Center was supposed to take place, but there was such a violent rainstorm raging that only a small number of the members came. Most of those who came did so because they expected that the question of my asking for a leave of absence would be brought up, and they were determined not to allow the trustees—i.e., J. H. Cohen—to give me a leave for a year.

When the number of those present reached about twenty-five I suggested that we postpone the meeting to some day next week, and that those present discuss informally Center matters. We went upstairs to the dining room. Fischman no sooner opened the meeting than questions began flying from different quarters as to the rumor of my asking for a year's leave

---

24. Julian Mack (1866–1943), lawyer and judge; national, communal, and Zionist leader.

25. Shemaryahu Levin (1867–1935), Zionist leader; Hebrew and Yiddish author; opposed Uganda scheme; one of the founders of the Technion; founded Dvir publishing house.

26. Menahem Ussishkin (1863–1941), Zionist leader; member, Hovevei Zion; president, Jewish National Fund.

27. Probably Benzion Mossinson (1873–1942), Hebrew educator and Zionist leader; active in Zionist hierarchy; established a number of Hebrew periodicals.

of absence. Fischman and Cohen tried to avert the discussion but without avail. The air soon became supercharged with ill feeling and anger. I saw that the time had come for putting formalities aside. I got up and in a calm and collected manner set forth the issue raised by J. H. Cohen. I stated that I still believed that the question of orthodoxy was irrelevant to the larger purposes for which the Center stood, that so long as I did nothing in my own life or in the Center that could be objected to by the Orthodox wing, I should be allowed to work out those plans which I considered essential to the future of Judaism.

Despite my having spoken frankly and openly on the question at issue, Cohen for a long time refused to say anything in reply. But I and others insisted till he had to give way. What he said seemed to have made little impression. I felt constrained to reply. In the reply I brought out that the specific issue was whether the educational work in the Center should be dominated by the Orthodox point of view, or the point of view upon which I had been laboring all these years. I pleaded with those present not to attempt to settle the questions of fundamentals in the course of one or two meetings but to devote every Wednesday night of the coming year to discussing them. I doubt, however, whether very many of the congregation could be induced to take their Judaism so seriously. So long as they expect a fight they are interested, but discussion for the sake of finding out the truth they find too tame.

It was the expectation of a fight that brought S. C. Lamport[28] to the meeting at a late hour. He was more suppressed and sedate than usual, but his championing of my work makes me feel uncomfortable, for I know very well that he has not the least interest in Judaism.

Fischman came to see me at my request this afternoon. I wanted to persuade him to retain the presidency of the Center, for his giving up the presidency at this juncture would be interpreted as a protest of the Cohen faction. It appears, however, that Cohen gained a march on me and so impregnated Fischman's mind with the idea that he has no right to preside over the Center so long as my point of view is represented in the educational work, that Fischman seems immovable. In the course of my conversation I learned that one of the pupils of Kadushin's[29] class got into an argument with Fischman about some question involving the Mosaic authority of the Torah and that in the course of the argument she told F. that she had been

---

28. Samuel Charles Lamport (1880–1941), cotton merchant, communal leader, and philanthropist. His father (Nathan) and his brother (Arthur) were both active in the Jewish community. All of the Lamports belonged to the Jewish Center.

29. Max Kadushin (1895–1980), Conservative rabbi; scholar; educator; faculty, JTS; a loyal follower of Kaplan.

taught not to disclose to people at home the views on the Bible that she was being given in the classroom.

FRIDAY, MAY 6, 1921

A committee consisting of Rothstein, Unterberg, Judge Rosalsky and Asinof[30] came to see me last night. That committee was appointed by the Board of Trustees of the Center to take up with me the question of the leave of absence for a year. The committee realized, after what had been taken place last Wednesday night, that the majority of the members were strongly opposed to the Trustees' granting me the leave of absence, now that the real reason for my asking for it had become public knowledge. Instead of the Committee proposing to me a plan of action, they asked me to tell them what I thought was the best way out of the difficulty. I tried to convince them that Cohen had been pestering my life ever since we began to discuss the Center. I read to them what I had written into this record on April 15, 1916. My advice to them was that they should ignore Cohen, and promise me the cooperation which I needed to make the Center a success. I also told them that I thought Fischman ought to continue as president for another year at least. I cannot say that I got them to see my way, for when they left they still held to the purpose of continuing their parlays with Cohen. I know that unless something happens whereby Cohen's spell on some of the leading trustees will be broken it is useless for me to work in the Center. I am simply wasting my time and my energy for a lot of people who are spiritually and Jewishly beyond redemption. I do not mean to say that any one is theoretically beyond redemption, but speaking practically a good many of these prosperous Jews are too far gone to be shaken out of their spiritual self-complacency by methods such as I am able to employ. They need a man of deep spiritual nature ready to martyrize himself and his family. Such a one might be able to wring their hearts which seem to be made of flint.

Rabbi Leo Jung[31] *Denounces Kaplan*

FRIDAY, MAY 6, 1921

Rabbi Solomon Goldman of Cleveland visited me this morning. He graduated from the Seminary about four or five years ago. As a student he found my general approach to the problem of Judaism helpful to him and ever since then has been a zealous advocate of mine. He is at present occupant of an important pulpit in Cleveland where he has built up quite a following. He has his troubles but seems to be able to hold his own.

---

30. Probably Morris Asinof (1876–1950), clothing manufacturer, New York City.

31. Leo Jung (1892–1987), Orthodox rabbi; author; successor to Kaplan at the Jewish Center and critical of him; faculty, Yeshiva University.

In the same city where he is rabbi there is a young man of about 30—a Rabbi Jung who was imported from England. He is credited with having a good knowledge of Talmud, Poskim [Law Codes] and a general education as well. But having no capacity to think he is genuinely Orthodox. He professes to believe in the literal truth of the Torah having come from Heaven in the manner described in Exodus. This Rabbi Jung wrote an article in the *Jewish Forum* of last month entitled "Reform, Orthodox and Kaplanism" in which he denounces me as an *Epikuros* [heretic] though he gave me credit for at least being honest. Typical of that man's point of view is that following which he told Goldman: "I would rather have America with a mikvah [ritual bath] than Palestine without a mikvah." His main interest, Goldman tells me, is to institute a Mikvah in Cleveland.

The Crisis at the Center

MONDAY, MAY 9, 1921

Having been under a mental strain these last few days I was unable to deliver the sermon on "Society and the Individual" last Sabbath and to attend to my work at the Institute. Last night I was present at the celebration of Philip Weinstein's[32] silver wedding anniversary. Part of the strain under which I labored yesterday was due to my having to overcome the mental resistance which I naturally felt toward attending the affair. It seems to have required at least two days' effort on my part to work myself into a mood sufficiently charitable to be able to deliver the little address at the opening of the festivities. I have learned enough from my general reading to realize that a puritanical and narrow moralist attitude toward people who are after all in the grip of a social system far beyond their control is not becoming to one who really aspires to serve mankind. Yet I am thankful for the mental resistance in me which renders my charity toward men of the Weinstein type anything but easy and spontaneous for I would adjudge myself a hypocrite otherwise.

The celebration which took place at the Astor Hotel was attended by a good many members of the Center. Among them were Cohen *ve-siyato* [Heb. and his group, gang]. I made it my business to make peace overtures right there and then. While I am confident that, if, at the annual meeting which will take place on Wednesday the controversy between Cohen and me should be aired I would have no difficulty in getting a large majority of the members to support me, I nevertheless realize that it would be a Pyrrhic victory. Not only would the Center suffer, but the Jewish educational

---

32. Philip Weinstein (1873–1938), women's coat manufacturer, communal worker, philanthropist.

undertaking that is still in its initial stages and especially the Seminary and Institute would be made the butt of attack on the part of the Yeshiva crowd that is lying in wait just for such an opportunity. That crowd represents in this country the survival of what was worst in Medievalism. Lately these people have been gathering force through the support of the Travis[33] family, exploiters of natural gas and oil reserves in Oklahoma, Texas and Mexico. Once that crowd gets in the saddle, it is all up with Judaism in this country. Judaism will have lost its last chance to function as a vital spiritualizing energy in consonance with the needs and requirements of life in this country. It will exist for a while as a galvanized formalism only to drop off in the end into the oblivion of dead cults. God forfend such an outcome.

After the banquet Fischman, Unterberg, Rosalsky, Lamport and myself got into a small room to discuss the possibility of the two sides coming to terms. Cohen had to leave because his doctor advised him not to remain, and his wife was about to make a scene. (She it was who three months ago when the controversy first broke out went around saying that I will be her husband's death if I don't resign.) Rothstein also was unable to attend the improvised meeting we were holding because his wife either took sick or pretended illness.

In the discussion it appeared that the main bone of contention now was the point of view that should predominate in the instruction of the children and the young people at the Center. Fischman said that if he had a daughter going to the Center he would take her away, if she were taught that the Torah was not given by God at Sinai. What he wants then is to have a committee on Education that would safeguard the orthodoxy of the instruction. It took me considerable time to draw this out from him. As soon as I understood that this was his wish I thought it offered an excellent opportunity to bring about peace in the Center. I therefore stated that I would gladly consent to the appointment of such a committee. I hope that I am not compromising myself, nor with the principle of intellectual honesty by consenting to the appointment of a committee that would most likely render the instruction Orthodox. The people know my views and if they are liberal enough to tolerate me, why should I not be liberal enough to tolerate them? After all they have a right to believe a "Thus said the Lord" that is thousands of years old more than a "Thus said the Lord" that is three years old pronounced by a man whom they can see and can hear and know to be just as weak and human as they are. I am sure I am right and that they are wrong. But I am not their father, and even if I were, I have no right to prevent them from making their mistakes. I am convinced that they are

---

33. Travis family, related to Bernard Revel.

sincere because they are too ignorant to be insincere. Let them try out their method. I am sure they will find out before long that it does not work.

But all this is very petty theorizing. I am afraid we have reckoned without the host. Cohen is a host in more senses than one. What will he say to this arrangement?

WEDNESDAY, MAY 11, 1921

The meeting of the Board of Trustees called for the special purpose of considering the action to be taken on my request for a leave of absence took place last night. It was the best attended meeting in the last two years and began almost the minute it was called for. It proved as exciting an experience as I had expected it to be.

THURSDAY, MAY 12, 1921

The meeting opened with the report of Judge Rosalsky on behalf of the committee of four that had come to see me last Thursday. What he said in effect was that what had taken place on Wednesday night at the informal discussion of the members proved that this was an inconspicuous [inauspicious?] time for me to take a leave of absence. His committee, accordingly, decided that I should be asked to withdraw the letter asking leave of absence, and that no discussion of views should take place at the postponed annual meeting scheduled for tomorrow.

Rosalsky was no sooner through with his report than J. H. Cohen fired his first gun. "Let us not beat about the bush. Why veil the issues? Let us discuss this matter in our shirtsleeves. Dr. Kaplan stated clearly some time ago that for three years he tried our way in his work in the Center. Realizing that he did not succeed in accomplishing his purpose, he said he must try a new method. He wants to give us a new Judaism. We, however, cannot permit ourselves to be experimented with. We are bound by the constitution to be Orthodox." He then went on to relate how I at one time said to him that I was not Orthodox (or as he put it "unorthodox") and that when he heard that from me he said "You cannot be our rabbi."[34] This led to the negotiations with Charles H. Kauvar (See Vol. I, 339, 342).[35] What happened to have brought us together he could not exactly say, as he kept no memoranda and made no written contract with me. But he was under the impression that in accepting the rabbinate of the Center I was pledged to make it 100% Jewish according to the "Din Shulhan Aruch."[36]

---

34. Kaplan changed the text to read "I cannot be your rabbi."

35. This reference is to the first mention of Kauvar in vol. 1 of the written Diary.

36. Law of the Shulkhan Aruk." The *Shulkhan Aruk* is the most important code of Jewish law; it was edited by Joseph Caro in the sixteenth century. The expression here, "according to the law of the Shulkhan Aruk," has the meaning of the exact letter of the traditional law.

Last summer, however, I published an article in which I broke completely with Orthodox Judaism and in addition, organized a society whose platform distinctly violates the principles of Orthodox Judaism.[37]

My answer to this charge was as follows:

It was not a new Judaism that I was trying to formulate but on the contrary, that I was doing all in my power to enable traditional Judaism to live. As far as my relations to the Center are concerned I am prepared to uphold the Shulhan Aruch as the code to be followed in our practice inasmuch as we have no other authoritative code to go by. But on the question of orthodoxy, I want it clearly understood that my views are not Orthodox, nor do I consider myself bound to uphold orthodoxy in the Center, since there is nothing in the constitution which says that the Center must be Orthodox.

This, however, does not mean that I intend to do anything prejudicial to the orthodoxy of any one in the Center. Nothing is further from my thought than to ram my belief down anybody's throat. If the principal directors of the Center object to having such unorthodox ideas as I hold taught to the young people, they have a perfect right to appoint an Education Committee to supervise the teaching and see to it that it be conducted in the Orthodox spirit.[38]

Last night the annual meeting of the entire membership took place. It was the best attended meeting of its kind so far since the Center has been in existence though a good many of the Trustees, wearied out by the discussion of the preceding night, did not come. Fischman announced the decision of the Board. The members seemed satisfied with the outcome of the controversy. In my address to them I said to them in substance as follows:

I am grateful for the confidence reposed in me despite the fact that I hold views that are not in accord with those held by some of the leading men in the Center. In re-electing me as Rabbi they did as much toward initiating a new conception of the rabbinate as they did toward initiating a new conception of the synagogue when they built the Center. The new conception of the rabbi is that he has a right to his own point of view, and must not be expected to be simply the mouthpiece of his congregation.

I then urged upon them, if they mean to carry the work of the Center to a successful conclusion, to regard the Center as a necessity and not as a

---

37. The article Kaplan is referring to here is "A Program for the Reconstruction of Judaism," *Menorah Journal* 6, no.4 (August 1920): 181–96. The society Kaplan is referring to here is the abortive Society for Jewish Renascence. It consisted of rabbis and scholars, mostly from New York City, who met sporadically in 1919 and 1920 to draft a new program for American Judaism. See *Judaism Faces the Twentieth Century* for more information.

38. The meeting accepted Kaplan's proposals, including appointment of a committee which would "safeguard the orthodoxy of the teaching at the Center," and after a few more hours of discussion reelected him rabbi.

luxury. All the activities of the Center would take on new life, the financial problems would be solved, and a new spirit would prevail among them, if they would adopt the attitude that an institution like the Center is essential to their physical, social and intellectual development.

I also touched upon the proposal to organize a Jewish Business Men's Conference—a movement to apply the teachings of Judaism to the problems of business and industry. The initial impulse toward such a movement ought to come from the Center.

From remarks made to me after the meeting by Rosalsky and from the conversation I had today with Fischman I gathered that some of the trustees including Fischman took offense at what I said at the meeting in the opening remarks of the address.

On Resigning from the Center

TUESDAY, MAY 17, 1921

I am beginning to realize already what an anomalous position I am occupying in the group of people with whom I have been attempting to work the last ten years. Until recently when my views were unknown to them, I was an asset to them, but a hypocrite in my own eyes. Now that I am known as holding views that are absolutely nonorthodox I can be of no service to them. I make no attempt whatever to sail under false colors. The arrangement at the Center was suggested by me not because I actually believe it is workable. I am human and have sufficient pride not to allow Cohen and Fischman to compel me to resign. I want to resign from the Center, but I don't want anybody to make me do it.

It looks as though I can no longer expect to find my spiritual haven with the class of our people I have been associated with ever since I have been in the ministry. I shall have to break with them sooner or later. I am therefore laying my plans to do so with as little a jolt or shock as possible to all concerned.

Kaplan Contemplates Joining Stephen Wise at Jewish Institute of Religion

TUESDAY, MAY 17, 1921

I went to see Stephen S. Wise today about my becoming a member of the faculty in the rabbinical school which he is on the point of establishing. I spoke to him about this matter a year ago. He encouraged me very strongly but I was still hoping that possibly I might work out my spiritual destiny in the Center and the Seminary. But both of these institutions have wronged me, especially the Seminary. The coldness and hauteur of the faculty, the attack made upon me by Adler on Jan 16 at the convention of the United

Jan. 1920

A class from the Jewish Center in Central Park, January 1920. Far right,
Selma and Naomi Kaplan. (Courtesy Hadassah Kaplan Musher)

Synagogue, Ginzberg's unwarranted assault the next day, all this in spite of
my utmost endeavor to help the Seminary morally and financially have led
me to conclude that I must cut away from my moorings.

Wise showed himself very friendly. I have always admired and
believed in him despite the tradition among our people and especially in
the Seminary that you can not be a good Jew without disparaging Wise. If
God will spare me and give me health I may be officially connected with the
Jewish Institute of Religion by next year.

Brandeis versus Weizmann

FRIDAY, MAY 20, 1921

I attended yesterday the conference of a number of Baale-Batim
[community leaders] called for the purpose of hearing from Dr. Weizmann
and Judge Mack debate the issue of the controversy between the World Zionist Organization and the Zionist Organization of America.[39] The meeting

---

39. See preceding note 23 on Brandeis for an explanation of this controversy. Part of the
conflict had to do with the *Keren Hayesod*. Brandeis hoped that American contributors to

was held in a room belonging to the Arkwright Club, 320 Bway. Judge Rosalsky opened the meeting at 3:30 with a few remarks prepared for him by Dr. Benderly who has been doing the actual work of getting the conference together. There were present about thirty men, five women, and representing the W.Z.O. Weizmann, Ussishkin with two secretaries, and on behalf of the AZA. Judge Mack, Prof. Felix Frankfurther and two secretaries. The meeting lasted until 12 midnight.

Mack was called upon first. He spoke for nearly two hours. He began with a resentful denunciation of the charge made against the American Zionist leaders that they were not Jews, that they knew nothing, had read nothing and learned nothing. He did not make clear just what was the ignorance he was charged with. The controversy, he said, had arisen at Paris where the various representatives of the Zionist movement met in 1919 to obtain favorable terms in the peace treaty for the Jews of the various countries. It was there that Zionists like Ussishkin urged that Jews must demand not only political equality but national rights. It was this conception that underlay the interpretation that the W.Z.O. gave to the Keren Hayesod. They regard the K.H. as a State Treasury, and demand implicit obedience in contributing to it.

A Meeting with Weizmann

MAY 27, 1921

The next morning [a number of days later] we met Weizmann at the Commodore. We found him in smoker and slippers. He had gone to bed late after having come back from an out of town speaking tour. When we saw him, he still looked weary and wan. I no sooner made my prefatory statement than he laid it down as a sine qua non that the office of the K.H. at 55 Union Sq. must be allowed to continue its work. He would not even hear of the A.Z.O. instituting a K.H. campaign of its own. He had with him Schmarya Levin and Neiditsch,[40] the originator of the K.H. idea. Weizmann and Levine berated the leaders of the A.Z.O. as obstructionists. Finally in a very dramatic way Weizmann appealed to us as real Jews to help him against these obstructionists, instead of acting as impartial judges meting out judgment. He actually wept when he spoke of how he was sacrificing himself for the movement. He had nothing else in the world to live for. He

---

this Zionist foundation would be able to control their contributions. Weizmann believed all money should be centralized. Setting up an office of *Keren Hayesod* in New York was a declaration of war against the Brandeis forces. See diary entry for June 16, 1921.

40. Isaac A. Naiditsch (1868–1949), philanthropist and Zionist; manufacturer; donated large sums for promoting Hebrew culture; originator and one of the first directors of Keren Hayesod.

addressed himself to me in particular. Naturally I was very much overcome at this sign of weakness and helplessness on the part of Weizmann in the face of apathy and obstruction. As I left him I felt very much broken hearted at the thought that those among us who had the interests of our people at heart have become so alienated from each other in their *Weltanschauungen* and sympathies as to engage in bitter quarrels even when confronted with so urgent a task as the rebuilding of Palestine.

WEDNESDAY, JUNE 15, 1921 (Long Branch)
      A week ago last Thursday (June 2) seven of us (Benderly, Rosalsky, Rothstein, Rottenberg, Semel, Sam Lamport and I) went to Washington with the purpose of urging Brandeis to resign from the Supreme Court and to become the visible leader of the Zionist movement in this country. The seven of us were crowded into one compartment of a Pullman. We spent the greatest part of the time in telling all sorts of funny stories. Just about an hour before we arrived in Washington we began to discuss the purpose of our trip. We soon realized that there was no unanimity among us as to the fundamental issues involved in the controversy and as to the statement we were to present to Brandeis. The troublesome one in the group was Rottenberg. He showed himself a determined Weizmannist. Benderly hoped to bring the discussion to a head by pointing out that there were three distinct phases to the controversy—principle, policies, and persons. He suggested that I formulate the principles involved. Before I got very far we had to leave the train. We continued our discussion at the Hotel Washington where we were to stay overnight.

A Meeting with Brandeis

THURSDAY, JUNE 16, 1921
      The next morning the seven of us went to the home of Judge Brandeis. We arrived on the minute of 9:00 and we were ushered into his study. Judge Rosalsky made a few introductory remarks in which he alluded to our having been very much troubled by the controversy and to our efforts to bring about an understanding, which have failed. He then called upon me to set forth specifically the purpose of our mission. The following is a summary of what I said:
      We represent no organization and have not been authorized by any organization to carry out the missions for which we have come to you. We are a handful of Jews taken at random from the large mass of synagogue Jews who look upon the Zionist movement as a means of bringing about the fulfillment of our age-long prayer for the restoration of Zion. At the same time we recognize our indebtedness to America for having given us

the opportunity to achieve material success and the only way we can express our gratitude to her is by countenancing nothing in our lives that might in the least impugn our loyalty toward her.

We have had occasion to get an insight into the Zionist problem through our attempt to learn what was involved in the Keren Hayesod controversy. It did not take us long to realize that issues of a fundamental character divided the European from the American Zionists. After reflecting upon these issues we arrived at the following conclusions:

1. The integrity and authority of the World Zionist Organization as the political representative and economic agency of the Jews must be upheld.

2. We look upon the World Zionist Organization as a means to an end and not as end in itself. With this in mind we are bound to conclude that the policies of the W.Z.O. must be directed solely toward the accomplishment of that end. Nothing is so essential toward the achievement of that purpose as enlisting the aid of as large a number of our people as possible. To bring that about the lowest common denominator of Jewish interest should be sought out in all types of Jews and made use of for the upbuilding of Palestine. The lowest common denominator is the desire to establish in Palestine an economically self supporting Jewry. No Jew can possibly take exception to such an aim. That aim, therefore, should be the one to which the Z.O. should devote itself.

3. A second corollary which follows from our conception of the W.Z.O. merely as a means rather than an end in itself is the freedom of each local Zionist organization to further that end in its way, and in a matter compatible with the spirit of the country to which it belongs. Being only a means to an end the W.Z.O. must not take the attitude that loyalty to it is not merely a means of administrative efficiency but qualification for being a full fledged Jew. We regard such an attitude as productive of a type of Jewish chauvinism that might compromise our position in the countries of our adoption.

We consider the American Zionist Organization as being in a position to ward off the danger of making the Zionist Organization an end in itself. But to bring about that result it must be visibly directed and guided by you. This would involve your giving your entire time and energy to the movement. We feel we have a right to ask of you to make that sacrifice because nothing could be more calamitous than for the Jews to fail to take advantage of the opportunity to reclaim Palestine, an opportunity that may never come to us again. America too cannot begrudge your making such a sacrifice on behalf of the Jews, especially now that all the countries of the world, America herself included, have shut their doors against the Jews.

Brandeis complimented me on having set forth clearly the issues of the controversy. After making the same points as the foregoing in other language he stated that there was no need for his coming out openly as the leader of the American Zionists, since he gave to the movement all that was expected of a leader, that is, the laying down of policies and the direction of affairs. He stated that he gave all of his leisure time to Zionism. More he could not do. He did not care to come before mass meetings, for he was of the conviction that the time for mass meetings was over, and that no good could come out of them.

Some of the other members of the committee then took up the word. Benderly especially urged him to adopt our suggestion because of the effect it would have on the indifferentists. Sam Lamport put in a word. I made use of Brandeis' statement that England was watching to see whether the American Jews would succeed in having their point of view prevail in the reconstruction of Palestine, to ask him whether the failure of the American viewpoint at the Cleveland Convention that was to take place next Sunday would not produce a bad effect on quarters where it might harm the cause.

But all of our pleading was of no avail. He insisted that being convinced as we were of the justice of the American Zionist viewpoint we should go to Cleveland together with a few more of our original committee to put the case before the delegates of the convention. We would not be regarded as meddlers, since such procedure is customary in the political national conventions.

We had not come to Washington to be told to go to Cleveland for that purpose; so we immediately started for home. While on the train it dawned upon me that De Haas played a trick on us. He was anxious that we should go to Cleveland, to urge the delegates to uphold the administration. He thought that by getting Brandeis to talk to us, we would be persuaded to go to Cleveland for that purpose. But how was De Haas to get us to see Brandeis? This he apparently solved by leading us to believe that Brandeis' resignation depended upon our coming to ask him to make that sacrifice for Zionism and promising him support. If that was De Haas' game, it would be an excellent reason for our questioning the sincerity of the administration.

In my estimation Brandeis is a remarkable replica of Wilson as the latter is described in the recent book by Keynes. Though apparently high minded he is too much of a stickler for abstract principles. He seems more-over to suffer from the inability to emancipate himself from the influence of his minions, or to judge them at their true worth.

I came out with my family on Tuesday, June 7, 1921 to West End, N.J., 310 Norwood Avenue for the summer.

On Friday night, June 10, I received a telegram from Weizmann saying that he was anxious to get in touch with me. He spoke to me by phone on Monday at 2:35 P.M.

There were two matters he wanted to talk to me about. The first was the request he received from the British Government to name a Jew to serve on the International commission to take charge of the Holy Places in Palestine. He wanted me to consider accepting the position which might involve my living in Palestine. The Commission is to consist of six men, two Jews, two Christians and two Mohammedans.

The second matter had to do with the Keren Hayesod. He wanted to know whether I would consent to serve on the Advisory Board of the K.H. I gave my consent.

Organizing the Society for the Advancement of Judaism

WEDNESDAY, MAY 10, 1922 [INSERTED HERE AT A LATER DATE]
The Society for the Advancement of Judaism was organized on Tuesday, Jan. 17. We held our first services at the meeting house, 41 West 86 Street on Friday night, January 27, 1922. Was elected leader for life Feb. 12, 1922.

The First Bat Mitzvah

MARCH 28, 1922
Last Sabbath a week ago (March 18) I inaugurated the ceremony of the Bat Mitzvah at the S.A.J. Meeting House (41 West 86 St.) about which more details later.[41] My daughter Judith[42] was the first one to have her Bat Mitzvah celebrated there.

Kaplan Defends Himself to Seminary Trustees

MONDAY MAY 1, 1922
This afternoon I had one of those experiences with the Seminary authorities that make me wish I could throw my Seminary job into the faces of Adler and the Trustees.

In the last report I made to Adler of the work at the Teachers Institute I happened to include the curriculum of the Post Graduate Department I organized last year. In that curriculum mention is made of the fact that the courses in Hebrew are devoted to an intensive study of Ahad Haam and to extensive study of modern Hebrew Belles-Lettres. The mere mention of these facts to Adler is like waving a red flag before a bull. He is one of

---

41. Kaplan never wrote up the details of the Bat Mitzvah of Judith. This entry is the only one concerning Judith's Bat Mitzvah. Girls who became Bat-Mitzvah did not have Torah honors afterward. Calling women to the Torah began at the SAJ in the late 1940s. For more information, see *Judaism Faces the Twentieth Century.*

42. Judith Kaplan Eisenstein (1909–96), eldest of Kaplan's four daughters; Ph.D., author, expert on Jewish music; Kaplan's favorite philosophical companion. See *Judaism Faces the Twentieth Century* for more information.

those fanatical anti-Zionists who cannot bear the mention of anything that has to do with the modern Jewish Renaissance without getting hot under the collar. In presenting my report, therefore, at a meeting of the Board of Trustees about three months ago he raised the question why I permitted so much time to be spent upon modern Hebrew. He asked that the special committee in Teachers Institute which had not been functioning for the last few years to meet me to discuss this question. The meeting was to have taken place about six weeks ago but was postponed on account of Adler's illness.

After great difficulty it took place today at Stroock's[43] office at 2:00 P.M. Felix M. Warburg said he had only twenty minutes' time. The others, Judge Greenbaum,[44] Stroock and Adler remained throughout the meeting. Warburg was interested only in hearing what I had to say about the various Jewish educational organizations and their relations to one another. I presume he was approached in reference to giving support to the Jewish Educational Association which I was in a way instrumental in organizing, but from which I have kept away, or been made to keep away, ever since the trouble with the Center came to a head. Warburg apparently wanted to learn from me whether there was overlapping of educational effort.

In the course of my explanation I made mention of the License Board which worked out standards for the different grade of teachers and I added that the graduates of the Teachers Institute were granted "B" licenses upon their receiving diplomas from the Institution. This furnished Adler the clue to launch his attack against the practice of regulating our work by requirements set up outside of the Institute. He denounced such practice as yielding to the Soviet spirit which has been introduced by Benderly in conjunction with undue emphasis upon modern Hebrew and a secular tendency in all of the instruction. I could at once see what I was up against. The ghost of Schechter seemed to have returned to plague me for having taken advantage of his absence for a year when he went to Africa[45] and having formed an alliance with Benderly. The other members of the committee supported Adler's contention. Stroock seemed to have been of the impression that all of modern Hebrew literature is anti-religious and pornographic. Greenebaum saw no use in Hebrew. He was interested in religion and ethics. The fact that the Jewish *Vorwerts* [Yiddish newspaper—

---

43. Solomon Stroock (1874–1941), lawyer; communal leader; active at JTS and in American Jewish Committee.

44. Samuel Greenbaum (1854–1930), lawyer; state appellate judge; communal leader, New York City.

45. In 1910 Solomon Schechter, on sabbatical, visited his daughter Ruth in the Union of South Africa. While he was away Benderly organized the Bureau of Jewish Education under the Kehillah. Schechter thought that this organization should be run by the seminary.

The Forward] is written in Hebrew characters does not alter the fact that it is objectionable was one of Greenebaum's oracular sayings.

When I saw myself attacked and criticized I got into a temper and told them that I did not think it was right for them after displaying so little interest in the work of the Institute and never keeping in touch with it, to place me on the defensive every time they met with me. I told them bluntly that the Trustees of the Seminary did not interfere with the curriculum of the Seminary. I saw no reason why they should interfere with the curriculum that was worked out by the faculty at the Teachers Institute. They replied in kind, and said that they had a right to know the policy of the T.I. and that they were not merely rubber stamps. I told them that if they had no confidence in me that I was conducting the institution along the proper lines I was ready to resign.

After a while the heat of the discussion subsided. I grew calmer and so did they. Nothing definite was arrived at. I did not even get a chance to ask for a larger allowance for the extension courses which they seemed to approve of as doing just the work they would like to see the T.I. do in contrast with the intensive courses of the Teachers Training Department.

Here is my situation. I am in the center of a four cornered fight. At one corner the Orthodox abuse me and the Teachers Institute as turning out heretics and non-observant teachers. At the second corner are the Hebraists who claim that we send out men and women who are totally ignorant of Hebrew and Hebrew literature. Our teachers are only good for what they term the "religious schools of the 'Yahudim.' "[46] At the third corner are the members of the Faculty of the Institute who resent any kind of religious emphasis as being ecclesiastical and would have the Institute turned into a school for Jewish nationalism. And finally Adler and the Trustees who want the Institute to give public school teachers a few lessons in Jewish religion and ethics and lessons in translating the order of prayer. This is their idea of the type of teachers we ought to train.

SAJ Dinner Dance—Kaplan Bored

MONDAY, MAY 22, 1922

Last night the SAJ gave a dinner and dance. Before the affair began I was in good spirits. When I thought of the fact that at last I have succeeded in actually building up an organization that came as near to being my own creation as I could ever expect, I believed for the moment that my effectiveness was demonstrated. But my ardor cooled off when I came to the Meeting House. I was disappointed in the small attendance. The people

---

46. Yehudim: term used to refer to wealthy German Jews, most of whom were Reform.

with whom I sat at table never mentioned a word about the organization, as though it had never existed. The main topic of conversation was golf. I was bored to death.

When the dinner was over Harry Simmons[47] asked me to speak. He never so much as said a word about the organization. His main object in calling upon me was not so much to get them to think a little about our aims but mainly that I might humor them along preparatory to their leaving for their summer resorts. I was not in the mood for entertaining. Instead I was prosy and preachy. I went back home thoroughly disappointed.

Kaplans Sail for Europe

WEDNESDAY, JULY 5, 1922

I am now on the S.S. Philadelphia which is bound for Naples. Lena is with me.

Two weeks ago last Saturday Mr. & Mrs. Harold Spielberg[48] who are now members of the SAJ called on us. In the course of the conversation, Mr. S. mentioned the fact that he had gone into a new business venture. Not content with confining himself to the shipping business he has become part owner of the Philadelphia which had been used by the Government as a transport ship and was having it fitted out as a passenger ship.

"It will sail on Sat., July 1. Mrs. Spielberg is going to Europe with it. Go along with her, Mrs. Kaplan. There's a chance for you to rest up, and you will keep Mrs. S. company."

Lena at once accepted the invitation. When they left Lena urged me to join her. She was sure she could get passage for me as well. Next morning she did.

It was interesting to note the reaction of our kiddies when the subject of our going to Europe was discussed that Saturday night. When Lena stated that she was determined to go Selma burst out crying. When I demurred and Lena said she would not go without me Judith burst out crying. She thought I was cruel in depriving her mother of a remarkable opportunity to see Europe.

Truth to tell I was really reluctant to take the trip. I had planned to devote a good part of the summer to writing and here I was to be interrupted again. Neither was I in a mood to incur the inconvenience due to eating Kosher. But seeing that Lena was anxious to go I felt I had no right to deprive her of the pleasure that the trip would afford her. My earnings have not been such as to enable us to indulge in travel. To block her in the

---

47. Harry Simmons (?), a distant cousin of Lena Kaplan; in the fur business.
48. Harold Spielberg (1879–1940), lawyer; legislator; organizer, Equitable Surety Co.

attainment of her frequently expressed wish to see Europe again when all I had to do was to readjust my plans for the summer seemed hoggish to me, and I therefore yielded.

A week ago last Monday we visited the Spielbergs and after having heard from them they would make it possible for us to take the trip without paying anything for the passage, we decided to take advantage of their generous offer.

The ship was scheduled to sail on Saturday, 2:00 P.M. from Pier 18 Brooklyn. This necessitated our stopping at a Brooklyn hotel on Friday before sundown. Isidore[49] took us there with his automobile.

A Bat Mitzvah in Rome

Next morning I attended services at the synagogue. There were about a hundred men in the auditorium. The women sat in the gallery. The services were dull and mechanical. The people were not in the least interested in what was going on.

Tuesday morning on S.S. Arabic, August 22, 1922

A man who spoke English rather fairly had me sit next to him. He told me he came from Austria about thirty years ago, but that he was thoroughly italianized by this time. From him and from a few others that I interrogated, I learned that there were about 13 to 14 thousand Jews in Rome, some of them very wealthy but that there was no Jewish life to speak of. Very few keep kashruth or give their children a Jewish training. I understood that there was such a thing as a Talmud Torah, but that it was closed at the time on account of vacation. The Rabbi Sacerdote was also away on his vacation to Switzerland. No sermons are delivered at the synagogue except on holidays.

I was very much pleased to see that they had the custom of taking cognizance of a girl's becoming Bas Mitzvah. They call it entering "Minyan" at the age of twelve. The ceremony consists of having the father called up to the Torah on the Sabbath that the girl becomes Bas Mizvah. She accompanies him to the almemar [reading stand in the middle of the synagogue], and when he is through with his part, she recites the benediction of *She-hehiyanu* [Heb. blessing said on important occasions of transition].[50] Before Musaph [the additional service] the Rabbi addresses her on the

---

49. Isidore Rubin (1883–1958), gynecologist; researcher into female sterility; brother-in-law of Mordecai Kaplan.

50. Blessed art thou, Lord our God, King of the universe, who has granted us life and sustenance and permitted us to reach this time.

significance of her entering minyan.[51] On the Sabbath I was at the synagogue there were three girls and one boy who entered minyan. The assistant rabbi who was supposed to address them, read something to them out of a book in a very mechanical fashion. The fathers of the girls acted as if they were rather infrequent visitors at the synagogue.

Kaplan Consults Finkelstein about Omitting the Kol Nidre

THURSDAY, AUGUST 31, 1922

Last night Dr. L. Finkelstein and his wife paid us a visit. He and I got into a hot discussion as to the wisdom of my replacing the Kol Nidre[52] with a selection from a poem by Luzzatto[53] and retaining only the traditional melody. He considered such action on my part as destructive of Judaism, for if I were to carry out the motive that led me to take this step to its logical conclusion I would abrogate such a law as Halizah.[54] I contended that I regarded sincerity in prayer as superior to all other considerations. The substance of the Kol Nidre expressing disavowal of all promises and oaths was entirely unspiritual and unworthy of a place in the service on the most solemn day of the year. The reason it is permitted to occupy so important a place is that the people have no idea of what it is about. The pious emotions that it evokes, if it does that at all, have nothing to do with its contents. Such a state of affairs is deplorable in any religion since it makes for mummery and hypocrisy.

Finkelstein, of course, remained obdurate, but his wife (who originally was a Miss Bentwich)[55] seemed inclined to agree with me.

---

51. Minyan: literal meaning is quorum necessary for prayer. Ten men for the Orthodox. Liberal Jews include women. Here it means to enter the community.

52. Kol Nidre: prayer which is the centerpiece of the high holiday service on Yom Kippur eve. Prayer deals with legal matters and Kaplan was unhappy with it. Substituted Psalm 130 for it in 1925. Many at the SAJ protested and eventually Kaplan reinstated it, after a lengthy correspondence with Judah David Eisenstein. The present reformulation of the Kol Nidre reflects J. D. Eisenstein's understanding of the prayer. See *Judaism Faces the Twentieth Century* for details.

53. Moses Hayyim Luzzato (1701–46), kabbalist and author of the ethical work *Mesillat Yesharim—The Path of the Upright*, which Kaplan translated for the Jewish Publication Society. This translation appeared in 1936. Luzzatto also wrote poetry and is considered by some to be the first modern Hebrew author.

54. *Halitzah*: biblically prescribed ceremony (Deuteronomy 25:9–11) performed when a man refuses to marry his brother's childless widow. Symbolic of outmoded laws.

55. Carmel Finkelstein (Forsyte) (1898–) née Bentwich, sister of Lillian Friedlaender and Norman Bentwich, later divorced from Louis Finkelstein.

4

September 22, 1922–April 16, 1925

Questions and Answers — Why Remain a Jew?

FRIDAY, SEPTEMBER 22, 1922

On Monday, Sept. 11, I addressed a group consisting of about fifteen young men and one woman who intend to go into Jewish Welfare Work. The group had been given a course of lectures by Rabbi Max Kadushin on "The Jewish Social Heritage." He made use largely of the two or three chapters I succeeded in working out during the month of June. Having told them he was giving them the philosophy of Judaism that I had worked out, they were anxious to have me answer in person some of the questions that the course had awakened in their minds. Judging from the interest displayed and the questions asked the course that Kadushin gave them seems to have proved very successful. Here are some of the questions.

What justification is there from the pragmatic point of view for the continued existence of Judaism, i.e., how can the distinctly Jewish principles rather than the secular principles of social justice etc. be of greater service in contributing toward the upbuilding of a better society and a more spiritualized individual existence?

Answer: The moral and spiritual aspects of life cannot be built up in vacuo. The principles of right and wrong, belief in God, etc. cannot be transmitted without reference to some historic background. That historic background is moreover essential to give momentum to the tendencies within us that make for living on a higher plane of existence than that of the sub-human being. The choice in actual life is not between furnishing the historic background and momentum, on the one hand, and on the other hand relying on abstract principles, but between one historic background or another, between Judaism and Christianity, between Christianity and Americanism, etc. In giving first place to Judaism we are at the same time furnishing background to what is of permanent worth in Americanism.

Question: A more or less distinctive racial minority submerged in a dominant majority—a minority that cannot or will not merge—will always be open to distrust and suspicion. Will not, therefore, the growing race consciousness of the American Jew, expressed in the increasing number of distinctive Jewish centers, Y's etc. foster and sustain anti-Semitism?

Answer: I conceive Judaism as a socializing and humanizing influence in a person's life. If these institutions would live up to that purpose in Judaism they would go a long way toward counteracting anti-Semitism. The absence of such institutions would create the development of a type of Jew who would not only cause anti-Semitism but justify it.

Question: Other world races do not object to merging their tradition and social heritage in the common stream of American life. Why then should the Jews hold aloof?

Answer: Because the Jewish social heritage is not merely coordinate with American Culture as are the traditions and social heritages of other people. It is the spiritual background to all of the western civilizations.

Question: Is the Jewish social heritage chiefly literary, centering around a theological theme, or is it social and bound up in the mores of Jewish community life?

Answer: The Greek or the Latin Heritage is literary in character because there is no group in which the heritage is transmitted as a social requirement to which the individual is expected on moral ground to live up. A child that is born to Jewish parents is not asked whether he wants to be a Jew or not but he is brought up as one first and then cannot break away from Judaism without incurring the charge of disloyalty. This fact renders the Jewish heritage social.

There were other questions of the same high order. The discussion made it necessary for me to attempt to give my conception of God. Cosmically, I said, "God" means that the aspect of quality is just as inherent in and basic to reality as quantity. Humanly, "God" means that all that we understand by human differentia is of supreme importance. This is clearly conveyed if we transpose the term "God" from the subject to the attribute. Thus, instead of saying God is justice, courage, etc., we were to say Justice, Courage, etc. are God.

Remembering the Center—Kaplan Happy He Left

MONDAY NIGHT, OCTOBER 2, 1922

The high holidays are over. They were a source of anxiety to me in view of the fact that the SAJ was to hold services for the first time in a hall where the atmosphere is not calculated to inspire any sense of reverence or worship. Personally there was much of a comedown from the magnificent though small synagogue of the Center to the entertainment and wedding hall with the improvised ark on the stage and camp chairs on the floor. Yet when I recalled how narrowly I escaped the clutches of an ingrowing bourgeoisie hypocritical religiosity that is devoid of the least idealistic aspiration I thanked God that he delivered me from the Center. I know that I make this damning statement about a Jewish congregation on the night after Yom Kippur. But I do not say this in anger and indignation. I am convinced that they are unfortunate spiritually in having come from homes where religion and morality were treated as two radically different domains.

"Vos tsu Got iz tsu Got und vos tsu Layt iz tsu Laytn" [Yiddish "What is God's is God's and what is man's is man's"].

Religion was a matter of fearing God and morality a matter of fearing man. What God wants, according to their idea of Him, is simply to get enough praises and prayers said to Him, and certain ceremonies, which He had commanded, scrupulously observed. What man wants is regard from the rights of others, and a whole string of ethical duties that interfere with a man's success in business. Since it is only man that exacts ethical duties, one doesn't run great risks in disregarding those duties, especially when they have not assumed the form of legal enactments for the violation of which one might be brought to court. This is the kind of world outlook which they have drilled into them by the example of their fathers and mothers, and by the sanction implied rather than expressed of the spiritual leaders in the small towns of Eastern Europe.

Kaplan Loses His Temper

Tuesday, October 3, 1922

I have been disillusioned today about the success of the Yom Kippur service. My loss of temper on Kol Nidre night when I scolded the congregation for the cold and lackadaisical spirit in which the Maariv [evening] service was proceeding—the people even forgetting to answer Amen at the end of benedictions—and for the leisureliness with which the congregation was collecting—seems to have displeased a good many, especially my brothers-in-law. One of them—whose Hebrew name is Moishe Hayim, which is shortened into Moe, but which has been translated into Martin for the sake of the Goyim and for the sake of his wife—whose nature seems to have been soured a good deal, complained to my mother-in-law about my shouting on Yom Kippur eve. He has never talked to me about anything or anybody. In all the years that I have known him we have probably not exchanged more than five sentences, although we have never had a falling out about anything, and although hardly a week has passed except during the summer without our seeing each other. My mother-in-law is not a well woman and ought to be spared all knowledge of untoward happenings. But Moe never misses an opportunity to pour out his tale of woes to her. His tale of woe this time was that I was driving away customers with my rough treatment.

As a rule my mother-in-law who has a good deal of common sense never discusses with me matters pertaining to my work. She knows that I am very touchy on that point and am ready to explode at the least provocation. My own mother knows the same too about me and most of the time observes the same rule of avoiding flammable conversation, but she often forgets the rule and there is a scene. Both of them use my wife as the target of their complaints about me. This time it seems my wife advised my mother-in-law to bring the complaint to me directly. (Later on I learned I was mistaken in the surmise of mine.) I acted like a model son-in-law, listened to all that she had to say—and she had a good deal to say about her wisdom and foresight in getting all her nine children—God bless them—to be good Jews and marrying them all off successfully. Therefore, I ought to give heed to her advice and not permit men and women to sit together at the SAJ House during services, and to control my temper on the pulpit. I was non-committal on the former, and on the latter I promised her that next Yom Kippur I would demonstrate to her how even tempered I can be.

I had to make up, of course, for my good behavior during the interview with her, by indulging in an extra fit of the blues over the fact that my hands are tied by a number of women of both sexes.[1] The natural desire to return their good will prevents me from taking the only logical step that I ought to take—accepting Wise's invitation to join the faculty of his Institute of Religion.

Kaplan Discusses His Belief in God

FRIDAY, OCTOBER 13, 1922

Among the persons that came to see me this week were the following:

Miss Garfiel:[2] She gave me a glowing account of her experience for the first time with a group of about 25 young girls at the Downtown

---

1. This is the language of Kaplan's text. He is rarely sarcastic, so this may be an error on his part, but you can never tell. At the Jewish Center men and women sat separately, with women on the left and right and men in the middle.

2. Evelyn Garfiel (1900–1987) (eventually married Max Kadushin [see glossary]), psychologist; author; faculty, University of Chicago. Authored *Service of the Heart—A Guide to Jewish Prayer.* She believed Kaplan dominated her husband and may have been a factor in Kadushin's alienation from Kaplan. On her relationship with Kaplan, see *Judaism Faces the Twentieth Century: A Biography of Mordecai M. Kaplan* (Detroit: Wayne State University Press, 1993).

Jewish Center on Stanton Street. Although at first opposed to instruction on Jewish matters they were won over into an interest in those matters as soon as she made clear to them that it was possible to view them from a different standpoint from that which they had been trained to see them.

On asking Miss Garfiel what in my sermons on the first day of Succoth—"What Does God Mean to Us" displeased her as I had heard from Kadushin, she said that I did not make clear whether I conceived God as a being or as an idea, i.e., a generalization of the ideals to which we aspire. I explained to her that to me God was not a being, but Reality[3] viewed as an ordered universe. I believe with Spinoza in a Deus sive Natura. God was as much more than an idea as the ego is more than an idea representing the sum of psychic forces in the individual.[4] In fact, Deus and Ego are related to each other as the body and apex of a pyramid. In prayer the Ego becomes conscious of God. Through this awareness it sets into operation psychic forces that are otherwise dormant. Hence the value of prayer.

Examining Finkelstein for Rabbinic Ordination

TUESDAY, OCTOBER 17, 1922

A meeting of the Seminary faculty took place yesterday at which the question of examining Dr. Finkelstein for the *Hatarat Horaah*[5] came up. He is the first graduate of the Seminary to receive that degree. The giving of that degree is a concession to Orthodox legalism. It calls for the study of a good deal of Talmud and Poskim [codes]. Ordinarily Hyamson who is professor of codes should have been the one to conduct the work of preparing for that degree but he has not the necessary knowledge. Ginzberg took charge of it. He mapped out the course and periodically examined Finkelstein in the ground covered. Now that Finkelstein is ready for examination there is no one except Ginzberg who is qualified to examine him. No other member of the faculty is considered expert in the legalistic literature. I suggested that outside Rabbonim be invited, men like Rabbis Klein, Margolies, etc., so as to convince them that the Seminary can prepare men who are ready to meet the traditional requirements for *Hatarath Horaah*. To this those present demurred, and rightly so, on the ground that the leading Orthodox rabbis are unreliable and untrustworthy. They are likely to give out a false report of the nature of the examination and of Finkelstein's knowledge of the subject matter. What a commentary upon Orthodox Judaism that not

---

3. Kaplan originally wrote, "God was not a being, but the world viewed as ordered universe." He crossed out "world" and substituted "Reality." Kaplan reviewed the diary and frequently "corrected" what he wrote. The final version is the one cited, except where the difference is significant.

4. Sentence awkward here. Sentences which are grammatically incorrect are not altered.

5. Hatarat Horaah: traditional rabbinical ordination.

a single Orthodox Rabbi could be found in this entire city who could be invited to a fairly conducted examination for *Hatarath Horaah!* Is there not an intrinsic relationship between the spirit of the subject matter that has to be mastered for that degree and the kind of character which it permits to develop?

I am in the habit of writing regularly every Friday to mother who is now with my sister at Woonsocket. Last Friday I forgot to write. When I reminded myself it was already Sabbath. Knowing that mother would be very much worried and help to make Sophie's[6] life miserable if she were not to receive her usual Saturday morning letter from me, I went into the bathroom after supper and wrote a letter to her.

Granting Finkelstein Rabbinic Ordination—The View Backstage

SUNDAY, OCTOBER 29, 1922

Tonight I attended a gathering of Seminary faculty students and friends. That gathering was for a threefold purpose: to celebrate the opening of the Seminary; to bestow the degree of *Hatarath Horaah* upon Dr. Finkelstein and to witness the unveiling of a tablet in memory of Jacob H. Schiff. It took this triple celebration to bring out the one hundred people who were present.

Adler as usual said nothing though he spoke for some time. Ginzberg began well—the part of the speech that he seems to have memorized—and ended up poorly. Imitating Schechter's manner of address, he pointed out that there was a distinction between *S'michah* [ordination] in Judaism and the laying on of the hands in Christianity which ceremony was a mystic rite. *S'michah* was awarded for knowledge and not granted to those to whom Talmud and Codes were a mystery. This is a jest à la Schechter.

After he was through speaking, he fumbled in one of his back trousers pockets for a slip of paper whereon was written the formula of the *Hatarath Haraah*.

Hyamson who by right should have been the one to direct Finkelstein's studies for the *Hatarah*, that is if he were in any way qualified to fill the position of Professor of Codes—played a very humble and humiliating role in the entire procedure. He had to ask Ginzberg to show him the formula of the *Hatarah* just before the Faculty marched into the auditorium and Ginzberg handed it to him with his cynical smile as if in contempt for a

---

6. Sophie Kaplan Israeli (1879?–1950?), sister of Mordecai Kaplan; helped teach Kaplan Hebrew; married Kaplan's JTS classmate Phineas Israeli.

poor boob who has to make a pretense of knowing what it is all about. I can not see how a man with any sense of self respect can go through such humiliation.

The members of the Faculty who sat on the platform had to be dressed up in the medieval academic garb. Such were the acting president's orders. The incongruity of wearing the garb of Christian scholasticism that has kept back the world for a thousand years from making any progress in a ceremony connected with the conferring of the most traditional Jewish distinction.

But is not the very idea of granting the degree "Rabbi" to men, many of whom have scarcely a reading knowledge of Talmud, an absurdity in an institution that is dedicated to the upholding of "Traditional" Judaism?

Kaplan and His Daughter Judith—Some Problems

THURSDAY, DECEMBER 7, 1922

This has been one of the unhappiest weeks of my life. It began with Lena [née Rubin; Mrs. Kaplan] showing me what my Judith thinks of me whenever I find it necessary to insist upon her realizing that she is after all my child and that she still owes me a certain degree of filial obedience. God knows I do my utmost to develop in her a sense of self-reliance, but until I can be certain that she has the necessary reasonableness and self-control to make self-reliance safe I deem it my duty to exercise guardianship. She is only thirteen at present. Yet when upon a single occasion I crossed her will, she became so wrought up that she charged me in her diary with being a despot.[7] There are a number of irrelevant charges she brings against me in what she says there—which fact leads me to believe that I am bound to be disappointed if I look forward to having in her an intellectual companion. She does not seem to have the love for me that my other little ones have. If I do not engage her in conversation she is apt to ignore me for weeks as though I did not exist. There are probably explanations for all this coldness, explanations we may find in the books on adolescence. Nevertheless the experience of it hurts me to the core.

Kaplan and Judith—Scene II

SUNDAY, DECEMBER 10, 1922

The cloud that overhung my mind during the previous week is almost dissipated. Here are the gratifying experiences that have brought back the sunshine to me:

---

7. Kaplan had apparently discovered Judith's diary and looked into it.

Last Friday night Judith happened to mention her diary. I took advantage of what I thought might prove to be an opportunity of my getting her to understand my motive in having crossed her will the day when she indicted those bitter charges against me in her diary. This month there began to appear in the Atlantic Monthly excerpts from John Davis Long's diary which he began keeping when he was nine years old. I had the copy of the Atlantic Monthly brought to the table and asked Lena to read from it. When she came to the part where the father of John Lang inserted his comment after having looked over what his son had written, I said to Judith, "How about my seeing your diary?" She at first pretended that she did not know where it was. But when Hadassah[8] offered to get it Judith got ahead of her, and after a while brought in her diary with the pages in which she poured out her wrath upon me torn out.[9] She apparently tore them out before bringing it to me. Of her own accord she remarked that she had torn out some pages because they contained matter that she did not care to retain in her diary. Later on when Lena tried to find out why she had torn out those pages she asked Lena not to press for the reason, because she was far too ashamed to think of what she had written to want to talk about it. As soon as I realized that Judith's ill will against me was only momentary and superficial and that all traces of it were completely obliterated, I was myself again.

Finkelstein Speech Reactionary

DECEMBER 10, 1922

This evening I attended a Seminary dinner participated in by trustees, faculty and students of the Seminary. As a rule these affairs bore me. I was very reluctant to go tonight so as not to have to see Davidson and Marx who not only witnessed my discomfiture last Wednesday night, but even may have contributed toward it. Lena however insisted upon our going, and I am glad I went. Among the speeches delivered were those of Dr. Finkelstein whose star is in the ascendant just now—a fact that I would gladly welcome were it not for his taking a reactionary stand against an honest intellectual approach to the problems underlying Jewish belief and practice. I see in him a useful recruit to the forces of Jewish Jesuitism. In his remarks tonight he insisted that only Orthodox Judaism plus modern Americanism could prevent [the] disintegration of Jewish life. . . .

---

8. Hadassah Kaplan Musher, second-eldest daughter of Mordecai Kaplan; active in SAJ; organized Reconstructionist Women's Organization; educator; married to Sidney Musher (1905–90), food and pharmaceutical research; president, P.E.F. (Palestine Endowment Fund).

9. This author in interviewing Judith Kaplan Eisenstein was shown the diary with the page torn out.

Lack of Spirituality at the Seminary

WEDNESDAY, FEBRUARY 7, 1923

A student of the Seminary by the name of Herbert Parzen[10] came to see me today. He was very unhappy because he was not getting at the Seminary what he felt he needs to prepare him for the ministry—a spiritual outlook and spiritual enthusiasm. He visited the classes of the [Jewish] Institute of Religion and could not help noting the contrast. He asked my advice whether he should join the Institute next fall. Of course I would not think of giving such advice inasmuch as I do not know what the future of that institution is going to be and the direction it is going to take.

Seminary graduating class and faculty, June 2, 1918. Seated, from left: Moses Hyamson, Alexander Marx, Louis Ginzberg, Cyrus Adler, Israel Friedlaender, Mordecai M. Kaplan, Israel Davidson. (Courtesy Ratner Center, JTS)

---

10. Herbert Parzen (1897–1985), ordained JTS; author who wrote about Conservative Judaism; active in United Synagogue.

Mrs. Lindheim[11] came to see me last Monday and urged me again to ally myself with Wise. Apparently she came at Wise's suggestion. I put her off with all kinds of slim excuses.

S. Wise Invites Kaplan to Jewish Institute of Religion

FRIDAY, MARCH 30, 1923

Of late my mind has again been agitated by the problem as to whether I have morally and spiritually a right to continue teaching at the Seminary, or whether I ought to associate myself with Wise's Jewish Institute of Religion. Dr. Wise wrote to me again a few weeks ago asking me to give a course at his summer school on the psychology of religion. I refused on the ground that my colleagues on the faculty would consider my acceptance an act of disloyalty to the Seminary. In fact, I had asked Dr. Adler whether I should accept the invitation and he answered in the negative.

Some of Wise's friends approached me and urged me strongly to throw in my lot with his institution: Dr. George Kohut,[12] Mrs. Lindheim and Chas. Cowen.[13] I have not had the courage either to say yes or no.

Seminary Faculty Critical of Kaplan

FRIDAY, MARCH 30, 1923

In the meantime I learned that some statements in the booklet published by the SAJ[14] on the occasion of its anniversary have called forth unfavorable criticism. Wanting to test out my strength at the Seminary I gave Prof. Davidson a copy last Tuesday and at the same time had a long talk with him about the attitude of the Seminary toward the freedom with which I discuss traditional beliefs. At first he could not see why I invited all this criticism upon myself. When I explained how impossible it was for me to evade the problem of higher criticism in teaching the men what to preach, he seemed to be convinced. I also appeared to explain to his satisfaction why I organized the SAJ after I severed connection with the Center, instead of retiring to study and writing. At the end of the conversation we arrived at the conclusion that I should have been more intimate with the members of the faculty and have discussed these problems in an informal way.

---

11. Irma Lindheim (1886–1978), studied at Columbia and Jewish Institute of Religion; national officer, Zionist Organization of America; author.

12. George A. Kohut (1874–1933), educator, author, and scholar; rabbi; librarian, JTS; founder, Camp Kohut.

13. Charles Cowen (1880–1953), lawyer, Zionist administrator, author.

14. The booklet of twenty-five pages entitled simply "The Society for the Advancement of Judaism" contains the principles of the Society. Written by Kaplan.

That same evening I went to see Prof. Ginzberg on the same subject. Under the guise of friendship I could see that he was laying a trap for me. He tried to impress me with his sophistries which I punctured as soon as he uttered them. He tried to show me that the Seminary permitted the critical method only in the study of the Talmud, but not in that of the Bible. I replied that the curriculum included modern commentaries in the teaching of the Bible. He then turned to the booklet (SAJ) which I had brought along and began to find fault with the statement on the very first page that Judaism was a civilization. It made no mention of religion or theology. That was enough to condemn it.

Ginzberg was not satisfied with informal discussion of my problem. He advised that I ask Dr. Adler to call one or more meetings for the purpose of discussing the question as to the attitude of the Seminary toward free expression of opinion on matters affecting traditional belief. Next day I received a letter from him suggesting that I should send a copy of the booklet to every member of the faculty, so that they might discuss the subject intelligently. I imagine that he is preparing to bring heresy charges against me.

Weizmann Visits the SAJ

Tuesday, May 29, 1923

The SAJ has made considerable headway the last few months. The membership is approaching the 100 mark and I have succeeded in working up a great deal of spirit. Someone described it as the only Jewish organization of a religious character that had college spirit.

Dr. Weizmann is here a second time to get funds for the Keren Hayesod.[15] I felt it my duty to get the SAJ to contribute a sum large enough to justify the claim that it is dedicated to the restoration of Israel's ancient land. At first I was going to have the Society tender W. a banquet in the hope that this would lead to the members' taking part in the campaign. It developed, however, that it would be much better to have the Society take the initiative in interesting the various congregations of the West Side in the effort to collect funds for Palestine. After two or three conferences of members from various congregations with Weizmann, an inter-congregational Keren Hayesod Committee was organized with a view of raising $100,000 by May 13 at which time a reception would be given to W.[16] At that reception no funds were to be collected. . . .

---

15. See entry for Friday, May 20, 1921, in chapter 3 for more information.

16. There is a photo of the reception in *Judaism Faces the Twentieth Century*, p. 322. The fund-raising effort is an interesting example of cooperation among the synagogues on the West Side of Manhattan.

Last Shabuoth night [Sunday, May 20] we had a very successful Program meeting. After the services we had conventional Shabuoth cheese pancakes. With the collation over the meeting began at 9:30. Six of the members delivered short talks on different phases of the SAJ platform set forth in the blue booklet which had been given out as a souvenir at the anniversary gathering on March 11.

The interest of that meeting was enhanced through the presence of Dr. Weizmann, whom I had invited to come. He had supper at my house before we went to [the] Maariv [evening] service. In the course of the conversation at the house, he explained to me what the chief issue at the coming Zionist Congress would be, and intimated to me that I ought to attend the congress as a delegate in order to help bring about the organization of the Jewish Agency on the lines suggested by him and approved by me at the time.

At the meeting W. was called upon to speak. He expressed keen satisfaction at the attempt that we were making to adjust Judaism to modern life. He called us a society of searchers. Taking up the point that Judaism is a civilization and not merely a religion, he developed Renan's conception of the reason for the unique character of the Jewish civilization.

At the end of the meeting he was elected an honorary member of our organization.

(Mother Rubin, however, complained to Lena that it was wrong of W. to make notes in writing on Yom Tov [holiday] night.)

Kaplan to Attend Zionist Congress

Sunday, June 24, 1923

I am writing this in Room 436 on the S.S. George Washington on the way to Europe.

This opportunity to go to Europe presented itself to me through the close contact with Weizmann and the SAJ, or rather some of its leaders. . . . Weizmann mentioned to them that he would want me to be one of the American delegates to the Carlsbad Congress which is to take place on Aug. 6. They readily took up his suggestion and urged me to accept the invitation to go to Europe. They expressed their readiness to defray the cost of my trip. At first I was hesitant more out of mere inertia than for any definite reason. But when I received a letter from Weizmann requesting me to be delegate I decided to go. . . . Having made up my mind to take the trip to Europe I went to see mother and Sophie[17] at Woonsocket. I had Lena along with me and spent the Sabbath there quietly.

17. Sophie Kaplan Israeli, Mordecai Kaplan's older sister.

Kaplan at the Zionist Congress in Karlsbad

JULY 24, 1923

I have met here Ussishkin, the head of the Zionist Executive in Palestine. When I saw him two years ago in the Brandeis-Weizmann controversy he impressed me as a strong charactered man, self-willed and not of the kind to know how to make compromises. For some reason Weizmann is apparently trying to oust him from that post of responsibility. There is probably a good deal of truth about his being none too competent to handle the situation, though he is honest as the day.

At the suggestion of Sol Lamport[18] and though his mediation I have transacted a piece of business with him for the SAJ. The Hebrew monthly magazine "Hashiloach" which had been appearing for many years and which enjoyed great prestige among Hebraists has been discontinued on account of lack of funds. Dr. Klausner,[19] a great scholar of note who lives in Palestine and who was the editor of *Hashiloach* urged Lamport when he saw the latter recently, to secure the $5,000 which was necessary for the resumption of the publication. Lamport mentioned the subject to me. Ussishkin also asked Lamport to secure that amount. When Lamport mentioned these facts to me I thought that there was an excellent opportunity for the SAJ to take a start in carrying out its purpose to issue a magazine. While it is not in a position at present to defray the entire cost of a publication like the "Hashiloach," it could begin by defraying part. In time I hope that the interest in the work would grow and the entire publication might be taken over.

Sol Lamport undertook to raise $2500 provided I raise the other $2500. he himself promised to give $1200 toward the $5000 that the Hashiloach needs at present.

Spiritual Energy of the Zionist Movement

FRIDAY, AUGUST 17, 1923: ON BOARD S.S. GEORGE WASHINGTON

Fortunately I had an occasion to come in contact while in Karlsbad with few people who opened my eyes to the fact that the Zionist movement had really very little to do with the congress. I also happened to read these days a little book by Holitscher, *Reise durch das judische Palestina*.[20] From both of these sources I gather that Zionism is primarily vested in the haluzim [Pioneers] and in the creators of the new Hebraic culture. The young men and women who rival the early American pioneers in grit and daring, who

---

18. Solomon Lamport (1871–1936), communal worker; Zionist; philanthropist; member of the Jewish Center who followed Kaplan to the SAJ.

19. Joseph Klausner (1874–1958), literary critic, historian, and Zionist.

20. Arthur Holitscher, *Reise durch das judische Palestina* (Berlin: S. Fischer Verlag, 1900).

venture to settle in pest ridden lands where they are liable to be struck down at any moment by Arab bullets, and who can look to no such rewards as those that awaited the American pioneer, these Haluzim are proof of the physical vitality of the Jewish people. Men like Ben-Jehudah,[21] Bialik,[22] Ahad-Haam, Tchernichowski[23] and dozens of others testify to the spiritual vitality of the Jewish people. The question as to the raison d'etre of Zionism is after all a question as to whether the Jewish people has enough physical and spiritual energy to demand self-expression. Men and women of the *Haluzim* type prove that such energy is present. Such energy needs no self-justification. All arguments in favor of it are futile.

A *Young Physician Gives Kaplan Advice on How to Organize His Work*

MONDAY, AUGUST 20, 1923

On leaving Karlsbad Sunday Aug 12 on the way to Vienna Dr. Levinson[24] happened to be in the same train with me. We spent the entire seven hours of our journey discussing various matters with regard to the Congress, Palestine, the Seminary, etc. I was delighted to find in him a good nationalist Jew familiar with Hebrew culture and something of a publicist in both Hebrew and English at the same time that he had made his mark as a physician. He specialized in children's diseases and had written a text book and many articles in his special field and had done a good deal of original research. He had been in Palestine recently and he was remembered by some people there as the author of a series of articles that appeared in the *Hashiloach* in 1914 on Jewish institutions in America. He came to America as a lad of fifteen or sixteen. He is now only thirty-six. Alongside so much achievement what have I accomplished? Here was a man six years my junior giving me advice as to how I might manage to get done some of the literary undertakings I have been dabbling in for the last ten or twelve years. "Take up one thing at a time and work on it until you finish it," he said. I suppose that lack of will power had a great deal to do with my failure to produce any literary work. Nevertheless, I can not altogether blame myself. I was

21. Eliezer Ben-Yehuda (1858–1922), Hebrew writer and lexicographer; generally considered the father of modern Hebrew; contributed significantly toward making Hebrew a spoken language.

22. Hayyim Nahman Bialik (1873–1934), the greatest Hebrew poet of modern times; essayist, story writer, translator, and editor who exercised a profound influence on modern Jewish culture.

23. Saul Tchernichowski (1875–1943), Hebrew author and poet; major figure in modern Hebrew literature.

24. Abraham Levinson (1888–1955), U.S. pediatrician; had an excellent reputation as a clinician, teacher, and historian.

not fortunate enough to have masters and guides in my youth to teach me system or inspire me with their example. I lacked both the opportunity and the capacity to come in touch with men of note in the different walks of life. When I contrasted the narrow circle of my acquaintances with that of this same Dr. Levinson, I became aware of my limitations to such an extent as to feel discouraged. But of course, I will not submit and fight hard with myself to rise above them.

Kaplan Arrives Home—Everyone Cheers

Sunday, August 26, 1923

I was greeted at the pier last Friday when the steamer arrived by a large delegation of SAJ members. The entire SAJ review of that week was devoted to greetings to me. In all sincerity I feel that I do not deserve all that friendship which these people are manifesting toward me. I ask myself "Why are they so good to me?" Is it because they feel that I might emancipate them into the larger life of the spirit, into the life where they would be free from their petty cares and from the useless burdens that the past has imposed upon them? But God knows, I myself need the strength and the courage which it should be my business to inspire others with. I realized this when a few hours after I came home I was advised by Estelle Lamport who spoke to me on the phone to get Judith back from camp as soon as possible because one of the girls in that camp had died. Not knowing exactly the circumstances of the case I naturally imagined the worst and I trembled as a leaf as I held the telephone. It took some time for me to be convinced that Judith was alright, because I spoke to her by phone. But the interval was black with fear. This is your spiritual leader.

Kaplan Ponders Leaving JTS for JIR

Thursday night, September 20, 1923 [Heb. end of Yom Kippur, 5684]

These have been three stormy weeks for me. At one time it looked as though I was finally to accept Wise's offer when suddenly I made up my mind definitely to turn it down and carried this determination into effect. It appears now that my position in the Seminary will be rendered more tolerable to me as a result of the intervention of my friends of the SAJ. That sudden change came about in the following way.

When I returned from my trip abroad I learned that the *Jewish Light*,[25] a weekly periodical issued by a few job seekers who leagued them-

---

25. The private correspondence between Cyrus Adler and one S. A. Israel appeared in *Idishe Licht* (*The Jewish Light*), July 1923, p. 3, much to Adler's dismay. Mr. Israel, a New

selves with a few fanatics and which has been publishing articles for the last three months, calculated to pillory me as an arch heretic and menace to Orthodox Judaism—published an exchange of letters[26] that had taken place between a certain Mr. Israel and Dr. Cyrus Adler. I have since learned that this Israel is a usurer whose wealth consists in second mortgages, and who is at the same time a rabid fanatic. In those letters Adler included a statement which he had written to someone else saying that my position in the Seminary is that of Professor of Homiletics and as such I am required to teach only the construction of sermons but not the knowledge of Judaism that goes into the sermons. This statement aroused my indignation and I became more determined than ever to conclude arrangements with Wise. . . .

But as soon as I began negotiating with Wise I began to feel an uneasiness which is probably the main reason for my having rejected his offer a second time. He did not inspire any confidence in me when I met him after I came back from Europe. I was troubled by the fact that he did not see his way clear to come to the city to see me that week, though if I were in his place I would have considered the matter of engaging a member to the faculty important enough to come to town. Yet the illness of a member of his congregation did bring him to town. That sense of values on his part made me apprehensive of joining his Institute.

When I saw him during the last week in August—I believe Monday or Tuesday night—he did not impress me as appreciating the difficulty of the undertaking which he was going into with his Institute. It seemed all a simple matter to him. Whatever I asked for he immediately granted. I said that I preferred to occupy a chair in Jewish Theology and he at once acceded to my request. But then I happened to learn that Oberman[27] was to teach the historic development of Judaism, and Prof. Gutman[28] of Berlin was to give the philosophy of Judaism, I naturally realized that Wise was not even awake to the fact that there was a likelihood of duplication overlapping in the subject matter taught. When I mentioned to him that I should not like to have the rabbinic degree conferred upon the average graduate, he at once fell in with that suggestion. It did not occur to him to reckon with

York businessman, had called for Kaplan's resignation because of his "poisonous doctrines"; Adler reassured Israel that Kaplan taught only homiletics, not theology, and hence there was no cause for worry. See *Judaism Faces the Twentieth Century*, 208 and chapter 8, footnote 7.

26. This exchange came in part as a consequence of Kaplan's attack on Orthodoxy in his articles in the *Menorah Journal*.

27. Julian Obermann (1888–1956), orientalist; faculty, University of Hamburg and Jewish Institute of Religion; author; editor.

28. Julius Guttman (1880–1950), philosopher and historian of Jewish philosophy. His *Philosophies of Judaism* (Philadelphia: Jewish Publication Society, 1964) is a classic.

the fact that there were students in the Institute who had entered with the understanding that they were to be rabbis.

Kaplan Thinks about a New Denomination and Leaving JTS

SEPTEMBER 23, 1923

When I left the meeting[29] there was no doubt any more in my mind as to my accepting the position at the JIR. The next day, however, Benderly, who returned not long ago from Palestine, injected himself into the situation . . . Benderly maintained that it would be a mistake for me to join Wise's Institute. It would identify me completely with the Reform group. I was not convinced by what he said . . . The Friday night following (Sept. 7) Benderly had supper with us. After supper Lena, he and I took a long walk. It was then that he opened my eyes to the fact that I would be doing a more constructive work for Jewry, if instead of accepting the position at the JIR I were to resign from the Seminary for the purpose of being able to devote myself to the consolidation of the element that is neither Orthodox nor reformed, but is looking for a program that shall be both Jewish and modern. There is need for the formation of a third party[30] in present day Judaism and he argued that my resigning from the Seminary would create the psychological occasion for such an undertaking on my part.

This argument of his won me over completely. I vacillated for a while when I reminded myself of having to look to the SAJ[31] for material support. But I dismissed that objection from my mind when my brother-in-law Max, whom I met that same night or early morning, expressed his fears as to the reliability of Wise. My uneasiness which I had repressed throughout the discussion got the better of me this time. At last my mind was made up both to resign from the Seminary and not to accept Wise's offer of the position at his Institute.

As soon as Sabbath was over I hurried to Wise. There I met the Lindheims. She was dressed in "knickers" having come a few hours before together with Wise's daughter[32] from Lake Placid whence they had hiked to

---

29. Kaplan met with the board of the SAJ. They were "favorably disposed" to his resigning the Seminary and joining the Jewish Institute of Religion. This is the meeting mentioned here.

30. The seminary was viewed at this time as a training school for rabbis, not as the center of a denomination. Hence Kaplan thought of Orthodox and Reform and the need for a third way in between.

31. Kaplan received a salary from the seminary but not from the SAJ. The SAJ paid only the premiums on his insurance policies. At the Jewish Center Kaplan's salary was donated to the TI.

32. Justine Wise Polier (1903–87), daughter of Stephen Wise; LL.B. 1928; justice, domestic relations court; judge; author.

New York. I mention this to record how often I would have had many deeply rooted Jewish habits jarred by the class of people with whom I would have to associate if I were to have joined Wise's Institute. Miss Wise insisted that I see the painting of Mrs. Lindheim done by her mother Mrs. Wise.[33] Not being thrilled by the picture I was at a loss what to say. All these trivialities annoyed me. I came to talk about an important matter, and to state a decision that meant so much to me, and here I was called upon to fish out a compliment for something that did not interest or thrill me. I am afraid that being in Wise's company would have brought me into such irrelevancies time without number.

Finally Wise called me into another room where he was ready to listen to what I had to say. Before I began he asked me whether I cared to have Lindheim join us. At first I hesitated, but then gave my consent. I told him of my twofold decision. To confirm my statement as to my resigning from the Seminary I read to him the resignation which I had drawn up the day before. As I look back, I cannot forgive myself for having done so, but I hope to straighten this matter out before long. Wise seemed very much disappointed at my finally refusing the position at the JIR. He claimed I had given him the impression that I was determined to accept the position, and that it was only a question of arranging the details connected with the post offered me. But he was gracious in giving me the benefit of the doubt. On the whole I must say that his conduct that evening put a doubt in my mind as to whether or not I acted wisely in burning my bridges that way in front of me. I assured him that I was going to burn my bridges behind me; but subsequent talks with friends of the SAJ caused me to change my mind.

The next day (Sunday) Mrs Lindheim came to see me. She voiced her disappointment at my action and hoped that before long I could change my mind. She pooh-poohed the idea of my organizing a third party. She said I lacked the force and power and popular appeal necessary for swaying the masses. I could do such a thing only with the help of Wise.

On Friday, (September 14) H.L. Simmons[34] called on me, and told me of a conference he had with S.C. Lamport and Brown at which my problem was discussed. They came to the conclusion that it would not be right for me to send in my resignation just now, but that I should address a letter to Adler in which I would ask him to explain his statement which appeared in the "Light of Israel" to the effect that I was not teaching the knowledge of Judaism that was to go into the sermon.

---

33. Louise Waterman Wise (1874–1947), Art Students League, communal, worker and artist; president, women's division of the American Jewish Congress.

34. An SAJ member.

I realized that I could not play a lone hand in this matter. I accordingly accepted their advice and framed a letter asking Adler to reconcile his statement about my work in the Seminary with the description given of my courses both in the Seminary and the Teachers Institute Registers. I sent off the letter on Sunday September 16.

Today (Sat. Sept. 22) I received a reply.[35] The letter is conciliatory and implies that I can go on teaching as I had. He intimates that I represent the minority opinion at the Seminary, as my views differ both from his and from that of most of my colleagues. It therefore looks as though I am going on with my work in the Seminary as of old.

Interviewing Students for Rabbinical School

Saturday, September 29, 1923

A student of the Seminary, Simon Greenberg,[36] who has come under my influence as a result of his being a student of the Teachers Institute happened to be in Minneapolis some time ago. He had occasion to speak to a group of young people about the ministry and painted it apparently in such glowing colors that they decided to come to N.Y. and join the Seminary.

But upon coming here they met with rebuffs. One of them, David Goldstein,[37] was asked by Professor Israel Davidson whether he was observant of the ceremonies. Goldstein told him he hadn't been but he would like to be. Davidson, instead of encouraging him, replied that he ought to have applied rather to the Hebrew Union College. When this same Goldstein saw Adler and probably conveyed to him in implicit terms what he told me explicitly, viz., that he was not interested in Judaism but rather in Jewish culture, Adler told him that Dropsie was the right institution for him, but not the Seminary.[38]

Kaplan, another of the Minneapolis young men, who looks to be very earnest and spiritual type, has not received any knowledge of Talmud. Instead of helping him to make up his deficiency, Davidson told him to

---

35. For the full text of the letter see *Cyrus Adler, Selected Letters,* ed. Ira Robinson (Philadelphia: Jewish Publication Society, 1985), vol. 2, September 21, 1923.

36. Simon Greenberg (1901–93), ordained JTS; Ph.D. Dropsie College; Conservative leader; executive director, United Synagogue of America; president, Rabbinical Assembly; admired Kaplan but critical of him. Greenberg happened to be in Jerusalem when Kaplan was there for the opening of the Hebrew University in 1925. See below for Kaplan's reaction to this event and report of time spent with Greenberg. For a full report on Greenberg and Kaplan, see *Judaism Faces the Twentieth Century.*

37. David Goldstein (1902–90), ordained JTS; rabbi Har Zion Philadelphia; prominent in Conservative movement.

38. Goldstein was eventually accepted and went on to become a prominent Conservative rabbi.

come again next year, if he will have acquired in the meantime the necessary knowledge.

Is that the way to attract desirable young men to the ministry?

The Idea of Judaism as a Civilization Introduced at Friday Evening Services

DECEMBER 25, 1923

Yesterday my nerves were on edge all day by reason of the evident intent on the part of the authorities of the Seminary campaign to. . . . shelve me. [dots in the text]

I have introduced [a new idea] into the SAJ late Friday evening services. The first service was held on Oct. 13 *Parshat Noah* [Heb. Section Noah[39]]. I am utilizing the opportunity presented by these services to develop what I consider the only kind of feasible program for Judaism, a program based upon the conception of Judaism as a Civilization.[40]

Kaplan's Courses at the Seminary 1910–1924

DECEMBER 25, 1923

The following is a record of the courses I have given at the Seminary:

In Midrash[41]	Year	In Homiletics
Began teaching in Seminary	Janary 1910	
Selections from [H] *Gen. R.* till about [H] *Toldot*	1910–11	
Selections from [H] *Gen. R.* till end	1911–12	Study and analysis of model sermons
Selections from [H] *Ex. R.* and *Levit. R.*	1912–13	

39. The Pentateuch read each Sabbath in the synagogue is divided up into weekly sections called "sidrot or Parshiot." The weekly section mentioned here includes Genesis 5:9–11:32.

40. Kaplan first began to speak of Judaism as a civilization at the Jewish Center in 1916.

41. One of Kaplan's courses consisted of the teaching of the classical rabbinic homiletical work called the midrash. A particular midrash entitled *Midrash Rabbah* was the focus of most of his teaching. "R." in each entry refers to parts of *Midrash Rabbah*. For the names of the various *midrashim* mentioned in this list, see *Encyclopedia Judaica*, s.vv. " Midrash" and " Midrash Rabbah."

In Midrash	Year	In Homiletics
Selections from first two chapters of [H] *Presiqta de Rav Kahana* and from first part of [H] *Canticles R.*	1913–14	
Text of [H] *Gen. R.* as far as [H] *Noah*	1914–15	Gathering of sermon materials for sermons of week
Text of [H] *Gen. R.* from *Noah* to about [H] *Toldot*	1915–16	Practical sermon work, biographies and theological concepts
Text of [H] *Lament. R.* half of that book	1916–17	Detailed interpretation of Genesis
Text of [H] *Levit. R.* till about [H] *Tazria'*	1917–18	the psychologic and sociological aspects of the God concept
No Midrash on account of misunderstanding of registrar	1918–19	Practical sermon work with class on sermons preached that year at the center.
	1919–20	The problem of reinterpretation: Scripture and rabbinic writings
Text of [H] *Cantic. R.*	1920–21	Detailed interpretation of Genesis.
Text of [H] *Levit. R.*	1921–22	The Jewish sanctions, some of the current religious and ethical concepts (freedom, nature, etc.)
Text of [H] *Gen. R.*	1922–23	Technique of sermon—generalization, etc. Sermon material (notebooks)
Text of [H] *Lament. R.*	1923–24	The problem of reinterpretation: Scriptures and rabbinic writings (notebooks)

The SAJ—The Center for American Civil Religion

DECEMBER 26, 1923

I have come upon an idea. But the question is, is it feasible? If the very people who are associated as an SAJ were willing to change the purpose and the name of the organization and become a Society for the Advancement of the Religion of America I would be in a position to utilize the training the spiritual momentum of the years I have spent in Jewish study and foster a spiritual movement that would certainly grow from day to day as Judaism in this country is waning from day to day. In my own personal life I would live as a Jew, artificially maintaining all of the elements of Jewish civilization, but in my public work I would articulate the spiritual aspects of American life, and try to build up spiritual values in terms of the needs we experience here in America. Such a change of purpose to my public activity would be in line with my fundamental conception of religion as that element of a civilization which has to do with the sanctions for requiring the individual to conform to its customs, living up to its standards of duty and law, recalling its past and cherishing its future. Apart from a particular civilization a religion is a pious futility. So far I have been interested in Judaism as a civilization comprising both secular and religious elements, in the hope that there would be some Jews who would be ready to cultivate it. But the more I work, the less hope I have of seeing Judaism take root in this country. Under such circumstances there are only the following two alternatives before me, either to migrate to Palestine and there to die in a losing battle with the worst obscurantism in the world, or to continue working here and utilize contemporaneous American needs to develop such spiritual values as might enable us to meet those needs in a rational and humane way. After all God wants to choose America as the instrument of his will no less than he wanted Israel of old to act as an instrument of that kind. The nations of old rejected his Torah, but new nations have sprung up since. He certainly offers them too the chance of accepting and living in accordance with His law. Why assume beforehand that they are in no condition to accept it? I do not believe this of the American people. With all its faults I love it too dearly to affirm that it is doomed to sink into selfish materialism. Would to God that I were granted the opportunity to serve the American people by demonstrating even in a small way that it can become chosen of God as Israel of old was chosen, and even on a more comprehensive and significant scale.

The historical religions have only a value for the historian and archaeologist. Insofar as every cultured person must know something of history and archaeology he must be acquainted with the spirit and development of those religions. But to expect that they can function in a vital and telling manner at the present time is to fly in the face of facts.

A Dinner Dance at the Astor

SUNDAY, FEBRUARY 10, 1924

Last Sunday night (Feb. 3) we celebrated the second anniversary of the founding of the SAJ. The celebration was held at the Grand Ball Room of the Astor Hotel. There were about 420 guests. A "milchdig"[42] dinner was served so as to have it kosher and inexpensive. Most of the people who attended the dinner would not hesitate to spend on the average of $10 a person on a Sunday night at one of the "cabaret" places. But at a gathering where one must listen to speeches about Judaism in spite of the singing and dancing which are part of the affair, six dollars is considered by no means moderate. Those who managed the affair took special pains to emphasize the good time, the sociability and the dancing. When, therefore, an attempt was made to cut out the dancing between courses the table of "Juniors"—there were about fifty of them—sent a walking delegate to me to protest against the ruling. There were six speakers beside myself. Each of them spoke on the average of seven to eight minutes. While they were rather amateurish, I thought the mere fact of getting uneducated laymen to express themselves on the problem of Judaism was quite an achievement for the organization. But unfortunately the rest of the people didn't think so. They felt themselves cheated somewhat of the good time they came to have.

Of course the delay in getting together and starting the affair was partly the cause of the growing impatience of the people. We were supposed to start promptly at seven. Instead we began about 8:00. The speaking began at 10:00. I rose to speak at 11:30 and got through about 12:00. Fortunately I held the attention of nearly every one present. I had put a good deal of time into the preparation of the address. It was no easy matter to find something striking to say about the SAJ, considering the way I have been feeling about it of late. Nevertheless, I managed to formulate a real message. My effort having proved successful, the second anniversary of the SAJ is registered in the minds of those who attended as a triumph. As far as I am concerned, I see that the only thing for me to do is keep on jogging along like a drayhorse. So far it's all up hill. Maybe I'll get to level road some day.

Cyrus Adler and Kaplan Discuss Faith and Doubt

MONDAY, FEBRUARY 12, 1924

In the afternoon I attended the faculty meeting of the Seminary. For the first time I had occasion to learn what, according to Adler, the Seminary stands for. Ginzberg's suggestion to establish courses in Theology

---

42. Dairy.

and Philosophy of Religion was being discussed. It is hard to say what Ginzberg has up his sleeve. Anyhow I could see that Adler was trying to swing the discussion so as to inveigle me into making some statement that would compromise me. He began in his drawly [drawling][43] way to state what he believed to be the policy of the Seminary.

There are two kinds of people, he said, those who naturally accept tradition and who entertain doubts only when there is strong proof against what tradition affirms; and there are those who naturally disbelieve or doubt whatever is handed down by tradition unless they find strong proof to verify it. The policy of the Seminary requires that a man belong to the former of these types of mind. I interpolated that there was a third alternative, and that was to distinguish between such traditions as conflict with experience and those which are of the same character as the rest of human experience. I would not accept any tradition about some miracle without some proof to confirm it; whereas I would accept the stories which sound perfectly natural and in keeping with what else we know about the situations they describe.

Kaplan Writes First Chapter of Judaism as a Civilization

Tuesday, September 16, 1924

During the winter when I am occupied with my routine duties I look forward to the summer months to make up for the time spent on things of small moment and to concentrate on the effort to publish a detailed statement of my ideas on Judaism. The summer of two years ago and of last year I wasted in traveling. I therefore made up my mind that I would use this summer to good advantage. But as I consider what I have accomplished the last four months I am very much dissatisfied. I succeeded in writing one address for the Teachers Conference, in working up two essays as propaganda literature for the SAJ, and in sketching the rough draft of what is to be the first chapter of "Judaism as a Civilization." This time I have no one to blame, not even myself.

Kaplan Feels He Should Be More Focused

September 17, 1924

At times I imagine that if I had concentrated on the Institute I might have really developed it into a highly specialized teachers' training school. If I could have given myself up wholly to some of the better students I might have achieved what all great teachers have accomplished, but personal ambition did not let me work in so humble and circumscribed a field.

---

43. Cyrus Adler was born in Van Buren, Arkansas.

This ambition has been encouraged by the appointment to the chair in Homiletics in the Seminary. Had I possessed the proper moral stamina and had I possessed the devotion and fanaticism of a Benderly, I would never have accepted the position in the Seminary. I see my mistake after fourteen years of mental and spiritual dissipation. The philosophers tell us that vain regrets are worse than useless; therefore, let me go on with my tale of happenings.

A New Building for the Teachers Institute

SUNDAY, NOVEMBER 30, 1924

Is it possible that the dream of seeing the Teachers Institute housed in a building of its own will be realized? Some time ago my brother-in-law, Dr. Isidore Rubin, intimated to me that his father-in-law, Mr. Unterberg, had discussed with him setting aside various monies for his children and for purposes of a communal character. Mr. Unterberg then mentioned to him that he wanted to put away about $200,000 for Jewish educational purposes. If he was to contribute that money to the Seminary it was to go through me and to be used as a memorial for his parents. Last Tuesday morning Mr. Unterberg invited me to walk with him. At 8:15 in the morning I met him and we walked through the park. In his conversation with me he mentioned to me what Isidore had told me about. Having anticipated what he was going to tell me, I at once mentioned to him the advisability of putting up a building to house the Teachers Institute. He asked me to give further thought to his question and to see him as soon as I had a definite suggestion to make. This evening I went in to see him and repeated practically what I said to him last Tuesday in reference to the Teachers Institute. Moreover, I added that in view of the desire of some of the directors of the Central Jewish Institute to sell their 85 St building perhaps that building could be acquired for the Teachers Institute. That did not appeal to him. As reasons he mentioned first that there was need for the Central Jewish Institute in that locality; secondly he did not consider it right to disturb the memorial aspect it bore in being dedicated to the memory of Sam Hyman; and thirdly its proximity to the 85 St congregation which was hostile to what the Teachers Institute stood for. I really think he was right in each of these reasons. He was favorably impressed, however, by the suggestion of putting up a building that would house the Teachers Institute[44] and he promised to let me hear right after the first of the year definitely as to the proposition that he would like me to make in his name to the director of the Seminary. That looks good!

---

44. Seminary buildings including the Teachers Institute at 122nd Street and Broadway were opened in 1929. The TI building was financed primarily by Unterberg. Until that point TI met in a building in the East Village.

Kaplan Depressed about the SAJ

December 14, 1924

Since last Monday night my mind has been all awhirl again as to whether I should proceed with my work at the SAJ. The Board meeting which took place that night was so poorly attended and was carried on in such a lackadaisical spirit that I began to doubt whether I should permit them to think of purchasing ground for a building. After all, once they will invest in ground I am tied to them for life. So far they have not made good. They are not ready to make any sacrifices in time or money. Outside of two or three upon whom I might count for work, there is no one that can contribute anything toward the purposes for which the SAJ was formed, and these two or three and especially H. L. Simmons, are too preoccupied with their own business cares to have any energy left for this work. Just now, for example, Simmons is suffering a slump in his fur business. This means that he is doing absolutely nothing to carry out his own plan to increase the membership by reducing the dues to $25 instead of $75. The services are poorly attended, not more than fifty percent of the members ever visiting the services more than a few times on holidays. The program meetings upon which I had counted so much are not entertaining enough for them. They become easily sated. They have so many distractions, so many sources of diversion that they are blase. In this respect their children down to the youngest are even worse than they are. The few young people cannot be made to take an interest in anything intellectual or spiritual. They cannot even be induced to undertake anything of a social nature so tired are they of one another. They are just worm-eaten with boredom. Lately I have offered to conduct a group of men in the study of ethics and religion, provided I got at least 25 to come regularly. So far no one but the one who got me to make the offer—Dr. Brand, a dentist who is as ignorant of Judaism as he is of Chinese—is the only candidate for the group. With such deadheads I have been working for the last three years.

On the other hand, whenever I get a chance to concentrate on the problem of Judaism as a civilization, I see more and more light. I am beginning to find a workable formula for Judaism in the Diaspora. Only last week I hit upon the idea that Jewish nationality may function even in this country through a number of institutions (social practices) and agencies which the constitution of the United States permits to exist, and will probably permit for a long time to come. Chief among these are the prohibitions of intermarriage, an interest in the restoration of Palestine and in the synagogue. I am quite certain that if I could go on working uninterruptedly I might at least realize the dream of my life—to work out a clear formula for Judaism as a civilization both in Palestine and in the

Diaspora, before my mental powers will begin to wane; which I understand is normally the case at 55.[45]

Seminary Dinner—Kaplan Anxious

DECEMBER 14, 1924

This evening I attended what to me is a most boring function, a Seminary dinner. The mere apprehension that I might be called upon to say something keeps me on edge for a week before, because I am naturally a very poor after-dinner speaker, and the fear that in case I am asked to say something I might make a *faux pas*. This evening I was called upon, Ginzberg being the only other member of the faculty to speak besides myself, and managed to come off with flying colors. While I had actually tried to find something to say, I had not succeeded more than to put together a few desultory statements, but as soon as I entered the room I took note of a few odd situations which suggested some remarks. That, together with the request by Adler that I say a few words about the Teachers Institute, enabled me to hit it off at just the proper speed and with the proper touch.

I felt offended when Stroock in dwelling upon the greatness of the various members of the faculty, not even so much as mentioned my name. I wonder whether Adler called upon me to compensate for Stroock's failure to allude to me. Anyhow, there never takes place an affair in the Seminary without something to give me a sense of inferiority.

Adult Education at the Seminary—the Friedlaender Classes

SATURDAY, DECEMBER 20, 1924

Yesterday afternoon I presided at a meeting of the staff of the Israel Friedlaender classes.[46] Chipkin's[47] report of the work was encouraging. There are at present 290 students enrolled in the classes. A branch has been formed at Newark. The staff consists of nine men and two women all qualified for the work. If we had more money we could expand. The question of working out syllabi in history and Bible came up. With the continual change of teachers on the staff, it was difficult to maintain uniformity in method and point of view. With the members of the staff receiving nominal salaries they could not be expected to devote the time to the working out of syllabi. When

---

45. Kaplan lived to celebrate his 102nd birthday. His last work, a collaboration with Arthur Cohen, was entitled *If Not Now When? Toward a Reconstruction of the Jewish People: A Conversation between Mordecai Kaplan and Arthur Cohen* (New York: Schocken Books, 1973).

46. The Friedlaender Classes were adult education classes established in the name of Israel Friedlaender. They were held at various locations around the city in addition to the TI.

47. Israel Chipkin (1891–1955), communal educator, Bureau of Jewish Education; director of the Friedlaender Classes at TI; registrar of the TI.

Berkson suggested that he would undertake to write a syllabus on History I promised to get $1000 as remuneration for the work. Of course I still hope that the SAJ will get out of its present mess and will begin to function. When it does it will be the logical organization to pay for the syllabus and publish it.

Growing Pains at the SAJ

DECEMBER 29, 1924

I had to plead, to cajole, to growl, to get them [members of the SAJ Board] to understand me and one another, and to make them realize that if they want to hold a members' meeting on January 11 then the board must come with a definite plan as to where to build, the kind of building to be put up, and the method of financing. After we were nearly through Mrs. S. C. Lamport objected that we had no right to come with ready made plans. We must first learn from the members what they want. When I succeeded in getting her to realize that has been exactly the procedure which brought about the present state of confusion and aimlessness she popped up with the suggestion that we ought to consider renting or buying the Portuguese synagogue. When I questioned her as to the source of her information she named Mrs. Mendes[48] who happened to drop a casual remark about the Portuguese synagogue being for sale. After a great deal of effort, I succeeded in getting the Board to decide to call a special meeting for next Monday, preparatory to the members' meeting on January 11.

The worst feature of this struggle, as far as I am concerned, is the lack of understanding and sympathy even from my own family. Jake understands somewhat but is too powerless to do anything. Max is a good fellow, and so is Isidore,[49] but they have no interest whatever in the purpose of the society. They would like to see me make a big splurge, and if the society doesn't give me a chance to do it, I ought to get out from under it. My own wife at time displays a gleam of comprehension of what it is all about but suddenly that gleam is obscured and she attributes my difficulties to my irritability and to my inability to handle the members properly. She and I have never quarreled in all the sixteen and a half years that we have been married, but last Saturday when out of a clear sky, without any real provocation she burst out that my failure with the SAJ was due to my inability I was beside myself with rage and simply refused to discuss the subject any further with her. She

---

48. Rosalie Lopez Piza Mendes (Mrs. H. Pereira Mendes) (1869–1953), born in St. Thomas, West Indies; communal leader; author; co-founder, Y.W.H.A. Her husband was rabbi at the Spanish-Portuguese Synagogue in New York City, Shearith Israel.

49. Jacob Rubin, Max Rubin, and Isaac Rubin, all brothers-in-law of Mordecai Kaplan.

has so far not shown the least sign of regret for what she said. Her action has hurt me more than anything that strangers could have done to me. I have never felt so alone in the world. But I must learn to take my punishment like a man, and I shall try to refrain from self-pity.

Arguing with Judith about the Sabbath

DECEMBER 29, 1924

I derived a great deal of joy from the sweet reasonableness displayed today by my Judith in an argument with her tonight before the meeting concerning the question of riding on the Sabbath. At first I was inclined to give her leeway, but as I proceeded in the discussion it occurred to me that if what I am after is to develop Jewish consciousness through such elements of Jewish nationality as are still possible in America, we ought to maintain a folkway of that kind which is effective for the average Jew who otherwise at present has but little opportunity of expressing his Jewishness.[50]

Kaplan Visits Scranton: The Complications of Setting up a Chapter of the SAJ

THURSDAY, JANUARY 5, 1925

Last Sunday I was in Scranton. My coming to Scranton, like much of my effort in behalf of Judaism, was attended with unpleasantness due to the human element involved. Bernard Heller[51] has been the rabbi of the Reform Temple there for the last four years. He studied at the Seminary for about two years and then left it to study at the Hebrew Union College. He has been hanging on to me in all the years since he was graduated from the HUC. He is a very honest, conscientious fellow with no sense of humor. He tried a number of times to get me to come to Scranton. I finally consented to come Jan. 4.

In the same city one of the Seminary graduates occupies the pulpit of the Conservative congregation.[52] He is a rather able chap with a good deal of common sense. He has been in Scranton since last winter and has succeeded in building up quite a following among some of the young people in it. They have organized themselves as the Jewish Culture Group headed by a young man about thirty named Bloch who at one time attended the Teachers Institute.

50. Kaplan later refers to the commandments as customs and probably means here that the mitzvah (i.e., custom) of not riding on the Sabbath ought to be retained.

51. Bernard Heller (1896–1976), ordained Hebrew Union College (HUC); faculty, HUC; author.

52. Kaplan is referring to Max Arzt (1897–1975), ordained JTS; author; chancellor, JTS; president, Rabbinical Assembly.

Heller and Arzt worked together in the community in a genuine spirit of cooperation. Arzt has a home, whereas Heller is single. Heller used to come to Arzt almost every day in the week. Of late there has been something of a break in their friendship and my coming contributed to the widening of the breach. And this is how it happened.

Heller told Arzt that I was coming to address a group of people that might organize themselves as an SAJ and he wanted Arzt with the Jewish Culture Group to help him furnish the people. Heller realized that he had very few from his own temple that would be capable of being interested. A few days later Arzt came to see me and asked me why I had ignored him in all the negotiations in reference to my visit in Scranton. I told him the absolute truth that his presence in Scranton escaped my mind completely. He then explained the situation as to the Jewish Culture Group with many of whom Heller was a persona non grata. They would therefore not be present if I were to come merely in response to Heller's invitation.

This necessitated my revising my plans and asking Heller to come to an understanding with Arzt as to the auspices under which my appeal for the organization of an SAJ unit was to be made. After a considerable interchange of letters and telegrams, Heller wired that while he cannot come to an understanding with Arzt I should come out in response to Arzt's invitation. This I did in the hope that I would be able to effect a reconciliation when I would get there.

At the station I was met by both of them together with Mr. Bloch. The afternoon was spent in discussing the situation. I learned that the Friday before the Jewish Culture Group had met and decided upon a definite plan of organization, according to which plan the SAJ[53] was to consist of various study circles in the city. To become a member of the SAJ one would have to be a member of some study circle in addition to subscribing to the platform of the SAJ. The Jewish Culture Group sent out invitations to about seventy eligible people for the gathering which was arranged to take place at the Hotel Casey.

After I learned of these arrangements Arzt, Heller and I got together in Heller's study and I worked hard to reconcile Heller. He seemed to realize that his main objection against converting the Jewish Culture Group into the SAJ was upheld and that as a matter of fact the SAJ that would be organized would be a federation of study circles. But at the meeting proper it seemed he had forgotten that and began arguing from the very beginning

---

53. Obviously at this point Kaplan viewed the SAJ not just as a single congregation but as the center of a movement.

as through I hadn't said a word to him. So hard is it to get in an idea edgewise, once suspicion or fear obsesses one.

I was successful with my address before the group of about sixty people that were there and I was pleasantly surprised at the rather intelligent questions that were put to me after the address. After answering those questions to the satisfaction of all present, they proceeded to discuss the plan of organization. Here was where Heller had to be taken the ground all over again and even then he couldn't see the point, until I got a chance to explain the situation to him after the meeting. Even the fact that they had decided not to go on with the election of officers until other study circles besides the Jewish Culture Group would join, failed to convince him that the SAJ in Scranton was not to be limited to the latter group solely. In the end, however, the difficulties were smoothed out and I left Scranton feeling that Heller and Arzt would cooperate.

A Typical Day—Preparing—Teaching

TUESDAY, JANUARY 13, 1925
Spent greater part of the day till about 6:00 on Gen[esis] R.

6:00–6:45: Discussed sermon with Abraham Horowitz.[54] A former freelancer, attended three years at Dropsie. Had been in the army during the war. Talks with a decided foreign accent. Gestures all the time. Rather odd specimen. He said Seminary gives one less chance to loaf than most institutions of higher learning.

Have been working all evening on paraphr. Of Cant.[icles] R. I 3.[55]

Karp and Draxler wanted to come to see me today but had no time for them. Asked them to come next Tuesday.

This and That; Judith; A Seminary Afraid of the Truth

SATURDAY, JANUARY 31, 1925
Very much annoyed this morning at the difficulty Judith encountered in getting into Barnard. A mere trifle, but enough to upset me.

No minyan[56] this morning at Shaharit [morning] services. Small attendance; felt very blue. Administered a laying out to those present. Preached in choppy fashion what might have been a good sermon. Subject: The Divine Right of Kings.

---

54. Abraham Horowitz (1900–1957), social worker, executive, editor.

55. The midrash mentioned here is *Canticles Rabbah*, the homiletical commentary on the *Song of Songs*. Kaplan may have had a long-term project to write a paraphrase.

56. Minyan: quorum of ten men required for a traditional service.

SUNDAY, FEBRUARY 1, 1925

　　2:15–6: Classes at Institute.

　　The lecture to post-graduate class dealt with primitive condition of life and thought of Israelites as they entered Canaan. Goldstein, a graduate of institute, remarked after lecture that he was afraid of the truth.

　　Discussion meeting of SAJ members. Bromberg in chair.

　　Berkson gave clear outline of problem of private vs. public school. The discussion that followed was unusually good. While I was not as good as I should have liked to have been I threw out a challenge to those who glorify the public school system.

　　Miss Baum, who is an old school principal, charged me with knowing nothing about the school system. Berkson said I was muddle-headed. (A remark that left me dumbfounded.) Others again were struck by the novelty of my presentation.

Kaplan Depressed

WEDNESDAY, FEBRUARY 11, 1925

　　10:30–1:30 at the Seminary teaching

　　Crestfallen because of following incidents:

1. Forgot the verse in *Job* in conversation with Marx.
2. New student told me Davidson said to him he does not have to take Homiletics.
3. Was misled to believe slough of abusement was in Bunyan.
4. Finkelstein handed me copy of his book "Self Government."[57]
5. Have been working all the rest of the day in hope of writing out address in Hebrew, but had to give up.

Kaplan Invited to Dedication of Hebrew University

FRIDAY, FEBRUARY 20, 1925

　　Received invitation from ZOA to represent it at dedication of University in Jerusalem. Called up Cyrus Adler in Philadelphia for leave of absence. Said he would refer matter to Board. Meantime he told me he was invited but thought it more important to raise money also about confusion due to Hurwitz's[58] inviting S. C. Lamport to represent

---

57. Louis Finkelstein, *Jewish Self-Government in the Middle Ages* (New York: Jewish Theological Seminary, 1924).

58. Henry Hurwitz (1886–1961), educator; essayist; communal worker; Menorah leader; editor, *Menorah Journal*.

Menorah[59] and S. C. asking for privilege to represent various universities. In this Hurwitz anticipated action of special committee consisting of Warburg, Marshall, Marx and Cardozo[60] designated to invite the various universities to representation. Adler also asked me to call up Mack to tell him about my invitation, which I did.

8:00–10:30 A story by *Smilanski* [Heb.][61]

10:30–2:00 Preparation for sermon.

Kaplan Sails for Jerusalem

THURSDAY, MARCH 12, 1925 (S.S. Olympic)

On Board the Olympic which sailed from N.Y. last Monday midnight. I am on the way now to Palestine to represent the Zionist Organization of America at the dedication of the Hebrew University of Jerusalem. I do not feel that I owe this honor to real merit or achievement but simply to a combination of circumstances which have put in my way this extraordinary piece of luck. A few weeks ago on the Sabbath before *Tu Be-Shevat* [Heb. fifteenth day of the month of Shevat][62] I happened to preach a sermon on the importance of the Haluz [Pioneer] movement in Palestine. Among the listeners there happened to be a Mrs. Jacobs,[63] an ardent Zionist and Hadassah worker. Accordingly when at a meeting of the Zionist administrative committee the question came up about sending someone to the dedication of the University to represent the Organization, I understand that Mrs. Jacobs proposed that I as an American Jewish scholar (sic!)[64] and a Zionist ought to be asked to go to Jerusalem. Maybe I am wrong about Mrs. Jacobs being the one to have suggested my going to Jerusalem. Abe Liebovitz[65] informed me that the question as to whether I would be willing to take the trip had come up some time before that at a meeting of the Keren Hayesod Board. But it really makes no difference for the point that I want to make which is that I pass among

---

59. Menorah Societies on American campuses maintained a Jewish presence in the early twentieth century. The Intercollegiate Menorah Association published the *Menorah Journal*, which became the primary vehicle for essays by Jewish intellectuals.

60. Benjamin Cardozo (1870–1938), U.S. and N.Y. Supreme Court justice; philosophical jurist; trustee, Columbia and Jewish Welfare Board.

61. Moshe Smilansky (1874– 1953), immigrated to Palestine from Russia in 1890; active in farming; prolific author.

62. Minor holiday, usually occurring during the winter months. The New Year for Trees.

63. Rose Gell Jacobs (1888–1975), member of the original group that established Hadassah; president, Hadassah; active in Youth Aliyah project, establishing Hadassah hospital on Mt. Scopus.

64. In the original diary; not the editor.

65. Abraham Liebovitz (1878–1964), manufacturer; communal fund-raiser; a founder of the SAJ; officer, Jewish Reconstructionist Foundation.

the laity for a great scholar and therefore am being accorded an honor which I feel should have been bestowed upon some one far more deserving than I am.

When I received the invitation from Lipsky[66] on Friday, February 20, I hesitated for a while whether I should accept it or not, but I soon came to an affirmative conclusion. I got immediately in touch with Adler in Philadelphia to find out whether I would be granted the necessary leave of absence. He said he was not authorized to give me an immediate reply but he felt that I would get the permission asked for. It was only as a matter of formality that he had to get the authority from the Board. In the long conversation which he held with me on the phone he informed me that the whole matter of invitations to the dedication exercises of the University was being mismanaged and that as a result of this mismanagement S. C. Lamport took it upon himself to obtain letters of greeting from the various universities. It seems that whenever Adler has anything to say about Zionism or Zionists he must find some cause for complaint.

On Friday, February 27, Adler informed me that the Board had granted the permission I asked for, and that I was also to represent and bring greetings from the Seminary. I confess that I would have been extremely annoyed if the Seminary had not asked me to represent it. Whatever doubt I may have entertained about going was now completely dispelled. I at once called up Hyamson and Morris Levine[67] of the T.I. to ask them to take over my work at the Seminary for the rest of the term. From that moment to my departure the week following I was in a state of tension. I had to deliver a sermon on Sat., February 28, and a talk to the SAJ members about the building on Sunday, February 29, to write an article for the *New Palestine* and to deliver an address at the Third Anniversary of the SAJ. Originally the dinner was to take place on Purim (March 10) but it was transferred to Thursday March 5 so as to have it serve in addition as a farewell dinner to me in view of my departure to Palestine. There were also work to round up at the Seminary and Institute, calls to make and telephones to answer.

Everything was fairly well attended to. I was in too much of a daze to do justice to the subject of the University when I addressed the students and the SAJ members during the week. I was really unprepared for that outburst of genuine friendship on their part. At the Anniversary and Farewell dinner Weizmann and Lipsky were present and spoke of me in the highest

66. Louis Lipsky (1876–1963), life insurance executive; Zionist and communal leader; author; editor; officer, Zionist Organization of America.

67. Morris Levine (1881–1935), rabbi; faculty; JTS; primarily responsible for bringing Hebrew to TI.

terms. Harry Liebovitz,[68] the new and efficient chairman of the SAJ, actually embarrasses me every time he speaks of me. When I rose to speak I kept entirely to my notes which dealt mainly with the SAJ and hardly alluded to the University. I even forgot to thank Weizmann, Lipsky and the ZOA, and seemed to take no cognizance of the friendly spirit of the SAJ.

On Friday night a large contingent of the SAJ came to the boat to see me off. I got a number of gifts which I cannot receive without mixed feelings of delight in their possession and uncertainty as to my measuring up to the idea that the senders have of me. Mrs. Unterberg gave me a check for $500. The Darmans sent me a beautifully fitted leather bag. The Friedlaender Extension classes sent me a pair of field glasses; besides smaller gifts from other friends.

On board the steamer I have been busy working on the address I have to deliver at the opening of the University. I worked on it for almost four days and I am still in doubt whether it is any good. I am waiting to show it to Weizmann who is also on board. We do not see very much of each other here. I keep to my room working most of the time, while he works "prospects." We have had however two long intimate chats and two others in which some of our friends participated. I wish I could remember the talk on Purim afternoon which turned upon his experiences with Allenby[69] and the English Administration in March 1918, and with Briand[70] on the day before the San Remo[71] confirmation of the Mandate. His accounts of the hardships encountered, the obstacles put in the way, especially the Vatican, of the hairbreadth escapes from complete collapse and of the fidelity of Lord Balfour, would make much nobler reading than our present Megillah.[72] I wish the Jews were alive enough to replace our traditional Megillah with an account of some of the recent events which point to a divine providence that is making for the rebirth of the Jewish people. Weizmann repeated more than once that he was sure that a *Hashgaḥa Elohit* [Heb. Divine Providence] was directing the course of events in Palestine.[73]

---

68. Harry Liebovitz (1882–?), men's clothing manufacturer; a founder of the SAJ.

69. Edmund H. H. Allenby (1861–1936), British field marshal; commander of the Egyptian Expeditionary Force which liberated Palestine from the Turks during World War I.

70. Aristide Briand (1862–1932), French statesman; headed French government during World War I.

71. The San Remo conference of the Allied powers in 1920 decided on the allotment of the mandates in the Middle East, including the British mandate over Palestine.

72. Biblical book of Esther, read on holiday of Purim.

73. From March 16, 1925, until June 17, 1925, Kaplan wrote the diary in Hebrew. The translation of the selected passages is by the editor. Bracketed words, unless otherwise noted, are supplied by the editor.

Kaplan Visits the Weizmann Home

MARCH 16, 1925: LONDON

I arrived in London on Friday evening at midnight. In the morning I roamed around [the city]. At about four thirty I went with Fishman to Weizmann's house. There I met his family and some of his friends including the well-known Dr. Feiwel.[74] We drank a cup of tea as is the custom. Weizmann showed me his house. I was happy to see how prosperously he lives. I think he has about four servants. . . . If indeed Weizmann is so wealthy that he does not need to work in order to support himself and can devote all his energies to the Zionist movement he certainly is fortunate.

Kaplan Visits Chief Rabbi Joseph Hertz

MARCH 16, 1925: LONDON

I telephoned Dr. Hertz[75] the Chief Rabbi of the British Empire. I know him from America. He expressed a desire to see me. I spent almost two hours at his home on 48 Hamilton Terrace. I could have spent more time but I did not want to talk more about conditions in America. He has gained weight since the last time I saw him. He was wearing his rabbinical hat and robes, all of which state, "I am the Chief Rabbi." He sat next to the fireplace and offered me a chair next to it also. After a short time his wife entered, bringing us tea. We spoke about the college [university] and the arrangements for the celebration.

Weizmann on Board Ship Discusses Hertz

MARCH 19, 1925

Yesterday when I mentioned the college [i.e., the university] and the name of Rabbi Hertz while I was talking to Weizmann during the meal, Weizmann complimented Hertz. [He said that] Hertz dared to oppose the powerful English Jews because he supported the Zionist [position] when they with all their power were trying to prevent the Balfour Declaration.[76]

---

74. Berthold Feiwel (1875–1937), Zionist leader; one of Herzl's closest assistants. Key person in helping to bring about the Hebrew University.

75. Joseph Hertz (1872–1946), ordained JTS; served in Johannesburg; appointed Chief Rabbi of British Empire in 1913. Kaplan knew him from the Seminary. Hertz was the first graduate.

76. Non-Zionists and anti-Zionists were afraid that any recognition of the Jews as a people would threaten their status as loyal citizens.

Weizmann—The Mediterranean Will Be a Jewish Lake

MARCH 20, 1925

A very appropriate word came from Weizmann when we arrived at the port [of Naples]. He called Naples a remote city. He said this when we saw the small group of men and a few women who had come to welcome [us]. The young people among them had blue and white bands on their arms. Among them there were a few sea scouts. Immediately after the ship anchored the group boarded and met [with us] in the [ship's] salon. On one of the sofas sat the head of the [Jewish] community of Rome who came especially to welcome Weizmann. On one side sat Weizmann and on the other side Sokolow.[77] The head of the community spoke in Italian and expressed the joy of the Zionists and the Jews of Italy at the founding of the College. Weizmann then rose and spoke in French. He expressed his hope that the Zionists in Italy will recognize their responsibility to the movement. He also mentioned me in my capacity as representing the Zionists in America. Afterwards, Sokolow also spoke about the value of the College. The small meeting finished with the singing of *Ha-tikvah*. It was difficult for me to keep back the tears when the song was sung in hushed tones in such a strange setting. At that very moment I felt the [great] effort of our people to come back to life and the tragedy of a dwarf arousing his people against colossal forces.

Both yesterday and today Weizmann emphasized that the Mediterranean is closer to his heart than any other body of water. It is a Jewish sea. If it is not one now it will become one within time—a hundred years, perhaps less. The Romans called it "Mare Nostrum" [our sea]. An imperialistic attitude like this grated on my ears. If the rabbis were imperialistic I understand, because it was only a psychological compensation for the inferior condition of the nation. But imperialism in the mouth of a Zionist has a hint of the chauvinism which reigns among modern nations.

First Days in Jerusalem

WEDNESDAY, MARCH 25, 1925

We arrived at the Jerusalem train station, which is less impressive than some of the local stations which we passed, and were met by a man from the Allenby hotel. I was in the Hotel only a few minutes when I saw the Lamport children. They hugged me for joy. Their parents appeared immediately. . . . I was happy [when I learned] that Lamport met Magnes

---

77. Nahum Sokolow (1860–1936), Zionist leader and Hebrew journalist; general secretary, World Zionist Organization; key person in negotiating the Balfour Declaration.

in front of the hotel and told him that I had arrived. Magnes invited me to his house for lunch. As I was going out of the hotel I saw a large group of people standing next to the post office. I asked Magnes why they were there and he said he thought it might be some kind of demonstration. Afterward I heard that they were waiting for Balfour to appear there. From there [Magnes] took me to Jaffa street and from there into the old city through the narrow streets and alleys. All of the Arab stores were closed [and some of the Jewish ones nearby] as a strike against the coming of Balfour. The wagons and the automobiles of the Arabs were nowhere to be seen. . . .

At Magnes's house I found a few people, all well educated, who waited to confer with him or who wanted something from him. It was very pleasant. I played with his two young children. . . . Magnes asked them to tell me about what they had learned in their private lessons. They responded without complaining. I was startled at their good manners and also by their knowledge. . . .

We talked about the program for the dedication of the College and I saw that Weizmann erred when he told me that I would be among the speakers in the first session of the opening [exercises]. But the question of when I will give my lecture has not yet been made clear. . . . [78]

A Walk to the Wall

SATURDAY EVENING, MARCH 28, 1925

Yesterday on Friday evening I walked to the Wall with Greenberg.[79] After we passed through the dark and narrow alleys we came to the Wall. A group of people, men, women and children, were praying. I did not feel any sense of holiness. There were tourists there from France, among them soldiers and nuns accompanied by a Greek priest who was their leader. Their faces showed disgust as they approached the Wall. I was walking behind them and I heard the priest say to them that they were going to see the Wall where the Jews prayed. One of the nuns said to him, "I hope the Jews don't kill us."

I was not able to pray there and I went to an Ashkenazic synagogue nearby which is called the "Ruins of Rabbi Judah the Pious."

---

78. There were many days of speeches in the week after the dedication ceremonies. Kaplan spoke then. The text appeared in the American Jewish press. A summation is contained in *Judaism Faces the Twentieth Century*, 327–30.

79. Simon Greenberg. See glossary. Greenberg was in Palestine for a year, serving as an assistant to Magnes. Many years later I interviewed Greenberg and he remembered minute details of Kaplan's visit. See *Judaism Faces the Twentieth Century*.

Kaplan on a donkey in Palestine, 1925. (Courtesy Hadassah K. Musher)

A Tour of Bethlehem and Hebron

MONDAY, MARCH 30, 1925

Today Mrs. Lamport and Mrs. Silverman invited me to go with them in an automobile to Bethlehem and Hebron. We left the hotel about 9:30 and returned about 2:30. We stopped to see the Tomb of Rachel. Inside many Jews were sitting around and reciting the Psalms and praying for rain. The man in charge tried to prove to me that this really was the burial place of Rachel. In Bethlehem I visited a Christian shrine—the place where people say Jesus was born. I saw the marks from the conflagration that had broken out as a result of the arguments between the Greek [Christians] and the Armenians. I also saw the work [entitled] "The Mother of Peace."

In Hebron we stood at the place which is supposed to be the Cave of Machpelah.[80] Afterward the guide led us to the other side of the cave where there is a shrine and in the wall of the shrine a hole where Jews throw little notes on which they write a request. They throw these notes into the hole in the belief that the patriarchs will fulfill their requests. . . .

Opening of the Hebrew University—The Ceremony

WEDNESDAY, APRIL 1, 1925

I just came from the celebration which was held at the college [university] theater. I hired a carriage together with two notable university people, one from Kovno the other from Cairo. When I arrived at the college [university] I found that people had already begun to gather. Those who had places on the stage gathered in sections according to their part in the ceremony. Mr Bentwich[81] organized the order of our going out to the stage. All the important people came after us and the celebration began about five minutes late.

The program started with the singing of *Ki mi-tsion tetse Torah* [Heb. Isaiah 2:3 "For instruction shall come forth from Zion, The word of the Lord from Jerusalem"]. I was not able to hold myself back and I cried like a baby. The instrumentalists and the singers played and sang divinely. Then they sang *ha-shamayim me-saprim kevod el* [Heb. Psalm 19:1 "The heavens declare the glory of God"].[82] But the splendid impression was lost because of Rabbi Kook[83] who promised to speak about eight minutes but went on

---

80. Cave where, according to biblical tradition, Abraham and Sarah, Isaac, Rebekah, Jacob, and Leah are buried. Near Hebron.

81. Norman Bentwich (1883–1971), English Zionist; lawyer; scholar; attorney general of the Mandate government; biographer of Solomon Schechter.

82. The ceremony took place in the afternoon and the sky was clear.

83. Abraham Isaac Kook (1865–1935), rabbinic thinker and chief rabbi in Palestine; Zionist and mystic; reached out to the non-Orthodox; criticized for participating in the Hebrew University dedication.

for half an hour and more. When Magnes asked him to begin the [opening] prayer, Kook agreed only on the condition that he be allowed to continue speaking; but he tired out the audience. I don't know why but I felt that this man is a *fakir;* and this feeling grew today when I saw him and listened to him for the first time. Following him [Herbert] Samuel spoke simply and briefly as a British Jew.[84] Even though he did not say a word which assailed the dignity of nationalism [i.e., Zionism] he also did not say even a word in its favor. Weizmann [then] spoke, as is his custom, first in Hebrew and then he himself translated it into English. The content was good but [his speech] lacked a little warmth. When Balfour rose to speak the air was electrified; the audience was spellbound, myself included. He spoke without notes for forty-five minutes and only briefly at the end of his speech did he lose the attention of the audience. His voice was strong and he spoke clearly. I heard every syllable he uttered and his words absorbed me and delighted me fully. He spoke as a lover of Israel and as a righteous person. . . .

Two things made a very deep impression on me now that I have returned from the reception and I am summing up what was said. He pointed out [that from Mt. Scopus, where we were sitting, one could see] where Israel crossed the Jordon into the Land. And when he said this he motioned with his finger in that direction. On the other side of the Mount where we were sitting [one could see the place] where Titus planned to capture Jerusalem— the beginning and the end of an era in the chronicles of Israel. Secondly he pointed that here the Jews and Arabs worked together nine hundred years ago and that they will be able to work together again in the twentieth century. At the beginning of his remarks he emphasized that it is not only the beauty of the place which is outstanding but that this celebration signifies a new historical era.

What a pity that after the wonderful impression made on the hearts of the audience, the day was ruined again by the speech of Bialik, which was as long as the exile. He seemed to put in every rabbinical saying about the Torah which is in his Book on the Aggadah.[85] He spoke not as a poet but as a preacher and not even among the best. The people seemed not to be able to tolerate him but they acted courteously. Rabbi [Joseph] Hertz concluded the program with a short prayer. In the evening when I congratulated him on his prayer he said to me that he "saved the situation."[86]

---

84. First Viscount Herbert Louis Samuel (1870–1963), British Jewish statesman and philosopher, Zionist, and First High Commissioner for Palestine, 1920–25, under the mandate. Responding to Arab pressure, Zionist leaders criticized Samuel.

85. This is a compilation by subject of rabbinic legends translated into Hebrew. *Sefer Ha-Aggadah.* First Published in 1908 by Bialik and Y. H. Ravnitzky. Many editions. English translation: *The Book of Legends—Sefer Ha-Aggadah—Legends from the Talmud and Midrash,* trans. by William Braude (New York: Schocken Books, 1992).

86. Hertz's words are in English in the diary.

A few minutes later when I met his wife she also said to me that he "saved the situation."

Sokolow Speaks—A Gathering of the Famous

APRIL 16, 1925 [IN TEL AVIV]

On Tuesday evening after dinner, a party was given by the local Zionists in honor of Weizmann and Sokolow in the hall of the gymnasium [high school]. Wine, sweets, and tea were served. Among those present were Ahad Ha-Am, Bialik, Tcherikhovsky, Shneur,[87] and Thon.[88] Musical artists entertained those assembled. There were speeches. Sokolow spoke after the introductions. His talk was moving and filled with substance. The central point was that it was an affront to say that the opening of the university was political in nature. This event is beyond our ability to evaluate correctly. The first day of the celebration united both the natural and the historical. On the second day the representatives of all the nations came to pay homage— before what?—before a dream. It is impossible to escape the conclusion that the Hand of God is revealed here.

His words and his enthusiasm overwhelmed me. Fishman said to me afterward that Sokolow does not feel even part of what he was saying and that all this was only rhetoric [artistry]. I don't agree with Fishman at all.

87. Zalman Shneur (1887–1959), Hebrew and Yiddish poet and novelist who together with Bialik and Tchernichowsky is considered one of the three great figures of Hebrew poetry of his generation.

88. Yaakov Thon (1880–1950), Zionist leader, active in the organization of the Jewish community in Palestine.

5

June 27, 1925–February 23, 1927

The Secular versus the Religious

SATURDAY, JUNE 27, 1925

Had a meeting with the staff of the Teachers Institute on Tuesday morning (10:00 to 1:00). The main object of discussion was the work with post-graduate students. The difficulty with those who have been taking post-graduate work this year has been that they had forgotten a great deal of what they had learned in the Institute when they were undergraduates. Every time the subject of lack of knowledge on the part of the students becomes a matter for discussion, I groan inwardly at the realization that with the best of intentions the vast majority even of willing students cannot do justice both to their secular and to their Jewish studies. The rivalry between Jewish and non-Jewish culture goes on forever in the lives of these young people. Instead of sympathizing with them, most of our faculty members take the attitude of pedants who are interested only in their own subjects and cannot see the human side of the problem.

This same tendency on the part of most of the members of the faculty is apparent also in the exacting demands which they would make of those who would wish to work for the Master's and Doctor's degree. I am especially annoyed at the inflexible and unimaginative attitude of Rabbi Levine.

A Young Liberal Rabbi Attracted to Hasidism

THURSDAY, JULY 2, 1925

From nine to 11:15 I spent with Dr. Jacob Sonderling,[1] formerly of Hamburg. A man in the forties, well built, quite good looking, impressive

---

1. Jacob Sonderling (1878–1964), Ph.D., rabbi; early Zionist; faculty, Hebrew Union College; founder, Society for Jewish Culture.

features, longish and well trimmed beard, neatly dressed in frock suit. He came to ask me to help him find a position where he would be able to function as rabbi to the measure of his ability. He is occupying at present a position in Chicago. He is very unhappy there because he cannot bear the people. According to his description ethical considerations play no part whatever in their Judaism which is strictly orthodox as far as their avowals are concerned, while in practice they vary from strict observance to the most indifferent laxity. They give little thought to the Jewish upbringing of their children. Their grandchildren usually attend the Sunday schools of the Reform temples.

As far as I could make out, his approach to Judaism is very similar to mine. Our conversation at first turned, accordingly, upon the absence of any formulation of Judaism from a modern and national viewpoint, and the faintheartedness of the rabbis who are in sympathy with this point of view but who prefer to maintain the attitude of ignoring questions of principle. A year ago Sonderling stated at the meeting of the United Synagogue that its position is that of one who has given up Orthodoxy but who has not yet accepted Reform. It should have the courage to form and defend convictions of its own. To which R. Hoffman retorted that Sonderling was a German and therefore insisted on principles. We in American believe in doing work and not bothering about principles.

In his experiences as war chaplain with Polish and Lithuanian Jews Sonderling says that he found it necessary to give up the philosophy of Judaism which he had acquired as a disciple of Herman Cohen.[2] Contact with real Jewish life made him realize that most of Cohen's philosophy was cold and irrelevant.

Sonderling mentioned a "Rebbi" whom he came across in Europe and in whom he saw real evidences of spiritual exaltation. Joined to that spirituality was a deep sense of humanity. "Hasidism is nothing more," said that Rebbi, "than finding a place where people do not pass each other in cold indifference, but where they take a sympathetic interest in one another." This Rebbi of Bunyim happens to be in New York just now. Sonderling said he would make it a point to look him up.

In a conversation which S. had with Kaufman Kohler[3] he told the latter that Reform made a fatal mistake in seeking to adopt the prayer book to present day needs. According to Sonderling it is important that we preserve that which helps to maintain the unity of Israel, and as for the passages that

---

2. Herman Cohen (1842–1918), German-Jewish philosopher; founder of Marburg School of Neo-Kantianism; immense influence on Jewish thinkers.

3. Kaufmann Kohler (1843–1926), Reform leader; rabbi; theologian; scholar; author; president, Hebrew Union College.

cannot be accepted literally we can get ourselves into the frame of mind that can read those passages with the thought of their historical setting. Kohler replied that was sophistry. On another occasion when S. argued in the hearing of Kohler against rationalism as the supreme guide in Judaism, Kohler declared that he felt hurt by what S. said against rationalism, because he, Kohler, was a thoroughgoing rationalist. Yet he could not fail to depict a certain music in Sonderling's plea for irrationalism.

Studying Some Talmud in the Morning

FRIDAY, JULY 3, 1925

Studied a few minutes while in Tephilin[4] the treatise of Baba Mezia—Folio 2a.[5] Shocked by statement in Rashi[6] proving that the lost animal of a heathen should not be returned. The spirit of the law in Ex. 23 is certainly superior to that of rabbinic Judaism.

Preparing a Course for School of Jewish Social Work

FRIDAY, AUGUST 28, 1925

This is the first summer that I have spent entirely in the city. The main reason for my staying in the city has been that I had undertaken to give a course in Judaism at the new school which was organized recently known as the School for Jewish Social Workers.[7] Its director is Mr. Maurice Karpf[8] who at the suggestion of Alex Dushkin and Drachsler[9] met me a long time ago and tried to induce me to give a course at that school which was then in the process of organization. Little did I realize then that I would get so much out of the course personally. I do not refer to the honorarium attached to it which is more than I ever expected, twenty dollars per hour, but to the stimulus that it has afforded me to put into shape my ideas on Judaism as a civilization. It was the first honest-to-goodness course in which I was absolutely free to speak my mind. The result has been extremely gratifying to me. The students though having little Jewish background, with

---

4. Tephilin or phylacteries: two black leather boxes fastened to leather straps, containing portions from the Pentateuch, bound to the arm and the head during morning prayers.

5. Tractate of the Talmud dealing generally with damages.

6. R. Solomon Yizhaki (1040–1105), rabbinic scholar; wrote commentaries on the Bible and the Talmud still very widely used by students of classical Jewish texts.

7. For an account of Kaplan and social work, see Harriet Finer, "Kaplan's Influence on Social Work," in *The American Judaism of Mordecai Kaplan*, ed. Emanuel Goldsmith, Mel Scult, Robert Seltzer (New York: New York University Press, 1990), 357–70.

8. Maurice Karpf (1889–1964), Ph.D. Columbia; Jewish social work administrator; author; director, Training School for Jewish Social Work.

9. Julius Drachsler (1889–1927), sociologist; faculty, CCNY; author; director, Bureau for Jewish Social Research.

the exception of two or three, are all intelligent and interested. I have thus been able to accomplish this summer more than I did during a good many of the preceding summers.

I cannot say that my health has been satisfactory. Although I seem to have escaped the rose fever this year, I have been having aches and pains, especially in my legs. Although I hate the idea of giving in to myself and annoying the family with complaints, I deplore the fact that this continual ailing prevents me from putting in as much work as I should like to and especially from being exuberant and cheerful. Believing that bad tonsils were the cause of these ailments I had them removed. The operation took place on Thursday August 6 at Mt. Sinai Hospital. Dr. Kaempfler was the physician who operated with the aid of a local anaesthetic. I stood the operation very well and recovered rapidly. I resumed the lectures last Monday, August 24, after an interruption of only two and a half weeks.

TI Faculty Discussion on Instruction in Hebrew

FRIDAY, SEPTEMBER 11, 1925

Last Monday night I invited the Faculty of the Teachers Institute to spend the evening at my house by holding an informal discussion concerning conditions at the Institute, and how to improve them. It was not because there has arisen any crisis that I called them together. On the contrary, the work is running so smoothly that there is the danger of its becoming mechanized. Somehow I never found it necessary to call the Faculty together on the eve of our resuming the courses. This time, however, it occurred to me that the morale of the Institute would be benefitted by having them meet one another at my home before the term started.

Those present[10] were Honor[11], Levine, Scharfstein[12], Bavli,[13] Chertoff,[14] Bragin[15] and Ovsay.[16] Absent were Kadushin and Silk.[17]

---

10. Those named are all members of the TI faculty.

11. Leo Honor (1894–1956), Ph.D., communal educator, New York City, then Chicago; leader in Jewish education; author; Bureau of Jewish Education, New York City; College of Jewish Studies, Chicago.

12. Zevi Scharfstein (1884–1972), Hebrew editor, educator, textbook writer; Bureau of Jewish Education; faculty, TI.

13. Hillel Bavli (1893–1961), Hebrew poet, literary critic.

14. Paul Chertoff (1880–1966), rabbi; talmudist; faculty, TI; supporter of Kaplan.

15. Joseph Bragin (1875–1932), principal, Hebrew High School, New York City; faculty, TI. Died in an automobile accident.

16. Joshua Ovsay (1883–1957), Hebrew literary critic; translator; author; immigrated to U.S. 1918 and to Israel 1955.

17. Benjamin N. Silkiner (Silk) (1888–1934), prominent Hebrew poet; educator; translated *Macbeth* into Hebrew.

Most of the men, despite the fact that they have adequate knowledge of their respective subjects, have little mastery of the art of education and still regard the purpose of any kind of education as being ability to remember and quote text. In addition, being modern Hebraists, they are zealots for the employment of Hebrew as a medium of conversation. They almost refuse to recognize that we are living in an American environment and view the encroachment of Americanism into the lives of our students with a good deal of jealous hostility. I must confess that while on the positive side I am probably no less in favor of making as much use of Hebrew as possible, I part company with them when it comes to excluding the use of English. Being a compromiser and a syncretist by nature, I try to abide by the principle enunciated in *Koheleth* [Ecclesiastes] *Te-ehoz Ba-zeh ve-gam mi-zeh* [Heb. Ecclesiastes 7:18 "(It is best that) you grasp the one without letting go of the other"]. The only one on the Faculty who agrees with me in that respect is Honor. I should also mention Kadushin and Silk, but they wield little influence.

Accordingly the discussion took at first the nature of fault finding with the indifference of the students to the Hebrew, outside of their classroom and after they have graduated. Bavli was the chief complainant. That phase of the discussion petered down to the question whether it was feasible to use Hebrew in those courses which called for unrestrained self-expression on the part of the students. Honor and myself are the principal culprits. Later Bragin, who is more of a teacher than the rest, pointed out that everyone of us is taken up with duties outside of the Institute so that we cannot devote as much time to teach the students individually as we should. This led to the question how to guide the students in their meetings and literary efforts that ought to take the form of a periodical of some kind. Toward the end I timidly raised the question whether we were not laying altogether too much a stress upon language, at the expense of content. I believe that 42% is altogether too much for the language and modern literature part of the curriculum. Ovsay must have been shocked. Anyhow I shall try to push the matter of content the next time I get a chance.

On the whole, however, I consider the gathering to have accomplished its purpose in having established the proper kind of mutual understanding before proceeding with the work of the year.

Happiness with Daughter Judith

FRIDAY SEPTEMBER 11, 1925

I experienced yesterday one of the most serene and joyous moments of my life at the opening exercises of the Teachers Institute. Those exercises marked the opening of the seventeenth year of the Institute. Yesterday also

happened to be the sixteenth birthday of my daughter Judith. Judith sat at
the piano and played the music of the Hebrew songs which were sung by the
students. Israel Goldfarb,[18] the music instructor, led in the singing. I had
Dr. Gamoran,[19] who returned recently from Palestine, teach Judith the songs
for which she played the music. All he had to do was to sing them once and
she immediately wrote down the notes. I then had Goldfarb come and learn
them from Judith and transmit them to the students. Such joy as seeing my
darling child beautifully developed physically and mentally and spiritually
participating on her birthday in the exercises of an institution which I have
had the privilege of nurturing from its very infancy, and with the future bright
for both my Judith and the Teachers Institute, makes me wonder how much
of it I really deserve. I never feel so humble as at moments like these, and my
sympathy goes out to the mass of humanity who are deprived of all such pure
joy. At the same time the thought that the happiness experienced in such
moments is unstable and transitory makes it impossible for me to abandon
myself to ecstatic joy.

First Time—Speaking to TI in Hebrew

FRIDAY, SEPTEMBER 11, 1925
    What contributed this time to a sense of inner satisfaction was
the fact that I finally succeeded in carrying out a wish I had long been
harboring and that is to hold the opening exercises entirely in Hebrew. Every
year I would feel humiliated by the fact that I could not summon enough
courage to speak in Hebrew on these occasions, thus neutralizing the Hebraic
character which it has always been my ambition to give to these meetings. To
speak extemporaneously in Hebrew I would not dare with so many Hebraists
around. On the other hand, to prepare an address, I somehow never found
the time. This year, however, in view of my resolve of last year, I took the
time to write out a neat little address which made an excellent impression.
"Now my joy is complete."

Dr. Morgenstern, President of HUC, Interviews Kaplan

THURSDAY, SEPTEMBER 24, 1925
    Last week (Wednesday, Sept. 16) I met Dr. Julian Morgenstern,[20]
President of the Hebrew Union College, at the Pennsylvania Hotel at 10.

---

18. Israel Goldfarb (1879–1967), ordained JTS; rabbi; cantor; composer; author; faculty,
JTS.
    19. Emanuel Gamoran (1895–1962), Ph.D., noted communal educator; president, Na-
tional Council for Jewish Education; author; editor, *The Jewish Teacher.*
    20. Julian Morgenstern (1881–1976), rabbi; president, Hebrew Union College; biblical
and semitic language scholar; author.

The interview lasted exactly an hour. I found him to be very pleasant and congenial. He came to the point at once by referring to the fact that Idelsohn[21] had mentioned to him that he had spoken to me about accepting a position at HUC and that I was ready to take the matter under advisement. Morgenstern asked me whether I would be willing to accept the chair in Jewish education which theoretically had been occupied by Dr. Slonimsky[22] but which in actuality had never been filled. I explained that my main reason for considering a change was that I wanted to confine myself to work of a purely academic character. Since as occupant of the chair of Jewish education I would be expected to engage in administration work and to head a department for the training of principals and executive secretaries, I would simply be doing the same kind of work I am engaged in at the present time. The academic work which I want to devote myself to lay, as he himself clearly put it, between the domain of Jewish Theology and Jewish philosophy. There was at present no chair for that kind of work. It seems, however, that Morgenstern would like to have me join the faculty and that he will recommend the creation of a chair for the subject that I would be willing to teach. This is the impression he gave me, since he went so far as to ask whether after I shall have indicated my willingness to accept the position at the HUC he could ask Dr. Adler to release me. This action he felt was part of the professional ethics which he said was violated by S. S. Wise in the appointment of Slonimsky. Slonimnsky was to have been asked anyhow to resign since his work was unsatisfactory. But Wise anticipated the request for Slonimsky's resignation by taking Slonimsky away without saying a word to the HUC authorities.[23]

Incidentally I suggested that Dr. Dushkin would be the right man for the chair in education at the HUC.

A *Kol Nidre*[24] Student Sermon

WEDNESDAY, SEPTEMBER 30, 1925

Rabbi Paul Chertoff happened to have made a good impression with the sermon he preached Kol Nidre night at the Seminary. When he told me last week the main thought and text of the sermon I took it apart and made a completely new sermon out of it, retaining as an incidental

---

21. Abraham Z. Idelsohn (1882–1938), musicologist, composer, author; established music department at Hebrew Union College.

22. Henry Slonimsky (1884–1970), philosopher; author; faculty, Columbia, Johns Hopkins, Hebrew Union College, Jewish Institute of Religion.

23. Stephen Wise had established the Jewish Institute of Religion in 1922 in New York City. It remained independent until 1950 when it merged with Hebrew Union College.

24. Central prayer on eve of Yom Kippur asking that vows be absolved.

analogy what with him served as the main text. The result was the Y.K. [Yom Kippur] sermon. The form in which he had it was good enough for the average uncritical layman, but certainly could not be considered sound from a logical or homiletical point of view. Yet the fact that it won the approval of Davidson and Mrs. Ginzberg[25] was sufficient to convince Chertoff that he had the true secret of sermonizing and that I did not know how to sermonize. So Kadushin told me this morning, and I was fool enough to let such talk annoy me. Is K's object in telling me this *rekhilut* [Heb. gossip] to revenge himself on me for having made use of the sermon I worked out in his hearing? I wonder whether I am doing the right thing in permitting him to use the sermons I work out with him at present. His contribution is almost nil.

Kaplan Defends Judith's Behavior at Camp

THURSDAY, OCTOBER 8, 1925

This morning I was as unhappy as an adolescent. Whether it is due to my working continuously without taking any time off for vacation, or whatever else may be the reason—it may be the tiredness in my legs—I have not been as cheerful as I should by this time have learned to be.

Last night Berkson told me about his impression of Judith and of her work in camp. As usual he managed to rub me the wrong way by telling me that she was not altruistic, and a follower instead of a leader in ideas and ways of acting, and not always sufficiently informed about the music work she was doing. I know that he was talking "through his hat," but I made him believe I took him seriously. I hate to argue with wrongheaded people of his type. I have never known him to express a sensible judgment of people or to be able to work long with them. I therefore could not put much stock in what he said about Judith, especially as in some of the conversations she had with me I could see that judging superficially and wishing to pose as a judge of human nature he would be easily misled by some transient symptoms which she, no doubt, manifested.

A Shivering Holiday

THURSDAY, OCTOBER 15, 1925

The Shmini Azereth[26] services were marred by the sudden cold weather which set in that day. With the building in a state of disrepair and with no heat to keep it warm the people shivered. I went home during

---

25. Adele Ginzberg (1886–1980), influential figure in Conservative movement as wife of Louis Ginzberg.
26. Festival of the Solomn Assembly, the eighth day of Sukkot.

the reading of the Torah to put on an extra pair of socks. I gave the sermon on Education for Character which took me fifty minutes to deliver. Common sense should have told me to cut it out altogether or at least to abbreviate. But I simply could not resist the momentum of three and a half days of work on it. The gun being primed it had to go off.

Kaplan Discusses God with a Reform Colleague

SUNDAY, NOVEMBER 1, 1925

A most unexpected development of my recent interview with Morgenstern, Pres. of Hebrew Union College, took place today. Last Thursday I received a letter from Dr. Samuel Schulman asking me to make an appointment to have a chat with him. I at once surmised that his desire to see me must have something to do with the interview that I had with Morgenstern a few weeks ago. The letter said that he wanted to get my impression of the Hebrew University in Palestine, but I knew that this was merely camouflage. The appointment was for Saturday, October 31 at 4 P.M. I found him and his wife in his apartment at the Olcott Hotel into which he moved recently. The first part of the conversation was a monologue by him, and a very long one at that, on his recent formulation of the attitude of the Rabbinical conference toward the question of the conflict between religion and science. He is an excellent talker, in the sense that he is fluent, but he usually moves on the plane of what I might call high class banalities. Never does a pithy saying or epigram light up his conversation; never a profound thought to provoke counter thought in you. The impression one gets when talking with him is that he uses you as a dummy to practice his sermons on. I bore it all patiently because I knew from the moment I entered what he was going to talk to me about, as he had opened the conversation with the prefatory remark that he did not want to be guilty of Geneivat Daat [Heb. deception] by giving me the impression that the letter conveyed the real purpose for which he wanted to see me. He promised to touch upon the real purpose of our interview later. Later meant one and a half hours afterwards.

I could see toward the end of his monologue that he was picking up a thread of thought which would give him a chance to evoke from me an expression of my view as to whether I identified God with the social phenomena of life, or believed in the reality of transcendent Being apart from such phenomena. I made my position clear to him that while I believed in God as a transcendent Being I could not conceive of that Being having any meaning for us except through and in terms of human experience. The more real and immediate such experience is of the realities of life the more can we appreciate the spiritual values that signify God. The experience of reality is, in my opinion, as essential to experiencing God as the harp is for the production of music. The music is not evolved out of the harp but is conditioned by it. So our appreciation of the reality of God is not evolved out of our every day experience but conditioned by it.

At that point in the conversation—for such it became by this time—he asked his wife to leave the room as he had to take up with me a confidential matter. He then came out with the question whether I was ready, as Morgenstern had intimated to him, to become a member of the Hebrew Union College Faculty if I received an invitation to some chair in that college. I explained my situation to him in the same terms I had to Morganstern. "I could go on working unhampered at the Seminary," I said, "but I feel that the Seminary was not altogether happy about my views on Judaism. I wanted, therefore, a more congenial atmosphere, and thought that in view of the presentations made to me by Dr. Idelsohn I might find it in the Hebrew Union College."

He then told me that when he was in Cincinnati a week ago on the occasion of the fiftieth anniversary,[27] Morganstern told Schulman about the interview he had had with me at the Pennsylvania Hotel, and he asked Schulman what he thought of the idea of my going on the Faculty. Schulman told him that he thought very highly of me, but that he wanted to have a talk with me before he would express himself as to the advisability of inviting me to the College.

As a result of our conversation Schulman was satisfied as he said that I "could bring a great deal of Jewishness to the College" and that from the standpoint of outlook upon Judaism I was perfectly satisfactory. He didn't state the latter part of his impression, but I could easily see that was in his mind. The main question into which the last part of our interview turned was the name to be given to the course. He of his own accord suggested that it be designated a course on the Philosophy of Judaism. That name had my hearty approval. A difficulty suggested itself in view of there being at present a chair in Jewish Theology occupied by Cohon.[28] The question was how to avoid trespassing on his field. The matter was left in abeyance. He thought it could easily be straightened out. Toward the end he promised he would write to Morgenstern the coming Wednesday. I left him at 6:50.

Lack of Faith among Seminary Students

SUNDAY, NOVEMBER 1, 1925

This evening I met for the first time this year a group of Seminary students with whom I am taking up the reading and discussion of books on

---

27. Fiftieth anniversary of the founding of the Hebrew Union College.
28. Samuel S. Cohon (1888–1959), ordained Hebrew Union College; theologian; faculty, Hebrew Union College; editor; helped draft Columbus Platform of 1937.

religion. The book reported on tonight was Shotwell's *Religious Revolution.*[29] Goldman gave a summary and criticism of it. The greater part of the session however was spent in the discussion of the indifference displayed by the students toward the problem of religion as such. Of the ten men that were present the majority admitted that they can't pray, that the term God is empty of content for them. They see in the ministry nothing but an occasion for preaching nationalism and social service. I was terribly upset by this failure.

To Go to HUC or Not to Go

SUNDAY, NOVEMBER 22, 1925
Dr. Schulman told me that he had written to Morgenstern that in view of the friendly relations between himself and the two seminaries, he was not in a position to make any recommendations that might be prejudicial to the interests of the Seminary. He accordingly confined himself to an objective description of what he regarded as my qualifications. From what I could gather he gave Morgenstern quite an accurate account of my views on the Bible, God, Israel, etc. He made it clear to Morgenstern that the impression that I had weakened on my nationalism and that I had lost interest in the SAJ was unfounded. Personally Schulman told me that if I would make up my mind to go to Cincinnati I would revolutionize the HUC. Nevertheless he warned me that I must be prepared for a great deal of unpleasantness. A man like Philipson,[30] if he would understand me (by this statement S. meant to imply that Ph. was not over intelligent) and would realize how intense a nationalist I was would go up in the air.

Kaplan and Hebrew Union College—Scene II

TUESDAY, DECEMBER 15, 1925
About two weeks ago I received a letter from Morgenstern which put an end to any illusions I may have entertained of emancipating myself from the spiritually stifling environment of the Seminary. The letter reinforced my fears which I began to harbor ever since I had the interview with Schulman that I would be even more alone and unhappy in the Hebrew Union College than I am here. Morgenstern's letter is quite frank though friendly. He says, "I have very reluctantly come to the conclusion that we are still too far apart in our envisaging of Judaism's problem and in the solution of it which we would offer, to permit me to do that which my own personal feeling makes

---

29. James T. Schotwell, *The Religious Revolution of Today* (Boston: Houghton Mifflin, 1913).

30. David Philipson (1862–1949), rabbi; Reform Jewish leader; faculty, Hebrew Union College; active anti-Zionist.

no desire strongly to do." That conclusion, he says, he arrived at after having carefully read the little book which I published last year. *A New Approach to the Problem of Judaism* pub. by the SAJ.[31]

Dedication of the SAJ and the Thirteen Wants[32]

THURSDAY, FEBRUARY 18, 1926

On the occasion of the dedication of the new quarters of the SAJ at 13–15 W. 86 St I formulated the principles of the SAJ in terms of thirteen "wants." My purpose in those principles is to convey that at the present time it is impossible to agree upon abstract principles, but it is possible to agree as to what differences in our lives the fact of being Jews should make. I believe that stating the principles of Judaism in that way should prove an excellent means of transferring the interest from something that can no longer function to something that can. Beliefs cannot function as a means of Jewish unity. Let us, however, learn to make demands upon Jewish unity and Jewish unity will be strengthened through the effort to have it meet those demands.

God as the Living Universe

THURSDAY, FEBRUARY 18, 1926

The work at the Seminary this year has given me an opportunity to organize more clearly my conception of God. I find myself at present believing in God as the Living Universe. The evil in the world is due to chance, which is as necessary to reality as the negative is necessary to the positive. Is God finite or infinite? The question is either meaningless or irrelevant. God is all that there is. God grows and can never attain the limit of his growth for there is nothing to limit that. Growth means invading the domain (if such it may be called) of non-being.

It appears to me that God feels with infinitely greater keenness whatever of evil there is in the world, for the more life or mind the more pain. Why should the fact that God suffers in any way prevent me from trusting in him? Would the infant when sick be justified in not looking to its mother for help if it were to know that its mother suffers more keenly than it does?

---

31. Reprinted under title *A New Approach to Jewish Life* (Bridgeport: Hartmore House, 1973).

32. The Thirteen Wants can be found in the 1945 Reconstructionist *Sabbath Prayerbook*, ed. Mordecai M. Kaplan and Eugene Kohn (New York: The Jewish Reconstructionist Foundation, 1945). The "Wants" are entitled "Criterion of Jewish Loyalty" and may be found in Hebrew and in English on pages 562–63.

The group of about fifteen who have been coming every other week to my house and with whom I have been reading "Hocking"[33] as a result of the discussions seem to become imbued with an appreciation of what the rabbinate should mean.

Conversion—Accepting Women as Witnesses

MONDAY, FEBRUARY 22, 1926

A certain Miss Ziegler, who is a nurse by profession, came to see me with reference to inducting her into the Jewish faith. She was born a Christian to parents of Pennsylvania Dutch extraction and she is now engaged to be married to a Jewish physician, Dr. Horowitz. She gave as her reason for wanting to become a Jewess the fact that she realizes that if there are to be children they would have to be given some kind of religious upbringing. In order that there be harmony in the home both father and mother had to be of one mind on the question of religion. Since she sympathized with the Jewish faith, she was willing accept it, and wanted me to proselyte her.

Disinclined as I am to making conversions, not as a matter of principle but simply out of an inborn inertia, I could find no excuse for referring Miss Ziegler to any one else to proselyte her. I therefore gave her certain books to read—Goodman's History of the Jews, Greenstone's on Jewish religion, and Bildersee on Jewish History[34] and told her to come see me again together with Dr. Horowitz. They called last night. From what she said to me the first time I gathered that her fiancé was indifferent whether she accepted the Jewish faith or not. It seems that he was afraid I might resent his attitude, and therefore spoke as though he was very much pleased at what she was doing. He mentioned that an uncle of his who was strictly observant of Jewish practice approved of his marrying this girl since she was willing to accept Judaism. That uncle is using his influence to persuade the doctor's mother to give her full consent to the match.

The doctor told me that he wanted his fiancée to acquire a knowledge of Yiddish. His folks speak Yiddish and he did not want that his fiancee should misgive that anything ill was being said of her in the course of their Yiddish conversation.

---

33. Probably William E. Hocking, *The Meaning of God in Human Experience—A Philosophic Study of Religion* (New Haven, Conn.: Yale University Press, 1912). This was a favorite book of Kaplan's.

34. Paul Goodman, *A History of the Jews* (London: J.M. Dent, 1921); Julius Greenstone, *The Religion of Israel—A Book for Use in Religious Schools and the Home* (Philadelphia: Hebrew Sunday School Society, 1923), many editions; Adele Bildersee, *Jewish History—Jochanan ben Zakkai Through Moses Mendelssohn* (Cincinnati: Union of American Hebrew Congregations, 1920).

This is the second case of conversion that I have had in the course of my rabbinic experience. The first case occurred during my ministry at the Jewish Center. Drs. Kotkov and Jacob Kohn together with me constituted a Beth Din [rabbinical court]. The immersion took place in the pool of the Center. In order to conform to the letter of the law that two men witnesses must testify to the immersion, the young woman was garbed in a loose bathing suit. This time I expect to accept the testimony of women witnesses. I am not certain that I shall get two rabbis to act as a Beth din on these terms.[35]

Talking about God with Alice Seligsberg[36]

THURSDAY, FEBRUARY 25, 1926

Last Monday Miss Alice L. Seligsberg called to discuss the following questions:

"Desire for belief in—but inability to believe in—mercy as an attribute of God.

Overwhelming consciousness of the cruelties of God and man toward man and helpless animals.

Question whether there is any way of righting oneself with one's own sense of justice; and of making one's love of mankind sincere to the utmost degree."

These questions gave me an opportunity to test out my latest formulation of the God idea. Miss Seligsberg is a social worker, highly intelligent and beyond middle age in years. In her younger years she was a follower of Felix Adler's but Zionism brought her back to Judaism.

I explained to her that we must give up the habit of thinking of God as a being—absolute, perfect, omnipotent—standing outside of the universe. God is the universe viewed as a living organic reality. As the living universe God is infinitely more susceptible to pain and suffering than any of its infinitesimal elements. The evil is simply the imperfection of the universe. It is nobody's fault. The universe is not so perfect or so potent as to have averted the evil which is simply the product of its own shortcoming plus the negative effect of chance. I gave her the analogy of the child and mother. It occurs to me that I might have added that the child no doubt at first thinks of its mother as all-powerful. When it is disillusioned it does not cease loving or appealing to its mother for help when in need. Why then should we cease turning in love and prayer to the Life and soul of the

---

35. According to rabbinic law, women were not accepted as witnesses.

36. Alice Seligsberg (1873–1940), B.A., Barnard; Zionist leader; social worker; writer; national president, Hadassah.

universe, so as to feel that we are not alone in an empty wilderness, so as to make some of the strength that upholds the universe part of ourselves.

Miss Seligsberg went away much comforted.

Purim—Kaplan as the Grand Koogle Does the Charleston

WEDNESDAY, MARCH 3, 1926

For the first time in years I really enjoyed myself on Purim. The fact that I had gotten through satisfactorily with my sermon (the seventh of the series on the "Thirteen Wants") on Saturday morning and that I had no classes the day following at the Institute on account of the Purim festival made it possible for me to enter into the spirit of the day. I did something I had never done before. I masked at the SAJ masquerade given on Saturday night. At Judith's suggestion I wore the uniform of the KKK. On the hood I had a Mogen David instead of a cross. In it I had three "kofs"[37] over the chest I had in red letter Grand Koogle. Although a few had a suspicion that it was I who was masked as a KKK, they were thrown off their guard when I Charlestoned down the room once or twice. I was even awarded a prize, a silver pencil. This tomfoolery went off without impairing my dignity in the least, even in the estimate of my friends who are overzealous of the proprieties touching my person.

God as Mystery—Questions from Rabbinical Students

WEDNESDAY, MARCH 3, 1926

This morning I took occasion to answer some of the questions contained in the work handed in weekly by the Seminary students on the lectures I give this year in Homiletics. I am lecturing on the pragmatic interpretations of some of the outstanding attributes of God. The questions which I tried to answer were brutally frank in their spirit of negation. One man asked "Why appeal to people to do their duty on the ground of a belief in God? Why not appeal on the basis of the mere worthwhileness of life?" Another man asked "Why should we be grateful for the forces in society that make for our happiness when those forces operate that way unintentionally?"

In my answer I had occasion to make the following points:

1. God in his essence is transcendent. As such he represents the mystery which we cannot help sensing behind the phenomena of the cosmos. Through his attributes, however, he is immanent. The ethical implications of religion are derived from God as immanent.

---

37. Letter of the Hebrew alphabet that has the K sound.

2. The attributes of God are simply aspects of reality which are inferred from the attitude of worthwhileness with which we face life, when we face it in a spirit of religion and moral responsibility.
3. The so called ethical inferences from these attributes are not inferences in the logical sense, for then they would not be known before the premises from which they are inferred. As a matter of fact these ethical inferences are nothing more than the implications of the attributes stated explicitly. How little they are inferences in the logical sense may be seen from the fact that they may serve in the capacity of premises. For example, the sense of responsibility may be treated as the premise whence we derive the notion of God as helper. That is what Kant has done in making the sense of duty the sole proof for the existence of God.
4. Both the premises and the inferences in our discourse of God are merely implications not of intellectual statements of fact but of affirmative acts of the will.

The Prophetic Mood versus the Rabbinic Mood

TUESDAY, MARCH 9, 1926

In my sermon last Sabbath I voiced the inner conflict under which I am laboring. Very few in the audience, I suppose, suspected that fact. I contrasted the prophetic mood with the rabbinic mood as expressed in the respective attitudes toward Israel on the part of the prophets and of the Rabbis. Moses, Elijah, Isaiah were very ready with their resignations. They despaired of Israel. The Rabbis glorified Israel and condemned the prophets for the lack of faith in Israel. When Elijah came to Horeb he handed in his resignation to God. The Rabbis characterized him as an informer for telling God that Israel destroyed his altars and killed his priests.

Which is the more ethical and spiritual course to follow? That is the problem with which I am forever wrestling.

Kaplan Meets H. N. Bialik and N. Sokolow

TUESDAY, MARCH 9, 1926

Today's meeting of the Trustees of the Matz Foundation[38] had an element of unusual interest due to the presence of Bialik, the great Jewish national poet, and Sokolow, the greatest Hebrew publicist. Bialik's talk savors of the poetic though in appearance he is very commonplace. Sokolow is an

---

38. The Matz Foundation for the support of Hebrew authors was founded by Israel Matz (1869–1950), a philanthropist who founded the Ex-Lax company. Kaplan was a member of the foundation board.

inexhaustible fountain of causerie and wit. Bialik not only recognized me but recalled distinctly having met me in Jerusalem as well as in Tel Aviv. For the moment I thought he had made a mistake, then I recalled having met him at the reception given by Herbert Samuel[39] on the eve of the opening of the [Hebrew] University. Sokolow seemed hurt that I had not come to see him in all the weeks that he had been here. He is leaving for Africa in three days. He is certainly a marvelous man. Among great nations he would have figured as one of the great makers of history. Among us, especially here in America, he is hardly understood, much less appreciated. When I think of H. L. Simmons turning up his nose at the suggestion I made a couple of weeks ago that Sokolow be met by some of our people, I say to myself "What a stupid people our Jews are. They don't deserve a man like Sokolow. Give them some leather lunged mouthing orator who talks well with the Goyim, [non-Jews] but who otherwise has not an original idea in his head, and they will dance around him as our ancestors did around the golden calf."

Kaplan Offered the Position as Head of Education in Palestine

THURSDAY, MARCH 11, 1926

This afternoon I called on Sokolow. His daughter was present and later Van Vriesland[40] turned up. Van Vriesland alluded to the fact that the educational work in Palestine was still without a head, and asked me whether I was at all desirous of coming to Palestine to take charge of the schools under the auspices of the Zionist Organization.

The conversation was entirely in Hebrew. Sokolow showed himself very friendly and even deferential to a degree that embarrassed me, as when he insisted upon helping me with my coat.

Rav Tzair Agrees with Kaplan

TUESDAY, MARCH 16, 1926

Dr. Tschernowitz (Rav Tzair)[41] called on me last Saturday night. We spent about three hours discussing the question as to the next step in Judaism. I naturally find him congenial because he takes the same attitude toward Judaism as I do, so that I do not have to go over the same ground with him as I have to do with those who are either too orthodox or too radical

---

39. Herbert Samuel (1870–1963), British statesman and philosopher; first Jew in the Cabinet; high commissioner for Palestine, 1920–25.

40. Siegfried Van Vriesland (1886–1939), Zionist leader and executive; Dutch; lawyer; settled in Palestine in 1919.

41. Chaim Tchernowitz (pseud. Rav Za'ir) (1871–1949), Ph.D., Talmud scholar; Hebrew author; Zionist; faculty, Jewish Institute of Religion; editor, Bizaron.

to see any need for reconstructing Judaism. He frankly denies (to me at least) any belief in *Torah min ha-shamayim* [Heb. divine origin of the Torah] and follows me a long way in my theory that the ritual practices cannot be continued in the legalistic spirit in which they have been observed hitherto. I believe that they must be converted into folkways, and very much developed and enriched both in content and in symbolic significance.

I am sorry for Tschernowitz personally. He is in Wise's JIR where the atmosphere is entirely too unJewish for him to feel at home. In addition Dr. Obermann[42] is unfriendly toward him. Obermann, I was told, hates the Talmud and would like to remove it from the curriculum. (This is on the authority of Dr. Kohut.)

Cecil Roth Calls on Kaplan

MONDAY, MARCH 22, 1926

Last Wednesday Dr. Cecil Roth[43] called. He is a young scholar from England who is specializing in medieval Jewish history, particularly Italian. He probably learned about me from George Hyman[44] who must have told him of my efforts to interpret Judaism as a civilization. Not long ago at one of the Menorah[45] journal dinners Roth happened to make the statement that Judaism wasn't a religion but a civilization. It was that fact probably which led George Hyman to call his attention to my endeavors.

I tried to draw out from Roth what in the course of his studies of Jewish medieval history did he find in the Judaism of the Middle Ages that might help us in meeting the problem of Judaism at the present time. He was unable to point to any specific method or principle or world outlook of that time as still valid for us. The mere fact that Judaism functioned then as a civilization was to him all sufficient. I contended that if the Jewish Middle Ages are to live in the soul of the Jew they ought to yield some fundamental value or values analogous to those of the prophetic age. Dubnow[46] tries to elicit a value of that kind when he proposes martyrdom for a civilization as the outstanding trait of the Middle Ages (cf. his philosophy of Jewish History). To me there is nothing distinctively Jewish in martyrdom, nor anything helpful as far as our present day problem is concerned.

---

42. Julian Obermann (1888–1956), orientalist; faculty, University of Hamburg; Jewish Institute of Religion; director, Judaica Research (Yale).

43. Cecil Roth (1899–1970), prominent Jewish historian; editor, *Encyclopedia Judaica*; prolific author; English.

44. George Hyman (1900–1936), communal, social, and educational leader; executive director, Central Jewish Institute, New York City.

45. On the *Menorah Journal* and Menorah Society, see above, February 12, 1914.

46. Simon Dubnow (1860–1940), historian; wrote ten-volume universal history of the Jewish people, emphasizing social factors.

I also suggested to him to find out to what extent otherworldliness characterized the outlook of the average Jewish layman of the Middle Ages. He had never thought of otherworldliness as the all dominant motif of medieval Judaism.

On the whole I enjoyed the two hours or so of conversation with him. Like so many other visitors the large number of Jews one sees here and the hubbub of Jewish organized [life] give him the illusion of an active if not promising Jewish life. Would that it were so. I know otherwise.

Kaplan's Ambivalence about Jewish Life

Monday, March 22, 1926

It has become clearer to me than ever that I am a veritable Don Quixote. Beguiled by the delusion that I can help to render Judaism permanent, or even temporarily safe, I fight against windmills which always worst me. That is why I am the Knight of the long face, always grumpy, always in bad humor.

The calculation is as simple as an example in subtraction. Any Jew that is worth his salt is engaged either in Palestine Work, Federation, Joint, CJI,[47] Jewish Center of the East Side, Home of Daughters of Jacob, Jewish Education Association and a thousand other organizations. People have to go to a show once in a while too. Business is strenuous. Why should they be expected to take an interest in the SAJ and its purposes? On the other hand, if Jews keep out of all these activities have they a right to call themselves Jews? Do I myself know whether the campaigns, drives and national organizations are upbuilding or destroying Judaism?

The vortex into which I have been drawn in is whirling me about with accelerating speed. I am dizzy. I pray to God to give me strength to tear myself away from this whirlpool to where the river of life runs smooth and straight. The worst of it is that I am at a loss how to bring up my children. The more Jewishness I inculcate in them the more I am drawing them too into their fatal vortex. Today I purposely put into Judith's hands the lengthy debate carried on in the English pages of the Yiddish *Vorverts* concerning the Jewish prospect in Palestine. I am afraid that she too is mesmerized by the romance and tragedy of the Jewish struggle. I want her to think for herself. I thought that the arguments against Zionism would shake her in her faith in Palestine. Instead she seemed as ardent in her faith as before. Of course it is too soon to judge.

---

47. Central Jewish Institute: A social center with an educational structure at its center. Directed CeJwIn Camp. Joseph Schoolman, a friend of Kaplan, was the director for many years.

Ginzberg Fumes over Kaplan Sermon

THURSDAY, MAY 20, 1926

An indication of Ginzberg's attitude towards me—on Sat., April 24 (Heb. Aḥrei mot kedoshim)[48] I preached on Religion vs. Superstition. David Goldstein, a third year student who comes frequently to the SAJ services heard the sermon. When he went to see Ginzberg that same afternoon, Ginzberg asked him where he had attended services as he does most of the students when they come to him. Goldstein told him that he had attended the SAJ services and heard me preach on Religion vs. Superstition. Ginzberg no sooner heard these words from him than he flew into a rage and delivered himself of a diatribe against drawing any distinctions between religion and superstition. The people had too little religion as it was and such talks were bound to deprive them of the little that they had. For half an hour he kept on raving and literally foaming [original has fuming] at the mouth. Rabbi Kadushin was also present. It was Kadushin who first reported this outbreak to me though he did not mention the violent form it took. He did remark, however, that Ginzberg was certainly no friend of mine. Not long after I chanced upon Goldstein and got from him more of what actually happened. Mrs. Ginzberg, rather embarrassed by her husband's conduct, and with a woman's intuition of pretending that the report of it might reach me tried to explain to them that Ginzberg hadn't slept that week for several nights and that his nerves were on edge. This is not the first time that the mention of my name to him was like waving a red flag in front of a bull.

Kaplan and Ginzberg at the Rabbinical Assembly

TUESDAY, JULY 6, 1926

The annual convention of the Rabbinic Assembly took place this year at Long Branch [New Jersey] at the Scarborough Hotel beginning last Wednesday, June 30, and continuing till Friday afternoon. I believe I missed the last three conventions of the Assembly. With the Assembly controlled by such reactionaries as Epstein[49] and Drob[50] these conventions were utilized by Ginzberg and Adler to repress by sarcasm and ridicule all attempts to get away from the beaten path of non-committal Judaism. This year I had

---

48. Kaplan wrote about April 24, 1926, on May 20, 1926. *Ahrey Mot Kedoshim* refers to the Torah section of the week. It was Leviticus 16:1–20:27.

49. Louis Epstein (1887–1949), ordained JTS; authority on Jewish law and marriage; president, Rabbinical Assembly.

50. Max Drob (1887–1959), ordained JTS; founder, United Synagogue; president, Rabbinical Assembly.

no excuse for staying away. I was not in Palestine as I was last year, nor did I have tonsillitis, as I did a year or two ago. Besides, I did not want it to become an established tradition that I kept aloof from the councils of the Seminary graduates. If the idea that I was a sorehead should come to prevail I would be playing into Ginzberg's hands. In fact, unfriendly as I know Ginzberg to be toward me, I am now trying to draw the teeth of his hostility by seeking to conciliate him. Despite the diatribe that he delivered against me in the hearing of R. Kadushin and the student David Goldstein I visited him during the week before I knew I would have to meet him at Long Branch. In fact I went so far as to tell him that I would deem it a favor if he would help me with the work I am doing on the Rabbinic conception of God. Of course he was glad to be treated as master, and promised to guide me in the work.

I can well understand why Ginzberg should feel hostile toward me. He cannot help realizing that if not for me he would have had the undivided allegiance of the graduates. If not for my encouraging the majority of them to insurgency against the policy of invasion he would have had his way with them in intimidating them into a slavish fear of rabbinic law, and here comes along Kaplan who hasn't any pretensions even to Jewish scholarship and tries to overthrow his authority and influence. Yet I can't see how I can act otherwise. My heart bleeds as I think of the tremendous opportunity that Ginzberg has had to put new life into Judaism, an opportunity that he abandoned simply out of some underlying selfishness or perversity which I have never been able to fathom. With the vast fund of Jewish and general learning at his command he could afford to be intellectually honest. Instead he uses his very cleverness to befuddle the minds of the students and to foster in them a cynicism and intellectual dishonesty.

On my way to Long Branch I found myself in the same seat with R. Benjamin Cohen[51] who is assistant librarian to Marx. I tried in vain to persuade Cohen that the policy of evasion in Jewish belief and practice was doing Judaism a world of harm. But he seems to have fallen victim to the Marx-Ginzberg influence. The dust of the books that he continually handles is beginning to settle on his soul. I realized that it was futile for me to get him as an ally. He told me however a bit of interesting information about Schechter which I am going to note down. Marx had told him that when Schechter came to this country and assumed the presidency of the Seminary he was about to draw up a platform which would set forth his conception of Conservative Judaism. In that platform he intended to state clearly wherein he differed from those who professed either Orthodoxy or Reform. But he

---

51. Later known as Boaz Cohen (1899–1968), ordained JTS; Ph.D. Columbia; rabbinic scholar; librarian; faculty, JTS.

was strongly advised by Adler and the late Judge Sulzberger[52] against coming out with such statements, on the ground that he would be sure to alienate the Orthodox Jews.

As usual instead of beginning at the time scheduled—10:30 in the morning, the Convention opened after lunch about two in the afternoon. Ginzberg was introduced as the first speaker to deliver an address of greeting. He spoke from 2:15 to 3:35. I can't help saying that he gets on my nerves, with his patronizing air, satirical side thrusts and medley of sophistries with which he dazzles the half awake minds of the majority of his listeners. There is no illuminating truth, there is no flash of genuine wit, there is no spiritual passion or fiery indignation in anything that he utters. Thinly covered pretense of humility, affected nonchalance to give the impression of indifference to what you think about him, caustic ridicule and occasionally a splutter like that of wetted fire crackers in the process of exploding. These are the varying moods of his talks. Every time he delivers one of these addresses I have the feeling that I heard him say these things and tell those stories time without number. Every other sentence is sure to have in it the word historical. He usually starts out with a long introduction about his having run for the train and having stopped on the way to join a crowd that had gathered because of an automobile accident and the policeman saying Damn it, if the man who drove the car had not gone to the right or to the left, but had kept straight ahead of him the accident wouldn't have happened. (I swear that I heard him tell this story once before as having happened to him.)

Then comes, of course, the rabbinic passage about avoiding the path of fire and the path of ice, etc. Then a jab at Adler by claiming to see no reason why he should be asked to greet the assembly since he is neither president nor dean. This is followed by some loosely relevant story or two, then the remark that he taught every subject at the Seminary (which means that he should have continued teaching theology) except Homiletics, and we all know why (half joke and half jab at me). This is followed by the statement that he was not prepared to speak, but having noticed in the train that some of the men who were going to the convention took out big manuscripts which they had prepared he thought he too ought to jot down some notes. Accordingly he has to refer to the notes which he hopes he will be able to read—at this point he drops out from a coat pocket large yellow foolscap[53] sheets which he holds with an air of indifference. This performance lasts for half an hour.

---

52. Mayer Sulzberger (1843–1923), jurist, scholar, Hebraist, Philadelphia; organizer of the JTS.

53. Foolscap: here a size of paper.

Then began the talk proper. It dealt with a few principles or rather generalizations concerning the need of judging the worth or truth of tendencies and institutions in the light of the circumstances out of which they arise. It is evident that this method of reasoning lends itself easily to one's purpose to condemn whatever one is prejudiced against, or praise whatever one is in favor of, especially the former. I cannot imagine Ginzberg praising anything. He vented his spleen against the objects of his hatred by subsuming each such object under some generalization to which he gave the air of a newly discovered truth. He did not fail to find some historical principle to put me in the wrong; and he also found another such principle to express his opposition to Adler's plan to combine the Seminary work with the Yeshiva. In the main he contended that rationalism was good in the days of Saadia,[54] and mysticism in the thirteenth century and nationalism in the prophetic period; the only implication that one could draw from his address was that at the present time rationalism and mysticism and nationalism are out of place. What is in place he left me and others like me guessing.

WEDNESDAY, JULY 7, 1926

After Ginzberg's address Levitsky[55] and Arzt read papers on the methods of organizing and holding adult study groups. The discussion of those papers was then thrown open to the floor. I happened to go out for a short while to answer a telephone. When I came back Epstein, who was in the chair, called upon me to express my opinion of the matter before the convention. I am at my worst when taken unawares. I proved it by making a stupid remark about my not having been asked in time to formulate any ideas on the subject. At this point Drob snapped back that I had been asked through Kadushin to read a paper on any subject I chose but that I had refused. The discussion proceeded. Jacob Kohn could not go on, it seems, with what he had to say without referring to the fact that although he had not been prepared to speak on the subject he had some suggestions to make. Seeing that I had to extricate myself from the thunder that I had made I asked the privilege of the floor to explain that I had misunderstood the purport of the discussion. My impression was not that each one was to give an account of his own experiences, but to express what general ideas he had on the subject of adult education. I felt that more important by far than the question of technique is that of the content of study. Lacking as we do such content due to our tendency to be satisfied with the archaeological viewpoint and to our failure to relate Judaism of the past

---

54. Saadya (Ben Joseph) Gaon (882–942), greatest scholar and author of his time; philosopher; leader of Babylonian Jewry.
55. Louis Levitsky (1897–1975), ordained JTS; president, Rabbinical Assembly; author.

to life of the present all efforts at perfecting our technique are mere gestures in the void.

It is evident that subconsciously or semi-consciously I was trying to get even with Ginzberg who seems to have become an obsession with me as I have with him.

Self-Doubt—Kaplan Muses on His Education and Ability

MONDAY, AUGUST 9, 1926

This is the first time that I am writing in this diary, early in the morning, even before saying my prayers—and a Monday morning at that. Behind my doing this peculiar thing there is the mental struggle that has been going on for years and that at times reaches an acute point. It is the struggle for self-expression by means of the written word. I remember as a small boy always looking up with admiration to any one who had the gift for writing. Lewis N. Dembitz[56] was at that time a visitor to our house. From what I know now, he was little more than a semi-educated moron. He used to write some stupid squibs for children. The thought of his having his ideas in print made me look up to him as to a great man and I used often to ask him whether he expected to write books.

But unfortunately although I had this urge to self expression there was nothing in my home atmosphere to stimulate, nor did any of the schools or even the college I attended afford me the least stimulus and direction. As a matter of fact I consider myself extremely unfortunate in the kind of so called higher education that I am supposed to have received. My years of adolescence were practically wasted, although I worked rather hard those years in cramming text for the classroom in City College and for the chronic examinations. But there was not one teacher among all the thirty-five or forty who taught me there that took the slightest interest in my mental development. All that they did was to assign so many pages of text to be gone over and next day they would make sure whether I knew it, not for the purpose of helping me in case I did not know it, but simply to make me. Very often I was given text that with all that I tried to understand it, simply eluded me. That was the case when in my Junior year I was given Dewey's psychology. I had not the least idea what it was all about. They had a young fellow just graduated from college teach it. I dreaded his hour for fear that he would call on me. I lived in fear all of that year. The same was practically true with Economics. They gave us a thin dry little text book and a fat professor named McNulty whom we nicknamed McBulky. The only redeeming feature in his case was that he seldom called on the students

---

56. Lewis N. Dembitz (1833–1907), lawyer; scholar; communal and civic leader; author; helped establish JTS.

but just wasted the hour palavering. Another source of dread to me was Geology. The man who taught it was Stratford, a big tall strapping man, broad-shouldered, heavy face and Kaiser Wilhelm mustache. The class met in the large anatomy hall or museum. I sat way back in the room in order not to be called on and the professor stood on the platform and in a thin little voice mumbled things that I assumed had some reference to the daily assignment. Then all of a sudden he would call on some one, the student said something, the professor nodded his head, raised his hand as though he were taking an oath in court, wrote down some mark on the list of names before him and proceeded mumbling until he called on the next one, and so on. Once a month my turn came. The subject, much as I would have loved to understand it, was a total mystery to me. I would simply repeat something from the daily assignment as a matter of wild guess. Physics I was so fond of that I managed to understand some of the facts mentioned in the book; and the man who lectured on it—mind you *lectured* on it—was somewhat human. He was a little old wizened man but with a fine spiritual face, way in the seventies, teaching a class of about fifty young fellows at a time. I was one of the fifty in the far end of the room, though there I often did want to sit in front to gaze admiringly at the instruments on the instructor's desk.

I hated City College then, and I hate it still for having robbed me of my best years. Of course that is totally unreasonable on my part, but when one feels as I do the consequences of an institution failing in its supposed task of educating the young, one cannot but recall the words in Proverbs "Arur oseh melekhet 'd remi'ah" [Heb. Jeremiah 48:10 "Cursed is he who is slack in doing the Lord's Work"].[57] And during those miserable years I attended the Seminary whose faculty consisted—as far as I was concerned—of Speaker,[58] Drachman,[59] Joffe,[60] each more or less of a moron. I learned practically nothing. I recall distinctly the feeling of having forgotten the little knowledge of Talmud and Bible I had come with. The former I had acquired from Father and the *Yeshivat eits hayim* [Heb. Yeshivat Etz Hayim][61] and the latter from a private teacher, Allen, who used to teach me two hours

---

57. A favorite verse of Kaplan's (see also entry for April 21, 1921). Here Kaplan mistakenly noted the source as Proverbs.

58. Henry Speaker (1868–1935), ordained JTS; educator; author; prinicpal, Gratz College, Philadelphia.

59. Bernard Drachman (1861–1945), ordained JTS (Breslau), Conservative leader; educator; author; founder, JTS, New York City.

60. Joshua Joffe (1862–1935), Talmudic scholar; rabbi; faculty, old JTS. Joffe lived at the old Seminary where Kaplan was one of the dormitory students. For more information, see *Judaism Faces the Twentieth Century: A Biography of Mordecai M. Kaplan* (Detroit: Wayne State University Press, 1993).

61. This is the elementary Yeshiva which Kaplan attended on the Lower East Side. It later became part of Rabbi Isaac Elhanan Theological Seminary.

a day and about four to five times a week for the munificent sum of four dollars a month. Father was then earning forty dollars a month. We were a family of four.

(At this point I had to interrupt my tale of woe to eat breakfast.)

Kaplan Helps out Recent JTS Graduates with Holiday Sermons

SEPTEMBER 12, 1926

Beginning Tuesday, Aug. 19, I met a number of the Seminary students and recent graduates in session several times to discuss the sermons for the high holidays. About twenty men attended each of the sessions. They seemed to find my suggestions helpful. I gave them as the main theme for Rosh Hashanah—Self-criticism, and for Yom Kippur—the Need of Standards in Jewish Life. I did not work out the sermons in detail. Preaching on these subjects myself I found I had a good deal of work to do on them. There is another source of discontent—preaching. Whenever I measure the results by the amount of time and effort expended on the sermons I become thoroughly disheartened. If I worked hard during the last two summers I have at least something to show for that work but of all the effort that I put into sermonizing there is hardly a page that I would consider worth while publishing. It seems that all of the energy goes into working myself into a mood wherein I can overcome the sense of doubt and the pain of self-repression. It takes much longer to achieve a mood which at best lasts about an hour or two than to formulate an idea which may have permanent value.

I am often thrown into a fit of anger when I see the SAJ building. The ugliness of the structure and utter indifference of the members have made the SAJ House to me a Heartbreak House.

Kaplan Seeks Ginzberg's Advice

SEPTEMBER 12, 1926

Last night I visited Ginzberg. Lena went along with me. During the first part of the evening he listened to the small talk between Lena and Ginzberg's wife. He hardly looked at me, and had not a word to say to me. He sat sideways from where I sat so that he shouldn't even feel the necessity of addressing me. But I overlooked his boorishness toward me, because I had come for a purpose. I want his help in the work I am doing on Rabbinic Judaism. While I am aware that a good deal of his scholarship is full of flaws and sophistries, yet I appreciate that his learning is so vast that he can well afford to be guilty of many an intellectual misdemeanor. Moreover, in the awful loneliness in which I find myself I am ready to embrace even a porcupine of an individual like Ginzberg if he only wouldn't stick his needles into my flesh.

After half an hour of listening to Mrs. Ginzberg's palaver I asked Ginzberg to take me into the library. There, after some questions on one of his notes in Vol. V of his Legends, I mentioned that I had with me the outline of work that I was doing in the concepts of God, Israel and Torah. I then took out my notebook and read to him parts of what I had written.[62] He seemed to be well impressed. On one point in particular I found that I had more exact knowledge than he did, and by no means an unimportant point at that, viz. The relation of *Yemot ha-Mashiah* [Heb. Days of the Messiah] to *Olam ha-Bah* [Heb. World to Come]. He first maintained that they were identical and tried to prove it by saying that the manna[63] was promised for the *Yemot ha-Mashiah*. I said at once that the manna was promised for *Olam ha-Bah* because the messianic era and the world to come were different, and phenomena of a supernatural character could take place only in the world to come. When he looked up the passage in the Mekilta[64] he saw that I was right.

Gloomy over Lack of Achievement

SEPTEMBER 25, 1926

On Tuesday, Sept. 21, I concluded 40 hours of instruction at the Training School for Jewish Social Workers. The ground covered extends as far as the Rabbinic conception of Israel. It is the one piece of work from which I get most satisfaction. On the other hand it serves to accentuate the undue proportion of time and effort I spend on the SAJ to the detriment of more permanent work that I might do by myself. Hurwitz and Cohen of the Menorah Journal have read what I have written on Orthodox and Reform Jewry and they found the material to be just what they want for the Journal.[65] I would have to write two more articles, one on the traditional conception and one on the proposed reconstruction to make it worth while for me to air my views again in the *Menorah* as I did some ten or eleven years ago.[66] But somehow I am thwarted by the tasks at the SAJ. The consequence was that

---

62. For a detailed discussion of this session with Ginzberg, see *Judaism Faces the Twentieth Century*, 222, where I discuss the Talmudic issue about which Kaplan and G. were talking. Ginzberg was a greater Talmudic scholar than Kaplan, hence Kaplan's pleasure at being "right" here.

63. Miraculous food which appeared during the sojourn in the desert.

64. The *Mekilta* is a midrashic commentary on Exodus. Kaplan does not mention the passage, but the one he looked up is probably *Mekilta-de-R. Ishmael*, ed. Jacob Z. Lauterbach, (Philadelphia: The Jewish Publication Society, 1949), Massekhta Vayassah, vol. 2, chap. 5, 119.

65. See Kaplan's article, "Toward a Reconstruction of Judaism" *Menorah Journal* 13 (April 1927): 113–30.

66. For complete bibliographical information on the early articles in the *Menorah Journal*, see Emanuel Goldsmith, Mel Scult, and Robert Seltzer, *The American Judaism of Mordecai Kaplan* (New York: New York University Press, 1990), 416.

the last few weeks I have been very gloomy. The only thing that prevented me from giving in altogether too much to self-pity was the theme I had to preach on during Succoth, namely, gratitude. I could not help realizing the spiritual value of gratitude which, as I thought about it, came to mean to me the art of discovering the good in every situation in life. Certainly I have enough to be grateful for, despite my inability to achieve certain literary and scholarly ambitions that I cherish.

Unhappy with Holiday Sermons

SATURDAY NIGHT, OCTOBER 2, 1926
I've been through hell again these last few days. Having done a little work on my "Reconstruction" during the week of Hol-Hamoed,[67] I was unable to give sufficient time to the Sh'mini Azereth[68] sermon. The result was a half digested idea on Public Worship. If everything had gone right that morning I might have gotten away with it. But I was physically on edge. In addition some women came and sat down in front just as I was beginning to speak. Before I plodded through about four sentences a barrel organ began to play. I could not find the right word for what I wanted to express. Although I managed to work myself into some kind of strained enthusiasm, sweating all the time not only perspiration but blood, I was unhappy that I spoiled what might have been a good sermon.

[Shabbat Bereshit][69]
This morning the attendance dropped down to about 85, as compared with about 225 of Sh'mini Azereth. Again I came but half prepared with a talk on Creation vs. Evolution. My mind kept on working to the last minute before going onto the pulpit. In addition I was debating with myself whether or not I should preach altogether. My mind was torn between fear that I might again preach a poor sermon and the desire to redeem myself. The small attendance militated against my speaking, the fact that I had spent the whole of last night preparing drove me on to speak. In this frame of mind I was up to the time when the congregation was chanting the last verse before the closing ark. I had to make a choice. In one second I could either tell the cantor to resume the service, or I could step into the pulpit. I finally decided for the latter. I made a brave attempt to set forth a most complicated theme before a motley crowd consisting of people of limited understanding. It seemed to have gone clean over their heads, but at least it went.

---

67. The intermediate days of the Festival of Sukkot.
68. Feast of the Solemn Assembly: the eighth day of Sukkot.
69. Sabbath when the reading of the Torah starts over again with the creation story.

Belief in God and Palestine

NOVEMBER 30, 1926, 2:30 A.M.

I have gotten into the habit of working far into the night. The work is piling up more and more and nothing seems to be getting done. It seems to me there is nothing more essential to a feeling of serenity than getting things done. Small tasks, undertakings of limited scope, are therefore more likely to produce a happy and contented disposition than undertakings of vast dimensions. Mine being that of reconstructing Judaism, God knows when I shall begin to see some tractable formulation of the main ideas I wish to set forth, among which are (1) the importance of realizing that religion in the future must mean not subscribing to any definite dogma about God, but an unceasing and strenuous search after God (a vital and active interest in the meaning of God in human experience).[70] To seek God, i.e. to want to know what God is, is more important than to believe in God. (2) The part to be played by Palestine is to be not that of a center radiating influence, but a central project eliciting the interest of the Jew in a common creative task. (3) The substitution of the folkway conception of the ceremonies for the legalistic attitude which is tenable only upon the assumption that they are [not] of divine origin.

Unfortunately there are so many disturbing and distracting duties that prevent me from concentrating all my thought and effort on this the most burning problem in the life of the Jew today, that I have to do all I can to control myself from giving way to the mulligrubs [the blues].

Going to the Theater and Feeling Guilty

DECEMBER 1, 1926, 12:30 A.M.

Tonight as I walked out of the house with Lena to take my usual stroll we met Max and Sarah[71] waiting for a taxi to take them to theatre. I was too weak willed to say no. They took us to a show called "On Approval."[72] It was a comedy farce full of clever repartee enjoyable while one listened to it but soon forgotten. I could ill afford to spend the three hours, and I feel like kicking myself for having yielded. But I am tired and at times I do yearn for a change but not that kind. Unfortunately I do not have the opportunity to enjoy the company of intelligent friends or to take part in scintillating

---

70. The material in parentheses was crossed out.

71. Probably refers to Max Rubin (1875–1955), Kaplan's brother-in-law, who lived next door on West 89th and Central Park West. He worked in textiles. Sara was his wife.

72. On Approval" by Fredrick Lonsdale. A farce concerning English society, "where everyone is too selfishly jaded to humor his neighbor," according to Brooks Atkinson, *New York Times*, October 19, 1926.

conversation. That is why I go to see shows. But every time I come back I swear off seeing another for a long time: but I do not stick to my resolution.

Reorganizing the ZOA

WEDNESDAY, DECEMBER 22, 1926

Last Sunday afternoon Dr. Weizmann asked me to meet him in conference together with Unterberg, Semel, and Judge Rosalsky. Unterberg came but left before I arrived. The conference took place at the Hotel Ambassador. Weizmann unfolded the story of the critical situation which confronted the Zionist movement at the present time, and of the tremendous burden that he had to bear.

Weizmann was mainly interested in getting Rosalsky to accept the chairmanship of the N.Y. campaign for the United Palestine Appeal. Incidentally he was also anxious to have Bernard Semel and Judge Otto Rosalsky undertake to organize the so-called "Baale-Batim" [community leaders] the substantial Jewish business men who were in sympathy with the Zionist movement into a group that might act as a mediatorial body between the Zionist organization and the Marshall group.[73] In fact he alluded to the part we played a few years ago when we tried to mediate between him and the Brandeis group as having put the idea into his head that we might play a similar role at the present time.

Neither Semel nor Rosalsky had anything constructive to suggest. The former merely dwelt upon the rift between the ZOA and the Marshall group. He excused himself from assuming any new responsibilities in view of the manifold communal tasks imposed upon him. Rosalsky spoke in a similar vein. Incidentally I learned of J. H. Cohen's part in preventing the Orthodox Union and Aggudath Ha-rabbonim[74] from being represented at the fiftieth anniversary celebration given to Rosalsky by the Jewish Education Association. At Cohen's instigation these organizations demanded as a condition of their being represented at the celebration the J.E.A. pledge itself to give the Orthodox authority over the educational policy of the Talmud Torah and Religious schools. They were refused, and therefore did not appear at the banquet.

When Weizmann asked for my opinion I said that the only way in which the present situation in the Zionist movement could be saved was

---

73. Louis Marshall, leader of American non-Zionists, was being courted at this time by Weizmann, who wanted to bring the non-Zionists into an enlarged Jewish Agency. By August 1929 Weizmann had succeeded.

74. The rabbinical association of the most traditional among the rabbis in the United States.

by having a sort of business men's council who by their very interest in the movement would impress and impel the attention of the Marshall group. Once that was effected a way would be found for ironing out the differences that have arisen between the ZOA and the Marshall group. I furthermore added that Semel was the only logical man to bring about the organization of such a group.

This suggestion of mine cost me a good deal of time last week. It gave rise to three subsequent conferences and numerous telephone conversations. Semel held out against my and Weizmann's pleadings. At the conference I had with him and Unterberg on Wednesday he suggested Morris Rottenberg.[75] Accordingly another conference was held at Unterberg's home on Thursday night. At this meeting there were present Weizmann, Unterberg, Samuel Rottenberg,[76] Semel, Harry Liebovitz, Albert Rosenblatt[77] and Rosalsky. By that time I had evolved a clearer idea of what I was to advocate. Instead of a Business Men's Council as a mere emergency measure to bridge the gap between the ZOA and the Marshall group I suggested that the Zionist movement be reorganized on entirely new lines from those which characterize it at present. In fact it was this plan to reorganize the entire movement which took up a good deal of my time last week. I had become convinced that the main reason for the Zionist movement failing to make sufficient headway in this country was due largely to the anomalous type of organization. Judging by all types of organization whether it be a peace movement or the JDC [Joint Distribution Committee] the administration consists of business men who in addition to furnishing the resources carry the responsibility for the success of the movement. It seems to be a principle that there can be no continuous taxation without responsibility. In the Zionist movement, however, the ones who first joined it because of its appeal to them have both assumed charge of it and have to earn their livelihood from it. This exposed them to the charge, which in itself is quite unjustified, that they were not and could not be disinterested supporters of the movement. My feeling is that this form of organization is not likely to inspire confidence either in the non-Jewish authorities that have to treat with the sponsors of the movement or with the doubting Thomases among the Jews themselves. A far healthier type of organization would be one in which the men of means would assume charge and make themselves responsible for the administration of

---

75. Probably Morris Rothenberg (1885–1950), lawyer; Zionist leader; city magistrate; national chairman, Palestine Foundation Fund, New York City.

76. Samuel Rottenberg (1873–1958), knitted wear manufacturer; director, Federation of Jewish Charities.

77. Albert Rosenblatt (1872–1944), clothing manufacturer and SAJ member.

the movement, and men like Lipsky Neumann etc. would act in the capacity of executives.

Weizmann recorded my analysis of the evil inherent in the Zionist work at the present time, and approved of the remedy I suggested. Semel presented difficulties in the way of carrying out such a remedy. The others accepted my plan with qualifications. The upshot was that those present organized themselves as a committee primarily to negotiate with Marshall for the purpose of bringing about peace between him and the ZOA and secondarily to further the United Palestine Appeal, and possibly also to look into the possibility of putting the ZOA on a more efficient basis.

Weizmann Tells How He Helped the Orthodox

SATURDAY NIGHT, DECEMBER 25, 1926

    . . . stories [were] told by Weizmann the last time I saw him at the Unterbergs.

    It was toward the end of the war—during the High Holiday season—Weizmann was in Palestine seated in a train that was to take him to Egypt from where he was to go to the Continent. There were two old Austrian Jews with long beards and earlocks. He told them that he was leaving Palestine. "But how can you leave us in the lurch at this time of the year?" they asked. "What is the trouble? What do you refer to?" "Why don't you know that Succoth is coming and there are no *Hadassim*[78] to be had?" "What can I do in the matter?" "We used to get the Hadassim from Trieste. If you would use your influence with Allenby he would see to it that we get them." "But don't you know the English are at war with the Austrians?" That was a revelation to them. When W. came to Alexandria he met Allenby there. The latter showed him a letter he had received from certain Jews in Palestine that he secure *Hadassim* from Trieste. "I can't get them from 'Trieste," said Allenby "but I can remove the quarantine from Egypt and have them sent from here." Those Jews got their *Hadassim*.

Kaplan Decides to Join Wise at the JIR

WEDNESDAY, JANUARY 12, 1927

    The incredible has happened. Wise once again asked me to join the faculty of the JIR. This time I finally said Yes. And this is how it happened. A week ago last Saturday night, Jan. 1, George Kohut called me up on the phone and told me that he had apprised W. of the conversation he had had with me recently, and that I should expect to hear from Wise himself within

---

78. The myrtle, one of the four species of plants tied to the palm frond (Lulav) which is used on Sukkoth.

a day or two. On Monday, Jan. 3, asked me to meet him, Judge Mack and Kohut at his office. W. opened the discussion by telling Mack that he had learned from K. that I was not altogether unreceptive to an invitation from the JIR to join the faculty. I explained why I was willing to consider leaving the Seminary. It was mainly due to my disappointment in finding that the graduates who theoretically were entirely in sympathy with my views showed no inclination to help me in putting them into effect. In the Seminary itself the attitude toward me had not grown in the least bit friendlier. I was therefore prepared to consider accepting W's offer, provided I would not encroach in the teaching of my subject "the philosophy of Judaism" upon the territory of any of the men who are there now. I also wanted to be assured that my position would be secure. The three of them, Wise, Mack and Kohut made it clear to me that they were anxious to have me join their faculty and that they would do everything in their power to meet my wishes in every respect, salary, congeniality and permanence. Mack expressed himself to the effect that he was especially interested in having the JIR produce scholars even more than rabbis and nothing would please him more than if I were to publish and stimulate creative work in the institution.

I went to see W. again the next day (Tues. Jan 4) to have some questions about the position cleared up in my mind. When I left him I felt that I had no right to hesitate any longer about accepting his offer. In the course of the conversation he said to me, "Kaplan you will be the first man on the faculty for whose sake students will join our institution."

Kaplan Resigns from the Seminary

WEDNESDAY, JANUARY 19, 1927

Last Wednesday night at 7:30 Wise called me up to tell me that the Board of Trustees and the Faculty of the JIR voted unanimously to extend the invitation to me to join the faculty. My coming was acclaimed with joy. Next morning Kohut told me the same thing over the phone.

Yesterday I showed Wise a draft of the resignation. He thought it was admirable. Today I mailed it to Adler and a copy of it to Judge Mack at Wise's suggestion. It reads as follows:

"Ever since I have been associated with the Jewish Theological Seminary of America as a member of the Faculty I have been pursuing various studies with the object of formulating a teachable program of Jewish life. In my opinion, neither the Orthodoxy of Samson Raphael Hirsch and Sabato Morais,[79] nor the Reform of Abraham Geiger and Kaufman Kohler,

---

79. Sabato Morais (1823–97), Sephardic rabbi, Philadelphia; founder and first president, JTS; friend of Mazzini.

offers a satisfactory program. But what those leaders proposed has at least the merit of being definite and consistent. It is such definiteness that I have been anxious to find in what is usually called Conservative Judaism.

In my humble way I have worked out a conception of Conservative Judaism to the teaching of which I should now like to devote myself. That conception is based upon the principle that both the national and the religious element in traditional Judaism must be conserved and developed. By omitting either of these elements we are bound to break completely with the Judaism of the past. It is not merely in regard to the rebuilding of Palestine as a Jewish Homeland that Conservative Judaism should differ from Reform, but also in regard to the retention of all that social content and cultural activity which go together with the traditional conception of Israel as a distinct people. Furthermore, Conservative Judaism should also differ radically from Orthodox in being prepared to reckon courageously in all of its educational and religious activities with the established conclusions of comparative religion and Biblical scholarship. Certainly no study of Judaism can call itself scientific which seeks to evade those conclusions.

It was inevitable that some of the ideas which had taken root in my mind should color my teaching both at the Seminary and at the Teachers Institute. This was known to the late Dr. Schechter, and has also been known to you and other members of the Faculty. Though seldom was anything of a disapproving nature said to me on the subject, I could not help but sense a feeling of opposition to the spirit in which I have been teaching. A few years ago, when I published some of my views, and organized the Society for the Renascence[80] of Judaism that opposition bore down on me quite heavily. Since then I have felt it my duty to avoid publishing anything that might embarrass the Seminary.

As a consequence, I have gotten into a state of mind which is by no means conducive to such creative work as I should like to do in the field of Judaism. Yet I cannot reconcile myself to a policy of drift. Being passive at the present time is not a case of letting well enough alone. In my opinion, the condition of so-called Conservative Judaism is far from being well enough. That a Conservative Jew is one who has ceased being Orthodox, but has not yet become Reform, though said in jest, is largely true to fact. It is high time that some steps be taken to develop the theoretic and practical implications of Conservative Judaism. My usefulness, however, in that capacity is bound to be curtailed unless I be free to voice my opinions concerning the spiritual

---

80. The Society for Jewish Renascence was organized by Kaplan in 1919 in order to formulate a progressive program and to implement it. It lasted two years. The members were mainly rabbis and scholars from the New York area. The Society published a list of its principles, which can be found in *Judaism Faces the Twentieth Century*, 185–86.

needs of Jewish life, without continually having in mind that I might be jeopardizing the interests of the Seminary.

In view of all this, I deem it advisable to tender my resignation from the Seminary both as a professor of Homiletics and Principal of the Teachers Institute, the resignation to go into effect at the end of the academic year, or at the pleasure of the Board of Trustees.

I am deeply appreciative of all that I owe to the Seminary and it is my heartfelt prayer that its future be glorious and blessed. I shall always be grateful to you and the other members of the Faculty for the courtesies and good will shown me during all the years I have been at the Seminary. Though we may differ in our views, I hope that I shall always deserve your confidence in my sincerity and devotion to the cause of Judaism."

Kaplan Withdraws His Resignation

WEDNESDAY, FEBRUARY 23, 1927

Events moved pretty fast last week. The Executive Committee of the Rabbinical Assembly bestirred itself and sent out notices for a meeting to consider a "serious situation which had arisen in the Seminary." The meeting took place last Thursday and they unanimously adopted a resolution that they would do everything within reason to prevent my severing connections with the Seminary. They lived up to that resolution. Right after the meeting they came in a body to ask me to withdraw the resignation. I took into consideration the fact that after all it was a composite statement representing views of men who were motivated by conflicting reasons for asking me to remain in the Seminary. Like all such composite statements it was bound to be weak. That the Executive Committee should take a hand in the matter altogether, and that men like Drob and Jacob Kohn should come to see me, the latter actually having come three times within three days, was the most that I could ever have a right to expect. The only argument that had any weight with me was the one used by Simon Greenberg to the effect that if I went to the JIR the liberal forces in the Seminary clientele would become demoralized, since they could not possibly follow me to Wise's Institute. Their resolution was forwarded to Adler.

On Saturday I received a copy of a letter signed by the students of the Seminary which had been sent to Adler. That letter had teeth to it. In fact I considered it a bit impudent. It had evidently been composed by Henry Rosenthal[81] who can write in vitriolic style. I felt compelled to call him up and ask him to tone down one paragraph in particular.

---

81. Henry Rosenthal (1906–77), ordained JTS; author; faculty, Hunter College; philosopher. A favorite of Kaplan's.

Last night the Seminary Board met. Adler did not present my resignation but had decided to confer with me. This morning when I came to the Seminary he asked me through Finkelstein to see him today. I met him this afternoon. The conference lasted nearly two hours. He began by saying that he had received word from the alumni that I was ready to withdraw my resignation. I replied that my action depended upon the result of our conference. He then took up my two letters point by point. He certainly showed a decided tendency to yield though he tried to keep up a bold front. The main points of interest are the following:

1. He tried to question my statement about there being established conclusions of biblical scholarship and comparative religion. I told him that in my opinion there was no disagreement among biblical scholars as to the non-Mosaic authorship of the Torah, nor among scholars of religion that there was no possibility of a pure monotheism having existed in the days of Moses. While non-committal himself, he said that there was room in the traditional conception of Judaism for both of these negations. Of course I disagreed with him emphatically.

2. He agreed with what I said in the second letter that in my opinion the Seminary was not committed to either Orthodoxy or Conservatism but to a maximum program on the Jewish mode of life and for a maximum knowledge of the sources as a prerequisite to spiritual leadership.

3. He said that he was not aware of any one having pried into the way the students observed the Sabbath. Only once did it occur that a Trustee— one of the left overs of the JTS of NY—told him about a student riding on the Sabbath, but nothing came of the affair.

4. As regards my apprehension that the Seminary would merge with the Yeshiva, there need be no fear of that on my part for negotiations have been broken off definitely. Even when he had contemplated bringing together the two institutions he had in mind the possibility of keeping two distinct families, one representing the Orthodox and the other Conservative Judaism. As precedent for such cooperation he cited the instance of the University in Strassbourg where theology is taught both by Catholic and Protestant professors. Such a scheme amused me inwardly, for I would never have thought Adler so naive and impractical as to dream of two kinds of Jewish theology being officially recognized in the same institution.

For the first time in all the years that I have known him did he display a trace of unofficial humanness in his makeup. He mentioned that for two nights his sleep was troubled on account of my resignation. He confessed to something like a note of doubt as to the wisdom of the course he had pursued during all the years he had worked for the Seminary. He was getting old and began to entertain fears that his life work had been all in vain.

I yielded and withdrew my resignation. He handed me back both letters. Then he said that if ever I felt like resigning I should first come and talk the matter over with him, implying that he had felt hurt at my having kept him at arm's length. Likewise if I ever did anything which would make my stay impossible, he too would have a talk with me instead of writing letters. Personally I thought that these remarks were totally inappropriate at that moment, and they left a bad taste in my mouth. But this is typical of the kind of thing I must expect for the rest of my days at the Seminary. At bottom Adler and I do live in different universes of discourse.

At eight o'clock this evening I called up Wise and told him that I wanted to speak to him. He was ready to see me at once. I went over the entire situation with him and told him that I had withdrawn my resignation. He took it in the magnanimous spirit despite the keen disappointment he felt in having to give up the idea of my coming to the JIR. He repeated twice what he had said today at lunch to his wife, that if in the course of a year or so I would accomplish one tenth of what he hoped for from me he would have me appointed to the presidency of the JIR. While it was certainly a high compliment that he paid me, nevertheless that is the one outcome of the conversation with the JIR that I least regret having missed. Somehow presidencies and deanships don't tempt me.

Another chapter of my struggle for freedom and self-expression as a condition of serving the cause of Judaism has come to an end. What this signifies only time will tell.

6

May 15, 1927–November 24, 1928

"Forty-Six and Still Not a Book to My Credit"

MAY 15, 1927

On the whole I have behaved pretty well the last two months. Except for an occasional attack of the blues I have been working quite steadily. Nothing of any account has happened to me during the interim. It seems that I am beginning to get tired of this journal. Everything is so commonplace and the little spare time that I have left I want to devote to serious writing. I shall soon be forty-six and not a single book to my credit. What a shame! Still, I must not give up.

On Being Mediocre and Ambitious

JUNE 9, 1927, 1:40 A.M.

I do not know why I find it so hard to write about myself. But as I think of it I really do know why. It is this terrible urge to do something worth while which leads me to regard as wasted every movement that I spend without improving my knowledge or mental power. I live inwardly as though I had but a short time to live and wanted to accomplish something substantial before it was too late. I suppose most people who combine mediocrity with inordinate ambition are always in a hurry. My mind is as littered and haphazard as my desk is now. Just to give an idea how I spent my day, one of those precious days when I am free from the routine of preaching and teaching. I rose at 8:30 after about 6½ hours sleep. Got down town to the Teachers Institute at 10:30 to attend a meeting of the T.I. Faculty. The meeting lasted till 4:15 P.M. Chipkin kept me till 4:45. Got home by 5:15; had appointment with Dinin[1] till 5:30 then with a representative of Macmillan's

---

1. Samuel Dinin (1902–72), Ph.D. Columbia; communal leader; editor; executive director, SAJ; faculty, JTS.

(not about book of my own) which lasted till 6:30. Supper and lolling about till 8:00, visited a sick member.

Conservative Rabbis Meet at Asbury Park

THURSDAY, JULY 7, 1927

I returned this morning from the convention of the Rabbinical Assembly which has been taking place at the Brunswick Hotel in Asbury Park. I arrived there Tuesday noon and found about fifty of the members present. After lunch was over, which was about 2:30, the convention opened with a prayer consisting of three short sentences, delivered by the local rabbi, Davidson.[2] Drob, the president of the Assembly, read a twelve minute paper from which I remember only two things, one, that the Assembly ought to work out some kind of pension plan and two, that we cannot expect to achieve uniform philosophy of Judaism, though we may and should have a uniform system of practice. He didn't state the matter quite as plainly as all this. I believe however that this is what he wanted to convey, because he clapped on to what he said the verse *Ha-nistarot la-'d Eloheinu Veha-niglot lanu ule-vaneinu . . .* [Heb. Deuteronomy 29:28 "The secret things belong to the Lord our God: but those things which are revealed belong to us and our children forever that we may do all the words of this Teaching"]. I stayed for a while after that to listen to some of the reports that were rendered, but having a headache I went to my room to take a nap. When I came down again I found Adler reading a paper on the Rabbinate. I learned that he had been preceded by Israel Goldstein[3] who had read a paper on the need for the Rabbinical Assembly to define more clearly the meaning of conservative Judaism, so as to establish a raison d'etre for our constituting a third party. The discussion which followed had to do only with Goldstein's paper. Jacob Kohn opened the discussion with a question which it took him fifteen minutes to state. The question was "Is it true that we constitute a third party or that we want to be known as such?" Hoffman then arose in all his solemnity and bellowed forth his stereotype speech about Morais and Schechter having dedicated the Seminary to Historical, traditional Judaism, and that we cannot and need not have anything that defines our position more clearly and satisfactorily. Then some one spoke who said nothing except that Goldstein's paper was excellent. Just wherein its excellence lay I could not discover either in the discussion that it elicited or in the summary that appeared in the Jewish Daily Bulletin. If anything it seems to have been

---

2. Max D. Davidson (1899–1977), ordained JTS; Ph.D. Columbia; drama critic; president, Rabbinical Assembly.

3. Israel Goldstein (1896–1986), ordained JTS; Jewish historian; New York Board of Rabbis; officer, Zionist Organization of America.

Rabbinical Assembly convention, 1927. First row: far left, J. Hoschander, and Kaplan; fourth and fifth from left, C. Adler, I. Davidson. (continued)

based on a wrong assumption as to the constitution and function of the Rabbinical Assembly and based its appeal for a definition of Conservative Judaism to the most unworthy element in our nature, collective selfishness.

At this point I got up to make my little speech. I gave credit to J. Kohn for having asked the proper question and to Hoffman for having correctly stated the general principles represented by the Seminary and the RA [Rabbinical Assembly]. Then I went one step further and argued that we should not expect all the members of the Assembly to agree in the

Second row: third and fourth from left, *Louis Finkelstein, Moshe Levine;* far right, *Max Arzt. (Courtesy Ratner Center, JTS)*

application of those general principles. We are a compromise organization, just as England is a compromise nation, understanding by compromise the willingness to cooperate on those things which we hold in common and to tolerate each other in things concerning which we differ. I pleaded for an attitude of mind on the part of the RA that would permit any group of members who happen to agree in some of the specific applications of those general principles to put those applications into practice without being designated as insurgents by those who differ with them.

Tuesday night Dr. Greenstone[4] led a discussion on the place of religion in the Hebrew school. The discussion meandered over the old familiar ground. At no point in the discussion was there the least intimation of the fact that we are all at sea about what we ourselves should believe. How, then, can we be expected to know what to teach? Assuming that as the head of the Teachers Institute I was expected to say something I made the point that psychologically the teaching of religion as such cannot begin nowadays before the years of adolescence. . . .

Kaplan's Rabbinical Disciples Meet

THURSDAY, JULY 7, 1927

Yesterday Rabbis Rubenowitz, Solomon Goldman, Kadushin and Eugene Kohn spent the afternoon at my house and also a goodly part of the evening discussing plans of cooperating in behalf of progress in Judaism from the point of view of Judaism as a civilization. Rubenowitz favored employing the SAJ form of organization to get our ideas across to the laity. The others felt that there were not enough men and women among their members who were ripe for the SAJ movement. We finally decided to issue a volume of essays to consist of articles by the five of us and by the two others whom we are willing to include in our number at the present time, namely Aaronson[5] of Minneapolis and Alex Burnstein[6] at present of New Bedford. These articles should deal with applications of our points of view to various phases of Jewish life and thought.

The Problem of Evil

WEDNESDAY, JULY 20, 1927

The death by drowning of Montague Lamport, the twenty-four-year-old son of Sol Lamport, last Sunday morning has brought me once again face to face with the fundamental problem of life's meaning and purpose. The few remarks that I knew I would be asked to make at the funeral made it necessary for me to rethink the meaning of *Tsidduk Ha-Din* [Heb. acknowledgment of (divine) justice].[7] Fortunately I am unable to get away with a few stereotype phrases which clergymen of all denominations use

---

4. Julius Greenstone (1873–1955), Ph.D., ordained JTS; religious educator; principal, Gratz College; roommate of Kaplan at JTS.

5. David Aronson (1894–1988), ordained JTS; rabbi, Minneapolis; president, Rabbinical Assembly; called for abolition of Second Day of holidays such as Passover and Sukkot.

6. Alexander Burnstein (1900–1980), ordained JTS, New York City; active in interfaith concerns.

7. Kaplan had in mind the issue of theodicy, or justifying the ways of God to man. The burial liturgy refers to God's justice.

upon such occasions. To say anything to the point upon so tragic an occasion involved my organizing once again my ideas concerning God. What I did say was completely subversive of the traditional notion of *Tsidduk Ha-Din*, Yet Rabbi Drob who is a fundamentalist and who officiated together with me, complimented my upon my remarks.

This is the idea I developed: Vindicating the ways of God as a means of taking up life's task in spite of the catastrophe which has occurred cannot take place in the traditional way of regarding calamities as punishment for sins. We must learn to vindicate God by conceiving Him as the general who orders the vast army of the living in its combat against blind chance and the unconscious cruelties of nature. When our beloved falls at our side the thought that there is a God who is a *Mefaked Tsevah Milhamah* [Heb. military officer] who is leading us on in this warfare against the evils of mere chance should hearten us to keep on fighting. As such [a] leader of the forces of life, God grieves with us over those who perish through no fault of theirs. Even over those who die for and through their sins, God is said to mourn *kalani me-roshi kalani me-zero'i* [Heb. Mishna Sanhedrin 6:5 "My head hurts my arm hurts"];[8] all the more over those who pay with their life for their courage and virtue. *Yakar be'einai 'd . . .* [Heb. Psalms 116:15 "The death of His faithful ones is grievous in the Lord's sight"].

This conception of God is undoubtedly heretical from the standpoint of Jewish thinkers of the past. But the fear of being guilty of heresy does not affect me in the least. I am chiefly interested in having a conception of the universe and of God which can give me courage to go on fighting against the terrible odds of unwarranted suffering and meaningless death. I prefer God without perfection [more] than perfection without God. The God of philosophy is perfection with a capital P, cold, impersonal, immovable, infinitely negative.

It is because God is to me the warm personal element in Life's inner urge to creativity and self-expression that I can conscientiously employ the name YHWH when praying. Although I would not dream of implying that our ancestors had any such conception of God as I stated above, or that they used the name YHWH for such a conception, I do believe that the ancients in general with their polytheisms and henotheisms had a far more correct intuition of the God-idea than the philosophic monotheists or deists.

---

8. The full Mishnah in the Danby translation (H. Danby, *The Mishnah* [London: Oxford University Press, 1933], 390–91) reads, "R. Meir said: When man is sore troubled, what says the Shekinah? My head is ill at ease, my arm is ill at ease. If God is sore troubled at the blood of the ungodly that is shed, how much more at the blood of the righteous."

Worship at Camp—Not for Children

SUNDAY, AUGUST 21, 1927

On Thursday, August 11, Lena and I left for Camp Modin,[9] Canaan, Me., where our children are spending their vacation.

In camp we found our children in good health and all but Judith utilizing their entire time in camp activities which are for the most part of an athletic nature. There is entirely too much devotion to athleticism in the camps and the mental life of the children is permitted to remain in abeyance practically the entire nine weeks that the children are out there. I was especially annoyed at seeing Judith devote her time to a handful of rather pampered children. I am sure that she derived little satisfaction from her work. She directs the singing and the religious services. As for the former it is of a rather elementary character; as for the latter she gets very little cooperation from the other counselors and little response from the children. Then again how can one expect children to appreciate the purpose of worshiping a God whom they do not see in a language they do not understand? I think that those who are really anxious to promote the spirit of worship are foolish for cheapening the practice by urging all and sundry to worship. Worship ought to be absolutely forbidden to most people on the ground that they are taking the name of God in vain. Certainly children and morons ought not to be permitted to worship and mature persons should be permitted only on condition they concentrate their thoughts on what they are saying. If I had my way I would prohibit keeping our eyes open while praying. Closing the eyes eliminates a goodly portion of the things that distract. If praying had been treated as a privilege, then there is no doubt that more people would have prayed and more sincerity might have been developed in prayer.

Seminary Student Life

THURSDAY, DECEMBER 15, 1927

The hour in Homiletics yesterday was an exciting one. Instead of proceeding with the lecture on Orthodox Judaism, I called attention to the wide diversity of opinion and attitude reflected in the papers handed in to me by the men. Some verge on atheism, others avow ultramontane Judaism. The men had no common denominator to which I could address myself with much profit to them. Hence it was my opinion that they must do something to effect among themselves a meeting of minds. This

---

9. Camp Modin was founded in 1922 by Albert Schoolman, Alexander Dushkin, and Isaac Berkson, who wanted a camp with a Jewish content. It was a private camp.

could come about only through discussion and interchange of ideas. The tendency of the body of students to break up into small cliques of two or three is not helpful. Every man must be in a position to discuss the various phases of the Jewish problem with all the other men in the seminary. If they would read and discuss among themselves the very papers which they have handed in to me much good would result. As I recall the best, and for that matter, the only training I ever obtained at the Seminary was not in any of the classrooms but in the discussions I carried on with my fellow students. . . .

After I spoke to them in this vein there broke out a veritable storm of complaints against the Seminary as a whole, and the Faculty in particular. I met the usual charge against the Seminary that it is non-committal in its attitude toward Judaism, by saying that such a charge was unjustified. The Seminary spells three outstanding principles: nationalism, religion, development. The very fact that it does not take a definite stand as to whether men and women may be seated together, or the prayer for sacrifices be omitted, etc. constitutes a principle in itself. That principle is that given those three elements, nationalism, religion and development, we must permit a certain amount of freedom and spontaneity to individuals and groups in the detailed applications of them to ceremonies, worship, etc. Nothing is to be so strongly deprecated as a regimen that made provision for every move a person has to make. This narrowly legalistic conception of Judaism is no longer tenable or desirable.

What shocked me most, however, was to learn that the greater obstacle in the way of a free exchange of ideas among the students was the heresy hunting which prevailed among them. Students, especially Freshmen, who venture to express a radical opinion are given to understand by the older students that they dare not harbor such heresies. What is worse, it does not take long before students venturing to speak their minds are betrayed to members of the Faculty. In my own days, of course, there was no occasion for such slander, since we practically had no Faculty. That practice of "making up" to a professor by bringing tales about other students was introduced into the Seminary with the advent of Schechter. He and especially his wife, had in them a good deal of that European ghetto trait of spying and gossiping. Prof. Marx told me that Jacob Kohn used this method of ingratiating himself with the Schechters. That is why he never realized his ambition of becoming a member of the Faculty. Kohn would talk about the members of the Faculty as well as about the students. The saying went that before a member of the Faculty formulated an idea in his own mind, Schechter was already aware of it, so perfect was the line of communication maintained by Jacob Kohn.

A Heart-to-Heart Talk with Judith on How to Meet Men

THURSDAY, DECEMBER 15, 1927

This evening I took Judith in hand and spent with her more than an hour in a heart to heart talk. Lena was present. Judith has been showing evidences of repressed unhappiness. Assuming that it was due to the lack of men's company, I drew that fact out from her and actually suggested to her what to do to meet young men who might take her out of an evening.[10] I suggested that she join young peoples' organizations which are both intellectual and social in character. This is certainly a better way of solving her problem than to go away to Palestine for a year where she thought she would escape from the surroundings in which she moves at present. In these surroundings she encounters young girls half of whom tell her of all the young fellows they went out with and the other half of whom bewail their lot continually that they have no one to go out with.

Supports Assisted Suicide

DECEMBER 19, 1927

It is horrible to go through the agonies of death. I hope that the time is not far distant when it will be legitimate for an expert physician to grant the prayer of those who *want* to be spared such agonies and to prescribe for them some euthanasic drug. I cannot see any possible justification for insisting that the victim of a mortal disease must endure the tortures of the damned. Of what good is he then to himself or to his family whose happiness is temporarily eclipsed. The dread of the sin of suicide is about as reasonable in a situation such as this as is the dread of the sin of murder in resorting to contraception to prevent pullulation [to breed, to swarm].

Thoughts about Death and Faith at the Death of His Mother-in-Law

SATURDAY, JANUARY 14, 1928

At the time I wrote down the above item I was going to describe some of the incidents in the closing days of my mother-in-law's life, the death bed scene, the funeral and the Shiv'ah Days [seven days of mourning] following, but I was interrupted, and now I haven't the patience to go into those details. On the whole as I look back to the entire episode I feel that the shallowness of our living extends to our dying as well. It appears to me that even death makes no impression upon our type of people. And fool that

---

10. Judith was about seventeen at the time.

I am I expect a sermon of mine to leave a lasting impression! Outside of the sense of loss experienced at the moment when Dr. Ira Kaplan pronounced my mother-in-law dead, next day when her body was taken into the SAJ House, and later when it was placed in the cold earth, it seems to me that her death in no way has made the least difference in the lives of all her children, except perhaps to give them a sense of relief, non-confessed, of course. I must admit that I was so struck by the fact that in her last conscious moment she repeated with all the fervor of her soul the prayer for universal peace and well-being, which she had been in the habit of doing throughout the greater part of her life, and by the further fact that she followed that with a conscious and deliberate pronunciation of the benediction *Shehakol Ni'heye Be-devaro* [Heb. "That everything should be according to His word"] before taking a sip of water, that I have not stopped thinking about the truly magic power of faith no matter how blind and uneducated that faith be. On the other hand I have since been puzzled as well. Since it is possible for faith to be so genuine and sincere as to constitute a source of strength in one's dying hour, why is it of so little help in adding to the joy of life? I do not recall that my mother-in-law was particularly cheerful or radiated happiness as a result of her faith. Moreover, why did she hold on so desperately to life? Unless, probably, she believed literally that as soon as she died she would have to confront some huge monstrous being whom she thought of as God. Is not this why R. Yohanan wept so bitterly when he was on his death bed?[11]

Anyhow, while it is difficult to puzzle out the train of thought that goes on in the mind of the untutored person, it is no less difficult, in fact, much more so, to arrive at any definite idea of what the tutored mind should think concerning the fact of death. As for the agonies accompanying it, I for one would plead and beg that every one of us be spared. If I were to devise some Utopia of my own, I would provide it with an institution where those whose days are numbered and who wish to be spared the mental tortures which they and their relatives have to endure, could go and have themselves dispatched in short order. I almost begrudge such miserable criminals like the man and the woman who were executed because of the murder they committed in cold blood, the quick and beautiful death by electrocution. Why should good and worthy people whose last days are a hell on earth be denied such euthanasia?

---

11. The story is told of R. Yohanan Ben Zakkai, who wept so bitterly on his deathbed. When asked, he said that he would be afraid to come before a king of flesh and blood, but before the King of kings who decided whether he would go to the Garden of Eden or Gehenna (hell)—how much more so? Berachot 28b.

And the "minyan?"[12] What a useless institution! Imagine to what excellent social and spiritual purposes all that energy which goes into rushing early morning to daily services could be applied. If, for example, every time the mourners came together they were to read or recite something instructive and inspirational, by the end of eleven months they might really be better for that experience. The stupidity and wastefulness of the human animal are even more conspicuous than those of animate nature.

Being Tormented over a Public Mistake in Hebrew

SATURDAY EVENING, JANUARY 14, 1928

Now to return to my own "dear" self. During the Shiv'ah week after my mother-in-law's death, I went to pay a condolence call to Prof. Marx who had lost his father. The time we pay such calls is usually toward dusk, so that we might help out the mourner with "minyan." Marx is strictly Orthodox in his mode of life. Accordingly when "minha" [afternoon] service was over he asked me to read a selection from the Mishnah.[13] It is customary to select a "mishnah" beginning with one of the letters of the name of the departed. Opening at random I began to read from the treatise of *Ketubot*.[14] I recalled the text quite well, but not having had occasion to read Hebrew out loud for a long time I wasn't sure at the moment whether the opening word for "I was captured" should be read with a "patach" or a "tsere."[15] I was misled by the fact that the book in which I was asked to read had the word (p. 266) *nishbayti* without a "yod"[16] between the "beth" and the "taf." Consequently I read it *nishbati* instead of *nishbayti*. This faux pas preyed on my mind for over a week. Of course it was in the presence of Hoschander[17] and Higger[18] that made me painfully conscious of the mistake I had made. I myself would have found fault with both of them, if they had read the word they way I did. To me it would be an evidence of ignorance of elementary grammar. Hence I felt that what they probably thought of me was not too complimentary. This upset my equilibrium for a good many days.

---

12. Kaplan is referring here to the daily prayer service and the traditional requirement for the mourner to attend and say Kaddish.

13. A Jewish legal text edited around 200 C.E. It is a common traditional practice to study from the Mishna in a mourner's house.

14. The tractate from the Mishna having to do with marriage contracts.

15. The text Kaplan used obviously lacked vowels. He had forgotten whether the word began with an "ah" sound or "aye." "Nishbati" means "I have sworn."

16. The presence of the letter yod would have told Kaplan that the word was to be read with the "aye" sound.

17. Jacob Hoschander (1874–1933), biblical scholar; Assyriologist; faculty, JTS.

18. Michael Higger (1898–1952), ordained JTS; Talmudic scholar; author.

Being Grateful for the Greeks—We Ought to Laugh at Our Gods

SUNDAY, JANUARY 15, 1928

I was far from being in a happy frame of mind when I left for Chicago on Sunday, Jan. 22, on my first lecture tour. As soon as I got on the train, however, I relaxed and began to read Aristophanes' Frogs in Gilbert Murray's translation. It acted like a sedative on my mind. I felt as though I had moved into a different world and breathed a freer air. What a relief from the morose and oppressive atmosphere of the Hebraic past and the Jewish present. How grateful we ought to be to the Greeks for having shown us that we can laugh at our gods! How we ought to bless those ancient Greeks for having had the good grace to disappear from the world! I came across the expression "humorless prigs." That hurt terribly. How well that described the *Tannaim* and *Amoraim* [Talmudic authorities]. If they only had a sense of humor! I would have forgiven them the discussion whether or not it is permitted to walk out with a wooden leg or to kill lice on the Sabbath.

Midwest Conference—Expanding the SAJ

MONDAY FEBRUARY 6, 1928[19]

The conference which I asked Dushkin to organize took place in Chicago on Tuesday and Wednesday Feb. 21 and 22. I arrived at Chicago on Tuesday morning and opened the conference with some remarks on the question wherein existing systems of Judaism were not satisfying.

FRIDAY, MARCH 23, 1928

I made it plain from the beginning that I did not want the discussion to be merely of an academic character but that it should lead to some plan of action. It was well that I said that because from what I learned later some one, I believe Kadushin, had suggested that they keep the SAJ out of the discussion. I have a feeling that he like so many among my colleagues, balk at the idea of being identified with the SAJ. They regard the Society as a personal creation of mine, and therefore apprehend that with it back of me I might become domineering. Moreover they claim that so far the SAJ is the name for nothing more than the local congregation to which I am ministering. As soon as I discovered that Dushkin had been diverted from the original purpose of establishing an SAJ branch, I began arguing him back to it. Of course that was done between sessions. During these sessions with him I became clear in my own mind just what the status of the group that was meeting in conference should be. It was then and there

---

19. Kaplan sometimes wrote about the events of many days without listing a new date. Thus he wrote about February 22, but the listed date is February 6.

that we evolved the plan of an SAJ council to consist of rabbis, directors of social work, educators. Later I suggested the inclusion of men and women of creative ability who would subscribe to the SAJ program.

The Purpose of the Diary—To Keep the Past from Dying

WEDNESDAY, APRIL 12, 1928

It seems like a century since last I wrote in this book. The longer the period during which I fail to record my experience the harder I find it to resume the practice. But I must keep up this diary. It is the only evidence I have that I have existed. I need it to counteract the feeling of blankness with which I am often seized. My past is as though it was not so that I feel forced to turn the pages of the diary to convince myself that I have lived. I sometimes feel that we don't have to die to know what death is—in fact, it is then that we don't know. The time that we know it is when we are alive and we try to keep our own past from dying; yet no matter what we do it dies on our hands.

I have been very much in the dumps of late. The longer I live the more alone I feel. I have not a single friend or companion in the world with whom I can share my interests and problems. What can wife and children do for me? They have their own lives to live. Of course they love me and I love them. But all they can do is to sympathize with me. What good can sympathy do me? In all the years that I have worked in the field of Judaism I have not succeeded in finding anybody who would be willing to collaborate with me on any project for the advancement or reconstruction of Judaism. So much could be made of the latent good in the Jewish heritage, yet it is allowed to go to waste. Some of the sermons I develop enable me to uncover veins of spiritual gold. Each time I come upon such a discovery I thrill with joy. To whom shall I announce the good news? A handful of simple untutored men and women who constitute my audience at the SAJ Services? For the moment I manage to forget how dull and lethargic they are. I delude myself into believing that they will receive with joy the news of the meaning I have discovered in life or in a text and, who knows, may even act on it. No sooner am I through speaking than the scales fall from my eyes. When the services are over they don't even take the trouble to bid me "Gut Shabbos" or "Gut Yom Tov." It is only when they get to the door and happen to turn around and see me standing near them that some of them give me their clammy handshakes and fishy looks.

Taking a walk tonight with Lena and feeling depressed as my mind revolved on these thoughts it occurred to me I might be able to shake off this mood of mine by stopping in at the Century Theatre to listen to a musical comedy. But I was almost bored to death by what went on the stage and had to leave during the first part of the performance. Coming back I resumed reading Willa Cather's *Death Comes for the Archbishop*. When I came across a passage which expressed my present state of mind more accurately than I could hope to with my half articulate style I was moved to take up the pen and to write down what was passing through my mind right now. Here is the passage:

"He was lying in bed with the sense of failure clutching at his heart. His prayers were empty words and brought him no refreshment. His soul had become a barren field. He had nothing within himself to give his priests or his people. His work seemed superficial, a house built upon the sands. His great diocese was still a heathen country. The Indians traveled their old road of fear and darkness, battling with evil omens and ancient shadows."

In the effect which this paragraph had upon me I experience the value of art. This passage gripped me, or rather it enabled me to take a firmer hold on myself. The ancients had an idea that to know the name of a thing or person was to be in a position to exercise control over that thing or person. Somewhat akin seems to be the work of art. Its points describe and articulate the innermost aspects of the environment and of our own natures, thereby enabling us to put them under our control.

The particular passage which had such a momentary therapeutic effect on my mind reveals to me a very interesting fact. It shows that discouragement need not arise necessarily from doubt as to the intrinsic value of the work that one may be doing. The main source of such discouragement seems to be the apparent futility of one's efforts, the failure to make an impression. For surely, the Bishop in question never for a moment questioned the divine truth or the intrinsic value of what he had to offer the people. Withal that, he was disheartened, because his efforts seemed to bear no fruit. Likewise in my own case, I have not the least doubt as to the intellectual and spiritual superiority of the doctrine I advocate to any of the current conceptions of Judaism. But the greater the conviction in my own mind, the more maddening the apathy and stupidity of our people.

Lunch with Weizmann

April 12, 1928

Dr. Weizmann lunched with me and the family yesterday (the seventh day of Pesah). He had promised to come to the services at 10:30. He came, however, about 11:15 after I had begun to speak and the janitor would not permit him to go in while I was speaking. After lunch he asked my advice as to what should be done with the ZOA now that it was being violently attacked by the Brandeis group. I reiterated my suggestion of last year that the movement be directed by a lay body which should employ the professional Zionists to do the actual work. He thought that I was right.

Laments Discrimination against Jews

Friday, April 20, 1928

Little as I can afford the time I cannot refrain from recording the devastating effect on my spirit of the facts which I learned from Mellville I. Rappaport of the Merit Employment Bureau. The difficulties experienced by Jewish young people who try to find employment are indescribable. At every agency the applicant is expected to state his religion. As soon as they state that they are Jewish they are told that no position can be gotten for them. In some agencies they actually tear up the application as soon as it is filled out by a Jew. Jewish firms often insist upon getting Christian help. A huge organization like the General Motors will not employ Jews. When Rappaport applied to the N.Y. Foundation (Warburg, Schiff, Lehman, et al.) for a loan of $2000 the one who prevented that loan from being made was Lee K. Frankel. The Insurance Co. Of which he is vice president hardly has any Jews in its employ. Rappaport showed me cards made out by Jewish applicants in other agencies than his own. On those cards they are registered as of "Catholic" or "Gentile." One said she was of French religion.

Seeing an O'Neill Play—A Transvaluation of Value—Judith

Thursday, April 26, 1928

Yesterday I attended O'Neill's play "Strange Interlude." By the time I got to the intermission I realized that O'Neill dramatized in that play the need for transvaluation of values. Instead, however, of doing what Nietzsche did, and attempting or suggesting the overthrow of the moral law, O'Neill is interested in subordinating it to the creative instinct. Religiously this transvaluation would imply the conception of God as more truly expressed in the mother principle than in any of the cold metaphysical abstraction of the theologies. It has occurred to me since that O'Neill's underlying philosophy seems to be the same as that of Havelock Ellis by whom he was no doubt influenced in his whole world outlook.

I saw the play with Judith. She has the kind of a mind that is challenging and provocative. Some of the most fruitful thoughts I have hit upon are due to conversations with her. If she goes to Chicago next year, as I believe she will, I shall certainly miss her.

A Discussion with Judith about Her Future—Is It Advisable for Her to Enter Jewish Work?

SUNDAY, APRIL 29, 1928

Last night Judith engaged me in a lengthy conversation about her going to Chicago. It seems that the effect of her trip to Chicago has been to rob her attempt to make her way in the world alone of all the glamour that the thought of such an attempt had previously possessed for her. Moreover as a result of her learning the nature of the work that she would have to do, the horizon of possibilities seemed to narrow instead of widen. These doubts were supplemented by one which I shared with her, namely whether it was advisable for her to throw herself entirely into Jewish work with the demand for Jewish culture being so limited. Why seek to impose on the public something it does not genuinely want? Why, then, should I sacrifice her future and her happiness to a purpose of doubtful value? Of course, if I could see the least indication of the demand for Judaism waxing instead of waning, I should not hesitate to advise her to confine herself to Jewish work. So far, however, I have found that only those who have a vested interest in Judaism are anxious to see it live. The handful of laymen who have the future of Judaism at heart are the fundamentalists. I have yet to meet an enlightened Jewish layman who would go out of his way to insure the existence of Judaism in this country by means of a deliberate effort at constructive re-adjustment.

Judith and I arrived at the conclusion that it would be best for her to establish a private studio. She could get a position in the school system. That certainly holds out no attractions. The room for initiative and originality is extremely circumscribed. In addition she would have to train the children for Christmas and Easter celebrations in which she could not put her whole heart.

This is the paradox of all social work, that the only value of going into it is to use for the purpose of changing the social mind and social habits. But how can one do that who has to depend for his living upon the people who engage him with the view of maintaining the status quo?

The Menorah Society Board Meeting—Lucius Littauer [20]

MAY 2, 1928

The other letter was from Henry Hurwitz in reference to the Dinner meeting of the Board of Governors of the Menorah, which I attended last

---

20. Lucius Littauer (1859–1944), A.B. Harvard; congressman; glove manufacturer; philanthropist; founder, Littauer Foundation, Littauer Professorship at Harvard.

Monday night. Among the persons present were Stroock (brother of Sol Stroock and apparently more human than he) and Littauer (the man who endowed the chair occupied by Wolfson[21] at Harvard). . . . Littauer who, by the way, said that it was fifty years since he was graduated from Harvard, stated in the course of his remarks that the reason the Menorah work with the undergraduates had suffered a setback in the last few years, was that it lacked a spiritual objective. This remark seemed rather strange, coming from a man who said that was the first time he had participated in a meeting for a distinctly Jewish purpose. I then explained in calm and dignified fashion that the Menorah was performing a great spiritual service in doing what no other institution in Jewish life was doing, humanizing the content of Judaism. It was probably with reference to this point that Hurwitz wrote in his letter to me "I am most grateful to you for your attendance at our Board meeting last evening, and for your gallant talk which made a profound impression." This time I feel that I deserved the *Yeyasher Koaḥ* [Heb. congratulations].

Forty-Seven and Feeling Depressed

Tuesday, June 12, 1928

    Personally I feel as totally demoralized and as much agitated by a civil war in which one part of myself is engaged against the other, as the Zionist movement. Intellectually I know I am all wrong for being so unhappy; I am fully aware that it is nothing but selfishness and greed for abilities which have been denied me by heredity and upbringing and yet I cannot get hold of myself to overcome this gnawing discontentment. What a wonderful subject for study and analysis I would make for one who has a descriptive ability. The special occasion for my present moroseness is the fact that I had promised to be ready for my 47th birthday on June 11 with the translation of the "Mesilat"[22] and the introduction and I am as far from being through with it as ever. The whole business doesn't amount to very much, and yet it has been on my hands for the last dozen years. When I see how men write one book after another and how I am struggling with a measly piece of work like this, I naturally have good reason to be disheartened. Then again I realize how foolish it is of me to be forever champing at the bit that holds me back from getting anywhere. I should really like to think and feel ethically and philosophically. I should like to be able to resign myself to my

---

21. Harry Austryn Wolfson (1887–1974), Ph.D. Harvard; scholar; historian of Jewish philosophy.

22. Kaplan translated, provided critical notes for, and wrote an introduction to Moses H. Luzzato's *Misilat Yesharim*. The book was part of the Schiff classics series and was published by JPS in 1936. Solomon Schechter made the original request of Kaplan in 1915, a few days before he died.

limitations. But there comes along the psychologist and tells me that such acceptance of one's limitations is nothing but a trick of the imagination. He labels it the compensatory tendency implying that I would be a fool for resorting to it.

"Judaism as a Civilization"—A New Thought Tool

FRIDAY, JUNE 15, 1928

The significance of the conception of Judaism as a civilization is that it provides us with an effective instrument for so ordering Jewish life that not only shall its continuance be assured, but also that its raison d'etre be fully vindicated. All thought which is not mere day dreaming is part of the process whereby a living entity, whether it be an individual or a group, strives to effect an equilibrium between itself and the environment. A concept is a thought tool or an instrument to facilitate the establishment of equilibrium between life and environment. The need in Jewish life for a new concept or thought tool to establish and maintain the equilibrium itself between itself and the environment is due to the inadequacy of any of the conventional concepts, the concept of religion being no more adequate than that of race. Recently even Claude Montefiore felt constrained to admit the need for a concept like Jewishness. The reason for such inadequacy becomes apparent when we analyze the nature of the present day challenge to Jewish life. The challenge itself contains factors which are not new. There is the factor of religious doubt, the questioning of tradition and the undermining of authority. There is the factor of migration with its accompanying evils. But taken as a whole it is of an unprecedented character and includes factors which are entirely new.

Being a Jew presents difficulties never experienced before, first because the social and cultural interests of the Jew are pre-empted and crowded out by the life of civic community of which he is a part; secondly, because even if he can spare the time, energy and resources for the cultivation of his spiritual heritage, he finds that heritage challenged by the general trend of modern ideology. Unfortunately these two causes are seldom thought of as two distinct factors to be reckoned with in our attempt to counteract the difficulty of being and living as a Jew. The tendency to escape Judaism or to find loyalty to it a burden is ascribed to some general deterioration in the stamina of the Jew, or to the spirit of the age. It is, therefore, hoped that by appealing to the courage, self-respect of the Jew we shall be able to evoke from him the self-sacrifice necessary to live as a Jew. This method of solving the problem of Judaism I believe to be ineffective and futile. The solution depends upon our realizing that the problem is essentially that of restoring the equilibrium between the collective life of the Jew and his environment. The solution will therefore depend upon the deliberate effort to modify the environment or reckon with it, even more than upon any repentant mood on the part of the Jew. Such an approach is itself novel and calls for a conception of Judaism which would warrant it. In viewing Judaism as a civilization we have such a warrant, for a civilization is necessarily determined by environmental influences. When it is on the wane we must look for the cause to some maladjustment between all those elements that constitute the civilization and the conditions that obtain in the environment.

The RA Law Committee

TUESDAY, JUNE 26, 1928

The Rabbinic Assembly began its sessions yesterday at Long Branch. I am scheduled to read a paper tomorrow on Judaism as a Civilization, which by the way, I consented to do only after a great deal of pleading on the part of Levitsky who had arranged the program. Although I could stay only for a part of the sessions yesterday I considered it proper to come even for a little while. Moreover I had to report to the committee on Law my opinion on the question put by Jacob Kohn concerning the possibility of circumventing the Law prohibiting a rabbi who is a "Kohen"[23] from officiating at funerals. From my own point of view any attempt to keep alive the institution of the "Kehunah" [priesthood] is ridiculous, but in order to act in unison with the other members of the Law Committee I was willing to discover some loophole that would justify us in abrogating the prohibition in such a way as not to constitute an absolute break with the tradition concerning ritual impurity. This necessitated my going to the rabbinic sources from the first hand contact with the Jewish legalistic literature, and I realized what a joy it would have been to me and others who are similarly minded if we had occasion to go to Jewish sources to arrive at decisions that really counted instead of such a decision of such trivial importance.

Folkways: A Talk to the RA

FRIDAY, JUNE 29, 1928

Last Wednesday I went for a second time to Long Branch to read my paper on Judaism as a Civilization at the convention of the Rabbinic Assembly. I embodied in that paper most of what I had read at the second conference of the Midwest Council of the SAJ about the distinction between

---

23. Jewish law prohibits descendants of the ancient priestly families from entering a cemetery for funerals outside their immediate families. The cemetery would contaminate them.

personal and folk religion. I doubt whether I would have cared to broach that view a few years ago, or whether I would even have done it this year if Ginzberg had not left for Europe. I confess that the apprehension that Adler would be present and attack me for holding such views had been in the back of my mind. That Adler stayed away from the sessions on that day I believe was by no means unintentional. To say nothing after such a paper would imply either assent or inability to refute the ideas I set forth. On the other hand he evidently does not cherish the notion of getting into polemics with me. He escaped this dilemma by not coming at all although I understand he is spending the summer somewhere in the vicinity of Long Branch. Yet I may be mistaken.

In the course of my reading the paper I made the statement about the *Mitzvot* [Heb. commandments] being treated merely as folkways which should not be dealt with in the same legalistic spirit as the civil law. Drob, who was the chairman of the meeting, whispered to me that I should repeat that statement so that the listeners might take note of the full extent of my heresy. I disregarded him, but the antagonism he displayed annoyed me. I felt that quite a few in the audience agreed with him. When I got through the question arose whether the paper should be discussed. Drob tried to choke off discussion, but had to concede to the wishes of the majority to allow a half hour for discussion. Hoffman (Senior) delivered a tirade in which he intimated that views such as expressed in the paper were incompatible not only with what the Rabbinic Assembly and the Seminary stood for, but with traditional and historical Judaism. He was followed by Jacob Kohn, who while approving the modernist approach implied in the paper, took strong exception to my treating the Jewish religion as a phase of the Jewish civilization. While considerably superior in his thinking to most of the men in the Assembly, he is nevertheless too obsessed by preconceptions to acknowledge the value of a new idea proposed by a colleague. The other men that raised questions contributed nothing to the discussion. I was given a chance to answer the objections. Toward the end of my remarks I let myself go and talked with a good deal of warmth. Whenever Chertoff hears me speak in that vein he remarks "I like to hear you when you get angry."

Giving a Belief in God Back to the Students

AUGUST 30, 1928

I am enjoying as usual my work with the class in the Training School for Jewish Social Work. I imagine that the students experience a feeling similar to that of beginning to learn a new language. Not having known anything to begin with the amount learned is perceptible and the sense of power gained is appreciable. As a consequence of their having practically no idea of Judaism, or what is worse, a very much distorted notion of it, when they first come to me I can notice from lesson to lesson how they grow in their understanding of Judaism.

This morning I explained to the class the typical fallacy of the child mind and of the minds of the ancients—who with a few exceptions racially speaking were children—that of hypostatising abstract phases of reality, cosmic or social. I showed how this fallacy gave rise to the anthropomorphic conception of God and to the literalistic conception of the Messiah. I usually begin by an analogy from any of the conceptions of truth, justice, liberty which have been personified and represented by means of symbolic figures. Suppose we were to argue that because there are no such personified realities as these symbols imply, would we have a right to assert that truth, justice, etc. do not represent any real forces in social life, forces that determine action? Yet this is exactly what all who deny the existence of God do when they become aware of the absurdity of the anthropomorphic representations of Him; they deny the existence of any reality whatever which might have given rise to the erroneous conception of God. In my opinion this is a more fruitful way of dealing with the problem of religion than is suggested by Santayana's definition of religion as poetry, which takes itself as science.

When the hour was over some of the students expressed satisfaction in having their ideas clarified. One man said "You have given me back the belief in God."

Finally! Conducting a TI Faculty Meeting in Hebrew

THURSDAY, SEPTEMBER 6, 1928

This afternoon the Teachers Institute faculty met. For the first time in my career I conducted the entire meeting in Hebrew. I hope that I shall be able to carry out my resolve to speak at the opening sessions next Thursday night in Hebrew without having my talk written out beforehand. This will give me courage to carry out the promise I made at the meeting that I would henceforth conduct my courses in Hebrew.

Ambivalence—Wants to Quit SAJ, but Can't

SUNDAY, SEPTEMBER 9, 1928

These are the days when I am forming momentous decisions by my very indecision. How I would love to be able to come before the Board of Trustees tomorrow night and say to them, "Gentlemen, you have not given the cooperation necessary to put the SAJ movement on the map. I have to quit." Whenever I am depressed these days I comfort myself with the thought that I am at last to be free and live my own life without worrying what is to become of Judaism. But then I realize how integrated my work at the SAJ is with all the rest of my work. I would be deprived of the backing without which I would scarcely venture to assert myself and speak my mind freely. I would also not have the mechanical help of secretarial service. So I yield to the inevitable and decide to remain in harness. Such are the conflicting sentiments that agitate me from early morning until I fall asleep.

Spinoza and the Belief in God

MONDAY, SEPTEMBER 10, 1928

Two interesting ideas have come to me lately, one while discussing Maimonides with the class of the Training School, the other while working on the sermon for Rosh Hashanah.

1. The fact that Maimonides points out that the order of the world which proves God is not the order visible in physical laws of nature but in mathematical and logical laws of reason, and moreover that even God cannot change the mathematical and logical laws of reason, enables me to understand the main point in Spinoza's philosophy. I see now that in the same way as Maimonides identifies the functioning of God with the mathematical and logical laws of reason so Spinoza goes one step further and identifies God with the physical laws of nature.

Lately there also dawned on me the true significance of Spinoza's philosophy in relation to religion as a whole. When I read again some of the Jewish ethical texts of the middle ages I become convinced that the protagonists of religion consciously and fervently uphold the theurgic and naturalistic conception of the world. While I realized in a general way that the reason the Jewish philosophers take such pains to emphasize the doctrine of *creatio ex nihilo* is that only such doctrine is compatible with the possibility of miracles, the full force of their insistence upon that doctrine did not strike me until recently. As I see it now the belief in creation *ex nihilo* is basic to the conception of a theurgic God, the God of all ancient and traditional religions. No wonder the medieval Jewish philosophers spent themselves defending that belief.

This of course brings into bold relief Spinoza's contribution to the development of religion. In the negation of a theurgic God he was not setting up anything new. All of Greek philosophy had practically achieved that. What Spinoza really did was to shatter once and for all the pretentious claims of the philosophers of the traditional religions that they were able to harmonize the theurgic conception of God with the philosophic conception. And his second achievement is in demonstrating that the philosophic conception of God can serve as the basis of an ethical program. To be sure even in this respect he was anticipated by the Stoics. But there is a difference between saying a thing for the first time, and reaffirming it in the face of universal denial and opposition.

2. The second idea is in a way an outgrowth of the preceding reflections. I have always found it difficult to reconcile what to me appear as two self-evident truths: one is that once we eliminate the God-idea from Jewish life there is practically nothing of value left in it; the other, that no modern culture can afford to commit itself to any particular God-idea however plausible it may seem. And I believe I can resolve this contradiction by maintaining that Jewish life calls for our identifying as God whatever *experienced* fact or process enables us to feel at home in the world and to live wisely. It makes no difference whether we accept Spinoza's, Comte's, Matthew Arnold's, Wall's, Hocking's, Royce's or Wieman's conception of God. The point is that each of these men suggested some identifiable experience as the source of our belief in God, in place of the revelational and theurgic conceptions offered by tradition. So long as the intellectual development of mankind made it possible for the God of tradition to be also an object of experience, insofar as the human imagination untrammeled by intellectual strictures could keep the image of Him sufficiently vivid to influence the rest of one's idea complex, there was no need to urge the adoption of one or the other philosophic view of God. Note, however, that the greater part of our people are too sophisticated to retain the idea of a theurgic God, they must fill the void with some one of the suggested conceptions, or if these do not satisfy them with one of their own. It is not even essential that a Jew should commit himself to one particular philosophic conception of God. Much depends on one's mood and state of mental development. But so long as a Jew will not rest content unless some experienced fact or process stands out in his mind as so all significant that it is identified with God, and becomes an incentive to his giving of the best that is in him, and to his enduring the worst that may befall him, he is fulfilling the sine qua non of Jewish life.

Henry Rosenthal—A Most Unusual Person

WEDNESDAY, SEPTEMBER 12, 1928

I do not think that I have so far said anything in this diary about Henry M. Rosenthal. If that is the case it is a serious omission because he is one of the very few extraordinary men that have walked into my life. When I first met him as a student about three years ago, he was a thin, somewhat ungainly youth, medium sized then, sallow complexion with a small and irregular-featured face. His heavy lidded eyes were shielded by glasses and only when in his nasal voice he shot out some brilliant epigram did those eyes light up for a moment signal-like. The course which I was then giving at the

Professor Henry Rosenthal. (Courtesy Abigail Rosenthal)

Seminary dealt with the reinterpretation of the three main attributes of God as a helper, as sovereign and redeemer. He and Milton Steinberg[24] continually belabored me with questions. His especially were like rapier thrusts. Time and again he challenged my attempt to stamp modernist concepts with an ancient terminology. In the end both he and Steinberg seemed to be convinced. So impressed was I then with his literary talent that I discussed with him the feasibility of employing him as a collaborator on a book to be based on the lectures that I was then giving. (I even suggested having his name appear as co-author.) The difficulty was to get the funds. He would have to be paid for his part of the work.

I remember how a remark of his made in the course of the conversation I had with him concerning this plan hurt me. I happened to say something about the need of embellishing the style of the material that I had been giving in the class, when he blurted it out that the style was rather crude. It may be that the fear that he might claim too much credit for any work on which we would collaborate deterred me from going on with the

24. Milton Steinberg (1903–50), ordained JTS; prominent author; Zionist instructor, CCNY and JTS; editorial board, *Reconstructionist*.

negotiations. Whatever the case may have been then by now I have grown somewhat more confident myself and less petty about acknowledging the help received from others. I had him help me with the editorials of the SAJ Review ever since it has appeared in print. I give him the substance and he writes it out in proper form. It is only occasionally that he fails to catch the proper slant of what I tell him. He told me that it takes him variously from three to five hours to write out the editorials. He is paid by the SAJ at the rate of $4000 per annum. Without such assistance as I get from him I could never have gone on with the Review.

I also had him revise my translation of the "Messilat."[25] He spent on it forty hours for which I paid him eighty dollars.

About a year and a half ago having been told by Steinberg that Rosenthal had become so disgusted with the Seminary that he was on the point of giving up the idea of studying for the rabbinate, I invited Rosenthal for a long chat with the view of persuading him to stick. I believe it was immediately after the examination period. He seemed to have crammed himself full of Talmudic lore which was too gritty for his honest intellectual stomach, and to have been overcome with a nauseous and retching sensation. From what happened subsequently I also infer that he was at the time also in love with Rachel Tchernowitz[26] whom he married this summer a year ago. Whether my words had any effect on him I have no way of knowing; but the fact is that he is still at the Seminary.

He met Miss Tchernowitz at the Hebrew School in Flushing where they both taught daily and he fell madly in love with her. He married her apparently without going into the kind of careful calculations as to the responsibilities involved in supporting a family. Never any too cheerful by temperament, he must have passed through some excruciating states of depression last year as he realized his limited earning capacity. I cannot say how well he will manage to get along with the $2000 he will get from the SAJ. It looks as though a baby is on the way.

What started me off on this rather lengthy account of him is a story which he finished at the beginning of the summer and which he gave me to read. It is entitled "With a Cigarette Behind a Door." He offered this story to the *Menorah Journal* but they have been hesitating about accepting it. They said that while it has intrinsic merit they were afraid it would be incomprehensible to the readers. Being curious to know what kind of writing it could be that the Menorah would refuse to accept anything of

---

25. Mesillat Yesharim: the ethical treatise which Kaplan translated. See November 25, 1928.

26. Rachel Tchernowitz was the daughter of Chaim Tchernowitz (pseud. Rav Za'ir) (1871–1949), a noted Talmudist who taught at the Jewish Institute of Religion.

Rosenthal's, I read the story immediately after he handed it to me. I found it to be a very remarkable account of his inner struggles not only with the God idea but with God. From the story and from the discussion which I had with him afterwards I became aware that Rosenthal is not only a man of unusual literary gifts but of extraordinary spiritual insight and courage. One statement that he made to me has a bearing on the article and on his general attitude toward religion. He said that it was blasphemy to believe that it was possible to blaspheme God. This is a mystic observation worthy of the greatest kabbalists. (I am thinking of course, of philosophic kabbalists and not of the Jewish magicians.)

Speaking Hebrew Extemporaneously in Public

FRIDAY, SEPTEMBER 14, 1928, 5:00 P.M.

The opening of the T.I. was scheduled for last night. I had made up my mind to speak extemporaneously in Hebrew no matter whether I acquit myself creditably or not. Despite all the interruptions that I have had this week I went primed to speak in Hebrew. When, however, I saw the small number of students—there were about sixty present—that came for the opening exercises, I was going to postpone the opening exercises for a later date. I had never postponed these exercises. Two factors contributed to the attendance being poor. First, the fact that no new freshman class had been admitted; and the second, the proximity of Rosh Hashanah eve. The instructors, especially Morris Levine, advised against postponement and suggested that the program be carried out in less elaborate fashion than usually. I acted on the suggestion and gave only part of the talk that I had intended to give. In order to counteract the frigid atmosphere that prevailed at the assembly I resorted to the matter of breaking up my remarks by questions. It worked quite well, and while I cannot say that I at last scored a victory against the element of fear of speaking in Hebrew publicly lest I make mistakes or be at a loss for a word, I succeeded well enough to want to try again.

Meeting Harry A. Wolfson

THURSDAY, SEPTEMBER 20, 1928

(Sidney) Matz[27] brought with him Prof. Wolfson[28] of Harvard. The first time I caught a glimpse of him about thirteen years ago was when I

---

27. Sidney Matz (1899–1946), M.A. Harvard; business executive; a founder of the American Economic Committee for Palestine.

28. Harry A. Wolfson (1887–1974), Ph.D. Harvard; scholar; historian of Jewish philosophy; faculty, Harvard. One of the great scholars in Judaic studies and an early appointee in the field.

delivered a lecture before the Menorah Group at Harvard. He then appeared very shy and unimpressive. But having heard since so much about his wonderful influence on some of the Jewish students at Harvard, and having read some of his writings I had imagined that he must have acquired in the meantime dignified presence. I was disillusioned, however, when I saw him again for the second time last night.

SUNDAY, SEPTEMBER 23, 1928
Wolfson remained for a while after Matz left. We discussed the question of what would be an ideal service. Some time ago he tried to establish a rational type of service for the Jewish students in Harvard. Those who attended came either from Orthodox or from Reform homes. The service accordingly appealed to neither element. As far as he himself is concerned, he told me, some time ago he went into an Orthodox shul on the first day of Rosh Hashanah, and was so disgusted that he has not gone into a synagogue since.

He expressed himself favorably with regard to the parochial schools and yeshivahs. They were the only guarantees of the traditional Jewish learning being kept up. His early Yeshivah training and probably also a sentimental temperament are responsible for his taking that attitude.

Personally I have of late evolved a new theory with regard to the place of Orthodoxy in the scheme of Jewish adjustment I have formulated in my mind. My theory is as follows: When Judaism came into contact with modern life and thought, the Reformists were the first Jews to achieve a new Jewish synthesis. Being the first they were bound to go down in defeat, not so much because of the inadequacy of their solution—though a good deal was due to that—but because in all social readjustments the first generations must be expected to lose out. It is like taking a fortress. The shock troops are thinned out, and victory depends upon the ability to supply reserves. In case of Jewish life, the reserves following upon the Reformists ranks are the Jewish nationalists. But even the nationalists despite the more adequate character of their solution will for the most part give way to assimilation. They too belong to the shock troops. Fortunately we can count on a reserve that will finally come to grips with the assimilationist forces and win. They are at present the Orthodox ranks who in a generation from now will adopt the nationalist solution and live by it as Jews.

In the extemporaneous sermon which I preached yesterday morning I interpreted the *Haazinu* Song[29] as expressive of the urge to discover some reasonable ground on which to base the hope that Israel will survive. The

---

29. The poem in Deuteronomy 32 usually read in synagogue at this time of year.

ancient poet believed that he discovered such a basis in the fact that the honor of Israel's God was at stake. At the present time too we crave for a reasonable basis for a belief in Israel's ability to survive the present crisis. The fact that the Jewish people is committed to the task of demonstrating the validity and supremacy of the spiritual is our guarantee, provided of course, we have intuitive faith in the ability of the spiritual to function as an efficient cause in human life.

The Sukkah — Symbol of a Simpler Life

TUESDAY, OCTOBER 2, 1928

The sermon on Saturday, the first day of Sukkot, was an interpretation of the Sukkah ceremony as a symbol of the simple life. Insofar as the Bible represents a revolt against the artificialities of civilization that ceremony can become a means of accentuating this "tendency" in the Bible. The two elements in civilization that give rise to the yearning to go back to nature are artificial wants and artificial social distinctions. A want is artificial when it can be supplied only at the sacrifice of honesty and justice. A social distinction is artificial when it is not based upon functions but upon such adventitious factors as possessions, parentage, etc.

This thought ought to prove fruitful insofar as it implies the identity of natural and moral. But I did not venture to point out this implication to the audience for fear they would scarcely understand it and would therefore be bored. As it was I was no means pleased with the reaction of the people. Perhaps I was too stilted in my delivery, due to the fact that I had not given sufficient preparation to the sermon, or to some temperamental indisposition that I had not taken the trouble to overcome. I suspect that the latter cause rather than the former was responsible for my stilted delivery, for on the second day of Sukkot (Sunday) when I had a much smaller attendance (about 110–120 people) on account of the rain, I spoke with far more fluency and ease on the subject of organization of Jewish life. On the other hand, the frequent iteration of the ideas in the second day's sermon may have much to do with the ease with which I spoke it.

Daughter Selma Has a Fright

TUESDAY, OCTOBER 2, 1928

This morning I had the fright of my life. As I was eating breakfast and Lena was having her cup of coffee, Selma ran in in a terrible fright and said that she swallowed a needle. Lena at once got hysterical and I ran down for the doctor on the ground floor of the house. When I was downstairs Lena called down that the needle was found. Selma imagined that she had swallowed it.

How in one moment all that which constitutes our life may tumble about as like a house of cards! The thoughts that naturally passed through my mind in those few minutes of the fright are too horrible for words.

Zionists Give a Reception for Allenby

MONDAY, OCTOBER 8, 1928

Last Thursday morning the Z.O. tendered a reception to Viscount Allenby who stopped for a few days in this city on his way to the Annual Convention of the American Legion, which is to take place at Houston, Texas. Herman Bernstein, who is a member of the Admin. Com. was entrusted with the task of arranging with Dr. Finlay[30] to make it possible for the Z.O. to arrange this reception for Allenby. When the question arose as to who should represent the Z.O. on that occasion Mr. Leaf[31] of Philadelphia nominated Judge Lewis.[32] The reception was scheduled for 9:45 in the morning.

I am such a greenhorn at these functions that I imagined there was to be a breakfast and that I might be called upon to give some opening prayer or benediction. Of course I went to the trouble of formulating what I would say, in case I would be called on. When I came to the Ambassador Hotel where the ceremonies were to take place I was surprised to find no tables, but simply a lot of chairs arranged in regular order for a meeting, with a dais and speaker's table at the head of the room. When Herman Bernstein arrived with Allenby, he invited the speakers to the platform. Although I took no part in the program I was also asked to sit on the platform. The speakers were Herman Bernstein, Masliansky,[33] Judge Lewis, Louis Marshall, Nathan Straus. Harry Sacher[34] and Dr. Finley were also on the platform.

Benderly Critical of TI Faculty to Their Faces

MONDAY, OCTOBER 8, 1928

Friday morning I had a conference with Dr. Benderly. I had Dr. Honor with me and I also asked Bragin whom I happened to meet at the Bureau to sit in. The main subject for which I called this conference was the question: How the work which Benderly was doing with his select group of Hebrew High School graduates would affect the progress of the Teachers

---

30. Abe Finley (1898–?), Lehigh University; tobacco and wholesale confectioner; Zionist leader; national executive board, Zionist Organization of America.

31. Samuel Leaf (1875–1938), Zionist leader; publisher; co-founder, *The Jewish World*.

32. William Lewis (1884–1939), municipal judge; civic and Zionist leader, Philadelphia.

33. Zvi Hirsh Masliansky (1856–1943), noted Zionist orator in Yiddish and Hebrew; teacher; editor, *Die Yidishe Velt*.

34. Harry Sacher (1881–1971), British Zionist and lawyer; Zionist executive; known for policies of economic efficiency

Institute. Honor had pointed out to me before I came to the conference that Benderly was taking away the best material from the TI and that, in addition, the proportion of male to female students was growing dangerously small. As a matter of fact, the decreasing number of boys that are taking advantage of Jewish educational courses is an evil that is flagrant already in the High School classes. But with this course which Dr. Benderly is conducting personally, and for which he takes the pick of the boys, the TI is apt to become a mere girls' seminary. (Incidentally, I may mention the fact that the predominance of the feminine element in the TI has prevented me from making the TI my chief interest as it should have been. Girls in the home, girls in the school. That was too much for me. I want to come to grips with the tougher human material present in the male.)

When I told Benderly of my fears about the TI and asked him whether it would not be possible to have the special group he is training also do work at the TI he broke out into a harangue in which he pooh poohed the suggestion I made. He was quite angry at the thought that he should be asked to surrender that group to the TI and asserted that he alone was qualified to give them what they needed in order to become leaders in Jewish life. He characterized Levine and Chertoff as unfit to teach and inspire the young people in the Institute. He told Bragin and Honor to their faces that they lacked the necessary personality to exercise the proper influence upon such as those whom he undertook to train. I squirmed in my seat to hear men so characterized to their faces. The very fact, however, that they had nothing to say in reply, proved the truth of his characterization. He said that I did possess the necessary qualities to train these people but that I did not have the time to give to them. He continued in this strain for half an hour quoting me in the course of his remarks against myself, by reminding me that I had always agreed with him that the Seminary was incapable of giving its students the proper kind of guidance and inspiration for their calling, and that if I had the chance I would have taken a few of the best students in hand and trained them myself. He certainly had the better of me in the argument. There was nothing further to be said. He's got to have his way. It is only a question of how he can possibly carry such a tremendous burden. My admiration and love for him have not been diminished in the least, although he refused to grant my request.

Visiting the Eldridge Street Synagogue—Memories from Boyhood

MONDAY, OCTOBER 15, 1928

This last weekend has been crowded with activity. As a result of the successful performance of the tasks that devolved upon me I feel considerably stronger and more self-confident than usual. The tasks I refer to were the following:

Friday night I spoke at the inaugural Friday night services at the Educational Alliance Building, E. Bway and Jefferson St. I enjoyed the experience immensely, not only the speaking, but my stay Friday night at the lower East Side. I visited the synagogue on Eldridge St. near Division where I had celebrated my Bar Mitzvah and where I had attended services and studied with my father from my twelfth to my fifteenth year. I fed my eyes on every part of the building. There were the same lofty vaults in the ceiling, the same stained glass windows, the same lighting fixtures, with the large chandelier suspended from the center of the ceiling by a long thin pipe which I used to be afraid would snap. On the almemar I recognized the bench which served as a container for talethim and prayer books. Boys rushed up now and then to snatch a prayer book as of old. The box of snuff tobacco was still there, and every once in a while someone would help himself to it in the course of the prayers. In fact the atmosphere was so strong with the smell of snuff tobacco that my nose was irritated. This sensation I do not recall having felt there as a boy. I also walked down to what is usually called the vestry. It was there I used to pray week days and study Talmud with father. I looked long at the seat near the Ark where he and I used to sit and engage in involved Talmud discussions. I recalled the joy and pride that would fill his heart when I would put a question to him that had been asked by some of the famous commentators. As I try to note specifically the peculiar nature of the sadness which overcame me during my visit to the synagogue I find that it had much in common with what Aristotle says is the effect of seeing a tragedy enacted on the stage. There seems to be much in common between the sense of the bygone and that experienced when seeing a tragic play. There is something histrionic [sic] in living over mentally the experience of one's childhood and youth, and it is naturally of a sad character since no achievement can measure up to the dreams of the possible.

I had been provided with a "meal ticket" which entitled me to a free meal at the vegetarian restaurant, 171 E. Bway. I enjoyed the unusualness of the meal and the strangeness of the surroundings. From time to time a little boy or girl with copies of the Jewish Day would come into the restaurant to sell papers.

After that I rested for an hour on a bench in Seward Park. Near me sat an old man who was telling his neighbor all about his children, their business, their troubles, their indifference to things Jewish, and he ended up singing to himself in a low tone melodies from the liturgy, and folk songs in Yiddish, and ended up with the sing-song of the magician intoning some of his own concoctions.

At the Educational Alliance there were seven and eight hundred people. The majority were young men. I learned later that most of these young men belonged to Young Israel, an organization of Jewish fundamentalists. There were about fifty old women, and the same number of old men. Of young women there must have been about 75 to 100. My talk was a summary of the sermons I had given on the holidays at the SAJ. I called it "The Test of Jewish Loyalty." I held the attention of the audience, yet when Lasker who conducted the services called for questions no one asked any. That was probably due to their not having been given a chance to collect their thoughts after I got through.

I had intended to walk back as far as I could, thinking that if I would find the walking a strain I would ride back the rest of the way. I personally did not believe that there was any value in insisting upon prohibitions like carrying and riding. It is only out of a desire to be in a position to work in the field of Judaism that I conform to the usual practice of abstaining from riding. At the conclusion of the service Lasker made the gratuitous remark to the people that I would walk all the way home. In addition, one of the graduates of the Seminary, Ed Horowitz,[35] insisted upon accompanying me home. I therefore had to walk, whether I wanted to or not.

RA Committee on Law Discussed Priesthood and Funerals

Wednesday, October 17, 1928

The Committee on Law appointed by the Rabbinical Assembly met this afternoon. It continued the discussion of the questions raised by Jacob Kohn concerning the right of "Kohen"[36] rabbi to officiate at funerals and study medicine. Finkelstein had sent around a memorandum giving his opinion from a legal standpoint. I presented my paper in which I took the attitude that the status of the priest should be maintained only for purposes of services in the synagogue and for the ceremony of *Pidyon Ha-Ben* [Heb. redemption of the first-born].[37] The maintenance of impurity laws was not defensible in view of our giving up the belief in the restoration of the sacrificial system. I was glad to see that I was able to give expression to such views without being regarded as disloyal to the principles of the Seminary.

---

35. Edward Horowitz (1904–?), ordained JTS 1927; author on teaching Hebrew; from Horowitz—Margareten family.

36. According to traditional laws of priestly purity a descendent of the Aaronide priesthood is rendered impure by contact with or close proximity to a dead person. Exceptions are made, of course, for the immediate family.

37. Pidyon Ha-Ben is a ritual performed on the thirty-first day following the birth of the first-born son, where the father redeems his child from the kohen or priest. For a record of the discussion on this matter see *Proceedings of the Rabbinical Assembly 1929*, (New York: Joseph Zukerman, n.d.), 155–65.

Reading Klatzkin at Coney Island

THURSDAY, OCTOBER 25, 1928

Lena and I spent the greater part of Friday and Saturday in Coney Island at the Half-Moon. The freedom from routine gave me an occasion to read Klatzkin's *Teḥumim* [Heb. boundaries].[38] I cannot say that his presentation of the Jewish problem added to the pleasure of my vacation. The conclusion which he arrives at that the Jews in the Diaspora ought to enter upon no compromises with their environment (and that all such compromises are only a means of hastening the death that is inevitable) had the depressing effect of the reminder that a day must come when each of us will be laid in his grave. Like the latter reminder, there are certain logical and physical inevitables which life must forget most of the time, if it is to carry on at all. That is the very trait of life to ignore, to mock at, to leap over death and not to allow itself to be obsessed or paralyzed over it. Klatzkin would have the Jewish people so obsessed by the thought that it must die everywhere except in Palestine; that it is bound to become too faint to survive even in Palestine. His strictures on Ahad Ha-Am are based on his misinterpretation of what Ahad Ha-Am attempts in his various generalizations concerning the spirit of Judaism. Misinterpreting Ahad Ha-Am to mean that these generalizations, which ascribe to Judaism values of a universal character, constitute the raison d'etre of Judaism. Klatzkin has no difficulty in proving that Ahad Ha-Am repeats the mistake of the Reformists. But that is not the case at all. Klatzkin first puts up a man of straw and then makes much ado in knocking him down. As to Klatzkin so to Ahad Ha-Am the justification in Judaism is in its individuality. That should not prevent him from discovering in Judaism values of a universal character. Klatzkin forgets that the more truly universal the spirit is in its functioning the more individual it is. Klatzkin still labors under the mistaken identification of individual with individualistic.

There are, however, a good many stimulating notions in Klatzkin's analysis. He is right in stressing the fact that no achieved value in Judaism can constitute a raison d'etre for remaining a Jew. The conclusion which I have been in the habit of drawing from this fact is that the raison d'etre of the Jewish people is to be found not in what it has achieved but in what it promises to achieve if given a chance to function normally. Insofar as a living being needs justification that justification must be based upon the future and not upon the past.

What he says about Jewish law is vitiated by his failure to distinguish

---

38. Jacob Klatzkin (1882–1948), author, philosopher, and Zionist whose collection of essays, *Teḥumim*, appeared in 1928.

between ceremonial and civil law. Nevertheless he senses correctly the part that ceremonies played in preserving Jewish life, though in his entire treatment of the subject he seems to be entirely unaware that the hold which the mitzvot had on the Jew was due to his belief that there were an indispensable means to salvation. For that matter, Klatzkin overlooks entirely that the real crux of the problem of Jewish life is the desuetude of the conviction that only through the Jewish people could any one achieve salvation. Nowadays the Jew, like most thinking people in the world, has changed his conception of salvation. How to relate remaining a Jew to salvation as we now conceive it—that in essence is the problem of Judaism.

Another thought to which I was led in reading his book was that by stressing the Jewish civilization rather than the nationality of the Jewish people as the object to be conserved and developed we might avoid being driven to the repugnant conclusion that sharing in the life of the nation of which we are citizens we are sinning against the Jewish people. I am sick and tired of this business of loyalties. Loyalty is absolution in the field of morals. It is that which prevents morality from ever having an aesthetic appeal. I am interested in conserving and developing a civilization because in being the unique incarnation of the collective life of a people it is as much an aesthetic object as any living thing or work of art. To be sure there are certain conditions that have to be met in order to render a civilization creative, the chief one being social interaction and organization.

On the other hand I avoid the mistake against which Klatzkin warns us, that of basing the raison d'etre of the civilization upon certain universal values. I agree with him in accepting a civilization as an end in itself.

Saturday night I saw the performance of Sholom Asch's[39] Kiddush Hashem at the Jewish Art Theatre, under the direction of Maurice Schwartz.[40] It is remarkable how much aesthetic potentiality lies dormant in the Jewish civilization. If we only had a few more men of the type of Maurice Schwartz it would not be so hard to be a Jew.

The Council for the Advancement of Judaism

THURSDAY, OCTOBER 25, 1928

The one achievement which holds out promise of proving in time to be of utmost significance is, I believe, the formation of the Council for the Advancement of Judaism. This morning the committee of nine appointed

---

39. Scholem Asch (1860–1957), Yiddish novelist and playwright.
40. Maurice Schwartz (1888–1960), actor, producer, and director; one of the leading figures of the American Yiddish stage. Founded the Yiddish Art Theater in New York in 1918.

at the suggestion of those who took part in the conference which took place at the SAJ House last June met at the Sulzberger Room of the Federation Building, 71 West 47 Street. Present were Benderly, Honor, Jacob Kohn, Max Raisin,[41] Henry Hurwitz, S. J. Karpf, Z. Scharfstein and I. The only one that had promised to come but was unavoidably prevented was Lowenstein.[42] In my opening remarks I set forth that the aim of the Council should be to maintain Jewish life whole and creative. This time I seemed to have struck it right. That purpose was adopted without any discussion. We then proceeded to formulate a plan or organization. We agreed that we want to limit the Council only to those who had something to say and were not afraid to say it. The publication of the views expressed was emphasized as of paramount importance. It should be our aim to develop into an organ of Jewish opinion. Hurwitz suggested that we should call in from time to time those at the helm of Jewish affairs to exchange ideas with them.

The question of the name was settled without much ado. Kohn objected to our being identified as an SAJ group. In order, however, that our connection with the SAJ be retained and somehow indicated we should adopt the name Council for the Advancement of Judaism. I readily assented to this suggestion, but stipulated that the SAJ Review be accepted as our official organ.

Which Is More Significant—My Theory about God or My Private Mental Tortures?

WEDNESDAY, NOVEMBER 21, 1928

The habit of writing this diary has grown on me to such an extent that I enjoy it as much as reading and derive much more satisfaction from it than I do from reading, because I feel, to use an expression that I heard from Dr. Schulman a long time ago, that I am engaging in an act of self-revelation. These things that I write up ought to have the value of a human document. Since God has not endowed me with a creative gift in the field of literature or art I think I might as well exploit myself as a means of giving expression to the creative urge. What I write down in obedience to this urge should have the same relation to what the gifted ones of earth do—say a man like Romain Rolland[43]—as the drawings of the cave dwellers to the paintings of Raphael. The only trouble is that I can ill afford the time I spend writing

---

41. Max Raisin (1880–1957), ordained Hebrew Union College; Zionist; author; director, Matz Foundation; rabbi, Paterson, N.J.

42. Probably Solomon Lowenstein (1877–1942), ordained Hebrew Union College; Zionist; executive officer, Federation of Jewish Philanthropies.

43. Romain Rolland (1866–1944), French novelist, playwright, biographer, and musicologist.

this diary. I imagine that I ought to use every spare moment to complete the articles I ought to have ready for the SAJ Review, or the books that are still in the process of gestation. I wonder, however, which is more worth while. Writing which records first hand experiences, however crude it be, it seems to me ought to have more value than formal writing in which we merely add to the endless discussions about this or that abstract concept. A detailed description, for example, of all the mental tortures I went through before and after the talk I gave last night should, it seems to me, be more interesting than my theory about God. But that detailed description must remain buried for a long time whereas the theory about God would make necessary copy for articles. To indulge in the former is therefore a luxury which must not be permitted to take up too much time.

A Banquet at the Astor Hotel—Social Discomfort

WEDNESDAY, NOVEMBER 21, 1928

I should like to describe the banquet which took place last night at the Astor. I thought I would come after the speaking had begun, because I was anxious to avoid being called on. Unfortunately they were still eating the fish—it was, of course, a kosher meal.

I was given a place at the head table next to Judge Lewis. Weizmann came over to greet me; Warburg happening to pass my way stopped to converse with me; other people also came over. Then Rottenberg served notice that I would be called on as the first speaker. From that moment my nerves were on edge. Lipsky's reference to indigestion that he developed as a result of his anxiety at banquets occasioned by his having to make speeches was not calculated to give me any encouragement. When Joe Levy came over to me I suggested momentary aphasia and forgot Judge Lewis's name so that I was unable to introduce him to Levy. It is this aphasia that accounts for my inability to draw on a sufficiently large vocabulary in developing my thought. When I begin to speak I feel as though I was trying to swim with a cramp in my leg. Now and then the mind cramp leaves me and I launch out with some vigor, but soon it comes back again.

Every time I go through such an experience I become disgusted with life. In my attempt to take the matter philosophically I begin to act silly when no one is around. I make grimaces and all kinds of odd gestures and emit words like one who is gone out of his mind. The effect of this reaction went so far last night that I thought that I better get hold of myself before it got the better of me. Even when I woke up this morning I still was under the spell of that reaction. It wore off only after I read in this morning's Yiddish paper the report of what I said. From the report it seemed that the impression I made must have been passable, to say the least.

What especially unnerves me on these occasions is that I am absolutely tongue tied when it comes to handing out compliments of a personal character and expressing the appropriate good wishes. This time I did not say a word about Weizmann's returning to Europe or about Mrs. Weizmann. Every other speaker had some gracious things to say about Mrs. Weizmann. Warburg called her W's minister of the interior. This awkwardness and mental inflexibility are no doubt due to my retired and unsocial life. But what am I to do if I have to be continually on tap and my memory is so poor that I have to be constantly replenishing it in order not to run out of supply?

Dr. Finkelstein failed to appear at the meeting of the committee appointed by Adler at the last Faculty meeting to consider the problem presented by the inadequate homiletic training of the Seminary men. Dr. Hyamson who besides myself is the other member of the committee insisted upon discussing the problem despite Finkelstein's absence. I mentioned Davidson's suggestion. Hyamson at once proposed a compromise plan, one year instead of two, to be devoted to the specific work of the ministry.

The following are the conclusions we arrived at:

1. Each student shall be required to write four sermons during each year of his stay at the Seminary.
2. That one whole year be devoted to studies that have a direct bearing on the work in the ministry.
3. That the department of Homiletics be given the full time service of the man at the head of it and that in addition he be given an assistant.

A Messy Desk Means a Confused Mind? — Kaplan at Home

THURSDAY, NOVEMBER 22, 1928

My desk has been so littered up of late that many important letters and other material to be looked over are misplaced and I have to waste precious half hours excavating some needed letter or document. This disorder on the desk reflects itself in the disordered state of my thoughts every time I sit down to work. Last year I managed to clear my desk every night before I went to bed, but this year with the unprecedented amount of details I have to attend to I get to bed between one and two every night. I do not feel then in a mood to spend an hour or two clearing up a desk. When I get up the morning is so far gone that I hate to use up any of it on merely putting things away. In the meantime the additional mail is deposited on the amassed heap and I haven't the courage to attempt bringing order out of the chaos. The fact is the room is too small and crowded for the amount of reading material I keep on getting all the time.

At times, however, the confusion on the desk reaches a stage which simply makes is impossible for me to go on with my work. This was the case this afternoon. I had been very eager to sit and write up quite a few incidents and thoughts, but I found myself unable to budge unless I brought some order on my desk. This led to my discovering letters I had forgotten about, and picking up articles in the *Nation* and other periodicals which I could not pass over without reading. Although most of what was on the desk is now below it I shall have to spend much more time before my mind will be sufficiently composed to go on with my routine.

I have to stop at this point because Lena keeps on nagging that I go to supper. The children have to eat earlier than usual in order to be able to take their music lesson in time (6:30 P.M.).

Meeting Tchernichowski—The Pagan

FRIDAY, NOVEMBER 23, 1928

I went to see Saul Tchernichowski, who recently arrived in New York and who is stopping at the Ansonia, Broadway and 72 St., to invite him to visit the Teachers Institute and to address the students. Knowing that I would converse with him and his secretary Dr. Feldstein in Hebrew, I read this morning some of the articles in the *Reshummot* [Heb. Record or Gazette].[44] So as to get into a Hebrew frame of mind. On the way to the hotel I was trying to formulate the answer I would give Dr. Feldstein who, I expected, would ask me to help him to interest some of my friends in the Tarbut in whose interest Tschernichowski came here. I thought I would tell him that although he probably hears my name mentioned as an *askan tsiburi* [Heb. community worker] and therefore as one of the *penei ha'ir* or *penei ha-kehillah* [Heb. city official or community official][45] I am in reality not of the *penei* [Heb. face] or *Einei* [Heb. eyes] but merely a *masveh* [Heb. mask] behind which some people hide to give the impression that they are doing their share of Jewish effort. Being merely a *Masveh* [mask] and not of the *Penei* or *Einei* I can not exercise any influence on those amongst whom I move.

I found Tch. dressed in a sweater, a jolly blond haired heavy mustached slav featured man in the fifties. He was combing his bushy hair with a small comb all the time I was with him. I had met him in Jerusalem and therefore found it easy to fall into conversation with him. He asked many

---

44. Reshummot: a Hebrew journal dealing with folklore published in Odessa between the wars.

45. The Hebrew here is an idiomatic expression which literally means the "face of the city" and refers to officials. Kaplan intends a play on words in what follows.

questions about the T.I. He wanted to know what was the subject that I taught. When I told him *Emunah* [46] (religion) I purposely avoided the use of the word *Dat* thinking that he would realize that I wasn't teaching merely the ceremonies. He expressed astonishment. I found it necessary to explain to him that I was teaching my subject from the evolutionary point of view and that I regarded it as necessary to help the students to adjust themselves to the problems of modern life. It seems that Tch. is so much of a Hebrew pagan in its aboriginal sense that I wouldn't be surprised to see in his home the images of Baal and Ashtoret and him burning incense before them.

Thoughts on Art, Gandhi, and Ice Cream Soda

Saturday, November 24, 1928

There seems to be much promise in the idea of approaching both religion in general and Judaism in particular neither with the creedal nor with the rational but with the poetic state of mind. Today I gave the third sermon on that idea. There were only about 100 people present due to the weather being gray and raw.

This afternoon I visited with Lena the art studio of the Palestinian artist Rubin.[47] I was able to appreciate his landscapes more than his portraits which are done in what I believe to be impressionistic style. I confess that I am a consummate Am-Haarez [ignoramus] in matters musical and artistic.

As I was working this evening alone in the house I felt that I would like to walk over to Schrafft's for an ice cream. But then there occurred to me what I read the other day about Gandhi's asceticism and I thought perhaps I ought to try to emulate his example and refrain from gratifying my want. On reflection, however, it appeared that I would be so busy the rest of the evening fighting off this particular desire that I might be distracted from my work. So I went and I had my ice cream soda. Was this merely "rationalization"?

---

46. The Hebrew word *Emunah* is usually taken to mean faith or belief. Kaplan translated it as religion here. The word *dat* which refers to religion has the connotation of law.

47. Reuven Rubin (1893–1974), Beaux Arts (Paris); LL.D. Jewish Institute of Religion; artist and author, Tel Aviv.

7

November 25, 1928–March 9, 1929

Tchernichowski

SUNDAY, NOVEMBER 25, 1928

As I sat down to work this evening on comparing Wohlgemuth's edition[1] of the Mesillat with the first Amsterdam edition of 1740, my mind kept on reverting to what I ought to say next Sunday in introducing Tchernichowski. It occurred to me that in view of his pagan proclivities I ought to say that Tchernichowski's service consists in so retrieving the fascination of ancient idolatry that one can understand why it was so hard to wean away the ancient Jews from it. I hesitate however to pay such a left handed compliment to Tch. who is, after all, to be the guest of the Institute. As this conflict was going on in my mind I came across the following passage in the Mesillat:[2] "They who praise the wicked man despite his wickedness, instead of censuring him to his face for his transgression, are themselves guilty of forsaking the Torah and permitting it to be profaned. On the other hand, they who keep the Torah and exert every effort to maintain it are unable to restrain themselves and be silent."

Dilemma of Introducing Tchernichowski — Praying and Hebrew

MONDAY, DECEMBER 3, 1928

Lena and I left last Thursday (Thanksgiving Day) for Long Beach where we stayed till Saturday night. I enjoyed both the change and the rest.

---

1. Joseph Wohlgemuth (1867–1942), rabbi, educator, and theologian; translated *Mesillat Yesharim* into German in 1906.

2. Kaplan noted the full passage from Mesillat Yesharim in Hebrew in the diary. The translation comes from Kaplan in the edition that he edited. Moses Hayyim Luzzatto, *Mesillat Yesharim — The Path of the Upright*, ed. Mordecai Kaplan (Philadelphia: Jewish Publication Society, 1936), 175.

There were few people about both in the hotel Frontenac where we stopped and on the paved walk near the sea over which we strolled back and forth. The pleasure of not having to prepare any sermon and of being spared the insufferable annoyance of witnessing the moronic looks on the majority of the audience was indeed a treat. But although I was not engaged in routine mental labor I used the time to read up the articles in the *HaTkufa*[3] about Tschernichowski whom I was scheduled to greet at the Teachers Institute last Sunday. I also read some of Tschernichowski's and Jacob Cohen's[4] poetry.

I cannot say that I have adjusted myself mentally to Tch's. poetry. No doubt it is vigorous, elemental and passionately sincere in its sensuousness, whenever he sings of life and the flesh. His idylls abound in beautiful pictures. But why must he offend and blaspheme and demolish all that piety and devotion and self sacrifice have striven to create? The self-suppressions and fanaticisms should not to the true poet be objects of hatred or even pity, but manifestations of life to be understood. To me this recrudescence of paganism, this self-identification not with the Maccabees but with the conquerors of Canaan appears as nothing more than infantilism. Are we Jews so senile that we take pleasure in imagining ourselves wading through the blood of the Canaanites? Too bad, that when at last there does appear among us one who is articulate and has the gift of song, he should prove to be nothing more than an overgrown adolescent destined never to attain maturity.

Seldom did I recite prayers with such gusto as I did after I read Tch's poetry and the poems of praise in honor of the 25th anniversary of his literary career. But I have not yet come out of the saddening effect produced on me by the thought that at a time when we Jews are struggling to eke out some good from the thirty centuries that we have been blundering and sinning and dreaming and suffering, there should come along one of our own flesh and blood and tell us that our entire history has been a cosmic illusion. Tch. with all the simplicity and fervor of a Rousseau but with what in him is unforgivable ignorance and immaturity, would have us apparently become primitive idolaters. And for this our Hebraists applaud and adore him.

And since it is the fashion for the Teachers Institute to honor those whom the Hebraists honor, I had to arrange a meeting of the students and graduates to greet Tch. My heart wasn't in the effort, but a mediocrity like me must not think of obeying the dictates of his heart. How I toiled Saturday night after I came back from the meeting at Cooper Union and Sunday morning over the few sentences that I was to speak at the meeting!

---

3. *HaTkufa*: a Hebrew literary journal published in Moscow, Warsaw, and Berlin.

4. A minor Hebrew poet whom Kaplan read in order to put himself in a "Hebraic" frame of mind.

This business of teaching in Hebrew and speaking in Hebrew which I am gradually acquiring some fluency isn't making me overhappy either. Chertoff was not altogether wrong when he said to me last Sunday that we have become addicted to a new idolatry. No matter how fluent we become in the use of Hebrew, the fluency consists very often in the ability to find readily something else to say besides what one originally intended, for in a foreign environment and with so inflexible and limited a vocabulary as the Hebrew possesses it is impossible to express all shades of thought. It is certainly next to impossible except for those who read and teach the language every day of their lives to think so freely in it as to have its words call up new ideas. The students certainly are prevented from discussing freely the subject matter studied. And worst of all this importance which the Hebrew schools attach to the ability to speak the language prevents the students from ever knowing the parts of the Bible which are interwoven with the life of the Jew—Torah and the earlier prophets. Not a single student in the Junior Class—after ten years of Jewish education—had the least idea about the brazen serpent which Moses made in the wilderness. The nearest that one got to it was it had something to do with the miracle that he worked in Egypt.

I feel that someday I shall create a scandal among the Teachers Institute staff by declaring war against this miserable slavishness to mere language regardless of the cost in genuine knowledge that the students might otherwise attain.

Last night I gave a lecture at the Zionist Centre of the First District (52 St. Marks Place). The audience was more attentive and interesting than any that I have occasion to address in this part of the city. Certainly the questions asked were far more to the point than I have ever gotten from the people I addressed at the SAJ.

Unevenness of the Inner Life

Thursday, December 6, 1928

I cannot understand why of late I find it so hard to record my experiences. Only a week or two ago I actually found pleasure in writing this diary, but lately the pleasure seems to have evaporated and I have to labor on each sentence. If it were not for the momentum which I have acquired from the habit of keeping my diary I surely would have given up in disgust the attempt to write any further.

There are no two days in which the "tenor of my way" is even. My inner life is much more like a landscape in which heavy autumnal clouds are being driven by a strong wind. For a moment it is luminous with golden sunshine, but for long stretches of time the sun is shut out by the long leaden clouds which wrap the scene in wintry melancholy.

Whenever I feel to write up my experiences immediately after their occurrence I find it difficult to do so late, especially if at the time that I take up my pen to record them my mood has changed. Many happenings which seem important for a few hours after their occurrence often appear trivial after a few days.

A Hanukah Sermon — Past Does Not Give Guidance

THURSDAY, DECEMBER 6, 1928

Here I am sitting and cudgelling my brain what to talk about before the SAJ congregation on Saturday morning—Sabbath Hanukah. The people naturally expect the regulation type of propaganda sermon to tell them to emulate the example of the Maccabees etc. But it is impossible for me to give that kind of sermon because there is very little analogy between the Jewish situation then and the Jewish situation today. The Hanukah festival is a striking instance of the fact that however much inspiration the past may afford us it can give us but little guidance in solving the problems that confront us. Why not then take that idea itself as the theme of the sermon and deal with the problems presented by the circumstance that the past should inspire us to live as Jews, but should not be expected to help us out of our difficulties. That we have to think out anew.

What is the significance and what is the value of inspiration as applied to the Jewish heritage?

This reminds me of the sermon preached by the student at the Seminary last Wednesday. He kept on reiterating the importance of being true to the past. I should have asked him whether he expected to Jews to be loyal to that past which was so silly as to eliminate the Book of the Maccabees. Perhaps I should take as my subject the strange circumstance that we owe to the Church the recovery of the history of that period and therefore the self-respect which that recovery has brought us. Likewise we owe the biblical scholars the more intelligent reconstruction of the biblical past. But there still remains the humiliation that we have not had sense enough to appreciate what we have. We must live down that humiliation by making it possible for Jewish scholars to work freely and devote themselves to the reconstruction of the entire past and the proper interpretation of it in terms of human experience.

FRIDAY, DECEMBER 7, 1928

This morning I worked out the outline of a sermon on moral courage. The point I make that it was the lack of moral courage in the wealthy and influential Jews that brought on the Jewish people the tyrannical decrees of

Antiochus to suppress the Jewish religion. Jacob Grossman[5] came to learn what I had to say. Signer[6] had intended to come but was prevented.

It took me some time to persuade Grossman that the action of Antiochus was the culmination of a campaign against Judaism carried on by the Hellenizing Jews, and that the latter were more to blame for the danger which then confronted Judaism than Antiochus. The only version of the events leading up to the victories of the Maccabees, with which he was familiar, was the one he got from the Sunday School Hanukah plays.

Celebrating Hanukah — Tchernichowski Attends a Congregational Party

TUESDAY, DECEMBER 11, 1928

Last night the SAJ congregation celebrated Hanukah with dinner entertainment and dancing. There were about 140 people present. For the first time in the history of the SAJ there was no need of calling up the people by phone to make their reservations. The meal was satisfactory hence the evening was considered a great success. It is remarkable to what extent our people insist upon being amply fed, and with real red meat in plenty too.

And who should be among the guests there? No less a person than Tchernichowski. I think he was brought by Dr. Einhorn. Like all the other men he put on the chef's garb of white apron and cap and seemed to feel at home, though his lack of English prevented him from being communicative. I do not think he possesses any sense of humor, certainly not of satire or cynicism. The more I see of him the more I find him to be an overgrown boy, a typical poet. He seemed to have taken a sort of idyllic delight in the decorous fashion in which those present joined in the singing of the Hanukkah hymns and the recital of the grace, though, as he remarked, they did not understand the meaning of the words.

Solomon Schechter's Wit

THURSDAY, DECEMBER 13, 1928

Schechter was certainly a man of extraordinary wit. This morning Jacob Grossman mentioned two of Schechter's sayings. One was to the effect that "he was going to have his greatness cut off" meaning that he was going

---

5. Jacob Grossman (1886–1970s?) Columbia B.A.; JTS 1911; rabbi, New York City and Flushing, N.Y.; helped found Camp Tabor; frequented Kaplan household to discuss sermon material.

6. Isador Signer (1900–1953), ordained JTS; rabbi, Brooklyn and Bethlehem, Penn.; executive committee, Rabbinical Assembly.

to the barber; the other in which he spoke indulgently of my "epikursos" as helping me more than anybody else.

Writing the Diary in the Third Person — The Ego and the Observer

TUESDAY, DECEMBER 18, 1928 [KAPLAN WRITING ABOUT HIMSELF IN THE THIRD PERSON]

In a fit of curiosity he asked Judith the other day what she thought of his idea of having his diary written in the third person. She told him she had once tried using the third person in her own diary but she soon gave it up because it sounded artificial.

He reflected, "It may be so. But there seems to be a good deal more to this attempt of making use of third person in telling a story about oneself than appears on the surface. It cannot be merely a whim. It may have something to do with the fact that each one of us is intrinsically a dual personality; one the actor, the other the onlooker. Our self knowledge would have been much further advanced, if language had evolved two forms of the personal pronoun which denote the first person, one form to designate the self in its extrovert capacity of being absorbed in and identified with a thousand and one things; the other form to designate the self in its introvert capacity acting as the detached onlooker and judge, evaluating the preoccupied ego, approving or disapproving of it, sympathizing with it or ridiculing it. Metaphysicians, of course, long ago recognized the difference between these two kinds of ego. It is only the scientific psychologists with their mechanical categories who have only confused matters by obliterating the boundaries between these two selves.

One thing is certain that the onlooker-ego is much more the product of deliberate cultivation than the active ego. The onlooker ego transcends the limits of the body to which alone of all bodies it has entree to the same extent that the life process does which makes the heart beat and awakens the physical hungers. The question then arises "what relations subsist between the life's process and the mind process?"

He began to grow dizzy as he contemplated the cosmic implications of his own ego and his mind reverted to his latest fad, filling his diary, postponing for some more leisurely hour the attempt to arrive at some working formula which might solve the metaphysical problem which he set before himself. He had a weakness for formulas. Never having had the fortune of experiencing the thrill of firsthand contact with things he lived in a universe of words. His greatest of all bibles, the source and fount of all that which is worthwhile in human life was—the dictionary. But he never lost sight of the greater reality of the universe of things which was denied to him. He never heard the phonograph, radio or telephone without wishing it were appropriate to kneel down and worship. If he had his way he would have created a ritual and recommended specific benedictions to be recited before making use of these great products of human ingenuity.

All these thoughts crowded into his mind as he was sitting on the train bound for Schenectady where he was scheduled to lecture in the evening. He began to wonder what this craving to write was which seized him like a madness. To be sure he had always harbored the ambition to write, but never was he so obsessed with it as of late. Not having any writing paper on which to jot down his thoughts he wrote on the back of a circular which he happened to find and when the blank part of the circular gave out he continued to write between the lines of the text. After every such writing spell he would experience a sense of calm as though he had succeeded in accomplishing something that had permanence to it, something, therefore, that rescued his life from the vortex of time. But before long that feeling would vanish. "How insecure is our sense of security, how transient our experience of permanence" he said to himself.

Rebelling against Parents

Tuesday, December 18, 1928

On the other hand, there were some people, two women (of the Sisterhood of one of the synagogues) who approached the lecturer after he was through to get his advice about securing a rabbi who could help to put some life into the community. He gave the man to understand that if he will try to cater to the older people he will destroy the community. It was evident to him that the younger people were suffering from an overdose of *kibbud av* [Heb. Honor thy father] which was responsible for their doing nothing to reconstruct Jewish life in accordance with their outlook. They are afraid of hurting the feelings of their narrow-minded bigoted parents whom they regard with a degree of reverence which those parents never merited. It dawned on him that numerous other congregations in this country are suffering from the evil of exaggerated filial piety. He recalled that in the first congregation where he ministered that condition obtained. Much as many of the younger folks had agreed with him as to the need of meeting the problems of Jewish life in a new way they never supported him in any of his suggestions because they would not think of displeasing their elders. Some one, he thought, ought to write a book that would deal with Jewish life in the same spirit as Butler's *The Way of All Flesh* deals with English life. That book exercised an emancipating influence upon him. Although he never had been an idolatrous worshipper of his parents, he could not in his younger days help doubting the rightness of his attitude toward his parents in oft questioning their wisdom and even their authority. He ceased to be troubled by such compunctions after he read Butler's book. That is why he now felt the need of such a book for Jewish life.

Thoughts on Jewish Nationhood

TUESDAY, DECEMBER 18, 1928

He stayed overnight at Schenectady and took the train for New York. After whiling away an hour or two on the three outstanding humorous periodicals which did not succeed in evoking from him more than one or two faint inward smiles, he betook himself to thinking about the question of Jewish nationhood which was to be the subject of his third lecture the coming Thursday night before the Avukah.[7] He worked out the following outline:

1. At the basis of the impassioned belief that the time will come when God would in extraordinary miraculous fashion lead His people back to their land was the irresistible call to nationhood, a call which the Jews felt in their blood and in their souls to a far more intense degree than the members of any other people.
2. The important question upon the answer to which will depend whether that call should be heeded now that it has grown fainter and that is being gradually silenced by other claims and distractions, is whether the call of nationhood is the call of the wild or the call of the spirit.
3. The answer must be based, *first,* upon proof that nationhood is so much part of human life that not only can it not be suppressed but that it crops up in the most unexpected quarters, in other words that it is inevitable. This is borne out by the following historical facts: a) The birth of modern science instead of retarding national development by reason of its giving rise to better means of communication and to transnational interests, was simultaneous with the birth of modern nationalities, English, Dutch, French, German, etc. b) The War which seemed to have been precipitated by national animosities should logically have given nationalism a set back. Instead it was followed by the birth of new national ties and the intensification of national sentiment. c) The Soviet Republic which has been established on an anti-nationalistic ideology, recognizing in that ideology a means of diverting the mind of the workers and the peasants from the class struggle, has nevertheless had to reckon with the various national groups and cultures that go to make up the Russian Republic. These national groups have far greater

---

7. Avukah: U.S. students' Zionist federation established in 1925 with the support of the Zionist Organization of America. It carried on important educational work.

freedom than they ever had under the Czarist regime. To be sure, the Communists try to save their face by claiming that they are only utilizing the national sentiment to destroy the capitalistic system but in the meantime they are fortifying nationhood. Likewise Russia as a whole is developing a national sentiment of its own.

Secondly, upon a rationale of nationhood. Its rationale is the fact that association based upon geographical propinquity is the indispensable prerequisite to all those efforts by which the human being endeavors to transcend the limitations of his physical nature. Of course if we take the view that the human being is only another species of animal and that life and thought are only so many additional manifestations of a complex mechanism, the only factor that should be reckoned with is the food supply. Not only an army but the whole of mankind marches on its stomach. The only divisions that really matter are divisions of class, the exploiter and the exploited. This is in brief the philosophy of economic determinism. But if we hold that values are just as real as so called facts, and that they have a share in the determination of human life, then we must look to geographic grouping as the main source of values, or spiritual factors. *Nationhood* has produced religion and the arts. The conventional idea that religion produced the arts views the matter from the wrong perspective. If religion were the parent of the arts, the arts would not have flourished when religion is in decay. The only religion that makes a difference in the life of its adherents is the religion that is associated with a history and not merely with a philosophy, and a history means the history of a geographic group. Christianity was victorious over the philosophic religions mainly because it adopted the history of the Jews and interpreted it to refer to the Christianized Roman Empire.

At the present time with the increasing tendency to have labor so divided and mechanized that very few human beings could possibly find their spiritual self-fulfillment in their labor, nationhood is becoming all the more important as a compensation for the fragmentary life of the worker. More than ever will he have to live vicariously through the other members of the nation, in order to round out his own limited existence. How is it possible to compare the opportunities for vicarious living presented by so variegated and permanent a group as one's nation (or geographic entity) with those offered by one's industrial group which is never more than transient and to which one belongs only for a limited number of years, or those offered by any other purposive group?

Thirdly, upon a rationale of Jewish nationhood. Such a rationale must consist of a workable plan that will indicate how the nationhood of the Jew is to function in view of its present dissociation from territory. That the functioning of nationhood is inconceivable without some territory is now quite self-evident. Assuming, however, that such a territory will be set aside for those who want to get back to reinstate Jewish nationhood, what is to be the status of those Jews who will remain in the Diaspora? There can not be one answer for all the Jews in the Diaspora. In the minority countries the Jews will exercise a large measure of cultural self-determination. In America the nationhood of the Jew will have to be limited to such cultural life as effective communal organization that exercises a disciplinary, educational and palliative control over the individual Jew.

SAJ as a New Denomination

THURSDAY, DECEMBER 22, 1928

Alexander Dushkin called this afternoon. In discussing the SAJ Council he stated that neither the Reformists nor the Conservatives seemed to be convinced of the need of having a special group or movement to sponsor the program of reconstruction. Freehof[8] speaking for the Reformists maintains that this program can be dealt with directly by the Central Conference of American Rabbis for Reform is not committed to any static program. Likewise Kadushin maintains that the Rabbinical Assembly can be gotten to accept the program of reconstruction by those of us who subscribe to that program working from within.

If that is true I ought to give up the prospect of ever seeing the SAJ develop into a national movement. Judging, however, by the reactionary spirit which dominates the counsels of the Rabbinical Assembly there seems to be little likelihood of the progressives in the Assembly carrying their policies. The same is probably true of the CCAR. There is certainly a need of some concerted action on the part of some self-conscious group to compel both organizations to give heed to the demands of their progressive members.

Lecturing in Savannah, Georgia — A Description of the Jewish Community

THURSDAY, DECEMBER 27, 1928: ON WAY TO JACKSONVILLE[9]

I got to Savannah yesterday at 5:00 P.M. and was met at the station by Mr. Pinsker,[10] the executive director of the local Educational Alliance.

---

8. Solomon Freehof (1892–1990), ordained, D.D., Hebrew Union College; authority on Responsa; author; faculty, Hebrew Union College.

9. Those interested in local Jewish history between the wars will find much material in the original of the Kaplan Diary. He traveled widely on speaking tours and gave detailed accounts of the places he visited.

10. William Pinsker (1896–?), social work administrator, communal worker, Boston; Educational Alliance, Savannah; worked in Brockton, Mass.

I learned from him that the population was 100,000 divided into Whites, Negroes and Jews. Till about two years ago there were 5000 Jews in Savannah, but recently more than 1500 left Savannah because of the decrease of business. With the transfer of cotton to the southwest, Savannah instead of shipping 3,000,000 bales per year shipped only 600,000 last year. Savannah has a number of survivors of old Jewish families of Sephardic descent. Most of the members of those families intermarried with the gentile population. The Jews take pride in a family by the name of Sheftel[11]whose founder fought in the Revolutionary war. Today there are three branches to that family, Jewish, Christian, and colored. During the latter part of the nine-teenth century there was an influx of German Jews and during the first part of this century Savannah was utilized as a way station by the agency which tried to distribute the Jewish immigrants among various smaller cities in this country. A goodly portion of this last element belong to the Arbeiter Ring.[12]

The only congregation there is the one that was founded by the Portuguese Jews almost 200 years ago and which is now Reformed. It numbers about 1200 souls. The rabbi is Solomon,[13] a graduate of the Hebrew Union College. He called on me at the hotel. He is not a well man, just having returned from Mayo's Sanitarium where he had gone to be cured of a malignant case of anemia. He looks to be a man of about 50. He has been occupying the position in Savannah since he graduated from the HUC 25 years ago. He deplores his having remained so long in Savannah where he has been unable to find any one with whom he could establish intellectual contacts. The only time he had an opportu-nity to engage in serious study was when the Orthodox element had as their rabbi a Dr. Goldberg, a Seminary graduate, who died about fifteen years ago. Rabbi Solomon used to study Hebrew from four to five hours daily with Dr. Goldberg. He put aside all communal work to take advan-tage of Goldberg's companionship which he knew could not last long. He was anxious, as he put it, to make hay while the sun shone. It was pitiable to see the frustrated look in his eyes. He was as a young man one of those who go into the rabbinate with the expectation of intel-lectual growth only to find themselves disillusioned before long. I could see how eager he was to have a long chat with me about some of the

---

11. Mordecai Sheftall (1735–95), born in Savannah; merchant; rancher; prisoner of British during Revolution.

12. Arbeiter Ring (also known as the Workmen's Circle): a fraternal Jewish labor society formed in the United States in 1900 with emphasis on Yiddish culture.

13. George Solomon (1873–1945), ordained Hebrew Union College; rabbi, Savannah; leader, Reform rabbinate; promoter of racial understanding.

fundamental problems of life in general and Judaism in particular, but unfortunately there was no possibility of my remaining over for any length of time.

The descendants of the Sephardic Jews in Savannah have been decreasing in number because those who were loyal to Jewish tradition refused to intermarry with the Gentiles; nor would they intermarry with the German Jews whom they considered their social inferiors. They did not admit German Jews even as seat holders of the synagogue. It took ten years for the latter to get a foothold in the synagogue, and another ten years before they were admitted to membership. At present these German Jews outdo their Sephardic predecessors in their exclusive attitude toward the more recent arrivals. They do not look with favor even upon Rabbi Solomon's participation in the Jewish communal matters outside of their own congregation.

The Educational Alliance Building where I gave my lecture is a sort of communal center where Jewish young folks meet for recreational and sport activities and to a limited extent also for literary activities. Despite the lack of positive Jewish content there is apparently fostered considerable Jewish consciousness which is chiefly race consciousness. There is no Hebrew school in the building nor do I believe there is one anywhere else. The non-Reformed elements are without a rabbi. Not long ago the Orthodox element had the man whom they had engaged as a Hebrew teacher to function as rabbi, although he admitted frankly that he did not believe in religion. Pinsker, the present executive director of the Educational Alliance, comes from Wilkes Barre. He has held his present position for the last eight years and seems to be largely responsible for the racial Jewishness which is the only bond that holds some of the young people to Judaism. But he is already impatient of small town limitations and contemplates giving up his position to go into publicity work. Unless some unforeseen cause should stop the process of attrition it is difficult to see how Savannah Jewry can last more than two or three generations.

There was a small attendance at the lecture which I gave last night because, as Pinsker explained, a mid-week night is a very poor one for lectures. The main lecture evening is Sunday. Moreover this week there has been taking place large social and sports events. At the game (basketball) played between the Jacksonville and Savannah Jewish athletic groups there were about 450. At my lecture there were about 100. Personally I think this is a good percentage. As for fostering Jewishness I believe the basketball game can compare very favorably with my lecture. My theme was "Toward a Reconstruction of Judaism." The lecture was listened to with understanding by an appreciable part of the audience. I think only one person slept.

A Sense of Beauty

THURSDAY, DECEMBER 27, 1928

I've just come across an extremely interesting observation by Santayana in *The Sense of Beauty*[14] p. 62. "Man unlike some of the lower animals has not his instincts clearly distinct and intermittent but always partially active and never active in isolation."

If that be the case the departmentalized mind is more akin to that of the lower animals than to what the mind tends to develop into in the human being. Likewise the division of labor in isolating abilities and interests in order to render them efficient is bound to push down the human mind to the level of the minds of lower animals.

SATURDAY, DECEMBER 29, 1928: ATLANTA, GA., ANSLEY HOTEL

Somewhere in this book I complain of a sense of aloneness in the very midst of the little world in which I move. That sense of aloneness is only a subjective state. It is paradise compared to the oppressive solitude which is real and objective when a person finds himself as I do now away from his little world in a remote city where he has not a single acquaintance to talk to. During all the hours that I have had all to myself my imaginative experience has been rich and satisfying. Between drinking in the delights of the scenery that I saw from the train window as I rode from Jacksonville and having my aesthetic faculty sharpened by my reading of Santayana's *The Sense of Beauty*, my imagination has veritably been having a royal feast. Uncultivated as my mind is in the appreciation of musical form, my enjoyment being limited to the content of the music, I am happy that at least natural scenery affords me not merely the calm serenity which derives from its mere mass, color and infinite variety, but also that exquisite joy which comes from the knack which I have acquired of spontaneously dividing up that scenery into unitary landscapes.[15] As I looked out of the train window yesterday I had the sensation of passing through an immense picture gallery hung with painted landscapes, depicting the infinite variations of the bronzes and greens of the earth, and the blues and ambers of the sky made luminous by the fiery gold of the afternoon sun. As my eyes wearied through the abundance of seeing, I took up Santayana's book and there my imaginative faculty was being schooled to know itself and to function adequately. With all that I have been restless and unsatisfied because I miss my world. Sant. is right

---

14. George Santayana, *The Sense of Beauty—Being the Outline of an Aesthetic Theory* (New York: George Scribners Sons, 1899).

15. Kaplan tried his hand at the plastic arts. He painted and sculpted. A photograph of a bust of his father which he created can be found in *Judaism Faces the Twentieth Century: A Biography of Mordecai M. Kaplan* (Detroit: Wayne State University Press, 1993), 350.

when he says "Social needs are almost as fundamental as vital functions and often more conscious." The very pleasure which I derive from reading is due not only to the feeling of discovery experienced in becoming aware of new truth, but mainly to the anticipation of employing those truths to help others find life—and Jewish life in particular—interesting and beautiful.

Jewish Life in St. Louis

DECEMBER 31, 1928: ON THE TRAIN FROM ST. LOUIS TO KANSAS CITY, 5:20 P.M. C.T.

The pulse of Jewish life in St. Louis is not as weak as I have found it in the smaller towns. The Jews are said to number 50,000 out of a population of 1,000,000. There are four Reform congregations with a total membership of about 1700 families. A merger of these congregations is contemplated at the present time. There are only two functioning rabbis there just now. One is R. Thurman,[16] a pushing energetic young man of the Litvack type. He is one of those younger Reform rabbis who if they have any Zionist leanings are sure to have them figure as little as possible in their practical work in the ministry. The second is R. Miller who is said to be a rabid anti-Zionist.

When R. Halpern[17] came to St. Louis twelve years ago he found the Orthodox Jews in a very disorganized state. His congregation consisted then of sixty members and all that they had was a small rudely built synagogue without facilities even for a school. It now numbers 400 members with a week day school of 150 children and with about as many additional children in the Sunday school. Until this year R. Halpern used to conduct Friday night services, but he found that the attendance dwindled down to 75 to 100. He therefore transferred his sermon to Saturday morning. The average attendance is between four and five hundred. Most of those who attend live far away from the synagogue and therefore have to come with their automobiles. It is interesting to note the matter of course spirit [text not clear] with which a congregation that claims to be orthodox permits what legalistically is tantamount to the utmost violation of the Sabbath. Yet were the least innovation suggested in the ritual or manner of service it would be sure to call forth the most violent opposition.

R. Halpern is neither a scholar nor a thinker, neither an orator nor an administrator. But he possesses just enough ability and application to attend to the detail duties of his calling and by dint of these qualities he

---

16. Samuel Thurman (1882–1963), B.A. Harvard; ordained Hebrew Union College; rabbi, St. Louis; contributor to local press.

17. Abraham E. Halpern (1891–1938), ordained JTS; president, Mid-West Rabbinical Assembly; executive board, United Synagogue.

worked himself up from a salary of $1500 to one of $9000. He is liked by his people and his position is secure—something which can be said of very few of the Seminary graduates. He knows how to get along with people and has contributed considerably to the fact that the Reform element reckon with the Orthodox in their communal undertakings. He succeeded in having a kosher kitchen introduced into the $2,000,000 Jewish Hospital in St. Louis. He is consulted by the directors of the YM with regard to activities to be conducted on the Sabbath, etc.

The YM & YWHA building was put up two years ago at a cost of $600,000. Harris[18] who is the executive director comes from a Reform home. It was mainly through his efforts that the institution was established. He impressed me as a fine type of young gentleman. The annual budget of the institution is $100,000.

The Zionist group is stronger and more active there than in most towns. In that result too it seems R. Halpern has a considerable share.

Impressions of Jewish Life in Small Town America

JANUARY 3, 1929: ON THE TRAIN FROM KANSAS TO CHICAGO
In view of the fact that I have to preach Saturday morning I thought instead of giving a sermon I might organize the impression of Jewish life I gathered in the course of the trip so as to give the audience at the services next Sabbath an idea of the destructive and constructive elements in the American Jewish scene.

A Survey of Jewish Life in Six Typical Communities

The Jewish population in the smallest of these communities is 3000; in the largest 50,000. Nearly every Jew belongs to one of the following groups:
1. The Orthodox—They have no conception whatever of the Jewish problem as one of adjustment. Goyim and Goyishness are to them the same all the world over both past and present. Their psychology is entirely that of the small town in the Jewish Pale of twenty-five years ago. They are completely nonplussed by the attitude of their children whom they try in vain to drag to "shul" [a traditional word for synagogue] and a few of whom learn from the Shoket [ritual slaughterer] how to davin [pray]. For themselves they want a "shul" where they can "davin" on Sabbaths and holidays and where they can occasionally listen to a "maggid" [preacher] or an itinerary "Rav" [here meaning traditional rabbi].

18. Gilbert Harris (1894–?), B.A. Washington University (St. Louis); communal executive and leader during World War I of the Jewish Welfare Board.

When one of these "Rabbonim" [rabbis] come to them they do not inquire as to his authority or qualification. They are impressed by his long beard and rabbinic looks and receive him with a great deal of satisfaction because he represents to them the old home associations which they cherish. They cannot afford to support an old time "Rav" and they find compensation for their lack of a permanent "Rav" by the occasional visits of these itinerary rabbonim. Among the latter are emissaries [meshulohim] of the NY Yeshiva. These emissaries obtain funds for the Yeshiva, from fifty to sixty percent of which constitutes their commission. The main practical objective upon which these Rabbonim concentrate their efforts is to instigate their listeners to oppose the efforts of the so-called modern orthodox and conservative congregations. Quote the case of Jacksonville where the name Jewish Center is regarded as goyish. The only redeeming factor in the case of the larger Jewish communities is the interest in the Zionist movement through affiliation with the Mizrahi.[19]

2. The Reform Jews constitute socially the most influential element of the Jewish population. They are devoid of all Jewish background and Jewish sympathies. The only sense in which they are Jews is that they are not goyim and do not yet intermarry on a large scale with goyim. They will not be gotten too easily to contribute to the upbuilding of Palestine even through the non-Zionist group. The Zionists look with a great deal of apprehension to the practical outcome of the extended agency. This antipathy against Palestine is to be traced directly to the active propaganda of the Reform rabbis of the old school and the disciples that have bettered the instruction to such a degree that they will hardly listen to either their old or new spiritual guide when urged to participate in the redemption of Palestine. So far the chorus of approval from the Reform camp consists mainly of the younger rabbis who came from orthodox homes and to whom Zionism has supplied with the main raison d'etre for their rabbinic calling.

Especially noteworthy is the racial Judaism which the Reform Jews are cultivating. It satisfies the inherent demand that Judaism be something more than abstract religion and is used at the same time to offset the national expression of Jewish life. The hospitals and the Y's are the visible expression of their Jewish racial zeal. Any one with Jewish sensibilities is even more offended by the goyish Jewishness of those who attend the Y's than by Jewish goyishness one finds in the temples. The executive directors who are young men too much in contact with Jewish life to have altogether escaped

---

19. Mizrachi: abbreviation of the Hebrew *merkaz ruhani*, spiritual center. Refers to the Religious Zionist Organization founded in 1901.

the influence of the national reawakening would like, if they only knew how, to put some Jewish content into the activities of the Y's. But they have neither the background, the knowledge nor the fervor to exert themselves seriously in behalf of intensive Jewishness.

3. The only Jewish groups that evince a tendency to deal with Jewish life as a problem in social and spiritual adjustment and that hold out promise of evolving as complete a type of Jewish life as we can hope for in this country are the so-called enlightened Orthodox or Conservative. The extent to which they will attain that goal depends upon the number of high calibre men that the Seminary will graduate and the amenability of these groups to influence at the hands of these men. There are many towns with Jewish populations between 3000 to 50000 without this third group. Those are in a most hopeless condition from a Jewish point of view. On the other hand where these groups exist we have at least the making of a Hebrew school that is training a future generation of Jews. There one finds a stirring of Jewish interest among the young people.

It is almost pathetic to note to what extent the entire Jewish situation hinges upon the presence and ability of the young rabbi. The moment there is an interregnum all his work is undone. This very type of community is as likely as any of the Y's to have a dance on Christmas eve. The worst drawback in the progress of Jewishness of these groups is the uncouthness of the lay-leaders. It seldom occurs to them to look to their rabbi first and foremost as the man to build up the inner life of their people in accordance with the highest conceptions of Judaism. Learning, piety even probity are never the qualities that these lay leaders ask for when they seek a rabbi for their congregations. The chief consideration with them is that they should be able to have their rabbi represent them to the Goyim by addressing meetings of the Chambers of Commerce and the Rotarian Clubs, so that they shall feel themselves the social equals of the Reform Jews.

4. Another element that is seldom reckoned with by the foregoing three groups is the Arbeiter Ring.[20] They represent the radical wing among the Jews. They differ from the other Jewish radicals in wanting to remain Jews and in having a constructive Jewish philosophy formulated by Zhitlowsky.[21] They are ardent upholders of Yiddish (as against Hebrew) as the national distinctive language of the Jewish masses. Toward religion they take a negative attitude. At tremendous sacrifice and in the face of tremendous

---

20. Workmen's Circle (in Yiddish *Arbeiter Ring*): formed in 1900 and actively assisted in formation of unions. Emphasized Yiddish.

21. Chaim Zhitlovsky (1865–1943), philosopher and essayist; socialist activist in Russia and the United States; advocated Diaspora nationalism, socialism, and Yiddishism.

odds they maintain afternoon schools where they translate their philosophy into an educational program.

Not in any way coordinated with the four groups enumerated but one which has potentialities for Jewish survival and growth is the Zionist group. It is exceedingly small, numbering from 50 to 450 and a somewhat larger number among the women.

Here and there one meets groups spontaneously organized like some oasis in a wilderness: a Bible study group of women who for more than seven years have kept up the study of the Bible with commentaries and have by now covered Genesis to Chronicles; a young people's group led by a few college men of intellectual ability.

In sum I venture to estimate that if the Jewish situation is to be saved it will be in the main through three agencies: 1) the conservative rabbi and 2) the Zionist movement and 3) the communal centers.

It is now 11:20 P.M. I want to note that with the help of God, the Life, the Love and the Intelligence of the Universe, I have been able to turn to good account the hours I am spending on this train. I thank thee, O God for the blessings which I enjoy. Amen.

FRIDAY, JANUARY 4, 1929: BEFORE LEAVING TRAIN
I was kept for a long time from falling asleep last night by the thought of the striking contrast between the way the lower East Side audience listened and reacted to my talk on the poetic approach to Judaism and the way the Kansas City audience listened and reacted. With the former I felt as though I were in my own camp, with the latter I felt as though I visited an enemy camp offering terms of peace. The cold impassive stare of the K.C. audience still lingers in my mind.

In former days when dogmas were regarded as the essence of religion and whispering campaigns were prevalent in religious circles some heresy hunter would surely have pounced upon the phrases by which I designate the divine aspect of existence and would have cried out "Eureka. I always knew Kaplan was a Christian at heart." Why, could you want a more certain affirmation of the Trinity? Life, the father, Love the son and Intelligence the Holy Ghost. By all that is sacred I would declare such a heresy hunter a fool and a mischief maker. Heartily repudiating as I do Christianity and all its works I have nevertheless always maintained that the same theological doctrines appear in different and the most hostile religions simply under different names. There is nothing philosophically wrong with a rationally conceived Trinity. But my gorge rises as I think of the Son. Mind you, not the poor simp Jesus, but the Son!

Reflections on Traveling

MONDAY, JANUARY 7, 1929: AT CANTON, O: 5:50 P.M.

It was certainly a joy to get back home. I kept on calculating the number of days and hours that I had to be away from home. What an ordeal it must have been for husbands and fathers to leave their families in the Old Country to seek their fortunes in America, not knowing when they might be in a position to send for their families. It is remarkable how readily on the one hand the human being becomes softened and in need of all the comfort and love and happiness that fall to his lot, and on the other hand, how with all his pain in missing what he has become accustomed to he is strong enough to endure the ordeal of privation when driven by necessity.

Here am I again sitting all alone in a hotel in Canton. What was all this traveling necessary for? How ridiculous it would be to account for my having consented to go on these lecture tours by any single motive! To earn a few hundred dollars? Am I as greedy as all that? To come into first hand contact with Jewish life? To some extent. To spread the idea of Judaism as a changing civilization? If I hadn't what to say I would not have undertaken to lecture to unfamiliar audiences. More than anything else it is the restlessness of soul due to my having to live continually on faith and not seeing any tangible results of all Jewish effort. I am like a feverish patient turning from side to side.

Saturday morning I gave the survey which is outlined a few pages ahead. There were 125 present. It seemed to have pleased the audience.

Spiritual Jews Need Wealthy Jews

TUESDAY, JANUARY 8, 1929, 2:00 P.M.: ON TRAIN TO ROCHESTER, NY

Somewhere in this book I refer to Luther as having had to rely upon the backing of worldly powers to achieve his reforms. This is verified by the following: "Martin Luther left to his own fate would be known today as a courageous but misguided monk who had tried his hand at playing reformer and who had been burned at the stake for his troubles. M.L. supported by a few landed proprietors might have survived a few years longer, but sooner or later his political friends would have been compelled to make peace with the Emperor and the Pope and would have been obliged to surrender their spiritual advisor to the worldly hangman. M.L. backed by a prince who through the recent invention of new mining machinery had become one of the wealthier individuals of northern Europe, was invincible." (*Whither Mankind*, p. 5a). This verifies my conviction that no spiritual or religious ideal stands the least chance of materializing without the backing of the moneyed powers. Not having a single friend among the rich Jews with whom

I ought to be on intimate terms I can see no likelihood whatever that my program for Judaism would come to be adopted.

Jewish life bears out the truth of the above generalization. There would not have been even a pretense of conservative Judaism in America if Schechter had not had a friend in Schiff. There would have been no Hebrew University if Magnes had not had a friend in Warburg. The reason there is no Jewish education in America is that Benderly has not been able to find a rich Jew to back him. Knowing that it is useless for me to expect even to interest any of the outstanding rich Jews in my program I was in the hope that a group of moderately well-to-do Jews might equal in influence one of the prominent figures in Jewry. So far my expectations have been sadly dispelled. The middle class rich will seldom initiate any esthetic or spiritual undertaking without the incentive coming from the very rich. Besides our type of Jews who have managed to succeed financially are too preoccupied with their business affairs, or too outworn by business cares, to have much energy left for undertakings to appreciate which they lack the background and education. Nevertheless it seems to me just now that if I am to give up my connection with the SAJ I shall be left without even the semblance of a backing and without the hope of ever getting one. On the other hand in case I succeeded in putting out a book which would set forth in elaborate form the ideas I have in mind, would I not then get one of the more influential ones to become interested in my program? This explains why I am again in the throes of doubt whether or not to continue with the SAJ.

Shalom Spiegel—Thoughts on a Play

SUNDAY, JANUARY 13, 1929

Dr. Shalom Spiegel[22] called this afternoon with reference to the publication in book form of his articles on the Hebrew Renaissance.[23] While I believe they are very much worth while I do not think that I could get the money from the SAJ for that purpose. I do not know why I am postponing publishing my own material.

SUNDAY, JANUARY 13, 1929

Last night I saw the Guild Theater Play "Wings Over Europe."[24] Although from the standpoint of dramatic technique it was adequate it

---

22. Shalom Spiegel (1899–1984), Ph.D., University of Vienna; scholar of Hebrew literature, Jewish Institute of Religion; faculty, JTS; lectured at the SAJ.

23. Shalom Spiegel, *Hebrew Reborn* (New York: Macmillan, 1930).

24. *Wings Over Europe* by Robert Nichols and Maurice Brown. A scientific genius discovers the secret of atomic energy and gets himself into trouble with the British government. He believes it can be used for the benefit of mankind.

somehow annoyed me. As I listened today to the very excellent talks on the play given under the auspices of the Guild Theater I realized why it had a disconcerting effect on me. It deals with the main problems of modern life, namely how to qualify man from the proper use of the tremendous power he had acquired through his control of the natural forces. Since the main object of a play is to entertain and not to call attention to social problems especially of so all embracing and urgent a character, I am afraid that the ultimate effect of a presentation on the stage is to give the people the illusion that by enjoying the play (assuming that they have understood it) they have actually wrestled with the problem. In that respect a play which deals with a social problem is as useless if not as harmful as a sermon. Both the uselessness and the possible harm are due to the problem being posed in such general terms or in terms of some imaginary situation that the question of what to do about it never arises in the mind of the audience. The situation in this play turns upon the hero Lightfoot who discovered the method of dividing the atom and thus gained control over a power wherewith he might blow up the earth. The very remoteness of such a contingency leaves the listener indifferent to the real problems due to the actual inventions of invisible death dealing rays and poisonous gases. On the other hand the latter kind of problem is so real that it is too late and too serious a matter to play with it on the stage and make it a subject for entertainment. I think I can understand now why Ibsen's plays which deal with social problems, or for the matter Shaw's, are out of place on the stage.

The foregoing is entirely my own opinion and was not voiced by any of the speakers I heard this afternoon.

S. Spiegel and Modern Hebrew Literature

Last Saturday Dr. Spiegel handed me a Hebrew article which he said I could publish in the SAJ Review if I wanted. It is entitled *Neged Yerushat ha-hemshekhi'ut be-ḥinukh ha-ivri* [Heb. "An (argument) Against the Heritage of Continuity in Hebrew Education"]. It is so entirely in accord with my own opinion as to what is radically wrong with the Teachers Institute curriculum that I hope to avail myself of the first opportunity to reorganize that curriculum. If a man who grew up in the environment of modern Hebrew literature finds that literature practically bare of permanent values I am convinced that it is my duty to compel the instructors of the Institute to lay less stress on the modern Hebrew writers and more on the rabbinic and medieval. It is positively sinful to have our students read Erter,[25] Y. L.

---

25. Isaac Erter (1791–1851), Hebrew satirist of the Jewish Enlightenment (Haskalah). His work satirizes the traditional Jewish society of his day.

Gordon,[26] Feierberg[27] and Brenner[28] when they ought to be studying Bialik's Aggadah[29] collection.

Jabotinsky a Hero?

TUESDAY, JANUARY 15, 1929

I cannot read anything about Jabotinsky[30] without being profoundly stirred by the sheer heroism of the man, a heroism that in his case is shared to an equal degree by body and spirit. He is not merely a talker of big words but a doer of great deeds. In his defiance of governments and majorities both of his own people and of other peoples he has displayed a courage the equal of any displayed by a Ghandi or a Lenin. Unfortunately he seems to have something of a Mussolini streak in him. Moreover he is too much of a secularist to be capable of voicing the innermost Jewish aspiration. Yet I shall avail myself of the invigorating influence of his message on his assuming the editorship of the *Doar Hayom*.[31] It is quoted in the Ha Olam[32] of December 28, 1928. . . .

Rabbinical Students at JTS—Irritating

WEDNESDAY, JANUARY 16, 1929, 8:20 P.M.: JUST BOARDED TRAIN FOR CINCINNATI

I have been on edge most of the time today. Wednesday is my day at the Seminary. When I start out from home I forget all my former irritations at that institution and look forward to communicating some of the ideas on Midrash and Bible interpretation I work out the night before and to receiving some inspirational challenge from the students. For fear that I might be a few minutes late I take a taxi instead of the street car. No sooner do I enter the building than I begin to feel annoyed. The students loiter in the hallway

---

26. Judah Leib Gordon (1830–92), Hebrew poet and one of the leading writers of the Haskalah in Eastern Europe.

27. Mordecai Z. Feierberg (1874–99), Russian Hebrew author best known for his novel *Le'an* (Wither?) expressing the struggle of East European youth at the end of the nineteenth century.

28. Yoseph Hayyim Brenner (1881–1921), Hebrew author; his short stories and novels realistically depict contemporary Jewish life.

29. H. N. Bialik (see glossary) together with Y. H. Ravnitzky produced *Sepher Ha-Aggadah*, a reworking of midrashic literature.

30. Vladimir (Ze'ev) Jabotinsky (1880–1940), writer, orator, and Zionist leader; militant revisionist leader; founder of Betar and spiritual father of the *Irgun*, both activist Zionist organizations.

31. *Doar Ha-Yom*: newspaper produced in Jerusalem from 1919 to 1936, edited by Jabotinsky and supporting the Revisionist ideal.

32. *Haolam*: organ of the World Zionist Organization.

with not a sign of making a move to enter the classroom although the bell has rung for the session to commence. I rush up the stairs into the faculty room, put away my hat and coat, and from there into the classroom. Fully fifteen minutes are gone before the class is assembled. For some reason a goodly number failed to show up today at the Midrash hour. Then come questions which I suspect have more of a filibustering purpose than that of getting information. Before much headway is made the bell to end the session rings. I continue regardless of the signal. The men become restive. The bell for the next session is sounded. I have to let the men go. The same dawdling takes place during this interval as in the preceding. When I inform the men of the reading they have to do for the session following there follows half-suppressed groans and protests. Then someone pipes up about having to prepare for this or that examination. And before I get a chance to complete a thought this hour is over too. The third session is usually spent in listening to a sermon by one of the men. It is usually so hopelessly devoid of all ideas and form that I am totally at a loss what to suggest as to how it might be improved. There is absolutely no room for improvement. The students who are asked by me to criticize it usually make fools of themselves, which, of course, affords the rest an occasion for loud guffaws. The elocution teacher, Robinson,[33] usually makes some inane remarks about the preacher's voice and pronunciation. Thus the three hours pass without a momentary gleam of intelligent or serious consideration of any of the intellectual or spiritual problems which these men ought to be preparing themselves to deal with.

Reading and Reminiscing about European Yeshivas

THURSDAY, JANUARY 17, 1929, 2:45 P.M.: ON TRAIN TO CINCINNATI
  I have begun reading I. Nissenbaum's *Alei ḥeldi* [Heb. *Leaves from My Life*][34] which I received from the author about two weeks ago. When on my returning from my western trip I found a package from Nissenbaum I did not even make the trouble to open it because I assumed that it contained some book of sermons by him. However, when I chanced to open the package Tuesday night I discovered that the book was his autobiography. The mere thought that I shall enjoy reading in Hebrew an autobiography written by a man whose life from a Jewish point of view is a link between the life of the old time Rov and my own contributed to my being unable to fall asleep till after 3:00 in the morning. The discovery of the book came on

---

33. Walter H. Robinson served as the teacher of elocution at the seminary for many years.
34. I. Nissenbaum (1868–1942), rabbi, Hebrew writer, and religious Zionist; work cited here is his autobiography.

top of the thrill which I got from reading Jabotinsky's statement as editor of the *Do'ar Ha-yom* [Heb. Daily Mail]. The realization that Jewish life is productive of outstanding personalities who are at last becoming articulate gave me the feeling that the cause of the Jewish people is far from being a forlorn hope.

No less important than literature for the renascence of our people is the emergence of articulate personalities. No matter how humble or undistinguished the person be so long as he succeeds in giving an integrated account of his life he transmits as permanent record a body of experiences that is just as unique, interesting and valuable as a new book or poem, insofar as that account of his life represents a combination of experiences that cannot be duplicated by the member of any other people. If Jews of the past had sense enough to write autobiographies like Nissenbaum's what a wealth of historical material we should have possessed. It is evident why biography or autobiography was a totally inconceivable art among the Jews of the past. Man counted for nothing; this world was only a preparation for the life in the world to come. Hence why bother with human trivialities of the here and the now? Is it not clear that the outstanding task for us Jews today is gradually to build up a humanist Jewish civilization? Therein lies the Redemption of Israel.

I have read as far as p. 93 in Nissenbaum's book. Seldom has a book kept me so spellbound. I would have continued it to the end without interruption if I had not had to get ready for the lecture this evening. Though the style is rather thin it is more than compensated for by the inherent interest of the narrative. That interest is due not to suspense in the unfolding of a tale of heroism or adventure but rather to the recognition and identification of fugitive impressions of life in the small towns in Lithuania gained from conversations heard by me in my childhood years. I had often heard my father refer to his experiences in the Yeshibah of Wolozhin and to Rabbi Yehuda Lieb Berlin[35] who was at its head when he studied there. But never did I get a full and complete picture of how a Yeshiba young man came to the Yeshibah, what he did before he got there and similar detailed facts necessary to give vividness to the picture. Nissenbaum's book fills out those gaps in the picture. Moreover in the part of the book I have read so far I got the background of personalities that entered into my own life. Rabbi Jacob Joseph was chief rabbi of a number of downtown congregations when I came to this country at the age of eight. My father was at first a "Dayan" [judge] in his house and then broke with him only to be reconciled to him after R. Jacob

---

35. Naphtali Zevi Judah Berlin (1817–93), ha-Neziv; leading rabbi; head of Yeshiva at Volozhin for forty years.

Joseph[36] became partly paralyzed. For many years the only impression I had of R. Jacob Joseph was that of an old time Rav who had not the least conception of the new world into which he was transplanted. In Nissenbaum's book, however, I see that he must have played an important role in the spiritual life of the Wilna community. Another personality is the "Ridwaz" or Rav from Slutsk[37] who helped to render the congregation Kehilat Jeshurun (the first congregation where I functioned as minister and later as associate rabbi)[38] proof against adjustment to present day spiritual needs. I was twenty-three years old when he was brought by the elders of the congregation to supply them with the spiritual authority and sustenance which they would not think of deriving from me. My business was to be entirely with the children and the young people. As soon as the *Ridwaz* was injected into the situation I was up in arms. The experiences which my father underwent in his relations with R. Jacob Joseph and other rabbis planted in my mind a distrust of that species of rabbis, a distrust which in all the years since has seldom proved to be unwarranted. Somehow their ethical standards never correspond with what has a right to expect from men who are considered spiritual leaders. To this day the *Ridwaz* lives in my memory as a good deal of a bully and shrewd business man. The reference to him in Nissenbaum's book while not derogatory is compatible with the impression he made upon me.

I am confirmed in my opinion that the monopolistic and tyrannical influence of Talmudism is responsible for the sterility of Jewish life in Eastern Europe. In the account of Nissenbaum's life during the first twenty years there is not a single suggestion of any original thought or aspiration. The greater part of those years are devoted to the one object of acquiring familiarity with [the] text of one treatise after another. The greater the familiarity and the ability to remember the source of any passage the greater the social prestige. It was that which not only saved him from starvation but gave him a wife. What a paralyzing influence this glorification of passive absorption of totally useless and beautyless ideas must have had upon the thousands of able young men who, had they not been allured by the social prestige of all that learning, might have left us a great heritage! This is not said in the spirit of the Maskil[39] to whom the alternative to Talmudism was complete westernization. I have in mind the kind of

36. Rabbi Jacob Joseph of Vilna (?–1902), installed as chief rabbi of New York to aid in regulation of kashrut.

37. Jacob David Ben Ze'ev Willowski, Ridbaz (1845–1913), Lithuanian talmudist and *rosh yeshiva* in Palestine.

38. In 1904 the Slutzker Rav preached on Rosh Hashannah at Kehilath Jeshurun though Kaplan was the rabbi. Kaplan was hired to preach in English. The Slutzker believed that preaching should be only in Yiddish. Eventually he settled in Palestine. For a detailed account of these events, see *Judaism Faces the Twentieth Century*, 71–73.

39. Maskil: an enlightened or rational person.

intensely Jewish civilization in which religion and art and Hebraism could have been completely synthesized.

Being in a Turbulent State

SUNDAY NIGHT, FEBRUARY 3, 1929, 1:00 A.M.

My mind has been in a turbulent state although outwardly I have appeared calm. When I woke up it was to worry over the tendency to forget the names of people I know very well. Later it was to feel upset about Lena's trouble with her eyes. I know that she worries. A certain degree of insensibility in the left side of her head which she experienced this morning made her wish that she had made the appointment with the nerve doctor for today instead of tomorrow. I myself felt physically indisposed and absented myself from the classes at the TI this afternoon. Instead of helping me, the failure to attend to my work only made matters worse. But I managed not to betray my state of mind. Lena and I visited mother, Sophie and Phineas[40] this evening. We stayed only long enough to eat supper because I wanted to do some work before I went to bed. With all my efforts to buckle down to some definite piece of work the days pass by like so many telegraph poles past a speeding train with nothing to show except this tale of woe. All my time goes into indiscriminate reading. For example I read Einstein's article in today's N.Y. Times[41] on his recent publication. I understood enough of it to wish that I had the time to give to the study of physics and mathematics and to deplore bitterly the fact that I never had any one to teach me to understand those subjects. I am quite sure that if I had had the opportunity to delve into higher mathematics I might have been able to discover some new formula which might have thrown light upon some of the fundamental problems of reality. Then I turned to Siegfried's *America's Coming of Age*[42] to find some material for the paper which I have to get ready for next week's SAJ Review. What I read was interesting, but it had no bearing on the purpose which I had in mind. Then in the course of clearing up the desk I read a number of articles in Hebrew and in English upon such a variety of subjects as the task of the Zionist Organization, a review of a play on the boards called "The Street Scene"[43] and an article on the question "Can

---

40. Phineas Israeli (1880–1948), ordained JTS; rabbi, Des Moines, Iowa; brother-in-law of Mordecai Kaplan. Pulpits also in Brooklyn and Massachusetts.

41. *New York Times*, February 3, 1929. A long article by Einstein himself explaining his latest theories against the background of his other work. A rather technical article.

42. Andre Siegfried, *America Comes of Age—A French Analysis* (New York: Harcourt, Brace, 1927).

43. "Street Scene," a play by Elmer Rice, is a realistic drama of tenement life in New York City.

the Prosperous Be Religious?" I cannot but view that way of spending a day as mental dissipation which has as much of a debilitating effect as a physical debauch. But what am I to do if I must be constantly on the alert for ideas that will help me in my work as a popularizer of commonplace truths? I would have given anything in the world to be able to work out a paraphrase of the Midrashic and Aggadic Literature or to complete any of the other pieces of work in which I have a genuine interest. No one realizes the extent to which the task of popularizing knowledge of any kind can be pursued only at the cost of any genuine thinking. I assume that to be the tragedy of all literary and artistic effort which is paralyzed by the need of supplying pot boilers. It is only genius which is sufficiently confident that it can achieve results worthy of the sacrifice of income and comfort that can give one the courage to refuse to waste itself on pot boilers. Lacking such self-confidence I have divided my energies between trying to do some original work and learning the art of popularizing. Not that the SAJ work which consists of popularization of Jewish teaching has brought me fabulous sums. Per contra, the very smallness of monetary gain—the seven years of toil, not counting the three and a half at the Center—have brought me little more than twenty thousand dollars and is the cause of my regret for having foolishly given up a good part of the last ten years to no worthwhile purpose. On the other hand small as that income is with the possibility of having to meet greater obligations than those I am called upon to meet at present I would be taking a great risk were I to let slip even the modest income which the SAJ brings me. The trouble is I know that such petty calculations are unmanly and bespeak a spirit of very small proportions which in turn is a reason for feeling contemptible and unhappy.

One might ask why waste time writing this stuff instead of concentrating on the tasks which might have some objective value? The only answer I can give—and it is no mere excuse—is that for those tasks I need long stretches of free time. Such time I am precluded from having by reason of my being continually on the lookout for sermon and lecture material. Whereas for this diary any spare half hour or hour is sufficient. Rather than reading another article I resort to this means of preventing some portion of my consciousness stream from disappearing into immediate and total oblivion.

Thoughts on Mysticism—Some Distinctions

WEDNESDAY, FEBRUARY 13, 1929

This morning I came to class at the Seminary without my lecture notes but fortunately Kollin put a question to me which gave me a chance to telephone to the house and have the lecture notes brought to me by the time I had to make use of them. Kollin's question was "What truth is there to the allegation that the Judaism of the Bible is lacking in mysticism?" This led me to point out that when we speak of mysticism we must distinguish the following three types which as a rule are either praised or condemned promiscuously: 1) Theurgic mysticism which is the survival of the primitive religion and being out of harmony with the advanced thought of the race should be designated superstition. 2) Philosophic mysticism which embraces all types of philosophy in which the mind recognizes its limitations and which in the knowledge of ultimates accepts intuition as a truer guide than reason. This is represented by thinkers like Al Ghazali, Halevi, St. Augustine, Kant, Bergson. 3) Saintly mysticism which is the state of mind attained through a sense of divine presence and which gives rise to various emotional experiences varying from serenity to ecstasy and to actions testifying to such experiences. The psalmists, the saints and the ascetics manifest this type of mysticism. It is the last type which we should mean and aim for in public worship and private devotions. To cultivate it deliberately by reckoning with the psychological laws that underlie these states of mind is just as legitimate as using our knowledge of psychology of childhood to cultivate ethical character in the child.

Mistakes Philosophy Makes Concerning God

SUNDAY, FEBRUARY 24, 1929, 12:00 MIDNIGHT

The mistake in the philosophical approach to the conception of God has been to ascribe attributes to God. This mistake has reduced the philosophers to the necessity of interpreting all attributes negatively for if those attributes were to be taken in a positive sense they would place God in the same category as created beings which possess those attributes. The philosophers would have been more successful in emphasizing the unique character of God, if they had said that God is attributeless, and had rather put the question concerning the nature of God thus: What attributes of the universe, as we know it, point to a reality and meaning beyond themselves? Much confusion would have been avoided if the attributes of divine significance were ascribed not to God but to the universe.

A Dinner for Cyrus Adler—Mixed Feelings

WEDNESDAY NIGHT, MARCH 6, 1929, 12:20

This evening I have been having a spell of tiredness, a tiredness that is more of the mind than of the body. I do not think it is the after effect of work that I have done but rather the fore effect of work that I ought to be doing—work not altogether to my liking, answering letters, a talk on "Wings Over Europe"[44] to be given Sunday night, and a sermon Saturday morning.

This has been rather an exciting week. Sunday night Adler was dined by the Faculty in honor of his trip to Palestine. Suspecting that I might be asked to speak I dawdled away a good part of the morning trying to think what I could say. I resumed thinking about it after I got through teaching. When I arrived at the Seminary no one said a word to me about my having to speak. I therefore ate my meal in peace and conversed with those at my table. Just as we were about to say grace, Marx came over to me and notified me that I would be called upon. I categorically refused on the ground that I should have been informed beforehand, since as I learned they had decided last Friday that I ought to speak. When Marshall was about to introduce me he was told by Marx not to call on me. Finkelstein was next. He spoke very well, the best up to that time. In the meantime Marshall was called away and turned over the toastmastering to Davidson. Davidson believing that I would feel hurt if I wouldn't be called upon announced me. Fortunately I had formulated in my mind the main idea of what I was going to say and spoke well and to the point. It was assumed by everybody that I got up my talk on the spur of the moment. It probably wasn't nice of me to play the comedy of refusing at first when Marx asked me. But I was honestly and sincerely reluctant to speak so that I am not altogether the villain that I make myself out to be.

I must say I liked Adler's reply to the speeches very much. He deprecated the eulogies and the expectations raised by the idealizations of him conveyed in the remarks of the various speakers.

Last night I gave the third lecture at the Brooklyn Jewish Center. The subject was the Three Types of Medieval Jewish Adjustment. The audience was small, due partly to the very inclement weather, but I was spiritually satisfied with the new light in which the preparation for the talk led me to see mysticism in general and Jewish mysticism in particular.

Kabbalah and the Control of Nature

THURSDAY, MARCH 7, 1929

My recent discovery that the Kabbalists and mystics were aiming at exactly the same goal as the scientists and inventors of today, control of the forces of nature (except that the former based all their reasoning on the assumption that the world was governed by personal instead of impersonal forces) seems to me to have very far reaching implications for

---

44. See diary entry for January 13, 1929, and note 24 above.

the proper understanding of religion. Kabbalah is the transition between ancient magic and modern science. It is all wrong to imagine that because kabbalah engaged in elaborate theories about God (theosophy) it had the same purpose in mind as Aristotelian metaphysics, namely, the knowledge of truth with a view to the contemplation of and communion with Deity. Not contemplation or passive perfection but power to control the forces of the environment was what kabbalah aimed at. Its theosophy was only a prolegomenon to its theurgy. This is why its theosophy was based upon the emanation theory of God, for only upon the basis of such a theory could God logically be brought down to the practical every day needs of man. So viewed religion is nothing more than primitive science, and modern science is the child and heir of ancient religion. The scientist of today is the son of the mystagogue of yesterday and the grandson of the medicine man of the day before.

Cyrus Adler on Cyrus Adler

FRIDAY, MARCH 8, 1929, 3:15 P.M.

A few personalia of interest: In his talk at the banquet last Sunday Dr. Adler said some interesting things about himself. He stated that there was a tradition in his family not to have any eulogies delivered when any member of the family dies. This was said apropos of the eulogies addressed to him by the speaker of the evening. As a young man he was in Palestine in the interest of archaeological research in behalf of the Smithsonian Institute. He then had occasion to acquire some experience in diplomacy in the course of his contacts with high officials of the government. His interest in specifically Jewish work, which led him to give up his position at the Smithsonian, was aroused in him by a gentile physician who treated him when as a young man he was seriously ill. The physician who had knowledge of the chaos that existed on the Lower East Side of N.Y. some forty years ago said to him that a man of his administrative ability was needed to bring some order out of that chaos. That administrative ability he acquired as a librarian, and had occasion to use at one time or another as curator of a zoological garden.

He stated very frankly that throughout his life he was fortunate in earning the friendship and cooperation of people of high standing and ability (these were not the exact words) and that in actuality he was a man of very moderate learning and moderate ability.

Judith Gets Angry

SATURDAY NIGHT, MARCH 9, 1929, 1:00 A.M.

The night before last Judith came home tired and moody. Lena happened to mention Atlantic City as a place where Judith might go to over the weekend to rest up. At this suggestion Judith snapped back "I don't want to go to A.C. That's a place for fat old Jews." I expressed my resentment at her using that phrase and she half-explained it by saying that I shouldn't have taken her remark seriously. Last night another incident took place in which I displayed undue sensitiveness. Judith was reading the current number of the SAJ Review which contains the article by Jacob Kohn. When Lena suggested to her that she should read the article she remarked she wouldn't read anything by Kohn. It irritated me to note how unsympathetic she was toward things Jewish; how totally devoid she seemed to be of that Judenschmerz which any Jew who is not ignorant, selfish or a Philistine ought to experience. What contributed to my irritation was the belief that this hard-heartedness was induced by the only intimate friend she has, Helen Cohen, Isaac Cohen's daughter. It is strange how uncomfortable I feel about this Helen Cohen. She strikes me as one of the Jewish Jew-haters that curse their parents for having brought them into the world. I realize that I may be mistaken, but I have noted so many evidences of her antipathy against Jews and none of any sympathy that I cannot help believing about her what I do. It is natural therefore that I should imagine that she is exercising an anti-Jewish influence upon Judith. Accordingly, when I was exasperated by Judith's second remark into which I read a derogatory connotation with regard to matters Jewish I let her know that I attributed her attitude to Helen's influence. At this Judith became frenzied with rage, madly flung away the book she had been reading, and burst out of the room screaming. Lena joined her. I was not a saint either, but with sharp cutting retorts I countered the accusatory epithets they both hurled at me. This storm, however, which is the first of its kind in our home, did not last long. After an hour it blew over and the three of us realized that we had made fools of ourselves, and continued to love each other with greater intensity than ever.

8

March 10, 1929–July 22, 1929

The Diary Saves Kaplan from Oblivion

SUNDAY, MARCH 10, 1929, 12 MIDNIGHT

Here for instance is a very specific question I should like to have answered. For the last hour and a half I have been writing aimlessly [in the diary] only to find some compensation for my frustrated hopes and ambitions. Would I not have employed that time to better advantage if I had worked on the paraphrase translation of the Midrash of Shir Hashirim [classical rabbinical commentary on The Song of Songs]? From one point of view the answer should be an emphatic yes. A well worked out paraphrase translation would open up new territory to those who are interested in exploring the field of Jewish knowledge. From another point of view the answer should be in the negative. For anyone who has a fair knowledge of rabbinic style and a sense of the English language could do that work. On the other hand no one but myself could write my diary. Whether what I have to say is wise or foolish, interesting or boring, it is the attempt of a personality to save itself from inarticulateness and oblivion by the mere skin of its teeth. Its struggles are entirely its own and no other person in the world could know them and record them. That fact makes of this kind of writing an actual addition to the sum of sense or nonsense that constitutes man's literary heritage. Now that I have stated both sides of the case I find that the hour is 1:45 A.M. and that it is time to go to bed.

Nincompoops at the Seminary

SATURDAY NIGHT, MARCH 16, 1929, 1:30 A.M.

The Seminary faculty meeting which took place last Wednesday was presided over by Marx on account of Adler's being away. R.'s request that he be given the rabbinical degree came up for discussion. It did seem a pity that he should be the first victim of the faculty's determination to cut down on the number of nincompoops it graduates annually. No one could conscientiously say he was worse than at least fifty of those the Seminary has inflicted on the community. But we can't be moving in this vicious circle forever. Davidson argued that if we were consistent we would refuse to graduate K. and W. Every time K. opens his mouth, Davidson said, he makes a fool of himself. Davidson was undoubtedly right. Although K. has carried off honors one year after another because of his capacity for hard work the fact remains that he has an addled pate and is lacking in personality. But the line has to be drawn somewhere. The vote was 3 against 3. I was among those that voted against R. being graduated as Rabbi this year. Marx cast the deciding ballot as opposed to R.'s graduation.

In the course of the discussion Davidson referred contemptuously to the demand of the students that the studies be coordinated to some extent with the practical work of the ministry. Marx referred in the same vein to the request they had made that the lectures be mimeographed and distributed before each session so that the session could be devoted to discussion. "The brazen impudence." "The idea!" "They want to tell us how to run the Seminary!" When Davidson spoke of the wild demand of the students for coordination of the work, he looked quizzically at me as though I had primed them to ask for such an unheard of thing.

Judaism as a Civilization—*Beginning the Book*

SUNDAY NIGHT, MARCH 17, 1929, 2:00 A.M.

Of late I have been experiencing difficulty falling asleep when I get to bed. It must be due to nervous tension. I have been giving a good deal of thought to what I hope will some day appear as a book entitled "Judaism as a Civilization" (I prefer it by far to the title "Whither Judaism?"). The surge of ideas on the subject and the prospect of putting out at last a respectable piece of work make me all agog with excitement. How comparatively easy it would be to put that conception of Judaism into effect once it were defined and rendered capable of transmission to Jews of creative ability. For example an editorial of mine in the SAJ Review on the possibilities of Jewish art brought me the acquaintance of an interesting person who might prove of great help in giving concrete form to the program of Judaism as a civilization.[1] Leaf (whose former name was Lipschitz) of 188 Columbus Ave. is engaged in Jewish art work for synagogues and homes. The editorial I referred to was shown him by somebody and I received a letter from him written in Hebrew

---

1. Reuben Leaf (1889–?), artist, Imperial Art School (Vilna), Bezalel Art School (Jerusalem); cartoonist, teacher, New York City.

thanking me for stimulating Jewish art. With my dilatoriness in answering letters especially in Hebrew, I found another means of letting him know that I appreciated his communication. One of the members of the SAJ is about to contribute a curtain for the ark. I had Lena recommend this Mr. Leaf to him. This is how Leaf happened to call this morning. I was glad to find him a likeable person with a good deal of knowledge and fine judgment on matters of art. I was especially interested to learn that he had experience in teaching arts and crafts in Simon Ginzburg's[2] school. There at once opened up before me the vision of having him teach his students of the Teachers Institute that type of work, and help to make of the TI building which I hope will be completed for next fall a center of Jewish art.

The more I think on the problem of Judaism the more convinced I am that the only possibility of saving Judaism in this country and for that matter anywhere, even in Palestine, is making it the theme of as many and varied aesthetic creations as possible. If I had the genius of a William Morris[3] I would have been able to demonstrate in a practical way what I have in mind. As it is I must content myself with acting as impresario of existing artistic Jewish talent. If I could corral a group of creative artists, poets and writers and actors—say men like Kuttai, Leaf, Simon Ginzberg, etc.—I would begin by planning two definite lines of effort, one would be to Judaize the home, the other to create new aesthetic forms for worship such as pageant, dramatic music, pantomime, the dance and music.

Judith Reading Autobiography of Isadora Duncan—Kaplan Concerned

Monday, March 18, 1929, 1:00 p.m.
     Among the books I got recently is Isadora Duncan's "My Life." Formerly a book like that would have been regarded as dangerous reading for a young girl. Still laboring under mid-Victorian fears (there ought to be a Jewish equivalent for mid-Victorian, but among Jews such books were not written or circulated) I was anxious to keep the book out of Judith's sight. I was careless, however, and so she got hold of it and read it. I confess that I was annoyed at the idea of her reading it, but when afterwards she expressed her opinion of the book I felt relieved. It seems that her aesthetic taste was revolted by the deliberate attempt on the part of Duncan at publicity and self-exposure. Judith correctly remarked that Duncan's defense of free love

---

     2. Simon Ginzburg (1890–1944), Ph.D. Dropsie; poet; translator; educator; editor, Hebrew journals.
     3. William Morris (1873–1932), theatrical, civic, and communal leader; president, Jewish Theater Guild, New York City.

and promiscuity is nothing but a rationalization. It thus looks that Robinson who helped to introduce the concept of rationalization did good as well as harm. The harm comes of the way in which many callow youngsters use "rationalization" to pooh pooh many an honest spiritual reaction to life. But the good that rationalization does is in opening their eyes to the hollowness of the arguments in defense of licentiousness may compensate for the harm.

Bodily Discomfort

TUESDAY, MARCH 26, 1929, 7:45 P.M.

I have not accomplished a thing since last week. I am not lazy nor given to dawdling but from time to time my system gets out of order, due mainly to constipation from which I am a chronic sufferer. Whenever I am physically affected that way my mind is dulled, my memory goes back on me and I feel generally out of sorts.

Believes His Religious Convictions Are "Freud Proof"

THURSDAY, MARCH 28, 1929, 1:00 P.M.

The one fortunate element in my makeup, an element which to some extent compensates for my many handicaps and frustrations, is the consciousness of being anchored to certainties about religion and the future of the Jewish people. Those certainties at least give me the satisfaction of being able to play my part in life with a greater measure of sincerity than most people in my position. I became convinced of my possessing this advantage as I read Freud's "The Future of an Illusion." The fact that my religious convictions are Freud-proof is a great source of comfort to me.

I do not mean to imply that I subscribe to the kind of religion which Freud describes as an illusion. In fact the premises upon which he bases his conclusions have long been known to me. But granted those very premises I draw entirely different inferences. The force of his argument rests upon his gratuitous and unwarranted assumption that God must be conceived in the traditional fashion or not believed in at all. The distinction that he draws between error and illusion is a very fruitful one. In contrast with error which is a mistake in judgment, illusion implies the existence of some wish which seeks satisfaction. Then why identify God with the being fashioned by the imagination and not with the universe as it expresses itself through the wish that is back of the various god ideas? This is so simple a jump that anyone with average intellectual ability should feel bound to take it of his own accord. That Freud refuses to take it I can only ascribe to some complex against religion which he must have developed in his youth or to a mental inflexibility which is characteristic of the oriental mind that has never been impregnated by Occidental thought or impregnated under circumstances of protest, fear and secretiveness.

The trouble with Freud's interpretation of life is not that it is incorrect but that it is one sided. It is undoubtedly a great contribution to truth to know the seamy side of our existence, of our virtues, arts and ideals. But it is nonetheless a falsification of life to give the impression that the seamy side is the only side and that the beautiful appearance of the garment or tapestry is an illusion.

Seeing a Yiddish Play with Lena and Judith

Monday, April 1, 1929, 11:30

Saturday night Lena, Judith and I went to see a Yiddish play called "Der Golizianer Chasuno" with Satz[4] as principal actor at the Public Theatre, Second Ave. and 4 St. It had little value from a dramatic or musical standpoint although it managed to be somewhat entertaining. It gave however enough features of the life in Hassidic Poland to arouse in a Jewishly attuned mind a sense of homesickness for the colorful Jewish life of the old world. It portrayed, for instance, the passionate idealization of the value of Torah, and although it introduced a fragment of American Jewish life with a strident and jarring effect, the contrast between the old and new Jewish life was saddening. When I learned that Judith felt exactly as I did I was convinced that the Judenschmerz [Jewish pain] has gotten hold of her too. Should a Jewish father be glad or sorry that his child is also a victim of the Judenschmerz?

Student Religious Observance at TI: Some Issues

April 1, 1929, 11:30

One of the main reasons probably for our being always on edge, teachers as well as students, is that there is so much self-suppression, hypocrisy and inconsistency in our mode of life. The following will serve as an illustration. The Seminary register states that the students are expected to observe the Sabbath and Kashrut. Since the TI is part of the Seminary its students ought to be expected to live up to that rule. Yet if we were to do that we would have to expel some of our best and most earnest students who are compelled to work on the Sabbath to earn a living. The TI faculty happened to touch on that question but I think it was shunted for fear that it might lead to violent disagreements.

---

4. Ludwig Satz (1891–?), immigrated to United States; studied at Columbia; Yiddish actor; director; founder, Yiddish Art Theatre.

Yesterday Ruffman, one of the best students of the senior class, asked me whether he did wrong in riding to the SAJ services last Saturday. He has to work Saturdays to support himself and his parents. Last Saturday being before Easter he had the day free. Being very anxious to attend services of the kind I had talked about he came to the SAJ House. Although he ordinarily rides to his work (because the place he works at is far from his home) he was afraid he acted improperly in riding to the services. I set his conscience at ease by telling him that circumstanced as he was he could not have acted differently. Did I do the right thing?

Henry Rosenthal—A Rabbinical Student with "Beauty of Soul"

THURSDAY, APRIL 4, 1929, 1:00 A.M.

Henry Rosenthal delivered the student sermon at the Seminary yesterday. He cast a spell upon the class by the wizardry of his style. Taking the subject that I had suggested to him last Thursday night and drawing upon the interpretation that I gave in class of the meaning of God as liberator, he delivered a sermon that throbbed with emotion. It was not the kind of cheap emotion displayed by the popular orator, but the restrained and highly articulated emotion of the poet. The one word that he uses most frequently is rhythms as though he were passionately striving to catch and express the deepest rhythms of the cosmos as they find expression in human life. The other word which he is fond of using is "troubled," indicating his sensitiveness to whatever interferes with the rhythms of reality. He certainly possesses an inner beauty of soul which spurns the ugly and the spurious in art, morality and religion, and which reveals itself in new incisive and most surprising association of ideas. Most remarkable is his attitude to Jewish life. Fully alive to its vulgarities and its sterility he is nevertheless deeply in love with it. If he will retain that love he will undoubtedly make some valuable contribution to its future development.

Reconstructing the Jewish Past—A Religion of Inwardness

SATURDAY NIGHT, APRIL 6, 1929

This morning I stayed away from services so that I not be tempted to preach. . . . [5]

In the meantime I had the chance to think about the article which is to give a reconstruction of the Jewish past. The following are some of the ideas that occurred to me:

In general the task of reconstructing Jewish life calls for 1) a new philosophy of Jewish life and 2) a new program which is to be based upon

---

5. Kaplan was not feeling well.

that philosophy. In the new philosophy of Jewish life the first important step is achieving a correct perspective of the Jewish past. Formerly every Jew had a definite idea, wrong as it may have been, how Judaism happened. After all whatever place in the world we assign to the people we belong to depends upon how we conceive that people to have come into being. Nowadays the Jewish past is a mere smudge to most Jews. They do not accept the traditional version neither have they been given any new version that might help them orient themselves in their environment. The modern Jew will never be able to utilize his past as a means of rendering the present significant unless the traditional ideas that have accumulated about the past will be disentangled and there emerge out of the confusion an orderly succession of three distinct types of civilization which have hitherto been reckoned with as one uniform type. Each type passed into the one that followed it so gradually and unconsciously that it takes a long time to overcome the shock of discovery that Judaism has been identified with three different modes of civilization.

The first type of civilization was theophanic. Its social habits, institutions, sanctions, literature and arts were permeated with the assumption that the God whose people they were was wont to manifest himself to those that sought Him and ever ready to make His will known to them. Theophany while an extraordinary experience was not an unusual experience. In fact without it they would have felt completely at a loss how to live with one another and would not have had the courage to fight their enemies. The center of gravity of their spiritual interests was entirely this world and the now. That type of civilization lasted during the first five or six hundred years of Israel's stay in Canaan.

The second type was theocratic. Theophany as a normal experience was a thing of the past. Instead of theophany the Jews had the Torah which was regarded as having been given by God. In addition there was the Temple where it was believed God was somehow present in a truer sense than elsewhere. All the social habits etc. were dominated by the belief that the low estate of the Jewish people was only temporary due to God not yet having manifested Himself as the prophets had presaged but that as soon as God saw fit He would manifest Himself through some extraordinary act of power, that all of Israel would be gathered from the various lands of the dispersion and that the nations would come to recognize the hegemony of the God of Israel. The center of gravity was no longer in the here and the now nor was it definitely removed from the here and the now. In this state of suspense Judaism found itself until the beginning of the common era.

The third type has been other worldly. This world and this life are treated in all the constituents of the civilization as an interim state between the past when men lived in the sight of a self manifesting God and the future when men shall again live thus. The center of interest is definitely shifted to the hereafter when God will bring back the order of life which obtained before man corrupted the world, etc.

The type of civilization which Judaism will develop into will be the spiritual. It will in many respects be a return to the first period but of course on a higher level. Its center of interest will again be the here and the now since the best way of providing for the future is to realize to the full the opportunities of the present. Likewise the assumption that communion with the divine is a normal experience will become operative again, except, of course, that instead of the divine manifestation taking on the form of an outward visible experience it will be looked for in the inwardness of the mind and heart.

Witnessing an Automobile Accident

THURSDAY, APRIL 11, 1929, 11:30

As I was taking a walk on Central Park West on the east side of the street two automobiles collided at the 77 St. crossing. One was a private car driven by a chauffeur, the other was a taxicab. There were two men in the taxicab besides the driver. I was walking south (that was about 10:30 P.M.). My attention was attracted by the private car speeding at what seemed a breakneck rate. There were no other cars on the avenue within a block or two either way. As I turned to look at the speeding car the taxicab emerged from the street that runs through the park. It was traveling at a much slower pace than the private car. They both collided on the west side of the avenue circling around till they came to a stop at a point in 77 Street somewhat west of the avenue.

I gave my name to the taxicab driver because I felt indignant at the reckless speed with which the chauffeur had driven down the avenue. Upon second thought, however, it occurred to me that the taxicab driver should have stopped to let the car pass. Both the chauffeur and the taxicab driver were at fault.

Salo Baron Comes to the House for a Visit

SATURDAY NIGHT, APRIL 13, 1929, 11:30 P.M.

This afternoon I had as visitors Dr. B. Elzas[6] and Dr. Salo Baron.[7] I met them last week while visiting Dr. Tschernowitz at the Mt. Sinai and

---

6. Barnett Elzas (1867–1936), rabbi; historian; chaplain, New York City Department of Correction.

7. Salo W. Baron (1895–1989), Ph.D., ordained JTS (Vienna); historian; faculty, Columbia; major author and editor in field of Jewish history.

invited them to the house this afternoon. We discussed the conception of Judaism as a Civilization. Elzas wasn't able to articulate his objections against that conception except to mention that any attempt to formulate a conception of Judaism that rules out from Judaism any one who feels as a Jew is to be condemned. In addition he repeated the irreverent jest about eating "gefilte fish" as being a part of Jewish civilization. Otherwise he left the field all to Baron and me. To this moment I don't know what Baron was driving at by trying to corner me with his "Socratic method" of questioning. For a long time we engaged in futile logomachy[8] at the end of which Baron admitted that I must be correct since I hold the same views as he does. Our discussion lasted two hours.

Kaplan Entranced with the Jewish Sculptor Enrico Glicenstein[9]

SATURDAY NIGHT, APRIL 13, 1929, 11:30 P.M.

This evening I had the treat of my life. I visited Enrico Glicenstein at his studio at 65 W. 56 St. Little as I am able to appreciate sculpture and etchings I could not but marvel at some of his work. I thought his "Jeremiah" superb. I probably reveal an uncultivated taste in admiring his "Sphinx" but I cannot see wherein it is inferior to Rodin's much cried [proclaimed] of "The Two Natures" (or some such name). His illustrations of the Book Samuel were infinitely more challenging to me than Dore's.

Then the talk. As he showed me some etchings dealing with Christian themes he remarked "I have to be a Marrano. I find it necessary to express my Jewish feelings through Christian themes because the Jews do not give me a chance to work only in Jewish subject matter." The greater part of our conversation turned upon the blindness with which our people are afflicted, the blindness to the dependence of the Jewish future upon the creation of permanent art values. He did not allude to the destructive influence of the traditional prohibition of the plastic arts, but I cannot see how one can forgive the many generations of teachers this stupid error by which they have impoverished Jewish existence. I was always wondering what became of all the latent genius for the plastic arts, which must have existed in large measure judging by the sudden outburst in recent years. Glicenstein answered that question tonight. He said that formerly anyone who possessed artistic ability accepted Christianity and usually employed his talent to create anti-Jewish art. I shouldn't be surprised that there is a great deal of truth to that statement.

---

8. War of words.

9. Enrico Glicenstein (1870–1942), sculptor, painter, etcher, woodcarver; noted for his portrait busts.

N. H. Imber[10] and Hatikvah as a Metaphor

SATURDAY NIGHT, APRIL 20, 1929, 12:00 MIDNIGHT

If people would realize what rich treasures lie hidden in Judaism they would tear their hair for their failure to exploit them.

It is said that Imber the author of Hatikvah in a state of drunkenness passed by a meeting hall where the Zionists were singing his Hatikvah. The rain was coming down in torrents and he wanted to enter the hall, but it was crowded and the man at the door, not recognizing Imber, refused his admittance. I want to use this incident in the concluding chapter of "Judaism as a Civilization"[11] as an analogue to what might happen to the Jewish people. Having given to the world its history and ideals as articulated in its Sacred Scriptures, it is liable to be reduced to the necessity of standing as a neglected outsider hearing the chorus of people as they take up its noble strains, but unable to join them in their song.

False Prophets in the Bible?

SUNDAY, APRIL 21, 1929, 12:30 P.M.

Is it possible that I have made a discovery? I have a hunch that the writings of the "false" prophets have been incorporated into the Bible. I could never find a satisfactory background for Isaiah 13 and 14. Does it not seem plausible to assign these chapters to the "false" prophets whom Jeremiah denounced (Jer. 29,8)? May this not be the reason for the anonymity of these prophecies? If it should turn out that the "false" prophets were the authors of the anti-Babylonian prophecies, they would have to be credited with the new consolatory trend that we find in biblical prophecy. It does not seem plausible to ascribe such lofty style and diction to any but the survivors of the great prophetic movement, who had been carried captive into Babylon.

Does the Passion to Achieve Equal the Creative Urge?

WEDNESDAY, MAY 1, 1929, 1:00 A.M.

Tonight belongs to the eighth day of Pesah. My thoughts are all a tangle and I find it hard to unravel them. Having saved for tomorrow the sermon which I should have given this morning I spent a good part of the evening reading Stefan Zweig's *Adepts in Self Portraiture*.[12] The reason for my interest in that book is apparent. I am trying to measure my pygmy self

---

10. Naphtali H. Imber (1856–1909), poet; Hebrew nationalist; wrote "Hatikvah" (Zionist and later Israeli national anthem).

11. So far as I can determine, Kaplan never used this story in his book.

12. Stefan Zweig (1881–1942), Austrian author; published poetry, novels, and biographies.

alongside the giants described in that book. I want to discover what it is that disqualifies me for noteworthy achievement. It is not lack of sensibility. In fact I become so choked up with emotion at the slightest provocation that I become even less articulate than I ordinarily am. Nor is it the lack of analytical power. My misfortune is a treacherous memory.

What is this passion to achieve? The psychologists give it a name, egomania, and imagine they have dismissed the question. This habit of laying the ghost of problems by the utterance of a name goes back to the days when medicine men would lay the ghosts of ancestors by some incantation with names. I find much more meaning to the surmise that this passion to achieve is the manifestation through the bodies of human beings of the creative urge of the universe. Why does this passion fulfill itself in a few and is frustrated in most human beings? Because apparently the physical structure of a few is more adapted to the self-fulfillment of that passion. The nervous system of these superior men is undoubtedly better organized to retain impressions and to react to the environment than is the case with most people.

But why is it that we of inferior breed should be afflicted with this passion to achieve? Why do we not resign ourselves to our limitations? Because life is not organized on a principle of economy. In its spendthrift fashion it wastes itself in infinite futilities. In the form of lust it lives on in those who can no longer procreate. In the form of passion to achieve it manifests itself in the vast multitudes who are too impotent to achieve. If one accepts his limitations and contents himself with passive enjoyments of the achievements of others he is forever pilloried by these superior men and their imitators as a stupid clodhopper. If, on the other hand, he struggles to overcome his limitations only to end in frustration, he is made to appear ridiculous. So long as people of mediocre ability are not asphyxiated or oslerized [meaning unclear], they should be informed by these same superior men of the proper role for them. With all the great things that all the great men have achieved, they have only succeeded in making their own names illustrious, but as far as telling us inferiors how to live, they might as well not have existed. Nor do I believe that with all their greatness they will ever be of much help to us. They only know how to make us feel cheap in our own eyes, how to make sport of our little ambitions and irredeemable frailties.

It is surprising that there hasn't arisen a Karl Marx to preach class war between the genuinely superior and the genuinely inferior human beings, for in actuality there is such a war going on all the time. It is just as real as the war between the capitalists and the proletariat. As I think of it the Russian communists seem to have declared war on intellectual superiority. Of course they have to retain in their service men who are naturally gifted or else they could not exist. But I suspect that they regard submission to men of that type as a necessary evil. Anyhow the facilities made possible by invention so augment the powers of the ungifted as to encourage them into believing that they might gratify their passion to achieve. Disappointed as they must ultimately be in this hope, they feel themselves despoiled by fate, and by those whom fate has favored with a greater measure not merely of the passion but the power to achieve. Such frustration is likely to make for war against inherent superiority. To be sure, such war is bound to be suicidal, but when one is faced with frustration he is not daunted by the possibility of self-murder.

Where does all this lead to? It indicates the need of training mediocre men not to cherish impossible ambitions, and superior men to help their mediocre fellow beings to adjust themselves to their limitations instead of adding to their sufferings by holding them up for contempt.

A Hasidic Story at the Seder

THURSDAY, MAY 2, 1929

At the second Seder we had Glicenstein, the sculptor, with us. This fact was responsible for Sokolow speaking in plain Yiddish.

When I omitted in the Haggadah the sentence *ve-nochal sham min ha-zevahim u-min ha-pesahim* [Heb. "And we shall eat there from the sacrifices and from the Pascal lambs"][13] he demurred and characterized my omission as a criticism of the ancients.

At the table he told an interesting story about the Maggid [preacher] of Dubnow and a rival Maggid who being more learned in the law was popular with the scholars but not with the masses. Once they both happened to come to the same town on a Friday afternoon and repaired to the local rabbi for permission to preach in the synagogue the Sabbath following. The rabbi refused to show any preference. So both were scheduled to speak. First came the rival of the Dubnow Maggid and took as his text *eftehah ve-mashal pi abi'ah hidot minei kedem* [Heb. Psalms 78:2 "I will open my mouth with a parable: I will utter riddles concerning ancient times"] which he explained as follows: There are some maggidim who preach in *meshalim* [Heb. parables]. Such preachment is mere blabber. But I shall preach to you of the mysteries of the Torah which have their source in ancient truth. After the introduction he proceeded with the main theme of his *Drush* [talk, homily]. When the turn came for the Dubnow Maggid to preach he took the same verse which he interpreted as follows: It is true that I preach in *meshalim* but they are at

---

13. This statement from the Haggadah refers to the ultimate return to Jerusalem and the rebuilding of the Temple where the sacrifices will be offered.

least my own. There are *maggidim* [preachers] who make it their business to preach the mysteries of the Torah, but those are old things and everybody knows them.

The People of Israel and the Land of Israel

SUNDAY, MAY 5, 1929, 12:00 NOON

I have to prepare for next week's SAJ Review the concluding part of the chapter on the Revaluation of the Concept Israel. The first part of the article is to be devoted to proving that Judaism has always contemplated Israel's original function and destiny entirely in terms of nationhood, i.e., in terms of collective life associated with a specific land. There is therefore nothing in Traditional Judaism to suggest what Israel could do in the world as a landless people.

This seems to be so self-evident that there should be no need of proving it, were it not that the Reform movement has repudiated nationhood from the role which Israel is to play. My task, therefore, is to prove the self-evident, which I find extremely difficult because of my inability to harp on a theme for any length of time as professional writers usually do. I have been cudgelling my brain for hours how to elaborate on so axiomatic a fact and yet have not found the way to do it. I shall try to write down in this book whatever comes to my mind on the subject since I have no one with whom to discuss the matter.

The main point I want to make is that Israel was highly conscious of its relationship to the land in which it developed its national life. It did not take that relationship for granted as most nations do, but wove out of that relationship the main texture of its career in the world. It is true that in the Bible Israel is now and then spoken of as a nation before it entered the Land of Canaan. It is this fact which has misled Samson R. Hirsch into arguing that the Land was a mere incident to Israel's career as a nation, that career, according to him, being entirely determined by the Torah. But when we note the nature of the national consciousness which Israel is alleged to have possessed while it was in Egypt or in the wilderness we find that it was permeated with a sense of homelessness, of being not actually a nation but a nation in the making. There is nothing that so stands out about the Israelites in Egypt as that they regarded themselves as temporary sojourners there destined to be led to the Land which their God has sworn to grant them. If the Torah is to be regarded as the principal instrument whereby Israel was molded into a nation, Israel was surely not a nation in Egypt. And although the Torah was granted, according to the traditional view, to the Israelites in the Wilderness, it was not in the Wilderness that it formed them into a nation since the greater part of its contents point to the Promised Land as the theatre of Israel's life. The years spent in the wilderness are represented as preparatory to Israel's career as a nation.

8:00 P.M.

It is impossible to read the stories which tell of the Patriarchs without being impressed by the fact that the basic theme is how God enabled the Patriarchs to take formal possession of the Land of the Amorite and how He reassured them again and again that He will enable their descendants to take actual possession of it. On the basis of a few aggadic passages which reflect the religious polemic interests of rabbinic times, Abraham has been wrongly pictured as having been called by God by virtue of his having discovered the truth about the one and only God. The Torah knows nothing about Abraham as a religious philosopher. It is mainly interested in giving an account of the way God went about creating a people that would acknowledge Him as its God and obey His laws. It informs us that God chose Abraham to be the founder of that people. To achieve that purpose He commanded Abraham to leave his home and kindred (among whom he would naturally have had to worship other gods) and He directed him to the land of Canaan, promising at the same time to make him into a great nation, great by reason of prosperity and prestige. Abraham no sooner arrived in the land than God appears and says to him "To thy seed will I give this Land." This promise is reiterated ten times in the course of the Patriarchal epic. Why did not the Patriarchs enter into actual possession forthwith? There were two conditions that had to be met. One, Abraham had to prove his worth as a faithful and obedient vassal of God. Second, the Amorite who held the land had to fill the measure of sin before he could with justice be deprived of his land. This latter condition necessitated the sojourn of Jacob, his children and their descendants in Egypt. God's purpose with regard to forming the descendants of Abraham into a nation had to be suspended, as it were. When Joseph adjured the children of Israel to take his remains to Canaan when the time for their return came he said, "God will surely remember you," etc. (Gen. 50, 24). It was in this spirit of waiting to be called to their land that the Israelites are presumed to have lived in Egypt.

When the time for the Exodus became ripe God sent Moses to lead the Israelites out of Egypt and to bring them to the Land (Exod 3,8 and 6,7–8).[14] In the song which celebrates Israel's victory at the Red Sea it is made apparent that the main significance of the redemption from the yoke of

---

14. Exodus 3:8 "I have come down to rescue them from the Egyptians and to bring them out of that land to a good and spacious land, a land flowing with milk and honey. . . ."

Exodus 6:7–8 "And I will take you to be my people, and I will be your God. And you shall know that I, the Lord, am your God who freed you from the labors of the Egyptians. I will

Pharaoh lay in the fact that it enabled the Israelites to enter into possession of the Land that is described as God's own. (Exod. 15, 15b–17). It is on their way to the Land where they are to live as a nation that they received the laws which were to govern them. Those laws (except for the directions concerning the Tabernacle) contemplate the Israelites in possession of the Land. Their sojourn in the Wilderness would not have lasted longer than was necessary to effect the passage between Egypt and Canaan, and to prove their qualification as the people of God by bearing patiently under the trials which they had to incur in the journey. They fail in every one of the trials, they violate outright the prohibition against making an image of the Deity. Yet they would have entered the Land after having covered the distance that separated them from it. But they committed one sin which more than any other called forth the divine wrath. They sent spies to reconnoiter the Land and those spies brought back an evil report which threw the people into a panic of fear and despair. In expiation of that sin the Israelites had to journey about well nigh forty years in the Wilderness until the entire generation that left Egypt after the age of twenty-one died out including Moses, Aaron and Miriam.

In the same way as Genesis unfolds the epic of adventure which had to be incurred by Israel's forebears to win the Land, so *Deuteronomy* plays variations on the theme of what their descendants will have to do to hold the Land. From the beginning to the end of *Deuteronomy* the one great concern is that Israel shall not forfeit its right to the Land. It is as though Moses were bringing the significance of Israel's experiences in the wilderness to a focus by pointing out their bearing upon Israel's destiny as a nation in the Land of which they were about to take possession. The first oration opens not as we might expect with a description of the Exodus but with a reference to the divine command to start on the last stage of the march to their destination. In section after section, Israel is reminded that all which it has gone through has been to train it and give it the wherewithal whereby it might be able to attain its goal as a people in the Land. The aim and reward of its obedience to the laws of God are interminable possession of the land and the enjoyment of the wealth of its blessings in which it excels, even the watered shores of the Nile. On the other hand in case of disobedience the Land will be forfeited and every conceivable disaster which was wont to follow in the train of invasion and conquest by enemy peoples would befall Israel. Thus in one uniform strain does *Deuteronomy* interpret Israel's fortunes and failures in terms of the part that it is to play in the Land.

---

bring you into the land which I swore to give to Abraham, Isaac, and Jacob, and I will give it to you for a possession. I am the Lord."

If we were to take a survey of the other books of the Bible we would invariably meet with the same tendency to define Israel's experiences, backslidings, its failures and its hopes in terms of its relationship to the Land. Some of those writings belong to an earlier period than the Torah, some are contemporaneous with it, and some belong to a later period. But no "value" is so uniformly interpreted and emphasized as the "value" of the Land in its relation to Israel. The Torah however embodying as it does the teachings of the earlier prophets and enjoying as it does preeminence among the sacred writings of the Jewish people, its influence must be regarded as most decisive in the shaping of Judaism. When therefore we find the Torah intent upon making Israel's relationship to the Land its principal motif we cannot conceive how it could ever have been possible for the Jews to contemplate their functioning as a group without association with the Land. Tautological as all this may sound, we find it necessary to harp on this fact in view of the opinion which is widely held among modern scholars that when the civilization of the Jewish people entered upon its theocratic stage during the period of the second commonwealth the Jews ceased to be a nation and became a church, an ecclesia. These scholars accustomed to thinking of nationhood as the product mainly of political government and statehood, and finding that from the return to the inauguration of the Maccabean Dynasty the Jews were a vassal state with a minimum of political machinery, conclude that the Jews became a Temple-community and passed into the class of organization best designated as church. Assuming that a church is a social or spiritual organization upon which territory exercises no determining influence (which fact is far from being admissible) they conclude that after the Return the life, the habits and the hopes of the Jews were accordingly an ecclesiastical entity, a Kingdom of priests. This view totally misrepresents the facts. Apart from what we would infer *a priori* from the nature of the Torah which dominated the life of the Jews that they could not possibly have thought of their future in any other but national-territorial terms, the actualities of Jewish history during the entire period of the second commonwealth confirm that inference.

The main support relied upon by those who imagine they can find a precedent in the past for divorcing the destiny of Israel from its local associations is the collection of prophecies contained in the latter part of Isaiah. While it is true that to the Torah Israel is inseparable from its Land, it is otherwise with the author or authors of those prophecies which speak of Israel as the servant of God destined to bring the light of truth and justice to the nations. That author may have been far ahead of [his] times. His universalism ill comported with the narrow nationalism of the lesser spirits fettered by the bonds of legalism. But now he can be appreciated and his teaching adopted as the correct interpretation of Israel's mission to the peoples of the earth, a mission that is unhampered by the limitations of territorial interests. This type of argument is blithely oblivious of the facts with regard to the anonymous author of the mission idea. Never did it occur to him to picture Israel as destined to achieve the goal as a landless people. On the contrary, like all the seers and lawyers of Israel, he cannot help viewing the dispersion of the Jewish people with concern, except that instead of losing heart as most of his contemporaries did who imagined that the dissolution of Israel was at hand, he in the firmness of his faith in the God of Israel concluded that even the dispersion was serving the purpose of acquainting the nations with the God of Israel. But that purpose was by no means to be final. It was only a mediatory step to the attainment of the final goal, that of Israel's restoration to its land. (Isaiah 49, 18–19).[15]

I do not know why I couldn't have written the formation of my thoughts on ordinary paper, or what it is about this book that has stimulated me to put down my thoughts which would otherwise have remained in potentia. The one striking fact which I hit on in the course of my writing out the above was the one about the Book of Deuteronomy. I had never realized to what extent it is devoted to the interpretation of the significance of the Land.

This afternoon I worked out a very interesting lesson with the Senior Class of the Teachers Institute. I took as my clue the definition of Torah as civilization. I defined civilization as aiming at the self-fulfillment of the individual through the various relationships which constitute human life. The place of art in civilization is to accentuate the element of worthwhileness in those relationships. Originally man found worthwhileness only in the relation of the individual to the cosmos. Then art was confined to religion. With the democratization, as it were, of worthwhileness, art has invaded the fields of the specific relationships.

Max Kadushin Invited to Be Rabbi of the SAJ

THURSDAY, MAY 16, 1929, 12:30 P.M.

I am sending the following letter to Rabbi Kadushin. It took me more than an hour to write it. As I was writing it I thought to myself "You no sooner try to work with somebody else than you have to be wary of what you say. This business of weighing words takes up a lot of time and energy."

"Dear Rabbi Kadushin, You know, I presume, that much as I have tried to interest the members of the SAJ in the furtherance of Jewish cultural

---

15. Isaiah 49:18–19 "You shall don them like jewels, / Deck yourself with them like a bride. / As for your ruins and desolate places / And your land laid waste— / You shall soon be crowded with settlers, / While destroyers stay far from you."

undertakings for the community in general as the main raison d'etre of the organization, they insist upon regrading themselves as organized mainly for congregational purposes. That being the case, I consider the rabbinic services which I am in a position to render entirely inadequate. They need the services of a rabbi who could give all of his time to them. He would have to preach, take charge of the Hebrew School, and direct the activities of the adults, in other words, do exactly what you are doing now for your congregation. They could then dispense with the services of an executive director, since the membership is comparatively small and there are no communal center activities being carried on in the building of the SAJ.

"What I would like to know is, first, whether you would care to fill that position in the SAJ; secondly, what salary you would expect and thirdly, what, in your opinion, should my position and function in the SAJ be so that you might feel that you are aided in your work by reason of your association with me.

"Kindly let me hear from you if possible by Monday morning.

"With kindest regards to you and Evelyn, Yours sincerely . . ."[16] .

A good deal of the time in formulating the letter was taken up with the first of the three questions. I am not satisfied even now with the way it reads, but I have to let it go as it is.

"My Powers Are Not Equal to My Goal"

Thursday, May 23, 1929, 5:00 p.m.

No words could state more accurately the arguments that make a coward of me than those in the article in Harper's Monthly Magazine (June 1929) by Harold J. Laski: He writes, "One who seeks to work for the acceptance of truth rejected by the powers that be, embarks upon a voyage where he can be certain his ship will be wrecked. The authority of existing interests is so strong that it is folly to rebel against their compulsion. . . . We have our own happiness to achieve; we are not, in any case, our brother's keeper. What profit does a man have who sets himself up for Athanasius? *It is rare that his powers are equal to his self-appointed task.* He will earn only bitterness and disappointment from effort of which the world is careless. Those whom he loves will only too often pay the price of his sacrifice to his conscience. His spiritual urgency will, to the generality, seem no more than a special form of egotism or stubbornness."

---

16. Kadushin was one of Kaplan's most devoted disciples. He taught for Kaplan at the Jewish Center. Kaplan influenced him profoundly, but eventually Kadushin became alienated from Kaplan. For more information on Kaplan and Kadushin see *Judaism Faces the Twentieth Century the Twentieth Century: A Biography of Mordecai M. Kaplan* (Detroit: Wayne State University Press, 1993), passim.

The sentence I've underlined hits the bull's eye. Had I possessed a facile pen or an eloquent tongue I would have dared Satan himself. It is the fear that if I were involved in a conflict I would find myself short of ammunition, or incapable of using the little I have with telling effect, that has prevented me from declaring war against the intellectual dishonesty of the Seminary and United Synagogue cohorts.

Family Complications

SATURDAY NIGHT, MAY 25, 1929

I have hardly ever written a word about my mother. Convention and taboo demand that we be silent about our parents unless we can speak of them in a laudatory view. Probably there is some value to the interdict so long as one receives from one's parents the slightest evidence of unselfish consideration. When a parent displays towards his child signs of meanness toward him he forfeits any claim to respect from him. This is unfortunately how I feel about my mother. I know she is a sickly woman, yet her ailments do not prevent her from coming all the way from Brooklyn to see the jeweler about an old candelabra of hers and not stepping into my house after an absence of months, although the jeweler's store is around the corner from where I live. Today I went with Lena to pay a condolence call at Mrs. E. L. Solomon's. There I learned that mother and Sophie were there two days ago. The Solomons live only a few blocks away from us. I really don't know whom to blame—Mother or Sophie. I feel in my heart that Sophie doesn't like me. She wishes me well—at a distance. She hates me because I do not bend heaven and earth to get a congregation for Phineas. The fact that I cannot conscientiously recommend him or make use of his services is of no consequence to her. Brotherhood in her opinion must override all other considerations.

Feeling Spiritually Starved

SUNDAY, MAY 26, 1929, 11:15 A.M.

The exigencies of my work prevent me from giving as much time as I should like to the reading and study of Hebrew subject matter. Time and again I am overcome by a feeling of homesickness for Hebrew. If I yield to that feeling and spend some time reading Hebrew I am rewarded by a sense of at homeness as though I were once again among my own. It is then that I also enjoy a good dose of pious sentiment and prefer it to the modern pragmatic claptrap. I just picked up, for example, Bahyas's Duties of the Heart[17] *Sha'ar Ha-behinah* [Heb. examination. (Second treatise in

---

17. Popular ethical treatise written in the eleventh century.

Kaplan's sister, Sophie Kaplan Israeli, ca. 1910.
(Courtesy Hadassah K. Musher)

the Duties of the Heart)]. I drank in every word as though my soul had been parched. The few opening paragraphs put me into a spiritual mood such as I seldom experience. Very often as I put on my tephilin (of late, somehow, I have allowed days and recently even a whole week to pass without putting on the tephilin—I can't account for these omissions) I search about for something that might put me into a prayerful mood, but without success. When I pick of the Bible I fall into the study mood, which is just what I want to get away from. When I turn to the little books issued by the Association press, I am revolted by the Christology in them. The result is that I am spiritually starved.

Being a *na va-nad* [Heb. wanderer] from one culture to another, being an exile in English culture (as one can see by my labored style) and being without a home in Hebrew culture, is not calculated to promote in me that unity and integration of personality which is said to be a prime requisite to happiness.

Some hours have passed since I wrote the foregoing and I am still sucking as it were, in the juicy morsel of an interpretation I came across in the *Hovot Ha-levavot* (Heb. *Duties of the Heart*) where Bahya renders *divrei ḥakhamim ke-darvonot* . . . [Heb. Ecclesiastes 12:11 "The words of the wise are like spurs, and like nails (well driven in are the sayings of the masters of collections)"] as implying that the written word is so much more valuable than the spoken word because it has permanence.[18]

Thinks He Always Looks Angry

MONDAY, MAY 27, 1929, 9:45 P.M.

I took this picture this morning on the way from Dr. Spivak to the library of the Union Theological Seminary. I suppose it is vanity that prompts me to have my picture taken or my bust made or to have a phonographic record made of my voice as I tried last Friday. But is there not also an innate desire to want to know more about oneself? Perhaps also the wish to snatch from the ravenous maw of Time something that might endure—if at least for a little while. I notice that I aged quite perceptibly within the last year, judging by the previous picture in this Diary. After listening to the "cheering" remarks by the physician about the blood becoming acidy when it secretes a good deal of water on account of a running nose caused by the hay fever, signs of aging do not exactly predispose one to being gay. I have to laugh at myself when I recall what passed through my mind when I caught sight of the series of snapshots of which the foregoing is one. I said to myself

---

18. R. Bachya Ben Joseph Ibn Paquda, *Torat ḥovot HaLevavot —Duties of the Heart*, trans. Moses Hyamson (New York: Feldheim, 1970), 1:128.

"No wonder young people take me for a bear when they first meet me. I can understand now why people say I always look angry. I recall Schechter applying to me the Yiddish epithet A *berogezer misnagid* [Yiddish: an angry anti-Hasidic type]. I there and then made up my mind that I must assume a pleasant expression. During the rest of my walk I must have looked as though I was obeying a photographer's order to look pleasant. During the rest of the day, however, my shoes pinched me so savagely that I forgot all about the resolve made in the morning, and continued to look probably like a Male Niobe.[19]

Seeing a Movie and Feeling Guilty

THURSDAY, MAY 30, 1929

I took this picture last night on 42 St. as I was walking home from the Teachers Institute. I first stepped into one of the vaudeville-movie places to overcome the sense of boredom which is one of my principal afflictions. I may have one or two friends but I haven't a single colleague with whom I might read, study, discuss or work together. An anchorite could not be more solitary than I am. Once in a great while I seek escape to a movie picture place only to come out even more bored and vexed than before. Vaudeville holds my attention somewhat; I enjoy the occasional dialogue, articulate clever thought or repartee more than anything else in the arts. For that matter any kind of skill captivates me. Some of the vaudeville artists appear to me to be super-men and women. They represent to me manifestations of human power, power highly organized and developed to the point of utmost skill. There was a young fellow, for example, who mimicked various dialects, sang, danced and played on a one string violin improvised out of a cigar box. I imagine that he too is often bored by the monotony of the few tricks which he has to perform, but seeing and hearing him as I do for the first time, I look upon him as a demi-god. After an hour of this kind of entertainment I get restless. The thought of being a passive spectator of the powers of others while not exerting my own drives me out of the theater. I walk further. Feeling thirsty I stop in at Schrafft's to take a soda. Not far away is a photomaton. I remind myself of the gloomy looking photo I took yesterday and how I have tried (when I thought of it) to look pleasant. Isn't it only natural that I should want to know how I look when I look pleasant? And here is the photomaton ready to give you an idea of the difference between your natural and your assumed self. Before I know it the series of eight snapshots is ready and I allow myself to be persuaded

---

19. Niobe, a woman in Greek myth punished and changed by Zeus into stone, who yet continued to weep for her lost children.

by the young fellow who is in charge of the machine to have one of the snapshots enlarged.

Now, would it have been making a better use of my time if instead of writing the foregoing I would have read a folio of the Talmud? I honestly do not know. And we are talking about freedom of the will. Assuming even that we have freedom even forty-eight years (or nearly that) of life doesn't give one any idea what to do with it or how to apply it to the best advantage.

In yesterday's paper (*N.Y. Times*) there is a news item from Paris about a young Englishman who after having given his mother a sleeping draught shot her dead to put an end to her suffering from cancer. According to his account she had repeatedly asked him to do so, and it was only when all hope of her recovery had been abandoned and when the agony from which she was suffering became unbearable that he took his decision. Then he tried to commit suicide. He is now recovering. Recently he sent a letter to the editor of the *Matin* in which he called attention to the problem of putting an end to the suffering of incurables at their own request. "It should never be done by private people," he says. "It should be done by the State. But when the State fails in its duty, then sometimes there is an excuse of those who themselves assume the responsibility."

I myself have often been thinking about that problem. I waive as untenable the argument that a person's life belongs entirely to him and he should have the right to do with it what he pleases. It is not from the standpoint of the sufferer that this question should be discussed, but from that of those who witness his suffering. What ground can they have for allowing a person to undergo physical and mental torture other than blind and unreasoning taboo which have no capacity for distinctions? To break down that taboo in the case of those who pray to be relieved of a living death would be the greatest act of mercy to the millions whose cry has ever gone up to heaven. *Lama yitein le'amel or* . . . [Heb. Job 3:20, 21 "Why does he give light to the sufferer/ (and life to the bitter in spirit;/ To those who wait for death but it does not come,/who search for it more than treasure)].

Wearing a Tallit Katan[20] *and a Conversation on Heresy*

FRIDAY, MAY 31, 1929, 3:15

This morning I sat, or rather I stood, for the bust Glicenstein is working on. When he talks about things in general I like to listen to him. Thus when he asked me to open my shirt he noticed my small "tallit." "That

---

20. Tallit Katan: a small undergarment with fringes at the four corners of the garment worn by observant men to fulfill the commandment in Numbers 15:39.

tallit is *posul*, [unfit from a halakhic point of view]" he said. The commandment concerning "zizit" reads "and ye shall see them and remember." Of what use are they when they are out of sight?[21] A mezuzah that's hidden is "posul" [unfit]. My reply that when I put on the small "tallit" I am conscious of their significance made no impression on him.

He then continued to talk about what happened to him when after being away many years from home he returned to his native town and his father gave him "tallit" [prayer shawl] and "tephilin" [phylacteries] to put on which he refused to do, adding that he would be making them "posul" by donning them. It is not easy to follow his conversation because the sentences do not come in regular sequence.

He then went on to speak about a Hassidic Rebbi of Kotzk who had apparently arrived at heretical conclusions which prevented him from donning the "Tephilin" for a number of days in succession. Those who had charge of visitors, fearing that rumor of his heresies might get abroad, made it a point to keep visitors away during those periods when the Rabbi seemed to be lost in philosophic contemplation. Reverting then to his own life, Glicenstein went on to say that when he came to Munchen [Munich] to study his fellow students would not let him don "Tephilin." "We are living in a different world," they said "what have you to do with these ancient customs?" When Sabbath came they made him go on with his work. Afterwards he himself came to the conclusion that as the sun went on shining it was his task to go on working day in and day out. Creativity is the sabbath of the soul. When he told this to his father who was himself a Hassid (and apparently earned his livelihood from writing scrolls of Torah and of "Tephilin") his father understood. Never did his father say to him "Observe the Sabbath for my sake." The father realized that his son adopted his mode of life not in a spirit of lightheartedness or irresponsibility but with "Toharah and Kedusha" [purity and holiness]. In Glicenstein one can see the humanist development of Hassidism, a development which there seems to be little trace among the dry pilpulistic [scholastic] "mitnagdim" [opponents of Hasidism].

Receiving an Honorary Doctorate from JTS

Sunday, June 9, 1929, 6:00 p.m.

I have just come back from Town Hall where the Seminary Graduation exercises were held. I was awarded the DHL honoris causa. It has become a custom in the Seminary to award an honorary degree to graduates of twenty-five years standing who have in some way distinguished themselves

---

21. The custom for modern Orthodox Jews in the early twentieth century was to not allow the fringes of the Tallit Katan to be seen.

in their career. I should have or would have been given the honorary degree two years ago, but at that time I was not persona grata. The cloud that had hung over me by reason of my contemplated resignation[22] from the Seminary had not yet been dissipated. The basis of the award, as Dr. Adler stated, is the service I have rendered Jewish education by having contributed to the growth of the Teachers Institute.

Could Work Harder

TUESDAY, JUNE 25, 1929, 2:30 P.M.

During the winter I look forward to the summer months with the expectation that I will fill reams of paper with the multitude of ideas which do not get a chance to be articulated owing to the press of routine duties. The many books which I have begun will at last be finished and will see the light of day. The languages which I should have cultivated will receive a good deal of attention, German, Latin, Greek, French. I will gain fluency in Hebrew. I shall take up Arabic and Syriac. All this I plan to do without forgoing the recreation that I need and that the summer heat renders necessary. No sooner, however, does the summer season arrive than all this turns out to be a pipe dream. The greater part of June is taken up with numerous appointments and meetings to label and appraise the work of the past academic year and to set the machinery for the coming academic year. It is also the season when I have to see the doctor three times a week to be inoculated against the hay fever. June being the month of weddings and wedding anniversaries I come in for three or four such occasions. The first week of July is usually taken up with the meeting of the Rabbinical Assembly. I imagine that in terms of actual reading and writing I achieve less during these weeks than at any other time of the year. This fact is not calculated to put me into a cheerful frame of mind, but I do all I can to overcome the moodiness to which it gives rise. I am well aware how ridiculous it is of me to complain that I am frustrated in my ambition to inscribe my name on the rock of permanent accomplishment, when so many of those I know are the victims of ill-starred fate and are engaged in a life and death struggle for sheer existence. There is poor Morris Levine[23] who has been in the hospital for the last four weeks, unable to take any food, suffering the tortures of hell, and fearing that he is stricken with cancer. What joy has that man gotten out of life? For more than a decade his wife was suffering from the fatal ailment which reduced

---

22. Kaplan had handed in his resignation to Cyrus Adler in January 1927 with the intention of taking a position at the Jewish Institute of Religion with Stephen Wise. Many protested, and after three months Kaplan withdrew his resignation. See *Judaism Faces the Twentieth Century*, chapters 7 and 8.

23. A TI faculty member.

her to the state of a living corpse. In addition to the many hours of teaching he would spend at least two to three hours daily in the subways. With an exaggerated conscientiousness he would give himself to the correction of the students' compositions in Hebrew.

I am not of those who when they note that good men suffer at once fall to taking God to task. I am not altogether sure that Levine himself is not a good deal to blame for assuming that it is proper to blame anyone, having brought a good deal of the trouble on himself. Even his friend Chertoff [24] tells me that Levine was too proud to accept any assistance that might have somewhat eased his lot. He had something of that proud asceticism which the Talmud ascribes to Samuel or to a R. Piṇhas ben Yair. I do not suppose I ought hold the Talmud responsible for Levine's failure to order his life more intelligently and to realize that he was doing neither himself nor God nor anyone else any favor by bearing unnecessary burdens, yet I cannot help feeling that much of Levine's gloom and austerity can be traced to Talmudic influence.

On Being Immortal through One's Writing: The Diary

TUESDAY, JUNE 25, 1929

Not having recorded my experiences since June 9, all that I lived through and participated in seems like a confused mass of fading impressions. If I should want to revive them I would have to exert mental energy for the purpose of giving them some logical order and proper evaluation to say nothing of trying to recall incidents that have sunk below the threshold of consciousness. That is asking too much. This is not meant to be literature, and does not deserve that mental strain and concentration which I ought to reserve for more serious tasks.

I cannot give any account of myself for this untamed urge to feel that I have lived. May it not be due to the fact that life after death is to me as inconceivable or as meaningless as white blackness or black whiteness? In the sense that whatever energy—and I certainly believe in the reality of spiritual energy—is represented by the term ego or selfhood goes on functioning in the life of mankind, I certainly subscribe to immortality. But that the individualized ego survives the death of the body and of the various personalities with whose life it is integrated is to be simply unintelligible. May it not be therefore that because I am so categorically certain of my personal non-existence after I am gone from this world that I want to make sure that I have been alive while I lived? Is that why more people write diaries than ever did in the past? Does that mean that with the waning in

---

24. A TI faculty member.

the belief in personal immortality the world will be flooded with diaries? There may come a time when the world will be cluttered with so much of this kind of writing that juries will have to be established to decide which diaries may be destroyed. I can't imagine that any one would have the heart to deliberately destroy a document in which the poor human ego flees as to the last refuge from complete death. When the need for breathing space will simply make it impossible for all diaries to be preserved, a process of condemning the trashy ones will have to be instituted, and it will probably assume the seriousness of consultations which will then be in vogue whether the victim of an incurable disease should have euthanasia administered to him.

Giving a Sermon—Kaplan Remembers His First

MONDAY, JULY 1, 1929, 12 MIDNIGHT

The most unwelcome interruption in my work is having to officiate at weddings. I have as a rule very few weddings, but those that I have are generally attended by the limited circle of SAJ members. This involves my formulating anew each time I officiate the remarks I address to the bride and groom. With but one main idea to harp on—viz., the spiritual significance of marriage—and with the few tense moments when attention of the guests is riveted on what the rabbi says—I find it rather difficult to introduce sufficient variety of form to prevent the listeners from saying, "I have heard you say that before." I suppose I ought to be insensitive to what people think of the way I officiate, but the fact is that I am just as nervous today as I was twenty and twenty-five years ago each time I have to address a bridal couple. I imagine it is due largely to my having practically to memorize my remarks, and there is nothing that I find more difficult than memorizing for public address. I shall never forget the ordeal I went through when as a student of about twenty I tried to deliver a memorized sermon before the students of the Seminary on a Sabbath afternoon. When I got to the middle of the sermon I completely forgot what I had to say, and being unable to go on I went down from the pulpit. It was as a result of that bitter experience that I made up my mind to learn to speak extemporaneously. During the summer months following that episode I would spend daily two hours reading and then repeating aloud the substance of what I read, in paraphrased form. Two months of that practice gave me sufficient self-assurance to speak extemporaneously. But to this day I need a full outline before me, if I want to be free of a sense of anxiety before I get up to speak, although some of my most powerful sermons have been those which were delivered without the aid of notes, and which I had to mull over in my mind until I rose to speak. But the energy and the time that go into the latter kind of sermon are too large a price to pay for the more effective delivery.

The Diary as Other

WEDNESDAY JULY 3, 1929, 11:30 P.M.

That after so many years of thinking on the subject of Jewish nationalism I should experience difficulty in setting forth my ideas on that subject in presentable fashion has a very depressing effect on my spirit, and it is with the greatest exertion that I barely manage to retain my courage in the face of the odds against me, to wit, a poor memory, lack of intellectual comradeship, and absence of any demand for the values that I am dying to create.

As on previous occasions I shall resort again to this diary as though it were an intelligent friend to whom I could communicate what I am struggling these days to formulate.

Meaning of Nationhood

JULY 5, 1929, 12:45 P.M.

I am still very far from being out of the woods with my discussion of the meaning of nationhood. The greater part of the day I dictated on the outline of the talk I am scheduled to give before the Rabbinical Assembly. That outline has put me off the track, somewhat, because I have had to formulate an introduction to the main thought which is a link in the argument that I am developing in the book. I shall now try to organize my ideas on the subject as an integral part of the discussion in the book.

Finding ourselves obliged to retain our affection for Palestine and yet accepting the condition of diaspora not as a state of exile but of permanent domicile we Jews are compelled to find a formula for nationhood that shall meet with following requirements: a) It shall indicate the basis for that moral evaluation of nationhood which justifies us in holding on to our status as a nation against all odds. b) It shall indicate the basis for that political conception of nationhood which permits affiliation with more than one nation.

    a. The basis for moral evaluation is the fact that nationhood is the sense of unity with the group which contributes, etc.
       a. It is a moral law to elicit the best from given conditions.
       b. In being the first influence (on) the human being nationhood is the most important determinant.
       c. Historically nationalism functioned as a means of transforming dominion into commonwealth.

b. The basis for the political conception etc. is the fact that nationhood does not coincide with statehood plus the fact that statehood does not imply absolute sovereignty.

A nation must have a degree of autonomy but not absolute autonomy. If it can establish a modus vivendi with another nation it can place itself in a position of equality or subordination without jeopardizing its own existence. This of course means the eliminating of any possibility of military conflict. In the latter case one could not be a member of two nations at the same time. Thus we can be a member of the Welsh or Scotch nation and at the same time of the British nation. But one cannot today be a member of the German and of the American nation because the possibility of war is a real one. On the other hand the situation is different with the Jews. This means that Palestine cannot permanently remain a mandatory country of Britain so long as war with Britain is a possible contingency without compromising the citizenship of the Jews under other governments. Either war with those governments would have to be completely outlawed or Palestine would have to become a protectorate of the League.

I am simply astounded that no one has taken the trouble to think out these problems which are so vital to the civic status as well as to the spiritual development of Jewish life.

Randomness and the Problem of Evil

THURSDAY, JULY 11, 1929, 10:30 A.M.

The Tuesday morning session also had a rasping effect on me. Again it was humanism that came in for a lambasting. Strange to say Jacob Kohn, who read a paper on the Spiritual Element in Judaism, was mild in comparison with the two speakers who followed him, Israel Goldstein and Friedman of Phila. It strikes me that the trouble with J. Kohn's approach is not that it is inherently wrong. On the contrary, he must be credited with enough common sense to realize the need for revaluation of traditional values, and with enough intellectual acumen to hit off occasionally a correct revaluation. But he distributes his emphasis in such a fashion as to gloss over the element of revelation and to abet the reactionaries in their cry against modernization. Like those of us who are abreast of the times he is influenced by liberal Christian theology, but he always manages to select the most conservative and theologically phrased reinterpretations. For example, in his paper which he read he made a point of retaining the fear concept of God. He repeated almost verbatim the statements I have so often come across by Christian preachers protesting against the tendency to identify God with love only and urging that we should behold in the consequences of sin the punitive aspects of God's dealings. To me the very idea of a punishing God is perfectly abhorrent. All punishment is nothing but revenge and therefore belongs to the same class of evils as sin, suffering, cruelty, disease and death. I might as well think of God as deliberately sinning or committing cruelty as to attribute to him the will to punish. God is not concerned in seeing to it that the consequences of sin shall be suffering. The consequences of sin are part of the sin which caused them, and like the sin itself possible in the universe because the domain of chance and accident still occupies a tremendous part of that universe and has not yet come under the dominion of God who is synonymous with whatever there is of order, purpose, intelligence and love in the universe. From a historical and psychological standpoint one is certainly more justified in applying the term God to Wells' "Invisible King" than to Spinoza's Substance. As for the old question, how can we pray to any but the God of tradition, the answer of course is that it all depends on what you conceive to be the function of prayer.

Kohn evaded all of the more fundamental problems in the conception of God though he gave the impression that he was taking deep soundings in the sea of religious thought. He certainly could not let the occasion go without mentioning something I had said about nationhood being a means to self-realization to indicate wherein he disagreed with me. He can never speak to me or of me without assuming an air of patronizing snobbishness that offends me to the quick. Why is it that whenever these colleagues of mine mention anything of Adler's or Ginzberg's, to say nothing of Schechter and Friedlander, it is always in a spirit of assent and approval. Whenever they mention anything I say it is always in a spirit of dissent and attack. And yet it is a fact that of the ideas which Seminary men make use of in public many more are those which they have gotten from me than from Adler or the others. I daresay that even J. Kohn has swung over toward humanism and has become more outspoken in recent years as a result of my continually hammering away at the self-complacent evasion which had been entrenched at the Seminary. I am sure that he got more out of my Judaism as a Civilization than out of Schechter's "Catholic Israel" which is as illuminating as a fog.

Loses His Temper and Some Thoughts on Being a Rabbi

Friday, July 12, 1929, 10:30 a.m.

I began the account of the convention with the statement that I did not come out of the ordeal unscathed. Being under the continuous strain of having to appear calm and benign despite provocation to anger cannot have a wholesome effect on the nerves, and when an explosion does come it is bound to wreak havoc in the relationship with my colleagues. The last session was over, everybody went his way and I had just telephoned for Vivian Bachrach to call for me with the automobile. While waiting I happened to sit down near Finkelstein and Boaz Cohen. Before I knew it I found myself almost shouting at the top of my voice that "I deeply resent Adler's attitude. Every time I read a paper he finds it necessary to poke fun at it. There is a limit to my patience. It was the fact that my patience reached the breaking point two years ago that led me to send in my resignation." I probably would have gone on and talked more foolishness, but fortunately the automobile arrived just then, and the harm wrought could not have been serious.

It is apparent that although I am middle-aged I have not yet come to terms with the Cosmos. A convention such as this is enough to start me dreaming about the possibility of disentangling myself from the mess of conventional lies and group of persons that constitute the Seminary universe. But to whom should I fly for refuge and with whom is there any hope of being able to work *le-shem shamyim* [Heb. for the sake of heaven]? Perhaps the very idea of having people devote themselves to the religious ministry as a life calling is so inherently wrong that under the best of circumstances abuses are bound to creep in. The real difficulty with the ministry as a calling is that the people in engaging a spiritual leader officially entertain expectations which are a survival from the days of magic and which are sincerely met only by the Catholics and fundamentalist Protestants. The spiritual leader is still officially regarded by the laity, Jewish as well as Christian, as the intermediary between them and God, a view consistent with the traditional anthropomorphic conception of God. He is still credited with authority to give sacramental validity to religious acts. So long as men naively hold to the magico-sacramental character of the rabbi or clergyman it is incorrect under the circumstances to speak of him as leader, for he is then in verity nothing but a minister or servant—and if [the][25] rabbi or clergyman is sufficiently unsophisticated to believe himself endowed with that supernatural gift, then he is fulfilling within the limited scope of his and his people's intelligence a normal and honest function. But among Jews other than those of Hassidic sects with their Zaddic cults even before the advent of enlightenment the magico-sacramental conception of the rabbi had long disappeared. Instead of intermediary between God and man the rabbi came to function as judge and mediator between men. His business was to interpret the law. With that function gone as a result of the abrogation of the Jewish civil code and the habit of engaging a rabbi persisting, the question as to what his function shall be in the future was answered by placing him in the same category with the priest and clergyman, especially as it is in that category that the

---

25. Word here is smudged.

gentiles place him. But that answer is a misfit in the case of the enlightened who have given up the idea that here is the domain of the supernatural over which certainly trained and ordained people can exercise control. The only other function which the rabbi could rightly fulfill now that he is deprived of his earlier one as judge and mediator, would be that of teacher and educator. Not as moral and religious exhortor, but as moral and religious teacher, i.e., as one who would keep his people informed as to what goes on in life from the standpoint of man's spiritual development, the rabbi would find his calling the most useful in the world. But the trouble is that the people have not the least understanding of spiritual development as a matter of general education. Neither have they the leisure or patience to acquire the ability to appreciate how much more interesting life would be to them as a result of that kind of education. It therefore never occurs to them to look to their rabbi for guidance in the process of social and spiritual self-education.

If the rabbi had been honest with himself and not given to careerism he would continually be holding up before his people and before himself this conception of the rabbinate. He might not be earning much in perquisites. He could not be continually visiting people promiscuously under the guise of affording them pastoral aid but in reality to get their sacramental trade when there are weddings to be celebrated, funerals to be held, memorial stones to be set up. One such rabbi makes it his business to visit every sick person to whom he has ever been introduced, so that in case the person dies he would be called in to officiate at the funeral. In case the sick person is an old bachelor he might even come in for a respectable bequest of some kind. All these things he would have to forgo but he would himself be growing mentally and spiritually, and actually succeed in building up the House of Israel. But what is to be done when today as in the days of Jeremiah *Ha-nevi'im nib'u va-sheker* . . . [Heb. Jeremiah 5:31 "The prophets prophecy falsely, / (And the priests rule accordingly; / And my people like it so. / But what will you do at the end of it)"]?

Instead of honestly appraising the situation and trying to find some cure for the prevailing evils, my colleagues urge each other to compel the people to regard them as authorized and capable of controlling the supernatural forces that govern men's lives. They want power, and since they cannot obtain that power through money or through ability to render services which are in demand, they want the people to get back the superstitious fears which made them turn to medicine men for help. This was the wish that one could discern in all the papers in discussions of the convention. The only exception was Eugene Kohn's comment on Finkelstein's paper.

I have my luminous moments when I realize how absurd it is for me to be deploring the way I am treated by my colleagues. That treatment is the height of kindness and considerateness as compared with that meted out formerly by rabbis to any colleague of theirs who dared to show the least sign of independent thought. They would not have stopped at murder if they were not afraid of their own lives.

The only happy thought I gleaned during the three days of the convention was the one that suggested itself to me when one of the recent graduates, Fisher[26] of Arverne, mentioned to me a curious fact about the Englishmen who go to India. Although in his native land an Englishman will not always be scrupulous about shaving every day and putting on his dinner clothes for dinner, when he gets to India he makes it his business to observe these details of etiquette in order to feel and assert his English nativity. . . . It is chiefly the desire to do something each day that is concretely and distinctively Jewish that is at the bottom of my keeping up those practices.

Solomon Goldman—A Court Case in Cleveland Regarding Orthodoxy

MONDAY, JULY 22, 1929

This morning's *Jewish Daily Bulletin* reports the decision of the Ohio Court of Appeals as upholding the Orthodox contention in the celebrated Cleveland Jewish Center case. According to that decision the synagogue was a trust formed for Orthodox purposes. Its trustees, therefore, could not without violating the trust change the synagogue ritual from Orthodox to Conservative. To Rabbi Goldman this decision would have been a severe blow, had he not given up his Cleveland position to go to Chicago where he is said to receive a salary of $18,000 per year. Goldman is no doubt a man of considerable ability. Had he placed the cause of Judaism above careerism he could have helped to bring some order out of the spiritual chaos which has settled down upon Jewish life. But he was too much infected by Talmudism to be straightforward in his attack upon Orthodoxy. Instead of openly avowing that he broke with Orthodoxy he tried to prove that the course he pursued, the changes he had introduced into his synagogue, were in accord with traditional Judaism, and that, therefore, he had a right to call himself Orthodox.

I am very happy that the decision of the court made it clear that Conservatism cannot hide under the skirt of Orthodoxy. Perhaps this decision will have the effect of ultimately breaking up that unnatural alliance between reactionism and progressivism which has paralyzed the Rabbinical Assembly and placed it in a position where it can do absolutely nothing of any account.

---

26. Henry Fisher (1903–?), ordained JTS; M.A. Columbia; officer, Rabbinical Assembly.

9

August 5, 1929–November 26, 1929

Benderly and the TI

MONDAY, AUGUST 5, 1929

On Tuesday, July 16, and on Tuesday, July 23, I went to Arverne[1] to ask Dr. Benderly's advice in reference to the Teachers Institute. I was hoping that I might succeed in persuading him to incorporate into the TI the groups of boys and girls whom he has taken out of the Hebrew High School and whom he is attempting to train in accordance with his own ideas. By selecting the best boys and girls for his groups he is undermining the prestige of the Institute. I had hoped that I might get him to conduct this work of his as a department of the Institute. Knowing however how sensitive he is on the subject I didn't even dare broach it to him outright but looked for a favorable opening that might present itself in the course of the conversation with a plea that with the funds now available in the TI there is an excellent opportunity presented to us to bring about a considerable improvement in the Jewish educational situation. The budget granted me for next year is about $67,000 of which $47,000 is to go to the TI and the rest to the Israel Friedlaender classes. I told him that he should look upon the TI as though he had charge of it and that he should feel free to make any suggestions he likes and I shall do all in my power to put them into effect after he and I weighed them carefully. He seemed to be careful not to allow the conversation to drift to the subject of the relation of his groups to the TI but kept it confined to the question of the critic [?] teaching and the negotiations with the United Synagogue whereby it is hoped that the TI would find an outlet for its graduates.

---

1. A seaside resort near New York City.

Not being in a position to discuss details the first time I went to see him I arranged for another meeting the week following. This time we had Dinin with us. The upshot of the discussion the second time was that I should get Adler's permission to transfer about $5000 from the Friedlaender Classes to the TI budget to be to the supervision, training and placing of teachers and graduates of the TI and that I should try to get Gamoran to head that work. Only at one point in the discussion did I have occasion to take issue with him. That was when he implied that no one but he has succeeded in developing men qualified to do constructive work in Jewish education. He intimated that through the groups which he was conducting he would succeed to make up some of the boys and girls into the kind of personalities that would impress their stamp upon Jewish life. I told him that neither he nor any one else was able to transform the nature and character of young people. The most we have a right to hope for is to discover the right kind of young people. We are merely impresarios as far as training leaders for Jewish education is concerned.

What the outcome of his obduracy will be it is hard to say. He has a great deal of contempt for the teachers of the High School classes. This year he has them come to camp but two or three times a week instead of having them live at camp as they did last year. He tries to do himself as much of the teaching as he can utilizing whatever text books and methods he likes without consulting the teachers. He works very hard and makes his wife a slave with him. He seems to lack the essential qualification for organizing work, that of delegating tasks. He is essentially an artist in the art of education and not an organizer. Visualizing finished results he has all the impatience of its artist to see them embodied at once, and not having faith in the capacity of anybody else to achieve those results, he deems it necessary to tackle the task himself.

Utilizing the Summer for Jewish Renewal

THURSDAY, AUGUST 8, 1929: WEST END, N.J.

The suspension of Jewish activities during the summer has something ominous about it. It accustoms the Jew to look upon Judaism as dispensable, so that when those activities are resumed Judaism seems all the more burdensome. Jewish life is vacuous enough the rest of the year, but during the summer it seems to have gone entirely dead. Very few of those who are accustomed to attend services during the other seasons of the year do so during the summer. In any plan of reconstruction considerable thought must be given to this problem. Summer ought to be the time for synagogue conventions. A real Jewish Chatauqua ought to hold its sessions then. Conferences to discuss Jewish problems, analogous to the

Williamstown Conference, and similar means might at least keep Judaism alive as a topic of conversation.

At the CeJwIn[2] camp—Teaching and Thinking

THURSDAY, AUGUST 8, 1929

Last week end I spent at the Central Jewish Institute Camp which is situated near Port Jervis, N.Y. The children who spend part or the whole of their vacation time at this camp come for the most part from Orthodox homes of the lower middle class. The children are accustomed to attendance at Hebrew schools about four or five times a week. The main purpose for which the camp has been established is to utilize the summer weeks for as much of Jewish training as it is possible to crowd into the program of the usual camp activities. The training is of the same character as that given during the rest of the year at the CJI which means that it is effective with children of quick grasp and who come from homes where intensive Jewishness is taken for granted. The fundamental problem of coping with the readjustment of the religious notions of the children is not even touched. There are many boys, more than 100 out of the 350, who balk at any attempt to shorten or modify the routine of daily and Sabbath services. They are permitted to hold the traditional type of service in a different building.

Two of my former students are in charge of the camp. Schoolman[3] who is the organizer and director, and Golub[4] who conducts the Jewish educational work. They were both anxious that I meet and discuss with the counselors some of the moot questions pertaining to Judaism. One such meeting took place at Schoolman's bungalow Friday night. Golub started the discussion by putting the following question to me: "What value is there to teaching the children the prayers?" In the answer I developed the following ideas: 1) the function of Jewish education is to inculcate habits of Jewish living. 2) One of the important habits is that of assembling with fellow Jews for Jewish purposes. 3) The Sabbaths and festivals afford the most natural occasions for such assemblies. 4) The liturgy is the best means we have of getting those assembled to be in rapport with Jewish aspirations.

---

2. CeJwIn Camp: established in 1919 at Port Jervis, New York, by the Central Jewish Institute of New York City, the camp was originally called C.J.I. Camp and was one of the first Jewish culture camps. This author first interviewed Kaplan in 1972 when he was at Cejwin.

3. Albert Schoolman (1894–1980), M.A. Columbia; JTS Teachers Diploma; president, National Council for Jewish Education; Kaplan disciple.

4. Jacob Golub (1895–1959), LL.B., Ph.D.; communal education administrator; author; educational director, Zionist Organization of America.

It became clear to me as I was speaking that another obstacle in the adjustment of Jewish life is designating the liturgy as prayer. This designation creates wrong expectations in the minds of those who take part in services. The element of magic helps, of course, to add to the confusion. It were well, therefore, that the articulate part of the service be designated ritual or liturgy and not prayer. "Prayer" should be limited to those devotions which voice a person's individual needs of the spirit. We have at the present no Jewish prayers, in that sense of the term. This fact ought to be emphasized again and again until the demand for inspiring devotional prayers would prompt those who have the gift of spiritual expression to create a literature of devotion.

Saturday morning I attended the children's services. The service was very dry and formal. I felt I had to say something to the children. Fortunately I thought of an excellent idea. The Sidrah [Torah portion of the week] was *Matot-Masei* [Heb. Torah portion in Numbers 30:2–36:13], the Haftarah [prophetic portion read on the Sabbath] was the second chapter of Jeremiah, and the Zionist Congress was at the time meeting in Zurich. These three facts formed the background of the proposition that the Jews are a chosen people not in the sense that they are better than any other people, but a more interesting and more dramatic people by reason of the remarkable ups and downs which it has experienced. Act I Moses dividing the Land among the twelve tribes; Act II Jeremiah prophesying exile; Act III The Zionist Congress deliberating how to reclaim Palestine.

Saturday afternoon I met a group of young people, counselors in training, who wanted me to answer some fundamental questions which had been troubling them.

1. Why be a Jew? Because the Jewish people is as much part of my being as my body is. I have to accept my body with all its limitations and powers. My task as far as concerns the body is to acquaint myself with the laws of its behavior, thereby learning to control it. So with the fact of Jewish affiliation. By learning to know the nature and possibilities of the Jewish people, I shall be able to make of it what I should want it to become.

2. The second question dealt with the conception of God. I do not recall how it was formulated. But I remember that in the answer which proved quite satisfying I pointed out that God is to be identified with that aspect of reality which causes it to be reckoned with as a unit the parts of which are interdependent. Active reckoning with that aspect of reality leads to a most satisfactory type of human life.

On Sunday morning I was present at the session of the boys and girls delegated by the rest of the camp to discuss the distribution of the money collected for the Keren Ami [Charity Fund]. This Keren Ami is a project which I believe was started by Dushkin in Chicago to train the children for active participation in Jewish communal life. I suggested that they utilize these occasions to acquaint the children with various passages from our literature that have a bearing on the duty of helping the needy.

During my stay in the CJI camp I saw a good deal of Golub and spoke with him at great length about the problem of Jewish education. He tried to impress upon me that I would and should stimulate those who are at present in control of the Jewish educational situation to come to grips with the fundamental problems of content. So far the actual subject matter of History, Religion, Ethics, is in an inchoate state in need of being amassed and organized. After considerable discussion it occurred to me that it might be advisable to organize an Academy of Jewish Education which is to consist of those who might reconstruct the content of Jewish education in accordance with acceptable values of modern Jewish life. The winter vacation might be used for holding the sessions of such an Academy.

I came away from these talks with Golub feeling that I should like to devote myself to Jewish educational work, and that it might even be worthwhile to give up teaching Homiletics at the Seminary. . . .

Making Jewish Civilization Significant and Some Thoughts on Felix Adler

MONDAY AUGUST 12, 1929: WEST END, N.J.

I am at work at the present time on a chapter in which I want to point out what the Jewish civilization is in need of nowadays in order to acquire something of that significance which it had for the Jew when he regarded it as divinely revealed. Among the things it is in need of are 1) literary material, occasions and intellectual leadership that will stimulate the cultivation of an ethical outlook, and 2) a code of law which will enlarge the scope and bring up to date the enforceable standards of social behavior. The need of expatiating on the first requirement had led me to read Felix Adler's *An Ethical Philosophy of Life*[5] and the need of dealing with the second, Cardozo's[6] *The Paradoxes of Legal Science*.[7] I haven't finished reading either of those books but I have read sufficiently to note that Cardozo has great legal learning and a philosophic grasp in addition to the power of clear exposition. Adler is, on the whole, ethereal, elusive and mystifying, though at times he is highly edifying and even inspiring. Instead of having thoroughly digested, assimilated and forgotten Kant he still belches Kant's philosophy. I have

---

5. Felix Adler, *An Ethical Philosophy of Life* (New York: Appleton-Century, 1918).

6. Benjamin Cardozo (1870–1938), LL.D., U.S. and N.Y. Supreme Court justice; author; philosophical jurist.

7. Benjamin Cardozo, *The Paradoxes of Legal Science* (New York: Columbia University Press, 1930).

never understood what he means by the universe of infinite spirit although I heard him speak about it twenty odd years ago when I listened to the first course of lectures that he gave at Columbia.[8] What he speaks of as Universe he could very well have designated as God. The fact that it is at variance with the Theistic conception of God should not have stood in the way, any more than the Theistic conception of sin stands in the way of his using the term sin. When he is off his guard he will resort to the most extravagant homiletic license to establish identity between a thesis of his and a biblical thought. Compare, e.g. his interpretation of the "Tree of Knowledge" that made man like unto God. I must therefore ascribe his refusal to apply to the God idea the principle of identity in change to some extraneous personal cause. The entire get up of the book shows poor taste and poor judgment, the former in the obtrusion of his personality, the latter in the insertion into the text (like his argument with Kant) what should have formed a postscript or note and placing as notes what should have formed part of the text.

Now to proceed with my own work: Judaism as a Way of Life

Having interpreted the ascription of supernatural origin to the Torah as pointing (from a pragmatic point of view) to the sense of supreme worth with which the Jews regarded their civilization we are confronted with the task of either perpetuating our spiritual heritage in the form in which it has been handed down to us or developing and enhancing it to the point at which it will evoke from us that high regard which our fathers entertained for it. (In rewriting this I have omitted the first three pages. Being the first draft it naturally began with a lot of redundancies. April 8, 1930.)[9]

Reconstructing Jewish Civilization

MONDAY, AUGUST 12, 1929: WEST END, N.J.

We have thus arrived at the conclusion that a civilization like Judaism which incorporates so high a sense of worth as that symbolized by the doctrine of divine origin indicates an intensive will to live which must necessarily find expression not only in discovering the civilization's inherent worth but also in adding to that worth wherever the civilization happens to fall below the standards of universal fitness.

From the standpoint of inner worth Jewish life and thought constitute far less of a problem in revaluation than in augmentation. It is not the

---

8. Adler's lecture notes for the courses Kaplan took are in Adler's papers at Columbia. See *Judaism Faces the Twentieth Century the Twentieth Century: A Biography of Mordecai M. Kaplan* (Detroit: Wayne State University Press, 1993), 80–82.

9. Kaplan sometimes reread what he had written and made additional entries, which he entered under the later date.

out-of-dateness of Jewish values that endangers Judaism, but their paucity. A civilization must not only be true and good but also adequate. Adequacy means that if a person chooses to live by that civilization only, he can find in it enough opportunity for self-expression to become the equal of the human product of any other civilization. The task for the Jewish people today is to render the Jewish civilization so adequate that if any Jew would choose to be a Jew only, he would find in the Jewish civilization sufficient means to become the equal of the child of the English, French or German Civilizations. This adequacy the Torah possessed for the Jew in the past. To possess it now it must be conceived humanistically as a civilization and supplied the territory which can afford that civilization sufficiently free scope to be at least as humanizing as the most progressive civilizations of the present time. If for the third time in this argument (the other two times being in the course of revaluation of the Israel and the God idea) we are driven to the inevitability of Palestine as a Jewish homeland, it is because we feel keenly the poverty of Judaism for life today, even assuming we have succeeded in bringing its traditional values into line with the highest aspirations of modern times. The spiritual heritage of the Jew may be compared to wealth in the form of foreign coin. The first step is to exchange it into current coin. But even current coin cannot feed or house a person. The necessaries of life have to be procured. Torah corresponded in ancient times not to current coin but to the necessaries of life. Likewise its equivalent, Judaism or Jewish civilization, must embrace all that a Jew requires to become a fully civilized human being. It is evident that to become that Judaism must have a land of its own.

The survival of Judaism in the Diaspora is contingent upon the Jews outside of Palestine endeavoring to live Judaism as a civilization to the maximum degree compatible with their physical, economic and mental powers as well as with the national spirit of the countries they live in, assuming that spirit to be fashioned by the ideal of internationalism. With the infinite diversity of temperament, training, beliefs, callings and interests and with the wide range of conceptions of life, the universe and God that are bound to obtain among Jews, Judaism must afford as vast a variety of opportunities for self-expression as a Jew as other civilizations afford to those that live by them. It is not to be expected that even under the most favorable circumstances that rich variety in content which Judaism will henceforth require will be fed by Jewish life in the Diaspora. Language, literature, the arts, social standards and values which are to constitute Jewish civilization will thrive chiefly in a Jewish Homeland. But it would be a serious mistake to assume that Judaism in the Diaspora can afford to become a passive reflection of Judaism in Palestine. There is room for creativity in many fields of Jewish life even if it be to a limited degree, in the Diaspora, creativity which in some instances may even influence Palestine Judaism. If Palestine Judaism is to be exposed to and influenced by the best of cultural life in the world at large, it should certainly be receptive to Jewish achievement in other lands. Wherever Jews are they should apply themselves to the task of increasing the content of Jewishness to the maximum degree so that there shall be no lack of variety in occasions for self-expression, and in appeal to the manifold spiritual interests of the modern man.

In sum, the principal prerequisite to the Jew valuing Judaism as of any worth, to say nothing of supreme worth is abundant, diversified and satisfying content. The enhancement of content should take place principally in the fields of a) ethics, b) jurisprudence, c) folkways and d) the arts.

Commandments as Folkways

FRIDAY, AUGUST 16, 1929

The new category "folkways" is one of the conspicuous corollaries of the elimination from Judaism of the theurgic element. In Jewish tradition all accepted customs are designated as commandments. The first distinction introduced was that between "commandments between man and God" and "commandments between man and man." Later a further classification was introduced to distinguish those of the "commandments between man and God" which were based upon some understandable reason from those which had no such reason. The term "commandments" (Mizwah) should continue in Jewish usage in the revaluated sense of being in conformity with the spiritual essence of the world, as far as we Jews have been able to sense that essence, it being at the same time definitely understood that should life necessitate any changes in the customs the fact that they are designated "mizwot" should not act as an inhibitive influence. But it is of vital importance to have a significant term besides *mizwot* [commandments] or those customs which were hitherto designated as commandments between man and God. We need a term that would indicate a totally different psychological approach from that with which we come to positive law or jurisprudence. That term is folkways. In the traditional literature the term *minhag* [custom] denotes a variant of customary practice, the variant being due to spontaneous, unaccountable popular approval. It is never applied to the customary practices which are urged in the Torah or in rabbinic literature because it would impugn the imperative character of those practices. From the point of view of the new stage upon which Judaism is entering we should extend the use of the term *minhag* to all customary practices which do not involve the conflict of interest and rights of individuals. The designation of the commandments between man and God as *minhagim* [plural of minhag] or folkways will carry with it a twofold implication. One, that the legalistic treatment of these "commandments," the duty of strict conformity to the letter of the "commandment," the fear of tampering with the forms prescribed, the quibbling and pettifogging that would begin when life rendered the strict observance of those commandments untenable would all be eliminated. The other, that not only should as many of these "commandments" as in no way offend the spiritual sensibilities of the modern man be conserved and further developed, but Jewish life should be stimulated to evolve new and additional folkways. *Folkways are the social gestures whereby a people externalizes the reality of its collective being.* The more alive that being is the more will it abound in folkways. The trouble with Judaism is not that we have too many commandments but far too few, of the folkway type as well as of the juristic type.

The revaluation of the commandments between man and God as folkways will not only displace the legalistic approach but will cause us to abandon the futile attempts to find a rational basis for each specific commandment. Ever since Judaism encountered the challenge of philosophy, opinion has been divided as to whether the species of religious *mizwot* should be subjected to rational interpretation, some holding that to subject any *mizwah* or divine command to the test of reason is to question the truth of tradition or the wisdom of God and others assuming that to give a rational interpretation to the religious *mizwot* is to insure their observance. But even those who assumed the propriety of rational justification befitting the religious commandments have not been uniformly successful in the application of their method. The one classic and large scale attempt to establish a detailed rationale for the religious *mizwot* was undertaken by Maimonides. The very conception, in fact, of *Taame Hamizvot* [reasons for the commandments]—like the phrase—is usually associated with him. This attempt, as is well known, utterly fails in the case of the sacrificial *mizwot*, for having first established that the sacrificial system was a concession to the strain of barbarism in Israel at the time of the giving of the Torah, Maimonides is yet constrained to hope for their restoration and perpetuation in a restored Jewish commonwealth—the reason being that the *mizwot* of the Torah are meant for all time. The inconsistency is glaring. But since even with the Jewish philosophers reason was merely the handmaiden of faith and her position was one of sufferance, they were not too much disturbed by the lack of logical integrity to their system.

Reconstructing the Concept of Torah

MONDAY, AUGUST 19, 1929

Torah as a habit of study occupied in traditional Judaism a position of primacy. It was not regarded as a form of intellectual activity, but as a spiritual experience. The interest in the knowledge of reality as an end in itself, the kind of interest that was shown only by some of the Greek philosophers, was practically unknown among the Jews as among all ancient peoples. The fascination which Torah study had for Jews derived from the belief that the Torah was the revelation of God's will and purpose with regard to man. To acquire the knowledge of its teachings was to be certain what a man had to do to achieve salvation, fullness of life and a share in the world to come. The importance of study was paramount because it was presumed to issue into the practice of the right. The naivete which enabled the Jew to accept the contents of specific writings and traditions as supernaturally revealed has departed. If, however, we cherish the wish to maintain the continuity of the Jewish civilization there is very little in that civilization that so lends itself to being continued that in itself is so much worthwhile, and that can be the principal means of adding new worth to Judaism, as the habit of study associated with Torah. To pursue knowledge of human nature with the end in view of discovering how it may be improved and of the knowledge of human relationships with the end in view of rendering them a means of eliciting the best that human nature is capable of, is to carry on in our day an activity similar in function if not in form with the study of Torah. The intellectual concern in the problem of Jewish life, a concern that aims at rendering the Jew a source of blessing to the world by enabling him to be true to himself, comes as near being a continuation in spirit and purpose of the study of Torah as it is possible for any element of a past civilization to be continued in modern environment without being out of joint in that environment. The significance of this fact is that we have by reason of it a ready means to promulgate the reconstruction of Jewish life. The first step in bringing about the reconstruction should be a movement the momentum of which the traditional attitude toward the study of Torah carries with it to the study of whatever the new knowledge has to offer toward enabling the Jew to play his part in the world with credit to himself and usefulness to his neighbor. That same fervor and desire for illumination, that same spirit of edification and inspiration which accompanied the study of a folio of the Talmud and commentaries can be made to accompany the study of a chapter in history, in psychology, in ethics or in law for the purpose of comprehending the Jewish past or planning the Jewish future. We would not in any way deprecate the study by Jews of the human sciences in a purely objective spirit. Nothing is further from our thoughts than assenting to such doctrine as propounded by Hirsch[10]

---

10. Samson R. Hirsch (1808–88), German leader of Jewish Orthodoxy; advocate of rigorously observed traditional Judaism.

that study as a means of satisfying intellectual curiosity is a sin. But we are addressing ourselves to the specific task of bringing order into the House of Israel. For that task the most important requisite is bringing to bear all of the enthusiasm which the Jew developed in the pursuit of the study of Torah upon the study of whatever the human sciences place at our disposal today for our self-knowledge and self-improvement as Jews.

Finding Relief from Writing in Sculpting

TUESDAY, AUGUST 27, 1929

To find relief from solitude and monotony while at work on the foregoing outline I played with clay and tried to make a portrait bust of my brother-in-law Jacob H. Rubin. I had only a small snapshot to guide me and I found it entirely unsatisfactory. After spending almost ten hours on modelling the head I succeeded in getting something that remotely resembled Jacob. Lena then suggested that I should take the bust with me to West End where Jacob was summering and make the necessary corrections with Jacob posing for me. In the meantime we would again have a chance of spending the weekend outdoors and rest up from the work we each had been engaged in; she with putting things in order and I on the chapter in the preceding pages. On Thursday morning I took the clay head with me on a plate in a hatbox and set out for West End. During the entire trip I was debating with myself whether I should turn back or not. It seemed altogether too ridiculous for me to take this playing with clay so seriously as though I knew what I was about. And suppose after having Jacob sit for me I would turn out something that had no resemblance to him whatever, what a fool I would be making of myself. Nevertheless I kept on my trip, got to West End and after lunch I started working. With an hour or two I managed to bring out a strong resemblance. From that time on I was surer of myself and with every additional hour I worked on the bust I improved it. I worked on it Friday, Saturday night and Sunday till four in the afternoon. Outside of reading a number of the *Moznaim* [Heb. *Balance*][11] and fifty pages of Benet's *John Brown's Body*[12] I did no intellectual work during the entire four days. The change from the effort to spin a Jewish Utopia out of the frailest cobweb of possibilities and the pleasure my attempt at modelling afforded every one of the folks in West End were extremely invigorating to me.

---

11. A literary weekly of the Hebrew Writers Association.

12. Stephen Vincent Benet, *John Brown's Body* (Garden City, N.Y.: Doubleday, Doran & Co., 1927).

A *Zionist Protest Rally against the Arab Massacre of Jews*

FRIDAY, AUGUST 30, 1929

The mass meeting at Madison Square Garden last night exceeded all my expectations. It was as effective and dignified a gesture of protest against the Arab outrages and of resolve to go on with the rehabilitation of Palestine as one could possibly conceive. The message from Hoover, the presence and pointed address of Senator Borah (who is now head of Foreign Affairs Committee), the presence and speeches of Lieut. Governor Lehman and Mayor Walker will no doubt open the eyes of the Arab leaders to the fact that they can expect little sympathy among Americans for their attempt to make England retract the Balfour Declaration. It will undoubtedly also stiffen England's determination to stand by the Declaration.

There was something of spiritual exaltation about the meeting. Thank God the meeting did not degenerate into a spectacular display of public lamentations. The meaning of Palestine for the Jews could be no better illustrated than by the contrast between the nature of the mass meeting after the Kishineff pogroms in which the number of Jews killed and wounded was less than the number of victims of the outrage in Palestine and that of the meeting last night. The temper of the meeting then was that of helplessness and despair; the temper of the meeting last night was that of courage and resolve to carry on. It may be that this outbreak against the Jews will fortify our position and future in Palestine more firmly. The one fear that I had always entertained was that the Arabs might succeed in inducing England to allow a representative assembly or parliament to be established in Palestine without insisting upon their formal recognition of the Balfour Declaration, or that they might give such consent and, after the representative assembly would be established then, ignore the Declaration. Had such an assembly been established before the Jews constituted a majority of the population the likelihood of a Jewish national homeland would have been destroyed forever. The actions of the Arabs during the last two weeks will probably defer for a long time the granting of a representative assembly for Palestine. They have shown themselves unfit and incapable of self-government as any tribe of savages in the heart of Africa. This will give the Jews a chance to settle a sufficiently large number of their own people to be able to hold their own against the Arabs both politically and if need be also belligerently by the time Palestine will be ready to have a representative assembly.

In the light of these significant happenings I feel almost ashamed to make mention of the fact that I did not deliver the speech which I prepared for last night's meeting. With all the travail I experienced in preparing it and the excitement arising out of the delay in having the typewritten copy of it sent me in time for the meeting it remained stillborn.

I am reading at the present time Walter Lippmann's *Preface to Morals*.[13] The word "reading" hardly expresses the mental activity which is set in motion in me by a book like that. That activity resembles rather the physical process which takes place in a starved person who is given delicious and wholesome food to eat. I feel new mental and spiritual vigor pouring into my whole being with every page that I read. It is not so much by reason of what the book says as by reason of what it suggests to me that I find it so invigorating.

Among the ideas it has suggested to me is one with reference to the need of introducing the proper classification into the discussion of religion as an aid to clarity. In what is generally spoken of as religion we must distinguish three distinct strands, viz.: popular religion, folk religion and personal religion.

1) Popular religion is the government of human conduct in all its relationships by means of assumed supernatural sanctions of reward and punishment.

2) Folk religion is the system of practice by which the individual identifies himself with some group in such manner as to affirm that that group is necessary to his salvation or self-fulfillment.

3) Personal religion is the achievement of a philosophy of life whereby the individual is enabled so to adjust himself to the world as to find himself at home in it. . . .

Incidentally it has occurred to me that in the use of liturgical formulas as part of Jewish folk religion it will be necessary to reinterpret the term YHWH to mean "the power manifest in the spiritual aspirations of Israel as making for human self-fulfillment." This may seem a rather cumbersome "Kawanah" to read into the Tetrogram[14] yet it is no more cumbersome than the "Name of Seventy-Two Letters," which consists of an entire verse.[15]

Such reinterpretation is a more plausible way of overcoming the difficulty presented by the traditional conceptions of YHWH than adopting what my Naomi told me tonight is the practice of some Palestinians,

---

13. Walter Lippmann, *A Preface to Morals* (New York: Macmillan, 1929).

14. Tetragrammaton: the four-letter name of God—YHVH—not pronounced by traditional Jews. "Kawanah" means "meaning."

15. Apparently a reference to the belief that the verses in Exodus 14: 19, 20, 21 are each an allusion to the name of God. Each verse consists of 72 letters. See B. *Sukkah* 45a Rashi loc. cit. Others hold that the verse in question is Deuteronomy 4:34. See Judah Theodor's note to page 442 of J. Theodor and Ch. Albeck's edition of *Midrash Bereshit Rabba*, Jerusalem, 1996.

omitting the Tetrogram from benedictions and reciting the "Birkat Ha-Mozi" *Barukh ha-motsi leḥem min ha-arets* [Heb. Blessed is the one who brings bread from the earth.][16] as a benediction of those who labor to produce bread. In retaining the Tetrogram I bless the power in the world which makes possible that cooperation among those who labor whereby bread is produced.

Speaking of benedictions I want to record my rejoicing and gratitude to God for my darling children Judith, Hadassah, Naomi and Selma and for the perfect love they cherish for Lena and me. Hadassah, Naomi and Selma came back today from Camp Modin. I am waiting impatiently to see Judith back from the CJI Camp.

Reconstructing the Jewish Religion

SUNDAY, SEPTEMBER 8, 1929

A workable description of a religion (not of religion in general) is the following: The sum of ideas, feelings and practices in a civilization which are related to God, a god or gods. The character of a religion changes with the changes in men's ideas, feelings (emotional reactions) and practices. In the flux of religion in the past we may distinguish two distinct stages: 1) the theophanic and 2) the theocratic. The type of religion which is evolving now may be designated as 3) the spiritual.

1) The theophanic stage is one in which God, the god or gods to whom the ideas, feelings and practices are related is regarded as communicating His will by supernatural means or signs in response to present inquiry on the part of the pious.

2) The theocratic stage is one in which the theophanic stage is interpreted as having been the golden age, the religious experiences of which constitute the guides and the divine revelations of which [are] the norms for all time.

3) In the spiritual stage both previous stages of religion are recognized as necessitated by man's limited knowledge of reality, but as representing man's attempt to form an indispensable adjustment to life, the type of adjustment becoming the more correct one with the growth in knowledge and experience.

The content of a religion in its first stage consists of a) magic, i.e., ideas, etc. which have as their object bringing that part of the environment under control which cannot be brought by empiric means, and b) affirmation of worth of objects, places, events, qualities, ideals or tendencies in man and in his environment.

---

16. The traditional form is "Blessed art thou oh Lord our God King of the Universe who brings forth bread from the earth."

In the second stage a religion has the same two orders of content but a change is effected 1) in the conception as to the part and nature of the environment which may be brought under control by magic means, and 2) in the objects etc. whose worth is affirmed.

In the third stage the order of magic is eliminated and its place is taken by mental phenomena which are to be controlled by such laws of the mind as have been discovered; the second order consists of a more conscious and concentrated emphasis on the order of worth-affirmations. This time the change in objects etc. whose worth is affirmed is recognized as a necessary principle of human growth.

Prayer, which may be defined as religion in action, varies in its function in correspondence with the variation in religion.

The basis of worth-affirmation is continuity and conservation, hence the tendency to cultural continuity and the discovery of a common element between the earliest and latest stages of a religion's evolution. This is both the psychological and the religious reason for the content of the past so far as it lends itself to assimilation with the latest mental and spiritual development.

(Spiritual will be used throughout of any mode of life or thought which is characterized by the tendency to reckon affirmatively with the aspect of worthwhileness.)

In this third stage it does not matter how the metaphysical nature of God is conceived intellectually, though it is essential that some conception be held for the sake of intellectual integrity. (At this point name some of the outstanding concepts of God from a cognitive standpoint.) Of primary importance is the selection as worthwhile of those objects, places, etc. which by being recognized accepted and reckoned with as worthwhile are conducive to the enhancement of human life.

The foregoing is the outline of the opening lecture of the course in Homiletics I expect to give the coming year at the Seminary. If I will have the courage to complete the book in Judaism as a civilization, that outline will be elaborated into the section dealing with the Religion of Israel, in place of the material which I have there now. That material is irrelevant and confusing, because it consists of essays written independently of the thesis which I am trying to develop in the book.

How the students of the Seminary will react to the course as outlined above it is difficult for me to prognosticate. There is no denying the fact that the congregations to which most or all of them are called to minister to are altogether unprepared for an evolutionary conception of Judaism. For the kind of work our graduates have to do the other courses in the Seminary are antiquated, and mine premature.

The Death of Louis Marshall

WEDNESDAY, SEPTEMBER 11, 1929

Louis Marshall's death which has seemed imminent since last week, coming on top of the tragic happenings in Palestine, could not have been more untimely, or from the standpoint of an angry Deity who had an old score to pay off to His people, more timely. If events will develop as I surmise it will be necessary for us Jews to defend our historic claims to Palestine against those of the Arabs, I can think of no one who could have done that better than Marshall. The service which he might have rendered us will be needed even more sorely than that which he gave at the Peace Conference [after World War I] to secure minority rights for our people in the East European countries.

On the other hand for himself he could not have chosen a more timely death. Having consummated the [Jewish] Agency he will go down in Jewish history as having done a heroic piece of work for which he will be ever remembered gratefully. He was as good a man and as good a Jew as the Jewish German laity could ever be expected to contribute to Jewish life. *T.N.Ts.B.H.* [Heb. acronym, May His Soul be Bound up with the Bond of Life].

Spiritual Religion — Outline for a Course in Homiletics

WEDNESDAY, SEPTEMBER 11, 1929

Spiritual Religion

1. Characterized by a passion for facts (inquiry vs. faith) and an antipathy against illusions—present and past (historical criticism)

2. It treats ultimate facts as incapable of change, hence it is for man to change himself (Man can change himself individually and socially) self-discipline

3. It regards no one method of adjustment as final and universal.

4. It attaches more significance to the present and future than to the past. Its attitude toward tradition

5. Its values are not such as transcend the practical needs but as are immanent

A Man Named Schneersohn Comes to Dinner—The Enjoyment of Hasidic Melody

SUNDAY, SEPTEMBER 15, 1929

Living as I do in an intellectual desert the acquaintanceship of Dr. F. Schneersohn[17] has been to me a veritable oasis. He is a descendant

---

17. This man is not the Lubavitcher Rebbe but perhaps a distant relative.

of a long line of Hassidic Rabbis, the first one of whom founded the Hassidic sect dedicated to the cultivation of H.B.D. [Heb. Habad],[18] a sort of intellectual mysticism. In addition he is a trained psychiatrist who has evolved a method of his own in which the long heredity of a penchant for the mystic is represented by an axiomatic assumption of the reality of personality. However skeptical I may be as to the strictly scientific worth of such a procedure I am fascinated by the pragmatic conclusions which flow from that assumption. His analogical reasoning (and that is the main method by which he deduces his inferences) casts a spell which I presume is a sort of wish fulfillment with me. To hear a man of his type suggest the very thing I do in the article on Torah written up in this book to the effect that the dance normally belongs to worship, is evidence to me that at last I have found a man with whom I move in the same universe of discourse.

Sometime ago I tried to help him by having Spielberg[19] and a few others extend to him a loan of $1500 with which to open an office as a practitioner. He probably got others to give him an additional loan and he opened an office at 22 W. 88 St. I have no idea how he has been making out. But whenever he calls at my home he always leaves me enriched in ideas and religious inspiration. I invited him to Friday night supper last week. While I enjoyed every minute of his conversation and especially the new Hassidic melodies which he sang, the children were unable to understand him because he spoke in Yiddish for Lena's sake. (When I am alone with him we discuss in Hebrew.) They found it very trying to keep quiet. They have no idea of what it is to discipline themselves to learning to understand. Whatever doesn't come to them without effort is at once ruled out as undeserving of attention. Of course they are young children, yet in my opinion old enough to possess something of that cultural curiosity and respect for culture to be eager to adjust themselves to a new cultural situation. The fact that few if any people of culture come to my house and that the entire environment in which we move is permeated by the most sterile of babbitries,[20] the babbitry of first generation Americans, are far more potent influences with my children than all my efforts to civilize them.

---

18. The acronym which is the name of the Lubavitch movement stands for Ḥokhma (wisdom), Binah (understanding), and Daat (knowledge).

19. Harold Spielberg (1879–1940), LL.B., NYU; lawyer; legislator; officer, Equitable Surety Co.; member, SAJ.

20. An allusion to the main character in Sinclair Lewis's *Babbit*—a businessman who adheres slavishly to social and ethical standards of the group. A philistine.

Helping Young Rabbis with Holiday Sermons—First Mention of Ira Eisenstein [21]

MONDAY, SEPTEMBER 16, 1929

This morning I met a large group of Seminary students for the purpose of helping them prepare the sermons which they will have to preach in the various communities during the coming holidays. Fortunately in the course of my reading and thinking during the summer I thought of a number of subjects for holiday sermons. Otherwise I would have found it difficult to elicit any ideas from the men themselves. Much as I try to develop in them a certain degree of cooperative thinking I do not seem to succeed. Outside of one or two men like Eisenstein and Peter Halpern,[22] they come with absolutely blank minds and refuse to exert themselves mentally.

This afternoon I attended the meeting of a committee organized by the United Synagogue to take charge of the special page and supplement in the Tribune, that page to be devoted to the United Synagogue articles and news. Israel Goldstein had been appointed chairman. The others present were Elias Margolis,[23] Sam Cohn, Louis Finkelstein and Mrs. Spiegel.[24] Before Mrs. Spiegel came into the room Margolis held forth in a violent tone in his determination not to serve on the committee if Mrs. Spiegel will be on it. After she entered the room he took part in the discussion and acted as though he had never mentioned a word about Mrs. Spiegel.

Problem of Speaking Hebrew—Opening Exercises at TI

THURSDAY, SEPTEMBER 19, 1929

At the opening exercises of the TI tonight (which I conducted for the twenty-first time) I spoke in English. My enthusiasm about conversing in Hebrew is at present at a low ebb. Even Benderly who originally was fanatical on the question of *Ivrit B'Ivrit*[25] and who was regarded fifteen years ago as the father of that method in this country said to me tonight as he had said many times before, that the insistence upon Hebrew prattling is largely

---

21. Ira Eisenstein (1906–), ordained JTS; leader, Reconstructionist Movement; leader, SAJ; president, Reconstructionist Foundation; founder, Reconstructionist Rabbinical College; Kaplan's son-in-law and most important disciple.

22. Peretz Halpern (1905–88), ordained JTS; rabbi, Rockville Center, N.Y. and Massachusetts; RA Joint Committee on Jewish Education.

23. Elias Margolis (1880–1946), ordained Hebrew Union College; Ph.D. Columbia; Zionist; president, Rabbinical Association of America; rabbi, Mt. Vernon, N.Y.

24. Dora Spiegel (1879–1948), daughter of Rabbi Daniel Rosenberg; B.S. Teachers College; president, National Women's League.

25. Hebrew in Hebrew. A pedagogical method which advocates that students be taught Hebrew using Hebrew.

responsible for the failure of the Jewish training in the Hebrew schools. But he prefaced this confession of his with the phrase *Al Tagidu be-gat* [Heb. 2 Samuel 1:20 "Tell it not in Gath"].[26] When I asked him "Why not proclaim it?" he answered that the Vogelsteins[27] and other assimilators would exult and say, "Aha, haven't I told you that before?"

In the talk which I gave to the students I pointed out that it is the function of the TI to make of them Jews by conviction, assuming that they were already Jews by habit. Unlike other training schools we wanted them to air to us their doubts and questions, and neither to be ashamed or afraid of them. We expect that they would become convinced Jews by learning to appreciate the past as containing permanent values and therefore not to be ignored or forgotten, and by learning to realize that Jewish life gives promise of being creative and productive in the future. This creativity consists of a) upbuilding Palestine; b) renaissance of language letters and arts, and c) reconstruction of ethical and religious values. [Morris] Levine complimented me highly on my remarks.

Teaching Religion at the TI

SUNDAY, SEPTEMBER 22, 1929

I began today my courses on religion at the TI. It is unfortunate that I cannot work with sufficient rapidity to plan out these courses carefully with the view of publishing a book on how to present the problem of Jewish religion to young folks. The main thesis which I developed with the Senior class dealt with what constitutes the proper approach to the study of the authoritative literature of Israel. So long as that literature was believed to derive its authority from its supernatural character, it was regarded as containing the last word in religion and morality. Adopting however, as we do, the evolutionary conception of that literature, our task consists in finding anticipatory intuitions of what we now accept as the ethical and spiritual norms, norms evolved out of the general experience of the human race.

In the Junior class I developed the thesis that Jewish religion has become differentiated as a subject of study apart from the rest of the content of Jewish life and thought because the entire complex of conduct, emotions and ideas associated with the belief in God is being challenged. The essence of that challenge consists in questioning the reliability of the tradition that the reality of God has been demonstrated by His self-revelation and his

---

26. The Hebrew phrase here is from the dirge of David when he hears of the death of Saul and Jonathan. The verse is "don't tell it in Gath lest the Philistines rejoice."

27. Ludwig Vogelstein (1871–1934), Reform Jewish leader; anti-Zionist philanthropist; board member, World Union for Progressive Judaism.

revelation of his will to man. The challenge is being met by a study of religion from a philosophic, psychological and historical point of view.

This is as far as I got with the class. Year in and year out after the first lesson or two I give in religion one or a group of students would come to me complaining that my ideas shock them. The same thing happened today. This time it was Rudelnik who said that the students were totally unprepared for such ideas as I expressed. These ideas should have been inculcated in their minds as far back as the Talmud Torah[28] years.

The difficulty I am experiencing in writing out in full the part of the book which is to deal with the religion of Israel is driving me insane. Why should I have to toil over a task which has been so excellently performed by Julian Huxley in his book "Religion Without Revelation.?"[29] That book expresses so clearly and trenchantly what I am struggling to articulate that I wish I could use it as a text book both in the Seminary and in the Institute. Yet if I were to attempt to introduce it as a text book I would be set upon by the whole pack of rabbinical and lay hounds regardless of the particular creed they subscribed to. It isn't that I am afraid of having to give up my livelihood. What I am certain is that the effect would be a total victory for the forces of reaction. The only time I would be prepared to lose my livelihood for the sake of my convictions would be if my convictions would get a chance to be heard. That can only be the case if I write them out with the necessary clarity and power to make an impression. I would lay down my life if I knew that by such a sacrifice I could indite a clear and compelling statement of my views. And why can't I do what Julian Huxley did? Because I haven't his heredity. In my immediate ancestry there were no Thomas Huxleys, and Matthew Arnolds and Mrs. Humphrey Wards. My ancestry consists of very ordinary folk who never achieved distinction in learning, business or saintliness. Why then do I not accept my limitations and try to lead a calm and peaceful inner life instead of forever boiling within like a volcano?

Louis Marshall's Funeral — R. M. Z. Margolies Attends

Tuesday, September 24, 1929

As I came to the Seminary yesterday to attend the Faculty meeting scheduled for three o'clock Dr. Adler apprised those of us who were present of the fact that working men were about to place the cornerstone of the new

---

28. These words, meaning the learning of Torah, refer to an elementary school in the Jewish community.

29. Julian Huxley, *Religion Without Revelation* (New York: Harper Brothers, 1927).

Seminary buildings. He asked us to go with him to watch the cornerstone being swung into place. We stood on the corner of Broadway and 122nd St. for about half an hour chatting about different things and then returned to the Faculty room of the old building.

The meeting opened with a few remarks by Adler concerning the last days of Louis Marshall. According to Adler's account Marshall never seemed to be in better health than on his trip to Europe and all through the days of the Zurich conference. It was in the course of that trip that Marshall informed Adler that he had just written a twenty-eight page letter to Rosenwald[30] about the importance of strengthening the cause of Jewish education by making it possible for the Seminary to do more effective work. In response to that letter Rosenwald donated $500,000 to the Seminary in memory of Marshall.

Today I attended Marshall's funeral at the new Temple Emanu-El.[31] The building impressed me more as a lavish display of wealth than as expression of aesthetic taste or spiritual yearning. It is devoid of artistry, humility and aspiration. I could not but think of the stage temples that are often seen in operas depicting the worship of ancient oriental gods. The music was in keeping with the operatic effect which the building had on me. Mammon is written over every square inch of wall space. The temple just glitters with gold. The mechanical contrivances whereby the voices of the rabbis could be plainly heard throughout the huge structure was another of those histrionic features that made me feel as though I was witnessing once again Reinhardt's production of the "Miracle."[32]

When I compared the vastness and cost of the structure, the effort that went into the production of the organ, orchestra and choir music with the few biblical verses which constituted the entire service, it seemed to me as though a whole museum were built to preserve a few simple flowers dried between leaves. The poverty and sterility of Jewish religion were strikingly conspicuous on this occasion. Is it worth while I asked myself, to build such gorgeous and expensive temples to hear those few timeworn verses? Are these verses written centuries ago all the Jewish religion has been able to offer us when facing the problem of death? Neither high philosophy or stirring poetry nor intoxicating music have we Jews produced since those

---

30. Julius Rosenwald (1862–1932), merchant; philanthropist; with Sears Roebuck, established Rosenwald Fund.

31. Temple Emanu-El, the flagship New York Reform synagogue, to which Kaplan is referring, was constructed in 1929. The previous synagogue building was at Fifth Avenue and 43rd Street and had been constructed in 1868.

32. Max Reinhardt (1873–1943), staged a religious spectacle of colossal proportions done in pantomime with musical accompaniment entitled "The Miracle." The theater was actually turned into a giant cathedral.

ancient days wherewith the articulate or satisfy the yearning to catch the meaning of death in life and of life in death.

I learned of a curious incident in connection with the funeral. Among the honorary pallbearers Rabbi M. Z. Margolies, the rabbi of the 85th St. Congregation,[33] was invited as representative of Orthodox Jewry. Never having entered a [reform] temple before in his life (he is now in the far seventies) he was about to refuse the invitation. When Polstein the former president of the congregation learned of Margolies's attitude he went with a committee to urge Margolies to consent to act as an honorary pallbearer since it was not as an individual but as representative of Orthodox Jewry that Margolies had been invited. Having such pressure brought to bear upon him Rabbi Margolies began hunting for some way of getting around the ban against all reformed temples. He finally found a loophole in the fact that the Temple had not yet been dedicated and was therefore no temple.

Judaism and the Sacred

Friday, September 27, 1929

We assume that neither the Orthodox conception of Judaism as a supernaturally revealed religion nor the Reformist conception of Judaism as religious philosophy can provide the Jew with a plausible program of Jewish life. The Orthodox conception regards as a true religion only that which is supernaturally revealed. According to the Reformist conception a true religion is a religion based upon a true idea of God. They both agree that a religion to be valid must be true, and since there can only be one truth there can be only one true religion. That conception of religion reduces the principle of tolerance to an inescapable modus vivendi.—No good.

In reconstructing Judaism as a modern civilization the most perplexing problem we have to deal with is to determine the place of religion in it. The factors that complicate the problem are the same as those that complicate the problem of church and state (1) The necessity of having a religion if the civilization is to conform to the conclusion of the psychological study of religion. (2) The necessity of reckoning with diversity of opinion.

The solution consists in adopting the distinction between folk religion and personal religion.

The psychological study of religion discloses the fact that in all religion there is the element of appreciation other than that of an aesthetic type—sacredness. The sense of the sacred has produced values in its own right apart from being an incentive to aesthetic values. A civilization must

---

33. Kehilath Jeshurun, the synagogue where Kaplan had been rabbi from 1903–9. Magolies became rabbi in 1906. Kaplan admired the elder rabbi but resented his intrusion. On their relationship, see *Judaism Faces the Twentieth Century.*

possess objects which for its adherents possess the element of sacredness. It must have places, heroes, events which furnish it with occasions for celebration and apotheosis.

This psychological aspect of religion will help us understand the problem of church and state. Civilizations recognizing to what extent the sense of the sacred contributed to their perpetuation, cultivated specific objects as occasions for celebration. The confusion of peoples ultimately led to the break up of ancient civilization and the attempt to establish a Roman civilization—Christianity. The visible Church is the detritus of the Roman Empire. The states represent the rise of new civilizations. The two systems of sancta under which most people live nowadays. Protestantism illogical.

The suggested solution is the recognition that a person may observe two or more systems of sancta. Folk religions must adopt tolerance not merely as an inevitable policy, but as an ethical principle, etc.

Hebrew High Schools and the TI

MONDAY, SEPTEMBER 30, 1929

This morning Rabbi Levine, Messrs. Bragin, Dinin[34] and I met to discuss what we should demand of Dr. Benderly in order that the graduates of the Hebrew High School qualify for the Teachers Institute. Bragin unfolded a tale of chaos that exists in the High School as a result of the so-called Dalton method[35] which has been introduced there without the necessary text books and facilities that that method demands. We decided that we shall demand that during the last two years of the High School course those who are likely to qualify for entrance into the TI should be given a curriculum of studies in line with our requirements for admission. Levine and Dinin wanted me to take up the question of the K'vuzah [group] and to insist that Benderly should not be permitted to select the best of the senior and junior classes in the High School for the group which he himself wants to train.

Making a Bust of His Father

TUESDAY, OCTOBER 1, 1929

Yesterday the painter Tepper[36] called. He asked me to write a letter to Miss Szold[37] to sit for a painting he wants to make of her. She is now in

---

34. All members of the TI faculty. See glossary.

35. An experimental teaching method where the classroom functions as a laboratory. Students work independently on long-term projects which they contract with their teachers. It originated in Dalton, Massachusetts.

36. Joseph M. Tepper (1886–?), came to United States in 1926; School of Fine Arts, Odessa; Beaux Arts, Paris; portrait and landscape painter.

37. Henrietta Szold (1860–1945), national Zionist leader; author; founder, Hadassah; editorial secretary, JPS; aided resettlement of Jewish refugee children in Palestine.

the country and he wants to seize the opportunity. When I showed him the plastiline bust I modeled of father he pointed out the faults in it. I at once took to remodeling it. Faults or no faults before I started remodeling it it bore a perfect resemblance to father. Since yesterday I spent about twelve or thirteen hours on it. I was up till 3:30 in the morning. I simply could not tear myself away from it until I managed to retrieve the resemblance to father, and in this I succeeded only by restoring the very face lines that Tepper criticized most severely as not being human. I wish my literary tasks and studies could have such a grip on me as this modeling.[38]

A *Biographical Confession*[39]

FRIDAY, OCTOBER 4, 1929

"I was born in a small town in Russia. My father was a very learned Talmudist but was unable to make a living. When I was a young boy the family migrated to America.

"I was intellectually alert as a student and might have gone into the study of law or medicine or worked my way up in business but my parents' hearts, especially mother's, was set upon my being a rabbi because in that calling I would be leading a Jewish life, and furthering the spiritual welfare of my people.

"I attended the Seminary for a number of years. During the last three years when my "Sturm and Drang" period was on I couldn't make up my mind whether to go into the rabbinate or not. In my second year at the post-graduate course in Columbia I had a chance to accept an Ethical Culture Fellowship at Harvard and commit myself to Ethical Culturalism.[40] But when I saw that my classmate Kauver was accepting the position in Denver, I was afraid that I would be losing a desirable opportunity in giving up the ministry.

"A short time afterwards I accepted the pulpit of the 85 St Congregation. I had my unpleasantness with the Slutzker Rav[41] and his followers. I was about to take up the study of law, when again the thought of what a

---

38. For a photo of the bust and a photo of Kaplan's father, see page 351 of *Judaism Faces the Twentieth Century*. The resemblance is good.

39. Kaplan's intent in this entry is unclear. Although he uses the first person, and clearly the experience is his own, the account uses quotation marks, as if it were a story told by someone else.

40. Kaplan continued under the sway of Ethical Culture though he resented Adler. His first idea for the SAJ was to call it the "Society for Jewish Ethical Culture." For the complicated relationship between Kaplan and Ethical Culture, see *Judaism Faces the Twentieth Century*, passim.

41. Jacob David Ben Ze'ev Willowski (Ridbaz) (Slutzker Rav) (1845–1913), Lithuanian talmudist; author, Talmudic commentaries; in United States briefly then moved on

great opportunity I would be surrendering, if I gave up the ministry, wedded me to it completely.

"In time I became a member of the Seminary Faculty where my commitment to the rabbinate became even more confirmed. Then came the plan of writing a new interpretation of the Torah, of revising and revaluating the conceptions of Jewish theology, etc., a kind of intellectual children. Much unpleasantness as I encountered in the Seminary, I continued with my rabbinic work for the sake of the children, incurred further ministerial duties such as preaching and wasting time with people who never learn or grow up, for the sake of my mental children. But in all that time I have missed the joy of honest creative effort which is possible only when one is free from the senseless taboos that shackle the mind and stifle the soul.

"But of course I couldn't tell that to the members of the Seminary faculty or the SAJ Board of Directors. They wouldn't understand. They are blind and will not see. They say I am cold and unsentimental. I wouldn't dare tell them why.

"Recently I learned of an excellent opportunity that presented itself in the field of insurance. I am a great believer in insurance from a practical and spiritual point of view. I regard it as the one invention in which man has put into practical effect the urge to cooperation and to security. My heart is very much drawn to that kind of work. But how can I engage in it without aspersing the children I've brought up—I mean, of course, the ideas and plans about Judaism? I become very much depressed at times. You see me now, an unhappy man, the victim of devotion to the children of my brain."

Judaism as a Civilization—*The Contest Spurs on the Book*

SUNDAY NIGHT, OCTOBER 6, 1929

This evening Phineas showed me a statement which appeared today in the *N.Y. American* about the Rosenwald prize[42] for the best essay about Judaism in America. That means that if I want to stand a chance of trying for the prize I must be up and doing and no longer postpone the formulation of my program based on Judaism as a civilization.

So far the outlines I have sketched of the discussion of the place of religion in Judaism as civilization have proved unsatisfactory. Perhaps I shall have better luck next time.

---

to Palestine. For more details on the conflict with Kaplan, see chapter 7, notes 36 and 37. See also *Judaism Faces the Twentieth Century*, 71–73.

42. Kaplan won the contest and used the money to publish *Judaism as a Civilization*. The judges split the prize money among the three finalists. It was probably because of Kaplan's philosophy that he did not get all the money. See glossary on Rosenwald and *Judaism Faces the Twentieth Century*, 338 for details about the contest.

A modern civilization differs from ancient civilization in being based on tolerance. If Judaism is to be a modern civilization we must conceive it as capable of harboring all kinds of religion and no-religion. There must be room in it for Orthodoxy, Modernist religion and mystic religion. The only kind of religion which a modern civilization cannot tolerate is one which would urge the destruction or suppression of that civilization. Hence it is not conceivable how a Jew can accept Christianity or Mohammedism and still be a Jew.

Getting Closer to Judith

MONDAY, OCTOBER 7, 1929

Judith is encountering challenge in her work at the school of the Jewish Center of Brooklyn, challenge on the part of the fourth and fifth grade pupils who resist her efforts to teach them Hebrew songs. This challenge is apparently doing more to intensify her Jewishness than any Jewish inspiration or instruction that either I or the Teachers Institute might afford her. This challenge brought her closer spiritually to me. She seemed to snuggle to Lena and me this evening when she asked to take a walk with us. While walking, I unburdened myself of the grievance that I had against the children for the kind of conversation in which they indulged at table both days of Rosh Hashanah. I certainly feel in better spirits now.

Kol Nidre at the SAJ—To Reinstate or Not

WEDNESDAY, OCTOBER 9, 1929

I have just come from a member's meeting of the SAJ. Much as I had wanted to avoid the discussion of the Kol Nidrei question[43] I could not refrain from bringing it up because I began to feel very uncomfortable under the pressure that Rosenblatt and Klein[44] (who is chairman) were beginning to bear upon me that I should cater to the Orthodox element in our membership body. They wheedled out of me the consent to permit the cantor to recite the K.N. on condition that I would announce beforehand that this was done out of regard for those who insist upon saying the K.N. If I had done that the word would have gone out that I retreated from the position I had all along taken. After heated discussion it was decided to abide by the status quo and not have the cantor recite the K.N.

I hope that the experience I went through again with the K.N. this

---

43. In 1925 Kaplan eliminated the Kol Nidre from the Yom Kippur service. He retained the tune with Psalm 130. He reinstated it only after a correspondence with J. D. Eisenstein on the matter. For his final version of the K.N. prayer see Kaplan's High Holiday Prayerbook for Yom Kippur. See *Judaism Faces the Twentieth Century*, 289–90 for more details.

44. Jacob Klein (1890–1946), U.S. attorney; chairman, SAJ Board of Trustees, 1927–44.

year will teach me to be firm in my dealings with the members and trustees of the SAJ and simply insist that I must have my way or get out.

THURSDAY, OCTOBER 10, 1929
Although I was aware before I went to the meeting last night that I would be called upon to say something there was nothing I could think of as a topic of interest. The halcyon days when I dreamed of establishing a group that would be dominated by the conspicuous purpose of enriching the Jewish aspects of their lives are long past. Bitter disillusionment is the only term that describes my reaction to the SAJ. Every time I enter the building I feel as though I moved among the ruins of a sanctuary which I had toiled to rear. But hope will not die down in the human heart. When I descry the slightest evidence of yearning for the truth or holiness my old illusions come to life.

This is what happened last night. Klein called upon Rosenblatt to speak. R. played—and for an untutored layman quite skillfully—upon his one string, the synagogue as the fountainhead of Jewish interest and activity, and appealed to those present to strengthen the SAJ synagogue or congregation. After he was through K. called for discussion, but not a soul responded. Seeing that the meeting might end in a flop Rosenblatt sprang his idee fixe of strengthening the congregation by holding a $100 dinner. He was aware that it would call forth opposition. H. Liebovitz voiced the opposition and there the second firecracker burned out. Again it looked as though the meeting would die a natural death. Up there spoke Starr,[45] the only other member besides Sol Lampert who understands Hebrew, and something of a "nudnick" and said that we ought to utilize the member's meeting to become acquainted with the aims of the SAJ, especially as the members seem to have forgotten all about them. I caught upon these remarks as a drowning man catches upon a straw and I tried to explain to those present that I agreed with R. that the synagogue ought to be the fountainhead of Jewish inspiration but that in actuality the synagogue is moribund. The movements that make for constructive Jewish effort have not emanated from the synagogue. There is need for vitalizing the synagogue. The only way to vitalize it is to have it function in a spirit of intellectual honesty and consistency. This led me to touch upon the question of Kol Nidre. After that the meeting was alive.

It may seem absurd to make so much ado about a matter that in itself is so trivial. Rosenblatt seemed convincing when he argued that it was like the fly which was the cause of the Israelites coming to Egypt. This time his attempt at cleverness miscarried because I turned the story against

---

45. Probably refers to Jacob Starr (1889–1976), business executive; philanthropist; founder of Albert Einstein College of Medicine.

him. If it suited God to accomplish great purposes by means of a fly why should he condemn means apparently small in order to attain large ends? The K.N. question was in my opinion merely an entering wedge to larger and more important improvements in the service. Once a trifle becomes an issue it ceases to be a trifle. Jews are commanded to martyr themselves for the manner of tying a shoelace, if a Gentile makes an issue of that.

On Not Putting on Tephilin and Feeling Guilty

SUNDAY, OCTOBER 13, 1929

I have again allowed a good many weeks to slip by without putting on the Tephilin in the morning and reciting the Hebrew prayers. When I had to address the *Bar Mizvah* yesterday morning I was naturally unable to make Tephilin the theme of my remarks to him. In the afternoon a young man by the name Stocker called on me. I had invited him to come so that I might discuss the possibility of organizing a group of lay students to take up the study of modern philosophic and religious problems. He too asked me "Why put on Tephilin?" I justified the ceremony on the ground of the four biblical sections contained in the Tephilin, assuming, of course, that those sections be reinterpreted in terms of modern spiritual aspirations. I couldn't wait till this morning to make good by act what I justified so glibly by talk. The fact that it is Erev Yom Kippur has added to my desire to act as well as to feel Jewishly. But the formal prayers did not satisfy so I turned to "A Book of Prayers" by McComb[46] and there I found the following which just suited me in my present mood.

"Help us to make religion a thing so beautiful that all men may be won to surrender to its power. Let us manifest in our lives its sweetness and excellency its free and ennobling spirit. Forbid that we should go up and own the world with melancholy looks and dejected visage, least we should repel men from entering Thy Kingdom. Rather, may we walk in the freedom and joy of faith and with Thy new song in our mouths so that man looking at us may learn to trust and to love Thee."

Teaching and Publishing and Lack of Support at JTS

FRIDAY, OCTOBER 25, 1929

When I received a facsimile copy of the last part of Marshall's letter[47] to Rosenwald I lived through the mental tortures which the Seminary

---

46. Samuel McComb, *A Book of Prayers for Public and Personal Use* (New York: Dodd Mead, 1912). Kaplan did not hesitate to borrow from Christian prayers, changing the language where necessary.

47. See diary entry for Tuesday, September 24, 1929.

authorities mete out to me from time to time whenever they fail to include me among the members of the faculty who add prestige to the Seminary. At every Seminary gathering at which special mention is made of Marx, Ginzberg or Davidson my name is ignored. No matter how little I may amount to in the world of scholarship, I believe I have done more to direct the minds of the students to the fundamental problems of Jewish life than the other men with their scholastic achievements. And I surely could have contributed a great deal more, if I were given the opportunity to teach what I am entitled to teach. I cannot of course blame the trustees. Men like Marshall and Stroock are impressed by the sight of the many books which the others publish, regardless of the value which those books have for Jewish life. The thought in the minds of these trustees is that when Gentile scholars will see these books they will be impressed. What greater service can one render Jewish life? The fact that these members of the faculty take smug and cynical attitude toward the future of Judaism, that they do not make the least attempt to correlate what they teach with spiritual needs of the Jews at the present time, isn't even suspected by the trustees. It's all wrong.

I'm a failure not only in the Seminary and in the S.A.J. but even in my own home. Despite all my yearnings to beautify Jewish life, to enrich it with song and poetry and dance, I do not get the least cooperation from any member of my family. I had hoped that Judith with her knowledge of music would bring the Shekinah into our household on Friday nights. I thought that my children would ask me to read or speak Hebrew with them. All these dreams of mine have proved to be nothing but illusions. It seems that I am doomed to live out the rest of my days in a sort of prison made for me by aspirations and tastes which separate me from my own wife and children.

SUNDAY, NOVEMBER 3, 1929

I keep on working steadily so long as my health is good. In my eagerness to get in as much work as possible I would like to take an hour off from my sleep or to skip a meal, but the moment I deviate from the routine of 7 ½ hours sleep and three meatless meals a day I am rendered unfit for the next two to three days.

I have not been able to do any studying of Bible and Talmud for the last few months. All my time is taken up with reading and thinking about the problem of religion. Whenever I allow a long time to elapse without the study of Hebrew texts I experience a sense of inferiority especially when I come to the Seminary. The fact is that the Hebrew texts do not furnish ideas to live by. They merely furnish the problem [of] how to render them vital and significant. But to one like myself who is sensitive to the opinion of others, they are indispensable as a means of maintaining my standing among those who put a premium upon text knowledge. It's the old story of idolatry over again. My colleagues are worshippers of dead letters just as our ancestors were worshippers of lifeless images. To be a prophet one must not only be an iconoclast but also be able to speak in the name of the living God. Since in spite of all my strenuous searching I have not yet found Israel's living God and cannot speak in his name, I must abide with the idolaters and imitate their ways.

In a book which has appeared recently "The Ascent of Humanity" by Gerald Heard,[48] there is an analysis of the inner experiences of the leader in whom the phenomenon of human individuality comes to light. That analysis is a true picture of what I have to put up with (especially p.73). It explains quite clearly why I am so lonely.

Incidentally, I want to say that the idea developed in that book has been one of my working beliefs. I touched upon it in the conception of God as Redeemer, where I treated the emergence of individual personality as an evidence of human progress and of the meaning of history.

The Value of the Philosophical and the Value of the Spiritual

MONDAY, NOVEMBER 18, 1929

On the way to Woonsocket[49] and back I read Whitehead's new little book "The Function of Reason." It was an eye opener to me. I find Whitehead's philosophy fills the void created by Dewey's Pragmatism. It comes in very handy at the present time when I am working on the problem of spiritual religion. I am at present in the process of changing my mind about the relation of religion to philosophy. I have for many years been working on the assumption that the function (pragmatic significance) of the philosophic conception of God is different from that of religion. The conclusion which is crystallizing itself in my mind at present is that philosophy which is the expression not of the group but of the individual mind represents the principle of progress, reason and individualism in the religion of the group. If there is to be such a thing as spiritual religion it has to consist mainly in permitting the last two of the three functions which religion had in the past (1. to transform the environment; 2. to inculcate and substantiate it by an ethical order of life; 3. to bring salvation) to be reevaluated in terms of the

---

48. Gerald Heard, *An Essay on the Evolution of Civilization* (New York: Harcourt Brace, 1929).

49. Woonsockett, Rhode Island, where Kaplan's sister, Sophie Israeli, and her husband lived. Kaplan's mother lived there also.

ever increasing experience not of the particular group which professes the religion but of the human race as a whole. If then faith and salvation are to be proved tenable as matters of individual conviction it is essential that we have resort to philosophy and metaphysics for a conception of God compatible with our present knowledge of the universe and of human nature. A thinker like Whitehead contributes considerably in some of his other writings I read to a metaphysical conception of God. From "The Function of Reason" I have learned to appreciate the importance of the Greek contribution to the conception of God.

As I analyze the reasons for my having held out so long against recognizing the religious value of the philosophic conception of God I find that they arose from the reluctance to surrender the notion that the Jews have contributed to the God idea more than the Greeks. I confess that it was the Jewish chauvinism in me which blinded me to the appreciation of the fact that it is after all Greek philosophy which has both criticized traditional religion and has evolved rational substitutes for the traditional God idea. It is indeed a great blow to my Jewish pride to have to admit that in the formulation of spiritual religion of the future we have to fall back upon the method of individual reasoning on the basis of human experience to arrive at a conception of God. Maimonides with his lack of historical background was at least able to ascribe to tradition a value coordinate with that of philosophy. We, however, are constrained at best to prove that tradition has vague intuitions and subconscious anticipations of that which the method of philosophy has enabled us to grasp consciously and clearly.

Palestine as a Cultural Center — Support for Magnes

WEDNESDAY, NOVEMBER 20, 1929

My warmest admiration for Magnes. Would that affairs in Palestine would take a turn that would bring him and his policies to the top! He can count upon me as a loyal supporter. At last I see the light. The Balfour Declaration has been like a foreign body in the system of Jewish revival, causing irritation and liable to set up a dangerous poison. I must have recourse once again to Ahad Haam to see to what extent he thought out clearly his program of Palestine as a cultural and not a political center.

Spiritual Values

SUNDAY, NOVEMBER 24, 1929

I see in this morning's Jewish Journal that Magnes denies the interview reported in the Jewish Daily Bulletin in which he is alleged to have favored the abrogation of the Balfour Declaration.[50] I am more mixed up than ever about this Zionist business.[51]

This afternoon I was in better form with my classes at the T. Institute than last week. I have worked out a series of spiritual values which I shall take up with the senior group. They are:

1. The universe is so constituted that it plays helpfully into man's needs
   a) Man the center of his world—he possesses worth
2. Man's cardinal sin is playing the god
3. The universal code a) sacredness of life; b) sacredness of the person negates moral impunity
4. The unity of mankind and moral significance of division into nations
5. The ideal type of devotee—Abraham—who lends himself to God's purpose
6. The actual [? word unclear] type of devotee—Jacob—impatient of God' purposes and frustrated
7. How man plays with the hand of God (The Joseph story)
8. God the Redeemer (The Exodus)
9. God the Lawgiver (The law code)
10. God the Upbringer (The trials in the wilderness)
11. The meaning of holiness (Leviticus and Numbers)
12. The meaning of Israel's nationhood (Deuteronomy)

Robert Gordis Calls—Thoughts on Palestine

TUESDAY, NOVEMBER 26, 1929

Last Saturday night Robert Gordis[52] called. He is a young man about 29 graduate of the Yeshivah Teachers Institute and has his Ph.D. from Dropsie. He is teaching in the Teachers Training School for Girls under the auspices of the Women's Organization of the Orthodox Union. That

---

50. The Balfour Declaration issued in 1917 declared that the British government favored "The establishment in Palestine of a national home for the Jewish People . . . it being clearly understood that nothing shall be done which may prejudice the civil and religious rights of existing non-Jewish communities in Palestine. . . ." Magnes was critical of the Declaration because he thought it encouraged the idea of "the Jewish relationship to Palestine, rather than emphasizing the nature of Palestine itself as an international Holy Land. . . ."

51. Magnes believed that Jews had the right to be in Palestine and supported a bi-national state where Jews and Arabs would rule equally.

52. Robert Gordis (1908–92), ordained JTS; biblical scholar; Zionist; faculty, JTS; author; editor, Judaism. Gordis admired Kaplan but was critical of his philosophy. As a young faculty member in the thirties and forties he did not stand up for Kaplan against faculty criticism. See *Judaism Faces the Twentieth Century*, 226, for more information.

school is another competitor of the Teachers Institute. Its raison d'etre is the Orthodox point of view which is supposed to prevail in its courses. Yet this teacher is no more Orthodox than I am. He came to ask me to have him in mind in case there was an opening at the Teachers Institute. He therefore made no secret of his unorthodox views about the Bible, though in practice he claimed he was entirely Orthodox. When I tried to point out to him that for the school to engage him as a teacher was an anomaly he tried quite eloquently to make out a case for the right of the Orthodox to permit a large variety of views ranging from those held by Jung[53] and Goldstein[54] to those held by himself. He pointed to the Seminary as equally vague about its views though it claims to stand for traditional Judaism.

I doubt whether a man who does not admit that the evolutionary conception of the Jewish religion gives one a radically different attitude toward everything Jewish from that which is bound to be held by one who subscribes to the traditional conception is fit to be a teacher in a training school for teachers. A man of that type is either muddleheaded or a cynic.

Mrs. Brodie called yesterday morning for the purpose of finding out where her two daughters, 16 and 17, might continue their Hebrew education. She returned lately from Jerusalem where she had spent 18 months with her five children. If the spirit of determination which she spoke of actually exists among the Jews of Palestine then there is hope that Jewish life will ultimately take root there despite the tremendous odds. The heroism displayed by the Jews and the efficiency of the Haganah [Jewish defense forces] are to me not only a guarantee of ultimate establishment of the Jewish Homeland, but also a demonstration of the working of the divine destiny in the history of our people. Incidentally I want to note that the gathering which took place in Washington last Sunday and at which Brandeis spoke out openly as willing to take a leading part in the reconstruction of Palestine is to me another indication that the fate of the Jewish people cannot be appraised in terms of the ordinary historical forces that operate in the life of nations.

According to Mrs. Brodie the greatest contribution to Jewish education in Palestine is being made by Miss Kallen. Why should a Miss Kallen have devoted herself at the greatest possible sacrifice of her health and peace of mind to working out a modern system of education in Palestine?

---

53. Leo Jung (1892– 1987), ordained Berlin; Ph.D. University of London; Orthodox rabbi and spokesman; author; succeeded Kaplan as rabbi at Jewish Center; major critic of Kaplan's ideology.

54. Herbert Goldstein (1890–1970), ordained JTS; Orthodox; founder, Institutional Synagogue; faculty, Rabbi Isaac Elhanan Theological Seminary (RIETS); president, Rabbinical Council of American (RCA).

Why should the Brodies look forward to settling in Palestine? These and thousands of others like them are being led or driven by that mysterious will, a people's will to life, stronger and more insistent than that possessed by any other people.

But would to God that this same unrelenting will were illumined by an intelligence commensurate with its drive. A more muddle-headed people there can scarcely be found in all the world. We haven't the power to think out any idea to its consequences and implication. Shouldn't we have insisted from the very start that an instrument like the Balfour Declaration should be definite and lucid? Talk about not looking a gift horse in the mouth. The Declaration isn't even a horse; it is a hypogriffe or a centaur. Why haven't we ever sat down to puzzle out the question "How is it possible for the Jews ever to constitute a majority in Palestine? And not having a majority how can we have a national homeland in Palestine?" Why have we never asked, or why asking it have we dismissed all too easily the question "Is it possible for the Arabs also to have a homeland in Palestine?" These and similar questions were regarded as too intricate and therefore to be avoided. Likewise the question of religion to state, etc. etc. Of course we were afraid that to discuss these questions would destroy our capacity for action. That is exactly what I mean when I say that as civilized peoples go our collective intelligence is of a very low order.

Here is now friend Magnes whom I could never credit with the ability to think out the plan that he proposes in the statement which appeared in today's Jewish Bulletin. He is and always has been even more muddleheaded than the other outstanding personalities in Jewish life. How does he come to so logical a plan as that suggested by him? The answer is Philby.[55] All he does is merely to adopt Philby's carefully thought out proposition.

But while I agree that such a plan is the only feasible one I cannot make up my mind whether Magnes should have come out with it at the present juncture. His statement has already precipitated a lot of aimless discussion and we shall be overwhelmed by a tidal wave of words when the all important thing now is to plan quietly and act quickly. Why in the world didn't he speak up at the last Congress and at the Agency meeting? It is alright for Philby to talk now but I am afraid that Magnes's Amen will stop our ears to reason.

There are a good many passages in the writings of the Anonymous Prophet [Deutero-Isaiah] that will come to plague us—Cf. Is. 60:12, 16 and plenty others in a similar and often in a vengeful strain.

---

55. Harry St. John Philby (1885–1960), British diplomat, Arabist, and author; supported a strong interpretation of Balfour Declaration recognizing rights of Jews and Arabs. See Arthur Goren, *Dissenter in Zion* (Cambridge: Harvard University Press, 1982), 282–85.

How does the Jewish will to live function in me? I do not yearn to live in Palestine. I detest oriental life and manners. The ignorance and fanaticism that thrive so luxuriantly under oriental skies are as hateful to me as the hot breath of the hamsin [hot winds from the desert]. Before the days of monoxide infested streets I used to love New York as I shall never love the Emek. A soil that is soaked with so much human blood will need long centuries of expiation by peace and security to atone for the cruel deeds that have been committed there.

How then does my Jewishness express itself? In a desire to move mentally in the fields of Hebrew literature both ancient and modern. That this is a matter of will is attested by the fact that the large tracts of desert in which these fields abound do not daunt me. A little snatch of English verse is as gloriously fertile as an English landscape, but I have the feeling that it is not mine or my people's spiritual territory. It is otherwise when I read a piece of Talmud, Midrash, medieval poetry or philosophy. Much of it is arid, barren, even ugly, but it is my cultural home, and this feeling of at homeness is more to me than the actual worth of the ideas or the beauty of their expression. I am utterly miserable when a long period of time elapses without my having an opportunity to read Jewish text, and I am equally miserable when I do read it, because of the awful solitude in which I find myself. I feel like one who comes back to his home town and finds it completely deserted.

10

November 28, 1929–July 30, 1930

Preachers in Training: A Proposal

THURSDAY, NOVEMBER 28, 1929

The experience which the seminary students acquire in public speaking when they preach on the High Holidays or when they take what are known as "weekend positions" is of questionable value in itself and is more than counterbalanced by the harm they do in corrupting the taste of their audiences. The practice of sending out raw youths to foist their spiritual crudities upon the general community indicates the cynical attitude of the institutions that are supposed to train these men for spiritual leadership. It is inconceivable that a medical school would permit its students to practice in communities where there are no physicians. If preaching were taken seriously by the preachers and by the institutions that train them, it would be considered as a method of dealing with social and religious ills, as demanding a knowledge of social and religious diagnosis and therapy. The practical problem, of supplying communities which cannot afford to engage a preacher permanently with some religious inspiration, could be met by having the students deliver sermons of a general nature furnished them by the Seminary, and which would be known as such by the audiences. Those sermons should be read from manuscript and not delivered by heart. It is not difficult to teach the students to read such sermons effectively.

Rabbis Distort the Bible and the Prayers

THURSDAY, NOVEMBER 29, 1929

The Talmud is an excellent thesaurus of instances proving that time is as likely to bring about deterioration as well as progress in ideas. Take, e.g., the following in Berachot 17a:

The bitter invective of the prophet *Nashim Sha'ananot komnah shema'nah koli . . .* [Heb. Isaiah 32:9 "Rise up you women that are at ease, hear my voice, you complacent daughters, give ear to my speech"] is inanely adduced by the Rabbis as proof that *Gedola havtaḥa she-hivti'aḥ h'k'b'h' le-nashim yoter ma-anashim* (Heb. The promise which God made to women is greater than the promise to men.)[1]

The beautiful prayer *Ve-nafshi ke'afar la-kol tehiyeh* [Heb. "(To such as curse me let my soul be dumb) and let my soul be unto all as dust"][2] is distorted by the Tosophists to mean *Yehi ratson she-zar'i lo yekhaleh le-olam* (Heb. "May it be thy will that my seed will never be cut off").[3]

On that same page even Rashi manages to take all the spiritual beauty out of a prayer that the students of Jamnia were in the habit of reciting.

A Sermon about Fear

FRIDAY, NOVEMBER 29, 1929

An interesting example of the way I manage to preach only what I believe in with all my heart and yet have something to say that is entirely acceptable is what I did with the sermon which I worked out for tomorrow. I happened to come across a book on Fear written by a religious psychiatrist. The author tries to prove that preaching [practicing?][4] the presence of God is effective as a protection against fear. He urges the reading of the *New Testament, Imitatio Dei*[5] and similar literature. It appears that he is a Catholic trying to win his reader for the Christian religion as a means to peace of mind. Having promised to base my sermon upon the book I was at a loss at first what conclusion to draw from it. I could not get myself to urge the reading of religious literature mainly as a means of counter-suggestion against fear. There was not enough truth in that fact for me. Upon further reflection, however, I drew the following inference from it: Since the main function of religion is to cast out our fears, then the criteria whether a religion is alive or not is its efficacy in discharging that function. Insofar as Jewish religion fails to do that at present it is our business to bring it up to that point.

---

1. There is a significant disparity between the meaning of the verse (i.e., reproach) and the interpretation in Berachot (i.e., promise of reward), which Kaplan is noting here. Men are not mentioned in this verse, hence the promise to women.

2. This prayer is found after the "Amidah" in the paragraph beginning "O My God Guard my tongue from evil. . . ."

3. This statement is found in Tosaphot to Talmud Bavli, Berachot. 17a.

4. Manuscript not clear.

5. *Imitatio Dei* (Imitation of Christ), fifteenth-century devotional work, still popular, attributed to Thomas a Kempis.

Incidentally I thought of other ideas concerning religion, e.g., in relation to ethics, which are both true, interesting and in need of being pointed out. All in all I do not regret having had to organize the sermon on Fear. It has helped me clarify my own ideas on the subject. May the time come when I shall be able to add *Darashti et 'd ve'anani . . .* [Heb. Psalms 34:5 "I sought the Lord, and He answered me, and delivered me from all my fears"].

Saturday night, November 30, 1929
    God is that element in the universe which makes it safe for life, intelligence and good will. This is the conception of God which I formulated in the sermon on Fear. Would to God that I could put into practice all that I preached today. It seems as though I am the psychiatrist in that book "Fear." I can help others without being able to help myself.

Dr. Faitlowitch,[6] *the Falashahs, and the Reality of God*

Saturday night, November 30, 1929
    I had Dr. Faitlowitch for dinner today. Although I am bored when he begins to speak to me about his difficulties in getting money to carry on his activities with the Falashas, I love to hear talk about our duty as Jews to do missionary work. When he mentioned the subject at the table neither Lena nor Judith could see the point. Judith seemed to think he was either a fanatic or a lunatic. I on the other hand feel like one who is numb with cold and who is anxious to warm himself at the first fire he comes across. One seldom meets a person in Jewish life in whom there burns the fire of religion. The rabbis and other professional teachers of religions are like paintings of coals aflame. This Faitlowitch actually feels the reality of God. Anyone who feels that way seems to me to possess a beautiful soul which not even the ugliest face can obscure. In fact the very ugliness of Faitlowitch's face compels me to think of his soul only. But so prosaically babittian, so narrowly slavish to the conventional good looks that even my own Lena and Judith seem to have not the slightest appreciation for a man like Faitlowitch who in his way has displayed as much heroism and endurance as some of the Jesuit missionaries who came to this country to convert the Indians to Christianity. Is this insistence upon fair looks the product of the modern education which tries to transmit the Greek ideal of beauty? Then Judith has hardly caught the true spirit of Hellenism at its best. Plato and Alcibiades who were prepossessing and who had been imbued all their lives with the ideal of beauty disregarded the ugliness of Socrates' face and could

---

6. Jacques Faitlovitch (1881–1955), orientalist; devoted to Falasha research and rescue. Falashas are black Jews of Ethiopia.

see nothing but the beauty in his soul. To me one of the most spiritual facts about Jewish life in the past is this very trait of setting a high value on the inward beauty of the spirit, a trait that has often been lampooned in the following: Many a Jew whose eyes were rheumy, whose nose was bulbous, who had a couple of warts on his cheeks would be described by those who knew him as "a schoner yid" [Yiddish: a beautiful Jew].

A Bad Dream — Feeling Depressed — A Prayer

THURSDAY, DECEMBER 5, 1929

The following prayer from "The Temple" by W. E. Orchard fits my present mood:

"O God, Life Eternal, my days are speeding fast away. The things I meant to do are still undone. What I meant to be I feel I never shall be. O leave me not. Sometimes I fear that life itself is dying down within me. Learning no longer comes easy to me. Change makes me afraid. Enthusiasm fades. Resolve proves impotent.

"O take not Thy holy spirit from me.

"I have so carefully husbanded my resources, yet they have steadily declined. What I kept I lost, only what I gave remained my own, and that is oh so small. I have sheltered my soul from the chill of criticism and daily have grown weaker. I have excused myself from arduous tasks only to lose my rest. I have shrunk from pain only to find the fear of life invade and terrify my heart.

"O cast me not away from Thy presence."

Just before I got up this morning I dreamt that I suddenly departed for Palestine and coming to Jerusalem I found that another Arab pogrom was going on. An Arab tried to stab me but I escaped. As I passed through the University halls I felt that the Jews were organized but were poorly armed. I lived through all the tension and fear of an actual Arab attack.

The Yarmulke as a Sign of Respect

THURSDAY, DECEMBER 5, 1929

When Rabbi Kasher was about to come I felt that it would be inappropriate for me to receive him with uncovered head since I was sure he would be wearing a skull cap. But this was something more than a sense of impropriety in the feeling I had about the matter. Rabbi Kasher somehow impressed me as a man deserving of high respect because of a certain spiritual light that seemed to shine in his face. Whether my reaction was natural or atavistic I experienced an inward desire to express my regard for the man by wearing a cap.

This experience led me to conclude that I ought not to sit with uncovered head at any time if I wanted to sense the holiness of life or the presence of God. Logically it seems ridiculous to connect the wearing of a skull cap with a sense of God's presence, but psychologically that connection can be accounted for. The sense of God's presence requires as a prerequisite some outward action that on the one hand serves no utilitarian purpose and on the other is a fitting symbol of humility.

TI Faculty Debates the Place of Hebrew Literature in the Curriculum

THURSDAY, DECEMBER 5, 1929

At the meeting of the TI Faculty today I suggested the revision of the entire curriculum. The present curriculum omits entirely the study of Aggadah [rabbinic legends] and Medieval Jewish Literature. I pleaded for an organic curriculum in which the thought life of the whole of Judaism be given a place. My contention was that it should be our aim to develop in the students a Jewish consciousness which is both national and religious. The circumstance that about 30% is devoted to modern Hebrew literature produces in our students a distorted type of Jewish consciousness.

The arguments advanced against my suggestion were 1) (Scharfstein) that an attempt to give the students a conception of every element of Jewish culture results in a superficial knowledge of each of those elements and a thorough knowledge of none. 2) The purpose of the courses in modern Hebrew is not merely to teach literature but to use it as a means of cultivating the use of Hebrew in speaking and writing. 3) (Bavli) Jewish consciousness is not acquired through comprehensive knowledge but through ability to use the media of Jewish self-expression. Moreover the question of inherent interest is a primary consideration. 4) (Dinin) Courses in belles lettres include study of authors whose writings came under that head only and not those whose writings have a value for content only.

Every one, however, conceded that the study of Aggadah was indispensable (despite the difficulty presented by the unorganized condition of the material.)

Sexual Thoughts Displace Torah Thoughts

TUESDAY, DECEMBER 10, 1929

I spent a good deal of time today looking through a number of prayers to be incorporated into the Supplementary Prayer Book which I am planning. It occurred to me that almost all of the prayers by Orchard lend themselves into arrangements for responsive readings.

I wonder whether the language and ideas of those prayers exert any affect upon my mind. Abstractly speaking they ought to be refining and spiritualizing. They ought to free me from anxiety, render me patient and unselfish. Yet should anything go wrong at the very time I read them the old Adam in me breaks out with all his wonted fury. Of course I am ashamed of myself but that does not prevent me from being upset and in a temper.

Why should I have read "The Chronicles of a Gigolo" by Julian Swift,[7] after having read all those prayers? I knew when I took up the book that it would only titillate the sex hunger. Of what earthly good all such literature is I cannot for the life of me make out. If I had the courage I would have come out boldly in favor of censorship. I do not deny that I would favor the prohibition of such books because of their harmful influence upon me. But I am no worse than millions of others nor even than those who would let the bars down entirely and frown down upon the very suggestion of censorship. These very people who refuse to exercise any restraint in the description of sexual gratification do so on the ground that the mind should be aware of the realities of life. Yet these very people are the ones who bewail the fact that the human being is too self-conscious or over-conscious. There are certainly many things which it is not good for the mind to be too conscious of or conscious of for too long a time. Except when the sexual impulses should be aroused—and there are times when they should—it is best for the mind to shut out all sex suggestions. I think one of the most remarkable statements in the Midrash is that one in Canticles Rabba which compares the mind to a beaker filled to the brim with oil into which water is spilled; for every drop of water there comes out a drop of oil. So for every sex thought there is displaced a thought of Torah (in the most general sense of the term).

God as an Attribute of Reality

Tuesday, December 17, 1929

In the past religion was based upon the conception of God as an identifiable being. In the future religion will have to be based upon the conception of God as a particular attribute of Reality or of the Universe. From an intellectual standpoint there is an unbridgeable gap between Reality or the Universe as an attribute or creation of God and God as an attribute of the Universe. But from an emotional and volitional standpoint there is *enough in common* to justify the use of the term God and of the traditional manner of personal address to him in prayer.

---

7. Julian Swift, *The Chronicles of a Gigolo* (New York: H. Liveright, 1929).

Perhaps the following diagram will illustrate the pragmatic reasoning which justifies the use of the term God despite the altered cognitive content of that term.

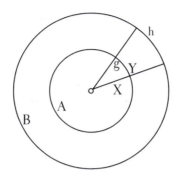

Let A represent the circle of emotional and volitional implications of a God concept whose intellectual implications are equal to X. Let B represent the circle of emotional and volitional implications of a God whose intellectual implications are equal to radius Y. (The justification for making them concentric is their being alike in their affirmative attitude toward life.) It then follows that arc H is parallel to and in proportion to the rest of one's emotional and volitional implications equivalent to arc g.

In traditional religion God is spoken of as the creator of the world. In modern religion God is the name of the creative principle of the universe. That creative principle, as far as human life is concerned is incompatible with arrogance, greed and uncontrolled sexual desire and is compatible only with intelligence, courage and good will. Emotionally and volitionally we get exactly the same type of practical and socially valuable results as could ever be obtained through the traditional idea of God as the creator of the world. Since however from an aesthetic point of view it is not feasible to speak of the creative principle except in the language of personification, we shall always find ourselves compelled to resort to the traditional content and formularies whenever we shall want to worship. This, of course, assumes that the tendency to worship is not determined or called forth by the assumption of human like personality in the object worshiped. First comes the tendency to worship, then the personification of the object worshiped. The creative principle in human life, especially in the manifestation of intelligence, courage and good will, can best be called into play through that self-conscious act for which there can be no better name than worship.

The worth of man derives from the fact that he possesses the creative principle to a far greater degree than any other being. This is the reason for describing him as godlike or as being made in the image of God.

Last night I met for the first time this year a group of four picked students of the Seminary for the purpose of interesting them in the study of the conception of God. The students are Eisenstein, Zwelling, Boxer[8] and Gelb.[9] I am taking up with them at present Hocking's *Meaning of God in Human Experience*.[10] They came prepared on the first three chapters of the book and made it impossible for me to add my bit to the ideas advanced by Hocking in those chapters.

God Declares All the Ten Commandments at Once

WEDNESDAY, DECEMBER 18, 1929

Except for the momentary embarrassment which I experienced this morning when I gave a wrong interpretation to a midrashic text and had to admit that I was wrong and that those who took issue with me were right, I enjoyed the sessions at the Seminary today. I am proud of the two ideas I hit upon in the homiletical rendering of the text. One is the idea that in the statement that God simultaneously calls the hosts of heaven by their different names there is adumbrated the notion of the one in the many. Likewise in the statement that the power of God was displayed when he simultaneously uttered all the ten commandments, we have the foreshadowing of the notion that there is one moral impulse behind the various and varying moral laws. (Both Midrashic statements referred to are found in Sifre on *Ve-Yasem Lekha Shalom* [Heb. Numbers 6:26 "(The Lord shall lift up his countenance unto thee and) grant thee peace"]. The other homiletical rendering had to do with the statement in Sifre 77 which reads *hamlikhu alekha tehilah* [Heb. Take God's rule on yourself first . . .].[11] I rendered it as follows: Prayer to be valid presupposes the acceptance of the spiritual order of existence.

---

8. Ben Zion Bokser (1907–84), ordained JTS; Ph.D. Columbia; author; rabbi, Forest Hills, N.Y.

9. Max Gelb (1907–87), ordained JTS; rabbi, White Plains, N.Y.; active in Rabbinical Assembly (RA); member, New York Board of Rabbis.

10. William Ernest Hocking, *The Meaning of God in Human Experience* (New Haven, Conn.: Yale University Press, 1912).

11. The question in the midrash has to do with the order of the additional service on Rosh Hashannah and why we say the sovereignty prayers (malkhuyot) before the shofar prayers. The midrash quoted literally reads "take God's sovereignty on yourself first and afterward ask for mercy. . . ."

His Own Decreasing Religious Observance Surprises Him

FRIDAY NIGHT, DECEMBER 20, 1929

I have been "evolving" pretty rapidly of late. Weeks have passed since I have recited the traditional prayers weekday mornings; neither have I worn the Tephilin during all this time. Here am I writing on Friday night without experiencing any moral compunction to speak of. This evening I asked Judith to improvise some music on the piano and I enjoyed listening to her giving renditions of "Ma'oz Tsur" [Heb. Rock of Ages][12] and "Adon Olam" [Heb. Eternal Lord. . . .][13] in the style of various great musicians. Where will this lead to? My reason urges me on to emancipate myself from the tyrannical bonds of traditional notions of prayer and Sabbath observance. But my moral sense upbraids me for being either a coward in not making known my change of views with regard to observances or a hypocrite in permitting people to entertain the impression that I still adhere to the traditional observances. I can advance enough reasons for letting well enough alone and not stirring up hornets' nests. Since nobody asks any questions of me, since no matter what I do is of little consequence to Jewish life, since all my being is sufficiently steeped in Jewishness without the need of submitting to an outworn system of taboos. And since this and since that, I ought to have long passed the stage of inner conflicts. But it is not a question what I ought to have felt. The fact is that I am undergoing excruciating mental torture in not being able to lead freely and openly the kind of life I should like to and that I know would be more beautiful and spiritual than even that which most people credit me with.

For a moment it occurred to me that I ought to pray to God to enable me to live openly as my conscience dictates to me, but then I realized that such a prayer would only be self-deception. The best kind of prayer in my case would be to plan seriously some way out of the present impasse. My mind, when confronted with this problem, always reverts to the desirability of linking up with Stephen Wise and his Institute. But the dread of moving into an environment where the desire to escape Jewish life is far stronger than it is in my present environment checks all further dreams of joining Wise. Besides I would find it much more difficult to formulate a rationale for his kind of Jewishness than for my own with all its paradoxes and heartburnings. The essential difficulty of my position as an upholder of Judaism is that the Jews themselves are getting to want it less and less, and I am reduced to the necessity of promoting spiritual values by means which are cumbrous, unintelligible and highly expensive.

---

12. Rock of Ages": a traditional Hanukah song, sung with the Hanukah candle lighting.
13. Adon Olam": a hymn sung at the end of the service.

Judith Kaplan, ca. 1930. (Courtesy Hadassah K. Musher)

Suppose I were completely free to do as I liked, what would I do? Would I join John Haynes Holmes?[14] Not by a long shot. If I am not mistaken he too is unhappy because he senses the futility of his endeavors. That sermon of his "What Shall I Preach On?" betrays an inner tragedy which I do not think even his tremendous literary output can make him forget. And no wonder, because even his experiment in making the religious organization non-sectarian and in the nature of a community church solves the problem. The reconstruction which the theoretic aspect of religion is undergoing must be reflected in a complete reconstruction of the organized expression of it. A few years ago I indicated in some of the lectures I gave at the SAJ that the organized expression of religion must follow the vocational organization of society. Each vocation must have its own religious institutions—religious places of meeting and religious spokesmen. On certain days of the year like Thanksgiving, New Year, etc., there might be inter-vocational meetings for prayer, song, music and drama. It is through meetings of that kind that religion would assume its folk character. In this scheme there is no room for churches or synagogues.

In the meantime I must stop writing (it is two o'clock in the morning) because I must get up in time to go to services and deliver a sermon on the subject "The Jewish People—A Study in Dual Personality"!!!

The Effects of the Crash on Kaplan

SUNDAY, DECEMBER 29, 1929

When I preached on the First Day of Succot concerning the need of using religion as a means of fortifying ourselves against the insecurity and precariousness of modern life, I little realized that I as well as the people I spoke to would soon have occasion to put their religion to the test. It was only two or three days after that the big crash in Wall Street took place. Some of my friends and relatives lost heavily. Brous who was about to be married to my niece Harriet Baron, lost about $300,000. Not having dealt on margin there is a possibility of my recovering some of the money that was invested for me. In the meantime the value of my investments shrank from about $85,000 to $45,000. I had hoped that in the course of a few years by saving and investing in stocks that would rise in value I would save up sufficiently to be able to give up all institutional connections and strike out boldly upon some program of spiritual reformation of Jewish life. Although

---

14. John Haynes Holmes (1879–1964), very liberal nondenominational clergyman; helped create NAACP and ACLU; strongly identified with the Community Church in New York City, which he served for many years. A pacificist in both World Wars.

that dream has now vanished I dare not complain. There are thousands of people who are in dire straits as a result of the crash and would consider themselves the happiest in the world if they were economically even half [as well] off as I am.

"*The Story of My Life*"

TUESDAY, JANUARY 7, 1930

The story of my career is the story of the application to Jewish life and problems of a deep aversion for fragmentariness and a fervid passion for wholeness or integrity. Thus when I began as an Orthodox rabbi I was emotionally devoted to tradition but intellectually I was a modern. This division in my being made me unhappy. I accepted the principalship of the Teachers Institute. That allowed me to reinterpret tradition in the light of modern thought. Then I became aware that the problem of education divorced from the problem of environment was fragmentary and insoluble. I therefore applied myself to the task of urging the instruction of a Jewish environment. This is how I became interested in the Center movement. But then I discovered that the attempt to construct an environment without a philosophy of Jewish life was again a fragmentary affair. The Center can not function as it should. It is based upon a wrong philosophy of Jewish life. This drove me to the need of formulating a program based upon the principle of the completeness of Jewish life. Neither philanthropy alone nor worship alone nor ethical idealism alone nor Palestine alone nor Hebraic culture alone nor the past alone nor the present alone, etc. but all of these combined into one integrated unity in which each part is animated and informed by the life and the spirit of the whole Jewish people—this is the meaning of Judaism as a civilization.

A Family Tragedy—Feeling the Pain

WEDNESDAY, JANUARY 8, 1930

A tragedy such as that which occurred in the family—the father of one of my nephews by marriage was killed in an accident—has a crushing effect on me. It doesn't upset my theological views, because in my theology I do not consider God as the cause of tragic mishaps. They are chance and nothing more. I am just as irritated when I hear one referring to them as fate, as when I hear them ascribed to the inscrutable working of God's will. Yet I cannot assume the attitude of the stoic. My nerves are all exposed. How do men who command armies and who send thousands to their death or to what is worse a death in life, manage to exist? I wish I knew of a way of cultivating hardness.

Praying for a New Self

FRIDAY, JANUARY 10, 1930

When I take up a book of prayers like that of Orchard's or McComb's I feel as though I could go on praying for hours and hours *halevai*[15] *yitpalel adam kol ha-yom . . .* [Heb. Berachot 21a "Oh that a man should pray the whole day . . ."][16] (doesn't seem in the least absurd though of course extremely uneconomical.) Petitions like the following just fit my mood and needs: "Still every passion, rebuke every doubt, strengthen every element of good within me, that nothing may hinder the outflow of Thy life and power. . . . Transform me by the breath of Thy regenerating power. . . . Let me no longer be sad, downcast, despairing, vexed by remorse or depressed by my failures. Take from me my old self. Give me a new self, beautiful, vigorous and joyous."

How much I am in need of this new self is sufficiently attested by the contents of this journal. But it isn't altogether my own limitations that worry me. To a far larger degree it is the apparent hopelessness of the Jewish situation which as something of a spiritual teacher and leader I am supposed and expected to improve. From the standpoint of that situation I feel "like a polar bear on an ice floe that is drifting into warmer zones as he watches with growling impotence the steady dwindling of his home."

Twenty-Five Years in the Rabbinate—A Celebration

MONDAY, JANUARY 13, 1930

The silver jubilee dinner which the SAJ gave last night in honor of my twenty-five years in the rabbinate was attended by 700 people. It was not the purpose of honoring me that suggested the dinner, but that of increasing membership. Rosenblatt as chairman of the membership committee suggested that it would help matters if the dinner were arranged in my honor, and looking about for some reason to honor me he bethought himself of the fact that I had completed a quarter of a century in the rabbinate. Under these circumstances I did not think it right to invite any of the leading men in the community. I felt it would be exploiting these men for the purpose of getting members. Besides, I was a bit jealous for my own personality and message. If these were not sufficient to enlist people in the ranks of the SAJ I didn't want to resort to meretricious means to get people to join the SAJ. Besides very few of these leading men, especially my

---

15. Kaplan here uses the more common and colloquial expression. The original text reads *u-levai*.

16. The question here is if one is in doubt that he said the Amidah prayer, should he say it again?

colleagues in the Seminary, are entirely out of sympathy with my aims, and their presence would rob me of the opportunity to define those aims freely to the old and the prospective members.

Relaxing and Reading Whitehead

SUNDAY, JANUARY 19, 1930

Yesterday and today I spent with Lena at Long Beach. For two days I threw off all cares and ambitions and lived a passive life. In the mornings I read Hebrew and tried to repeat in paraphrase from what I read so as to acquire some fluency in the use of Hebrew in conversation and on the platform. (I thought I forgot all ambitions.) In the afternoon I read Whitehead's new book *Process and Reality.*[17] Only now and then would the thought of my impotence flash upon me. As I was trying to fall asleep last night the thought that I am already in my forty-ninth year almost frightened me. I couldn't endure this kind of passive existence for any length of time. It would drive me mad. That is why I dread the summer vacations. Why am I condemned to this life of loneliness? What are not men like Kallen[18] or Waldo Frank[19] or others of that type accessible to me?

Judenschmerz — or — Is Communism a Better Way?

SATURDAY NIGHT, FEBRUARY 1, 1930

I have by no means gotten out of the state of depression I was in when I made my last entry in this journal. If it isn't physical pain of some kind that puts me into the dumps it's the *Weltschmerz*[20] that agitates me and if it is not the *Weltschmerz* it's the *Judenschmerz*. A psychiatrist would probably probe beneath what I speak of as *Weltschmerz* and discover some nervous or mental maladjustment. Even though he were right that wouldn't prove me wrong. The psychiatrist taking a scientific view of a situation must necessarily abstract from it those phases he can speak about with some definiteness. He may be right as far as he goes, but he can never go far enough. I am in all truth and sincerity absolutely miserable at times over the evident incapacity of the human being to find a way to happiness and salvation. All I needed was to see tonight the play "Red

---

17. Alfred North Whitehead, *Process and Reality: An Essay in Cosmology* (Cambridge: The University Press, 1929).
18. Horace M. Kallen (1882–1974), Ph.D. Harvard; philosopher; author; New School Dean; ideology close to Kaplan's.
19. Waldo David Frank (1889–1967), M.A. Yale; novelist; critic; editor, *New Masses*; conscientious objector.
20. *Weltschmerz*: sadness over the present or future state of the world. Similar for Jewish situation to *Judenschmerz*.

Rust,"[21] written by two modern Russian playwrights and produced in Russia, to fall into a state of despair as to whether the human being will ever be able to order his life with any degree of success. Thoroughly dissatisfied with capitalist civilization I had been hoping that communism would point the way to a better world. The more I have been learning about what has been going on in Russia the more I have been disillusioned. One of the characters in the play makes the remark that for the communists the world began in Oct. 1917. Judging by the actions exhibited on the stage that is obviously true, for on the whole they behave like our first human ancestors. The picture presented of the life in present day Russia is a picture of a people half of whom have gone mad and the other half savage. And the background of it all, an idolatry that rivals the ancient worship of Moloch. The tomb of Lenin in the Red Square symbolic of the idolatry which called for human sacrifices—the sacrifice of feeling, the sacrifice of the individual, the worship of verbal formulas, the glorification by an act of specious sophistry of man in his most inhuman aspect—man in the mass. And all this travesty on human aspiration is the result of deliberate intent to bring the millennium.

I cannot afford to lose my faith in human nature, because then I would lose all faith in God, and the universe would fall, as it were, upon me and crush me. If I could find just three or four people with whom I [could] come to an understanding about these grounds for despairing of God and man, and who would cooperate with me in some literary social or spiritual enterprise to help us live down this feeling of hopelessness I would cease this continual whining.

Working on the Book—Knowing God

SUNDAY, FEBRUARY 2, 1930

The reason I haven't kept up my writing in this journal for the last ten days is that I have found that it interferes with the work that I am doing on "the book." The chapter on spiritual religion has given me a good deal of trouble and I am far from satisfied with its present form, but I can breathe a little bit more freely now that it is in shape for the lecture course I am giving at the Seminary. Having steeped myself in the question what to make of the God idea in the next stage of religious development, the God idea suggested itself as a subject for the sermon that I was to preach yesterday on *Va'era* [Heb. The portion of the week, includes Exodus 6:2–9:35] which opens

---

21. *Red Rust*, translated from the Russian. A Soviet "propaganda piece," a reviewer states, where a student spouts a "false" version of communism and is executed. Many quotations from Lenin. Reviewer found it difficult to take the play seriously. *New York Times*, March 17, 1929.

with an appropriate text. The subject was entitled "How do we know God?" I pointed out that since we have given up the idea that God is visible or audible or capable of being known by an unmistakable evidence of His intervention, it is important to learn how we may know God through the use of the mind. Rejecting the method of (ratiocination) inference as undependable I suggested the method of intuition. We can know God not by reasoning from effect to cause, but by contemplating mind itself. The significance of the marvels of nature attains its climax when we begin to appreciate the marvel of the mind which is experienced with a warmth of immediacy in the sense of personal unity. When in this experience of personal unity there is also borne in on us the unity of life and the world as a whole we have come face to face with God.

As a means of holding fast to this experience we have to resort to material analogies. The analogy which seems best suited for that purpose is the following: The vast expanse of ocean yields up an insignificant portion of its waters to the clouds. These are driven by the winds over the land. When they reach the mountains they precipitate into rain. The rain gathers in springs. Each spring begins to course down to the sea. They join and swell into streams and the streams that might otherwise lose themselves in the sands are enabled to continue their journey to the sea because they are joined by other streams and together they form into rivers. God may be likened to the sea, each human soul to the spring. The very earth which holds the spring and gives it form, permits it to rejoin the sea. So does the physical environment provide the conditions for the soul's development. In this it is helped by the other selves or souls as is borne out by the circumstance that it is through interaction and cooperation with our fellowmen that we each develop our personality and come to know God.

Working with the Committee on Law

WEDNESDAY, APRIL 2, 1930

Finkelstein is after me that I should work with the Committee on Law. At first I tried to put him off with excuses about my being unwell (which is true to a large extent), but after a while I explained to him that in my opinion the Committee was of too heterogeneous a character ever to arrive at anything like a unanimous opinion about any issue. I could not cooperate with men like Drob or even Greenstone. Secondly I could not sanction the legalistic attitude in questions of ritual and therefore if I am to cooperate with the Committee it would have to confine itself in matters of law only to civil and domestic problems. To my surprise he showed himself willing to meet me more than halfway. He too found it impossible to get along with Drob. He said that Drob was ready to resign and that his resignation would be accepted. Moreover, he would have all matters of ritual transferred to Dr. Ginzberg for decision.

Sacrifices: A *Sermon on* Sidra Vayikra

FRIDAY, APRIL 4, 1930

The Sidrah [Torah portion] of this Sabbath being *Vayikra* [Leviticus 1:1–5:26] I wanted to speak on the traditional attitude toward sacrifices. One of the loosest of loose ends in Jewish ideology is the matter of the sacrificial cult. They have eliminated every reference to it in the prayer book as being obsolete and beyond all desire of recovery or even remembrance.

When we come to non-reformists we note three distinct attitudes. 1) That of the traditional type who to all intents live mentally in the fifth or sixth century. Rabbi Kook has instituted an academy for the study of sacrificial laws. 2) That of the Orthodox who pray in Hebrew for the restoration of sacrifices, but don't lose any sleep over the fact that they won't be called upon in the near future to resume the practice. 3) That of the Conservatives who are annoyed when you ask them whether they really want to see sacrifices restored and grudgingly answer, "If you don't like them I'll print a special edition of the prayer book for you with the text changed from that of a petition for the restoration of sacrifices you will merely be mentioning them as having existed once upon a time." Of these three attitudes the conservative is the most contemptible. It is contemptible because it is non-committal and cowardly. It belongs to the unfortunate policy that has grown up in Jewish life of evading all matters about which there is a difference of opinion. Those who have instituted this policy have contributed a good deal to the growing indifference to Jewish religious questions. If you keep on evading those questions concerning which there is a difference of opinion it won't be long before those questions will become an object of indifference. Important issues are thus permitted to die from starvation and they are not even given a decent funeral but are allowed to clutter the highways of life and emit far from fragrant smells. This is the case with the question of the sacrificial cult.

Let me therefore try to clarify the issue by stating just what is the traditional conception of the sacrificial cult and by asking ourselves the question whether the choice is between subscribing to the traditional attitude or subscribing in to the attitude of the Reformists who would eliminate all reference to the cult completely because they can see no earthly or spiritual value to it.

The traditional attitude is properly described in the article on sacrifices in *Hastings Encyc. Of Religion and Ethics* (I refer to the part of the article on Jewish Sacrifices written by [Moses] Gaster. He seems to belong to the kind of scholars who are great in small things and small in great things. D. Hoffman,[22] Luzzatto[23] and a host of others belong to this group.) The points that Gaster makes are as follows: 1. "The destruction of the Temple in Jerusalem wrought a profound change in the religious life of the Jews" by bringing with the cessation of sacrifices the entire divine service to a standstill. "But divine ordinances cannot be abrogated. They are merely temporarily suspended until the time comes when they are again to be enacted."

The main point in the article is that traditional Judaism has not been content with mere prayer for the restoration of the cult. It has found it necessary to devise substitutes so [deeply] does it miss the institution of sacrifices. These substitutes are 1) prayer, 2) study of Torah, 3) fasting, 4) charity.

Would complete elimination as advocated by the Reformists be an anti-Jewish act? 1) They point to the prophets as having been violently opposed to the sacrificial cult. The fact, however, is that the prophets, not even the few who distinctly condemned the cult as practiced in their day, can be taken to mean that they objected to the cult as such. 2) They point to Maimonides and Ibn Ezra. But Maimonides and Ibn Ezra merely accepted alien philosophic assumptions without clearly analyzing the assumptions or synthesizing them with Judaism. They spoke in two voices, a natural and a falsetto.

The guiding principle is the fact that the Jews were passionately desirous of the restoration and insisted upon finding substitutes. This should lead to the question, Why were the Jews unable to surrender the sacrificial cult? The answer is that they were anxious to give expression to their awareness of God's presence not only by word but by gesture and outward action. There is a profound psychological justification for wanting to do something in order to feel more intensively the presence of God. It is the most effective as a means of experiencing the reality of God.

We have to forgo of course all desire of the restoration of the sacrificial cult but we should find some other tangible means of achieving the sense of God's presence. The substitute should be one of action. Already in ancient times Judaism discovered that the ordinary meal can be assimilated to the rite of sacrifice. The dietary laws surrounding the meal, the washing of the hands, the benedictions are intended to make of the meal a sacrament, a means of sensing the reality of God. In our occidental life where meals

NB !

---

22. David Hoffmann (1843–1921), rabbinic scholar; director, Berlin Rabbinical Seminary; opponent of Reform movement; author.

23. Samuel David Luzzatto (Shadal) (1800–1865), Italian scholar; wrote on Bible, Hebrew grammar, liturgy, poetry, and philosophy.

call up hotels, cafeterias and quick luncheons, where food is meant to be merely chewed and swallowed but not to grow poetic or spiritual about, this interpretation of the meal as a sacrament sounds bizarre. Yet with a little effort of thought and will we can get back into the god-conscious frame of mind of the traditional Jew. To achieve that experience is to conserve the most worthwhile contribution of traditional Judaism.

Doing a Conversion and Rabbis Who Have Little Faith

WEDNESDAY, APRIL 9, 1930

Just now a young woman, a Miss Ackerman, came to ask me to officiate at her wedding. I am very loath to officiate at functions and I therefore try to turn down requests from outsiders, especially from those who are not identified with Jewish religious life. The very first thing this Miss Ackerman said to me was "I know a number of rabbis, but you are the only one for whom I have any respect." This hurt me to the quick, although I did not show it. I only remarked gently "What you said about my being different from other rabbis sounds so much like what Goyim [non-Jews] say about a Jew they happen to like." In the course of the conversation she justified her statement by saying that she knows three rabbis quite well, all of the Reform wing, and elderly men with well established reputations, who not only do not believe in God, but in the imperative character of idealism. I distinctly asked her whether she meant that they failed to live up to the ideals they preached or that they did not even believe in the ideals themselves, and she reaffirmed that the latter was the case. If that is true, the sooner American Judaism will disappear, the better.

About Writing: "I Am Like a Woman Who Constantly Miscarries"

SATURDAY NIGHT, MAY 3, 1930

On Thursday night April 24 as I was taking a walk with Lena on W. 110 Street and Central Park I felt the onset of my annual affliction, the so-called rose fever. Although I had been taking inoculations regularly since the beginning of March I have not escaped being a victim of this annual plague. My nose kept on running incessantly and in addition I had a headache combined with neuralgic pains in my eyes. I had to miss teaching the classes at the Institute on Sunday afternoon, April 27th, in order to have some strength for the talk on marriage that I had been scheduled to give in the evening.

All in all I am in very low spirits these days, although I manage not to show it. The main cause is the hiatus in my writing, and the dissatisfaction with what I have so far written. When I think of all that could have been said on the subjects I am dealing with by one who is able to express himself adequately I could burst into tears. After all that I have been working on the subject I should have been able to depict vividly the centripetal and centrifugal forces in Jewish life. All that I have succeeded in doing has been to give a labored and rather abstract delineation of the principal disintegrating forces. Likewise in the discussion of religion, which necessarily takes me far afield, there is lacking that dynamic style which is necessary to place the entire system of Jewish ceremonial on a religio-aesthetic level. Last year I had gotten pretty far with the discussion of the aestethic approach to the problem of religion—but somehow I failed to clinch the matter. Another one in my place having all the idea material that I had accumulated would have been able to get out a respectably sized book on the subject. I am like a woman who constantly miscarries. Is it a wonder that I am green with envy when I see some of my younger colleagues spreading themselves out in numerous learned periodicals? My reason, of course, tells me that in giving way to such envy I am a darn fool, without a sense of humor and a self-centered careerist to boot. But those who know the agony of a frustrated will to create can appreciate how much I suffer.

The Plan of "The Book" — "The Future of Judaism"

THURSDAY, MAY 8, 1930

Last night I hit upon what seems to me an excellent idea that might serve as an ariadnes' thread to guide one in the argument of the book on Judaism as a civilization. It is the idea that our desire to remain Jews is waning. The first chapter sets forth the causes for this decline. The next four chapters, the programs which are expected to check this decline and the reasons why these programs fail to supply the necessary motive and direction to the desire to remain Jews. After that I make the point that we should take the case of those Jews in whom the desire to remain Jews is still alive, not because they happen to be Orthodox but for other reasons. By analyzing their reasons we find that Judaism is to them a civilization thus presenting itself to them in a way which motivates their desire to remain Jews. The next thing to do is to develop the implications of this motivation and to formulate directions whereby the purpose implied might be most surely and effectively achieved.

When I came upon the foregoing I was happy to the point of elation. I took a three mile walk last night. I felt as though I walked on air. After that I spent some time incorporating the idea into the text of the book. As soon as I was through the feeling of depression returned and was reinforced by a conversation I had this afternoon with Ira Eisenstein. He drew a gloomy picture of the prospects awaiting the graduates of the Seminary, in view of the limited number of available pulpits, the overproduction of rabbis and the inaction of the Seminary which has permitted the JIR[24] to preempt every opening in sight.

I could not help giving vent to my feelings and to charge Adler with being the main cause of the predicament in which our graduates are finding themselves. Instead of eliciting from the men powers of thought or activity, Adler has perhaps unwittingly done more to repress their spontaneity and innermost yearnings than any person or body of persons in this country. Many of these men have escaped the clutches of their fanatical parents, but they are helpless under the paralyzing spell which Adler has cast upon all the younger people who come within the purview of his religious authority. He represents all the forces making for inhibition that have been stored up by Morais, Schechter, Schiff and Ginzberg. It seems to me that the Seminary is doomed to permanent inefficiency, because the tradition he will leave behind will be taken up by those who are at present basking in the sunshine of his influence.

I have felt today the effects of the hay-fever, obstruction in the nasal cavity, occasional yellow discharge and general tiredness.

Lena's being unwell and staying in bed also contributed to my depressed state of mind.

Ira Eisenstein Comes on Board at the SAJ

WEDNESDAY, MAY 14, 1930

I spoke to Ira Eisenstein last Monday about the position of executive director at the SAJ which would be open because of Perlman's expected resignation. I told Eisenstein that if he will prove successful next year I shall recommend him for the position of associate rabbi the year after, and after two years' stay I shall recommend him for the position of assistant rabbi. The salary he is to get next year is $3000.

It appears that he will accept the offer. This makes me extremely happy because I have a feeling that he will help me to enlarge the SAJ and in time take it over entirely and have it function in the spirit of Judaism as a modern spiritual civilization.

---

24. Jewish Institute of Religion, founded in 1922 in New York City by Stephen Wise. On Kaplan, Wise, and the Jewish Institute of Religion, see *Judaism Faces the Twentieth Century: A Biography of Mordecai M. Kaplan* (Detroit: Wayne State University Press, 1993).

Getting Brandeis Back in the Zionist Movement

SATURDAY, MAY 24, 1930, 2:30 A.M.

At the last meeting which took place in A. Tulin's[25] rooms I intimated that I would try to be of service in helping to bring Brandeis back into the leadership of the Zionist movement. Tulin and Brody who have been meeting this week with Mack and others of the Brandeis group in reference to the negotiations being carried on between the ZOA and Brandeis called on me this afternoon and suggested that I together with a few others who are identified neither with the Brandeis or with the Lipsky group send cablegrams to European Zionists urging them to call upon Brandeis to step into the breach at the present time. They maintained that Brandeis would go to any length to be of help to the movement if he would feel that he is really wanted and that he has the Zionists back of him.

I undertook to get Pool[26] Tschernowitz, Goralnick and Emanuel Neumann[27] to send such a cablegram. When I called up Tsch. And Neumann I learned that they were out of town. Pool consented to add his name and suggested that a similar message be sent to prominent American Zionists asking them to urge upon Brandeis to assume leadership. Goralnick was rather skeptical about the whole affair but suggested that before going any further I together with one or two others find out from Brandeis whether he were to receive such requests he would be willing to assume the leadership. Otherwise we would merely be stultifying ourselves.

Brandeis and the Zionist Movement

WEDNESDAY, MAY 28, 1930

I realized that I was allowing myself to be dragged into Zionist politics by consenting to act on Tulin's and Brody's suggestion that I take steps to crystallize sentiment among Zionist leaders in this country and abroad in favor of Brandeis as a leader of the Zionist movement. I would not have minded the loss of Weizmann's friendship if I were sure that there was such sentiment waiting to be crystallized. Instead I discovered after the first few moves that I made that there was first the need of creating the sentiment. Life is too short for such a long-range proposition. Pool was the

---

25. Abraham Tulin (1883–1973), lawyer; Zionist leader; author; assistant, Herbert Hoover Relief Administration.

26. David De Sola Pool (1885–1970), Sephardic rabbi; Ph.D. Heidelberg; author; Zionist; Union of Orthodox Jewish Congregations, New York City.

27. Emanuel Neumann (1893–1980), Zionist leader; author; president, Zionist Organization of America.

only one who was apparently willing to go ahead. Tschernowitz, Goralnick and Emanuel Neumann showed themselves entirely too disputatious for me to be able to count on their cooperation. Consequently I called off the meeting which I have been trying to arrange for tomorrow 5:30 at my house. It appears that the statement issued by the Brandeis group recently in answer to the overtures made by the local Zionist Organization has lessened the chances of any get together between that group and the general Zionist body. It appears that there is absolutely no hope of Brandeis ever being rid of the evil genius that has gotten between him and the rest of the Zionist world—De Haas. How a man like Brandeis should have permitted himself to be mesmerized by De Haas is hardly understandable. And there is nothing to be done about it either because Brandeis is by this time far too much committed to De Haas ever to release himself from his influence. De Haas has written Brandeis' biography. That seems to have made Brandeis forever impossible as a leader of the Zionist movement, since he would never think of assuming responsibility without taking De Haas along with him as his chief counselor. Hence the future historian will have to record that the Zionist movement in America was wrecked by two people, by Lipsky who became disqualified for any gainful occupation by being too long in the presidency of the ZOA and by De Haas who believed that the movement owed him a life competence because he brought Brandeis into the Zionist movement.

On the Flyleaf:[28] *Kaplan Quotes from Books He Is Reading*

"To wear out our lives in the pursuit of worthy though imperfectly attainable ideals is the essence of human dignity."
[No Source] (Saturday Night, September 19, 1931)

"Perhaps I've never known reality as other human beings know it," he thought. "My life has been industrious, monotonous, patient. I've carried my load like a camel. And I've been able to do this because it hasn't been my real life at all! My 'Mythology' has been my real life."
From Wolf Golent by John Cooper Powys, Vol. 1, p. 13 (copied Wednesday, October 28, 1931)

"There is a lack of vicissitudes about them that is almost distressing."
"Wellington" by Philip Guedella, Friday, January 1, 1932

"The expression 'death in life' means living, even living passionately and in a way efficiently with a sense, nevertheless, underneath of the hollowness, the futility of the objects of pursuit."

---

28. At the beginning of each of the volumes of his diary, Kaplan was in the habit of writing quotations from some of the books he was reading.

Felix Adler in An Ethical Philosophy of Life, p. 225 (Sunday, January 24, 1932)

"Ay, think of it—wish it done—will it to boot

"But do it —! No, that's past my understanding." Peer Gynt. (May 21, 1932)

Can We Teach Honesty While We Deceive Ourselves?

WEDNESDAY, MAY 28, 1930

While we were discussing three or four students who had been reported as unpromising for the rabbinate because they were considered lacking either in personality or in mental ability, Morris Levine became very much wrought up. He communicated only to Finkelstein and to me what it was that excited him. "What are we doing," he said under his breath, "to give these men what they need most?" In the hubbub of the meeting the other members of the Faculty did not hear this question and went on stolidly with the discussion which ended in the decision to drop the men in question.

Worst of all a number of students in both institutions go to the extent of cheating at the examinations which are supposed to be conducted according to the honor system. This is true of those who are preparing themselves for the rabbinate no less than of those who are preparing themselves to teach Jewish children religion and ethics. But why should we be surprised? What are we doing to inculcate in the students a respect for truth? Is the entire approach to the fundamental problems of tradition marked by a spirit of truth? Even if we wanted to inculcate honesty we couldn't very well do it, because we would have to begin with ourselves. We would have to prove to them that we are doing and saying nothing to deceive ourselves and the rest of the world. That's expecting too much. Isn't it?

Rabbinical Students Found Wanting, but Not Felix Adler

THURSDAY, MAY 29, 1930

The five graduates of the Seminary this year had as their assignment in my subjects the preparation of five sermon outlines based upon propositions which they were to find in various books that I had suggested to them. If the seminary students had taken the proper attitude toward their studies they would have welcomed the opportunity of working out material they could make use of subsequently in the ministry. But unfortunately as victims of a lot of professional erudition which has not the remotest bearing on present day life, they are forced to skimp in their Midrash and Homiletics. Instead, however, of coming to me like men and placing their difficulties in the proper light they leave the task I assign to them to the very last minute and hand in some superficially thought out and hastily gotten up outline as the equivalent of finals in the subjects I teach. Sophomores in college would be ashamed to hand in that kind of stuff for their courses in English.

The Faculty meeting to pass on the candidates for graduation took place yesterday afternoon. Even this non-descript stuff which these men worked out was handed to me only a few hours before I had to go to the meeting. I was very much peeved at their inconsiderateness and general attitude and reported at the meeting that only one man's work was satisfactory. The Faculty decided that a telegram be sent to each of the men asking them to meet me this morning at 10.

I don't want to go through that kind of experience again. I felt as though I was a peddler trying to get these men to pay me enough to defray the mere cost of some article that I was trying to sell them, and as though they were haggling to force me to sell it to them at a cut-throat rate. I have seldom felt so cheap. They succeeded in cheapening themselves and me. The entire argument was on the lowest possible plane. An institution that can thus evoke the worst in people's nature is hardly qualified to train men for a high spiritual vocation.

This afternoon I attended the graduation exercises of the Ethical Culture School at Fieldston because my Naomi was one of the graduates. The exercises were simple and dignified. Felix Adler spoke. What he said was so much more spiritual and exalting and so much more beautifully expressed than anything I ever heard at the graduation exercises of the Seminary that I felt sad to think of our spiritual sterility. But what saddened me most was the striking contrast between the high minded elimination of all prizes and honors at these exercises and the petty spirited emphasis upon awards at our Seminary graduation exercises.

Shir Ha-Shirim Rabba[29] — *To Edit or Not to Edit*

SATURDAY NIGHT, MAY 31, 1930

When I visited Prof. Davidson last week he awakened in me that ambition to edit the text of *Shir Hashirim Rabba*. Last night was the first time I had a chance to take a look at the material I had collected a long time ago for that purpose. This led to my rummaging among my old papers. I came across a number of things I had done a good deal of work on but never consummated because of my lack of experience in publishing. This

---

29. While Kaplan was in Europe on his honeymoon in 1908 he copied a manuscript of the midrash on *Shir Ha-Shirim Rabba* (The Song of Songs) which he intended to use along with other manuscripts to publish a critical edition of this midrash. He also may have had this in mind as the dissertation for his doctorate. He never finished the project.

rummaging is like reminiscing with oneself. Once I get started I find it difficult to stop. It was 11:30 when I began and I stayed up till 3:30. My ambition cooled down a good deal as I studied the material once again. The difference between the reconstructed text that I might publish and the one extant now is so slight as far as the substance of the ideas is concerned that I fail to see why I should spend all the time that the editing would require. I feel certain that Jewish life and thought would be much more advanced if I were to continue working on Jewish ideology and relate it to questions of present import.

After having sat up so late last night I could not get up in time to go to services this morning, and if I had gotten up my mind would not work with sufficient rapidity to enable me to preach impromptu as I did last week. I therefore stayed in bed instead of attending services. But such is the force of habit that all day I have been feeling as though I had been out on a debauch last night. It takes me a long time to get over the ill effect of an omission in my routine activities.

A Conversation with Shalom Spiegel

SATURDAY NIGHT, MAY 31, 1930

A short while after . . . Dr. Shalom Spiegel called. His coming was a tonic. I talked my heart out to him, but instead of merely giving assent to my tale of woe, he made me feel that I was wrong in being despondent. His faith in the future of the Jewish people and in the ultimate establishment of a Jewish national home proved strong enough to silence my doubts. Without the least excitement he spoke in his fine musical voice and in a Hebrew that glowed with beauty concerning the eternal verities in the Jewish heritage and the love of the heroic that still lingers in many a Jewish youth. I suppose I wanted to be convinced that I was wrong in allowing myself to be disheartened. Anyhow, I consider every minute of the two and a quarter hours he stayed well spent.

He made an interesting point when he said that having women teachers in the Hebrew schools was a serious mistake. The most important element in education is the personality of the teacher. More essential than the knowledge which the school transmits to the child is the type of personality it can hold up to him as a goal for him to strive after. If we can get the child to be as ambitious of being a teacher as to be a policeman or fireman we have really achieved what we aim for. For that reason it is essential that the teacher should be a young man who possesses all the qualities of a successful scout master as well as those of a good pedagogue.

This leads me to the further conclusion that the most fundamental need of Jewish life is for the Jewish community to select a group of young men of unusual ability and train them for various positions of leadership in education, the rabbinate and social work.

A Religion Based on Experience—How to Teach It

FRIDAY, JUNE 20, 1930

In the future a religion will have to be based upon experience. This implies that a group which will express its life, its memories and aspirations in terms of religion will seek to establish the validity of its religion by upholding its universal character, by demonstrating wherein it conforms with the universal principles of human experience. The particularity of the religion will not consist in the profession of some truth or teaching that is necessarily defined by the religion of some other group, but in the fact that the experience upon which are based and in terms of which are expressed the teachings and practices of a particular religion are drawn from the life of the group professing that religion. Some such understanding of the mutual relations of religions to one another is indispensable to those who themselves adhere to and seek to get others to adhere to their inherited religion in an age as ours when religious tolerance has come to be adopted as an ethical standard and not merely as a political necessity. . . .

The teaching of religious folklore should be distinguished from the teaching of history not only in the nature of the content but chiefly in the type of approach. All that comes under the head of folklore should be treated as poetry and as the product of the imagination. The child nowadays is told in the course of his general education stories concerning which it never occurs to him to ask whether they were true or not. Although the division between fact and fiction is for him rather vague especially in his younger years, as soon as that division begins to be clearly perceived by him those stories which were not intended as an account of actual happenings fall easily into the category of legend or myth without his having to go through the process of mental struggle and readjustment. It is that very struggle and readjustment that we must spare the child when we teach him any of the narrative parts in which God figures as a participant or as interlocutor. All these facts must be given to the child as ancient religious folklore not as history fact. Why should not the child realize that the Greek myths he studies at school are the religious folklore of the Greeks? Our ancestors had likewise stories in which they tried to express their religious beliefs. But while the Greek myths have one kind of beauty, the Jewish myths have a different kind of beauty. If the stories of creation, the flood, the patriarchs, Moses, Israel in the wilderness, etc., were told in this spirit there would be once and for all an end to that mental conflict which has alienated our youth from the Jewish religion.

Gratitude as the Basic Religious Virtue—How to Teach It

SUNDAY, JUNE 22, 1930

But neither the history of the Jewish religion nor Jewish religious folklore constitutes religion. Those two subjects are necessary merely to clear the ground for the teaching of religion proper so that it be unencumbered by misconceptions. Religion proper consists not in talking or thinking about what other people believed, felt or acted but in personal experience. The problem before us is how to elicit from the child of today the kind of religious experience which makes for growth of personality and capacity for wholesome self-adjustment to life. Recalling that religion is essentially the experience of the worthwhileness and significance of reality as a whole of the individual human being and of the group to which one belongs our task is to foster in the child these phases of worthwhileness and significance. We are evidently confronted with a task similar to that of fostering in the child an appreciation of the beautiful in nature and in the arts. The initial step is to establish some point of contact in the inner life of the child to which we might transfer whatever of worthwhileness or significance we ourselves are able to discover. That point of contact is presented by the inherent capacity for thankfulness. It is as impossible for a person who is devoid of a native sense of gratitude to have religious experience as it is for the tone deaf to appreciate music. It is the capacity for thankfulness which enables a person to discern elements of worthwhileness and significance in life. Fortunately the average child possesses it to a sufficient degree to serve as starting point for the training in religion.

The training in religion may be divided into two parts, instruction and practice. The instruction should consist mainly of discussion between the teacher and class. Where the purpose is to produce not merely verbal knowledge but inner experience of some kind text books are out of the question, because inner experience can be called forth only by the teacher establishing a point of contact with the actual knowledge and interests of the child. The purpose of the discussion should be 1) to articulate the feeling of thankfulness; 2) to socialize it; and 3) to relate it to the conception of God.

These three purposes are not to be thought of as disparate aims but as constituting the elements indispensable to the translation of the capacity for thankfulness into religious experience. To articulate the feeling of thankfulness is to get the child to identify the specific facts in his experience he has reason to be grateful for. In order to enable each child to express himself fully and frankly it might be advisable to have them state in writing the things they actually and truly feel grateful for. It might even be necessary to resort to anonymity in order to break down all barriers of embarrassment. The teacher should then take up each specific statement and point out some of the larger relationships and implications of that which the child mentions as the object that evoked his gratitude. Let us say the child is thankful that he got a new suit. This should be the occasion for the teacher to point out some of the elements in the network of material labor exchange and good will which has made it possible for his parents to buy him the suit. All the knowledge that the child acquires in his general training should be brought to play in the process of articulating and deepening the experience of gratitude.

It is evident that it would be dangerous to emphasize the child's thankfulness for having his new suit without reminding him that there are numerous children whose parents cannot afford to buy for them new suits. A sense of thankfulness for the advantages one enjoys without sympathetic realization of the many who are deprived of that advantage begets a self complacency that is more offensive than ingratitude. To prevent any such self complacency from gaining headway the teacher should point out that the thankfulness which the little boy feels on account of his having gotten a new suit would remain a mere form of selfish indulgence unless it found an outlet in some kindly act or act of rectification so that when he will grow up he will be able to do his share toward widening the scope of human welfare.

After a while the child should be gotten to experience thankfulness not only for the good that accrues to him individually, but to all those to whom he is related by ties of blood and friendship. Gradually as the circle of social self-identification is enlarged through his general studies and contacts it is important that thankfulness for the good fortune enjoyed by those with whom the child learns to identify himself should be articulated and socialized. An example of that is the victorious outcome of a war about which he may have learned in the history of his country.

In the hands of an able teacher the child's capacity for thankfulness and for converting that thankfulness into creative energy will come to feed not only upon the limited range of the child's own life, but upon the wealth of human attainment which man has built up as a dyke to keep out the limitless chaos that threatens to engulf him. The entire range of things true, good and beautiful will come to be appreciated by the child in a spirit that will compel him to add to their sum in accordance with the gifts that are his. It is in this connection that the teacher will have occasion to place all outstanding individuals and movements that help to render life worthwhile in such a light as to enable the child to see in them the true index of what human life should strive to be and do.

Parallel with the widening of the relationships and implications of the objects that elicit gratefulness will be the deepening of the conception of God which will not be given to him in catechismic form, but in the form of ever renewed restatement. In each such restatement the teacher will have to counteract the tendency to anthropomorphism and accustom the mind of the child to associate a sense of reality with those tendencies in the world that call for and justify human gratitude. Conceived as belonging to the one organically inter-related world those tendencies in their togetherness constitute God. How all religions in general and the Jewish religion in particular have approximated this conception of God would naturally form an important part of these discussions after the pupil has become habituated to this kind of presentation of religious ideas.

Should it be said that it is impossible to expect of the average teacher who is used to having his subject matter all set out for him in text books and divided into lessons and who is helpless the moment he has to work out the subject matter himself, the answer is that the teaching of religion should not be entrusted to the average teacher. There is no reason why the average teacher should be expected to teach a subject which requires considerable specialization. We have special teachers for music and for arts and crafts. The master of the main results of research in the field of religion and the communication of it to others to say nothing of the possession of a special temperament and happy combination of sense of reality, a poetic sense and a highly ethical disposition, are possible only to those who would specialize in the science and pedagogy of religion. It would be a happy consequence of these our deliberations if they would have the effect of persuading rabbinical institutions to train their graduates in religion and a still happier consequence if they would ultimately induce men and women who devote themselves exclusively to teaching to qualify themselves as teachers of religion with that same concentration and attention to pedagogic details as those who qualify as teachers of a subject like music or the arts.

The instruction of religion must culminate in religious practice. Apart from the translation of the sense of thankfulness or of worthwhileness into conduct in all its aspects, a process which must be left to each child to work out for himself, it is necessary to train the child to translate that sense into the practice of worship. In the light of the distinction that we have drawn between religion of the past and the religion of the future, worship will henceforth not be used as a means of petitioning God as though he were a benevolent despot to grant us favors, to bring into existence such environmental conditions as are entirely beyond our control. Worship will have but the one function, that of imbuing us with the God consciousness, or the consciousness of life's worthwhileness. It will therefore express itself as it has expressed itself in all highly developed religion, namely in words and gestures of "tehillah" rather than "tefillah" of praise rather than of prayer. Worship is a sense of worthwhileness in action. That sense to become so potent as to function in times of stress and temptation must be cultivated by practice. The teaching and discussion of life's worth is after all confined to the hour of instruction, the experience of it is necessary at every moment of the day and every day of one's life. Hence the need of frequent acts of affirmation of the active principle that gives meaning to human existence. This is the function of the benedictions which formed part of the religious regimen of the Jew. If we do not deem it necessary as did the traditionalist to recite a hundred benedictions a day, the recital of some benedictions in the spirit of religion as we have interpreted it is spiritually rewarding. There is always the argument that routine deadens spontaneity, and the purely mechanical religiosity of the masses is held up as a warning of what the practice of such a religious device is likely to degenerate into. It is forgotten however that mechanical religiosity was the concomitant mainly of the traditional conception and practice of religion, when religion was for the masses a form of theurgy, and there was supposed to reside an inherent virtue in the religious act apart from the awareness of the one who performed it as to any meaning it was to have for him. Deprecating as we do any religion but that which is translated into terms of conscious experience, we have no fear that outward gesture will reduce the awareness of that experience.

But it is especially through religious service, participated in by large numbers of children, that the spirit of thankfulness which is the form which the child's sense of life's worthwhileness first takes can achieve that expression which will make religion a vital and interesting experience to him. It is through religious service that Jewish education should bring to bear upon the child all of those factors which influence not by means of ideation but by means of emotional impressiveness. All the artistic skills of the children should be enlisted in rendering religious service an occasion of joyous self-expression on the part of the children, in which the joy emanates not from the animal spirit of the child but from that distinctively human trait of human thankfulness. We do not in the least deprecate the joy which comes from the animal spirits, but we certainly need also the other which has its roots in the higher potentialities of the child. The distinctive mark of the latter kind of joy is that instead of expressing itself in hilariousness it expresses itself in the attitude of reverence. It is thus that we may hope to implant in the child a reverence which is genuine because it is an outgrowth of his own religious experience.

All this implies the need of organizing religious services for the children as an integral part of their Jewish training. To expect them to develop genuine religious experience of the kind that is compatible with our present ideas of religion by participating in adult services is to fly in the fact of all pedagogic principles. We have no right to draw any inferences from the influence exercised on children in former generations by the public worship of adults, for then the atmosphere was charged with the spirit of theurgy, and the influence was one which simply subdued or frightened the child into the vague fear of an anthropomorphic god. So long as people enjoyed having that kind of religion adult worship was the best thing for the child. But since the average adult service today has lost the spirit of theurgy and has so far evolved nothing to take its place, the child is merely bored and is forced to attend and is so fed up that as soon as he leaves his parents' home he gives the synagogue a wide berth.

From the standpoint of the need of revitalizing the element of religion in Jewish life, there is little hope that it will be possible to do very much with the adult. It is only a new generation brought up to look upon religion not as a matter of unassimilated and irrelevant tradition but of personal experience in which whatever tradition enters is related to the whole of one's outlook, that will be qualified to carry through the great spiritual reformation which Jewish life must undergo if it is to justify itself to the millions of Jews who are fated to remain in the Diaspora.

FRIDAY, JUNE 24, 1930

On Friday, June 6, I went to see a physician (Dr. Simon Ruskin of 351 West 86 St) about my right ear which seemed stopped up and caused a peculiar sensation in my head when I spoke. My ear annoyed me considerably when I had to deliver a sermon, making it quite difficult for me to concentrate my mind on what I was speaking. That condition of the ear had lasted for about two weeks when I thought that it was time for me to have it attended to. Several treatments which the physician gave me have done it good. I also want to record that I have been taking the hay fever treatment regularly about twice a week and that I have not been troubled by hay fever since the attack during the last week in April.

Work on "The Book" Going Well—Tasting "the Bliss of Serenity"

WEDNESDAY, JULY 16, 1930

I have been steadily at work the last few weeks on *Judaism as a Civilization* and could not get myself to spend time on anything else. This accounts for my allowing so long an interval to elapse without making any entries into the journal. Except for a day or two of depression caused by articles in this month's Harper's and Atlantic Monthly dealing with Zionism and unemployment, I have on the whole been in a contented frame of mind. On days like yesterday and today when the weather was ideal and I was able to work uninterruptedly from early morning till late at night except for swimming and occasional walks, I tasted the bliss of serenity.

Last Friday (July 11, 1930) I converted to Judaism Miss Yvonne Daget. Dr. Joshua Frankel and Samuel Dinin acted as witnesses. The ceremony and the immersion took place at the YWHA building on West 110 St.

In the afternoon I officiated at Miss Daget's marriage to Max Spielberg at 1 West 81 St. Everything went off well that day.

A Philosophical Dialogue on the Nature of Evil

THURSDAY, JULY 24, 1930

For want of any one to discuss with some of my ideas on religion and Judaism I have resorted to writing out my thoughts in this journal. The chapter I wrote last summer on Torah as a Way of Life and the one I wrote a few weeks ago on the teaching of religion will find their place in *Judaism as a Civilization* though in considerably reorganized and amended form. I should now like to engage my ego and my alter in a discussion on the problem of all problems "Has life any meaning?"

I am interested just now in developing the thought that modern religion cannot accept any of the traditional solutions of the problem of evil, and must therefore try some new way out of the impasse. Otherwise religion hasn't a leg to stand on.

A. What do you understand by traditional solutions?

E. According to the traditional approach evil is subject to one of three possibilities. One possibility is that suffering serves no good whatever; a second is that a certain amount of good results but far too small to be accounted as a compensation for the suffering; and a third is that the good fully compensates for the suffering. Traditional theology has been hard at work proving that the third possibility is the actual one.

A. What's wrong with that?

E. It falls back on the old fallacy which maintained that if you could prove that evil is a means to good it is evil no longer. Even on the assumption that evil brings about good the question still remains why should suffering be necessary at all in the scheme of things? Could not the good have been achieved without suffering being a necessary means? I am aware of the reply you have in mind. You probably want to say that we could not appreciate anything as a good unless there were evil to offset it. This is sophistry. For the question may again be put why is the mind so constituted that it needs suffering as a means to the awareness of the good? The main weakness of the traditional theology is due to the fact that it assumes that God is perfect. On the assumption that the world is not only divine or if you will divinely governed, but that the God of the world is also perfect, nothing is gained even if we succeed in proving that the existence of evil is a means to overwhelming good. But perfection is in my opinion a perfectly useless and gratuitous conception which is responsible for the snarl in our thinking about religion. What I am interested in is not to prove that God is perfect but that there is a God. It is immaterial to me whether He is perfect or not.

A. What do you gain by believing in God if you are not sure that He is perfect? And how would your belief in God help you to deal with the problem of Evil?

E. Since I am interested merely in proving the existence of God the important concept for me is not perfection but meaning. I do not feel called upon to argue away the existence of evil. On the contrary from the standpoint of meaning, evil which serves as a background for good may be an actual necessity. Meaning demands contrasts.

A. You read this morning about the earthquake in Naples and the neighboring sections of Italy where hundreds of lives were lost, thousands injured and many more thousands rendered homeless. You also read the long list of earthquakes in Japan, India, Portugal and Italy in which human beings by the myriads were crushed like flies. Do you want to imply that all that havoc was necessary in order to give meaning to your sheltered existence?

E. Now don't get indignant. I am only feeling my way. I am not making any dogmatic assertions, nor trying to come off easily. I want you to help me to think this through. Of the three possibilities I mentioned traditional theology has tried to prove that the last possibility corresponds to fact. It could do that because it knew so little about the world and allowed its imagination to run away with it when it spoke of God. If you feel that in order to have religion God must be shown to be perfect then you must show that every evil is a means to good, or is compensated by some good. But I feel no such urge. In order that the world shall have meaning I do not need to assume that evil is a means to good or is more or less compensated for. What I have to be sure of is that the evil in the world shall be somewhat more *counterbalanced* by the good. The evil instead of being a means to the good is merely an occasion. All that I have to be sure of is that the sum of existence is increasing in life and mind and not decreasing. If I can be sure that the direction in which Reality is moving is toward more order, more uniqueness and more love, then I am satisfied that Reality has meaning or pattern. It is that meaning or pattern which gives to Reality the character of godhood and which demands that my life fall in with it. This is what we understand by human life being spiritual.

A. This is too good to be true. At times you seem to be straining for gnats, and when it suits you to swallow whole camels. Do you think that I did not notice how you bootlegged an assumption which is no less pretentious than those you reject? You have assumed nothing less than the fact that in Reality there is more good than evil. Since when have you become so expert a cosmic accountant as to be able to balance the good against the evil and in such a confidence strike a balance sheet in which good is on the credit side?

E. Please don't impute me sins of which I am innocent. Did I not say "If I can be sure that the direction of Reality is such and such?" *I am merely stating what I need to be sure of in order to have religion.* In spite of your poking fun at my ability as a cosmic accountant I feel that I or any one with a sufficient knowledge of reality and a clear head could take cosmic stock much more readily than prove that every evil is a means to some good. Which means that to have religion we merely have to satisfy a reasonable and not an unreasonable demand. This is a considerable gain on the traditional theology.

A. What warrant have you for saying that what you demand is capable of being supplied?

E. Because the mere fact that there is now more of life and mind than there was let us say during the ice age, should make it easy to prove that the world is not running down.

A. But what about the return of the ice age which geologists foretell and the ultimate cooling of the sun that the astronomers prognosticate?

E. You can't squelch me with those prophecies. I can meet you on your own ground. If you want me to think in astronomical terms then I must set up the creation of new suns and new worlds to console us for the ultimate destruction of the one we belong to. I would advise you, however, to leave the dizzy spaces alone, come down to earth and see what the span of existence within our mental purview has to offer us on the question whether there is more than enough good in the world to counterbalance the evil.

A. I am impatient to know how you expect to proceed with your stock taking.

E. I hope you will not accuse me of juggling when I show you that the matter of stock taking is not as difficult as it seems. The reason it seems so overwhelmingly difficult to you is that you imagine I shall ask you to detach ourselves from our own lives and minds and stand as it were outside of the universe and then have some one reach over to us all the good things in it and all the evil while we keep piling them on the scales and watching which way the needle points. Dismiss that from your mind. That way of doing things was common with theologians. They pretended they were able to rise mentally above Reality and take it all in with one glance, until we came along and proved to them they were only kidding themselves.

A. Now you've got me all puzzled. I suspect you are actually guilty of the word juggling you are afraid I'll charge you with.

E. I have purposely forewarned you so that you might be on the lookout for anything that is questionable. What I want to make plain to you is that in order to find whether or not the good counterbalances the evil it is neither necessary nor possible to detach yourself from yourself to do so. Whatever we think about the world is inevitably conditioned by our own needs. Why hide that fact? Rather make use of it openly and accept its consequences unprotestingly.

A. I still don't see what you are driving at.

E. The point is this. If you want to know whether the good counterbalances the evil, ask yourself, Can human life be improved and enhanced despite all that we know of the evil which exists in the world? Is it possible for man to escape the dire consequences of such disasters as earthquakes and hurricanes? There can be no question of his ability to overcome all man made evils. There is equally little doubt that with the application of intelligence there is no natural catastrophe against which he cannot protect himself. Man can not escape death but with the proper mental and physical equipment he can anesthetize himself against pain and the fear of death. If these things are possible then the world, that is, man's world which is after all the only world he can know and care about, is so constituted that the measure of good more than counterbalances the measure of evil. A world so constituted can not be meaningless. Of course I realize that in asking you to contemplate the world, I am asking you not to limit your view to the past and present but to take into account the potentialities, the part of reality which is as yet beneath the horizon of actuality. But that is just what the religions of the higher type have always been trying to get man to do with their messiahism, otherworldliness and even nirvana.

A. You've talked a lot, but whether you've said anything I cannot tell you just now. Let me think it over.

WEDNESDAY, JULY 30, 1930

It appears that I have come to another turning point in the process of clarification in the following ideas:

Having reached the generalization that all religions in their manifold variety of self-expression have met the following four needs of the human being a) of controlling the physical environment, b) of discovering meaning in the cosmos, c) of achieving a sense of the supreme worth of personality and d) of being at home in the universe and finding meaning and worth in the civilization which supplies him with basis of personality or meaning in history, the next step is to point out that as a result of the challenge to religion the latter necessarily has entered upon a stage of self-consciousness, the effect of which is to become aware of the fact that the religions have functioned not only in meeting those needs, but meeting them in a spirit that treated those needs as interrelated organically, so that any one need cannot be met without the other. The attempt to ignore their organicity or to treat any one or two of them to the neglect or denial of the other needs always results in spiritual chaos and catastrophe. In other words, power, faith, salvation and loyalty which constitute the four satisfactions of the four needs that give rise to religion must form a pattern governing every act or thought that falls within the scope of any of the satisfactions.

11

August 1, 1930–October 18, 1931

On the Existence of God—A New Way

FRIDAY, AUGUST 1, 1930

The trouble with traditional religion is that it fails to distinguish between the language of fact and the language of aspiration. The statement that God is perfect if formulated accurately would read, "we want to find the world meaningful, and our place in it such as to give meaning to our lives." Traditional religion looks at the wrong end of the telescope. What we need is not a new philosophy of life but the proper code by which to decipher the eternal human quest in the various constructs called religions. The conventional approach consisted in proposing the assumption that there is a God and then spinning out of that assumption such qualities as we must affirm concerning Him. The typical inference that was thus spun out was that since God must be conceived as perfect otherwise he would not be God, and since perfection is inconceivable without existence therefore God necessarily exists. And so one quality after another. Such an absurd game (for such reasoning is nothing more than intellectual ping-pong) can hardly be taken seriously. Instead therefore of the conventional approach, the question we should seek to answer is "What is the actual need which has led man to affirm the existence of God, and to what extent is that need or any other reflected in the honorific attributes man was in the habit of ascribing to God?"

After having identified those needs and being assured that our well-being demands reckoning with them, the task of religion consists in pointing out how they may be satisfied—partly by ratiocination, but to a far larger degree by living on the assumption that the very existence of those needs implies that the world is inherently so constituted as to gratify them. To live on that assumption involves living a life of high idealism as articulated in the conscience of man's spiritual leaders. The art of religion is like the art of friendship. If I wait to have a friend I do not first develop a theory about some person that he possesses all the qualities that render his company desirable, only to find myself disappointed when actually meeting that person. Instead I am aware that my life demands the society of a person I can call my friend. I then proceed to make various overtures, act as friendly as I can toward the person whose friendship I wish to secure, and before I know it my purpose is attained.

Kaplan Annoyed at Kadushin's Criticisms of His MS

TUESDAY, AUGUST 12, 1930

I do not think I am so vain as to resent criticism. Nothing so bores me as unqualified praise of what I have said or written. Why, then, was I annoyed at the way Kadushin who stayed over the weekend at Long Branch and who spent some time reading my manuscript criticized some of the points developed in it? There is a certain note of captiousness in the way he states his opinions. It appears in his failure to get the full force of the point he criticizes, and more especially in his manner which betrays the apprehension that I do not like to hear any criticism.

As a matter of fact, I am very grateful to him for having called my attention to the unsatisfactory character of the chapter which deals with the Kehillah. After some effort he succeeded in making himself clear as to what he thought was wrong with it. He maintained that I failed to take advantage of present day organization of Jewish life and tried to construct something entirely new and artificial. I admit that he is entirely right in his contention. This means that I have to rewrite that entire chapter.

Idea of Judaism as a Civilization Taking Hold

FRIDAY, AUGUST 15, 1930

We should make part of our national literature the two books of the Maccabees, Ben Sirah and Philo's Commentaries.

SUNDAY, AUGUST 17, 1930

I experienced one of the greatest surprises of my life when I came across in the CCAR[1] report the following answer to a questionnaire sent to Reform Rabbis in 1925–26.

"Is the trend toward placing less emphasis on Judaism as a cult and

---

1. CCAR is the Central Conference of American Rabbis, the rabbinical organization of Reform Judaism.

more emphasis on Judaism as a civilization, i.e. identifying it with all the activities and relations of life?"

	North	South	West	East
Cult	3	8	4	15
Civilization	20	12	18	50

Yearbook Central Conference, American Rabbis 1926, p. 320

How Wonderful to Work

THURSDAY, AUGUST 28, 1930

This is a great life! To sit carefree in a genially warm sun the better part of the day and keep on reading and writing and to feel that one's ideas about life are falling into their proper places giving to life certain order and design and meaning—this is paradise. This is the way I have been spending my time the greater part of the ten weeks that I have been here in West End.[2] Not that this state of placid serenity is unbroken by the thought that this bliss cannot last forever, that millions of people are out of work or are afflicted with some fatal disease, that the status of the Jews throughout the world is still very doubtful. But I was at least able to shake off these thoughts for a time and to go on with my work.

I have just referred to my work. What is it? To help redeem Jewish life in this country from the primeval chaos into which it has been thrust. And then what? A strange simile comes to mock me. There is a craze just now known as Tom Thumb Golf, an imitation of what [sentence ends here].

"The Tradition is Untenable"—Explaining This to His Mother

MONDAY, SEPTEMBER 1, 1930

Last Friday I received a copy of the book on "Intelligent Philanthropy"[3] which includes the article on "Jewish Philanthropy: Traditional and Modern" which I wrote two summers ago. My mother, who was here in West End with us for the last five weeks, read the article with great avidity. I was afraid that as soon as she would start reading it she would take offense at my denial of the traditional conception of the Torah. She

---

2. Probably in New Jersey.
3. "Jewish Philanthropy," in *Intelligent Philanthropy*, ed. Ellsworth Faris, Farris Laune, and Arthur J. Todd (Chicago: University of Chicago Press, 1930), 52–89.

evidently read the beginning too hurriedly to grasp fully its meaning, and as she kept on reading was very much delighted with the number of rabbinic passages quoted in the text. In fact she repeated more than once that she was especially grateful for having been persuaded to remain over this weekend with us, otherwise she probably would not have known about the article. Yesterday, however, an hour before her leaving she seemed rather sad. When I came near she got up from the couch on which she was lying restlessly and said to me, "There is something in the book I don't quite understand and which I don't think I like." Then turning to the first page of the article and pointing to the sentence "We regard as untenable the tradition that Moses" etc. She asked me explain that sentence to her and to tell her the meaning of the word untenable. Of course I told her exactly what the words meant. The scales fell from her eyes. "That's the old trouble over again," she said bitterly.

A Shabbos *Afternoon with J. D. Eisenstein*

MONDAY, SEPTEMBER 1, 1930

The afternoon of last Saturday I spent also arguing that we should not base our right to existence upon our being a superior people. That time, however, it was against two men who believed that we actually were a superior people, J. D. Eisenstein,[4] the editor of the Hebrew Encyclopedia and compiler of ever so many other collections of Hebrew writings, and Rabbi Metz.

Incidentally I must add that when J. D. Eisenstein had told me in the morning that he would come to see me I was rather taken aback. I had always looked upon him as strictly Orthodox in his views and an outspoken antagonist of the Seminary. He is in his 76th year. Consequently I wondered what could he and I talk about without immediately clashing in our views. Then again there was mother sitting in the house near the window about which Eisenstein, Metz, Rabbi Eugene Kohn, Hyams (a fellow student at the seminary of Ira Eisenstein, a grandson of the old man) and a local Hebrew teacher, Kimmel, were seated. I was therefore more than pleased when I found that I could expound my views openly and frankly while the old man Eisenstein sat calmly listening. To what shall I attribute this change of attitude? To the fact that his grandson is a student at the Seminary and that I am taking an interest in him? That would mean that one ounce of friendship and personal interest is worth more than a pound of argument.

---

4. Judah David Eisenstein (1854–1956), Hebraist; author; encyclopedist; translator; grandfather of Ira and Myron Eisenstein.

"Jews Without Money"—A Great Book[5]

WEDNESDAY, SEPTEMBER 3, 1930

I have been in a black mood again the last couple of days. I have not been able to make any headway with my writing. On top of that came the letter from mother asking me to recant. The latter made me feel ashamed of her and her religion. In it she tried to bribe me with the promise of popular acclaim and to threaten me that I would be the cause of her losing her mind. In my reply to her letter I tried to be as restrained as I possibly could, but naturally I could not refrain from telling her that she was exploiting her weakness to the utmost in asking me to be false to myself and my convictions.

I seem to have reached for a while a saturation point in dealing with abstract ideas and ideals. Wanting to steep myself in the seething chaos of life but being condemned to a career of impotent spectatorship, the only thing to do is to pick up some book which might at least give me a picture of the grim realities. This is how, despite the approaching holidays and the multitude of perfectly stupid and useless things that will soon have to occupy my days, I put everything aside and read through today Michael Gold's *Jews Without Money*. And I am not in the least sorry that I did it. It has had the effect on me that Aristotle ascribes to Greek tragedy. The book had been in my house for the last few months, but I refrained from reading it because from the opinions that some people gave me of it I thought it was another one of those East Side literary garbage cans that Ornitz began parading with his *Haunch Paunch and Jowl*.[6] Instead I found myself reading a veritable martyrology of the Jewish people.

The book cured me of the superficial and light hearted tirade I was going to launch against our people for doing nothing to prevent gangsterism and racketeering. I realized as I never did before that these festering sores in the body of our people are the outcome of the American capitalistic order. If there is any charge that one has a right to bring against our people, it is the charge not of heartlessness but of stupidity. If as a people we possessed any gleam of intelligence we ought to have acclaimed a book like *Jews Without Money* as the outcry of a prophet whose heart writes with pain over the sufferings not alone of his people but of all suffering humanity. I would go out of my way to claim Michael Gold as a Jew of Jews much sooner than I would to claim Spinoza. How much pathos and passion for righteousness in the last page!

---

5. Michael Gold (Irwin Granich) (1893–1967), communist author; edited *Liberator*; author, *Jews Without Money*, one of best known accounts of Jewish immigrant life; wrote a column for *The Daily Worker*.

6. Samuel Badisch Ornitz (1890–1957), New York City social worker; author; wrote *Haunch, Paunch and Jowl*, a novel critical of upwardly mobile Jews; advocated assimilation.

"At times I seriously thought of cutting my throat. . . . I developed a crazy streak. . . . I prayed on the tenement roof in moonlight to the Jewish Messiah who would redeem the world. . . .

"A man on an East Side soap-box, one night, proclaimed that out of the despair, melancholy and helpless rage of millions, a world movement had been born to abolish poverty.

"I listened to him.

"O workers' Revolution, you brought hope to me, a lonely suicidal boy. You are the true Messiah. You will destroy the East Side when you come, and build there a garden for the human spirit.

"O Revolution, that forced me to think, to struggle and to live.

"O Great Beginning!"

Judaism and the World to Come

MONDAY, SEPTEMBER 22, 1930

I am just now trying to polish up the statement in the beginning of "Judaism as a Civilization" which bears on the question of exclusive salvation. The matter is as plain as a pikestaff. The Jews held in common with all Christian and Mohammedan believers that the goal of life was in the world as it will be after God will have changed the present order, and with them agreed that only those who gave their allegiance to the revealed will of God were qualified for life in the world to come. Yet simple as this fact is there is not a single Jewish writer past or present that seems to grasp it. Maimonides is so entangled in Aristotelianism that he can't see straight. To him *Olam Ha-Ba* [Heb. the world to come] is the doctrine of bodiless immortality which has come down from Greek philosophy. The modern writers fall over themselves trying to prove that the Jews offered free admission to everybody. N. Guttman and J. Z. Lauterbach[7] resort to all kinds of pilpulistic sophistry to prove their point. I actually tremble with indignation that men noted for scholarship should be so obtuse in so simple a matter. What then could be expected of them in matters that are inherently difficult and complicated?

I consulted the Jewish Encyclopedia to see whether it had anything on Olam Ha-ba or Other Worldliness. Not a word. Under the heading salvation, Emil G. Hirsch discusses the meaning of *Yesha* [Heb. salvation] and *Geulah* [Heb. redemption] and it never occurs to him that he was on the threshold of the most significant idea of the great traditional religions. What an idiot!

---

7. Jacob Zallel Lauterbach (1873–1942), Ph.D. Gottingen; rabbi; Talmudic scholar; faculty, Hebrew Union College; editor, *Jewish Encyclopedia*.

The Kol Nidre Caper

MONDAY, SEPTEMBER 29, 1930

But the greatest source of annoyance and vexation at this time of the year has been the SAJ. Like a harbinger of a plague Rosenblatt accosted me the Sabbath before Rosh Hashanah and started pestering me that I should compromise on the matter of Kol Nidre.[8] I told him that I regarded the question closed and begged him not to discuss it with me any further. For a few days after that I began to sense a storm gathering. A letter arrived from J. Klein in which he practically threatened that he would resign from the presidency if we will not restore the Kol Nidre. Then Joe Levy called on me last Sunday with the request that I do something to quiet the growing discontent. He and I finally decided that I should meet some of the ringleaders of the agitation and try to persuade them not to have the Kol Nidre restored. Harry Liebovitz had arranged for a dinner to take place tonight at the yacht room of the Astor Hotel to consider the financial situation of the SAJ. Levy arranged that I should meet those who expected to be at the dinner for an hour or so before the dinner. I followed his suggestion and came to the hotel a little before six this evening. . . .

This group of men went at me hammer and tongs for over two hours. They bullied, they cajoled, they flattered me to get me to yield. I held out to the end. At first the discussion turned on the Kol Nidre as such. Under no circumstances would I consent to its reinstatement. When it was suggested that only the first two words be retained and also the passage *Miyom Kippurim Zeh . . .* [Heb. From this Day of Atonement . . .] I replied in the same way as I had done in previous years, viz: that if an appropriate text can be devised I might acquiesce. They insisted that I adopt the text quoted in translation in this week's American Hebrew by Elbogen[9] and have it recited this very Yom Kippur. I told them that they had time all year to bring the matter up and to thresh it thoroughly. But it would be childish to act in so serious a matter as a change of the liturgy on the spur of the moment. We might introduce the new version next year. But this year we would have to adhere to what has now become officially the practice of the SAJ. Nothing would move me from that decision.

---

8. In 1925 Kaplan had eliminated the text of Kol Nidre and substituted Psalm 130, though he kept the tune. For more information, see *Judaism Faces the Twentieth Century: A Biography of Mordecai M. Kaplan* (Detroit: Wayne State University Press, 1993).

9. Ismar Elbogen (1874–1943), scholar and historian. See his *Jewish Liturgy—A Comprehensive History by Ismar Elbogen,* trans. Raymond P. Scheindlin (Philadelphia: Jewish Publication Society, 1993), 128.

Eliminating the Second Day of Yom Tov

WEDNESDAY, OCTOBER 8, 1930

Yesterday afternoon Mr. Abe Liebovitz and his wife and their son-in-law W. and his wife, a recently married couple, paid us a Yom Tov [holiday] visit. I think it is the first time in the history of the SAJ that parents have visited me together with their grown up children. Although I stand in well with the older folks of the organization, the young people keep entirely aloof from me, as if I belonged to a different world from theirs. There is more chance of parallel lines meeting than the interests I cherish with those which fill the lives of the sons and daughters of our members.

The conversation opened with their remark about the fine weather we have been having these holidays. For want of anything better to say I remarked, "Thank Goodness the weather isn't anti-Semitic." At this the company brightened up and we were faring capitally for a while, when without notice Mrs. Liebovitz popped the question What I thought of the possibility of doing away with the second day holiday.[10] I inferred from her question that she was in favor of abrogating useless and burdensome institution. Without further ado I blurted out my favorite plan to get the members of the SAJ to pledge themselves in writing to observe the first day of each of the holidays properly as a prerequisite to my abrogation of the second day. Abe Liebovitz expressed his assent, but his wife began raising all kinds of objections. The young people paralleled their elders. It was ridiculous of me to discuss such a matter with them, but what is one to do? Simply to sit back and do nothing?

Before long the conversation veered to the topic "why the young folks are indifferent to Judaism." It had no point. The young Mrs. W., a simpering feminine fop, launched into a tirade against the young folks. "They" and "they" and "they" as if she ever made the least attempt to do or learn anything Jewish in her capacity as one of the young folks.

When people fall into this vein of discourse I am totally nonplussed. How can one fight against a vacuum? Right after they left old man Siegel who is about to celebrate his 71st birthday stopped me on the street and began condoling with me about my trying to work with the wrong kind of people. When I asked him what about his own children—I think he has seven able bodied sons all successful businessmen and one daughter—he replied that they were affiliated with the Ethical Culture group. This irritated me and I almost went off the handle, but I checked myself in time. I could see that he

---

10. A number of Jewish holidays (Passover, Pentecost, and Tabernacles) involve celebration for two days; only one day is mentioned in the Bible. The second day was created so that Jews in the Diaspora would be celebrating the holiday at the same time as Jews in the land of Israel.

wasn't so happy about their ethical culture affiliation, yet I doubt whether he enjoyed having vinegar poured into his wounds.

Believe it or not there is a possibility of my changing my mind about the Kol Nidre and advocating its restoration in the Yom Kippur service. The correspondence between J. D. Eisenstein and myself especially the letter of Oct. 5,[11] has made me see the question in an entirely new light. I do not recall ever having heard or read anywhere an argument in defense of Kol Nidre that sounded so plausible as the one advanced in the letter of October 5. I intend to give further thought to the question and if after a few weeks I will find the argument as plausible as it sounds to me at present, I shall not hesitate to make known my change of mind regardless of the ridicule and disapproval and even insinuations of being vacillating in my views, or a "turncoat" when pressure is brought to bear.

The New Year—The Pull of Zion

SUNDAY, OCTOBER 12, 1930

This has been quite a full day for me. In the morning I dictated the outline for the Shemini Ezeret sermon on "The Meaning of Worship" after having worked on it with Leon Hurwitz,[12] Signer[13] and Jacob Grossman for about three hours last night. I like the idea on which it is based and it promises to turn out a good sermon. Then I read Hebrew for about 3/4 of an hour to get into a Hebrew frame of mind for my work at the Institute. I found no difficulty in teaching for three and a half hours in succession. I am greatly buoyed up by the feeling of at homeness in the new TI building. I experienced a novel and thrilling sensation when I walked over from the TI building to the old Seminary building by way of the colonnade walk. I felt for the first time the way a professor at one of the universities must feel, a sense of belonging and that to an academic institution that molds lives of young people. But I was not destined to enjoy this feeling very long. For when I heard Abraham Halkin[14] who had returned last week from Palestine after a summer's stay there I felt as though I ought to take up the wandering staff again. He emphasized the point that any

---

11. On this correspondence, see *Judaism Faces the Twentieth Century,* 289–90. Kaplan restored the Kol Nidre text but amended it in line with Judah Eisenstein's understanding that the vows in the prayer referred to statements people made in anger that they did not intend. For the amended text, see *Judaism Faces the Twentieth Century,* 290.

12. Leon Hurwitz (1900–), ordained JTS; rabbi, Brooklyn; active in World Jewish Congress, Zionist Organization of America.

13. Isador Signer (1900–1953), ordained JTS; rabbi, Brooklyn; active in the Rabbinical Assembly.

14. Abraham Halkin (1903–90), Semitics scholar; faculty, JTS, CCNY; author; editor, *Encyclopedia Judaica.*

Jew who really believed in Zionism must tear up his stakes and migrate to Palestine.

I am glad I have formulated my conception of Judaism as a civilization. I feel that it is a satisfactory answer to the extremists who insist that Jews must give up all hopes of any kind of Jewish life outside of Palestine. The answer I try to give in the book is that if we really had enough energy to betake ourselves to Palestine, we could use that energy to work out a satisfactory modus vivendi as a Diaspora Nation with Palestine merely as the center. I proceeded to act on this theory right after I was through teaching, for I met a committee of the students and suggested to them to work out a kind of model *minha* [afternoon] service to be conducted during the recess interval. I was happy to find myself using a good and fluent Hebrew and conveying concrete and helpful suggestions as to how they should go about their task and that without having devoted any time to thinking out the matter beforehand.

Being Happy—Set Realistic Goals

MONDAY, OCTOBER 20, 1930

Last Thursday night I enjoyed an hour or so [of] that serenity which I experience so seldom. The fact that I had completed the address I was to deliver at the dedication exercises in less time than I had expected, and that it turned out quite satisfactory, produced in me a state of self-conscious happiness. It was especially while returning from the Institute in the evening after having visited Chertoff's class and indulged in an analysis of the question that I was in an exalted frame of mind. As I was walking through Central Park I thought I caught the secret of happiness as being that of carrying out what you undertake, hence if you want to be happy first make sure of what it is within your power to achieve and work away at that.

Becoming Dean Instead of Principal at the TI—The Real Story

MONDAY, OCTOBER 20, 1930

Oh, yes, I forgot all about the great "honor" that was conferred upon me last night when Adler, in introducing me, informed the audience that the Board of Trustees had offered me and that I had accepted the honor of henceforth being designated as Dean instead of Principal. What a joke! I have an idea that the consent of the Board meant the whispered conversation that Adler had with Unterberg in the lobby of the old Seminary building while we were getting in line for the procession to the large tent in the quadrangle where the Dedication exercises were to take place. It was right then and there also that Adler called me aside and asked me whether I would accept the title Dean. So that's that.

Kol Nidre Again

FRIDAY, NOVEMBER 7, 1930

I was for a long time under the spell of J. D. Eisenstein's argument in favor of Kol Nidre. But with every statement in defense of Kol Nidre that I have had occasion to read recently my former attitude not only awakened but became more confirmed. Adler in the *Mahzor* [High Holiday Prayerbook], Davidson in the Jewish Year Book (5684), Greenstone in his *The Jewish Religion*[15] do not give the least intimation of any such rendering as that suggested by Eisenstein. It is evident that it was never with this rendering in mind that the mass of Jews ever recited Kol Nidre. The irrational attachment to it has all the earmarks of the kind of devotion that primitives entertain toward a fetish. One of the outstanding characteristics of Jewish religion is its abhorrence of fetishes. This is shown in the story of Hezekiah's shattering the brazen serpent (cf. The use made of that story by R. Judah the prince) and of Jeremiah's condemnation of the ark in the Temple.[16]

Taking Care of My Animal—A Typical Day

WEDNESDAY, NOVEMBER 12, 1930

No one, I dare say, could accuse me of not taking good care of myself. Realizing that my spiritual outfit is only of mediocre capacity I knew that I have to be a healthy animal as a prerequisite to being a passable sort of fellow. If what they say about Wilson having forever suffered from headaches and indigestion is true, his career might not have been cut short in its prime had he been in the habit, as I am, of taking a teaspoon of cascara [laxative] daily before going to bed instead of drugging himself with headache powders. I know all this sounds ridiculous, but it is strange what a change in one's Weltanschauung a teaspoon of cascara can effect.

So here is what I have done today to give that animal of mine a chance to thrive. I rose at 9:00 after a sound sleep of six and a half hours, took my daily cold shower (something I have practically never missed the last twenty years) and had breakfast consisting of orange juice, one egg, a cup of

---

15. Julius Greenstone, *The Jewish Religion* (Philadelphia: Hebrew Sunday School Society, 1902).

16. The serpent made of brass by Moses (Numbers 21:4–9) to heal the people was destroyed by King Hezekiah many centuries later (2 Kings 18:4) because "The Israelites had been offering sacrifices to it." Later R. Judah the prince and other sages approved of this action (cf. *The Mishnah*, trans. H. Danby Pesaḥim 4.8. On the ark see Jeremiah 3:16).

coffee and two rolls. I had to be at the Seminary at 10:50. Instead of taking either the subway or taxi I walked the distance which is two full miles in about 36 minutes. I then taught almost continuously till 1:20. The Midrash and Homiletics hours went off snappily. The men were delighted with the outlines of the sermons I gave them, both the oral one on Imperialism and the written one on Social Climbing. Miss May then brought me the 64th Report of the work of the Teachers Institute on which I spent 25 minutes making corrections and then I marched home again. The lunch I found at home was the ideal one for the appetite I had worked up on the walk, oatmeal porridge prepared at my suggestion, asparagus tips on toast in an ocean of cream sauce and a cup of coffee with the dried crumbs of chocolate cake.

As I sat alone and ate the lunch I said to myself, "This is a fair quid pro quo." I gave the world three hours of homiletics and the world gave me back a nourishing lunch. I can never cease marveling at the miracle of exchange of goods and services. Not all the Ten Plagues of Egypt with the dividing of the Red Sea thrown into the bargain can compare in marvelousness with the miracle of exchange that makes it possible for me to get asparagus on toast in exchange for the homiletic interpretation of a few paragraphs of Leviticus Rabba. It is for this marvel of marvels that I thank God whenever I say grace, and I say it quite often with cap on or without a cap.

At three I lay down to take a nap. I woke up at 3:25. I had to be at the dentist's at 4:00. I thought I would just rest another little while, but before I knew it I dozed off and when I woke it was 4:05. I made a dash for my shoes, collar and tie and managed to plant myself in the dentist's chair, five blocks away from where I live, at 4:15. This appointment with the dentist was for the purpose of filling a cavity which I had discovered in one of my teeth the night before.

I think I have justified my claim that I take good care of my animal.

The Kol Nidre—The Book—The Stock Market

THURSDAY, DECEMBER 11, 1930

The sermon on "Parable of a Nation that Forgot its Past" which I delivered a week ago last Saturday, and the one on "Why Religion Is Necessary" delivered last Saturday were very successful. I ascribe the success of the first one to my having based it on the story of the play Siegfried and the success of the second to my having connected it with Einstein's article which appeared recently in the magazine section of the N.Y. Times on Science and Religion. I doubt whether I could have managed to discuss the conception of God from the pulpit, if it had not become the subject of controversy in the press as a result of that article. On the other hand, I suspect that there was not a single person in the audience who really got the full implications of the idea that religion is now entering upon a third stage in its development by becoming cosmic. Anyhow Einstein has rendered us poor preachers a good turn by helping us put across a new idea in religion, something we could never have done ourselves. In playing this role he makes me think of Jacob easily rolling away from the well the huge stone which it required the entire gang of shepherds to remove.

An outcome of my ironic mood is the peaceful settlement which I believe I have finally arrived at in the Kol Nidre controversy. Last Saturday afternoon a committee of the SAJ headed by A. Rosenblatt and consisting of Semel, Jacob Levy, Schwartz, Segal, Thompson and Bromberg came to discuss the question of reintroducing the Kol Nidre. This committee was formed in accordance with my suggestion that the time to discuss the question was during the year and not immediately before Yom Kippur. Fortunately I had given the matter considerable thought. J. D. Eisenstein's interpretation of the Kol Nidre seemed plausible, but to restore the Kol Nidre as it is and merely add a rubric would have placed me in the peculiar position of not having thought of that interpretation in all the years that I am supposed to have studied the question, and would be taken as implying that I was merely yielding to pressure. A few weeks ago as I was about to fall asleep the idea occurred to me that to insert into the Kol Nidre words to the effect that all vows, etc. uttered in anger or undue provocation intended as punishment or revenge, these and only these vows should be null and void.

When I told this to the committee they felt very happy about it. The only man who persisted in asking that the text be left intact was Jacob Levy. Again he recited instances of the people in his acquaintance to whom Kol Nidre was one of the most sacred and solemn institutions in Judaism. He quoted the Grand Street Boys of whom he was one. I wish I had the literary gift to portray that gang. Haunch, Paunch and Jowl describes some of those "boys."

This time the other members of the committee sided with me and spared me the trouble of arguing with him. Semel and Rosenblatt finally squelched him.

The task of beating into shape the substance of the book on Judaism as a Civilization is not only taking up all of my spare time, but making me feel how deficient I am in the mental qualities necessary to clear and effective writing. There is no end to the number of times I have to rewrite a passage before it expresses what I have in mind. There are many factors which contribute to the difficulties I experience in writing. When I came to this country I was eight years old and began to attend public school at eleven. The schools I attended—both elementary and higher—did absolutely nothing for me in the way of teaching me to write or to speak. I was never trained or required to read English literature. These facts plus the lack of any native gift for language account for the tremendous effort I have to put forth to express myself clearly. As to being eloquent or being able to pull off platitudes in profuse and magnificent style—an art so essential in successful preaching and making speeches at banquets—that is out of the question. Realizing all this I am not apt to be in a very cheerful mood. I am therefore grateful to Bertrand Russell for having written his latest book on The Conquest of Happiness which I have been reading today. It has done for me what the Ethical treatises used to do at one time for the pious Jew. It made me realize that I ought to be ashamed of myself for not being happy. It has opened my eyes to those unethical traits in myself which stand in the way of my happiness, and to the advantages which I enjoy and which ought to banish from my mind all thoughts that mar my happiness.

In common with everybody who invested in stocks, Lena and I have suffered our quota of financial losses. We did not speculate on margin and we invested in bank stock which we had been assured was the safest of all stocks. As we stand today we have lost not only the twenty or twenty-five thousand dollars of paper profit we had made before the crash but an equal amount of actual hard earned cash which we had invested. Today the U.S. Bank of which stock we have ten shares closed down. The shares cost us $2080. That we are bearing our losses with equanimity is probably due more to the realization that there are thousands of people who are infinitely worse off than we rather than to any native or acquired ability to remain unperturbed.

God as Process

JANUARY 15, 1931

After all the years of thinking on the problem of religion I am still at a loss how to connect the conclusions I hold with the actual situation in which we find ourselves. I know very well what I mean by God. God to me is the process that makes for creativity, integration, love and justice. The function of prayer is to render us conscious of that process. I can react with a sense of holiness or momentousness to existence because it is continually being worked upon by this divine process. I am not troubled in the least by the fact that God is not an identifiable being; for that matter neither is my Ego an identifiable being. Nor am I troubled by the fact that God is not perfect. He would have to be static to be perfect. Nothing dynamic can be perfect since to be dynamic implies to be in the state of becoming.

But how shall I relate all these ideas to the problem of Jewish religion?

United Synagogue Problems

THURSDAY, FEBRUARY 5, 1931

Yesterday at the meeting of the Executive Committee of the Rabbinical Assembly which I attended for the first time this year, Finkelstein brought up the question of what can be done to have the laymen of the congregations affiliated with the United Synagogue display some interest in the cause of Conservative Judaism. What prompted him to bring up that question was the contrast between the successful convention of the Union of Hebrew Congregations held recently at Philadelphia and the dismal affairs which are meant to pass for conventions of the United Synagogue. His idea was that the Seminary ought to be made the object of a project for Conservative Jewry to work on. I, for one, couldn't see how the Seminary with its inflexible organization could fall in with such a project. I then held forth on what I believed would be the kind of project that would fire the imagination of those who are at present dissatisfied both with the Orthodox and the Reformist programs. I suggested that we call into a being an organization that would be representative of all aspects of Jewish life, religion, social work, education, creative endeavor. I spoke quite freely and warmly on the subject. The discussion was participated in by the few present. Israel Goldstein, Finkelstein, Israel Levinthal[17], Morris D. Levine, the younger Alstat and Landesman.[18] I hardly believe I won them over to my way of thinking, but I believe I made a dent in some of their preconceived notions.

The Value of Sermons

FRIDAY, APRIL 10, 1931

I am mentally and physically tired after the strain of delivering five sermons within eight days. As far as I can see, the only good resulting from the sermons is that it brings Jews together for worship, thereby keeping alive their Jewish consciousness. It is immaterial what I preach. There does not seem to be any relation between the ideas expressed in the course of a sermon and any tangible or visible action on the part of the listeners. In fact the very multitude of ideas with which the listeners are bombarded during such a barrage of sermons prevents any of them from being acted on. It is not without some effort that I myself recall the sermon before the last one. The main requisite of a sermon is that it should hold the attention of the hearers while it is delivered. Its function is mainly to enable those

---

17. Israel Levinthal (1888–1982), ordained JTS; author; rabbi, Brooklyn Jewish Center; Zionist; national executive, Zionist Organization of America.
18. Alter Landesman (1895–?), ordained JTS; rabbi, social worker, Brooklyn.

who come to synagogue to while away their time with the minimum degree of boredom. If a cantor and choir could keep the people interested there would be no need for sermons. This use of religious and ethical ideas as a means of helping people to while away their time falls under the category of *Halomade Lo Al Manat Lekayame* [Heb. He who learns (but) not for the sake of carrying it out]. The preachers are unmindful of the sterility with which such work is cursed; they prefer to act in accordance with the advice which cynics read into the dictum *Derosh VeKabel Sakhar* [Heb. Give an explanation and receive a reward].

To my shame and regret I am reading only for the first time the *Brothers Karamazov*. It is a veritable encyclopedia of problems dealing with society and the individual. How clearly and succinctly Dostoevsky states what I have been long struggling to express in reference to the relation between church and State! (Cf. Book II, Ch. 5).

A Conversation about Bialik and His Conversation

SUNDAY, APRIL 26, 1931

Pesah Ginzberg,[19] one of the younger Hebrew poets, who lives in Palestine, came to see me last Friday in reference to getting subscribers to the Moznayim.[20] His visit was preceded by a letter from Bialik urging me to do all I can for that magazine. Ginzberg spoke rhapsodically of Bialik's spiritual influence on the Jewish life of Palestine. As many as four thousand people came to greet Bialik on Simhat Torah. Aside from his greatness as a poet, he pours forth a continuous stream of conversation full of wit, wisdom and learning. If there were a way of recording that conversation the Hebrew literature would be enriched by several volumes of the most magnificent prose. There has developed, however, an opposition group which is combating in the magazine, Ketubim,[21] Bialik's efforts to renew interest in ancient Hebrew literature, especially the medieval poets. The Ketubim group hold in contempt everything preceding the literary endeavors of the present younger generation.

According to Ginzberg the Jewish community in Palestine is growing inwardly stronger and more self-reliant despite all the troubles it has been having the last two years. He described the efforts of Magnes and the B'rith

---

19. Pesach Ginzburg (1894–1947), born in Volhynia; studied in Odessa; settled in Palestine in 1922; night editor of Ha-Aretz; poet.

20. *Moznayim:* literary organ of the Hebrew Writers Association.

21. *Ketuvim:* weekly organ of young avant-gardists; published in Tel Aviv.

Shalom[22] as ultimately helpful to the establishment of friendly relations between the Jews and the Arabs. As he spoke I felt a yearning to visit Palestine this summer.

The Evils of Organized Religion — Louis Finkelstein and Other Problems

TUESDAY, MAY 5, 1931

The storm that is just now raging within me makes it difficult for me to set down in writing all that is in my mind just now. I wish my reason were able to cope with host of impulses, hungers, ambitions that sweep like hurricanes over my soul. My reason tells me that I ought to consider myself one of the happiest in the world. I have a home; my wife and children, thank God, are in normal health; I am free from organic disease; I make a comfortable living; I have won the right to intellectual freedom; I enjoy the good will and respect of a few hundred people; I have influenced the thinking of a good many men and women. Compared with the sufferings and deprivations which fall to the lot of the vast majority of human beings, my unhappy state of mind is merely a form of self-indulgence. But while it lasts it blots out all rational considerations and all sense of proportion. It was of course stupid of me to ascribe, as I did on the end of the last page, my eternal discontent to so simple a cause as that mentioned by Russell. The fact is that I am by nature too socially minded to be able to confine myself when weighing the pros and cons of happiness to the advantages of my own secure and sheltered life. The injustice, stupidity and cruelty that mark every phase of human life I come in contact with upset my peace of mind. Last night, for example, I went to see the play "Five Star Final."[23] On my way to the theater I passed the Christian Science church on Central Park West and 68th Street. I saw throngs coming out of the church and throngs standing in line waiting to get into a church. I immediately lost my mental poise. I became aware of the hopelessness of ever getting the masses to repudiate their superstitions. We are supposed to be living in an age of enlightenment and science and yet such a farrago of the most incredible nonsense as that which goes on to make up Christian Science has mesmerized millions of men and women who are generally regarded as intelligent and educated. These reflections

---

22. Brith Shalom (Covenant of Peace): formed in 1925, advocating absolute political equality between Jews and Arabs. Judah Magnes, Henrietta Szold, and other pacifists from the Hebrew University were members.

23. *Five Star Final,* by Louis Weitzenkorn. Elaborate exposé of a newspaper's persecution of a private citizen. The newspaper digs up an old murder case in order to boost circulation. Many suffer in the process. Reviewed by Brooks Atkinson, *New York Times,* December 31, 1930.

formed a fitting prelude to the play I saw last night which told the story of what goes on behind the scenes in a publishing house of a tabloid newspaper which caters to the moronic tastes of its readers by serving them with all sorts of scandal to titillate their suppressed sex desires. The play brought out the fact that the publisher compels those in charge of these papers to go to all lengths to secure circulation, regardless of the lives and reputations that they may be the cause of ruining. The central character of the play was the editor who had something of a conscience and who inwardly rebelled at the idea of raking up the story of an unfortunate young woman who had shot her betrayer. What led him to stifle his conscience was the fear of starvation. He rationalized his cowardice by persuading himself that "ideals don't patch pants," and when he would save up enough to live on he would turn his back forever on the vileness to which he was stooping. That was all I needed to lose the little self-control that enabled me to retain my balance. If I had a few bombs I would have gone right there and then and placed them beneath the homes of some of the owners of these filthy generators. I inwardly cursed a social order that permits such criminal dispensers of moral disease to flourish and batten. Of course my impotence and the impotence of the playwright who probably tried by means of this play to arouse the social conscience, and of the numerous audiences that probably included sensitive people like myself, only helped to deepen my gloom.

Life for me is not just a pedestrian affair as it is for most people; neither is it a matter of climbing mountains to some pinnacle of attainment as it is for the privileged few, but a continual learning to walk on a tightrope. My task consists in having to control my personality and my experiences so that I might retain my mental balance and sanity. I am pretty successful when I perform in public but when I am by myself I always slip. Fortunately there is always the net of habit to save me.

The source of all the social evil may be traced to organized religion. Those who are at the head of religious organizations are not inherently worse than other people, but they are far more blameworthy for the evil that they abet and encourage. After that upsetting experience of last evening, I had something additional to embitter me. I was looking over the work that the Seminary had handed in some time ago. In one of the notebooks I came across the note on Theology, the course given by Louis Finkelstein. I was completely amazed at what I read. In the first place the ideas were taken for the most part from the second hand sources dealing with reconstruction of the religion of Israel during the first commonwealth. Those ideas seemed (after discounting all the possible inadequacies due to the student who recorded them) detached from each other and from the context of the rest of Jewish life ancient or modern. The courses which I have been giving to the junior classes at the Teachers Institute represent much more original thinking and organization of ideas. And Finkelstein gives this kind of elementary knowledge, which he seems to be picking up as he goes along in his capacity as associate professor of Theology.

But it is not this that angers me. The main source of my being vexed by the contents of his course is that he openly disavows belief in revelation and at the same time poses before the world as an Orthodox rabbi and functions as the head of a strictly Orthodox congregation. Of course I am happy that he is contributing to the cause of enlightenment by teaching the way he does. I feel quite confident that I may take some of the credit for having made such frank teaching of the modern version of the development of Jewish religion possible in the Seminary. But why should all these concessions to modernism be denied, and their implications resisted by Finkelstein and the others who equivocate like him? When dishonesty is thus rife among the spiritual leaders what right have we to expect regard for the decencies and moralities from the harassed and fear driven multitude?

"I Should Have Gone into Philosophy"

SATURDAY NIGHT, MAY 9, 1931

The Sabbath service at the SAJ today was one of those occasions which belong to the ordeals which test my acceptance of my spiritual status quo to the straining point. On these occasions I have to forget all my doubts and despairs, suppress all my inward struggles and identify myself completely with the part that life has assigned to me, that of the preaching pragmatist. That is probably the inherent weakness of civilization. Civilization is a heroic attempt to fit the confusion of human existence into the framework of a drama with a purpose. The unfortunate thing is that most people are cast for parts for which they are not adapted. I am one of those people whom it is undoubtedly most difficult to cast for the proper part, because I belong to those whose reach far exceeds their grasp. I should have been a Morris R. Cohen.[24] That is to say my ambition lay in the direction of demonstrating the supremacy of reason. It is a philosophy such as he develops in his recent book *Reason the Nature of Things*[25] that I probably was most qualified to make a contribution to as far as my mental reach was concerned. But I lacked the mental grasp for the mastery of mathematics and science necessary nowadays to anyone who is to say anything philosophically authoritative. At the time he chose his career I was in a fair way to choose a similar

---

24. Morris Raphael Cohen (1880–1947), Ph.D. Harvard; philosopher; famous teacher, CCNY. Kaplan knew him when they were young.

25. Morris Raphael Cohen, *Reason and Nature—An Essay on the Meaning of Scientific Method* (New York: Harcourt, Brace, 1931).

career. But I was not sufficiently mature to overcome the pressure brought upon me by my parents to enter the rabbinate and the expectations aroused by my seven years of attendance at the Seminary. It was in 1901 or 1902 that Woodbridge[26] asked me whether I would accept one of the fellowships offered by the Ethical Culture Society to take post-graduate courses at Harvard. That was after I had come out second in line for consideration for a Columbia fellowship[27] in philosophy. I then regarded all contact with the Ethical Culture Society as treason to Judaism and would not hear of Woodbridge's suggestion. That choice was final. It shut me in forever within the narrow horizon of the rabbinical calling in New York City where that calling limits one to acquaintanceship with the most boring set of human beings in the world, all of the one species designated by Mencken as booboisie. I am perhaps a cad for speaking in that way of people who think well of me and respect me. But I can't help being resentful of their absolute irresponsiveness to anything worthwhile that I ever ask them to do. If, e.g., Finkelstein tells me a story that Maurice Samuel is hard up, and calls upon me that I should help him raise a fund of a thousand dollars as a loan for Maurice Samuel,[28] I naturally think of my many "friends" and "admirers." I meet the wealthiest among them, ask them what to do to get $500 for Samuel, whom they know very well and on whose literary talent I expatiate at great length. The answer I get is "Let Samuel turn to the Free Loan Association."

This is only one of the many instances of irresponsiveness I have to contend with. Instead of my being able to use them to carry out some of the cultural or Palestinian projects on which my heart is set they manage to exploit me to the full without giving me any moral or spiritual return. They come off rather cheaply with their Jewish religiosity. I cannot get them to spend a dollar on anything not connected with their own "shul" interests. Dushkin has been dunning me to get the SAJ to pay the National Education Association $50. I can't even bring up the matter because I know beforehand they will turn it down. And so on and so on. . . .

The Self and Civilization

THURSDAY, MAY 14, 1931

One of the most illuminating concepts in M. R. Cohen's "Reason and Nature" is that of polarity. I arrived at that concept independently and

---

26. Fredrick Woodbridge (1867–1940), philosopher; taught at Columbia 1902–12, also dean 1912–29.

27. Kaplan studied philosophy at Columbia and received his master's degree in 1904.

28. Maurice Samuel (1895–1972), noted author, lecturer, translator, Zionist.

have even gone so far as to work out somewhere its implications for Judaism. Polarity is an object of immediate experience in the conflict that goes on within us between the physical and social instincts, between the hungers and reason, or as the ancients were wont to put it, between the body and the soul. If this experience of polarity truly reflects the nature of polarity as such then polarity must be like the action of a scale trying to attain equilibrium. This means that to operate with the ego or Reason as though it could be isolated is absurd. Correspondingly the universe and God represent the polar aspects of the same reality, and to operate with the notion of godhood apart from its relation to the universe is like trying to operate with positive electricity to the neglect of the negative electricity.

How then shall we dispose of that unrelenting desire of the self for survival? It surely cannot survive as an entity independent of a physical counterpart. The answer that suggests itself is that the only way to satisfy that desire is to render self-aspect of our individual polarity transferable from our own bodies to other bodies. Through propagation the body aspect of our individual polarity is actually transferred to other bodies. The desire that our children should cherish our traditions and ideals is essentially the desire to transfer to them our self-respect as well as bodily aspect, thereby assuring ourselves a form of survival which is as near to personal identity and continuity as is possible in the face of the fact of death. The desire, however, to use our own children as a means of continuing our personal identity must necessarily result in two conspicuous evils; first, in assuming that the children are sufficiently docile to render the process successful, we are bound to reduce human life to a limited number of patterns which would keep on repeating themselves. And secondly, it is quite impossible to expect that the body-aspect of the child should be so much like our own that our soul or self aspect would match it accurately. This is bound to result in maladjustment and unhappiness. The progress of civilization consists in finding ways whereby the self-aspect might be rendered transferable without having to depend upon one's children to take it over. In all creative effort, especially art, the self-aspect is externalized and then adopted by those to whom it appeals.

As far as I am concerned, I am succeeding very little in getting my children to take over my self-aspect. I believe in letting them have their way; I, therefore, do not force them to cultivate a knowledge of Hebrew or to devote themselves to learning. On the other hand, I do not possess the ability to externalize my personality by means of song, story, poem or painting. The only kind of creative effort I probably might have succeeded in had I worked with the proper materials is in the domain of social adjustment. But to exert one's efforts in that direction with Jews in order to help them survive as Jews during the process of social self-adjustment is like trying to make ropes with sand. In my frustration, I turn to writing in this journal as the only means left me to externalize and render transferable that aspect of my being I experience as my soul, self or reason.

Mind and Body

THURSDAY, MAY 21, 1931

The analogy by which R. Ishmael illustrates the manner in which God will settle the dispute between the body and the soul as to which is to blame for man's sin (*Wayikra Rabba* IV, 5) hits off accurately what goes on in my mind with regard to the relation of the body to that something we call ego or soul. Speaking for myself my worst enemy is my body; I dare say that is the case with most human beings. I can very well understand why the ancients believed in the mortification of the body. The body is a continual drag on the mind. It interferes with the mind's work and enjoyment. It is in a continual state of dying and is forever in need of being replenished with food and drink. It is too lazy, generally, even to attend to its garbage and has to be prodded with all kinds of laxatives to keep itself clean. It is the nest of billions of microbes that are waiting to spring on the smallest lesion or scratch to manufacture their poisons and to kill it off altogether. Its living cells are centers of eternal hunger and they combine to produce those earthly desires that never know when they have had enough.

So long as we are young and our bodies don't interfere too much with our ambitions we regard them as our friends. While we enjoy enasthesia we identify ourselves so completely with our bodies that we and they seem indistinguishable. But as we get older and we have to waste our time keeping the body in order, bridling its appetites and curing it of its ills, we may well pray we were free from it. That people make such a fuss over the remains of those who depart this life is as intelligible as most of the things they do. The sensible thing would be to present the remains to the medical schools for dissection purposes. But it is not in the disposition of the body that I am interested. The other pole of its being—the ego—and as such logically bound up inextricably with it, that is the main object of these reflections. My intuition insists upon the separability and transferability of the ego despite the contention of logic that the ego is only one pole of which the other pole is the body. I am trying to habituate myself to accept what my intuition tells me and to live accordingly.

Eisenstein Becomes Assistant Rabbi at the SAJ — Kaplan Organizes the Seminary College

MONDAY, JUNE 2, 1931

It was not without difficulty that I got the Board to appoint Eisenstein assistant rabbi. They sent committees to confer with me and to urge me to try to get along without him, but I would not think of giving in to them, because I realize fully his worth to the SAJ. He, on the other hand, was being offered the position at Roxbury at a much more tempting salary. I had also to counteract the reluctance which the Board displayed in offering him the appointment. Fortunately I permitted nothing to swerve me from my purpose to have him associated with me in guiding the destinies of the SAJ. From the standpoint of the purpose of the organization he is worth more than a hundred additional members of the kind that we are likely to get. Since his appointment my mind is more at peace with regard to the SAJ and I am beginning to cherish the hope that some of the projects which will help the conception of Judaism as a civilization will at least be consummated.

Another matter upon which of late my heart is set is the reorganization of the academic department of the Teachers Institute into a College of Jewish Studies that would be authorized to give the Bachelor degree in Hebrew Literature. I urged that on various occasions in my conversations with Adler, and recently (Thursday, May 14) I appeared before the Trustees of the Seminary to receive the necessary authorization to proceed with the necessary changes. It looks as though the College of Jewish Studies will finally be realized. Many years ago I devoted the greater part of my address at the Seminary exercises to the need of establishing such a college. That was in Schechter's time. Then the time was not ripe for such an undertaking. Now it merely requires manipulation of means and resources present in the general community and in the Teachers Institute.

Biblical Criticism—A Summary and Evaluation

Monday, June 2, 1931

I was scarcely aware of the task I would have on my hands when I undertook to write the paper for the next convention of the Rabbinic Assembly on The Attitude of Conservative Judaism toward Biblical Criticism. My difficulty arises not from any inability to state what I actually believe ought to be the position taken by a Jew who has been brought up to think scientifically and who wants to remain a Jew. With the view that I hold concerning the place of religion in the Jewish civilization, Biblical Criticism presents no problem from the religious point of view. It is simply a matter of getting at the facts concerning the composition of the Bible. But when I come before the Rabbinic Assembly I come before people who still speak in the confused patois of people who live on the borderline between medievalism and modernism. How to disentangle their confused ideas for them so that they shall be in a position to have an open mind for what I have to say to them is the problem with which I have been wrestling these last few weeks.

At first blush it appears that biblical criticism is a direct attack upon the traditional conception of "Torah min ha-shamayin" [Torah from heaven or direct divine revelation]. There is no gainsaying the fact that the doctrine of "Torah min ha-shamayin" was in the past regarded as a sine qua non of Judaism. We must accept Orthodoxy if we subscribe to the assumption that the continuity of Judaism calls for complete identity with the past. On the other hand, Reformism recognizes that continuity does not call for complete identity, yet it fails to achieve sufficient identity with the Judaism of the past to warrant its being regarded as continuous with that Judaism. Conservatism takes the position that change there must be, hence complete identity is impossible. Yet there must be more of identity than provided for by Reformism. Applying this abstract principle to the doctrine of "Torah min ha-shamayim" Conservatism recognizes that it cannot deny the right of reason to question the tradition that the text of the Pentateuch was dictated in a supernatural manner to Moses by God and interpreted by God to Moses in the manner recorded in *T.SH.B.P.* [Heb. acronym: the oral tradition]. There are many distinct phases to that tradition. 1) The text known as Pentateuch was written entirely by Moses. 2) It was written entirely by Moses at the inspiration of God or the Pentateuch is divinely inspired. 3) This inspiration of God is to be conceived as literal dictation which took place in a supernatural fashion. 4) The meaning given to the text by tradition was also conveyed by God to Moses. 5) All of this is true of the text of Pentateuch which we now possess. To omit any of these five aspects of the doctrine is to be guilty of heresy, according to Orthodoxy. Conservatism as represented by the Historical School (Krochmal,[29] Weiss,[30] Frankel,[31] Schechter, etc.) subscribed only to the first two phases of that tradition. Although apparently retaining two phases or elements of the traditional doctrine they really retained nothing but a shadow of it. So at least the Orthodox might contend. To judge whether the substance of the doctrine is retained it is necessary to analyze that doctrine into its implications especially those of the pragmatic type. Let me try therefore to analyze each of the foregoing five aspects into its pragmatic implications.

The implications both positive and negative of the first element of the doctrine are a) The Torah is animated by a unitary purpose. b) Since

---

29. Nahman Krochmal (1785–1840), historian and philosopher; major author, " A Guide for the Perplexed of the Time."

30. Isaac H. Weiss (1815–1905), Talmudic scholar and historian of the oral law; major author.

31. Zacharias Frankel (1801–75), rabbi and scholar; directed JTS at Breslau; major figure in religious change in the nineteenth century.

that purpose deals with Israel it deserves to be adopted by those who are identified with Israel. c) The Torah is not necessarily infallible.

Of the second element of the doctrine: Since there is nothing in this element of the doctrine that limits us to any specific conception of God or of dictation by him the only implications to be drawn from that element are the following: a) The Torah constitutes the human formulation of the will of God. b) The Torah possesses a higher degree of sanctity than other writings. c) The Torah is not necessarily eternal and fallible.

Of the third element of the doctrine: a) The Pentateuch consists of infallible truth and unchangeable law. b) Every statement in it is equally authoritative and binding. c) There can be no contradiction and d) It is the only reliable proof of the existence and providence of God.

Of the fourth element: a) The oral tradition is equally binding and authoritative.

Of the fifth element: a) It is heresy to question the divine origin of the present text of the Pentateuch.

What are the implications of biblical criticism?

1. That the entire Pentateuch was written by Moses is a human tradition which we have a right to doubt and to subject to scrutiny.

The one element which biblical criticism leaves intact is that the Pentateuch is divinely inspired. Biblical criticism as science is thus true to form. It challenges human tradition and leaves intact the functioning of God in human life. Point out here the inconsistency of the historical school in limiting science to post-biblical literature.

Thus the implications of Biblical Criticism leave intact only elements of the doctrine itself.

What do the implications of Biblical Criticism do to the implications of the doctrine?

They leave intact the implications of element one and certainly of element two (cf. Spinoza who recognizes the inspiration of the biblical writers).

They work havoc with implications a) and c) but are neutral to b) of element 3.

They leave intact the implication of element 4.

They destroy implications of element 5.

The trouble with Reformism is not that it accepts Biblical Criticism but that it attacks all the implications of the doctrine with the exception of implication a) of the second element.

Conservative Judaism should therefore subscribe not to the conclusions of this or that Bible critic but to the implications underlying Biblical Criticism. It likewise accepts a sufficient number of important implications of the doctrine of Torah min ha-shamayim to feel justified in claiming that it is in continuity with Judaism of the past. Those are the implications of elements 1) and 2) of the doctrine.

TUESDAY, JUNE 3, 1931

The foregoing analysis worked itself out with an ease and spontaneity that surprised me. If I will follow it in the paper I expect to read at the convention I will have to preface my reading with remarks that will forestall Cyrus Adler coming out afterwards with cynical remarks about the attempt at accuracy in the definition of terms. I still recall his wisecracks about the paper on the attitude of Conservativism toward Jewish nationalism I read two years ago at the convention of the Rabbinical Assembly.

Biblical Criticism — A Lecture Not Delivered

TUESDAY, JUNE 9, 1931

After a violent inner struggle I decided not to go on with the preparation of the paper on "The Attitude of Conservative Judaism toward Biblical Criticism" which I had promised to read before the convention of the Rabbinic Assembly. This decision was motivated by so many reasons and of such complex character that I am not inclined to go to the trouble of stating them. If I do so it is only to illustrate the truth so often stressed that no act of ours, especially one involving choice, but is motivated by multiple causes.

One reason was the unduly slow progress I was making in the writing of the paper. That slowness was in turn caused by the awareness of having to address an unfriendly audience, or at least one that would number a good many who would take a hostile attitude toward my attempt to combat supernaturalism. Another reason was the apprehension that I might get myself in trouble with the Faculty who might even go so far as to ask my resignation. I would not mind if they would take such a step on the appearance of the book "Judaism as a Civilization." There my negations are given in a constructive and affirmative setting. But an isolated statement about Biblical Criticism which would have to be destructive of all that false front known as Traditional Judaism which the Seminary and the United Synagogue are putting up, would place me in a false light. Then again I found myself in the few pages that I had written not only saying the same thing I have said in the book but saying it in much more elementary fashion.

Thoughts on Dewey and Lenin

TUESDAY, JUNE 9, 1931

There have also been contributory reasons. I have been reading John Dewey's *Individualism Old and New.*[32] Every time I read anything

---

32. John Dewey, *Individualism Old and New* (New York: Minton Balch, 1930).

by Dewey I become painfully aware of the futility and irrelevance of most of the problems I am occupied with. Whereas most of the books, articles and essays I read furnish one with ideas I can utilize in the course of my teaching and preaching, his writings give me heartache. As I read this last book of his I said to myself "Why waste my energies trying to convince a few old fogies or challenging a handful of insincere so-called spiritual leaders whom no body takes seriously, to give up the dogma of supernaturalism, when there are such pressing problems as those Dewey suggests that call for a complete revolution in economic and political relationships, and upon the solution of which the immediate happiness of a whole world depends. And even Dewey is to be pitied for having to urge ideals that are being tried out on a tremendous scale in Russia today, whereas only a few thousand will take the trouble to read what he says. After they are through they will become all the more aware of their complete impotence to effect any change whatever in their own surroundings. So why should I subject myself to unnecessary strain to try to convince a small group of hopelessly complacent reactionaries that they are wrong when the only consequence of my attempt may be that I might have to remain without a livelihood?

I have also read through Irwin Edman's "The Contemporary and His Soul"[33] which was sent to me by his father at his request. Edman himself is at present in Rome.

In a sense he tackles the same problem as Dewey but is far less direct and transparent in his definition and treatment of it. There is too much straining after literary effect. He does not forget himself in his argument. The result is that he merely grazes the surface whereas Dewey delves deep into the heart of the matter. "Individualism" is a much clearer and more pointed conception of what the modern man is after than salvation of the soul. It is only in a remote literary sense that it is proper to identify the yearning after a share in the world to come with yearning for effectiveness and security which is really uppermost in the mind of the modern man. The strange thing is that the thing Edman finally offers as a means of stilling the soul's hunger for salvation is what Dewey really insists on as the future means of satisfying our yearning for individualism, namely accepting the environment instead of seeking to escape it. Edman seems to have forgotten that essentially the scope of his inquiry is much wider than Dewey's. The problem he poses is not merely what shall man do in the here and the now to realize his individuality, but what does he do to transcend the fear of death? That transcendence is the only possible denominator

---

33. Irwin Edman, *The Contemporary and His Soul* (Port Washington, N.Y.: Kennikat Press, 1931).

common to the yearning for salvation on the part of the ancient and of the modern man. Surely not by living a harmonious life can such transcendence be effected.

After I read books of that kind I feel that spiritually I am no worse off than men like Dewey and Edman who have a much larger audience for their message than I can ever expect to have. Of what use is it to have larger audiences, when the books they write and the theories they advance only help to accentuate their own futility and the helplessness of those they address? All of us white collar slaves are in the grip of the capitalistic system. We have not the courage to rebel against the tyrants that feed us. Dewey is a much better thinker than Lenin, but Lenin was a much better doer. Dewey will be celebrated as a great man by schoolmarms of both genders, but Lenin will be remembered by all mankind as the great Emancipator of the white race from its own predatory instincts.

On Being Fifty Years Old and Mediocre

JUNE 11, 1931

Why do we always look to other people's opinions before we form our own, if we regard our own judgments as sound? Why do we almost imagine that we would have been better off, if we had chosen another calling, or acted differently in a number of situations, if we are prone to consider our preferences just? Only a fool can succeed in deceiving himself about the nature of his passions. As to blameless errors, if we are at all given to being objective about the contributing causes of our errors and identifying those which are beyond our control, we are likely to do the same for others no less than for ourselves. Now on the eve of the fiftieth anniversary of my birthday I think I have a fairly correct idea of myself. I am not blind to the fact that my abilities are mediocre, and that I failed to utilize them to full capacity, especially during the adolescence and young manhood. If I had no teachers to guide and inspire me, it was because I did not put forth enough effort to win high position in college, or to secure the scholarships and fellowships that would have given me the advantage of the right kind of teachers. My first failure that condemned me to that most baneful of institutions the city College of the nineties was due to my inability to win the Pulitzer scholarship. But why go on recounting my failures and shortcomings?

Despite my mediocrity I have enjoyed a greater measure of success than many of my colleagues who possess decidedly greater ability. By a stroke of luck Schechter chose me to organize the Teachers Institute. That emancipated me from Orthodoxy. Despite my inability to read character, I was fortunate in getting a wife who possesses a character that is most ideally qualified to render our married life absolutely frictionless. I believe that I would have gone to pieces if she had not afforded me the physical and mental peace that acts like oil on troubled waters. Having led a sheltered existence I have managed to take myself more in hand as the years passed and have attained a certain degree of clarity and organization in my thinking. I am none too sanguine about the things I am doing, but I realize that the whole of American life, to say nothing of the Jewish element in America, is bound to be completely transformed before many years will have passed. The economic inequality and insecurity are daily growing more unbearable, and the reactionary forces are acting in the usual highhanded and stubborn fashion which is the forerunner of violent revolution. It is therefore impossible to build with the prospect of permanence. The most any individual can do is to perform his task from day to day until the volcanic forces which are gathering, the forces of social cataclysm, will break forth and usher in a new world order, an order similar to that which is now forming in Russia. The birth throes of the communist order will be most violent in this country, because of the bitterness with which communism is being presented here. The only possibility of averting the dreadful civil war that will be waged in this country between the capitalists and the proletariat would be to permit the communists to have their say and even to be represented in the political life of the nation. But such a thing is out of the question with the forces of reaction in command of all the resources of restraint and highly conscious of the danger that lurks in the ultimate success of the Russian experiment. The injustice and the suffering to which millions in this country are subjected and the inevitability of a world war that will exceed in its horror and devastation the last war have robbed me even of the desire to achieve anything lasting in the world of spiritual values.

—It is now June 11, 1931, 12:15 A.M. I am just fifty years old.

The Family Sings to Kaplan on His Birthday—In a G&S Mode

SATURDAY NIGHT, JUNE 13, 1931

I received twenty-seven telegrams of congratulations on my fiftieth birthday anniversary, the most flattering among them being Louis Finkelstein's, Shalom Spiegel's, Bernard Semel's and the one from the SAJ who also sent me a bouquet of fifty gorgeous roses. The greater surprise and pleasure, however, were afforded me last night by a skit which Judith and Al Addlestone[34] worked out for the occasion, and in which they together with Hadassah, Naomi and Selma took part.

---

34. Al Addlestone, lawyer whom Judith married and then divorced.

Though it is a hastily improvised sort of thing it is an excellent take-off on my problems with the organizations I am working with. The skit represented Lena admitting to the house a student of the Seminary, a student of the Institute and an SAJ member with all of whom I was supposed to have made appointments to come see me at 7:00. They are all kept waiting, and while they do so each one sings some lines suitable to the character he plays.

Here are some of the jingles sung to Gilbert and Sullivan tunes with the exception of the SAJ song:

Seminary Song:

O, I know that this sermon, my mark will determine
　　　　I've followed all rules homiletic
At the top is my text, my proposition comes next
　　　　Ah, my method is most systematic
To the troubles of Jews, to apply I would choose
　　　　A philosophy that is pragmatic.
From the poets I quote, with long words I emote
　　　　Bringing in a touch of the esthetic
To the prophets referring, my message is stirring
　　　　With metaphors strong or pathetic
Though I haven't, I fear, got a single idea
　　　　I can make all my gestures emphatic
And how hard do I try with his rules to comply
　　　　But alas! They are too enigmatic.

Teachers Institute Song (Reinterpretation of the Bible)

Everything is upside down, David never wore a crown
Shyster lawyers wrote the Torah, Psalms belong in the
Gemorah
　　　　Dearie me, can it be!
Revelation is not true, Abraham was not a Jew
Ezekiel was a prophet false, Miriam danced the Danube
waltz
　　　　So they say, anyway
Ten Commandments were lobbyed through by the WCTU
Evidence still remain that Yahweh rode by aeroplane
　　　　So what?

SAJ Kol Nidre Song (To the tune of Kol Nidre)

Times are hard!
      Business is bad!
The wolf! The wolf is knocking at my door
      Oi vey! Oi veh! The wolf is knocking at my door!
My pent-house is filled with weeping
      My stocks are downward creeping
All because we didn't say it!
      Ai, ai, ai, ai, etc.
Give us back this little thing we beg of you.

The following was sung by Al who impersonated me:

When I was a kid I would combat
      Any boy in the neighborhood at pussy-cat;
My mother would cry from the window high
      "Come Motle, and study Jewish histor-I

I studied so hard, I studied so well
      That I'm rabbi preacher teacher in Israel
In 85th Street shul, from the high pulpit
      I stole many glances like a shy culprit
To where a maiden fair, with golden hair
      Made me want to say things I didn't think I'd dare

I said them at last, I said them so well
      That now she is a Rebitzin in Israel.

And now with an air that is kind and wise
      She and I keep our tempers as we supervise
The wild careers with propriety
      Of our private Ladies Aid Society

But try as I may, I can't compel
      Any one of them to worry about Israel.

I think the last couplet is a gem. It sums up exactly how I feel about the unwillingness of my children to share my interests and my worries. I can't compel doesn't mean here that I try and do not succeed, but that I see no use in trying to compel them. If they can not manage to lead Jewish lives with some degree of spontaneity and naturalness, if they have to keep on denying themselves legitimate freedom of action, if they have to be forever poignantly and painfully conscious of their Jewishness, what earthly or spiritual benefit can they get out of it? As it is hard to be truly happy except in a happy world so hard is it to be a Jew except in Jewish surroundings. My entire striving with the concept of Jewish civilization has been to get my colleagues to realize the importance of building up in this country a Jewish environment and atmosphere, and stimulating Jewish creativity through freedom of thought and love of art. But if those who ought to engage in such work are too stupid to appreciate how urgent it is, or too selfish to forgo their own personal advantage or ease, why should the average Jew be expected to sacrifice himself on what must in that case be a hopeless cause? I want my children to be absolutely and unqualifiedly happy. I don't want them to do anything for my sake which they would not also do for their own sake.

A Birthday Note from the JTS Faculty

SUNDAY, JUNE 27, 1931
I was quite elated last week when I received the following letter from the Seminary faculty, dated June 19, 1931:

Dear Doctor Kaplan:
It is my great privilege and pleasure, as secretary of the Faculty, to convey to you mine and their heartfelt congratulations on your fiftieth birthday.
By your teaching with which you have inspired those who studied at the Seminary and by your public utterances, you have made your influence felt in the progress of American Judaism. May you be granted many more years of good health and vigor to carry on your work with distinction and success.
Very faithfully yours,
Israel Davidson

This letter put me in so ironic a frame of mind that I felt like asking them to forgive me for having acted as though it was my function to be a thorn in their side. I sincerely regretted all the caustic remarks I ever made about them or penned in this journal. It is remarkable what a cheering effect a kind word can have upon one who is unhappy and disgruntled.

When I told Eisenstein about this letter he confirmed the belief which had dawned on my mind, that it was probably dictated by Louis Finkelstein, with whom it is a matter of principle or policy to be lavish of praise, when praise is to be administered. Notwithstanding this possibility Davidson signed the letter, and the entire Faculty is represented as concurring with what it says. Why not, then, apply to it the kind of pragmatic interpretation by which I manage to raise the Pentateuch from the level of a composite document representing views of different writers to the level of a national instrument animated by a unifying aspiration? Interpreted pragmatically, or functionally, this letter is sent to me as an olive branch of peace. I shall accept it as such and do my best to live up to that spirit in which I now accept it.

Finishing "Judaism as a Civilization" — "But It May Be Too Late"

TUESDAY, JULY 14, 1931

I concluded today another revision of my "Judaism as a Civilization." I spent on it the greater part of the last four weeks. As I went over the book this time I felt satisfied that it offered the only plausible program for American Judaism. Much in it sounds like counsel of desperation, and I doubt whether very many Jews will be found who will be ready to pay the price in effort and sacrifice which such counsel calls for. It may be that the book is fifteen or twenty years too late. That, of course, is to be seen. Anyhow, I am glad it's off my chest. I even believe it is quite readable. The passages which I rewrote in the course of this last revision were improved at least a hundred per cent. So that's that.

A Candid Evaluation of Max Kadushin

TUESDAY, JULY 14, 1931

Kadushin is stopping in Long Branch this year. I am very sorry for the poor showing he makes every time I hear him. He certainly means well but he labors under both natural and artificial handicaps. Like all of us he has mediocre abilities, but in addition, he suffers from a sense of inferiority which prevents him from making as good a use of his abilities as he might otherwise. In his attitude toward me he seems to be obsessed with the idea that I am trying to crush his individuality. He therefore makes it a point to disagree with me, although he is completely in sympathy with my entire approach to the problem of Judaism. If, for instance, I organize my ideas about Traditional Judaism around the three categories of God, Torah and Israel, he finds it necessary to make a fourfold classification and to divide the category of the God idea into the justice of God and the mercy of God. He fights shy of the formula "Judaism as a civilization" and tries to be original by advocating Organic Judaism. Our common cause suffers through his taking that attitude, and he himself gains nothing by it. His paper on the attitude of Conservative Judaism toward Jewish nationalism which he gave in outline form on Monday was a flop. He said very little that was concrete, and introduced a lot of irrelevant matters from the thesis on *Seder Eliyahu* he has been working on the last few years. I think his wife, Evelyn Garfiel, is largely to blame for his acting that way. She is in some respects abler than he is and has her doctorate. She naturally wants to feel that she has married a great man and so she forces him to act unnaturally.

Working on Shir Ha-Shirim Rabbah

Tuesday, August 11, 1931: Camp Achvah, Avenue Beach, 694 Street

Whichever of the two preceding goals[35] I would adopt I would have to enter upon a long drawn out process of reading, thinking and writing for which I need much more time than I see ahead of me at present. I therefore fell back upon a piece of work in which I can see more immediate results, the editing of the Midrash *Shir Ha-Shirim*.[36] My plan is to follow Dr. Israel Davidson's advice of working out on cards a short eclectic text based upon the readings of the different manuscripts. At the rate at which I have been copying it would take me about 250 hours to complete the entire text of *Shir Ha-shirim Rabba*. The prospect however of going on with the critical apparatus and discussion of parallel texts does not altogether regale me. But I don't want to think so far ahead. Let me at least finish the text itself.

Writing on the Sabbath — Sinning in Private

Sunday, August 16, 1931

I do not see how it is possible to continue the prohibition of handling the pen on the Sabbath. Although I have abrogated for myself that prohibition I handle the pen only when unseen (*Betsniah* [Heb. in private]). Incidentally it is an interesting fact that Jewish ritual law makes a distinction between flagrant and secret transgression, regarding the former as far more reprehensible.[37] I suppose it is the tendency of all law to lay stress on outward conformity rather than on inner consent. Sumptuary laws are not bothered by the moral evil of hypocrisy. On the other hand, insofar as they frankly differentiate between flagrant and secret transgression they remove the very quality of hypocrisy from secret transgression.

---

35. Kaplan had been thinking about a large project that would incorporate the ideals of economic justice into Jewish education.

36. Midrash on Song of Songs. Kaplan copied a manuscript of this work while on his honeymoon in Frankfurt in 1908. He may have intended it for his doctoral dissertation. He never finished it.

37. In the margin Kaplan quotes Numbers 11:21, where Moses questions God's ability to provide food for all the Israelites. This questioning was in private, whereas Moses' doubting of God's ability to provide water by striking the rock at Meriba was in public.

J. D. Eisenstein Visits

MONDAY, AUGUST 17, 1931

J. D. Eisenstein paid me a visit yesterday. In spite of his seventy-five years he works daily on his various Thesauri uninterrupted by worries or illness. Having lived all his life in the narrow world of traditional and Orthodox Judaism he cannot be expected to be able to think straight, although he is by no means a fanatic. It seems that the object of his visit was to induce me to accept the Talmud as the basis of Jewish life. The Orthodox accept the Shulhan Aruk, the Reformists recognize no authority. I, as a conservative Jew, he argued, ought to recognize the Talmud as my authority. "Whatever changes or reform you have a mind to introduce," he added, "I can prove to you that you can find a basis for in the Talmud." He even thought he could find a way of getting the testimony of a woman to be accepted in court. But when I asked him how it is possible to find a basis for eliminating the prayers for the restoration of the sacrificial cult he was stumped.

His main assumption in urging the acceptance of the Talmud as authoritative in Jewish life derives from the belief, as he expressed it, that the ancients were more in contact with the supernatural than we were. This, of course, is part of the very mentality which the majority of mankind have had inculcated into them. To idealize the past was the very essence of piety. To lack that trait was to be impious. I do not mind seeing untutored laymen hold those preconceptions but when I find it in educated people I am exasperated. They necessarily become an element of obstruction by reason of that kind of prejudice.

Last week when Shalom Spiegel called we touched in our discussion on the question of Kabbalah. I expressed the belief that it was only a glorified form of magic and a rival of the rising spirit of science. He disagreed radically with this view. Kabbalah, he said, is essentially a yearning for communion with God. I wish I had thought then of the fact that the reading of the Zohar was regarded as having spiritual potency irrespective of the meaning it conveyed to the reader. Children from the age of ten were required to read it though they did not understand the meaning of a single sentence in it. I learned this fact from three different sources in one week, from Katzowitz's autobiography, from Benderly's account of his own childhood in Safed, and yesterday from J. D. Eisenstein.

Why People Believe in God—God as Sovereign

THURSDAY, SEPTEMBER 3, 1931

It seems a long time since I have been thinking about the conception of God. The only time during this summer I had a chance to discuss the meaning of God was when I visited the Kadushins. I made use of the analogy I had worked out long ago. I compared the God idea to the concept of sovereignty. This still seems to me a fruitful analogy. It furnishes what is tantamount to proof of the reality of God and it explains why mankind has been in the habit of identifying God with some concrete symbol or personification. I would define sovereignty as that in each human being and in their relations to each other (this latter element is very important) which makes for organized society and utilizes organized society for the highest good of the individual. Before the notion of democracy arose man himself was not in the least aware of sovereignty in this form. Yet his entire life as a human being was sustained by sovereignty which functions through what we now term symbols. Those symbols were to ancient man the very fact of sovereignty itself. It never occurred to him that the social order was maintained by the forces inherent in every member of society. He was certain that it was the king or chieftain who alone made society and the social order possible. Although man has acquired the ability to sense sovereignty in its true form, he still has to resort to symbols, such as kings, presidents, etc. where the kings and the presidents have no other function than that of being symbols, as is the case in England and France respectively. All except the simple minded are conscious of the symbolic function of these human figureheads. The case with godhood is entirely parallel. The godhood of the world is that quality in each entity and in the relations of all entities to each other which makes for an ordered and meaningful world and for the maximum of self fulfillment of each entity. Such godhood is as real as earth and sea and sky. Man, however, was unable until recently to conceive of the world in this fashion and to grasp the reality of this invisible aspect of it. Yet this unrecognized intuition found expression in the multitude of gods that he fashioned or imagined. Yahweh to ancient Israel was an identifiable being who represented to them all that there was of godhood, just as the king represented to the ancient man all that there was of sovereignty. But to the Jews Yahweh began to serve merely as symbol of the fact of godhood. They gradually refrained from pronouncing the name. They themselves accounted for this taboo of the Name in terms of their accustomed thinking. But unbeknown to themselves they were beginning to reckon with the reality of godhood as it inheres in the world and in man, apart from the symbol which their ancestors identified as the reality of godhood itself.

This analysis makes it just as necessary and as easy for us to use the ancient religious terminology in articulating our sense of godhood as it is necessary and easy for the Englishman to avail himself of the ancient trappings of monarchy in symbolizing the fact of sovereignty.

"What I Did on My Summer Vacation"

MONDAY, SEPTEMBER 7, 1931, LABOR DAY

The things are packed ready for the express man to come to take them to New York. Mother, Lena and I are leaving with the 5:25.

Thank G, my fear that I was getting late summer hayfever turned out to be groundless. It was just an ordinary cold that got me these last few days and I am glad to say I am nearly rid of it by this time.

As I review in my mind these summer months in West End I feel grateful for the little I have accomplished—the revision of the manuscript of "Judaism as a Civilization," the final touches on the translation of the Mesillat Yesharim,[38] the first draft of an essay on Jewish Dogma,[39] the copying [on] little cards of 1/3 of the *Shir Hashirim Rabba* text, the groundwork for a series of talks on a Program of Social Justice, and over 70 pages of this journal. In these distressing times I ought [to] deem myself fortunate that I am free from economic worries and am able to work without interruption.

Ritual Sheelot *[Questions] to Kaplan*

THURSDAY, SEPTEMBER 17, 1931

The following "ritual questions" which I was asked the days following all my explanations of the meaning of Rosh Hashanah prove conclusively how radically incommensurate what I teach is with the mentality of the people I deal with:

1. "My mother-in-law is sick in the hospital. She has asked that I come to see her. But I vowed some time ago that I would have nothing to do with her. May I break my vow?"
2. The second question was: "A pigeon blew into my house and I cannot get it out. I am not superstitious, but isn't there some omen attached to this fact? And to overcome that omen must I not have the pigeon slaughtered?"

The first question came opportunely on top of the new version that I have worked out for Kol Nidre as may be seen from the appended leaflet.

---

38. *Mesilat Yesharim—The Path of the Upright*, by Moshe Hayyim Luzzato, Critical Edition Provided with a Translation and Notes by Mordecai M. Kaplan (Philadelphia: Jewish Publication Society, 1936).

39. Probably the basis of "The Place of Dogma in Judaism," *Proceedings of the Rabbinical Assembly of the Jewish Theological Seminary of America*, vol. 4 (New York: Jewish Theological Seminary, 1932), 280–300.

Shalom Spiegel Is "Music to My Ears"

SUNDAY, OCTOBER 18, 1931

  Dr. Shalom Spiegel is a collyrium to my eyes, music to my ears and a challenge to my mind. He is good to look at. My ears drink in his musical voice as it intones the vibrant and colorful Hebrew diction he uses in speaking to me. I am both inspired and informed by his interpretations of the Jewish spirit. He called on me yesterday and in my labored Hebrew which only hampered the expression of my thoughts I tried to convince him of the idea which is uppermost in my mind these days: that it is more important for Jewish life to emphasize the break rather than the continuity with the religious conceptions that governed it in the past. If Jewish life will have the power and the courage to perform this surgical operation upon itself its future is assured. He kept on reminding me, however, that those to whom I appeal have first to be imbued with Jewish life, and that any such emphasis as I advocate will prevent them from wanting to live a Jewish life. This is as a matter of fact what I had hoped to accomplish when I organized the SAJ but it hasn't worked out. The layman is too ignorant to appreciate the distinction between Jewish life and Jewish religion, or too reluctant to bother with Jewish life unless it can give him immediately authoritative and acceptable religious values. It is impossible to make him realize that being a Jew at the present time means first, being willing to identify oneself with the life and career of the Jewish people and to adopt as much of its civilization as is feasible in a non-Jewish environment, and secondly, being willing to reconstruct the religious concepts and practices which constitute the central element in that civilization so that they may answer our present day spiritual needs.

12

November 17, 1931–December 19, 1932

A JTS Meeting from the Inside

TUESDAY, NOVEMBER 17, 1931

How I loathe those Seminary Faculty meetings! The moment I enter the room every part of me turns into raw flesh and every move of my colleagues somehow agonizes me. If I had the ability and the patience I would dramatize these meetings in the genre of the play "Wings Over Europe," where one whole set is devoted to a meeting of the English Cabinet.

The curtain rises on the meeting room at 3 P.M. with the following present:

Hoschander, Hyamson, Levine, the first and the last reading books and Hyamson the morning Times. Boaz Cohen sits and stares. The rest straggle in in the following order: Kaplan, Davidson, with his papers and Ginzberg who expects everybody to take notice of him. Then Adler slouches in with a loud greeting to the Faculty, immediately after him Finkelstein with his hair disheveled rushes in. After everybody is seated and the minutes are being read Marx enters and as soon as he sits down he begins to work at his pipe. (I have no time to go on with the description and will merely note the incidents that irritated me at the meeting which took place last Wednesday.)

1. Attention was called to the fact that of about 15 to 20 students who were awarded bursarships and scholarships many amounting from five to eight hundred dollars only one man acknowledged the award. This gave rise to the usual discussion about the need of teaching the students manners. From this the discussion passed over to the need of telling the men who are in the dormitories that they must not drop a nickel in the slot machine to telephone on the Sabbath nor turn on the light. It looks as though there is going to be quite a rumpus. Some one reported these "violations" of the

Sabbath to Davidson and Davidson turned over the matter to Finkelstein and Finkelstein himself is quite worked up over it and he is probably busy thinking up some sophistries by which to tie the students down to regulations which they must necessarily rebel against.

2. Adler read some letters from congregations before which the students preached the last High Holidays. A casual remark in one of those letters about a student's confining himself to preaching led to the usual inane discussion about the students' acting as Hazanim.

3. The assignment to Seminary graduates holding positions in New York of candidates for graduation whom they are to induct into the practical side of the ministry gave Adler an opportunity to tell the story about a woman relative of the late Mr. Bush who became a convert to Christianity. She had been a member of Temple Emanuel. When she moved out to Westchester she was at once looked up by the local clergyman who called on her. The late Rabbi Silverman of Emanuel happened to meet her. He admitted he had never met her mother. When he alluded to the fact that he understood she had accepted Christianity she retorted that one of the reasons she took that step was that in all the years that her people had been members of Emanuel Silverman had never visited them.

This story was intended to point out the main failing of the men who are graduated from the Seminary. But if that is the case, why doesn't Adler try to counteract that false and misleading standard glorified under the name of scholarship and continually held up before the men as the only worthwhile thing for a rabbi to engage in. Bibliotry—the worship not only of the book but even of useless manuscripts as though the salvation of Judaism depended upon them—is undoubtedly effective in augmenting the respect of the students and graduates for the bookmen on the faculty, but it undermines the self-respect of the majority who have not the time for those esoteric and irrelevant studies and distorts their sense of Jewish values.

S. *Spiegel Takes a Look at MS of* Judaism as a Civilization

Tuesday, November 17, 1931

I gave my book on Judaism as a Civilization to Shalom Spiegel which he kept for two weeks. He read it through carefully and made notes. Last Saturday night he came to speak to me about it. He seems to consider it an important piece of work. When I asked him what should be my next move, he hinted quite plainly that I ought to transfer my activity from the Seminary to the JIR. I would not have hesitated to take that step now or at any time before if Wise were free from the weaknesses so excellently described in an article about him which appeared in a recent number of the *New*

Yorker.[1] I am genuinely fond of him, but I doubt whether I could work with him in the cause of Judaism which, to be effectively promulgated, would have to absorb the whole of him as well as of me. I would deeply resent and be jealous of any outside interest to which he would continue to be drawn.

I have very little hope of being awarded the Rosenwald prize. I have to make up my mind what to do with the book. In the meantime there are other things to think about.

The Changing Functions of Religion — Outline of a Lecture

THURSDAY, NOVEMBER 19, 1931

The talk I gave this afternoon could very well serve as the outline of a course or of a book on religion. The following are the points I made:

1. Religion is beset with more misunderstanding than any other phenomenon of life because of prejudices entertained towards it and unwarranted notions about it held by believers and non-believers. Hence objective and dispassionate views are rarely reached.

2. The main source of confusion is the prevalent notion that religion is the relation of man to the supernatural. Religionists give that as reason for their adherence to religion and non-believers as reason for their indifference or opposition to religion.

3. The misunderstanding of religion may thus be attributed to the fact that religion is thought of as having but a single function. Failing that, it has no place in human life. A more correct way of viewing religion is to regard it as one of the outstanding attempts on the part of man to adjust himself to life. That attempt has found various expressions, one of which has been on the basis of a dichotomy of existence into the natural and supernatural.

4. This dichotomy has by no means been the only assumption upon which religion has sought to base itself. This becomes clear when we study religion from the standpoint of the uses to which it has been put in the course of its career. To study those uses we should ask the question: What functions were the gods of the various religions regarded as fulfilling in helping man in his struggle for existence?

5. From a survey of the history of religion we find that the gods were regarded as functioning in three capacities a) to help man satisfy his natural hungers; b) to help him maintain the integrity of his group; c) to sponsor civil law and social justice.

---

1. "Stephen S. Wise—Prophet," *New Yorker*, November 7, 1931, 22–25. The article praised Wise for his courageous code of ethics and his independence, but was critical of him and his sense of his own importance.

6. a) It is necessary to realize that to the ancient man the physical environment was completely animate. Its visible parts—trees, stones, rivers, springs—were entities that possessed personality. In addition there were invisible beings that were believed to manifest themselves occasionally to man. It is wrong to apply the term supernatural to these beings. They constituted for the ancients the conception of phenomena we now include in the term Nature. Insofar as man was dependent upon these putative beings (visible and invisible) for the satisfaction of his hungers, he employed devices which he regarded as essential to obtaining their favor and refrained from what he imagined would offend them. Thus arose the complex systems of practices and taboos which formed the most conspicuous element in ancient religions.

b. The god in his function as the guardian of the group integrity had to protect his worshipers against outside foes. He was thus the god of war. In that capacity he injected the tendency to arrange the various gods into a hierarchy. This tendency led to some one god coming to occupy a position of primacy. In addition the tendency to syncretism resulted from the need to merge different populations and cultures that the fortunes of war and migration brought together. Loyalty to the traditions that emphasized group unity was expected from every member of the group.

c. The god as sponsor of internal peace was regarded as sponsoring the civil laws by which men were governed in their relations to each other mainly as individuals. Insofar as internal peace made for group unity one would expect to find that the gods who led in war would usually lay down the laws governing men's relations to one another. Nevertheless these two functions must not be considered as identical.

7. The place of the Jewish religion in the history of religion. In working out this outline it would be necessary to illustrate at this point the way in which the foregoing functions were carried out in the beginnings of the religion of Israel.

8. It appears that as a result of historical circumstances and the extraordinary devotion of Israel's spiritual leaders to their own people and to the ideal of righteousness there was effected in the consciousness of the Jew a synthesis of the three functions. That synthesis derived from the belief that the three functions were inherently interdependent. Consequently the Jewish consciousness had to find rest in the conception of a god who united in himself all those functions.

SATURDAY NIGHT, NOVEMBER 21, 1931

This led to YHWH absorbing into himself all the three functions, although after the Israelites arrived in Canaan he figured chiefly as a war god.

9. Thus ethical monotheism which the Jews contributed to the development of religion has as its background the three functions which the various gods were associated with and resulted from the process of elimination that the Jews applied to them. That is sufficient to give to ethical monotheism an entirely different significance and function from those that properly belong to philosophical monotheism.

10. The next stage in the development of religion takes place when the expected harmony among the three functions is not borne out by experience. The natural inference from the belief in one god who provides well being, exacts loyalty and righteousness in that the latter two virtues would be rewarded by him with well being. Three solutions have been offered by mankind:

a. Zoroastrianism—Dualism or belief in two gods	This part I added
b. Judaism—Belief in two worlds	while I was writing
c. Buddhism—release or escape	up this outline.

(This of course assumes that, although there was no ethical monotheism which preceded Zoroastrianism and Buddhism among the respective peoples which adopted these religions, the stage of polytheism had already been outgrown by them and they would have adopted ethical monotheism had they not been too far advanced culturally to accept it in the simple form in which it first presented itself to the Jews.)

11. The solution of the "two worlds," this world and the next, gave rise to a new function for religion. The main interest of man came to be what to do or how to live in their world so that he might feel sure of salvation or a share in the world to come. It was assumed, of course, that one had to live in accordance with the will of god, and that God had declared His will in some unmistakable revelation. Jewish religion pointed to the Torah, Christianity to Christ and Mohammedism to the Koran. During this stage of religion when it was otherworldly (it still is with the Catholics today) God functioned as the creator not alone of this world but also as that of the world to come. It is through the latter that His godhood is to be chiefly manifested, hence its designation as the Kingdom of God.

12. With the Renaissance the three functions come to be regarded as within the province of human ingenuity and self-expression. Science and invention, patriotism and social legislation and reform are removed from the province of religion.

13. a. But as a consequence there is a resurgence of the need for that sense of the unity of life which would enable man's sense of loyalty and of righteousness to develop synchronously with that control over nature

which gives him the means to well being. Man has to learn to see life whole. The term God comes now to connote the totality of existence (interpreted pragmatically by Hocking and metaphysically by Whitehead).

b. The second danger is the sense of futility, impotence and vanity. If the age of deficit gave rise to otherworldliness in this age of surplus man becomes subject to failure of nerve and disillusionment. The apostles of this attitude are Schopenhauser, Spengler, B. Russel, Krutch and [illegible]. In the face of this danger, godhood is that quality of life which renders life significant and worthwhile despite all the evil that mars it and the function of religion consists in keeping us conscious of this worthwhileness.

Louis Ginzberg Pays Kaplan a Visit

Tuesday, December 1, 1931

Last Thursday night Dr. Louis Ginzberg and his wife paid us a social visit. My relationship to him is beset with so many inhibitions that I actually feel uncomfortable whenever his wife calls up Lena to tell us that she and her husband would like to visit with us. They tried to call on us last year but somehow I was never free when they could come. Instead I always prefer to call upon them as the lesser of two evils. The real reason for my regarding Ginzberg's visit as an ordeal is that I must restrain myself from touching upon any phase of the problem of Judaism when I am together with him, so impassable is the gulf that divides us in our thinking. Consequently I have to be at my wits' end to think up something to talk about. This time I thought perhaps an opportunity would present itself during our conversation for me to ask him to stop thinking in the indicative mood and the past tense and begin thinking in the imperative mood and present tense. But no such opening presented itself and we parted without any attempt on my part (and certainly not on his) to break down the wall of spiritual antagonism that exists between us.

What is the matter with these scholars? Do they have such contempt for a man like myself that they would not condescend to discuss with me the problem of Judaism? Or are they so unfeeling and unimaginative as not to realize how my soul cries out to them just because they possess mastery of details, to come out from behind the piles of information they have stored up, and to act and talk like Jews who are sensitive to the "Judenschmerz" [Jewish pain] and would use some of their knowledge for the purpose of healing that "schmerz" [pain]? There he sat all evening with a face like a mask. And mine too had to freeze into a mask. And there we talked to each other for two hours like automatons.

A Celebration: Finkelstein Speaks—And Praises Kaplan

MONDAY, DECEMBER 14, 1931

When I wrote the foregoing I did not have the faintest notion that I was to be the guest of honor at the Hanukkah dinner which the Seminary students had arranged for last night. If I had the slightest suspicion of what was going to take place last night I would not have spent any time writing in this journal, but I would have been working on the address I had to give in accepting the honor bestowed on me. Yesterday morning Lena apprised me of the fact that she had known for some time that the dinner was to be given in honor of my fiftieth anniversary, but she had promised to keep it a secret from me for fear that I might upset the plans of the students who were arranging it. They know how I hate and dread those functions, and they thought that the only way to assure my attendance was by springing the dinner as a surprise. I really do not know what would have happened to me if I had come totally unprepared. Lena could not have done a wiser and juster thing than to have informed me in time, although by doing that she broke the promise she had made to Harold Goldfarb, the chairman of the Students Committee who was in charge of the affair, to keep the matter secret from me. If she hadn't told me I would probably have come away so discomforted from the affair that I would have been miserable for months to come.

Every one of the faculty was present except Adler and Levine. Adler sent a telegram of congratulations. Rabbis Burnstein, Goldman and Eisenstein sent in very warm letters of greeting. The speakers were Harold Goldfarb, Walter Robinson, Robert Gordis and Prof. Finkelstein and Aaron P. Drucker.[2] Although most of what they had to say about me belonged to the type of inflated rhetoric which such occasions naturally call for, there was the ring of sincere friendship and appreciation to what each one said. Finkelstein went to great lengths to dilate upon how much he profited from his contact with me during the two or three years after his graduation from the Seminary. I could almost feel the way he was fighting an evil desire in himself to minimize my influence upon him. That is the only way I can account for the detailed and specific description he gave of his frequent visits to my house and for the odd remark that there are things one cannot say in private that one can say in public. Such a remark seemed to imply that he was making a confession, as it were, a confession in which one violently takes one's lower self and whips it like a dog till it goes off slinking in a corner. I know that Finkelstein has very fine qualities in him

2. Aaron Drucker (1876–?), attended JTS; business administrator; dean, Colorado College.

but unfortunately also a very strong "Yezer Ha-ra." How can I trust him if he doesn't trust himself?

All in all, however, last night's affair has had a purifying effect on me. It has purged me of a good deal of ill will that has been recently generated by my experience at the Rabbinical Assembly.

In my talk I made the point that I have been serving in the capacity of "Meturgeman" [translator] basing my remarks on the statement in *Hagigah* 24a [Heb. Talmudic Tractate—Festival Offering]. As the forerunner of the Aggadist the Meturgeman filled an important place in Jewish life. Every part of the passage in Hagigah from which that statement is taken fell in beautifully with the thought I developed and I concluded with the statement in *Taanit* [Heb. Talmudic Tractate—Fast Days].

I don't think I could have summed up my methodology better than by saying as I did in the course of those remarks that the two questions which I put to any statement or idea which is part of our tradition are: What does it imply? And How does it apply?

H. Kohn Talks on Arab Nationalism

MONDAY, DECEMBER 21, 1931

Tonight I listened to the talk given by Hans Kohn[3] before the group which is being led by Edwin Samuel[4] and which has now met for the third time at the home of Mrs. Jacobs.

Kohn sketched the nationalist movement among the Arabs. He described the movement as having received its impetus from the Russo-Japanese War, the Russian Revolution of 1905 and the Turkish Revolution of 1908. Britain and France are quite ready to allow the Arabs to achieve the unity and freedom they are seeking, provided they (England and France) can have control over the coastal countries. France needs the Christian Arabs of the Lebanon as a minority population to guard the French imperial interest in the Near East, and England needs the Jews of Palestine to do that for the British imperial interests. On the other hand the Arabs resent the French and British occupation of these coastal countries as interfering with the development of national unity and direct contact with European culture and commerce.

When he was through he was asked to point out the bearing of his analysis upon Zionist hopes. At first he demurred and said that he came with

---

3. Hans Kohn (1891–1971), Ph.D. University of Prague; historian; author; expert on nationalism.

4. Edwin, Second Viscount Samuel (1898–?), son of Herbert Samuel; Zionist; author; established Institute of Public Administration in Israel.

the understanding that he would not be asked to discuss Zionism. But since the question was asked, he felt he had to give some answer. It soon developed that there was a deep rift in sentiment and belief between him and the general body of Zionists. He displayed a good deal of passion in spite of his attempt to control himself when he touched upon the extravagant dreams of official Zionism. He definitely coupled the movement with Sabbatai Zebeeism.[5] He not only considers the possibility of the Jews ever getting a majority as illusory but he regards the fact of such an objective being basic to all of the constructive and educational effort in Palestine as distorting the moral and spiritual outlook of the Jews who grow up in Palestine. To him the very idea of the Jews striving to be a majority people in Palestine must necessarily give rise to belligerency on the side of the Jews and of the Arabs.

When he began answering the questions he said that he differed with most people as to the nature of Judaism and although I tried to gather from the various replies he made some idea of his philosophy of Judaism I did not succeed. All I recall was that he attributed his views on Judaism to Tschernichowski, Berditschewsky[6] and Buber, and that with Tchernichowski he regarded the binding of Yahwah with the straps of the Tephilin the nemesis of Judaism. At this point he seemed to glorify physical prowess and military power, while in the rest of his remarks he seemed to voice extreme pacifism.

But although I was mystified by his discussion I became convinced by his main talk that we Jews are in an awful mess with prospects in Palestine no less than with our economic and spiritual prospects throughout the world. As I was walking home the thought occurred to me that the Jews have gotten themselves into such a tangle that by persisting to stand out as a distinct group they are contributing in no small measure to the conclusion that human life is the most senseless and meaningless phase of reality. Such a conclusion is atheism. To be a Jew, therefore, is to further the cause of atheism. I do not care how wild and shocking these words may sound. They express exactly how I feel at this moment as I am still under the influence of the tragic spectacle that Hans Kohn presented to me tonight both in what he said about the nationalism of the Arabs and in his passionate condemnation of the Zionist futilities.

TUESDAY, DECEMBER 22, 1931

Hans Kohn said that until the age of eighteen Judaism meant nothing to him because he had come from an assimilationist background. At

---

5. Shabbatai Zevi was a seventeenth-century false messiah. Many Jewish leaders believed in him. He converted to Islam under pressure from the Sultan.

6. Micah Joseph Berdichevsky (Bin Gorion) (1865–1921), Hebrew novelist and philosopher; researched Hebrew and Yiddish folk stories.

every Christmas there was a Yule tree in his home and they sang Christmas songs. He ascribed his coming back to Judaism to two factors, one his coming across the allusions to Jews contained in the writings of the ancient classic authors, the other an address by Buber. The classic authors seemed to him to speak of the Jews in the same vein as Houston Chamberlain.[7] They were awed and repelled by them. That fact struck him as remarkable and awakened in him an interest in the Jews.

Solomon Goldman—A Critical Portrait

FRIDAY, JANUARY 1, 1932

I returned last night from the mid-western lecture trip. I left for the West on Wednesday night, Dec. 23. Rabbi Solomon Goldman met me at the LaSalle Station at Chicago the next day and took me to the Covenant Club. The conversation turned first upon his work in Chicago where he has been the last two years or so. To all appearances he is still drawing large attendances at his Friday night lectures, Sunday morning classes in Hebrew and History. I gather not only from his own account but from what I heard about him from others that he is an outstanding figure in the Jewish life of Chicago and is making an appreciable dent in the hardened indifference to things spiritual on the part of the middle class Jews in that city. It is too bad that this has to be achieved at the price of publicity that often borders on the sensational and theatrical. It is hard to say just how much of this sensationalism is due to his self-seeking and how much to the desire to get his purpose across.

Kaplan and Family—Difficulties at Home

SATURDAY NIGHT, JANUARY 9, 1932

I have felt quite depressed these last two days. Is there anything wrong with my glands or hormones? For otherwise I am in physically good condition. I have every reason to be contented in spite of the reduction in salary. A year ago at this time I had an attack of grippe which left after effects that last until quite recently. Now those after effects seem to be hardly perceptible. Then why am I so downhearted? It think it is due to the overwhelming sense of futility that overcomes me whenever I realize how irrelevant all my efforts to reconstruct Judaism are. If I do not succeed in my own home to make Judaism live, if it means so little to my own children, what can I expect of other homes and the children of other people? My Judith has been engaged to a young lawyer, Albert Addelston, for more than

---

7. Houston Stewart Chamberlain (1855–1927), anti-Semitic writer. His *Foundations of the Nineteenth Century* (New York: J. Lane, 1913) developed racial theories.

two years. Apart from the fact that he has to work hard merely to get his office experience, he has to be in the office on Saturdays. Judith herself has to take courses at College on Saturday morning. Today she came home all thrilled by the work she had seen being done at the preparatory music schools on Saturday mornings, and during dinner she remarked to Naomi and Selma, "You don't know what you missed by not attending the Saturday morning sessions in the preparatory school." At once Naomi's eyes filled with tears in resentment of the restraint which Judaism imposed upon her, and Selma uttered protest against our having deprived her of an educational opportunity. I suppressed my own rising anger against Judith, and in all calmness asked her how much more educated musically she would have been even if she had taken work Saturday mornings at the preparatory school.

This evening another incident of a similar character upset me. When I was called in for supper I said "Let us have Habdallah." "But Pearl (the maid) is frying eggs and they will get cold if we have Habdallah now," said Lena. When she went into the kitchen I remarked to the children, "If I wouldn't remind you each week about Habdallah you wouldn't think of it." "To tell you the truth, we didn't miss it" Judith snapped back.

JTS Student in a Traffic Accident—The Agony

SATURDAY NIGHT, JANUARY 16, 1932

I took advantage of the opportunity offered by the walk the Karpfs and I had after the Seminar was over to tell Karpf of my plan to organize a Council for the Reconstruction etc. He cannot, of course, feel any very strong urge to grapple with the problem of Judaism. His own studies are sufficiently preoccupying to eclipse whatever phase of the problem does not have a direct bearing on social work. Besides, the aspect of religion with which Judaism is generally associated probably plays no part whatever in his thinking. It will, therefore, be all the more interesting to get him to commit himself to the kind of platform which I am trying to formulate these days.

On Wednesday as I got through with the hour on Midrash—which happened to be a particularly interesting one on account of my discovery that Ben Zoma apparently used the term *Mayim elyonim* [Heb. the upper waters] as a synonym for *ruah elohim* [Heb. the spirit of God][8]—I was told that Phineas Kartzinel had been knocked down by an automobile on 110 St. near Fifth Ave. and seriously injured. It was impossible for me to

---

8. Apparently a reference to Ben Zoma's comment in Genesis Rabba, section 2, paragraph 4.

continue teaching. I immediately took a taxi and got to Harlem Hospital on Lexington Ave. and 135 St. where he had been taken after the accident. Louis Finkelstein and Morris Levine had preceded me. I then learned that Kartzinel was so badly injured that if both his legs were amputated he had a slight chance to live. By the time I saw him he had been given a blood transfusion and had strenuously refused to give his consent to be operated on. He had threatened the hospital with legal prosecution if the surgeon would amputate his legs. In the meantime Dr. Nathan, who is supposed to be an authority on such cases, came and confirmed the opinion of the hospital surgeon. It then devolved upon Levine and me to go and argue with K that he should submit to the operation.

We went into the operating room and found K lying on one of the hospital wagon beds with his head lower than the rest of the body which was raised almost at an angle of 30° to the bed. A nurse was standing by him and giving him every little while a few drops of water to quench his thirst. He recognized us as soon as we approached him and began to thank us profusely for coming. Then began the terrible tussle between him and us with regard to the operation. A hospital surgeon, apparently a Jew—was standing there with us and he kept on saying that every minute's delay lessens the chance of survival. There was poor K struggling with death debating with himself whether or not to permit the amputation of his legs. He could not get himself to believe the surgeon's diagnosis of his case. On the other hand, if their diagnosis was the correct one then he preferred death to surviving as a cripple. He countered every one of our pleas that it was his duty to try to save his life at all costs. With his body mangled with the pallor of death on his face, the energetic clarity of his mind presented a gruesome contrast. He kept on saying that he dreaded the thought of falling a burden on people, and referring continuously to the helplessness of his mother.

At one time he let drop the cruel remark, "It is easy for the one who is not the victim to talk." I say "cruel," because it sums up the horrible paradox in all manner of advice and comfort to sufferers. That was the cruelty which Job inflicted on his friends. After all what did he expect them to do? If they had not come to see him they would have been guilty of being inconsiderate and hard-hearted. When they tried to comfort him it was the only thing they could have done. And what they said at first was by no means objectionable. The average sufferer apparently wants everybody else to suffer with him. Words of consolation are to him irrelevant. The exceptional person doesn't need any consolation. This is why all *Tanḥumim* [Heb. comfort] is [are] *Tanḥumei hevel* [Heb. futile comfort]

K. finally yielded and signed his name to the statement authorizing the operation with the words "I know I am signing my doom." The fact was that he had been a doomed man from the moment the automobile struck him. He died an hour or two after the operation.

I knew K from the time I met him as a student in the Junior class of the Teachers Institute, that is about six or seven years ago. He had come from the Yeshibat Isaac Elhanan and brought with him all of the mental narrowness and confusion that reign supreme in the Jewish ghetto reenforced by the cynical fanaticism of the Yeshibah. His father who had been a "Rav" died when K was six years old and left the family in great poverty. K finally completed the courses at the Institute and entered the Seminary. His mentality was considerably improved, and he was able to appreciate the value of a rational approach to tradition. Throughout his student days he worked hard to maintain himself and his mother and sisters. He was graduated as rabbi last June and got a scholarship of $1000 to continue his rabbinic studies. He was busily engaged in the study of the principle of *Mitzvat asey shehazman geramah* [Heb. a positive commandment tied to a particular time frame][9] and was making considerable progress. The accident which put an end to his life happened while he was on his way to the Seminary library. "I thought," he said as he lay in the operating room, "that *Sheluḥay mitzvah aynan nizokin*" [Heb. those in the process of doing a mitzvah will not be injured].

The funeral took place on Thursday afternoon in the lecture hall of the old Seminary building. The students together with Finkelstein asked me to make the arrangements. I read the ninetieth psalm and followed it with the passage in *Midrash Shir Hashirim* which gives the funeral address that R. Zera delivered over R. Bun and concluded with a prayer. I was followed by Prof. Ginzberg who quoted the story about the sons of Aaron and pointed out that silence was the only thing possible in the face of such tragedy.[10] Then came Dr. Hyamson. I had asked him merely to read a prayer, but instead he launched forth into a stereotype *Hesped* [Heb. eulogy, but literally means a wailing] which he delivers indiscriminately at all kinds of funerals. He knew very well that every minute was precious because the funeral had been delayed over an hour and a half and the cemetery might be closed by the time the hearse arrived there. Hyamson himself had given me all the information before the services. Yet he could not withstand the temptation of going through the regular performance which he imagined was expected

---

9. Commandments which must be done at a particular time are not incumbent on women. So, for example, according to rabbinic law women are not obligated to pray the morning prayers because these prayers are tied to a specific time.

10. At the death of his sons, Nadab and Avihu, Aaron remained silent. See Leviticus 10:1 for details of this incident.

of him. It was for that he had come all togged up in ministerial vest and coat and high hat.

The family of K behaved hysterically. The mother and sisters kept on shrieking at the top of their voices and threw themselves on the ground and on the coffin. Pandemonium reigned for a while before I could begin the services, but Hyamson frightened the hysterical women into silence. It was with great difficulty that I succeeded in controlling myself from giving way to my emotions as I went on with the service. This is Saturday night and I still feel the effects of the strain. I can hardly walk.

Talking with S. Spiegel about the Origin of Monotheism

SATURDAY NIGHT, JANUARY 30, 1932

I just came back from Dr. Spiegel's with whom I spent two hours. The main part of the conversation dealt with the question whether or not the Israelites brought monotheism with them from the wilderness. We always find ourselves in fundamental disagreement on that question. He refuses to accept the evolutionary conception of monotheism. I asked him to explain to me the meaning of the sentence *Shemah Yisrael* [Heb. "Hear oh Israel the Lord our God the Lord is one"]. He labored very hard to bring it into consonance with his theory that *YHVH* [Heb. the Tetragrammaton: four-letter name of God here translated as the Lord] was not a proper noun.[11]

His approach to Judaism seems to be the same as that of Buber and Rosenzweig about whom I at present know very little. It is a pity that my time is so limited that I cannot get to them.

There is something in me that responds to the mysticism which Spiegel falls back upon whenever he discusses the Jewish conception of God. That idea of Israel's eternity as inherent in the very blood hypnotizes me every time he mentions it to me. I can very well understand how young people yield to its spell. But as soon as I am left to myself it works havoc with me. I simply cannot integrate it into my thinking, yet it creates in me a discontent with my own pragmatic approach.

The Threat and Attraction of Communism

SUNDAY, MARCH 27, 1932

Communism is eating into the vitals of rabbinic and social work. The students in the Seminary and in the Graduate School are seriously

---

11. In modern biblical studies some argue that YHWH is a name like Athena and therefore that YHVH is one among many. Others argue that YHVH implies uniqueness. Kaplan assumes the first position, Spiegel the second. In this passage Kaplan wrote out the Hebrew letters Y.H.W.H.

troubled about the contempt in which their respective callings are held in the communist philosophy of life. I have been trying very hard to find a rationale wherewith to counter this growing sense of inferiority in the rabbis and social workers, but I am fully aware that I am merely trying to rationalize something which at heart I consider untenable.

The main objection which I raise against communism is its advocacy of violence as indispensable in the overthrow of the capitalistic regime. When Rosenthal advanced the argument that the ruling classes resorted to violence as soon as they felt they were about to lose their throttle hold on the rest of society, I said that the habits of millennia cannot be overcome in a century. It will undoubtedly take a long time before education will become effective as a means of social reform, but education is a process which cannot be skipped. Even after violence attains its objects, education has to be imparted to prevent those objects from being lost and to learn how to use them properly.

Finkelstein and the Rabbinical Assembly

THURSDAY, MARCH 31, 1932

This morning Louis Finkelstein, Eugene Kohn and I met to see whether it would be possible to carry out the mandate of the Rabbinical Assembly to have a committee appointed to bring in at the coming convention some kind of Platform that would indicate the attitude of the Rabbinical Assembly on the fundamental problem of Jewish life. A committee of nine was appointed after that meeting of the Executive Committee at which I got very much excited about the way Levinthal and Finkelstein tried to kill the resolution which had been passed at the last convention. The committee met three times, I believe, and there have been subcommittee meetings besides. For a time it looked as though the plan of having a symposium would work out. But when it came to translating that plan into concrete form it broke down. The three of us who met today tried to save it but in vain. Finkelstein is hot upon one thing and that is to have the Rabbinical Assembly present a solid front to the outside world. I on the other hand could not see how that could be done. I hoped that it would be possible to have the Rabbinic Assembly accept the fact of its heterogeneous character and at the same time bring that fact under some larger category like that of Judaism as a civilization, thereby achieving variety in unity.

Louis Finkelstein is evidently very sure of himself as voicing the attitude of the majority of the graduates in matters Jewish. He challenged me, in the course of the discussion this morning, to put the matter to a vote among those holding rabbinical positions in and about New York.

The Frustration of Teaching in Hebrew

SUNDAY, APRIL 10, 1932

I find the teaching at the Teachers Institute Sunday afternoons quite an ordeal. In trying to conform to the wishes of my colleagues on the Faculty to foster a Hebraic atmosphere in the institution, I have been torturing myself into teaching in Hebrew and torturing a number of students in the class to whom it is as unnatural to think in Hebrew as it is to me. I suspect that the reason I find it so hard to think and express myself in Hebrew is due to some subconscious resistance to what I feel to be an unnatural procedure, or to the inner conflict and indecision of which I am the victim. After all these years I am still vacillating between emphasis on content regardless of language and emphasis on Hebrew as indispensable to experiencing as a Jew. In the meantime I am probably throwing away a golden opportunity to influence the lives of the young people I am teaching. If I could abandon myself completely to the ideas and values of Judaism or if I could devote part of the time to some actual experience of the mood of prayer, I might have left a lasting and wholesome impression on their lives.

On Feeling Dull

SATURDAY NIGHT, APRIL 16, 1932

What often worries and frightens me is the feeling of dullness I experience in my head when I find myself among a group of people whom I don't know very well and am in fear of being called upon to speak. I believe that feeling is due to a state of nervousness which inhibits the digestive process and causes gas to accumulate in my system. Whenever I feel that way I suffer a partial aphasia. I forget names, and I lose all power of giving variegated expression to what I want to say because the range of my vocabulary becomes shrunken.

Kindergarten Educator Y. Halperin Visits

SUNDAY, APRIL 17, 1932

Yehiel Heilprin called on me yesterday afternoon. He is one of the *Meshugaim ledavar ehad* [Heb. fanatics about one thing] who keep the world going. His particular *Meshugaas* [Heb. craziness] is Hebrew kindergartens. He worked his idea in Odessa, Palestine and lastly in Russia. Bialik, Ussischkin and Greenbaum were his most ardent supporters. He published with the assistance of the musician Engel and noted artists some excellent kindergarten literature. He edited a Hebrew magazine dealing solely with

Samson Benderly (center front) and, Kaplan (far right), with young people, early 1930s. (Courtesy Ratner Center, JTS)

kindergarten problems. He came to this country and after mediating and orienting himself to the American Jewish scene for about six months he has been trying to infect susceptible people like myself with his microbe. The first question I asked him was, of course, whether he had consulted Benderly. He told me that he had, but that he had not received any encouragement. Benderly's contention was that the problem of Jewish education is essentially with the adolescent and not with the young children. It seems to me that B. is wrong in transferring the center of interest entirely to the adolescent. Judaism is both experience and idea. To acquire Judaism as idea one must first have it as experience. Adolescence is altogether too late for the acquisition of experience. Childhood on the other hand is too early for the understanding of such ideas as constitute the thought element in Judaism.

Salo Baron and Putting on Tephilin while Studying Talmud

WEDNESDAY, APRIL 10, 1932

According to Eisenstein, Prof. Salo Baron, concerning whom I had gotten the impression from Shalom Spiegel, I believe, that he has no interest in religion, is said to put on Tephilin[12] daily. Whether that is true or not I have become convinced as a result of my work on the Pesah sermon that I ought to resume the practice of putting on the Tephilin daily. It is very evidently symbolic of freedom. The law in the Talmud is that a slave who is allowed to put on Tephilin is thereby manumitted. And freedom as I interpret it in the sermon is the indispensable prerequisite to experiencing the reality of God or the worthwhileness of life. Unless I record to the contrary, I will resume and continue the practice of putting on Tephilin daily.

SUNDAY, APRIL 24, 1932

Am just now following out what I had promised myself: sitting with my Tephilin on and reading Taanit.[13] I just came across a statement which indicates how dangerously Torahlotry borders on idolatry: *Lamah notnin efer makleh al gabei sefer ha-torah . . .* [14] [Heb. *Taanit* page 16/a Why do they put wood ashes on the Torah scroll? Said R. Judah B. Pazzi, this means to say: "I will be with him in trouble" (Ps. 91:15).[15] Resh Lakish said, it means to say: "In all their affliction He was afflicted" (Is. 63:9). Said R. Zera: When I saw wood-ashes put on the Torah I trembled in my whole body"].[16] To which I add : When I read the foregoing *Hava mizdaz'a . . .* [Aramaic. "I trembled in my whole body"].[17]

MONDAY, MAY 16, 1932

These last twelve days have been for me full of interesting activity. First came the experience of being a contributor to the Seminar Group which took place under the auspices of The Religious Education Association

---

12. Phylacteries: small boxes with quotations inside, mostly from Deuteronomy, held together with leather straps, that males traditionally wear during weekday morning prayers.

13. Taanit: Talmudic tractate which deals with fasts connected with drought in addition to historical public fasts. Kaplan was continuing a traditional custom of studying Gemorah after he ended his prayers and continuing to wear his tefilin while he studied.

14. The whole statement is in the diary in Hebrew and therefore is fully translated into English. The transliteration contains only the first few words of the passage.

15. This verse is often explained as saying that while God punishes His people on account of their sins, He at the same time sympathizes with them and says: "I am with them in trouble." The Torah-scroll represents God, and the ashes strewn on it symbolize his sympathy.

16. The English translation here is from Henry Malter, *The Treatise Ta'anit of the Babylonian Talmud* (Philadelphia: Jewish Publication Society, 1928), 110.

17. Kaplan repeats the last words of R. Zera.

on May 4th and 5th at the Casa Italiana on Amsterdam Ave. and 117 St. Dr. Limbert of the Religious Education Department at Teachers College who helped to organize the Seminar had invited me to take part in it. As a rule I keep away from discussions of this kind because I have the feeling that the mere fact of their being participated in by people of the most diverse outlooks and backgrounds is bound to prevent any searching analysis of the matters discussed or complete frankness in the statement of one's views. This time, however, the invitation having come to me in a personal form from Limbert with whom I was to be associated during the period that I was to give the unit course in Teachers College,[18] I could not refuse. And I am very glad now that I took part in the Seminar; in the first place because it afforded me an occasion to probe the fundamentals of the ethical life, secondly, because it broke me into the practice of exchanging ideas with Gentiles, and thirdly, because it taught me the use of the Seminar method for such purposes as I shall myself want to use it. . . .

Two sessions of the Seminar took place on Wednesday, May 4, one in the morning and the other in the afternoon, and a third session took place on Thursday morning. The last among the listeners to ask questions or raise objections in the afternoon session was Dr. Morgenstern of HUC who took exception to my emphasis upon personality. He showed that he possessed very little understanding of the problem under discussion.

For the next morning I came prepared with the following definition of personality:

Personality is the totality of one's being both actual and potential. That totality is not only conditioned but also conditions. It is not only the effect of action but initiates action. Personality is that inalienable untransferable element of singularity which renders an individual an unrepeated and unrepeatable entity in the entire universe, that selfhood whose essence it is to grow by assimilating an ever widening area of human experience, and by continually enlarging its sympathetic appreciation of what goes on in other selves.

The criterion of the normal functioning of the various relationships between the individual and his environment is the question: To what extent does the relationship make for the enhancement of personality?

1. Sex relationship; 2. youth adult relationship; 3. economic relationship; 4. political-citizen state relationship; 5. religious-individual cosmos relationship.

The question we should ask in religion is: Is God conceived in such a way as to make for the enhancement of personality? In fact we might

---

18. From time to time Kaplan taught survey courses about Judaism at Teachers' College.

define God (as he should be conceived) as that aspect of reality which in the individual human being makes for the enhancement of personality.

Kaplan Elected President of the Rabbinical Assembly

MONDAY, MAY 19, 1932

The most exciting part of the convention came Thursday night. The majority of the men had to leave Friday morning. The session scheduled for that time was therefore held on Thursday night. Even then very few had remained. The most important matter brought up at the closing session is the election which is usually steamrollered in regular political fashion. The Nominations Committee hands in its ticket and all the nominees are elected. This time there was a break with that tradition. Ira Eisenstein had been agitating for some time among the younger men that I should be elected to the presidency. A few days before the convention he and Boxer went to see Finkelstein and to tell him of their purpose to push my candidacy. When Finkelstein heard that they wanted me to be nominated he let loose an angry protest against them for daring to suggest such a preposterous idea. From that moment he was trying to maneuver the nominations so as to prevent the possibility of my running for the presidency. He at once told Levinthal about it who appointed on the nominating committee mostly those who were known as my opponents, with Louis Epstein as chairman. At F's suggestion apparently Boxer was also included in the committee so as to keep him from agitating for me on the floor of the convention. Finkelstein was busy instructing the nominating committee. Eisenstein, Laugh and Israel M. Goldman came before the committee and brought with them 23 signatures of men who petitioned that I be nominated. At this the committee waxed indignant and they worked up Morris Levine into an attitude of resentment against the electioneering methods to which my friends dared to stoop. Finally the ticket which the committee handed in was as follows: Jacob Kohn of Los Angeles, President; Max D. Klein of Philadelphia, vice president. This was a trick on the face of it to put Klein in office, because it would be impossible for Kohn to function as president. As soon as the ticket was presented the wrangling began. Schoenfel nominated me from the floor. I was then asked to leave the room and for over an hour there was violent debate whether I was the right man for the presidency. Finkelstein fought hard against my election and used every possible argument to defeat me. When the vote was taken I won by a majority of three, the vote being 16 for me and 13 for Kohn. The students of the Seminary who were eager to see me elected had also to leave the room while the debate and voting went on. They stood in the lobby awaiting the result. When it was announced that I won they raised a shout that was heard all over the place.

I must say that Eisenstein began well in his efforts to have me elected but he did not show very much political ability when it came to seeing things through. In fact after his conference with the nominations committee he was sure I had no chance of being elected. On Thursday evening just before the question of nominations was to come up Elias Margolis came up to me and took me aside to ask me whether I really wanted to run against Kohn. I answered in the affirmative. In that case, he said, he will run for the vice presidency. He at once passed the word to some of my friends and that is how I came to be elected.

The accompanying editorial in the *Jewish Morning Journal* explains why F. fought so hard against me. He is sure that my election will give the Yeshiba crowd a weapon with which to fight the Seminary and the Seminary graduates. While I too hate to contemplate the possible harm it might do some of the men I cannot help being satisfied that my election will begin to put an end to the policy (which Finkelstein, Epstein et al. are responsible for) of having the Seminary sail under the Orthodox flag.

This tendency to regard misrepresentation and sailing under false colors as necessary to save Jewish institutions is so deeply bred into the character of a man like F. that it breaks out even on uncalled for occasions. For example last night he and I happened to be at Mrs. Jacobs' home where Edwin Samuel was giving his concluding talk on the problem of Arab Jewish relations. In the course of the discussion the question arose as to what should be done to deflate the Zionist propaganda of the past years and to bring it into line with the realities of the situation. Finkelstein averred that such deflation meant death to the Zionist organization. To this Samuel had to retort "You've got to speak the truth even in public. You can't fool all the people all the time."

A Rebbe and Rabbis: Israel Levinthal and Max Arzt

THURSDAY, MAY 26, 1932

R. Louis Levitsky told me a Hassidic story which he had used in a sermon on prayer. The story runs that a Jew came to his "Rebbi" and asked him to pray in his behalf for sustenance. The "Rebbi" said "Why don't you pray to God yourself?" "I am not good enough to have God answer my prayers," said the Jew. "In that case, answered the "Rebbi, "you are in need of something that is more important than sustenance."

He told me another story not about a Hassidic "Rebbi" but an up-to-date modern Rabbi. The "hero" of this story is R. Israel Levinthal. Levinthal was invited by R. Arzt of Scranton to address his congregation. R. Arzt made quite a fuss about him in the community as the president of the Rabbinical Assembly and as an outstanding figure in the rabbinate. In the course of his stay Levinthal got to talking with the president of R. Arzt's congregation. The first question he put to the president was "Have you been paying your rabbi his regular salary?" When he was told that their rabbi's salary continued the same as what it had been before the crash, Levinthal said "Why, that's remarkable! I have had to take two cuts in my salary." Not many days elapsed before R. Arzt was notified that he too would have to take a cut in his salary.

Trying to Win over Simon Greenberg

THURSDAY, JUNE 16, 1932

I don't know why I went out of my way to take Greenberg to task for being unfriendly to me and why I tried so hard to win him over to my side. I spent several hours with him to prove to him that he had me all wrong in his notion of my theology. I took lunch with him, walked with him all the way to my house, took him upstairs and read to him portions from the book on Judaism as a Civilization. In the course of the conversation with him I learned the reason for his antagonism to me. Several years ago when I tried to organize a conference similar to the one I am organizing now I did not invite him to take part in it. I did not think he would be in sympathy with the aims of that conference. I had come to that conclusion from the controversy he had carried on with me in the SAJ review. When he asked me why I hadn't invited him I told him that I classed him with R. Charles I. Hoffman. He hasn't forgiven me since. If I had any political sense I should have known that by deliberately identifying him as an opponent I only intensified his opposition.

Courses for Rabbinical School Alumni

SUNDAY, JULY 17, 1932

For some time the Rabbinical Assembly has been talking about organizing courses for the graduates. Originally the idea was to get the Seminary Faculty to cooperate. In view, however, of the general slump in spirit and finances the Seminary Faculty was in no mood to cooperate. Finally Finkelstein and I formulated a tentative program of courses. This was sent with a letter to the graduates asking them to indicate which courses they wanted and the dates they preferred for taking those courses. Epstein and Finkelstein were on the tentative program but when it came to final arrangements they changed their minds. In that program I had myself scheduled to give a course in supplementary prayers. Of all the things I could profitably give the men that was the one I was least able to give and one that would have entailed the greatest hardship for me. Why then did I suggest it? First because there is a real need for supplementary prayers in our services which at present are dreary and monotonous for want of anything spiritually stimulating. And secondly, because I was afraid of giving the one course I had my mind set on, namely, the one dealing with the development of the Jewish religion.

Fortunately that inhibition was broken down through a request which I received from Rabbi Levitsky of Wilkes Barre. He came to see me just about the time the summer course was in the process of organization. For some reason we had not been as friendly with each other as we should have been. I was therefore very glad when about a month ago I got a letter from him saying that he had been trying in vain to reach me and asking for an appointment. Crowded as my time was then I made it my business to ask him to spend an entire evening with me. He explained in the course of the conversation that he had been making use for the last ten years of the material he had gotten from me at the Seminary but now he found himself in need of new material. I was both pleased and chagrined when I heard this from him; pleased at realizing the practical value of the courses that I was giving at the Seminary and chagrined that the Seminary authorities fail to appreciate the fact. I took Levitsky to task right there and then for never intimating to Adler or the other members of the Faculty whom he sees occasionally to what extent my courses have been helpful to him. He admitted he had been negligent and thoughtless and promised to make good his neglect.

It then occurred to me that instead of giving the course on the writing of supplementary prayers, I might give the course on the development of the Jewish Religion which the graduates could use as a guide in some of their work with adult groups. This course would provide the kind of material Levitsky wanted. There was no doubt other men would benefit equally by it. I at once notified Finkelstein of the change, and a sufficiently large number of men replied that they would take it.

I began the course on Tuesday, July 5, and completed it on Friday, July 15. Although there were only nine lectures altogether I gave the men such copious outlines that they will have enough material for at least two years' courses with adult groups. The average attendance was 28.

Reviewing a Book on Philo of Alexandria

FRIDAY, JULY 29, 1932

I am engaged at the present time in a task which I have undertaken mainly for fear that by refusing to undertake it I might read myself out permanently from the class of people who write for the Jewish Quarterly Review. About half a year ago Cyrus Adler who, in addition to his dozen other jobs, is also editor of the JQR, wrote to me asking whether I would review a book by Edmund Stein entitled "Philo und der Midrasch." I knew it meant spending a good deal of time on a matter that would divert me from my general interests, but for the reason stated above I consented to write the review sometime this summer. Of course, if I had felt that I would learn nothing from this task I would not have undertaken it at all. I knew that I would be compelled to read Philo not only in the translation but also in the original, and that I would become better informed about the whole problem of the relationship between Alexandrian and Palestinian Judaism. But unfortunately the little book by Stein is so impossibly stupid, so full of contradictions, and so far from proving his main thesis that the agada is a link between the literal and the allegorical interpretation that I am at a loss to find anything good to say about it.

I am grateful, however, for the many interesting books to which this task has introduced me. I learned about the edition of Philo by Leopold Cohn and Winland and of the translation into German by Cohen; I have read considerable parts of Frankel's writings on the subject Philo and the Septuagint; I have been introduced to Carl Siegfried's Philo. But as usual I miss in all that they have to say on the subject anything gripping or inspiring, anything that throws a revealing light on the inner life of the Jews either in Alexandria or in Palestine. The question whether Philo knew Hebrew is discussed at great length by these writers and withal that I am unconvinced by the arguments which they advance that he was totally ignorant. Edmund Stein in another little book by him on Philo as exeget makes him out to be nothing more than a collector of interpretations that he heard in the various synagogues. All of that is so depressing and disconcerting that I wish I hadn't dipped into these studies, because I hate to be left in suspense about all of these matters and yet I cannot afford to devote to them the time I would need to arrive at some more definite and constructive conclusions than I have been able to arrive at from my last two hours' reading on the subject.

Difficulties of Praying

SATURDAY, JULY 30, 1932

All in all, I am in an exceedingly wretched frame of mind these days as I witness the rapid breaking up of Jewish religious and cultural values. I feel like one who has been washed ashore watching the waves working havoc with his stranded ship. Some time ago I resumed the rite of tephilin, but I simply could not keep it up. After I would put them on I would find myself unable to recite the prescribed morning prayers because those prayers had palled on me. I would therefore turn to the Bible or the Talmud in the hope of getting into a mood that justified the wearing of the tephilin. Instead, I found myself looking up dictionaries and commentaries. So why do all that with the tephilin on, which made the looking up of the necessary information more difficult? The result is that except for grace after meals, I do not pray. This I consider as being totally incongruous with my innermost feelings about religion. I shall not be happy unless I succeed in formulating for myself a series of prayers that will express my own religious needs.

Formulating the Basic Principles of the RA—Disagreements with Finkelstein

WEDNESDAY, AUGUST 10, 1932

I made it a point to have Finkelstein go on with his plan to have the Rabbinical Assembly present its point of view in the form of a symposium on the various phases of Jewish life and religion. Yesterday I received a letter from him enclosing a detailed formulation of the questions to be discussed under each of the topics. I found his conception of each topic satisfactory except the one I had undertaken to discuss, the Place of Religion in Jewish Life. In my reply to him I am sending him the following reformulation of the questions under my topic:

"The article should discuss the conceptions which prevail at the present time among the different Jewish groups with regard to the relation of religion to the rest of Jewish life, and point out with which of these conceptions the RA is identified. It should grapple with the main issue which turns upon what each group understands by religion and how it conceives religion to be related to the various expressions of collective life, such as nationalism, language, literature, laws, mores, arts, etc. The discussion should also indicate some of the practical differences which the RA conception of the place of religion in Jewish life would make in the American Jewish scene."

I also write that while I thought his outline was excellent as a whole, there was one serious omission. "If the RA point of view differs both from the Orthodox and the Reformist—else why talk about it—that fact ought in some way to be made clear. Somewhere, therefore, in the description of each topic the writer ought to be asked to point out the special aspect which is indicative of the RA point of view."

I deliberately wrote the foregoing to Finkelstein because, unless I keep after him to have the symposium bring out the differentia of the RA, he is certain to have it consist of a lot of platitudes which Orthodox and Reformists alike would say "Amen" to. I shall not let him or any of the other two men who are to write for the symposium evade the issue if I can help it.

Rabbi Solomon Goldman arrived here this afternoon and we spent together about three hours talking about things in general. He, of course, did most of the talking. The two of us have so much in common ideologically that there is hardly any need for our discussing general principles. Of practical experience I have very little that is worth telling. He, on the other hand, comes in contact with all sorts of people in the course of a very active ministry. This is why he had to do all the talking.

Socialism and the Spiritual

SUNDAY, AUGUST 14, 1932

I just got through reading "Socialism: An Analysis" by Rudolph Eucken (1922). It is another of those books in which I found support for my ideology. Of course, I cannot say that I would have been able by myself to give so adequate a presentation of both the strong and the weak points of Socialism as Eucken does. But I have to a large extent felt all along that socialism was narrow and abstract in its conception of the human being. It is simply an elaboration of Adam Smith's emphasis upon the economic aspect of life, an emphasis that is as one-sided as Freud's emphasis upon the sex aspect of life. I think, however, that Eucken overstates the case for what he terms the independence of the spiritual. I never could understand that idea which occurs again and again in his philosophical writings. Likewise his conception of the Kingdom of God as transcending the complex daily living is to me incomprehensible. But he is certainly correct when he points out that all that renders life interesting, beautiful and significant cannot be accounted for in terms of economic determination. The qualitative or value aspect of life derives from Reality taken as a whole, and unless we contemplate man against a cosmic background his life becomes too unimportant to try to improve it. Socialism as an idealistic movement is compatible only with a spiritual outlook on life.

At Camp Modin—The Stench of Prayer

SATURDAY NIGHT, AUGUST 20, 1932

It is regrettable that the Dushkins, Berksons and Schoolmans who started this camp with high hopes of carrying on an experiment in Jewish education through Jewish living together, have not been able to develop anything new either in the technique or in the content of Jewish education in the summer camps. They are too much distracted by their main vocations to give the thought, time and energy necessary for so difficult an experiment which is complicated by the fact that they have to cater to children whose parents would have to be subject to a long process of education before they would consent to the innovations that the directors would wish to introduce.

This fact is brought home to me every time I witness the manner in which the children's services are conducted here. Although the ritual is very much shortened, the general traditional form is retained. The weekly Pentateuchal portion is adhered to. The children sing and recite very mechanically the parts of the service. As I sat at the services in the girls' camp this morning and watched some of the youngsters wriggling and talking and laughing it seemed to me that the whole performance was tantamount to blasphemy. By that I do not mean to imply that these children's services were worse than any conducted in the synagogues. They are all of the same deadening type. If I could express my feelings about all these traditional and conventional types of service I would speak in the following vein:

Friends, I find it very hard to stay while these services are going on. There is a terrible stench that pervades this atmosphere. I am surprised that you do not seem to mind it at all. In fact, you betray no signs of discomfort. I must therefore tell you where I think this foul smell comes from. It is said that prayer which lacks the spirit of devotion is like a body without a soul. By the manner in which you are satisfied to keep on saying words that have not the slightest meaning to you, you call into being this foul smelling carcass—lifeless and soulless prayer. For your own sakes and for the sake of Heaven, put an end to this mummery. Learn to have too much respect for your human dignity to be contented to chatter like apes, or to repeat like parrots. If you cannot put as much of yourselves into the words meant for communion with God as you do in your discourse with one another, better be silent altogether.

Jews and Negroes: Thoughts after Seeing a Musical on Negro History

SATURDAY NIGHT, SEPTEMBER 3, 1932

"*Tom-Tom* (written and composed by a Negro girl, Shirley Graham) is no less than a musical projection of the Negro race, from early seventeenth-century Africa to modern Harlem. The characters in it reappear, from the years of the first slave hunters through Civil War times, when Yankee armies trailed freedom in their tread, to these modern days when the race is seeking to find itself in a society to which it is still a stranger. The Voodoo man turns up in the third act as an idealist seeking to repatriate his race in its homeland. Need we add that Negro spirituals vibrate throughout the entire production and spirit of the work?" (The Stage, Sept. 1932)

Am I playing the part of the Voodoo man or is the Jewish situation radically different? "The things one feels absolutely certain about are never true." O. Wilde.

Justice O. W. Holmes[19] is one of the few men after my own heart. The kind of thinking we ought to cultivate seems to have reached in him its perfection. I gather that from the following description of his mind: "The keynote of his thought Mr. Laski[20] finds in his rejection of absolute concepts. . . . Holmes' scepticism, so modern in its refusal to take any idea as the last word, remains always robust. He has no faith in the narrower sense of the word; but abundant faith in the value of life itself, lived for its worth" (The New Republic, Sept. 7, 1932).

Thinking about Brooks Atkinson[21] on Shakespeare

SUNDAY, SEPTEMBER 4, 1932

In spite of my many notebooks I have nothing to fall back on every time I have to sermonize. And yet I cannot read for more than a few minutes before I come up against an idea that overpowers one with the wealth of its implications. The ideas which are thus selected by the mind as pregnant with suggestions are as much an index of the mind as the books of a library are of the interests of their owner. Then why not record in this journal the phrases and sentences which excite me into communicativeness as I come across them in the course of my reading? This morning, e.g., I picked up Brooks Atkinson's article in the N.Y. Times on William Shakespeare, Poet, and this is what I came across:

"More and more they find in him the wholeness that our scheme of living misses."

"This is an age as arrogant as it is dispirited. Having accumulated an enormous fund of knowledge, having superseded religious dogma with scientific discoveries, raised sturdy defenses against nature and thrown an entire world into a bondage of machines, it withdraws with a fine intellectual austerity from passionate avowals made in a simple world."

No, this won't do. I have overstepped the limits of what I ought to record. Only as much of an idea as I thrill to should find admittance here.

---

19. Oliver Wendell Holmes (1841–1935), lawyer; author; associate justice of the Supreme Court; legal theorist.

20. Harold Laski (1893–1950), English political scientist, economist, author, and lecturer; chairman of the Labor Party.

21. Brooks Atkinson (1894–), American journalist and reporter; drama critic for the *New York Times*, 1926–60.

I cannot afford to pack this journal with a lot of fine rhetoric. In the last paragraph, e.g., all that I should have recorded is the first sentence.

Nostalgia for a Traditional Way of Life

SATURDAY NIGHT, SEPTEMBER 10, 1932

I have repudiated many a belief which according to tradition is a sine qua non of salvation, but I have a nostalgia for a life marked by genuine piety and one steeped in Jewish content. I am, therefore, susceptible to the least intimation or sign of interest in the old Jewish way of life. Ever since I got that letter I have been studying Mekilta[22] and the treatise of Gittin including the Tosafot.[23]

SUNDAY, SEPTEMBER 11, 1932

On further thought it occurs to me that it is not merely nostalgia that draws me to the study of Rabbinics. A more powerful motive is probably the desire to derive some satisfaction from all the time and energy I have spent on Talmud and Midrash. It is a form of vested interest. I can therefore appreciate what a herculean task mankind has in ridding itself of habits and sancta which in those days served a useful purpose. In contrast with the extravagant waste of nature man is jealous of everything he produces. He projects his personality into whatever he creates, and he therefore experiences the agony of dying every time his creations have to be thrown into discard.

Helping Rabbis with Their Rosh Hashanah Sermons

WEDNESDAY, SEPTEMBER 14, 1932

Every year about this time I make it a practice to help the Seminary students with their sermons for the High Holidays. This year I announced that I would hold a sermon seminar today and tomorrow and I invited the members of the Rabbinical Assembly within the metropolitan area. The seminar is being held under the auspices of the RA and as one of its activities.

Between fifty and sixty men were present at the session this morning. I gave them the outline of the sermon "How We Come to Know God." Chertoff, who is one of those zigzagy Lithuanian Talmudists, kept on badgering me. It is impossible ever to get men of his ilk to let go either of the two horns of the dilemma by which they apparently love to be tossed about, the horns of fundamentalism and cynicism. But in trying to set him

---

22. Kaplan had received a letter from an Orthodox rabbi. *Mekilta de Rabbi Ishmael:* a rabbinic midrash on the book of Exodus. See English translation by Jacob Lauterbach (Philadelphia: Jewish Publication Society, 1949).

23. *Gittin* is a Talmudic tractate dealing with divorce. *Tosaphot* is a Talmudic commentary by French and German scholars of the twelfth to fourteenth centuries.

right, the point I was trying to make became all the more definite in my own mind. The following is the idea I developed:

The preacher should not enter the pulpit with the expectation of transforming the lives of his hearers by means of his sermon. He does not come with a truth which has been supernaturally revealed to him. He must realize the circumscribed function of preaching and set up only modest aims as are reasonably attainable. He should be aware that his own life is a mixture of all kinds of good and evil as is the life of every one of his hearers. He is desirous however of fortifying the good in himself and in others so that he and they might have the courage to face life with all its difficulties and the strength and patience necessary to better it. How is he to attain this purpose? By recognizing and focussing his attention upon his better self and his own higher yearnings. These latter he must strive to articulate. This consists in formulating them in accordance with their own logic. It will not be the logic of science, but it will justify itself by its effects in terms of greater courage and virtue.

Jewish Civilization over American Civilization

WEDNESDAY, SEPTEMBER 21, 1932

I count upon meeting with a great deal of opposition to the designation of Judaism as a civilization. People have become habituated to thinking of a civilization in terms of externalities and Judaism has at present a minimum of externalities. Nevertheless I am confident that the differentia of civilization is to be sought in those elements in it which are distinctively human and spiritual. The characteristic of a civilization is the possession of institutions that may with dignity command men's loyalty. Tested by this simple criterion American civilizations cannot hold a candle to the Jewish. No amount of gazing at the Empire State Building will thrill me as did the momentary glimpse of the little village of Anatoth from the tower in the government building in Jerusalem. Ex-governor Smith may be a very excellent man but when it comes to eliciting loyalty I much prefer Jeremiah.

Professional and Nonprofessional Jews—An Unfortunate Distinction

WEDNESDAY, OCTOBER 5, 1932

A new and vicious dichotomy is emerging in Jewish parlance, professional and non-professional Jews. Any Jew who makes his living out of Jewish activities is a professional Jew. He is regarded as having a vested interest in Jewish life and therefore bound to urge its cultivation. Nothing that he says in favor of advancing Jewish life can be accepted as free from self-interest.

This is perhaps the worst symptom of Galut Judaism. And there is no way of overcoming it. If one has a vested interest in urging Jewish life he cannot be taken seriously. If one has no such interest he cannot possibly be sufficiently interested in Jewish communal life to discover such latent good as might justify its continuance. The normal life of a people demands that every one in it shall have a vested interest in it. This is possible to all the members of a geographic unit, but not to those of an ideological group, such as the Jews in the Galut are bound to be.

On Wearing a Skullcap at the JIR

THURSDAY, OCTOBER 13, 1932

I forgot to include in the last item the curious fact that I wore a small skull cap throughout the [opening exercises of the JIR][24] and was the only one to do so. Originally Wise wanted that the Faculty and I should all wear academic dress. I begged off having to don those medieval rags and we were all in Tuxedo. Consequently the entire service was carried on in the usual manner of the Reformists with uncovered head. I keep up the practice of covering the head on every occasion which is of a distinctively Jewish character. I include among such occasions lecturing on religion. When it comes to meals I have no fixed rule.

Members of the RA Unhappy with Kaplan Speaking at the JIR

MONDAY, OCTOBER 24, 1932

At the meeting of the Executive Council of the Rabbinical Assembly at which I presided this morning, Israel B. Levinthal "lifted up his voice" in complaint against me for having delivered the address at the Opening Exercises of the Jewish Institute of Religion. He bracketed Prof. Ginzberg with me as having given aid and comfort to the enemy. The hour was too late to permit those present from going very deeply into the subject. Henry Rosenthal and Eugene Kohn sprang to my defense. Landesman joined in the attack and Morris Levine looked daggers at me. I tried to pour oil on the waters. The debate was postponed for the next meeting.

But what struck me later when I thought about what had happened was that Finkelstein withdrew from the meeting in time to be absent from the discussion of the propriety of my speaking at the JIR exercises. I am quite convinced that he had instigated Levinthal to voice the complaint, but preferred to stay away from the meeting so as not become involved in the discussion.

---

24. Jewish Institute of Religion: a rabbinical school in New York City founded by Stephen Wise, well-known Reform rabbi.

Teachers Institute faculty and graduates, 1932. (Courtesy Ratner Center, JTS)

Kaplan's Next Book, "The Meaning of God . . . ," Takes Shape

I've been making considerable progress on what is now emerging as a book to be known as "A Creed for the Modern Jew." I had started out with the idea of writing up the ideology of the Jewish holidays. But as I proceeded, especially of late, I realized that what I was actually doing was to formulate the religious creed for the modern Jew. I was especially elated over the ease with which I have been able to develop the function of Shemini Azeret and to fit the Simhat Torah into that function. I tried out that interpretation of Simhat Torah at the Seudah held this afternoon at the SAJ house in honor of the Hatan Torah and Hatan Bereshit (Dr. I. C. Rubin and Heller) and I got it across beautifully.

I saw tonight a performance of "The Good Earth" at Guild Theatre and enjoyed it very much.

Thoughts on the Meaning of Life in the Wake of a Terrible Accident

WEDNESDAY, NOVEMBER 9, 1932

Bragin who has been a member of the TI Faculty the last sixteen or seventeen years was taking a walk last Sunday night with his wife. As they were crossing the street near their home they were both thrown by a taxi. He was knocked unconscious and has remained in that state since. The doctors hold out little hope for his life. Knowing that such tragedies are but common daily occurrences, one has to be a brazen faced self-deceiver to make believe that one can find some meaning to human existence. What is religion if not a tissue of self-delusions, skillfully and transparently woven so as to seem part of the reality which they hide? Believing this about religion, you will ask, how do I come to pose as a believer in God and a teacher of religion? The answer is that no matter what I would do it would be nothing but a pose. Do I live because I choose to live? Do I breathe because I find it the wiser or preferable thing to do out of two courses of action, either of which I could choose with the same degree of ease? Why then regard the fact that I delude myself as more a matter of choice than the fact that I live? If it is impossible to live without deluding oneself or believing in God then one doesn't really delude oneself when one thinks one does; then one believes in God although one suspects oneself of not believing in Him. Is this kind of reasoning Kaballah or madness? Perhaps both. That is why it borders on the truth.

A Basic Question to Himself

MONDAY, DECEMBER 19, 1932

"Those engaged in the production of luxurious goods and personal services, carry heavy moral costs in the sense of their essential disutility or futility." (Ethics and Economics, J. A. Hobson, p. 209.)

Do I and my colleagues come under that category?

13

December 20, 1932–June 1, 1934

Benderly—Kaplan's Best Friend

TUESDAY, DECEMBER 20, 1932

Thank God there is at least Benderly. In spite of all that I may have said in the pages of this Journal in disparagement of him, I still love and admire him. The few hours that he spent with me at my house yesterday afternoon were balm to my soul. To see a man who can go through all that he does and still hold up his head and retain his faith in the worthwhileness of the cause to which he has given his life is a rebuke to my wavering vacillating weak spirit. But I revive under such rebuke.

Communism Will Not Save Mankind

SATURDAY NIGHT, JANUARY 28, 1933

One thing at least I have learned—that Communism or the Third International will not save mankind. Without minimizing the part it is playing in the destruction of Capitalism, and the inherent idealism of its program, I find that it is entirely too much bound up with the same kind of unreason that has actuated the historic religions to be acceptable to anyone who refuses to qualify his allegiance to Reason. Its philosophy is as orthodox and self-contradictory as that of the Catholic Church and its strategy is as cruel as that of the Jesuits. No doubt such a combination must lead to success, but the success can be only temporary, and even while it lasts only illusive. The high purpose and ultimate goal which Communism strives for can never be realized through the materialistic philosophy of history which it takes as its premise, nor by means of the ruthless use of violence which it invokes in its strategy.

The Essay Contest—Being Nervous and Anxious

SUNDAY, FEBRUARY 5, 1933

The judges who are to pass on the essay or book which is deserving of the Rosenwald prize[1] have been inordinately dilatory. They were supposed to announce their decision by the end of December 1931. At the beginning of January of this year I learned that they were finally to come together for the purpose of arriving at a decision on Sunday, January 29. The Thursday before that Sunday I called up Benderly[2] and asked him to wire to me to Atlantic City if he had good news for me. The picture of myself winning the prize and that of myself learning that somebody else had won it had kept on alternating in my mind during the entire month with greater and greater frequency as the day on which the announcement was to be made drew nearer. If there were to be the hoped for good news I was to have learned of it just as I entered the building of the Jewish Community Center where I was to give the lecture. When I came and there was no telegram for me I was upset, but I managed not to show the least sign of annoyance. Not a person in the world—not even Lena—has the least suspicion to the moment of this writing of the inner strain under which I labored that weekend. It was quite a task for me to put the prize award matter out of my mind and to concentrate on the lecture. The lecture came off very successfully, though it left me mentally very tired.

Witnessing a Divorce [GET] at the JTS—A Dismal Experience

WEDNESDAY, FEBRUARY 15, 1933

On Thursday, February 9, I sat in on the divorce proceedings of the Rabbinical Assembly Bet Din [Rabbinical Court]. I had made arrangements for these proceedings in behalf of Abe Liebovitz's daughter, Beatrice, from Laurence Wener. The rabbi who conducted them was Max Drob and his associates were Boaz Cohen and Higger.[3] He had a scribe and two witnesses. The lawyers of both the husband and wife were also present.

That was the first time I had ever witnessed a divorce procedure. It brought home to me the problem of the Jewish civilization trying to galvanize itself into life. After the state has threshed out the question

---

1. Kaplan won the contest and used the money to publish *Judaism as a Civilization*. See glossary on Rosenwald and *Judaism Faces the Twentieth Century: A Biography of Mordecai M. Kaplan* (Detroit: Wayne State University Press, 1993), 338, for details about the contest.
2. Benderly had been appointed executive director of the contest.
3. Michael Higger (1898–1952), ordained JTS; Talmud scholar; author.

whether the couple should be divorced or not and after it has rendered its solemn and binding decision along limps up the cripple Judaism to this couple and says to them you must get my consent too if you want to be divorced. And when for sentiment's sake they pretend that they take it seriously it proceeds to draw up a divorce with all the make believe of a serious legal enactment and in the manner of ancient formalities which are as much in place today as knee breeches and powdered wigs. The entire procedure that evening was in the spirit of the ancient law in which woman had hardly any rights of her own and according to which she can never divorce but can only be the divorcee. All in all the affair was to me very dismal and unimpressive.

Using Roosevelt Inaugural in a Sermon

SUNDAY, MARCH 5, 1933

This morning the first of the SAJ Forum meetings took place; it was a big success. Fortunately I had sense enough to change the subject which had been announced as the one I would speak on. I was to have spoken on "Is Judaism a Religion?" But when I pictured to myself a crowd of people hearing me for the first time speak on a question pertaining to the nature of Judaism, especially these days when people are in a semi-panicky condition, I was quite worried. I was certain that the people would be disappointed and it would be difficult to build up a well attended forum. As a last resort I pounced upon President Roosevelt's inaugural message to find there some peg upon which I might hang some of the ideas on economics which I have been mulling over of late. And sure enough I found the statement in which he speaks of facing the arduous years ahead of him "with the consciousness of seeking the old and precious moral values." This I thought gave me the necessary clue to the fact that he was a mere Babbit and a typical product of organized education and organized religion with their tendencies to incapacitate the mind for a profound understanding of the moral issues involved in the economic process.

The Hadassah choir, led by Mrs. Lubarksy, with a Miss Anthony at the piano, furnished the music which gave an esthetic touch to the Forum. The attendance was larger than I had expected—about 275 to 300. The basket was passed around in the approved Sunday morning service fashion and the leading members of the Tuesday night group who organized this Forum functioned as ushers. They were dressed in regular Sunday morning suits with striped trousers. The meeting passed off with clockwork precision as though it took place not the first but the hundredth time.

Jewish Education and the Economic Crisis

TUESDAY, MARCH 7, 1933

This entire evening was taken up with the meeting which took place at my house to consider what to suggest at the meeting scheduled for next Sunday at Vogelstein's house. Benderly, Semel, Chipkin and I took part in this preliminary conference. The greater part of the discussion was carried on between Benderly and Semel. Semel wanted Benderly to consent to work with the Jewish Education Association. Of course Benderly wouldn't even consider such cooperation. I acted as umpire of the debate between the two. I could see where both were wrong and where both were right. I finally succeeded in getting them to adopt my suggestion that we come to the meeting with the following three propositions:

1) Under the present economic uncertainty nothing should be done to tamper with the resources of the three organizations viz. Bureau of Jewish Education, Jewish Education Association and Teachers Institute,[4] especially in view of the fact that those resources are drawn from three different clienteles and in view of the fact that these organizations supplement each other's work without overlapping.

2) A letter should be addressed to Warburg to be signed by the representatives of the three organizations describing the nature of the work done by each of the organizations, pointing out wherein they serve functions that are supplementary to each other. Further more, mention should be made of the following constructive measure which will have emerged from the conferences:

3) Benderly, Semel and I representing the three organizations will undertake to build up a group of Jews who will make themselves responsible for the advocacy of Jewish educational endeavor in order to counteract the opposition to it, and who will later seek to synthesize and coordinate the efforts of the three organizations.

When the meeting was over I took Benderly aside to ask him about the Rosenwald contest. He wouldn't tell me much. All I learned was that Lehman[5] hadn't as yet sent in his letter to Benderly and that Heuhner[6] seemed to be fighting hard against awarding the prize to me. It seems that I

---

4. Bureau of Jewish Education: established under the New York Kehillah in 1910, the model for many later bureaus which attempted to standardize urban Jewish Education.

5. Irving Lehman (1876–1945), judge, state supreme court; legal philosopher; board, Union of American Hebrew Congregations (UAHC). He appreciated Kaplan's submission but thought that it had significant weaknesses. See *Judaism Faces the Twentieth Century*, 340.

6. Leon Huhner (1871–1957), lawyer, historian, and poet; a traditional Jew, he opposed Kaplan's receiving the Rosenwald Prize.

have a majority of the judges in my favor. I therefore cannot imagine where the hitch is.[7]

THURSDAY, MARCH 9, 1933

"He was sentimental, fussy, miserable"—this is a description of Cardinal Newman (Sat. Review of March 4, 1933). I never knew I was in such good company.

One Thousand Attend a Gala Dinner for Einstein

WEDNESDAY, MARCH 15, 1933

My present mood is that of a cold gray day, somber and leaden. Lena and I came not long ago from the Commodore Hotel where we attended the dinner given in honor of Einstein. The cost per plate was $25. We would never have even dreamt of attending had it not been for the kindness of Sol M. Stroock who had invited all the members of the Seminary Faculty and their wives as his guests.

Before the dinner began a certain Max Manischewitz[8] who had a large bust made of Einstein led me to the room to show me the bust. In a little while Einstein himself came into the room shepherded by Jacob Landau.[9] Landau introduced me to Einstein in highly flattering terms. Einstein made some comment which implied he took note of Landau's flattering characterization of me. In the meantime he was made to stand alongside his bust in order to be photographed.

The dinner at which there were what looked to me like eight hundred to a thousand guests was a very brilliant affair. The adoration accorded Einstein together with the large crowd of people among whom were men successful in the different walks of life gave me a sense of insignificance. When the Harvard astronomer sharply passed mentally in review the great universes and nebulae that swim in infinite space and reminded the hearers of the infinitesimally small atom which is man's world, he expressed in astronomical terms the awareness of inconsequence to which I felt myself reduced in the midst of such a gathering.

---

7. Unbeknownst to Kaplan the judges were indeed divided. They divided the prize among three contestants: Kaplan, Eugene Kohn, and Rabbi Lee Levinger. The opposition to Kaplan may have been ideological.

8. Max Manischewitz (1889–1947), industrialist; businessman; philanthropist; Zionist; president, Manischewitz Foundation.

9. Jacob Landau (1892–1952), journalist and publisher for the Jewish Telegraphic Agency.

Judaism and Social Revolution

FRIDAY, MARCH 17, 1933

The following is the outline of what I expect to say:[10]

We misunderstand the Jewish religion if we regard its main contribution as having consisted in the teaching of monotheism. The part which the Jewish religion has played in the history of mankind has been due to something which is seldom recognized or even associated with it, namely, the idea of social revolution. The idea implies that mankind cannot go on indefinitely permitting injustice, oppression and cruelty to exist. Sooner or later there must be an upheaval. Only those who repent of their ways will escape the calamities which will follow in the wake of that upheaval.

That idea began its career as the hope that before long Yahweh would manifest Himself in all His glory, the hope summed up in the phrase "the day of the Lord." Originally it meant the day of national triumph for Israel. When the Prophets came they interpreted it to mean not national triumph (Amos V, 18) but God's triumph (Is. II, 12, 17). For the nation it meant disaster, the downfall of the state, the disruption of the existing order and the emergence of a new and just order of things (Is. IV, 3–4). The prophet was the herald of the social revolution. His mission was to call upon those who wanted to escape its dire consequences to change their entire outlook and mode of life. Prophets ceased to arise when the idea of social revolution died down. That idea was driven underground and found expression in the Apocalyptic literature. It flared up in Jesus and gave rise to Christianity; it flared up in Mohammed and gave rise to Mohammedanism.

The idea was never entirely extinguished but kept on smouldering during the centuries under the ashes of religious beliefs and practices which had nothing to do with justice and goodness. As a smouldering flame it continued in the prayer for the coming of the Kingdom of God and the expectation of a hereafter in which all the inequities of this life would be righted.

The Enlightenment was the awakening of the human mind to the realization that man was not to play the part of a passive instrument, but of a co-creator with God in the shaping of his world. Man's salvation lay in the here and the now. This led to the dispersal of some of the ashes that had choked the fire of the idea of social revolution. The political revolutions which marked the end of feudalism and the advent of political freedom were the result.

But there were many thinkers in England and France who realized the superficial character of the political revolution. They maintained that

---

10. The place where this speech was to be delivered is not clear from the diary.

political revolution had failed to secure to each individual the inalienable right to life, liberty and the pursuit of happiness. Such right is formal and empty unless there take place a radical change in the economic principles and arrangements upon which our social order is based. These men attacked the principle of private property as the source of all social ills, holding that labor was the only title to property. Thus arose socialism.

A Critical Evaluation of Marx and the Jewish Alternative

SATURDAY NIGHT, MARCH 18, 1933

Only blind prejudice can lead one to underestimate Marx's epochal contribution to the understanding of the part played by the economic factor in human life. It has revolutionized the study of human history in the same way as Darwin's discovery of evolution has revolutionized the study of nature. But it is one thing to advance a scientific theory as a means of understanding phenomena of nature or history, and another to plan one's life and the life of society on the basis of a scientific theory. The fact is that life is altogether too complicated to be capable of being guided by a scientific theory, which if it is really scientific should have nothing whatever to do with any practical aim we may wish to further. It does not require elaborate analysis to puncture the scientific theory of economic determinism.

The way to appraise Marxism is by testing, not the soundness of his scientific theory, but the wisdom of what he regarded as the way in which the social revolution must come about. Marx's resort to science is only an intellectual fashion which fails to touch the heart of the matter he is really concerned with. It reminds one of Spinoza's resort to geometry's method to arrive at the idea that man's true freedom consists in an intellectual love of God.

What did Marx really want to say?

1) That social revolution is not a matter of choice, but is bound to come by virtue of the inexorable law of human history.

2) That the middle classes are totally powerless either to stop or to further the social revolution.

Both as Jews and as members of the middle class (though some of us have recently become proletarians, if not in sympathy, at least in pocketbook) we want to know how to take these two Marxian principles.

There can be no question that in emphasizing the inevitability of the social revolution Marxism is a much more vigorous and potent means of furthering it than Utopian Socialism. But as Jews we cannot be indifferent to the Marxist conception of the process by which it is to come about. It is conceived as a process of blind struggle of forces of might. Might makes right.

Our religion has a much wiser conception of that process. It conceives the struggle between the strong the weak, the exploiter and the exploited not as blind and purposeless, but as ultimately proving that the destiny of mankind is governed by a power that makes for righteousness. Righteousness is that norm of social life whereby all men shall realize themselves, or their highest capacities to the fullest measure. This norm of human equality must be translated into the means of subsistence of which there is ample. The God who manifests himself as the power that makes for righteousness is also the God who "openeth His hand and satisfieth every living being." This amplitude in the case of man arises from the intelligence wherewith he fashioned the machine. The machine precipitates the advent of the era where all men shall enjoy the security necessary to their complete self-realization.

As members of the middle class we refuse to accept the Marxist doctrine that we are lost souls, doomed to perdition. This refusal is based on the conviction that as human beings we are dominated by a desire in the long run no less potent than the need for sustenance, the desire to retain our self-respect, and our faith in the meaning and worthwhileness of human life. If the middle classes will have their eyes opened to the incontestable fact that a competitive economic order is incompatible with the essential dignity of man, then they will throw in their influence to replace it with one in which they would find it possible to live as human beings ought to live.

We are all guilty of violence. The fact that it is under duress does not exempt us from protesting, nor justify us in acquiescing.

Will the middle classes be awakened and realize their moral degradation? If not then the prophecy of Marxism will be fulfilled, because that prophecy is as old as the words of Scripture (Ps. 12, 6 and Malachi 3, 23–24).

Is All Effort Futile? — A Depressing Moment

MONDAY, APRIL 3, 1933
Yesterday I gave the concluding lecture of the SAJ Forum. The subject of the lecture was "Whither Judaism?" I set forth once more the program of reconstruction. This time I presented it as an answer to the question "What kind of Judaism can help the Jew to live creatively?" The attendance was about 300. I was in good form and as far at the lecture is concerned I have no regrets. But I cannot help feeling the heartbreaking futility of it all. All this work of mine is like pouring pails of water on hot desert sand with the expectation of rendering it fertile.

A *Talk with Benderly about the Orthodox*

TUESDAY, APRIL 4, 1933

I had a long talk this afternoon with Benderly. We both bemoaned our fate and the futility of our endeavors. He admitted for the first time in all the years I have known him that he had all along committed the serious mistake of not heeding my advice against trying to develop American-Jewish life with the personnel and institutions provided by the traditionalists and the Orthodox. He reminded me of a meeting which Magnes and I had with Rabbi M. Z. Margolies, Harry Fischel and a few other representatives of the Orthodox wing, and of my having tapped him on the knee and having said to him: "Why do we waste our time trying to work with these people?" He now realizes that all the years since have been wasted, and is looking about to start something entirely new.

Incidentally, he referred to Isaac Berkson as the only one, out of the entire group he trained during the first years of the Bureau's existence, who was capable of holding out in a crisis. All the rest—Dushkin, Gamoran, Golub, Schoolman—crumple up.

The main purpose of my going to see him was to obtain from him some information about the present status of the contest. I gathered that it had been left to Lehman to decide whether my book was good enough to get the prize, and that Lehman reported that he did not consider it as measuring up to the prize. The matter is therefore again in abeyance with Lehman continuing to act in dilatory fashion.

Rabbinical Students Protest the Curriculum

THURSDAY, APRIL 6, 1933

At the meeting of the Seminary Faculty there came up once again a petition from the students to bring the curriculum into line with the actual needs of the rabbinate. Incidentally their purpose is to reduce to a minimum the three courses from which they learn least, Hyamson's, Hoschander's and Davidson's. Two months ago they presented specific recommendations. At that time Davidson led the opposition to any change in the curriculum. It was then suggested that the recommendations be referred back to the students who were to be advised by a special committee consisting of myself, Finkelstein and Levine. Levine being sick, Finkelstein and I met with the students and we advised them to formulate their petition in form of general principles which, if accepted by the Faculty, would serve as a basis for specific changes.

At the meeting yesterday Davidson again tried to nullify their petition. He was abetted by Hyamson and Hoschander and to some extent by Ginzberg. It became clear that these men have no interest in correlating the curriculum with the rabbinical function of the students they are supposed to train. Each man considers the various problems which research has raised in his own particular subject an indispensable part of the knowledge that a modern rabbi ought to have. On that assumption even a ten year training would scarcely suffice.

This inability to formulate a satisfactory curriculum accentuates a seldom noted aspect of the problem of Jewish adjustment, and that is the difficulty in arriving at a reasonable minimum standard of what a Jew ought to know if he is to live his Jewish life intelligently and creatively. There is so much that one has to know to keep up with the times both in the world at large and in his own particular calling that there seems to be no time left for matters of Jewish interest.

Listening to a Lecture by George B. Shaw
THURSDAY, APRIL 13, 1933

After the second seder I listened in to the speech delivered by Bernard B. Shaw[11] at the Metropolitan House.[12] I was deeply impressed by the contents of the address as well as by the fact that a man of his age, experience and reputation should tell the American people what they ought long ago to have known. I was, therefore, keenly chagrined at the avalanche of abuse that has come down on his head in the general press. There is no hope for this country unless they come to realize the truth of two main points of his address 1) that the Constitution is a "charter of anarchism," and 2) that the financiers are the irresponsible rulers of this country. The first indispensable step in the socialization of wealth is the nationalization of the banks, which Shaw so ably advocated. If coming from such a source this common advice was so violently repudiated, what chance is there of getting the bourgeoisie to see the light?

Spirituality and Needing Others
FRIDAY, APRIL 21, 1933

When Whitehead said that religion is what a man does with his solitariness[13] he seemed to have had no conception of the devastating effect of solitariness on those who labor in the field of religion. Solitariness may

---

11. Kaplan meant George B. Shaw.

12. Metropolitan Opera House. Shaw left America the day after the lecture. He was interviewed by the press and said he saw America as the savior of the world, and "what he liked best about New York was leaving it." *New York Times*, April 13, 1933.

13. This famous remark is contained in Whitehead's book on religion, *Religion in the Making* (New York: Macmillan, 1926).

be as essential to the life of the spirit as sleep is for the recuperation of physical energy, but the time to experience the reality of God is when we are in the midst of those who are kindred to us in soul by reason of common hopes and difficulties. The psalmist was not advancing any general theories, but merely recording actual experience when he said that his doubts about the divine scheme of existence were resolved when he resorted to the sanctuary, or that he reached the height of ecstasy when he led a throng in pilgrimage to the temple. The Rabbis were not scientific psychologists. Yet they knew whereof they spoke when they said that those who studied the Torah entirely by themselves condemned themselves to sterility and frustration. The implication of the term *khaver* [Heb. friend][14] is that association with those who are engaged in the same spiritual pursuit is a prerequisite to spiritual attainment. It is this fact which makes our collaboration for common ends and our periodic getting together the very life breath of our calling. Spiritually speaking we are never so alone as when we are busy with the round of our duties of preaching, teaching, attending meetings, making calls, officiating at various functions. There is authority to uphold, the authority of certain truths and ideals, and authority of however attenuated a form always draws a circle around the one exercising it; there is a certain expertness to maintain, the expertness of the functionary, and expertness real or imaginary creates a laity who use the lack of it as an excuse for feeling apart and distant. There is the added circumstance in the case of the rabbinic office that the laity are entirely preoccupied with their own personal problems which the economic crisis has rendered more numerous and acute, in addition they are altogether devoid of a Jewish knowledge. This makes it necessary for the rabbi to think and work for the laity. Seldom does he have a chance to think and work with them. He has to come to them with plans, solutions and a fund of inexhaustible energy. The most fertile mind, the most sanguine soul and the most tireless worker is bound to find his powers ebbing as a result of this constant drain upon them. We need the replenishment which only contact and interchange of ideas with one another can give as one that is thirsty needs water.

(Now that the plane is off the ground, it shouldn't strike some wire or roof.)

As I suspected I got stuck at this point and couldn't write a line all afternoon. I was browsing among the papers and discussions of CCAR of 1931 and 1932. It is amazing on how much higher a plane most of their arguments move than do those of the Rabbinical Assembly papers and discussions.

---

14. Kaplan certainly had in mind the statement in *Ethics of the Fathers*, chapter 1:6: "Joshua Ben Perachya says: Find a Teacher. Acquire a friend. Give everyone the benefit of the doubt."

An Encyclopedia Article on Schechter

MONDAY, MAY 1, 1933

I wrote the letter to Alvin Johnson and Lena typed it. She objected to my sending it. I yielded to her objection and instead wrote the usual excuse of not having time.[15]

"I regret I do not see my way clear to writing the article on Schechter because I do not hold the majority opinion about him. I do not question his eminence as a savant and as an outstanding personality. He was a Jewish Samuel Johnson but I cannot act as his Boswell. While I consider his contribution to Jewish scholarship as worthy of the Historical School to which he belonged, I regard his contribution to the problem of Jewish adjustment as more confusing than helpful. He belonged to that school of thought which views life as something self-evident and to be accepted as a God-willed destiny and as bound to become soulless and meaningless as soon as it is treated as a problem. The social sciences were to him the work of the devil, and those who invented the Jewish problem, the devil's disciples. Since he probably classed me as one of those disciples, although we were always on the friendliest of terms, I feel someone else ought to do his biography."

A Negro Folk Drama and a Jewish Play Compared

TUESDAY, MAY 9, 1933

Last night I saw the play "Run, Little Chillun"[16] by Hall Johnson given at the Lyria on 42 St. It is described as "A Negro Folk Drama in Four Scenes." It has so many points in common with the play "Yoshe Kalb"[17] by I. J. Singer, which was produced in this city by Maurice Schwartz, that it set me wondering what possible implications can there be in the fact that Jews and Negroes resemble each other to so large a degree in their sufferings, in their yearnings and in the primitive force and character of their religiousness when untouched by the skeptical spirit of Western Civilization. "Yoshe Kalb"

---

15. Kaplan was asked to write an encyclopedia article on Schechter and refused. Instead of writing the letter recorded here, he simply gave the excuse of lack of time. For more information on Kaplan's relationship to Schechter, see my *Judaism Faces the Twentieth Century* as well as my "Schechter's Seminary" in *Tradition Renewed—A History of the Jewish Theological Seminary*, vol 1, ed. Jack Wertheimer (New York: Jewish Theological Seminary, 1997).

16. *Run Little Chillun Run* by Hall Johnson. A thinly disguised plot about conflicts between two churches becomes the background for a group of Negro spirituals which are superbly done. New York Times, March 2, 1933, 21.

17. *Yoshe Kalb* is a dramatization of a novel of the same name by I. J. Singer. The story revolves around a powerful Hasidic rabbi and his involvement with a woman much his junior who becomes his fourth wife. It was presented at the Yiddish Art Theater with Maurice Schwartz directing and in the title role.

might be described as a Hassidic folk drama. Both dramas exhibit the human soul being tortured by a sense of sin, in both it is illicit love which gives rise to the sense of sin, in both the heroine meets with tragic death and the hero finds redemption. The theme "Run, Little Chillun, run! Fo' the devil's done loose in de lan' " has its analogue in the search for sinners which is started when the plague breaks out in the town where Yoshe was expiating his sin. The conflict in Yoshe's soul finds a close analogue in the struggle which Jim, the son of Rev. Jones, the pastor of the Hope Baptist Church, undergoes on account of his love for Sulamai.

I must confess however that the Negro folk drama shows off to better advantage because the background of religion against which the story is enacted is of much finer stuff and a more spiritual texture than the background of religion in "Yoshe Kalb." In the latter, pietism with its high ecstatic moments and moments of deep depression is the only attractive feature which the religion of the Hasidim possesses. The rest is rendered repellent by fanatical punctiliousness, horrid superstition and, as in the case of Reb Melech, Yoshe Kalb's father in law, calculating worldliness. In the Negro Folk Drama we behold the struggle between the official religion which the Negro took over from the white man, and the religion which awakens in the Negro like a call from the primeval forests in which his ancestors dwelt. "The New Day Pilgrims" stand out against the conventional Baptist religion of their more staid brethren like the followers of the Baal Shem against the traditional religion of the Talmudic casuists. The native religion to which the Negroes revert has a high esthetic appeal but it culminates in orgiastic abandon. The self abandon of Hassidic religion acted as a release from the sex urge. That is of course the essential difference. That difference goes back to the days when YHWH's zealots, the Nazarites and the Nebiim with their ecstatic dances around YHWH's ark stood out against the orgiastic revelries in the temples and groves of the Baalim.

Anxieties about Judaism as a Civilization

FRIDAY, MAY 12, 1933

I was very much perturbed this morning when I read that Abba Hillel Silver had returned from abroad. Nursing a vindictive hostility against Sol Goldman, and knowing that Goldman derived the main impetus to his interpretation of Judaism from me, he takes every possible opportunity to attack me and my conception of Judaism every time he gets a chance to do so. He happens to be one of the advisory committee on the Rosenwald Contest. He will in all probability take part in the meeting scheduled for May 28 (according to what Benderly last told me). In that case the last ray of hope that I might win the award is extinguished.

Every time I look into the manuscript I submitted to the committee I am sorry for myself. In its way it isn't a bad piece of work. There is so much in common between my approach to Judaism and Spengler's to culture as a whole that I feel that I can't be altogether wrong. My version of Judaism is at least in focus with the thinking of the day, which is all that true interpretation or art can be expected to be.

Rise of Nazis Changes Study Plans for Kaplan's Daughter

WEDNESDAY, MAY 17, 1933

My Selma who attends the New College, Columbia, was advised some time ago by Dr. Alexander, the head of the College, to specialize in German, and for the purpose join the group that he was planning to take to Germany to study. With the rise of the Nazis to power I had Selma give up the idea of going to Germany. Instead she is to go to England and to specialize in English. But she was to have sailed with those who are to go to Germany on the Hamburg-American line, a German concern. With the strong boycott sentiment which has recently made itself felt among the Jewish people in retaliation for the treatment of the Jews in Germany it would have looked odd for me to allow Selma to travel on a German liner. She and three other girls of the group asked Alexander to allow them to get to England by another steamer. Their request came largely as a result of an effort made by the prominent lawyer Untermeyer to get Alexander to cancel his arrangements for all of the eight Jewish girls to sail on the German steamer. He even sent Alexander a check of $1000 to cover the loss which Alexander would sustain by making the change. Alexander was very much incensed by all these interferences with his plans but he finally yielded.

A Friendly Gesture from Finkelstein

The meeting of the Seminary Curriculum Committee headed by Prof. Ginzberg took place this morning. The main butt of attack was Hyamson. The problem was how to get the students to acquire some knowledge of the Codes in spite of him.

My courses were not disturbed. When the question arose of having each member of the Faculty give a Seminar in addition to his regular course I was satisfied not to give any, but Finkelstein suggested that I give one in the history and philosophy of religion. I regard this as a friendly gesture on his part.

Selma Kaplan Goldman, ca. 1936. (Courtesy Selma K. Goldman)

Kaplan and Louis Finkelstein, late 1930s. (Courtesy Library of the JTS)

Praying Is a Form of Thinking

SUNDAY, MAY 21, 1933

To say "I believe in praying" sounds to me as absurd as to say "I believe in thinking." The question whether prayer is effective is only a special form of the question whether thought is effective. And just as we make use of the best thoughts of others in order to channel our own thinking into the surest and most beneficent effectiveness, so should we make use of the most noble and sincere prayers of others to channel our own prayers into a life of the greatest nobility and sincerity. This is why I like to pray and why I frequently resort to the prayers of those who could speak their mind in the language of prayer. Unfortunately we Jews have limited prayer to the deadening routine of reciting the few meager passages which go to make up our official prayer book. If I had anything to do with the prescribing of rules for prayer I would have insisted upon living up to the principle of R. Eliezer *kol ha'oseh tephilato keva* . . . [Heb. Mishna Berachot 4:3 "Everyone who makes his prayer fixed (i.e., mechanical) his prayer is not deemed as supplication"] and ordained that the vast storehouse of religious poetry be drawn upon continually. That would have set the wealth of devotional literature into circulation. One can understand why it would have been difficult to live up to such a requirement in the past. But with the help of the printing press, it should be comparatively easy to place that devotional literature at everybody's disposal.

For the last ten years I have been in the habit of reciting a blessing or prayer at the end of the morning Sabbath service. From time to time I improvise something new. Yesterday, for example, I made use of three passages from the Haftarah[18] (Jer. XVI and XVII) which I paraphrased in translation and arranged in the following order *'d uzi umahuzi umenusi beyom* . . . [Heb. Jeremiah 16:19 "O Lord, my strength, and my stronghold, and my refuge in the day of affliction . . ."].[19]

O God, Be Thou our strength, our fortress and our refuge in these troublous days.

refa'eyni 'd ve'eyrafey hoshi'eyni venivasheyah [Heb. Jeremiah 17:14 "Heal me oh Lord that I may be healed; save me and I shall be saved: for Thou art my praise"].

Give us healing of body and mind so that we may be truly healed, grant deliverance to our spirit so that we may be truly saved.

Baruch   hagever   asher   yivtah   badonai . . . [Heb. Jeremiah 17:7 "Blessed is the man who trusts in the Lord, and whose hope the lord is"].

May we be of those who, having faith in Thee, merit thy gracious blessing.

The Bas Mitzvah Is Neglected

WEDNESDAY, MAY 31, 1933

The institution of the Bas Mitzvah which I introduced into the SAJ not long after the Society was organized had fallen into desuetude of late. There has not been a single Bas Mitzvah celebration during the last two years. This morning Shirley Lubell, the daughter of Sam and Jennie Lubell, celebrated her Bas Mitzvah. I hope that from now on that institution will be kept up regularly.

Songs about Kaplan from the Family

SUNDAY, JUNE 4, 1933

Last Thursday night all the members of the Rubin[20] family and mother, Sophie, Phineas[21] and Esther[22] came to our house to celebrate the

---

18. The prophetic portion read each Sabbath after the reading from the Pentateuch.

19. In each case Kaplan gives a translation slightly different from the original. We have included a more literal translation.

20. Kaplan's in-laws.

21. Sophie Israeli is Kaplan's sister; Phineas is her husband.

22. Esther Israeli (1905–94), daughter of Sophie and Phineas; schoolteacher; loved music.

silver anniversary of our wedding which took place on June 2, 1908. We were all happy and had a lovely time. Judith, Al and Harold Bernstein, David Baron's son-in-law, regaled us with songs which they wrote and set to music for the occasion. Here are two of them:

I Love to Lean on Lena

In time of strife, I need my wife
I always lean on Lena
In time of peace, my needs don't cease
I love to lean on Lena.

She'll protect me from an importuning guest
Who is likely to become an awful pest
And when the text is troubling me
She'll bring cherries and hot tea
To restore to me my intellectual zest.
      Refrain: In time of strife, etc.
She'll lay out my tie and handkerchief and shirt
And she'll look behind my ears for any dirt
And when homeward late I toddle
She'll become my artist's model
And assume a classic attitude and pert.
      Refrain: In time of strife, etc.
I adore to lean on Lena.

A Philanderer's Wife Leads an Arduous Life

A philanderer's wife leads an arduous life
The trials I've endured have been many
To Mordecai long I've been married, He's a man whose
      loves have been varied
A new love in his life every year.

For the first year his love just ran to
That language they call Esperanto
He talked and he muttered, he stammered and stuttered
My poor heart, it fluttered with each word he uttered
      Refrain: A philanderer's wife leads an arduous life,
As she waits for the next to appear

And next, to speed up the traffic, we wooed the art
      stenographic

He became so ambitious, my worthiest dishes
My food most delicious, he found meretricious.
   Refrain
He went on to mushrooms and toast
the food he declared he loved most
His constant petition for a repetition
Of this form of nutrition would embarrass a dietician
   Refrain
He declared this love's consummation was bound up with
   The League of Nations
That each nationality would achieve a personality
In the totality of Universality.
   Refrain
And every new love was the best,
Good grammar for instance he blessed
Studied Blackstone as well, lots more I could tell
What a man! What a life! It's just swell!!!
   Refrain

On Friday Selma sailed for England there to pursue part of her course at the New College, Columbia. God bless her and prosper her in her studies and in her friendships.

Last night the members of the SAJ gave Lena and me a surprise party. This was a surprise party for fair. Even for some time after I got to the SAJ Building, and found the people seated in the social hall I was under the impression that it was a surprise party for Ira Eisenstein on the occasion of his leaving for Palestine. Lena and I thought we were fooling him while he was all the time fooling us. The joke was surely on me this time. I had even thought of what to say in case I would be called upon to wish Ira Bon Voyage.

The Contest—A Disappointment

SATURDAY NIGHT, JUNE 10, 1933

Wednesday afternoon Lena and I went to visit the Benderlys at their recently acquired farm in Godefroy, NY. That evening and all day Thursday till 5:30 they spent with us showing us the various points of interest on their farm and the set up of the camp for the boys and girls who come there in the summer.

In the course of the conversation Wednesday evening I asked Benderly about the Rosenwald contest. He gave me practically the same information as E. Friedman[23] with the addition that I was to get $3500 and the other two $1500 and $1000 respectively. I am far from certain whether Rosenwald's son will be willing to give the money under those terms since he can avail himself of the loophole that the judges had evidently not found any of the essays worthy of being awarded the prize as originally stipulated.

Benderly admitted to me that I was right in my original contention that it was illogical to have expected judges holding such diverse views to come to an agreement on any essay that dealt with the problem of Judaism. Of the six judges, E. Friedman and Dr. Harry Friedenwald[24] are nationalists, Judges I. Lehman and Horace Stern[25] are Reformists and Prof. Isaacs[26] and Leon Huhner are Orthodox.

Great as is my disappointment in the outcome of the contest it is trivial compared to the feeling of hopelessness about the Jewish situation as a whole, which the attitude of the majority of the judges and the slipshod and dilatory manner in which they dealt with the entire matter have produced in me.

Organizing the Midwest

THURSDAY, JUNE 15, 1933

Immediately upon the conclusion of the exercises I made the train for Detroit to attend the conference of the proposed Council for the Advancement of American Jewish Life. The fact that a considerable number of those who were in sympathy with the aims of the Council were likely to be in Detroit to attend the conventions of the National Council for Jewish Education and the National Conference for Jewish Social Service led Honor, Dushkin, Goldman, Golub and Brickner to hold the conference to organize the Council for the Advancement of American Jewish Life. It was to be an all-day meeting at the Statler Hotel in Room 1230.

Among those present were Benderly, Dushkin, Honor, Golub, Brick-

23. Elisha Friedman(1889–1951), economist; investment banker; active in Joint Distribution Committee. The idea for the Rosenwald contest originally came from Friedman. See *Judaism Faces the Twentieth Century*, 338.

24. Harry Friedenwald (1864–1950), M.D., national president, Federation of Zionists of America; author.

25. Horace Stern (1878–1969), lawyer; chief justice, state supreme court of Pennsylvania; officer, Dropsie College, Jewish Publication Society.

26. Nathan Isaacs (1886–1941), Ph.D., LL.B., lawyer; faculty, Harvard; delegate, World Jewish Congress; Orthodox.

ner,[27] Karpf, Edidin,[28] Friedland,[29] Felix Levy,[30] B. Heller (of Hillel Foundation),[31] Dr. Gordon (of Minneapolis),[32] Gamoran, Chipkin, Dr. L. Bernstein (of Pittsburgh)[33] and a few more whom I can't think of just now. Felix Levy and I were the only ones who came to Detroit solely for this conference.

When I was called upon to state the purpose of the meeting I dwelt upon the fact that a sense of futility in all our endeavors should impel us to formulate a new orientation to Jewish life. Our problem as a group was how to introduce that new orientation into the various forms of Jewish communal effort. I was followed by Ludwig Bernstein who explained his attempt to organize a Jewish Community Council (or Kehilla) in Pittsburgh. Incidentally he mentioned the fact that both the Orthodox and Reformist rabbis were friendly disposed toward his plan. The only quarter where he encountered opposition was the group of Seminary graduates who head the so-called conservative congregations.

The discussion at the conference turned in the main upon two questions: 1) the purpose of the organization as set forth in its name and 2) the feasibility of engaging someone to give all his time to the organization.

Dr. Benderly argued that the council ought to supply Jewish life in America with the orientation that it lacks. He therefore advocated the name Council for the Orientation to Jewish Life. Brickner argued that we should come out boldly for the reconstruction of Jewish Life. Although I too argued for reconstruction as an avowed aim, yet when it came to a final decision, I advised the adoption of the name which had been agreed upon at the preliminary meeting last summer at Camp Modin, the Council for the Advancement, etc. I did not feel that our group measured up to so presumptuous a term as reconstruction.

The second matter which was debated at some length was the feasibility of engaging some one to devote all his time to the organization. It seems that Benderly had asked Dushkin whether he would be willing to give

---

27. Barnett Brickner (1891–1958), ordained Hebrew Union College; Zionist; president, Central Conference of American Rabbis (CCAR).

28. Ben Edidin (1889–1948), Ed.D. Columbia; Zionist; member, Board of Education (Tel Aviv); president, National Council for Jewish Education.

29. Abraham H. Friedland (1892–1939), Yeshiva College; Zionist; Hebrew author; director, Board of Jewish Education (Cleveland).

30. Felix Levy (1884–1963), Ph.D, ordained Hebrew Union College; president, CCAR, Zionist; College of Jewish Studies, Chicago.

31. Bernard Heller (1896–1976), Ph.D., ordained Hebrew Union College; Hillel Director; author; faculty, Hebrew Union College-Jewish Institute of Religion.

32. Albert I. Gordon ? (1903–68), ordained JTS; rabbi, Minneapolis; executive director, United Synagogue; officer, Zionist Organization of America.

33. Ludwig Bernstein ? (1875–1944), Ph.D., sociologist, Bureau of Jewish Social Research; Federation of Jewish Philanthropies (Pittsburgh).

up his position in Chicago to engage in this work and Dushkin consented, if we could subscribe $5000 to cover his salary and expenses. Benderly, Karpf, I and Dushkin pleaded for contributions by our own members that would make it possible for one of our number to give all his time to the Council. I went as far as to offer $200. But the others present felt they were not in a position to contribute large amounts. So the plan fell through.

The positive results accomplished were the following:

1) The Council was formally recognized. I was chosen President, and Golub, Secretary and Treasurer.

2) An Institute to be held during the last week in August or the first week in September to discuss the various aspects of the inner problems of Jewish life.

3) The symposium planned during the summer should be carried through.

4) Membership dues $25 per annum to defray cost of activities.

Reading Ezekiel Kaufman— "Golah ve-nekhar"[34]

TUESDAY, JUNE 20, 1933

I finished yesterday the second volume of *Golah ve-nekhar* [Heb. "In Alien and Foreign Lands"]. I find myself entirely in accord with his [i.e., E. Kaufman's] analysis of the beginnings of Christianity. He is the first writer among Jews and Christians that I have come across who understands correctly the part played by the belief in the world to come. I was happy to find my views with regard to the mission of Jesus entirely confirmed.

But the more I realize what appears to be the main thesis of his work, viz.: that the tragedy of the Jewish people has been due to its tendency to domicile itself within some non-Jewish group, that the only thing that has prevented the Jews from being absorbed by the various non-Jewish groups among which it has found domicile has been its religion, and that (I infer that this is the point of the next volume) with the breakdown of religion both among the Jews and the non-Jews this tendency must lead to the disappearance of the Jews unless (and this I think is the point of the last volume) they evolve the capacity to create an environment of their own which is free from the complications in which Palestine is entangled—the more I find my own solution to be what he would characterize as *peri kela'im shel she'efat hitbolelut veratson le'umi* [Heb. the fruit of the (strange) mixture of the desire to assimilate and the nationalist will.]

---

34. Yehezkel Kaufmann (1889–1963), biblical scholar; essayist; author of " A History of Israelite Religion" in eight volumes. "Golah Ve-nekhar" ("In Alien and Foreign Lands"): a two-volume sociological study of Jewish history.

I begin to question the validity of the thesis upon which I have been building all these years and which I have elaborated in the manuscript Judaism as a Civilization. It is when I turn to the manuscript and read some passages out of it that my confidence returns. The fact is that the question whether my thesis is true or not can be settled only in the way the Chinese say it is possible to settle the question whether or not there is a God. "If you believe in Him, he exists," they say. Likewise the truth of my thesis cannot be substantiated unless there will be found Jews who will believe in it to the point of translating it into a program of life. Had any group which I have tried to build up—in order to convince myself of the truth of my thesis— shown the least sign of translating that thesis into life, there would never have flitted across my mind the least shadow of a doubt as to its validity. But so far I have hardly had a moment when I did not feel as though I was surrounded by impenetrable gloom.

A Conference on Jewish Life Organized by Kaplan

Tuesday, September 5, 1933

The Institute which was held under the auspices of "The Council for the Advancement of Jewish Life" at the Cejwin Camps, Port Jervis, proved more successful than I had expected it to be. It was in session from Wednesday afternoon, Aug. 30, to Sunday evening, Sept. 3, morning, noon and night. The total attendance was twenty-five of whom only a few attended all the sessions. The following were the papers read and my impressions of them:

1. Solomon Goldman: "The American Jewish Scene" (Wednesday afternoon, Aug. 30)

A journalese jeremiad when what is needed is an objective analysis.

2. Maurice J. Karpf: Social Research and the Advancement of Jewish life (evening)

A dry as dust elaboration of a self-evident need and an impossible plan for meeting it. The paper was read by Signer.

3. My paper took both morning and afternoon sessions of Thursday.

The discussion was only on the first half. There was no time to discuss the second half.

4. S. Benderly: An extemporaneous talk on making the summer camp the chief instrument in Jewish education in America (Thursday evening).

5. Jacob S. Golub: "The Jewish School of Tomorrow" (Friday morning)

Analysis good; solution, the impossible one of making "Haluziut" the objective.

6. Friday evening: The organization of the Council was discussed by Dushkin, Gamoran, Golub, Edidin, Chipkin, Brickner and me.

7. Saturday morning before services B. Brickner gave a talk on "The Synagogue of Tomorrow."

Nothing new except that the synagogue should be expanded to the dimensions of community.

8. Abraham H. Friedland: "The Place of Hebrew in American Jewish Life." (Saturday afternoon).

The first reasoned statement on the subject.

9. Emanual Gamoran: "The Jewish Home" (Saturday evening)

A warmed over rehash.

10. Eugene Kohn: "Uniting World Jewry" (Sunday morning)

An excellent paper.

11. Edward L. Israel: "Participation of Jews in Radical Social and Economic Movements." (Sunday afternoon).

The makings of a good paper.

The outstanding fact in the Institute was the high level of the discussion from the beginning to the end. No one spoke unless he had something to contribute to the argument. I would find my own ideas undergoing changes as I listened, ideas with regard to matters I had been thinking about for a long time.

The next problem will be how to work out the material presented into a symposium.

Kaplan Writes a Birthday Letter to Cyrus Adler

MONDAY, SEPTEMBER 11, 1933

I have just now sent off a letter of congratulations to Dr. Adler on the occasion of his seventieth birthday. It took me one and three quarter hours to write it although it is little more than a page in length. The reason I had to labor so long on it is that I am a poor hand at saying or writing the conventional eulogies and good wishes, which most people roll off glibly because they have a good memory and can recite them by rote. Each time I have to praise somebody or wish somebody well I go through the agony of original creation. Secondly, I had to suppress my inner opposition to his, shall I say, fundamentalism or limited understanding, I really don't know which, and to center my attention upon that aspect of his character which I genuinely was grateful for. In spite of my irritation at his non-progressivism I am indebted to him for not only tolerating me but actually smoothing my way in my work at the Institute. It was for this that I was honestly able to write a warm hearted letter to him.

I still maintain that in the Seminary scheme I occupy a more important place than my colleagues or Adler would care to admit. The Seminary is designated "Seminary." They lend it academic dignity. Finkelstein as Professor of Theology justifies its being called "Theological." Upon me falls the burden of keeping it "Jewish" so that the students might carry away from it some knowledge of how they might direct the course of Jewish life in the future.

In spite of the many opponents that Benderly has managed to create for himself I still believe in him and in the single-mindedness of his purpose to find some way out of the apparently hopeless task of imparting to our children a Jewish training that will stick.

Hebrew in the Synagogue

MONDAY, SEPTEMBER 11, 1933
    What will become of Hebrew as part of American Jewish life if it is to be gradually eliminated even from the synagogue whose worshipers claim to be more intensely Jewish than those affiliated with the Reformist synagogue? Last Sabbath I read the story from Makkot 24 about R. Akiba,[35] passage by passage, first the Hebrew and then the English translation. Lena, who no doubt reacts the way most of the people at the SAJ services do, was very much annoyed at my reading the Hebrew. It interfered with her appreciation of the story.
    In the course of a conversation I had with Joe Levy in the evening of the same day we discussed the possibility of changing the services radically. What I had in mind was substituting the poetry of a Gabirol or Halevi[36] for the insipid parts of the liturgy. But he had in mind throwing out the Hebrew entirely. And that from a man who has been born and bred in the traditional synagogue, and who has been one of the pillars of the SAJ!

Kaplan Pays a Subsidy to Macmillan to Publish His Book

TUESDAY, NOVEMBER 7, 1933
    It is 10:30 P.M. I am now sitting all alone in the library. This apartment at 2 W 89 St (The St. Urban) into which we moved on Monday, October 9, is much more spacious than the one we moved from. Now that it is almost in order I can see what an improvement it is on the last one in which we lived for fifteen years. My only prayer is that we should all have

---

35. A rather long account in which other rabbis bemoan the fate of Israel whereas Rabbi Akiba rejoiced because of his certainty that Israel would be delivered.

36. Medieval Hebrew poets.

our health to be able to enjoy the pleasure which it can afford us. In all my days I never dreamed of ever being in a position to have such comfort. If I were a millionaire I shouldn't want anything more luxurious.

I just sent off to Macmillan's the signed contract for my book "Judaism as a Civilization" together with a check for $900 which I drew from the prize money. May God grant that the book appear and be well received.

It was my sad duty to speak this morning at the funeral of Benjamin Silk who died yesterday at the Beth Israel Hospital. He was a rare type of man, gifted and modest, a genuine poet with a beautiful soul which found expression in all that he did.

Both he and Hoschander were unknown, uncelebrated men yet far more noble and heroic than most of those whose names are on everybody's lips.

WEDNESDAY, FEBRUARY 21, 1934
I worked steadily on the manuscript of "Judaism as a Civilization" practically from the High Holidays till January 16 when I handed it in to Macmillans. Rabbi Jacob Weinstein[37] went over the text and suggested a number of verbal changes. Abraham Duker[38] went over the notes. Their assistance has so far cost me about $400.

So Much Misery! The Scottsboro Case

SUNDAY, FEBRUARY 25, 1934
I am having one of my usual spells of misery. Last night I saw the dramatization of the Scottsboro[39] case called "They Shall Not Die."[40] It upset me so that I was not in a fit mood to teach my classes at the Institute today. Man's cruelty to man, whenever it is brought home to me in anything I read or hear about, completely unnerves me. It dashes into pieces all my hopes and ambitions. In a country that can permit such violations of elementary justice as the Mooney and Scottsboro cases, in a humanity that can permit

---

37. Jacob Weinstein ? (1902–74), ordained Hebrew Union College; president, CCAR; editor, *Jewish Frontier.*

38. Abraham Duker (1907–87), Ph.D., author, librarian; faculty, Brooklyn College.

39. A famous case in Alabama beginning in 1931 in which nine black men were accused of raping two white women. Liberals felt the charges were racial. Long prison sentences were imposed.

40. *Thou Shall Not Die* by John Wexley. A play about unjustly condemned young black men assumed to be based on the Scottsboro case. "It is a play of terrifying and courageous bluntness of statement, thoughtfully developed, lucidly explained and played with great resolution." Review by Brooks Atkinson, *New York Times*, February 22, 1934, 24.

without protest the kind of wholesale slaughter that was perpetrated about a week ago in Vienna,[41] in a world that tolerates the ruthless extermination of half a million Jews in a country which they loved with every fibre of their being and which they enriched with their cultural contributions, what prospect can there be of human life ever becoming worthwhile? What is there to sustain one's faith in man, or one's belief in God? I am sure that if I had the courage to break with my professional ties and to ally myself with some kind of a fighting organization that would hold out the least promise of destroying the present crime infested social order, I would regain my faith in life. If I manage to go on with my work it is simply due to this hypothetical belief in God. There is the well known philosophy of "As if." Mine is at present the philosophy "That If."

The Attractions of Communism

SUNDAY, MARCH 4, 1934

The extent to which young people doing Jewish work or being trained for it are victims of inner conflict as a result of its irrelevance as compared with the more realistic approach to life's problems, offered by Communism, is brought home to me almost at every lesson I teach. Whether I am teaching a class at the Seminary, in the Institute or in the Graduate school for Jewish Social Workers, I am confronted with the problem of meeting the arguments presented by those with communist leanings. God knows I myself feel very much as the students do but what can I or they do about it? We are doomed to languish spiritually. We cannot be accepted by the communists, and I for one doubt whether I would be willing to give myself body and soul to a movement that calls on me to repudiate my entire past or the past of my people as having intrinsically nothing to give to the future.

Ira Eisenstein was over this evening. He bewailed his lot. I argued this way and that to make out some kind of case for our place in the world, but without conviction. The best I could do—and that with the help of Judith—was to maintain that since we were hemmed in and unable to work for communism we should accept our limitations and do the best we can under the circumstances. If we make a serious effort to predispose those who come within the ambit of our influence to a just social order we can afford to retain our self respect. To act otherwise and to give in to a feeling of being trapped and frustrated is to commit moral suicide.

---

41. In February 1934 there was an uprising in Austria against the Dolfuss regime following a decree dissolving all political parties.

Modern Rabbis and Social Justice

MONDAY, MARCH 5, 1934

It may be that we rabbis take ourselves too seriously. We experience bitter disappointment because we misconceive our calling and dream of achieving things way beyond our reach. We have talked it into ourselves that we are the successors of the Prophets and therefore believe that we are a failure unless we devote all our energies to the cause of social justice. It would indeed be wonderful if we could do that. But to be prophets we would have to be of the proletariat class, live and work with them and be able to be their spokesmen. But ours is an entirely different calling. We are not world reformers or improvers. As rabbis our function is to keep alive the culture or civilization of the Jewish people. That does not exempt us, to be sure, of the responsibility for the furtherance of social justice, but it is a mistake to treat us as if the furtherance of social justice was our only function.

To formulate a clear conception of the rabbinical office it is necessary to take into account the relation between culture and social justice. Culture is the sum of those activities which produce the human differentia. Social justice is the social conditioning which is necessary to render those activities productive of the human differentia. The very existence of a culture or civilization presupposes some degree of social justice. A time however comes when the institutions which are supposed to maintain social justice are not only corrupt but bound to be inadequate because they are based on outgrown ideas of human rights and privileges. It is then the business of those who foster the culture or civilization to denounce the perversion of justice even according to the old standards and to instruct their people in the newer and more adequate ideas of social justice. But they do that only as part of their more comprehensive task of keeping alive the culture or civilization as a whole. After all there is more to life even than the just distribution of wealth. There are art and literature and history and the attitude toward Reality. Who if not the rabbi is going to keep these things alive for the Jewish people?

It seems to me that if the rabbi teaches the kind of religion and ethics which are based on the principle enunciated in the manifesto "From each according to his abilities, to each according to his needs," he has no reason to find fault with himself for not giving up the rabbinate and joining the communist organization. In removing the prop of self-righteousness from the capitalist economy he is rendering a useful service. The fact that he derives a livelihood from people who thrive on that economy does not prevent him from being their gadfly and conscience. If he pursues his task honestly they will not come to regard their giving him a livelihood and their upholding religious institutions as an atonement for their sin of exploitation. The truth is that the mass of middle class people are as helpless as the rabbi. The only trouble with the people is that they seldom realize that they are doing anything wrong. It is for the rabbi to make them and keep them aware of their sin and urge them to support whatever movement might free them from the evil necessity of exploiting others.

An Example of Kaplan on Midrash and the Red Heifer

TUESDAY, MARCH 6, 1934

When I manage to develop interesting and fruitful ideas in the course of a lesson I give to one of my classes all my inner conflicts are resolved. This was the case this morning; during each of the three sessions at the Seminary I succeeded in bringing out one or more significant points.

In the Midrash hour I made the following comments on Gen. R XXIV, 2: The Rabbinic interpretation of Ps. 139[42] constitutes an attempt to find in it the metaphysical conception of man. That conception is associated with the creation of Adam. As developed in the Midrashic passage it is strikingly similar to the idea of man as developed by the Platonists. Not only is the heavenly Adam (Logos) represented as filling all space but we even find an allusion to *hulay* [Greek: wood, matter, or substance] in the term *golam* [Heb. unformed substance. i.e., in Psalm 139:17].

The significance of the Platonic doctrine of ideas is that Reality is meaningful and not chaos. It is intended to convey the religious affirmation of life's worth.

The statement that the Heavenly Adam had the book of subsequent generations of leaders unrolled to him implies that the leaders give significance to the cosmos of human society.

The notion of *shel ma'ala* [Heb. above].[43] *bet mikdash* [Heb. the Sanctuary, i.e., Temple], *Yerushalayim* [Heb. Jerusalem] *Yeshiva* [Heb. academy] *sefer toldot shel ma'alah* [Heb. The book of the generations which is above . . .] is again a transfer from the Platonic system of ideas.

During the Homiletic hour I stressed the point that a world-outlook is incompatible with collective or folk religion. I advanced first the argument

---

42. The midrash in question comments on Genesis 5:1 "This is the book of the generations of Adam . . ." and cites a verse from Psalm 139:16 which reads "Thy eyes did see my unshaped flesh, for in thy book all things are written. . . ." This verse is taken to mean that God saw the future even before Adam was fully formed. This midrash also describes Adam as being as large as the world.

43. Kaplan is referring here to the upper heavenly realm, which is supposed to reproduce the earthly realm. He proceeds to enumerate the heavenly Temple, heavenly Jerusalem, heavenly academy, etc.

based on the analysis of the meaning of world-outlook. A world-outlook has to be individually achieved and freely maintained, otherwise the truths or ideas which seem to express such an outlook are merely symbols or sancta. Then I proved from actual fact. With Maimonides holding a highly rational concept of Reality and Nahmanides a highly mystical, the Jewish religion which they both professed can hardly be said to have had a common world-outlook.

During the sermon hour I interpreted the statement of R. Johanan about the red heifer[44] to the effect that the laws pertaining to it should be accepted as divinely decreed to mean the following for us: To pass upon religious rites and observances whether they are to be continued or modified, and to find their inner meaning, we have to come to them with a spirit of piety and national loyalty. Otherwise they will seem superfluous and irrelevant *ki lo davar rayke hu* [Heb. Deuteronomy 32:47 "This is not a trifling thing for you (it is your very life)"].

. . . Considering that I had come to class this morning entirely unprepared and that all these ideas came to me in the process of teaching, this was quite a fruitful day.

Preparing the Book for Publication

FRIDAY, APRIL 13, 1934

On Wednesday, April 11, I returned the corrected page proofs of my book. This time I did not rely on Leo Schwartz but read the entire proof myself. I found it necessary to rewrite so many passages that the bill for author's corrections will probably be more than $300. I am unfortunate in not having anyone upon whose assistance I can rely. It is true that many of the changes I made in the text I could not expect Schwartz to make. But, on the other hand, there were many errors in the galley proof which he should not have permitted to go uncorrected. Likewise Duker who was trumped up to be a paragon of exactitude. The number of mistakes he allowed to remain in the corrected proof of the footnotes upset me. On the way to Macmillan's I discovered some of them and I had to sit in the 14 St. subway station of the BMT to correct some of those mistakes, with one express train after another stopping before me and the passengers crowding around me. The peace of mind I experienced when I returned the first proofs did not last very long.

---

44. Red Heifer (Parah Adumah): a sacrifice whose ashes when mixed with water removed impurity. Later generations found the ceremony incomprehensible but thought following it was the model for the nonrational law. See Numbers 19:2–10 and Rashi loc. cit. The reference to R. Yochanan Ben Zaccai is in *Numbers Rabbah* 19:4, where he put off a non-Jew with some lame explanation about the Red Heifer; later he told his students that they must observe it simply because God commanded it.

Ira Eisenstein and Judith Are Engaged

TUESDAY, APRIL 17, 1934

This is one of the very happiest days of my life—Judith has become engaged to Ira Eisenstein. Apart from the self-fulfillment which this union will bring to both of them I have the feeling that it harbors consequences of an auspicious character for the course that my life will henceforth take, and points to the ultimate establishment of Jewish life in this country.

Proofs for the Book—Questions

TUESDAY, APRIL 24, 1934

Today I went over the corrections in the third set of proofs of my forthcoming book. I am glad I am through with making changes in the book. I admit that I am afraid to look at the book when it finally does come out, lest I discover mistakes. Working on the manuscripts has made me realize how faulty my English is. I cannot write or say anything without being apprehensive of mistakes. I am all mixed up now about the use of the subjunctive and I have to be continually on the guard not to use the future after "when." Only the other day I permitted the phrase "when the Jews will have acquired" to remain in the text. I asked Ira whether that was correct usage and he assured me it was. Just a little while ago I came across the phrase "when the Jews have united they will etc." From this I infer that I should not have used the future plup. [pluperfect] with "when."

I realize how funny all this sounds, but when one is as handicapped as I am by a rather poor sense of language, it is a big nuisance.

THURSDAY, APRIL 26, 1934

As luck would have it I happened to glance at the page proof today and noticed that the title on the left page of Ch. XII read "Neo-Theology" instead of "Neo Orthodoxy." God knows how I would have felt if that had appeared in the book.

Max Kadushin's Thinking Irritates Kaplan

SUNDAY, MAY 6, 1934

Last Wednesday night Rabbi Max Kadushin called. He had come from Madison, Wisc. to work on texts of the *Seder Eliyahu*.[45] I like him very much as a person. That makes me all the more sorry for his self-entanglement in a methodology of interpretation of rabbinic thought, a methodology the

---

45. This midrashic work, also known as *Tanna De-Vei Eliyahu*, is a uniform work, perhaps by one author, dealing with ethical and religious values reflected in the lives of the patriarchs.

implications of which he does not fully comprehend. He calls it organismic. He is so obsessed with it that no one can engage in conversation with him for five minutes without becoming aware about something being organismic. But the worst of it is that he has become so "hipped" on "organismic" thinking that organized logical thinking is to him an inferior and artificial sort of thinking. Before you know it he will pronounce "Eliyahu" a superior thinker to Aristotle.[46]

Consequently during the greater part of his stay Wednesday night we wrangled and irritated each other.

Lenin and the Jews—A Critical Evaluation

SUNDAY, MAY 6, 1934

After I formulated the foregoing questions I picked up the pamphlet "Lenin on the Jewish Question." I felt as though a thunderbolt struck the whole edifice of my "Judaism as a Civilization" and shattered it to smithereens when I read the following:

"Whoever directly or otherwise puts forward the slogan of Jewish national culture (however well intentioned he may be) is the enemy of the proletariat, the defender of the *old* and *caste* element in Jewry, the tool of the rabbis and the bourgeoisie. On the contrary, those Jewish marxists who join up in the international Marxists organizations with the Russian, Lithuanian, Ukrainian and other workers (both in Russian and in Jewish) to the creation of and an international culture of the working class movement are continuing (in the teeth of Bundist separatism) the best traditions of Jewry, and struggling against the slogan of 'national culture.'"

That was written in Oct–Dec. 1913. It is unfortunate that I had kept myself ignorant of all these ideas. I would have made it my business to probe much more deeply into the problem of Jewish survival than I have done hitherto.

After all the case is by no means as simple as it first appears. Lenin, despite his great mental clarity, failed to realize that national culture in the case of the Jews possessed a variant which should have prevented him from treating it as no different from the rest.

Let me take as text something that he says in the same statement from which I quoted the passage on the preceding page.

"International culture," he says, "is not non-national. Nobody ever stated it was so. . . . In *every* national culture there are, even if undeveloped,

---

46. Kadushin published *The Theology of Seder Eliahu; A Study in Organic Thinking* (1932) and *Organic Thinking: A Study in Rabbinic Thought* (1938). Kadushin was a devoted disciple of Kaplan during and immediately after his years as a student at the Seminary. See my *Judaism Faces the Twentieth Century* for more material.

the *elements* of a democratic and Socialist culture, because in *every* nation there are toilers and exploited masses whose conditions of life inevitably give rise to a democratic and Socialist ideology."

"But in *every* nation there is also a bourgeois culture (and in the majority still a Black Hundred—clerical culture) which moreover is present not merely in the form of 'elements' but in the form of the *dominant* culture. Therefore 'national culture' generally is the culture of the landowners, priests, bourgeoisie."

There seems to be enough in the foregoing that makes being a Jew compatible with the acceptance of that in communism which is of permanent value. It also sets a task for anyone who wants to reconcile Judaism with communism. That task is to isolate from Judaism as of permanent value those elements in it which may be identified as democratic and socialist culture. It seems to me that this ought not to be difficult.

One has only to read Lenin's denunciation of the Bundists to realize how little he understands the essence of Jewish culture. He attacks their anti-assimilationism as though it implied the refusal to fight side by side with the proletarians of other nationalities, or the hatred of the proletarian culture of other nations. Nothing but sheer ignorance could have blinded him to the passion to devotion which the most ardent anti-assimilationist displays toward the ideal elements of the most hostile culture.

At Long Last the Book Is Out! Two Reactions

THURSDAY, MAY 24, 1934

At long last the book is out. I received the first copies of it yesterday afternoon. It looks good from the outside. But I am afraid of reading any part of it for fear I might find the style infelicitous. I can't read a sentence without feeling that I might have expressed the thought in better style. But for the sake of everybody concerned I must enter into the spirit of happiness which should naturally accompany the thought of having consummated an undertaking that has stretched over many years. In gratitude to God I record the benediction *Baruch atah 'd Eloheynu melech ha-olam shehehe'yanu ve-kiyymanu ve-higiyanu la-zeman ha-zeh* [Heb. Blessed art Thou O Lord our God King of the Universe, who has kept us alive, sustained us and allowed us to reach this time"].[47]

---

47. A general, all-purpose blessing for happy occasions.

TUESDAY, MAY 29, 1934[48]

Today Macmillan's published my book. I was very much chagrined to find no reference to that fact in today's N.Y. Times. It is the practice of Macmillan's to send in to the N.Y. Times the lists of the books they are about to publish. They certainly included mine in the lists they sent in, but somehow the one who edits the lists for the Sunday Book Review and for the daily account of new books deliberately refuses to announce my book. I called up MacMillan's to complain of what I thought was their fault. From what they told me I could see that they were not to blame. Nevertheless they promised to look after the matter and to see to it that a notice of the book gets in tomorrow's edition.

"Everyone Lives Happily Ever After"—Ira and Judith Married

MONDAY, JUNE 1, 1934

Yesterday Judith and Ira were married. The ceremony took place at the SAJ synagogue and the reception at the Hotel Brewster, the building adjoining the SAJ House. There were about 500 guests present. Cantor Nathanson chanted the Yemenite song *ahavat ra'aya* [Heb. The love of my sweetheart] set to music by Engel.[49] I was the *mesader kidushin* [Heb. performer of the marriage ceremony].[50] Louis Finkelstein delivered a very beautiful little address,[51] Israeli read the *Ketubah* [Heb. marriage contract] and I concluded with the benedictions and a special prayer. The floral decorations were in excellent taste and everything connected both with the ceremony and the reception passed off without a flaw.[52]

The members of the Institute Faculty sent me a beautiful resolution most handsomely engraved in honor of the occasion.

If I could only forget for a moment the threatening clouds of another war, I would be the happiest human being alive. How disappointed I was when three and four years ago Ira did not seem to show the least sign of interest in Judith. Although I was reconciled to the match with Al, it was because I wanted Judith to be happy and I thought she was happy. But I felt deeply frustrated in not getting a son-in-law with whom I could have some interests in common. And to think that in the end everything should turn out not—God forbid—as the canons of higher literary art command

---

48. On the date of publication of Kaplan's magnum opus this author was one day old.

49. Joel Engel (1868–1927), composer and music editor; pioneer of music in Erez Israel; special interest in Jewish folk music.

50. Strictly speaking, the word *Kiddushin* means sanctification or betrothal.

51. Ira Eisenstein remembered Finkelstein speaking of the wedding as a union of two "royal" families—the Kaplans and the Eisensteins.

52. Ira Eisenstein reports that everyone suffered in the great heat of that particular day.

*The Kaplan family, ca. 1935: Kaplan, Lena Kaplan, Judith Kaplan
Eisenstein, Ira Eisenstein. (Courtesy Reconstructionist
Rabbinical College)*

but rather as the popular taste demands, with everybody living happily—as I am sure—ever after! Excellent material for a novelist, with plenty of fact to prove no less exciting than fiction.

A Prayer for God Not to God

JUNE 1, 1934

At the services last Sabbath I delivered a sermon on the Meaning of God in Human Experience. Taking as my text *ve'ata yigdal nah ko'akh 'd* [Heb. Numbers 14:17 "And now, I pray thee, let the power of my Lord be great, according as Thou has spoken, saying the Lord is longsuffering, and great in love, forgiving iniquity and transgression . . ."] I developed the thought that when prayer (which is an expression of the God-consciousness) attains the level of development analogous to self-consciousness in the individual, it takes on the character of being a prayer for God and not to God. It is then an expression of a wish in which both God and man join, to see the wrongs and sufferings of life eliminated. It is just that type of prayer we are getting to be in need of as a means of experiencing the reality of God.

Sidney Musher, Hadassah Kaplan Musher, and Jane Fonda, Ben Gurion University Dinner, 1982. (N. Silverstein, photographer, Courtesy Hadassah K. Musher)

Glossary

Note: An asterisk indicates that more information may be found in *Judaism Faces the Twentieth Century: A Biography of Mordecai M. Kaplan* (Detroit: Wayne State University Press, 1993).

*Cyrus Adler (1863–1940), Ph.D. Johns Hopkins; national communal leader; president, Dropsie College, United Synagogue, JTS, American Jewish Historical Society; editor, American Jewish Yearbook (AJYB). Adler became president of JTS in 1915. He was traditional in his outlook and he and Kaplan had their problems.

*Felix Adler (1851–1933), Ph.D., philosopher; founder of the Ethical Culture Movement; faculty, Columbia. Kaplan studied with Adler and was deeply influenced by his concern for the ethical.

Ahad Ha-Am (Asher Ginzberg) (1856–1927), essayist and philosopher of cultural Zionism. A major figure in the development of Zionism. Opposed Herzl on many issues. Kaplan was his most important disciple.

Max Arzt (1897–1975), ordained JTS; author; chancellor, JTS; president, Rabbinical Assembly.

Hillel Bavli (1893–1961), Hebrew poet; literary critic; faculty, TI.

Salo W. Baron (1895–1989), Ph.D., ordained JTS (Vienna); historian; faculty, Columbia; major author and editor in field.

*Samson Benderly (1876–1944), U.S. educator who was born in Palestine and served as director of the Bureau of Jewish Education of the New York Kehillah. A major figure in American-Jewish education. He is the only person in the 1920s and 1930s that Kaplan considered a close friend.

*Isaac Berkson (1891–1975), communal educator, philosopher, Palestine, New York City; faculty, Jewish Institute of Religion and CCNY; director, Central Jewish Institute.

Herman Bernstein (1876–1935), journalist, editor, and diplomat; founder of *Der Tog* and editor, *American Hebrew*; war correspondent.

Hayyim Nahman Bialik (1873–1934), the greatest Hebrew poet of modern times; essayist, story writer, translator, and editor who exercised a profound influence on modern Jewish culture.

Ben Zion Bokser (1907–84), ordained JTS; rabbi, Forest Hills Jewish Center; author of popular and scholarly works.

Joseph Bragin (1875–1932), principal, Hebrew High School, New York City; faculty, TI. Died in an automobile accident.

Abraham Burstein (1893–1966), rabbi; ordained JTS; editor, *The Jewish Outlook*.

Alexander Burnstein (1900–1980), ordained JTS, New York City; active in interfaith concerns.

Paul Chertoff (1880–1966), rabbi; talmudist; faculty, TI; and supporter of Kaplan.

*Israel Chipkin (1891–1955), communal educator, Bureau of Jewish Education; director of the Friendlaender Classes at TI; registrar of the TI.

Boaz Cohen (1899–1968), ordained JTS; Ph.D. Columbia; rabbinic scholar; faculty, JTS; author on comparative law.

*Joseph H. Cohen (1877–1961), businessman and philanthropist. Born in Russia, Cohen came to the United States at the age of four. His business firm manufactured men's clothing, with stores throughout the northeast. He was the key figure in the founding of the Jewish Center and served on the Board of Beth Israel Hospital for many years. He had a rather complicated relationship with Kaplan, first as supporter and then critic.

*Israel Davidson (1870–1945), scholar of Medieval Hebrew literature; born in Lithuania; taught at the JTS. His magnum opus is a four-volume thesaurus of medieval Hebrew poetry.

Jacob De Haas (1872–1937), Zionist leader; journalist; associate of Herzl; introduced Brandeis to Zionism; founder of Zionist Organization of America (ZOA).

*Samuel Dinin (1902–72), Ph.D. Columbia; communal leader; editor; executive director, SAJ; faculty, JTS; faculty, TI.

*Max Drob (1887–1959), ordained JTS; founder, United Synagogue; president Rabbinical Assembly. Abraham Duker (1907–87), Ph.D., author, librarian; faculty, Brooklyn College; compiled index for *Judaism as a Civilization*.

*Alexander Dushkin (1890–1976), educator and rabbi; Ph.D. Columbia; communal educator, New York City and Jerusalem; became an important disciple of Kaplan; responsible for bringing Kaplan to Hebrew University to teach in 1937 and 1938.

*Ira Eisenstein (1906–), ordained JTS; leader, Reconstructionist Movement; leader, SAJ; president, Reconstructionist Foundation; founder, Reconstructionist Rabbinical College; Kaplan's son-in-law and most important disciple. Eisenstein served at the SAJ for many years.

*Judah David Eisenstein (1854–1956), Hebraist; author; encyclopedist; translator; Orthodox; grandfather of Ira and Myron Eisenstein.

*Judith Kaplan Eisenstein (1909–96), eldest of Kaplan's four daughters; Ph.D., author, expert on Jewish music; Kaplan's favorite philosophical companion.

Louis Epstein (1887–1949), ordained JTS; authority on Jewish law and marriage; president, Rabbinical Assembly.

*Louis Finkelstein (1895–1991), Conservative rabbi; talmudist; author; president, JTS, 1940–72. Finkelstein respected Kaplan but they differed on a whole host of issues and had a difficult time with each other from the start.

Abe Finley (1898–?) Lehigh University; tobacco and wholesale confectioner; Zionist leader; national executive board, Zionist Organization of America.

*Harry Fischel (1865–1948), philanthropist; supported many Jewish causes, including Hebrew Immigrant Aid Society (HIAS) and Yeshiva University; Jewish Center. Kaplan was highly critical of him.

*William Fischman (1867–1959), cloak and suit manufacturer; an organizer of the Down Town Talmud Torah; active in the Union of Orthodox Jewish Congregations.

*Israel Friedlaender (1876–1920), semitics scholar and community leader; born in Russia; in 1903 became professor of biblical literature at the JTS. He was killed in the Ukraine while on a relief mission. His philosophy has much in common with Kaplan's.

Emanuel Gamoran (1895–1962), Ph.D., noted communal educator; president, National Council for Jewish Education; author; editor, *The Jewish Teacher*.

Adele Ginzberg (1886–1980), influential figure in Conservative movement as wife of Louis Ginzberg.

*Louis Ginzberg (1873–1953), Talmud and Midrashic scholar; faculty, JTS; author; one of the founders of the Conservative movement; primary faculty critic of Kaplan. There was a complex relationship between the two.

Enrico Glicenstein (1870–1942), sculptor, painter, etcher, woodcarver; noted for his portrait busts.

*Solomon Goldman (1893–1953), Conservative rabbi, Zionist leader, and key disciple of Mordecai Kaplan.

David Goldstein (1902–90), ordained JTS; rabbi Har Zion Philadelphia; prominent in Conservative movement.

Israel Goldstein (1896–1986), ordained JTS; Jewish historian; New York Board of Rabbis; officer, Zionist Organization of America.

Jacob Golub (1895–1959), LL.B., Ph.D.; communal education administrator; author; educational director, Zionist Organization of America.

*Simon Greenberg (1901–93), ordained JTS; Ph.D. Dropsie College; Conservative leader; executive director, United Synagogue of America; president, Rabbinical Assembly; admired Kaplan but critical of him.

Julius Greenstone (1873–1955), ordained JTS, Ph.D.; religious educator and administrator, Philadelphia; author; friend of Kaplan.

Jacob Grossman (1886–1970s?), B.A. Columbia, JTS 1911; rabbi New York City and Flushing, N.Y.; helped found Camp Tabor; frequented Kaplan household to discuss sermon material.

Joseph Hertz (1872–1946), ordained JTS; served in Johannesburg; appointed Chief Rabbi of British Empire in 1913. Kaplan knew him well and thought him pretentious.

*Charles I. Hoffman (1864–1945), journalist; ordained JTS; journalist; friend of Solomon Schechter; Conservative leader.

Leo Honor (1894–1956), Ph.D., communal educator, New York City, then Chicago; leader in Jewish education; author; Bureau of Jewish Education, New York City; College of Jewish Studies, Chicago; trained by Samson Benderly

Jacob Hoschander (1874–1933), biblical scholar; Assyriologist; faculty, JTS.

Henry Hurwitz (1886–1961), educator; essayist; communal worker; Menorah leader; editor, *Menorah Journal*; friend and admirer of Kaplan.

Moses Hyamson (1862–1949), rabbi and scholar; chairman Beth Din of British Empire; faculty, JTS; taught Talmud and Codes.

Samuel Hyman (1870–1917), businessman, communal worker, New York City; one of the founders of the Jewish Center.

Sophie Kaplan Israeli (1879?–1950?), Mordecai Kaplan's older sister. She was well educated and helped teach Kaplan Hebrew.

*Phineas Israeli (1880–1948), ordained JTS; rabbi, Des Moines Iowa; brother-in-law of Mordecai Kaplan. Pulpits also in Brooklyn and Massachusetts.

Vladimir (Ze'ev) Jabotinsky (1880–1940), writer, orator, and Zionist leader; militant revisionist; founded Betar; spiritual father of *Irgun* (Jewish underground organization of the 1940s).

Selma Kaplan Jaffe-Goldman, fourth daughter of M. Kaplan; worked in television production and syndication; married to Saul Jaffe (1913–77), attorney, radio and TV production; married to Joseph L. Goldman (1904–91), M.D., chief, Department of Otolaryngology, Mt. Sinai Hospital.

*Max Kadushin (1895–1980), ordained JTS; scholar of rabbinic Judaism; author; educator; faculty, JTS; an important disciple of Kaplan but critical of him in later life.

Maurice Karpf (1889–1964), Ph.D. Columbia; Jewish social work administrator; author; director, Training School for Jewish Social Work.

*Charles E. H. Kauvar (1879–1971), ordained JTS; author; rabbi in Denver; president, United Synagogue of America; cousin of Kaplan. Inspired Kaplan to seek out the JTS and attend.

Jacob Klein (1890–1946), U.S. attorney, chairman, SAJ Board of Trustees, 1927–44.

*Eugene Kohn (1887–1977), rabbi; Reconstructionist and close disciple of Mordecai Kaplan; edited Reconstructionist prayer books with Kaplan and Rabbi Ira Eisenstein; rabbi in Baltimore and brother of Jacob Kohn, also a Seminary graduate.

*Jacob Kohn (1881–1968), Conservative rabbi who served congregations in Syracuse, Manhattan, and Los Angeles. While in New York Kohn served as rabbi of Ansche Hesed. He is the brother of Rabbi Eugene Kohn, a key disciple of Kaplan.

George A. Kohut (1874–1933), educator, author, and scholar; rabbi; librarian, JTS; founder, Camp Kohut.

Wilfred Kotkov (1885–1921), rabbi, instructor at JTS.

Arthur M. Lamport (1883–1940), investment banker, philanthropist, government advisor.

Nathan Lamport (1854–1928), merchant, philanthropist.

Samuel Charles Lamport (1880–1941), cotton merchant, communal leader, and philanthropist. His father (Nathan) and his brother (Arthur) were both active in the Jewish community. All the Lamports belonged to the Jewish Center.

Solomon Lamport (1871–1936), communal worker, philanthropist, New York City.

Alter F. Landesman (1895–?), ordained JRS; rabbi; social worker, Brooklyn; superintendent, Hebrew Education Society; author.

*Irving Lehman (1876–1945), judge, state supreme court; legal philosopher; board member, Union of American Hebrew Congregations (UAHC); judge in Rosenwald contest. He appreciated Kaplan's submission but thought that it had significant weaknesses.

Morris Levine (1881–1935), rabbi; faculty, JTS; primarily responsible for bringing Hebrew to TI; much respected at JTS.

Israel Levinthal (1888–1982), ordained JTS; Doctor of Hebrew Letters (DHL); author; rabbi, Brooklyn Jewish Center; national executive, Zionist Organization of America.

Louis Levitsky (1897–1975), ordained JTS; president; Rabbinical Assembly; author.

Joe Levy (?–1944), businessman, Crawford Clothes; one of the founders of the SAJ.

William Lewis (1884–1939), municipal judge; civic and Zionist leader, Philadelphia.

Abraham Liebovitz (1878–1964), manufacturer; communal fund-raiser; a founder of the SAJ; officer, Jewish Reconstructionist Foundation

Harry Liebovitz (1882–?), clothing manufacturer; president, Jewish Education Association; board member, SAJ.

Irma Lindheim (1886–1978), studied at Columbia and Jewish Institute of Religion; national officer, Zionist Organization of America; author.

*Louis Lipsky (1876–1963), life insurance executive; Zionist and communal leader; author; editor; officer, Zionist Organization of America.

*Julian Mack (1866–1943), lawyer and judge; national, communal, and Zionist leader.

*Judah L. Magnes (1877–1948), rabbi and president of the New York Kehillah; Zionist leader who later became the first president of the Hebrew University. Kaplan and Magnes knew each other well.

*Moses Sebulun Margolies (1851–1936), Orthodox rabbi and community leader; rabbi at Kehilath Jeshurun in 1906 along with Kaplan. Kaplan respected him though they had their differences.

*Louis Marshall (1856–1929), lawyer and community leader; one of the founders of the American Jewish Committee; served for many years on the Board of the JTS; important spokesman for Jewish rights and a key figure of the German-Jewish elite.

*Alexander Marx (1878–1953), historian, librarian, and author; faculty member, JTS; largely responsible for making Seminary collection one of the largest Jewish libraries in the world.

*Sabato Morais (1823–1897), Sephardic rabbi, Philadelphia; founder and first president, JTS; friend of Mazzini, the Italian nationalist.

Julian Morgenstern (1881–1976), rabbi; president, Hebrew Union College; biblical and semitic language scholar; author.

Hadassah Kaplan Musher, second-eldest daughter of Mordecai Kaplan; active in SAJ; organized Reconstructionist Women's Organization; educator; married to Sidney Musher (1905–90), food and pharmaceutical research; president P.E.F. (Palestine Endowment Fund).

Abraham Neuman (1890–1970), ordained JTS; author; president, Dropsie College; editor, *Jewish Quarterly Review*.

William Pinsker (1896–?), social work administrator, communal worker, Boston; Educational Alliance, Savannah; worked in Brockton, Mass.

*Bernard Revel (1885–1940), educator, scholar, and author who reorganized Rabbi Isaac Elhanan Theological Seminary and founded Yeshiva College, later to become Yeshiva University. Neighbor of Kaplan at one point.

*Otto Rosalsky (1873–1936), lawyer, judge, philanthropist; fund-raiser, Yeshiva College.

Albert Rosenblatt (1872–1944), clothing manufacturer and SAJ member.

*Henry Rosenthal (1906–77), ordained JTS; author; faculty, Hunter College; philosopher; favorite student of Kaplan's.

*Julius Rosenwald (1862–1932), merchant; philanthropist; with Sears Roebuck, established Rosenwald Fund, which ran a contest that Kaplan won. He used the money to support the publication of his book.

Abraham Rothstein (1857–1939), cotton merchant; labor arbitrator; active in the Jewish Center.

Samuel Rottenberg (1873–1958), knitted wear manufacturer; director, Federation of Jewish Charities.

*Herman H. Rubenovitz (1883–1966), rabbi and Zionist; graduated JTS in 1908; a disciple of Kaplan and one of his strongest supporters; rabbi of Temple Mishkan Tefila, Boston, 1910–46.

Isidore Rubin (1883–1958), physician, gynecologist, and researcher into female sterility; brother-in-law of Mordecai Kaplan.

Edwin, Second Viscount Samuel? (1898–?), son of Herbert Samuel; Zionist; author; established Institute of Public Administration in Israel.

Zevi Scharfstein (1884–1972), Hebrew editor, educator, and textbook writer, Bureau of Jewish Education; faculty, TI.

*Solomon Schechter (1847–1915), first president after 1902 of reorganized JTS; well-known rabbinic scholar who discovered the large cache of medieval Jewish documents in Cairo called the Geniza; primary force in creating Conservative Judaism in America; liked Kaplan but was critical of him.

*Jacob Schiff (1847–1920), financier and noted community leader; involved with virtually every major institution in the Jewish community.

Albert Schoolman (1894–1980), M.A. Columbia; JTS Teachers Diploma; president, National Council for Jewish Education; Kaplan disciple and friend. They spent many summers together in Camp CeJwIn.

Bernard Semel (1878–1959), businessman, communal leader, Zionist, New York City.

Benjamin N. Silkiner (Silk) (1888–1934), prominent Hebrew poet; educator; translated *Macbeth* into Hebrew.

Nahum Sokolow (1860–1936), Zionist leader and Hebrew journalist; general secretary, World Zionist Organization; key person in negotiating the Balfour Declaration.

*Shalom Spiegel (1899–1984), Ph.D. University of Vienna; scholar of Hebrew Literature; faculty, JTS; lectured at the SAJ; much admired by Kaplan.

*Milton Steinberg (1903–50), ordained JTS; author; Zionist; instructor CCNY and JTS; schooled in Jewish philosophy; disciple of Kaplan but critical of him in his later years.

Nathan Straus (1889–1961), department store executive (Macy's); public servant; legislator; officer, Jewish Institute of Religion.

Solomon Strook (1874–1941), lawyer; communal leader; active at JTS and in American Jewish Committee.

*Henrietta Szold (1860–1945), national Zionist leader; author; founder, Hadassah; editorial secretary, JPS; aided resettlement to Palestine of Jewish refugee children. Kaplan met her in 1903 when she came to study at the Seminary. She and Kaplan sat in Schechter's classes together. She greatly admired Kaplan.

*Chaim Tchernowitz (pseud. Rav Za'ir) (1871–1949), Ph.D., Talmud scholar; Hebrew author; Zionist; faculty, Jewish Institute of Religion; editor, *Bizaron*.

Saul Tchernikhowski (1875–1943), Hebrew poet and physician; revolted against moral emphasis in Hebrew poetry. Known for his poems of nature.

Abraham Tulin (1883–1973), lawyer; Zionist leader; author; Herbert Hoover Relief Administration.

*Israel Unterberg (1863–1934), wealthy clothing manufacturer and member of the Kaplan's congregation at the SAJ; strong supporter of Kaplan; donated money for TI building at the JTS.

Menahem Ussishkin (1863–1941), Zionist leader; member, *Hovevei Zion* [Lovers of Zion]; president, Jewish National Fund.

*Felix Warburg (1871–1937), banker and philanthropist; born in Germany, emigrated to the United States, and became a partner of Jacob Schiff in Kuhn Loeb and Company; married Frieda Schiff; a supporter of many agencies and causes throughout the Jewish community.

Naomi Kaplan Wenner (1914–97), third daughter of Mordecai Kaplan; M.D.; psychiatrist; retired 1982, then full-time sculptor; married Seymour Wenner (1913–93), administrative law judge at several U.S. government agencies.

*Stephen Wise (1872–1949), outstanding liberal rabbi; Zionist; founder of the Free Synagogue and the Jewish Institute of Religion. Admired Kaplan and hoped he would be associated with the JIR.

Index

Books in the American Jewish Civilization Series

Jews of the American West, edited by Moses Rischin and John Livingston, 1991

An Ambiguous Partnership: Non-Zionists and Zionists in America 1939–1948, by Menahem Kaufman, 1991

Hebrew in America: Perspectives and Prospects, edited by Alan Mintz, 1992

Judaism Faces the Twentieth Century: A Biography of Mordecai M. Kaplan, by Mel Scult, 1993

A Credit to Their Community: Jewish Loan Societies in the United States, 1880–1945, by Shelly Tenenbaum, 1993

The Forerunners: Dutch Jewry in the North American Diaspora, by Robert P. Swierenga, 1994

Isaac Leeser and the Making of American Jewry, by Lance J. Sussman, 1994

Rebecca Gratz: Women and Judaism in Antebellum America, by Dianne Ashton, 1997

Communings of the Spirit: The Journals of Mordecai M. Kaplan, Volume 1, 1913–1934, edited by Mel Scult, 2001

Jewish Voices of the California Gold Rush: A Documentary History, 1849–1880, edited by Ava Fran Kahn, 2001